THE
RANDALL HOUSE
BIBLE
COMMENTARY

THE
RANDALL HOUSE
BIBLE
COMMENTARY

THE BOOK OF ACTS

by
Danny L. Dwyer

FIRST EDITION

randall house
RANDALL HOUSE
NASHVILLE, TENNESSEE 37217

RANDALL HOUSE BIBLE COMMENTARY, ACTS
© Copyright 2018
RANDALL HOUSE
NASHVILLE, TN 37138
ISBN: 9780892659753

General Editor:
ROBERT E. PICIRILLI
Professor Emeritus, Welch College
Nashville, TN

Dedication

To Carolyn whose life models Christ in
all things and for her sacrifices as I wrote.

To our children and grandchildren,
our "Jerusalem" of witness.

To pastors and all who serve in ministry and their
proclamation of the gospel of Jesus Christ.

To all Christ-followers of "the Way" who
continue the witness of the risen Savior.

PREFACE

Here is yet one more volume—the penultimate one, as it happens—in the series known as the Randall House Commentary on the Bible: that is, on the New Testament. I refer the reader to the preface to the last commentary published, on the Gospel of Matthew, for more about the writers of this series and the aims of the publisher, Randall House.

It is a great honor and a serious responsibility to handle the Word of God, the Bible. Second Timothy 3:16 assures us that "All Scripture is given by inspiration of God." These last five words translate one Greek word in the original, a word that means God-breathed. It is the very breath of God, the person of the Holy Spirit moving or bearing along the human writers in such an overshadowing way that they were enabled to say exactly what He wanted said. As the late Francis Shaeffer used to express it, God is there, and He is not silent. He has spoken to reveal Himself and His provision for us. So to comment on the Bible is serious business. We want to know exactly what God said and what He meant by it.

Second Timothy 3:16 also assures us that "All Scripture … is profitable." The Lord did not give it to us just to impress us or to give us the intellectual pleasure of figuring out what it means. He gave it to us to be lived out. It is not enough to mouth what we believe about the Bible, we must also submit to its authority to rule our lives. When Saul disobeyed the Lord, Samuel said he had "rejected the word of the Lord" (1 Sam. 16:26). Really believing that the Bible is the Word of God cannot be separated from obeying it, from submitting ourselves to it as what Almighty God has spoken to us.

So anyone who preaches or teaches—or writes commentary—on the Bible is doing important work, in telling others what God has said and what difference that should make in the way we live. Not only is our eternal salvation at stake in this, so is the way we conduct ourselves day in and day out. Scripture is profitable, then: for teaching, for rebuke, for correcting us, for instructing us how to live righteously.

The Book of Acts is the last of the "historical" books in the New Testament, providing us with information about what happened following the ascension of Jesus Christ to His Father. It is exciting to follow the first disciples to the Upper Room, and from there to the heart of the civilized world as they proclaimed the gospel, brought many to Jesus, planted churches, and "turned the world upside down" (Acts 17:6).

We see many wonderful things in this book. The empowering of the church for witness. The fleshing out of the Great Commission. The transition from a primarily Jewish to a primarily Gentile church. The thrilling exploits of Paul as God's man to take the Good News westward to Rome. There are important lessons for us in these chapters.

Dr. Danny Dwyer, at the height of his ministry among us, has devoted months to giving us this commentary. He is well qualified in education and experience—as pastor and teacher. Those who read this volume will find that he is everywhere concerned to enable us to see our Lord at work, by His Spirit, to propagate the gospel and build His church. In every chapter, Dr. Dwyer is careful to make sure we understand what is happening, what it meant then, and what it means for us.

And at Dr. Dwyer's suggestion we have included a few pages of helps that are not like anything we have provided in other volumes in this series: a set of maps that will help the reader visualize the progress of Paul's travels; and a table that provides a chronological overview of the key events of the book. Do not overlook these helps; they will assist you both in grasping the "big picture" and in relating the details to each other.

Robert E. Picirilli

CONTENTS

COMMENTARY ON THE ACTS OF THE APOSTLES

INTRODUCTION

The Author of Acts

Although some dissent, scholars of all levels agree that the Gospel according to Luke and the Acts of the Apostles were written by the same person. That person was the close companion of the apostle Paul: Luke, the beloved physician (Col. 4:14; 2 Tim. 4:11). The supporting evidences for Luke as the single author are many. First, the language of both has a common style and vocabulary (Cadbury, *Making of Luke—Acts,* 113-154; Polhill, *Acts,* 24; Bock 13). The Greek used by Luke is common Greek, as would be spoken in everyday usage, but is regarded also as "educated, standard" Koine Greek (Schnabel 23). In other words, he writes as one who has been formally trained and is able to express articulately the common speech of everyday use.

Secondly, outside sources from as early as the second century writings of Irenaeus establish the tradition that Luke was the author of both the Gospel and the Book of Acts (Keener 1:410-411).

Thirdly, from the "we" sections of the Acts record it is clear that the writer was a close companion of Paul's. It may be argued (as does Haenchen 112-116) that the author used the person who wrote the "we" sections as his source and that the writer was from a genera-

tion later. But as Fitzmeyer (49-51) asserts this view would only arise out of reluctance to admit what is clearly the evidence in favor of Luke. The "we" sections have always been the crux of the matter about authorship. The first-person references put the writer in the mix with the apostle Paul in many of his travels, and they make the claim that the writer was present at the time. Unless one has clear evidence for an author other than Luke, there is no reason to propose another (Hiebert 248). Although Paul had other companions who could have undertaken the task, like Titus or Timothy, Luke is the preferred option.

The traditional authorship of Luke for the Book of Acts (and the Gospel of Luke) is assumed throughout this commentary.

Who Was Luke?

There are only three direct references to Luke in the N.T. (Col. 4:14; 2 Tim. 4:11; Philem. 24). What is known about him from these references and from what is written in Luke—Acts is: 1. He was a physician and probably well-positioned in society and well-educated (as Ramsay, *Luke* 56-59, attests). 2. He was a close companion of Paul. 3. He was a very capable writer. 4. He was a second-generation believer.

1

Luke's place of origin is uncertain. Some connect him with Antioch of Syria (Geldenhuys 17, 21). Since he joined Paul at Troas (16:10) he may have been from there. Since he stayed at Philippi when Paul moved on during the second missionary journey, he may have been from there. That he was well-traveled is reflected in his detailed knowledge of sailing, as noted in the record of the sea voyages and the sheer number of cities, towns, and ports he mentions.

Sources for the Writing of the Book of Acts

In addressing this area, I am assuming the superintendence of the Holy Spirit in all that Luke did to interview eyewitnesses, in the writing and preservation of his notes—particularly during the storm and shipwreck, in his own observances, and in the selection of key events and people to include in his account. I assume the special inspiration of the Holy Spirit in his writing of the original document we now call the Acts of the Apostles. Further, I assume the superintendence of the Holy Spirit in the preservation of Luke's writing through the copies that were made and available for the Church today. There is abundant manuscript evidence for the Acts record. As Bock (29) states, "The MS evidence for Acts is strong."

In reading Acts, one cannot help asking, "Where did Luke get his information"? After all, he wrote of people, events, conversations, sermons, and other details to which he was not personally privy. This is especially true until the first "we" text (16:10).

There were six main sources from which Luke drew information. First, he spoke with "eyewitnesses" (Lk. 1:2). He would have interviewed the original parties involved and taken careful notes of what they said. For example, from these he would have learned of the church's vote to replace Judas Iscariot. He would have been informed from Peter himself of the substance of his message on the Day of Pentecost, his confrontation of Ananias and Sapphira, his personal experience of the vision of the great sheet that taught him to regard no person as "unclean." He would have learned about the exchange with Cornelius and, later, his miraculous deliverance from prison and certain death at the hands of Herod Agrippa I.

From Philip he would have learned of the Samaritan revival and the conversion of the Ethiopian eunuch. Perhaps from Paul he would have learned of the incredible abilities and spiritual power of Stephen and his role in his death. From Ananias of Damascus he would have learned of the personal vision he had regarding Saul of Tarsus. From Barnabas he would have learned of his initial efforts with the newly converted Saul of Tarsus.

Second, he was personally present for events in the "we" sections of Acts from chapters 16-28. There are four views regarding how the "we" is to be understood (Polhill, *Acts* 36-38). The traditional view is that these indicate Luke's personal presence in the event. Some interpreters prefer to think he used a personal companion of Paul's as a source, keeping that companion's "we" in his record. Others suggest a written source in the form of a diary or journal adapted for the writing. Still others think the "we" was merely a literary device. Allowing for narrative differences to convey first-person presence and third-person identification, the "we" references are from Luke's first-hand experiences, reflecting his ownership for what he writes. He was there personally when the things he related happened.

Third, there were some written sources for Luke's information. These would include copies of documents that are quoted, including the decrees adopted by the Jerusalem Council (15:23-29), the letter written by the centurion, Claudius Lysias, regarding the rescue incident and transportation of Paul to Caesarea (23:25-30), and probably notes that were made of messages preached—from Pentecost on.

Fourth, there were details that would have been part of that day's pool of shared information. This would include the names of Roman Emperors past and present, seasonal changes, geographical references, calendar dates, etc. There are always many things that are common knowledge within the culture and populace.

Fifth, as most writers point out, there were traditions in the Christian community that became part of Luke's source material. Most of these would have been related verbally. There might have been some early, written traditions in the church, but these are more assumed than certain since none are preserved—except for hints in the text of Acts (1:26; 4:24-30; 21:8).

Sixth, it is possible that Luke read some of Paul's early letters and made subtle reference to particular themes found there. I say this in differing with Polhill (*Acts* 39). Paul used the term *justified* once in his recorded sermons in Acts (13:39), but often in Romans and Galatians. Paul's message to the Athenians references the witness of creation (17:24) and is similar to Romans 1:19-20. To be sure these are not direct quotes but show similarity and perhaps familiarity with these epistles.

The Date of the Writing of Acts

One assumes there were two stages in the writing of Acts. One would have been the compilation of notes from the sources named above. The other was when Luke actually penned the document. It would have taken Luke a number of years to compile his notes in preparation for writing, a process without which the final work would not have been possible. His travels with Paul and his companions—beginning with the Second Missionary Journey (16:10) and culminating with their arrival at Rome—would cover approximately ten years. This assumes the date of the Second Missionary Journey as A.D. 49/50 and the arrival in Rome as A.D. 60/61. Luke would have taken copious notes during all these travels.

There are breaks in the "we" connections with Paul. Luke was not always with him. For example, during Paul's two-year imprisonment in Caesarea, Luke could have easily used that time for research and interviews. That extends also to the two years of imprisonment in Rome.

Given the time needed for the compilation of his notes, the question of when he wrote Acts boils down to three opinions, but only two real possibilities (Bock 25-27; Polhill, *Acts* 29-31; Bruce, *Acts* 10-12; Fitzmyer 51-55).

First, the idea of a very late date of A.D. 150 should be excluded since it raises all kinds of questions about authorship.

Second, some argue for a date prior to A.D. 70 and perhaps even before A.D. 64. This allows for Paul's two-year imprisonment in Rome to precede the beginning of the persecution instigated by Nero in the fall of A.D. 64. This fits well with the actual chronology of the events and the sense of conclusion one gets with the ending of Acts. It is possible, perhaps likely, that Luke actually penned Acts in Rome during this imprisonment period. Given the "abrupt" ending of Acts, which does not cover Paul's trial before Caesar and death (after A.D. 64), it seems likely that Acts was penned in Rome at the end of that two-year imprisonment.

Third, some argue for a date after A.D. 70. Given the fact that Acts was written subsequently to the gospel, some interpret Luke's Gospel as showing an awareness of the fall of Jerusalem in A.D. 70. Those who hold this position point to the seeming vividness of Luke's descriptions of the fall of Jerusalem by the Lord Jesus. However, that is interpretative speculation. If Luke is careful to mention the fulfilling of the prophecy of Agabus (11:28), why would he not mention such monumental events as the destruction of Jerusalem and the death of the apostle Paul if they had happened prior to his writing (Geldenhuys 34-35)?

Those who hold to a date after A.D. 70 also point to the parallels of Luke with the Gospel of Mark. Most hold that Mark wrote his Gospel after the death of Peter, which probably took place in A.D. 65/66. They put the writing of Mark's Gospel sometime in A.D. 70. Some place it a little earlier. If Luke drew upon Mark's Gospel for his Gospel account, then that moves the writing of Acts to later. Picirilli (*Mark* 10-12) asserts that Mark was most likely written in the mid 60's, perhaps A.D. 65-67, soon after Peter's death—which would have taken place not long after the

Roman persecution began. Consequently, if Luke used Mark, this would coincide with the view that Acts was written in the mid to late 60's.

Considering all the issues, it is impossible to pinpoint just exactly when Luke penned Acts, but the period from before 64 to the late 60s seems likely.

The Title of the Book

By the end of the second century there were explicit references to Acts and to Luke as the author. However, there was no official title assigned to the book. In fact, it appears that Luke did not include one. Irenaeus (A.D. 180) referred to it as "Luke's witness to the apostles." Tertullian called it "Luke's Commentary." The present title "The Acts of the Apostles" has been its title since the second century (Bruce, *Acts* 3).

Major Themes of Acts

As one reads and gets acquainted with Acts there are several themes that become apparent. Here is a brief listing and synopsis of what I see to be the top ten.

1. The Ministry of the Holy Spirit. Beginning with the filling for empowerment on the Day of Pentecost, as promised by Jesus (1:8), a new era began that more clearly defined the Person and guidance of the Holy Spirit. That a person possessed the Spirit served as evidence to help the apostles determine the authenticity of saving faith (2:38; 8:15-17; 19:1-7). One can include accompanying miraculous events that sometimes (not always) evidenced the proclamation of the gospel and the ministry of the Holy Spirit.

2. The Gospel Message. Beginning with Peter's message there is a consistency of truths that make up the message of the gospel of Jesus Christ. The core of the message consists of five truths. (1) The O.T. prophecies of the Messiah are fulfilled in Jesus of Nazareth. (2) Jesus the Messiah was condemned to die by the leaders of Israel and Rome. (3) Jesus of Nazareth was raised from the dead. (4) Repentance from sin and saving faith in Jesus as the Messiah are necessary for salvation. (5) Salvation through Jesus Christ is offered to all.

3. The Church. With the gospel of Christ there was established a new community relationship of believers termed the *church*. Acts charts its birth, model, growth, organization, and renewal, beginning with the believers at Pentecost and highlighted in the missionary journeys.

4. The Persecution of Believers. The message of the gospel that proclaimed Jesus of Nazareth as the Jewish Messiah and Savior of all men was not met with enthusiasm or acceptance by the majority of Jews. Neither was it tolerated or merely viewed as a temporary diversion. The apostles were almost immediately threatened and beaten. Saul of Tarsus became the leading terrorist against the church until his conversion. Official Roman persecution did not begin, as such, until after the Book of Acts closes.

5. Prayer. From the first chapter, where believers are huddled in an upper room in a continual prayer meeting, the theme of prayer permeates the lives of believers and the church. They pray when threatened, for guidance, for strength and boldness, for the anointing of missionaries, when beaten and imprisoned, and on the deck of a storm-tossed ship. Sometimes the prayers are recorded for us. Most of the time they are not. But one cannot miss this theme.

6. Preaching. There are ten recorded sermons in Acts and seven sermon summaries. Of the one thousand and seven verses in Acts, two hundred and forty-seven of them are in sermons or these summaries. Most of the time the sermons are to those who have an O.T. background and reference the authority of the Scriptures. To Gentiles the messages utilize the themes of creation, the necessity of a Creator, God's provisions for the well-being of humanity, the resurrection of Christ, and final judgment. Preaching is the central method of communicating God's truth in the Book of Acts.

7. Missions. The specific intentionality of sending messengers with the gospel to win souls to Christ and establish local churches is highlighted in the three missionary journeys of Paul. This begins in a local church in Antioch of Syria with the Holy Spirit's call of Barnabas and Saul, the support they received, and returning to account for their ministry. The missions model is part of the Acts record.

8. The Strategies of Satan. Satan and demonic spirits are referenced a number of times in Acts. His evil hand is obvious even when his name is not called. There are four strategies that highlight this theme in Acts: intimidation (4:1-21), imitation (5:1-11; 8:9-24), intervention (13:8-11), and infiltration (20:28-31).

9. Problems That Arose Within the Churches. Contrary to the idealism of some about the early church, things were not always peaceful and unified. Problems arose over hypocrisy, accusations of favoritism, exclusiveness, and doctrinal controversy. These same continue today.

10. The Providence of God. One cannot miss the hand of God in leading, providing, preparing, and protecting. This is evidenced in, but not confined to, the conversion accounts of the Ethiopian eunuch, Saul of Tarsus, and Cornelius the Roman centurion. God's guidance and protection in Paul's imprisonments and journey to Rome are apparent. For every time we are aware of the providence of God, there are a thousand times we are not.

The Speeches and Sermons of Acts

One of the distinct characteristics of Acts is its record of speeches that make up nearly one third of its contents. Some of these are the speeches of political leaders and contributing characters that are part of the story. While these are important, the ones most important to the biblical narrative of the witness of the Church are the sermons and sermon summaries (Polhill, *Acts* 43-47; Bock 20-23; Keener I:258-319; Soards 18-20).

Not counting the individual speeches incidental to the occasion, there are ten sermons and seven sermon summaries. The longest is by Stephen. Most are presented to audiences that have some knowledge of the O.T. Only a couple are given to "secular" audiences. None of them takes more than a few minutes to read. What is their purpose? Are they to be understood as the complete message that was given? How did Luke know what was said if he was not there to hear the speaker? Any number of answers to these questions have been given.

Begin with the fact that the sermons are the central method of communicating the gospel and biblical truth. Recording them affirms the methodology (1 Cor. 1:18-24).

More was said than what is recorded (Acts 2:40). However, what is recorded is an accurate re-statement of what was said. The source information for the content of the sermons would have been the speakers themselves and the notes taken by those who heard them. Note-taking of public speeches both during and immediately following a speech were common to the day. In speech-oriented societies the ability to record and recall accurately has been well documented. I do not agree with those who propose that Luke constructed any of the sermons, sermon summaries, and other speeches (Ridderbos 6-11). It is Luke's claim that the speeches and summaries came from the person who spoke: "Peter...lifting up his voice" (2:14); "he (Stephen) said" (7:1); "Cornelius said" (10:30); "Paul said" (17:22); "Festus said with a loud voice" (26:24); "Agrippa said" (26:28), etc. Whatever comparisons may be made with other early writers (Thucydides, Josephus, Suetonius), it must be remembered that Luke had direct access to his sources for the sermons and speeches. He was not generationally removed.

The central purpose for recording the sermons and summaries was, at least, two-fold. One, to show the consistency of the core beliefs of Christianity. All the sermons that proclaim the gospel contain the same basic themes regardless of who the speaker is. This core teaching later came to be called "the Kerygma" (Dodd). A full proclamation of the gospel will contain these themes today.

Secondly, preaching was a tool of persuasion as well as a method of communication. Acts is not just a historical record, it is an apologetic for Christianity. Sermons were the central methodology in Acts of accomplishing this goal.

Each of the sermons and summaries will be analyzed in the commentary, explaining the contents as they were given.

The Literary Genre of Acts

Commentators are almost unanimous in agreement that Acts is unique in literary style (Polhill 42). Luke uses travel narrative, biography, speeches, conversations, historical references, and more in weaving together his work. In the attempt to categorize Acts, interpreters have given it many labels, but not one fits exactly. The most popular contemporary label is that Acts is a form of ancient historiography (Keener I:90). Bock (3) characterizes it as a "historical monograph."

Luke writes with style and flair. His sense of irony is second to none. His vocabulary is the largest of any N.T. writer. Together with the Gospel, the two volumes compose twenty-seven percent of the N.T. Acts is the longest single-volume Greek text in the N.T.

What is clear is that Luke intends to present to Theophilus, and to all who read, sufficient evidence of the validity of Christianity. In doing so he brilliantly weaves together theological, social, and historical themes to make his case.

The Text of Acts

For purposes of this commentary, I have primarily used the Greek text reflected in the KJV, with some clarifica-

tions from A. T. Robertson (*Word Pictures*), Bruce Metzger, George Ricker Berry, and *The Greek New Testament* edited by Aland, Black, Metzger, and Wikgren. I have not engaged in the discussion of the Greek texts themselves as to their credibility or comparative value. My focus for the purposes of this commentary is to give the sense of the words and terms for their interpretive meaning.

When referring to the Greek text, for the purpose of communicating the meaning more fully, on a few occasions I have adjusted the reference in a way that I believe will clarify it. Not all who read this commentary have a working knowledge of Greek or have the resources available to check; therefore, some may find it helpful to have such clarifications in the text.

Methodology of Interpretation

My purpose and goal in writing has been the discovery and explanation of the writer's intent. This is called historical-grammatical interpretation. My view is that the "literal" or "normal" interpretation of the writing is best (Forlines 51-53). In some cases, I have called attention to the theological theme and intent of the author, especially in the recorded sermons. Theological traditions vary and impact how we interpret some texts.

I have made some references to theological traditions that call into question the inerrancy and integrity of the Scriptures. I have done so to show contrast, not in approval or agreement. I am not challenging the sincerity of these writers, but I am challenging their conclusions. For example, Adolph Harnack (203-231) lists what he calls "Instances of Inaccuracy and Discrepancy." Having worked through these, I do not see any valid instances of either.

I have intentionally shown deference to varying theological traditions in explaining how that tradition would affect the interpretation of a text. For example, Acts 13:48 is widely interpreted according to ones perspective on Calvinism and Arminianism. I have gone into detail to show how each tradition may interpret this verse.

While making a theological judgment about a text, I do not want to be guilty of being judgmental against a writer or a theological position. I make no apology for the Arminian tradition, which I personally hold, and which influences my perspective. No one can come to a text with complete open-mindedness. We are products of our choices. To admit that is to be honest. To deny it is disingenuous.

Style and Structure for the Commentary

The historical and narrative nature of Acts dictates the style of writing I have chosen. With respect to devotional commentaries, I have chosen to address the text in its historical context. Because the Scriptures are intended to be preached and taught, I have included an exegetical outline and some applications as I see them. Applications should always be drawn from accurate interpretations of the text, but applications tend to be subjective. I may see applications that some do not, and some may see applications that I have not. I confess my weakness for both outlines and alliteration as tools of communication in preaching and teaching for these many years. However,

I have tried to keep accurate wording in the outlines according to the text.

The Time Period of Acts

The historical nature of Acts and the expansive geography it covers raise the question of how much time is involved in the story. It begins in Jerusalem and ends in Rome. It has in its "table of contents" (1:8) the goal of carrying the witness of Christ "unto the uttermost part of the earth." Even a cursory reading shows incredible movement and progress. This is especially significant in comparison to today's efforts of witnessing and church expansion. So how long did it take? How much time does the Book of Acts cover?

From the death and resurrection of Jesus Christ in A.D. 33 until the imprisonment of the apostle Paul in Rome in approximately A.D. 60-62, the Book of Acts covers about thirty years. That is a little less than one forty-year generation. Although the phrase is something of an exaggeration, and derisive, these followers of Jesus Christ did indeed "turn the world upside down" (17:6).

The commentary itself is but one man's opinion on the biblical text; the text itself is the important thing. If in writing or in reading Acts we miss this sense of witness as modeled by these Christ-followers known derisively as "Christians" (11:26; 26:28), we miss the main point and rob ourselves of the intent of the command of Christ (1:8) that remains as relevant today as it did when He gave it.

Christianity is rooted in historical facts. The people, culture, languages, political figures, and events of Acts are all part of the real world in which the early followers of Christ lived and shared the gospel. The resurrection itself is the ultimate fact that changed everything (1 Cor. 15:16-20). To the person of Jesus Christ and His Messianic work, the followers of Christ gave unflinching witness in the realities of their world.

Historicity is important, therefore, since all we believe theologically determines how we live out those beliefs in the realities of our world and have hope for eternal life (Rom. 8:24-25). The importance of Acts cannot be overstated. The book is an absolute in the canon of the N.T. as it, in follow-up to the Gospel accounts, shows the plausibility of living as Jesus modeled and taught. Without the Book of Acts, we would have less understanding of the power of the Holy Spirit necessary in witness for Christ. We would lack the testimony of courage and faith in the face of persecution as demonstrated by the apostles. We would not have essential doctrinal clarity of the Christian view of redemptive history. We would not have the consistent summation of the gospel (the "kerygma") as preached by Peter and Paul. We would not have the definitive model of missions in the winning of people to Christ and the local church organization needed to disciple them. We would not have much of the historical background of the Pauline epistles and the epistle of James. We would not have the testimony of the passion of the early disciples as they extended their incredible witness over most of the Roman empire in only thirty years! We would not have the model of authentic resolution of fellowship issues in the clash of cultures that find common cause as being part of the body of Christ (Eph. 2:13-22). Every major theme of biblical Christianity is proclaimed in Acts; hence, the record of the sermons.

The historical records of the past impact the present and the future. Secular historians commonly use the proverb, "The only thing we learn from the past is that we don't learn from the past." The exact opposite is to be true of Christianity. The historical records of the Bible, in particular the Book of Acts, provide the models we are to emulate (1 Cor. 10:11). In so doing, we find the blessings of God, who applauds and honors our obedience.

Overview of the Book of Acts

The Acts narrative is the longest book in the Greek N.T., longer even that Matthew though both are divided into twenty-eight chapters. Its length, however, is brilliantly presented according to Acts 1:8. The witness of the Church expands accordingly. An overview helps one grasp the contents of Acts. One can use this overview to browse through Acts while noting the progress and developments chapter by chapter. These are expanded in the commentary itself.

Acts begins with a transitional connection to the Gospel of Luke and the identification of the person to whom both were addressed (chapter one). The chief character of both volumes, the risen Messiah, Jesus of Nazareth, met with the apostles for one final word before departure to heaven. The apostles were to wait in Jerusalem until they were endued with spiritual power before they began the task of carrying the witness of the gospel to the "uttermost part of the earth." One hundred and twenty believers remained in Jerusalem in obedience to Jesus.

The Day of Pentecost occurred fifty days after Passover (chapter two). Jerusalem was filled with Jewish festival

9

keepers from many countries where many different languages were spoken. The sight and sound of the Holy Spirit's coming upon the believers marked the unique beginning of this new era and relationship. The evidence of the Holy Spirit's arrival and infilling was the miraculous enabling of the believers to speak in the foreign languages of the Jewish festival keepers. They marveled to hear the disciples speak in the languages of their birth and wondered what it meant.

Taking advantage of the crowd's curiosity, Peter explained what the sign meant and proceeded to proclaim its wider intention. Succinctly, he presented the message that Jesus of Nazareth was the long-awaited Messiah. He had been crucified by some who were present but had risen from the dead. With His resurrection, He offered forgiveness to all who would repent, believe in Him, and follow with believer's baptism. Incredibly three thousand stepped forward to signal their acceptance of Peter's message and forgiveness from the risen Savior.

The gospel message was attended by miracles, including the notable healing of the congenitally lame man who lay at the Gate Beautiful of the Temple. His healing sparked not only the curiosity of those in the Temple courts, but also raised the ire of the Jewish Sanhedrin (chapters three and four). These were some of the same men who had condemned Jesus to death a few weeks previously. They had little patience and mercy for the apostles, beating them and commanding them to cease and desist all further teaching and preaching about Jesus. The apostles refused to obey them and obeyed the Lord instead.

When all was going well in spite of the intimidating threats from the Sanhedrin, hypocrisy was discovered by Peter within the fellowship of the believers (chapter five). Ananias and his wife Sapphira died as a direct result of God's immediate judgment. This sent a note of reverence and fear throughout the body as they took notice that hypocrisy was a serious sin not to be tolerated.

As the body of believers grew and their mercy ministries increased, there arose a division over the feeding of widows (chapter six). With wisdom the apostles led in the choosing of seven Spirit-filled men to oversee this ministry. That became the door of opportunity for the ministries of Philip and Stephen.

Stephen's powerful witness in some of the synagogues drew the attention and hostility of some who charged him with blasphemy and heresy. He was brought before the Sanhedrin to account for his teaching. Stephen's message is not only the longest recorded in Acts, it is also the definition of the Christian view of redemptive history (chapter seven). His message so incensed the court that they stoned him to death. He was the Church's first martyr. The perpetrators of the stoning laid their garments at the feet of young Saul of Tarsus.

With the passion of a mad wolf, Saul began his legalized campaign of terrorism against the Christians in Jerusalem and Judaea (chapter eight). Many of the believers left Judaea seeking relief but proclaimed the gospel wherever they went. Among them was Philip, who went to the long-neglected area of Samaria. With spiritual power over demons, disease, and spiritual darkness, the people responded by multitudes. When the apostles learned of the work in Samaria they visited to confirm the work. While there the Holy Spirit also confirmed the re-establishment of the relationship with the Samaritans through the gospel. It was a historic moment of restoration. Philip's ministry was also crowned by the conversion of the Ethiopian eunuch as the first Gentile convert.

The conversion of Saul of Tarsus was historic as well (chapter nine). With legal authority to press his campaign of terror, Saul was on his way to Damascus to arrest and torture believers into denial of their faith. As he neared the city, he was confronted by the risen Lord Jesus. Saul was saved and strengthened with the initial assistance of Ananias of Damascus. Saul tried to minister in Damascus, probably after spending some three years in Arabia for personal instruction from the Lord. His testimony was so bold and effective that even the city officials sought his death. He had to escape under the cover of darkness. Coming to Jerusalem, the apostles would not accept him until Barnabas was willing to risk his testimony. With the help of Barnabas, Saul became a powerful witness in Jerusalem. Thing got too hot for him there, as well, so he was sent home to Tarsus in order for things to cool down.

The conversion of Cornelius the Roman centurion (chapter ten) was both the open door for witness to the Gentiles as well as a major learning opportunity for the apostle Peter. With complementary visions to both, preparing them to meet, Peter went to the house of Cornelius in Caesarea and proclaimed the gospel to him and those gathered to hear him. The result was the conversion of the entire household of Cornelius and the confirming outpouring of the Holy

Spirit at the next stage of witness to "the uttermost part of the earth."

Returning to Jerusalem, Peter was called to account for his ministry to Gentiles (chapter eleven) by the less tolerant believers there. When Peter explained how God prepared him and Cornelius, all concluded that the door of witness had indeed been opened to the Gentiles. That door of witness was further opened as believers made their way to Antioch of Syria where multitudes of Jews and Gentiles turned to the Lord. Barnabas was sent to confirm the work and was thrilled with what he found. The demands of the work were great, and Barnabas went to fetch Saul of Tarsus to come and help him. Finding him they returned to Antioch. Here the disciples were given the name *Christians*.

Bending to the malice of the Jewish elite in Jerusalem, Herod Agrippa had the apostle James killed and imprisoned Peter for the same purpose (chapter twelve). Peter was miraculously delivered from prison as the believers earnestly prayed. His appearance at the home of John Mark caught them by surprise. Peter left for parts unknown and became a fugitive from injustice. In the meantime, Herod Agrippa gave a speech after which he was proclaimed a god by the fawning multitude. God visited him with death judgment soon afterward. His unusual death is also confirmed in the writings of Josephus.

The church at Antioch became the church of focus in the next six chapters of the Acts narrative, shifting from the church in Jerusalem. In its atmosphere of worship and zealous witness, Barnabas and Saul were called by the Holy Spirit to extend the witness of the gospel even farther (chapter thirteen).

11

Barnabas, Saul, and John Mark began the first missionary journey, taking the gospel to chief cities where they first spoke in the synagogues to the Jews. In almost every city, there were notable conversions. When the door closed to the Jews, they turned to the Gentiles where they would find more success. However, their success was often met with hostility and rejection. Paul especially was targeted and in one city was stoned and thought to be dead (chapter fourteen). Working their way back through the cities they had gone to, they established the believers and further organized local churches. They returned to Antioch of Syria with great news of many being saved and churches established, but of hostile reactions from some.

Theological controversy arose when some Jewish believers came to Antioch proclaiming that Gentiles had to be circumcised in order to be saved (chapter fifteen). Paul and Barnabas seriously confronted this error and were commissioned to go to Jerusalem and to the apostles about the controversy. Peter joined in correcting the error. James, the brother of the Lord Jesus and senior pastor of the Jerusalem church, wisely concluded the discussions and offered four decrees to request of Gentile believers that would help with the cultural differences in fellowship. These were unanimously accepted. An official letter was drawn up to be carried to the Gentile churches with the confirming testimony of men chosen to represent the council's decision. Silas was among those chosen.

The second missionary journey arose with the best of intentions but saw the breakup of Barnabas and Saul as a missionary team. Paul chose Silas and Barnabas chose the restored John Mark, resulting in two missionary teams. The entire focus of the Acts narrative shifts to the ministry of Paul as the central leader. He and Silas, joined by Timothy and Luke, journey to Philippi (chapter sixteen) at the special direction of the Holy Spirit. Here they win Lydia and her household to the Lord. After confronting a demon-possessed girl Paul and Silas are cast into prison. A timely midnight earthquake loosens their bonds and gives them opportunity to win the jailer and his household to the Lord. Appealing to their rights as Roman citizens, Paul and Silas receive an apology from the city officials and move on.

Traveling south to Thessalonica they were able to speak in the synagogue for only three Sabbaths and with mixed results—as usual (chapter seventeen). When persecution arose, they were forced to move on to Berea where they were met with Jews who searched the Scriptures to verify the message of the risen Messiah. Many were converted but persecutors from Thessalonica followed them and Paul was forced to leave while Silas and Timothy remained to minister to the new converts. Paul traveled on to Athens where he was engaged by the philosophical Athenians and brought to the Areopagus for a hearing. Here Paul delivered his first message to a strictly Gentile audience, who had no biblical reference. Even with that a few responded in saving faith to the gospel.

Paul moved on to Corinth (chapter eighteen) for an extended and fruitful ministry. Here he met and joined with Aquila and Priscilla, who become faithful and trusted helpers. From here he determined to return to Jerusalem and Antioch of Syria, but he chose Ephesus as his next strategic city. Leaving Aquila and Priscilla there, Paul traveled on to Judaea in completion of the second missionary journey.

Meanwhile, back in Ephesus, a dynamic and brilliant Apollos arrived and caught the attention of Aquila and Priscilla. He needed grounding, so they helped him, and he moved on to Corinth. Paul had remained in Antioch of Syria for a while, then began his third missionary journey traveling alone and overland to the churches previously established. When Paul returned to Ephesus (chapter nineteen) he found some of the last disciples of John the Baptist. With Paul's instruction they were updated in their faith and the Holy Spirit was manifested uniquely to signal the end of the O.T. era. At Ephesus, Paul enjoyed another long and fruitful ministry but had to confront demonism and sorcery. The ministry was so effective, and so many were saved out of idolatry, that the guild of the silversmiths who made graven images for the Diana (Artemis) cult rose up in protest, threatening Paul's life. The city was stirred into chaos. Finally, the chief officer of the city calmed the crowd and dismissed them.

From Ephesus Paul embarked on a return trip to Judaea (chapter twenty), confirming the churches along the way. At Troas, he spoke all night and restored a young man who fell asleep and fell to his death while Paul preached. Moving on, Paul met the Ephesian elders on the shore at Miletus where he charged them with faithfulness and watchfulness. Here he informed them of the Holy Spirit's witness, that trouble awaited him in Jerusalem.

Paul traveled to Judaea, with his ship making port at Caesarea (chapter twenty-one). Here he met with Philip and others related, through the Holy Spirit, that they too were aware of the trouble that awaited him in Jerusalem. Paul insisted on going anyway, believing it to be God's will for his life. When he arrived in Jerusalem he met with James and the elders, reporting to them the results of the third missionary journey and delivering to them the famine relief offering that had been gathered from the Gentile churches for the Judaean brethren.

James informed Paul of serious rumors regarding him and counseled him to demonstrate his commitment to Jewish customs and practices. Paul agreed and began a period of observance and ceremonial cleansing in the Temple. While here he was recognized by Asian Jews who hated him. When they discovered him in the Temple they immediately incited efforts to kill him. Providentially, a Roman guard rescued Paul and removed him from the mob.

As Paul was being escorted up the stairs in custody, he was permitted to speak to the crowd who had beaten him severely. Here he gave the first of his testimonial defenses (chapter twenty-two). Paul was not released but kept in custody. The Jewish high court was assembled to deal with him.

When Paul appeared before the Sanhedrin (chapter twenty-three), he appealed to the belief of the Pharisees regarding the resurrection as the basis of the controversy about him. The court itself became so divided that Paul had to be rescued again by the Roman guard. When the Roman official learned of a conspiracy to kill him, he transferred Paul by night to Caesarea where he was kept until further notice. An official letter detailing Paul's arrest and innocence, written by the centurion in charge, accompanied him and was presented to the Roman Governor, Felix.

Five days later the high priest, representative elders from the Sanhedrin, and their professional prosecutor appeared before Felix in Caesarea to press the issue against Paul (chapter twenty-four). Paul successfully defended himself and was afforded the opportunity to witness directly to the Governor and his Jewish wife, Drusilla. Regardless of Paul's innocence of the charges, Felix was more motivated by political favor and left Paul imprisoned at Caesarea for two more years.

Chapter twenty-five records a change in Roman leadership with the appointment of Festus as the Governor. In a political courtesy visit to Jerusalem, the Jews re-introduced Paul's case to him and received Festus's promise that he would attend to it back in Caesarea. Paul had to defend himself again and was shown, again, to be innocent. Festus wanted to accommodate the Jews by having Paul return to Jerusalem for another hearing. To prevent what he knew would be a deadly trip, Paul appealed his case to Caesar. This set the arrangements that took Paul to Rome.

Though Paul was innocent of all the charges against him, Festus was at a loss of how to compose the official documents appealing to Caesar. When Herod Agrippa II and his sister, Bernice, paid a visit, Festus enlisted his help. For Agrippa to hear the case against Paul, the elite of Caesarea were called to a meeting where Paul was brought before them. Here he eloquently and brilliantly spoke for himself (chapter twenty-six) with his defense testimonial. He concluded his defense with an appeal to all present to believe savingly in Jesus the Messiah. His innocence was asserted

again, but the course had been set. He must be sent to Rome.

Paul's famous voyage and shipwreck is the subject of chapter twenty-seven. Luke accompanied Paul through the trip and recorded in great detail each leg of the journey. His narrative reads like a suspense novel as he charts the course, records conversations, and highlights the leadership of Paul through the storm. Providentially, God not only protected Paul but delivered all those on the ship even when it crashed on the rocky shoals of the Island of Melita (Malta).

As if deliverance through the storm and shipwreck were not enough, while helping with stoking the fires on the beach of Melita, a poisonous snake bit Paul (chapter twenty-eight). The islanders took this to mean he was a murderer and divine justice was being meted out. But Paul suffered no harm and the islanders changed their opinion, regarding him as a god. Such is the stuff of superstition. The "chief man" of the island attended to their needs as Paul was instrumental in bringing healing to many of the islanders. The entire manifest of the ship's passengers was treated with kindness and provisioned for the remaining leg of the journey to Rome.

Luke appears to regard their arrival at Puteoli in Italy as a victory of accomplishment. With the encouragement of believers they met along the way to Rome, they arrived in Rome itself where Paul was given much freedom though he was still in custody. From his own rented house, he met with and ministered to those who came. The Acts record closes with Paul living in his own rented quarters, free to minister but still in custody and chained to a Roman soldier.

ACTS

The Book of Acts is indispensable in the biblical narrative of what happened with the followers of Jesus of Nazareth, the risen Messiah. To know its contents is to appreciate the kind of faith demonstrated in the lives of those documented, who were willing to give everything to the cause of Christ. In the sermons and speeches of believers, Christianity is defined in contrast to the stagnant and lifeless Judaism that had become the religious establishment in Israel for centuries. The "hope of Israel" had been in its Messianic promises. When He did finally come, that hope had been so obscured that the Jews did not recognize Him. They rejected not only Him but His followers as well. Even so, His followers would not be silenced. That is the record of Acts that should continue in the Church until the return of Jesus Christ.

ACTS

Authorities and Events of the Time of the Acts (all years are A.D.)

Roman Emperors	Governors of Judea*	Key Events in Acts**
14-37 Tiberius		
	26 *Pontius Pilate*	
		30 or 33 The resurrection of Jesus and Pentecost (Acts 1-2)
		30-32 or 33-35 Early witness of the church in Jerusalem (Acts 3-5) (Acts 4:6: Peter and John before Caiaphas, Jewish high priest since c. 18, whose father-in-law Annas, high priest from c. 6/7-c. 18, was still influential)
		32 or 35 Martyrdom of Stephen (Acts 7) 32 or 35 Witness by Philip in Samaria (Acts 8:5-24) 33 or 36 Witness by Peter in Samaria (Acts 8:25) 33 or 36 Conversion of the Ethiopian Eunuch (Acts 8:26-39)
	36 Marcellus	33 or 36 Conversion of Saul of Tarsus (Acts 9:1-19a) 33-35 or 36-38 Sojourn of Saul in Arabia (Gal. 1:15-18\ 35/36 or 38/39 Witness of Saul in Damascus and Jerusalem (Acts 9:22-29)
37-41 Gaius/Caligula	37 Marullus	36-41 or 39-41 Silent years of Saul in Tarsus of Cilicia (Acts 9:30)
		36/37 Conversion of Cornelius (Acts 10:1-48)
		38/39-42 The witness of the church in Antioch of Syria (Acts 11:19-26)
41-54 Claudius	41 *Herod Agrippa I*	
		42/43 Famine predicted and relief offering begun (Acts 11:27-30) 42/43 Martyrdom of apostle James (Acts 12:1-2)
	44 Cuspius Fadus	44 Judgment-death of Herod Agrippa I (Acts 12:20-23) 44-51 Famine in Judaea (Acts 11:28) 45/46—47/48 First missionary journey of Paul (Acts 13:1-14:28)
	46 Tiberius Iulius Alexander	

	48 Ventidius Cumanus	
		49/50 The Jerusalem Council (Acts 15:1-29) 50-52 Second missionary journey of Paul (Acts 15:40—18:22) 51/52 Claudius expels Jews from Rome (Acts 18:2) 51/52 Gallio becomes proconsul in Corinth, rejects charges against Paul (Acts 18:12-17)
	52 Artonius *Felix*	52/53 Confirmation of Apollos by Aquila and Priscilla (Acts 18:24-28)
54-68 Nero		52/53—56/57 Third missionary journey of Paul (Acts 18:23—21:16) 57/58 Paul's arrest in in Judaea, sent to Caesarea (Acts 21:17—23:35) (Acts 23:2; 24:1: Paul before Ananias, Jewish high priest from c. 58-c. 59) 58/59 Paul before Felix (Acts 24:1-26) 58/59 Paul begins two years in prison in Caesarea (Acts 24:27)
	60 Porcius *Festus*	60 Paul before Festus (Acts 25:1—26:32) (Acts 25:13—26:32: Paul also before Herod Agrippa II, ruling part of Galilee and Northern Palestine and the Transjordan from c. 52, son of Herod Agrippa I) 60 Paul's journey to Rome (Acts 27:1—28:15) 60-62 Paul's two-year imprisonment in Rome (Acts 28:16-31)

* Those in bold italics are mentioned in the New Testament. All were Roman-appointed procurators except for Herod Agrippa I, who was a Roman-approved "client-king" over the Jews in Judaea.

** The two sets of dates (before the end of Paul's silent years at Tarsus) reflect differences of opinion about the date of the crucifixion of Jesus, whether early (30) or late (33). From about 41 on, the dates are fairly confident but are often less than precise.

This commentary includes maps of Paul's three missionary journeys and Paul's journey to Rome. Each map is located at the beginning of the corresponding Scripture text.

ACTS

OUTLINE OF THE ACTS OF THE APOSTLES

I. Prologue, 1:1-5
   A. Link to the "former treatise," 1:1-3
   B. The Command to Wait, 1:4-5
II. The Empowering of the Holy Spirit for Witness, 1:6—2:47
   A. The Purpose for Waiting: Empowered Witness, 1:6-8
   B. The Ascension of Christ, 1:9-11
   C. Obedient Waiting in an Upper Room, 1:12-14
   D. Selection of a Replacement for Judas Iscariot, 1:15-26
      1. The defection of Judas Iscariot, 1:15-20
      2. The election of Matthias, 1:21-26
   E. The Filling of the Holy Spirit, 2:1-13
      1. The miraculous event, 2:1-4
      2. The wider audience responds, 2:5-13
   F. Peter's First Sermon, 2:14-36
      1. Appeal to the prophesy of Joel: "this is that," 2:14-21
      2. Jesus of Nazareth, the resurrected Christ, 2:22-36
         a. His approval by God, 2:22-24
         b. Confirmation from Psalm 16:8-11, 2:25-31
         c. Proclamation of Jesus of Nazareth as Lord and Christ, 2:32-36
   G. Response to Peter's Message, 2:37-41
   H. Early Community Life of the Church, 2:42-47
III. The Church's Witness in Jerusalem, 3:1—8:1a
   A. Healing of the Lame Beggar, 3:1-11
   B. Peter's Second Sermon, 3:12-26
   C. Peter and John on Trial Before the Sanhedrin, 4:1-22
      1. The arrest of Peter and John, 4:1-4
      2. The arraignment before the Sanhedrin, 4:5-7
      3. The answers to the charges, 4:8-22
         a. Response from Peter and John, 4:8-12
         b. Response from the Sanhedrin, 4:13-22
   D. The Report to the Church, 4:23-31
   E. The Church Continues Community Life, 4:32-37
   F. The Deceit of Ananias and Sapphira, 5:1-11
   G. Further Signs and Wonders by the Apostles, 5:12-16
   H. All the Apostles Arrested and Arraigned Before the Sanhedrin, 5:17-42
      1. Arrested by the Sanhedrin, released by the angel of the Lord, 5:17-26
      2. Arraigned before the Sanhedrin, 5:27-40
         a. The testimony of the apostles, 5:27-32
         b. The reasoning of Gamaliel, 5:33-40
      3. The continuing witness of the Apostles, 5:41-42
   I. Further Organization of the Community Life of the Church, 6:1-7
   J. The Witness of Stephen, 6:8—8:1a

ACTS

1. Stephen's ministry, 6:8-10
2. Stephen's arrest, 6:11-15
3. The Message of Stephen to the Sanhedrin, 7:1-53
    a. The time of Abraham and the Patriarchs, 7:1-8
    b. The time of Joseph, 7:9-16
    c. The time of Moses, 7:17-43
        (1) The first forty years, 7:17-22
        (2) The second forty years, 7:23-29
        (3) The third forty years, 7:30-43
    d. The time of David and Solomon, 7:44-50
    e. Stephen's pointed application, 7:51-53
4. The martyrdom of Stephen, 7:54—8:1a
    a. Stephen's vision of Jesus, 7:54-56
    b. Stephen is stoned to death, 7:57—8:1a

IV. The Church's Witness in Judaea and Samaria, 8:1b-40
   A. Persecution and Dispersion Throughout Judaea and Samaria, 8:1b-4
   B. The Witness of Philip, 8:5-40
      1. Initial ministry in Samaria, 8:5-8
      2. The conversion of Simon the sorcerer, 8:9-25
      3. The conversion of the Ethiopian eunuch, 8:26-40

V. The Church's Witness "to the Uttermost Part of the Earth," 9:1—21:17
   A. The Conversion of Saul of Tarsus, 9:1-31
      1. Saul encounters the living Christ, 9:1-9
      2. Ananias sent to help Saul, 9:10-19a
      3. Saul preaches in Damascus, 9:19b-25
      4. Saul comes to Jerusalem as a Christ-follower, 9:26-31
   B. Peter's Ministry in Western Judaea, 9:32-43
      1. The healing of Aeneas, 9:32-35
      2. The raising of Tabitha (Dorcas) from the dead, 9:36-43
   C. The Conversion of Cornelius the Roman Centurion, 10:1—11:18
      1. The vision of Cornelius, 10:1-8
      2. The vision of Peter, 10:9-16
      3. Peter's witness to the household of Cornelius, 10:17-48
         a. Peter meets with the representatives of Cornelius, 10:17-23a
         b. Exchange between Peter and Cornelius in Caesarea, 10:23b-33
         c. Peter's message to the household of Cornelius, 10:34-43
         d. The Holy Spirit falls on the household of Cornelius, 10:44-48
      4. Peter's testimony of the conversion of the household of Cornelius, 11:1-18
         a. Contention with Peter at Jerusalem, 11:1-3
         b. Peter's testimony and the glorious agreement, 11:4-18
   D. The Establishing of the Church at Antioch, 11:19-30
      1. Many at Antioch converted upon hearing the gospel, 11:19-21
      2. The Jerusalem church sends Barnabas to confirm, 11:22-26
      3. The beginning of the famine relief offering, 11:27-30

ACTS

E. Herod Targets the Church for Persecution, 12:1-25
   1. James is killed, and Peter is imprisoned, 12:1-19
      a. The killing of James by Herod, 12:1-2
      b. Peter is imprisoned by Herod but released by the angel of the Lord, 12:3-19
   2. The death of Herod, 12:20-23
   3. The church continues in ministry, 12:24-25
F. The First Missionary Journey, 13:1—14:28
   1. The call and commissioning of Barnabas and Saul, 13:1-3
   2. Witness on the island of Cyprus, 13:4-12
      a. First witness, in the synagogues, 13:4-5
      b. The conversion of Sergius Paulus, 13:6-12
   3. John Mark abandons the work, 13:13
   4. Witness in Antioch of Pisidia, 13:14-52
      a. Paul's first recorded sermon to Jews, 13:14-41
         (1) The setting, 13:14-15
         (2) The sermon, 13:16-41
            (a) God's favor in choosing Israel, 13:16-25
            (b) God's promise of the Messiah fulfilled in Jesus, 13:26-37
            (c) Paul's appeal and warning, 13:38-41
      b. Gentile opportunity, Jewish opposition, 13:42-52
   5. Witness in Iconium, 14:1-7
   6. Witness at Lystra and Derbe, 14:8-21a
      a. Healing o the lame man, 14:8-10
      b. Barnabas and Paul proclaimed as gods, 14:11-18
      c. Jews from Antioch and Iconium stir opposition, 14:19-21a
   7. Paul and Barnabas return to Antioch, 14:21b-28
G. The Council at Jerusalem, 15:1-35
   1. The controversy, 15:1-5
   2. The consideration of the controversy, 15:6-12
   3. The counsel of James, 15:13-21
   4. The conclusion that was reached, 15:22-29
   5. Conferring with the church at Antioch, 15:30-35
H. The Second Missionary Journey, 15:36—18:22
   1. Division and separation of Paul and Barnabas, 15:36-41
   2. Return to Lystra and Derbe: Timothy joins the team, 16:1-5
   3. The call to Macedonia, 16:6-10
   4. Witness in Philippi, 16:11-40
      a. The conversion of Lydia, 16:11-15
      b. Deliverance of the spirit-possessed damsel, 16:16-18
      c. Imprisonment of Paul and Silas, 16:19-40
         (1) Arrested on false charges, 16:19-24
         (2) The conversion of the jailer and his household, 16:25-34
         (3) Humiliation of the city leaders, 16:35-40
   5. Witness in Thessalonica, 17:1-9

6. Witness in Berea, 17:10-15
7. Witness in Athens, 17:16-34
    a. In the synagogue and market, 17:16-17
    b. Challenged by the Epicureans and Stoics, 17:18-21
    c. Paul's message to the Areopagus, 17:22-31
    d. Response to Paul's message, 17:32-34
8. Witness in Corinth, 18:1-17
    a. Joining with Aquila and Priscilla, 18:1-3
    b. Witness to the Jews, 18:4-11
    c. Trial before Gallio, 18:12-17
9. Paul returns to Antioch in Syria, 18:18-22

I. The Third Missionary Journey, 18:23—21:16
    1. Strengthening the churches, 18:23
    2. Witness in Ephesus, 18:24—19:41
        a. Apollos, 18:24-28
        b. The Ephesian disciples and the baptism of John, 19:1-7
        c. In the synagogue and school of Tyrannus, 19:8-12
        d. Encounter with Jewish exorcists, 19:13-20
        e. Paul's intention to go to Jerusalem, then Rome, 19:21-22
        f. The riot of the cult worshipers against the believers, 19:23-41
            (1) The charge of Demetrius and the silversmiths, 19:23-28
            (2) The frenzied mob in the theater, 19:29-34
            (3) The town-clerk dismisses the assembly, 19:35-41
    3. Journey to Jerusalem, 20:1—21:16
        a. Paul returns to Macedonia and Achaia, 20:1-5
        b. Paul at Troas and the restoration of Eutychus, 20:6-12
        c. From Troas to Miletus, 20:13-16
        d. Paul addresses the Ephesian elders at Miletus, 20:17-38
            (1) Paul's personal ministry, 20:17-27
            (2) Charge to the elders, 20:28-35
            (3) Tearful farewell, 20:36-38
        e. From Miletus to Tyre, 21:1-6
        f. From Tyre to Caesarea, 21:7-14
        g. From Caesarea to Jerusalem, 21:15-16

VI. Paul's Witness Before Kings and Rulers, 21:17—28:31
    A. Meeting With James and the Elders at Jerusalem, 21:17-26
    B. The Riot Over Paul in the Temple, 21:27-40a
        1. Paul accosted and beaten by the temple mob, 21:27-30
        2. Paul rescued by the Roman guard, 21:31-40a
    C. Paul's Defense Before the Temple Mob, 21:40b—22:21
        1. His appeal to be heard, 21:40b—22:2
        2. His life before conversion to Christ, 22:3-5
        3. His conversion to Christ, 22:6-16
        4. His vision in Jerusalem and commission from the Lord, 22:17-21
    D. Paul's Exchange With the Roman Tribune, 22:22-29

The life of Jesus of Nazareth that culminated in His resurrection and ascension, as recorded in Luke and Acts respectively, raises the question, "What happened to the followers of Jesus Christ?" His was a life unlike any other. It culminated in an event unlike any other. It was the testimony of His followers that Jesus was literally, physically raised from the dead. They claimed to be eyewitnesses who saw Him, spoke with Him, interacted with Him, even ate with Him—for many days following their discovery that His body was not in the tomb where they laid Him. His appearances to them on that day when He had them physically touch His body (Jn. 20:24-29) were convincing proofs of His reality. That not only changed their lives, it changed everything.

How did it change everything? How did it change them? What did they do with that information? Did they follow His directions to tell the world about Him? Luke provides his answer to those questions in the Acts of the Apostles. His is an apologetic of the validity of Christianity on every level of faith and lifestyle, as demonstrated in the lives and messages recorded in the narrative. Although Theophilus is named as the recipient of the records Luke is presenting, it seems clear that a wider audience is also expected. This is intended by Jesus' command to witness this message "unto the uttermost part of the earth" (1:8).

I. PROLOGUE (1:1-5)

In beginning his writings, Luke, the author of the Gospel and the Book of Acts, uses a formal literary prologue unlike any other N. T. writer. Its usage is not without purpose and is, at least, two-fold. First, in using a literary structure, Luke distinguishes himself as more than just a keeper of diaries and a collector of interesting stories. Fitzmyer (80) remarks that Luke is a remarkable Hellenistic writer.

Second, the intentional use of a second literary prologue also serves as a clear connection with the previous volume, the Gospel of Luke, as well as an introduction to the present volume. Indeed, the two volumes by the same author have been acknowledged since the second century as a "History of Christian Origins" (Bruce, *Acts* 15).

A brief survey of commentators shows differing opinions on the length of the prologue to the Acts narrative (Stott 21; Bruce, *Acts* 30; Harrison 35; Fitzmyer 191). Beginning with a reference to the Gospel of Luke, then using a command from Jesus to transition to the Acts narrative, the most natural break in this opening statement seems to come at the end of verse 5. These first five verses establish a literary bridge that connects Luke's record in his Gospel—which concludes with the most miraculous event in history, the resurrection of Jesus Christ—to his record of what happened to the followers of Jesus Christ. These two volumes present the written apologetic of real people, places, events, and testimonials with which Luke wants to establish the faith of Theophilus and all who read his accounts.

A. Link to the "former treatise" (1:1-3)

1 The former treatise have I made, O Theophilus, of all that Jesus began both to do and teach,

2 Until the day in which he was taken up, after that he through the Holy Ghost had given commandments unto the apostles whom he had chosen:
3 To whom also he shewed himself alive after his passion by many infallible proofs, being seen of them forty days, and speaking of the things pertaining to the kingdom of God:

Luke begins his second volume with a reference to the first, the Gospel of Luke. In doing so, he clearly takes ownership of the writing and links the two together. Bock (51-53) lists five distinct links between the two volumes showing that the Acts of the Apostles is an essential outgrowth and continuation of the Gospel of Luke:

"First, Luke calls the first book a 'former account'... Second, the address to Theophilus recalls the figure introduced to us in Luke 1:3. The overlapping address shows that Luke composed Acts as a single story line extending from His Gospel...Third, this link to Luke's Gospel is further confirmed in Acts 1:4-5, which marks the connection with John the Baptist, the figure with whom Luke's Gospel begins...Fourth, the overlapping accounts of the ascension...Fifth, the direct allusion back to the instruction given...to await the Spirit and be witnesses."

The same person, Theophilus (meaning "lover of God" or "loved by God"), is addressed as the recipient of the book, only this time with no qualifying title ("most excellent" in Lk. 1:3). Geldenhuys (53) sees the title as indicat-

ing high political rank (compare 24:3) and suggests that Theophilus was but one of many high ranking officials of Luke's acquaintance. As the Acts record will show, Luke would have interaction with many such high ranking officials, especially at Antioch of Syria (13:1). Lenski (21) proposes that the difference in the uses of the name shows that Theophilus was not a believer when Luke wrote the prologue to the Gospel but now he is. This second volume would serve him as evidence of faith displayed in the lives of many others, including many of high civil and social rank such as he.

Some infer that the intent of the name usage is not personal but a general appellation with the sense of "dear Christian reader." However, the name "Theophilus" was an ordinary personal name found in common use as early as the second century (Bruce, *Acts* 29). There is no good reason to discount the personal relationship Luke had with Theophilus or that Acts was specifically addressed to him—as Paul addressed his letters. The personalization of the writing is appropriate because the Lord always targets the human heart with His truth. His design is to convince men of the spiritual validity of the words and works of Jesus Christ. In that sense, all of us are "Theophilus." The Book of Acts is addressed to us.

Luke uses the word *all* in his summary of the works and teaching of Jesus. Certainly this must be qualified to mean all that Luke chose to write for his purposes. (For a comparison of Luke's selection of the activities and teachings of Jesus with the other synoptic Gospels see Geldenhuys 43-44; Picirilli, *Mark* 1-5). According to the apostle John, there were many other things Jesus did that are not included in his Gospel (Jn. 21:35). Although John probably used hyperbole in saying this, Jesus certainly did many things not recorded in any of the Gospel accounts. One such statement by Jesus is recorded in Acts 20:35, when Paul was speaking to the Ephesian elders at Troas. We can reasonably assume that all He did would be extremely interesting to know about if there had been recordings made of them. However, there are no additional records and writings, awaiting discovery, that would add content to our Bibles or change what we know about the person of Jesus Christ. There have been many attempts throughout church history to alter and add to the Scriptures. Dozens of religious writings from the first three centuries and later, that claim some affiliation with Jesus and the apostles, have been known about and diligently studied. None of these have passed the tests of canonicity (EDT 140). But those things that are recorded for us should be considered as divinely selected (1 Cor. 10:11). When one reads the Book of Acts it must be remembered that these people, places, and events were indeed historically real in every sense of the word. They are recorded because in some measure they contribute to God's work in the world. These are models from which to learn and be established in our faith.

The statement "began both to do and teach" summarizes the actions and teachings of the Lord Jesus as recorded in Luke's Gospel. The word *began* should be noted. Luke selects events, people, sermons, conversations, etc., that help him achieve his purpose of showing the continuing work of Christ through His followers. In that sense, what Jesus began during His life and ministry continues in His church today (Bruce, *Acts* 30; Polhill, *Acts* 79-80; Stott 32; Bock 52-53; (Ridderbos 7). This will be addressed at the conclusion of Acts in commenting on Luke's seemingly abrupt ending.

The ascension of Christ into Heaven is a notable event for Luke in both Acts and his Gospel account. Lenski (21) refers to the ascension event as "the terminus of the Gospel." It is the culminating encounter of Jesus with His disciples just prior to His departure back into Heaven (Jn. 3:13). Of the Gospel writers, only Luke (24:51, Acts 1:2, 9-11) and Mark (16:19) record the ascension of Christ into Heaven as a separate event. Mark adds that, after Jesus ascended into Heaven, He "sat on the right hand of God" (16:19). Later, as Stephen was dying from wounds inflicted while being stoned (7:56), he was given a glimpse into Heaven where the Lord Jesus was "standing on the right hand of God." The exalted position of Christ is testimony to His finished work of redemption (Outlaw 239). Further, His continuing intercession for His saints shows that the Savior is neither removed from nor reticent about the needs of His followers.

As Luke records it, the ascension event at the beginning of Acts shows Jesus' place of authority and observation over the works of His followers. He is the Lord enthroned over us and over all the works of His hands. But He is not removed from us, as will be evident in His timely appearances to His witnesses in the Acts record and especially in the indwelling presence of the Holy Spirit.

The phrase *taken up* reminds us of two other figures who were transported directly to Heaven from earth, Enoch (Gen. 5:24; Heb. 11:5) and Elijah (2

Kgs. 2:9-11). While these were righteous men whom God favored in this unique way, Jesus was more than just a righteous man. He was (and is) the Son of God. Further details of that last exchange with the disciples will be added in vv. 6-11, but here it provides transitional context.

Luke provides an insight that the work of the Holy Spirit was directly connected with the ministry of the Lord Jesus in instructing His apostles: "he through the Holy Ghost had given commandments." He does not state this in the Gospel account (Lk. 24:44-49), but it certainly would be the case (Polhill, *Acts* 80). The work of the Holy Spirit had been an integral part of Jesus' teaching about His ministry (Jn. 16:7-15). It would be only a few days later that they would enter into this new era of relationship with the Holy Spirit.

That the apostles were aware of the Holy Spirit and His teaching ministry is clear from the Upper Room instruction they received earlier (Jn. 13—16). There had been, also, an initial receiving of the Holy Spirit into their own lives when Jesus appeared to them Sunday evening on the day of His resurrection (Jn. 20:19-23). This would culminate later in the incredible filling of the Holy Spirit on the Day of Pentecost. Stallings (281-282) discusses these separate, yet connected, experiences as an initial indwelling culminating in being filled.

Luke asserts the resurrection of Jesus Christ as tangible truth, not just a novel idea. That "he shewed himself alive" literally means He "presented Himself living" (Greek *parestesen heauton zonta*). The use of the term *passion* (Greek *pathein*, constative aorist) has the concept of suffering (Acts 17:3; 26:23) and often summarizes the events directly related to the death of Christ. It shows His suffering as completed. It is impossible to separate the provision of Christ for the sins of humanity from His suffering for those sins. He "shewed himself alive" only after He had suffered death, at the hands of men, in the most horrible and cruel form possible (Acts 2:23-24).

Christ did indeed suffer as no man has ever suffered before or since, taking upon Himself the penalty of death and hell for all men for all time (Rom 3:22-26; 5:17-19). His salvation provision was sufficient for all men, but efficient only for all who savingly believe. It was His unique, once-for-all *passion*, suffering for sin as our God-provided substitute, that forms the core of the gospel of Jesus Christ.

The unique message of the gospel of Jesus Christ, as opposed to all other religious systems and beliefs, is that He arose literally, bodily, from the dead (1 Cor. 15:1-4, 17). Indeed, this is the central foundational truth of the gospel of Christ, without which it fails (Forlines, *Quest* 181). This truth will be the central and unwavering motivation and message of the witnesses throughout the Book of Acts.

The *infallible proofs* (Greek *tekmarion*) mean things surely and plainly known. Those alluded to in Luke's Gospel would include the following: (1) the stone rolled away from the grave entrance (Lk. 24:2); (2) the empty grave (Lk. 24:3); (3) the discarded grave clothes (Lk. 24:12); (4) the appearance of Jesus to the two travelers on the road to Emmaus and their seeing Him, though at first they did not recognize Him (Lk. 24:13-29); (5) eating fish and bread with the Emmaus road witnesses (Lk. 24:30); (6) Jesus' personal appearance to the eleven apostles in Jerusalem and their seeing Him (Lk. 24:36-39); (7) touching His nail-scarred hands and feet (Lk. 24:39-40); (8) eating fish and honeycomb with the apostles in Jerusalem (Lk. 24:41-43); and (9) verbal communication with these witnesses. Seeing, hearing, touching, eating, all being done repeatedly, provided some of the proofs that He was the *living* Christ. These were entirely sufficient for the apostles and other first generation believers. They witnessed His living presence and boldly proclaimed its reality, staking their very lives on its validity.

One may add to that list the appearances cited by the apostle Paul in 1 Corinthians 15:1-8. The date for the writing of 1 Corinthians was somewhere between A.D. 55 and 56 (Picirilli, *Paul* 136). Even if the earliest date for the writing of Acts is correct, 57-59 (see Introduction), it is entirely probable that Luke was well aware of Paul's list. But Paul's list was not Luke's reference point. His perspective was the eyewitness account of one or more of the apostles and other witnesses who would have been present at the resurrection event and later. Luke was a second generation believer and would not have seen personally the risen Savior; at least, he does not record that he did.

The appearances of the resurrected Christ continued over a forty-day period between Passover and Pentecost. Apparently, He came and went (somewhere) continually during those forty days (Polhill, *Acts* 81; Bock 55) for the purpose of further instruction and confirmation, "speaking of the things pertaining to the kingdom of God."

The *kingdom of God* was a central theme in Jesus' earthly ministry. Luke uses the phrase some thirty-two times in

his Gospel and six times in Acts. Bock (55) summarizes the "kingdom of God" as "God's promised rule that comes with Jesus's messianic program and activity." The phrase *kingdom of heaven* is a variation of the same concept (EDT 607-608; Crabtree 49-50).

Although the apostles had literally lived with Jesus for over three years, heard Him speak, and seen His miracles, such a life as that which Jesus lived must have been overwhelming to them. Added to that was the culminating drama of betrayal, being forsaken by all of the apostles, trial, denial by Peter, scourging, crucifixion, and resurrection; all of this would have added to that sense of being overwhelmed. No wonder Jesus met with them for forty days to confirm and instruct! It was a time to regain perspective, to refocus, to prepare for the next step in redemption's plan. They needed all the instruction they could get for the task assigned to them.

B. The Command to Wait (1:4-5)

4 And, being assembled together with *them*, commanded them that they should not depart from Jerusalem, but wait for the promise of the Father, which, *saith he*, ye have heard of me.
5 For John truly baptized with water; but ye shall be baptized with the Holy Ghost not many days hence.

The specific place where Jesus met with the disciples is not stated. Since the Feast of Pentecost was approaching and Jesus had already instructed them to tarry in the city of Jerusalem (Lk. 24:49), the place of meeting might very well have been in the city of Jerusalem. Some take the occasion as one of table fellowship and perhaps spending the night with them (Polhill, *Acts* 82; Bock 59; Fitzmyer 203; Lenski 26). Of course, this would certainly be appropriate to the account of His actions following His resurrection, as both Luke and John record. But the occasion is not merely for table fellowship. The presence of the Supreme Guest hardly made this an ordinary meal occasion. It was primed with purpose.

In this setting, Jesus specifically commands the apostles to remain in Jerusalem and wait for "the promise of the Father." This was a promise of such great importance and impact that its implementation would not only alter their lives but would change the world forever. Table fellowship with Jesus was never trivial or boring.

It may be that the disciples had been coming and going to Jerusalem, some of which was in obedience since Jesus had instructed them to go to Galilee (Mt. 28:16; Jn. 21:1-22). Now they were to remain in Jerusalem (Polhill, *Acts* 83). They needed to adjust their activities: literally, "stop departing" (Greek present tense). Preparation for ministry always includes a time of "waiting" for God's Hand of power and favor.

The *promise of the Father* is defined as "ye shall be baptized with the Holy Ghost." It was a promise unparalleled yet expected (Ger 20-21). While the promise is a part of the message of John the Baptist (Mt. 3:11), it is a Messianic prophecy rooted in the O. T. (Isa. 32:15; 44:3; Joel 2:28-32). As John the Baptist heralded its soon fulfillment, the Messiah Himself was at that very moment coming down the road to be baptized. Later, Peter understood the O. T. prophecy

very well as he explained the experience of the descent of the Holy Spirit upon them at Pentecost. He declared the event to be the direct fulfillment of the Joel prophecy (2:16-21). In meeting with the apostles and disciples in Jerusalem, Jesus is preparing these chosen vessels for the next major phase of God's redemptive plan.

It is significant that Jesus connected the apostles to the ministry of John the Baptist when He said, "John truly baptized with water" (Lk. 3:16). Indeed, some of Jesus' apostles had first been close followers of John the Baptist (Jn. 1:35-40). John's message and baptism with water foreshadowed the baptism of the Holy Spirit and was preparatory (Bruce, *Acts* 35; Bock 57). John served as the Elijah-herald (Mal. 3:1, 4:5; Mt. 11:14) for the Messiah and had been confirmed as such by the Lord Jesus (Mt. 11:7-15; Lk. 6:19-30). The baptism of the Messiah, however, was greater and involved a new relationship with the very Spirit of God, the second person of the Triune God. Poignantly, Jesus specifically tells them that they personally would experience this baptism "not many days hence."

Summary
(1:1-5)

The first five verses of Acts are clearly transitional from the Gospel of Luke. Further, the address of the narrative to Theophilus and Luke's personal ownership of the writing ("the former treatise have I made") leave us with little doubt as to the authorship and integrity of the writing. These verses provide for us the principle of Christ's continuing interaction with His church ("began both to do and teach") throughout the Book of Acts and until today. It is absolutely clear that the first-generation followers of Jesus were fully persuaded of Christ's literal, bodily resurrection ("shewed himself alive after his passion by many infallible proofs"). This was the ultimate truth that compelled them to witness as they did. The promise of a special enabling relationship with the Holy Spirit of God ("ye shall be baptized with the Holy Ghost") would have given them encouragement and confirmation of the task Jesus assigned them. That event would soon take place in their lives. Reading these verses should leave one with a keen sense of anticipation of what the rest of the narrative holds.

Application: Preaching and Teaching the Passage

Exegetical Outline of the Text: 1. The Address of the Book (1:1a). 2. The Purpose of the Book (1:1b-2a). 3. The Apostles as His Chosen Ones (1:2b-3). 4. The Promise of the Father (1:4-5).

The Book of Acts abounds with material for preaching and teaching. One can "plug in" almost anywhere and find exciting events and excellent, relevant truth for Christian living. That is certainly true from the very beginning of the book. For example, one might consider a comparison of the introductory verses of both the Gospel of Luke and the Book of Acts to show the integrity and continuity of the gospel of Christ. Both are: (1) Personal (addressed to Theophilus); (2) Christ-centered; (3) Foundational to Christian faith.

Also, there is little doubt that these verses deliberately provide an apologetic for the resurrection of Christ ("many infallible proofs"). In fact, much of Acts is intentionally apologetic, as seen in the sermons recorded, the audiences addressed, and the narrative selections. See the commentary above for nine proofs of Christ's resurrection from Luke 24 and the connection with them in Acts 1:3.

The ascension of Christ is a key event. Luke addresses this further in vv. 9-11. One might study other texts, like Ephesians 1:20, Hebrews 4:14-16, 10:1, and others to show the development of this event for a lesson or message on the Person, Position, and Power of Christ Our High Priest.

An outline about the resurrection and ascension of Christ, as seen in His being "taken up" (Acts 1:2), "carried up into heaven" (Lk. 24:51) to the "right hand of God" (Mk. 16:19) could be: 1. The Conquering Work of Redemption (Eph. 1:19-22); 2. The Completed Work of Substitution (Heb. 10:11-13); 3. The Compassionate Work of Intercession (Heb. 4:14-16).

II. THE EMPOWERING OF THE HOLY SPIRIT FOR WITNESS (1:6—2:47)

A. The Purpose for Waiting: Empowered Witness (1:6-8)

6 When they therefore were come together, they asked of him, saying, Lord, wilt thou at this time restore again the kingdom to Israel?
7 And he said unto them, It is not for you to know the times or the seasons, which the Father hath put in his own power.
8 But ye shall receive power, after that the Holy Ghost is come upon you: and ye shall be witnesses unto me both in Jerusalem, and

in all Judaea, and in Samaria, and unto the uttermost part of the earth.

Luke records the final exchange between Jesus and His followers. They had a question and it was a big one. They wanted to know if the time (Greek *chronos*, from which we get "chronology") had finally come for Israel to be restored to a place of world prominence as prophesied. In essence, they were asking about God's chronological planning for this world. Was Jesus going to make Israel great again?

We should not be surprised with their question nor reduce it to some politically narrow sense of nationalism, though some allude to that (Fitzmyer 205; Lenski 29; Bruce, *Acts* 38; Sproul 26). Their question actually reached back into O. T. prophecy and connected with one of the common themes of Jesus' teaching concerning the national independence of ethnic Israel and the Kingdom of God (Ger 22-23). Even the model prayer included "Thy kingdom come" (Mt. 6:10). Earlier, they had interpreted His teaching to include them in positions of authority in His kingdom (Lk. 22:24-30). They were seeing hundreds of years of biblical prophecies fulfilled before their eyes, so one can understand their question.

Furthermore, there is no question that the O. T. Messianic kingdom prophecies included a restored, national Israel (2 Sam. 7:12-16; Isa. 9:6-7; Ez. 5:5; Joel 2:28-32; etc.). Israel's prominence in Messiah's kingdom was certain. With the resurrection of Jesus as the capstone event regarding His Messianic mission, therefore, it seemed to them, the Messiah's kingdom was imminent (Polhill, *Acts* 84) and their positions in it

needed securing. Perhaps this was a short-sighted question. It was one that needed clarification, certainly. But the question seemed pertinent to them. Is it not the same with all who study God's Word and His prophetic plan for humanity? We are gripped with a sacred curiosity. We want to know of God's work in our times.

Jesus does not reject or demean their question but directs them to the larger scheme of God's plan (Bock 62; Sproul 26). The two words used here (*time* in v. 6; *times* or *seasons* in v. 7—Greek *chronos* and *kairous;* see 1 Thess. 5:1) form a hendiadys, a rhetorical figure of speech to express a single idea. Jesus uses this expression to move from the Father's plan for Israel to the more immediate concern of preparing them to be global witnesses. He makes it clear that the Father reserves the *times or the seasons* of this world's future under His own authority. He only reveals such when He so determines, and the time for Israel's restoration had not yet arrived. Then He moves to the more immediate issue. They needed spiritual power to accomplish their mission. As true now as then! Spiritual work must be done with spiritual power. That kind of power comes from God (Ps. 62:11).

Jesus' statement to them, about being empowered to be global witnesses, is one of the most arresting and profound of the N. T. Almost all commentators agree that this statement serves as the scope of Luke's narrative (Sproul 27; Bruce, *Acts* 36; Fitzmyer 206; Polhill, *Acts* 86). It is something of a "table of contents" for the Book of Acts. Their witness begins in Jerusalem (chapters 2—7), moves to Judaea/Samaria (chapters 8—11), and continue finally to "the uttermost part of the earth" (chapters

13—28). The recorded sermons in Acts also correspond to these movements (Ridderbos 6-7).

Even so, Jesus' command was more than just marching orders. It was a truth that so powerfully rested upon them and in them that their voices and testimony, of the message of the resurrection of Jesus Christ and His gospel, would literally change the world.

To communicate to them this incredible truth, Jesus used another play on words with *power* (Greek *exousia*) in verse 7 and *power* (Greek *dunamis*) in verse 8. The first carries the meaning of "authority, the power of choice, liberty to do as one pleases" (Thayer 225). That certainly applies to the authority of the Almighty God regarding the ordering of *times* and *seasons*. The second word, used ten times in Acts, carries the meaning of "strength, ability to be able to do something" (Thayer 159). This is what the apostles needed and would have. He promised them that there would be a spiritual enabling, a heavenly strength for the mission they were commanded to accomplish. That *power* they would experience was directly related to the Holy Spirit's coming upon them. Without His power upon them they would not succeed (Harrison 39; Schnabel 77).

That power would be demonstrated in various ways in Luke's narrative. It was initiated on the Day of Pentecost as the unlearned Galileans spoke in multiple foreign languages. Then it was shown in the powerful testimony of the public preaching of Peter, Stephen, and Paul. Sometimes that power was demonstrated in miracles of healing, protection, and deliverance (Fitzmyer 205; Bock 63). Most of the time it was demonstrated in the changed lives of those who exercised saving faith in Jesus as Lord and Savior.

The purpose of the Holy Spirit's enabling was that they would be His *witnesses* (Greek *marturos*, from our term "martyr"). The concept of *witness* is rooted in the O. T. prophecies (Isa. 43:10; 44:8) of Israel as God's witness to the world. There was a unique sense in which the apostles were witnesses to the very words and works of Jesus as no one else was (Lenski 31-32; Bruce, *Acts* 39).

But those who embraced the witness of the apostles also were witnesses via the common, spiritual experience of conversion to the living Christ and the indwelling of the Holy Spirit. Furthermore, this witness would include the inspired writings of those authors of the N. T. who, like Luke, were second generation believers. The written witness of the apostles will therefore extend to the "uttermost parts of the earth" until Jesus returns at the end of the age.

The scope of their witness was staggering. It was an ever-extending outreach to the world they knew ("Jerusalem, all Judaea, Samaria"), and to the world they did not know ("the uttermost part of the earth"). Each area presented its own challenges. Given their limited knowledge, even of the Roman world, one can only imagine how strange and overwhelming this must have sounded to them initially. Luke records the incredible stories of just how that occurred in their obedience to the Great Commission. God's perspective is always bigger than ours. We tend to perceive as we obey.

It should be noted that their worldwide witness coincided with the worldwide provision of redemption secured by the Lord Jesus (Acts 10:35; 13:39; 17:30; 1 Jn. 2:2). Given the scope of the commission, the disciples could boldly proclaim to "all men everywhere" (Acts 17:30) the good news of the "Good News."

This commission stands, then, as the imperative of individual believers and the church as a whole. We are to have a worldwide vision of ministry. Every believer ought to be a soul-winner. Every local church ought to do its best to support, prayerfully and financially, the efforts of worldwide missions. We are *all* commissioned to be His witnesses.

B. The Ascension of Christ (1:9-11)

Before addressing the text itself, I note that some commentators, in recent years, have argued that Luke contradicts himself in the two records of the ascension of Christ. Stott (45-49) effectively counters such arguments, showing there are no contradictions.

Also, some commentators state that Luke is the only N. T. writer to address the ascension of Christ (Bock 68; Polhill, *Acts* 86; Stott 47). Those who say this accept the manuscripts in which Mark 16 ends at verse 8. Picirilli (*Mark* 21-22) gives reasons for the acceptance of the longer ending; in that case Mark, too, records the ascension of Christ.

9 And when he had spoken these things, while they beheld, he was taken up; and a cloud received him out of their sight.
10 And while they looked stedfastly toward heaven as he went up, behold, two men stood by them in white apparel;
11 Which also said, Ye men of Galilee, why stand ye gazing up into heaven? this same Jesus,

which is taken up from you into heaven, shall so come in like manner as ye have seen him go into heaven.

The final words of Jesus to His disciples were incredibly compelling and powerful. It may be because they had more questions to ask, but His time had come to return to Heaven and a new phase of God's plan of redemption was to begin. However, the work of Christ would continue through them (Ger 27; Polhill, *Acts* 86-87) in witness and for them in intercession at the "throne of grace" (Heb. 4:14-16).

Luke stresses the visual perception of the disciples about the ascension of Christ, using five different verbs: "while they beheld," "out of their sight" (v. 9), "looked stedfastly" (v. 10); "gazing," and "ye have seen" (v. 11). They also heard the voice of the angelic messengers and what was said to them. The point of this is that the ascension of Christ was a very real, very literal event (Stott 46-49; Fitzmyer 208-209), not just an idea developed by the apostles regarding the end of Jesus' ministry. Just as He rose literally and bodily from the grave, so the same Jesus was literally and bodily (and visually) *taken up* (vv. 2, 9, 11) from this earth in the most dramatic fashion possible.

Luke includes the fact that a "cloud" finally obscured their sight of Him. It is possible that it was simply a cloudy day in Jerusalem (Lenski 33), but some writers propose that the "cloud" was the Shekinah glory-cloud (Ex. 13:21-22), representing God's presence (Stott 50; Bruce, *Acts* 38). In that case, the scene reminds us of a similar one in Matthew 17:5.

The whole scene completely arrested their attention (v. 10). And whose attention would not be arrested in such a situation? Peter, James, and John had experienced something similar on the Mount of Transfiguration (Mt. 17:1-8), but there Jesus did not leave them alone. Here, they are left to themselves—but not for long.

The appearance of angelic messengers (v. 10) attests to the on-going visitation of angels in connection with the early establishment of the gospel message. Angels assist believers a number of times in Luke's narrative (Acts 5:19; 10:3; 12:7). Their appearance reminds us of the two who appeared at the empty tomb (Lk. 24:4), two being the number for credible witness (Bruce, *Acts* 38). The angelic messengers speak a mild rebuke (Polhill, *Acts* 87; Bock 69). The apostles' mission was not to be star-gazers but witnesses. The rebuke is followed by a reassuring promise that they have not seen the last of Jesus.

In verse 11, the angel messengers affirm the promise of Jesus (Jn. 14:1-3) and the major eschatological doctrine of the N. T. regarding the return of Jesus Christ. Note the words "this same Jesus...shall so come in like manner." What is not said is also interesting. There are no instructions about signs that signal His return, nor is there anything about dates and events. One can study other eschatological, biblical prophecies for such matters. Here is a matter-of-fact statement of a future event when this Jesus who rose from the dead and now ascends back into Heaven will come again. With that the angels redirect the attention of the disciples to the immediate task at hand. Heavenly visions and visitors are for the purpose of preparation for earthly ministry.

Summary
(1:6-11)

Luke reconstructs the last earthly meeting of Jesus with His disciples. They had an important question regarding God's plan for Israel at that time. But the Lord Jesus had a different plan regarding the world. In profound terms He defines their identity and their mission. Now they are His *witnesses* and their mission is to carry the message of His gospel to *the uttermost part of the earth*. Such a task would be futile without God's help. Consequently, He also promises them spiritual *power* in a new relationship with the Spirit of God. He would equip them for the task.

When the Lord finished His challenge, He did not hang around and make small talk. Instead, Jesus dramatically *was taken up* into Heaven. He ascended to the right hand of God. The event left them staring upward, even after the *cloud* obscured their sight. Angelic messengers got their attention and redirected them to the task at hand. They reminded the disciples that Jesus will, indeed, come again, but that time and season are under the Father's authority and timing. It was a promise that would be part of their motivation in ministry and of endless investigative interpretation for the church until the final return of Christ.

Application: Teaching and Preaching the Passage

Exegetical Outline of the Text: 1. The Curiosity of the Apostles (1:6). 2. The Command of Christ (1:7-8). 3. The

Ascension of Christ (1:9). 4. The Affirmation of the Angels (1:10-11).

This passage is full of great truth for teaching and preaching. One might consider an eschatological study stemming from the disciples' question about the restoration of Israel. What is God's plan for Israel and what is the timing for it to be fulfilled? That would have to be tempered by the eschatology of the Second Coming, but it would be a good study nonetheless.

The five references to the Great Commission (Mt. 28: 18-20; Mk. 16:15; Lk. 24:45-48; Jn. 20:21; Acts 1:8) are sufficient for several studies. A suggested outline could be: 1. The Savior and His Authority ("all power is given unto me"). 2. The Servants and their Responsibility ("witnesses"). 3. The Scope and its Challenge ("both in Jerusalem...uttermost part of the earth"). 4. The Strength and its Necessity ("ye shall receive power").

Another great area of study is the ascension of Christ. Beginning in Acts 1:9, other references to the Lord's ascension and His continuing work could be used (see the text above).

A study of the ministry of angels is always a blessing. They are "ministering spirits" (Heb. 1:14) whose work is an integral part of the resurrection event and at key events in the Book of Acts.

C. Obedient Waiting in an Upper Room (1:12-14)

12 Then returned they unto Jerusalem from the mount called Olivet, which is from Jerusalem a Sabbath day's journey.
13 And when they were come in, they went up into an upper room, where abode both Peter, and
James, and John, and Andrew, Philip, and Thomas, Bartholomew, and Matthew, James *the son* of Alphaeus, Simon Zelotes, and Judas *the brother* of James.
14 These all continued with one accord in prayer and supplication, with the women, and Mary the mother of Jesus, and with his brethren.

The ascension of Christ had taken place somewhere on the slopes of the Mount of Olives (literally, "Olive Grove"). It was a place of poignant familiarity to the apostles. Here Jesus had detailed the future in His "Olivet Discourse" (Mt. 24-25; Mk. 13; Lk. 21). Here He often came with them (Jn. 18:2) when they were in Jerusalem. And here, in the Garden of Gethsemane, situated on the side of the mount of Olives, He had struggled with the impending "cup" of suffering on the night of His arrest (Lk. 22:39-54). Here, just forty days prior to the ascension, all the apostles had forsaken Him, running in fear for their lives (Mk. 14:50). Specific places are often associated with significant events.

The reference to "a Sabbath day's journey" does not necessarily mean the ascension took place on the Sabbath. More than likely it did not (Polhill, *Acts* 88, Bock 76). Apparently Luke used the term merely as a measure of distance. He also referenced the town of Bethany (Lk. 24:50) as being in the vicinity that lay about a mile and a half from Jerusalem. A "Sabbath day's journey," according to rabbinic tradition, was figured by combining Exodus 16:29 with Numbers 35:5; this equaled 2,000 cubits, about three-fourths of a mile (Bock 76). Taken together we have a good idea of the vicinity where the ascension took place. Furthermore, according to Zechariah 14:4 this is the exact place where the Messiah will return.

Upon returning to Jerusalem the apostles secure "an upper room" where they will obey the Lord's directive to "wait." It is impossible, of course, to know whether this is the same "upper room" where Jesus had shared the Passover with them (Lk. 22:12-13), but the words certainly remind us of that. Polhill (*Acts* 89) remarks that it might have been "the top floor of a large Palestinian house."

It is significant that Luke records some of those who were present. At the top of the list are the eleven apostles, listed as in Luke 6:13-16, but with a slightly different order and one exception, Judas Iscariot. Peter, James, and John will be the only apostles referenced by name later in the Acts narrative.

Added to that list in verse 14 are "the women, and Mary the mother of Jesus, and...his brethren." Most agree that the "women" are those who ministered to Jesus, assisted in the preparation of His body, and discovered the empty tomb (Polhill, *Acts* 89; Bruce, *Acts* 41-42; Bock 77-78). Jesus' mother, Mary, is the only woman named in the group. Her role in the life of Christ was complicated, to say the least. Now, she is among the first community of believers (Fitzmyer 216). We would be completely surprised if that were not the case.

Jesus' brothers (Mk. 6:3) are also included in this first gathering of believers. There were four brothers, and since none are specifically omitted I take it that all were there. One remembers that they did not believe in Him previously (Jn. 7:5). That changed after the resur-

rection and His personal appearance to the next to the oldest of them, James (1 Cor. 15:7). Jesus was, of course, the oldest. Nothing is said of His sisters, though one may hope that they were included among the women mentioned.

Their time of waiting for "the promise of the Father" (Acts 1:4) was spent in continued, steadfast ("devotedly continuing," ESV) "prayer and supplication." Bock (77) characterizes this as, "piety and unity." Great spiritual events require humility, surrender, unity, and prayer. With few exceptions, prayer and unity among the Lord's followers characterize the church in the Book of Acts.

D. Selection of a Replacement for Judas Iscariot (1:15-26)

1. The defection of Judas Iscariot (1:15-20)

15 And in those days Peter stood up in the midst of the disciples, and said, (the number of names together were about an hundred and twenty,)

16 Men *and* brethren, this scripture must needs have been fulfilled, which the Holy Ghost by the mouth of David spake before concerning Judas, which was guide to them that took Jesus.

17 For he was numbered with us, and had obtained part of this ministry.

18 Now this man purchased a field with the reward of iniquity; and falling headlong, he burst asunder in the midst, and all his bowels gushed out.

19 And it was known unto all the dwellers at Jerusalem; insomuch as that field is called in their prop-

er tongue, Aceldama, that is to say, the field of blood.
20 For it is written in the book of Psalms, Let his habitation be desolate, and let no man dwell therein: and his bishoprick let another take.

In the ten days between the ascension of Christ (v. 3) and the Feast of Pentecost, the followers of Christ not only met in prayerful waiting, they addressed the issue of replacing Judas Iscariot. Apparently, they felt it necessary to reconstitute the original number of the apostles. Peter is the one who took leadership in the matter. That he would do so in light of his own recent denial of Jesus may seem presumptuous. Indeed, it would have been presumptuous had not Peter been confronted and restored by the Lord Jesus (Jn. 21:15-19) and commissioned to shepherd the church (Ger 30). Here is His first opportunity for leadership. With that said, one cannot help wondering whether Peter felt somewhat awkward as he addressed the situation. After all, both he and Judas had denied the Lord the very same night. But Peter was restored to fellowship and position, unlike Judas who would forever be a spiritual enigma.

There are many reasons they would consider replacing Judas Iscariot and completing the number of apostles. First, Jesus had chosen twelve men from the hundreds of followers and called them *apostles* (Lk. 6:13; Mt. 10:2; Mk. 3:14). The word *apostle* (Greek *apostolos*) means one sent forth with orders (Thayer 68), used in distinction from *disciple* (Greek *mathetes*), which means a "learner" (Thayer 386). *Apostle* carries the idea of one to whom is given authority in representation. Most agree

that the number was representative of the twelve tribes of Israel (Fitzmyer 221; Bruce, *Acts* 44; Sproul 35). The apostles represented the new "Israel" (Lk. 22:30). These men would be the "founding fathers" on whom the future of the church depended (Geldenhuys 205).

Second, these men had been with Jesus for three years as intimate eyewitnesses. They would be responsible to insure the integrity of the words and works of the Lord Jesus Christ (Stott 58). This becomes one of the qualifications (in their view) for the candidate to replace Judas (vv. 21-22).

Third, as Luke will show in the developing witness of the church, these men would constitute the authority sometimes needed in appeal (Acts 6:1-4; 8:14-17; 11:1-18; 15:2). For the first few years, the Jerusalem church was regarded as the standard-bearer of truth and practice. However, as the church confirmed its theology in key decisions and expanded its territory in mission, their role as "the Twelve" declined in reference but not in effect. They are not mentioned by Luke after Acts 15:22 and the historic Jerusalem Council. But the standard of truth and practice had been established in the unanimous agreements of the apostles by then. One can therefore see why they believed replacing Judas was an important decision to make at the outset.

The first mention of the number of disciples in the church is in verse 14. There are one hundred and twenty disciples gathered in waiting. Some writers believe this is more than just a specific number (Polhill, *Acts* 91; Lenski 43-44), and that it only refers to those present in Jerusalem at that time. The apostle Paul lists "above five hundred brethren" as eye-witnesses of Jesus' resurrection (1

Cor. 15:6). For whatever reasons, these one hundred and twenty disciples were the ones who waited in Jerusalem for "the promise of the Father." One hundred and twenty people would be a large number for an upper room of that day (Ger 29), but some events are worth packing the house!

Peter's proposed resolution to complete the number of the apostles begins with the Scriptures that specifically point to the defection of Judas Iscariot. He ends with a recommendation of who qualifies as Judas's replacement. The whole process is not viewed negatively by the church (Bock 79), and they proceed to follow Peter's lead in the matter. Sometimes tough decisions have to be made even when it involves someone who has been close and well known. This incident may very well be a precedent for dealing with denial and betrayal in the church since Peter had to face this again in a later situation (Acts 5:1-11).

Three Scriptures in the Psalms are referenced, all written by David himself (Ps. 41:9; 69:25; 109:8). Peter equates the Scriptures with the authority of the Holy Spirit, and rightly so (Bruce, *Acts* 45; Lenski 45). Interestingly, he says these were "concerning Judas." In what way did these verses apply to Judas Iscariot, since they were written several hundred years earlier and with a different context for each one? The answer is that Peter uses theme and terminology from each one to relate to Judas and an aspect of the situation (Bock 82; Shires 49-51). Peter's reasoning is: Judas was one of the twelve apostles and an integral part of the ministry (v. 17; Ps. 41:9); Judas rejected his position (v. 20; Ps. 69:25); his position needed filling (v. 20; Ps. 109:8).

Peter notes the following about the actions of Judas in his betrayal. First, he was a *guide* (Greek *hodegos*) to those who arrested Jesus. In a city crowded with Passover worshipers, Judas would have known where Jesus and the other apostles were likely to be since they often went there when they came to Jerusalem (Jn. 18:2). He led the arresting soldiers, authorities, and assorted gawkers to the very place. In the darkness of the Garden of Gethsemane, with a kiss of feigned friendship, he indicated which one of the men there was Jesus.

Second, he was "numbered with us." He was one of "the Twelve" and participated in all that group represented. "He had received from Jesus this highest station which was graciously bestowed on so few" (Lenski 45).

Third, he "took part of this ministry." Judas was not only there to hear Jesus speak the most famous words ever spoken, he saw people raised from the dead, multitudes miraculously fed, raging seas calmed by the voice of the Master, demons subdued, and a thousand other incredible deeds. He himself was endued with spiritual power to preach the gospel, subdue demons, and heal the sick (Lk. 9:1-6).

Fourth, he "purchased a field with the reward." Matthew 27:3-10 records the details of Judas' returning the blood money of betrayal. In a causative sense (Bock 84) the "blood field" (v. 19) was purchased.

Fifth, note the phrase, "falling headlong...all his bowels gushed out." Of interest is the additional information about the gruesome details of the death of Judas. Matthew 27:5 only states that Judas "went out and hanged himself." What can be made of these differences? Fitzmyer argues for discrepancies in the accounts (219-220, 224). It is possible that the reference is meant as a figurative exaggeration to demean even the body of the one who betrayed Jesus. However, it is entirely reasonable to assume that after he hanged himself, his body was not immediately discovered. The effects of death upon the body, and the eventual disposal could easily explain what happened to it (Stott 55-56; Ger 31). The accounts differ because the authors are emphasizing different points (Bock 655). They are complementary not contradictory.

One cannot help noting the contrast shown between the body of Judas and the body of the Lord Jesus. The body of Judas is described as gruesome, disfigured, and discarded in a "field of blood," purchased with the price of betrayal, bound to hell forever. The body of the Lord Jesus is living, glorified, perfect, and ascended to Heaven.

Perhaps there is also the note of a grim sense of justice in Peter's extended details about Judas. The consequences of the betrayal of the perfect Son of God are seen even in the body of the ultimate traitor. The name of Judas Iscariot has historically become synonymous with the worst kind of betrayal.

Although the *Gospel of Judas*, recently discovered, seeks to improve on the reputation of Judas, it cannot be trusted as anything more than fanciful literature that tries to soften his image (Bock 80).

2. The election of Matthias (1:21-26)

21 Wherefore of these men which have companied with us all the time that the Lord Jesus went in and out among us,

22 Beginning from the baptism of John, unto that same day that he was taken up from us, must one be ordained to be a witness with us of his resurrection.
23 And they appointed two, Joseph called Barsabas, who was surnamed Justus, and Matthias.
24 And they prayed, and said, Thou, Lord, which knowest the hearts of all *men*, shew whether of these two thou hast chosen,
25 That he may take part of this ministry and apostleship, from which Judas by transgression fell, that he might go to his own place.
26 And they gave forth their lots; and the lot fell upon Matthias; and he was numbered with the eleven apostles.

Peter concludes his address with a directive for specific action (v. 21). In effect, he says that one of the men present who met the qualifications should be chosen to take the place and position of Judas Iscariot as one of the twelve apostles.

Three very restrictive qualifications were required for the replacement of Judas Iscariot. One, he must have been among the followers of Jesus from the beginning, i.e. from the day when John baptized Jesus to the ascension (Sproul 36; Polhill, *Acts* 93). If it referred to the very beginning of John's ministry, prior to the baptism of Jesus, some of the other twelve apostles might not qualify. Bock (87) alludes to a figure of speech regarding the phrase "from the baptism of John unto that same day he was taken up," which is similar to our saying "from A to Z" and includes everything of significance in between. The phrase "companied with us" indicates that they should know the man personally and be able to verify his qualification. It is possible that he might have been one of "the seventy" (Lk. 10:1).

Two, he must be an eye witness to the resurrection. The resurrection was the capstone event of the gospel. It was the ultimate confirmation of the life and ministry of Christ. It defined the very reason for the gospel message. The replacement must be able to verify personally this historic event in order to be an apostle. This qualification alone may have been paramount to all the rest. One's personal witness of the resurrection of Christ was integral to the initial authority of the gospel message.

Three, he must be one whom the Lord chose (v. 24). This would be a direct link to the original selection of the twelve apostles by Jesus Himself (Lk. 6:13-16). In this situation, they equated the casting of the lots with the Lord's personal choice (v. 26). Their selection at that time would be tantamount to the personal affirmation of Christ.

Out of the assembly of disciples, two men were put forth as meeting those qualifications, Joseph called Barsabas (lit. "son of the Sabbath"), "whose surname was Justus" (a Gentile name), and Matthias (meaning "gift of God"). Apparently, both were well qualified. Either of them would fit the bill. Not all selections or elections have such worthy candidates.

It is interesting that this is the only time when they replaced one of the apostles. Even though James would be killed later (Acts 12:2), apparently no efforts were made to replace him. After the Jerusalem Council in Acts 15, there is no further mention of the apostles. Founding fathers are limited in number, function, and longevity. However, "the

names of the *twelve* apostles of the Lamb" are inscribed on the twelve foundations of New Jerusalem (Rev. 21:14).

Later, Paul, would set forth his claim as an apostle (Rom. 1:1; Gal. 1:1; etc.). As a result, a good question arises: namely, whose names are inscribed on the foundations of New Jerusalem? Eleven of them are certain but who is the twelfth man, Matthias or Paul? Morgan argues that the church was presumptuous in choosing Matthias (19-20). Stott disagrees (58). Any number of arguments can be made for either case. Ultimately, we will just have to wait and see for ourselves!

Although they had decided to replace Judas, they were not through speaking of him. Peter had previously noted the physical death of Judas; now they comment on his spiritual destiny. First, they concluded that "Judas by transgression fell" (Greek aorist of *parabaino*), which includes the implication that he abandoned his trust (Thayer 478). The language is clear that Judas himself made the choice to reject his privileged position and all its benefits (Lenski 44).

Furthermore, they stated that he went "to his own place." Most writers agree that this phrase is a euphemism meaning that Judas went to hell (Bock 89; Lenski 53; Barnes 17; Polhill, *Acts* 94; Robertson, *Acts* 18). Lenski states without qualification, "The fact that Gehenna or hell is referred to is beyond question" (53).

Casting lots to determine the will of God was a practice in Israel going back centuries (Lev. 16:8; Josh. 18:6; 1 Chron. 26:13; etc.). The results of the procedure were viewed as the decision "of the Lord" (Prov. 16:33) and one that settled differences (Prov. 18:18). (Josephus, *Wars* VII.IX.1, includes an interesting, extra-biblical account of the use of lots among the Jews.) Different types of lots were used, including bones, stones, and wood (Bock 90). These were placed in a bag and the one that was drawn out, or fell out as the bag was shaken, decided the issue. In this case, the process began with a specific prayer (v. 24), asking the Lord to oversee the process and use it to reveal His will in the matter. The names of the two men (or representative colors) were put on markers and placed in a bag. The marker that came out determined who was chosen. The result was that Matthias "was numbered with the eleven apostles."

This is the only time in the Book of Acts when lots were cast as a means of determining the will of God. Hereafter, decisions were made by verbal input and vote.

Summary
(1:12-26)

In verses 12-14, the disciples dutifully obeyed the Lord in returning to Jerusalem after His ascension from the Mount of Olives. In an "upper room" reminiscent of a previous quality time spent with Jesus (Jn. 13-14), they joined with other disciples to begin their vigil of waiting "for the promise of the Father." It was a time of unity ("one accord") and continual prayer.

With the apostles short one man because of the choices and actions of Judas Iscariot, they determined that someone should fill the spot (vv. 15-26). Here Peter began asserting his leadership. In his statements to clarify the reasons for such a decision, Peter tied the situation to specific biblical principles and prophecies. He proposed three

qualifications for such a unique position. Two men were put forth, prayer was offered, lots were cast, and Matthias was deemed to be the one chosen by the Lord as the replacement.

Application: Teaching and Preaching the Passage

Exegetical Outline of the Text: 1. A Prayerful Assembly (vv. 12-14). 2. Some Pertinent Business (vv. 15-22). 3. A Particular Process (vv. 23-25). 4. A Prominent Position (v. 26).

The spiritual focus of the disciples is remarkable. They were a diverse group in a multitude of ways. From Mary, the mother of Jesus, to the siblings who previously did not believe in Him, to the several apostles with their wide backgrounds, there was much that could have separated them. However, the effects of the resurrection of Christ, its life-changing impact, and the pending promise of the Father were greater than their differences. So, it is, and should be, with the makeup of a local church. This could be the basis for a great study about the local church and what unifies believers.

This is the last listing in the N. T. of the apostles. A study of the selection of the apostles and who they were would be excellent material for several messages and lessons on leadership. One could extend the study to the other mentions of the apostles in Acts. Such a study could be supplemented with materials written about them by noted authors.

Of particular interest about the apostles would be a separate study on Judas Iscariot. Though he presents a negative role model, he presents the realistic possibility of human free will even with the best of all possible role models to follow, the Lord Jesus Himself. While the others continued to follow Jesus, though they had their failings as well, he totally abandoned his calling and paid the ultimate price for his choices. The study would certainly include the death of Judas and harmonizing the Gospel accounts of the details provided. One must be careful not to assume that all suicides are Judas-like in choices and spiritual destiny. That is certainly not the case.

A study on Peter himself would be most beneficial. Such could include his personality, his qualities, his denial, and his restoration to leadership. This could easily lead to studying Peter's leadership in the rest of the Book of Acts.

The disciples trusted the casting of lots (v. 26) to reveal to them the will of God regarding the replacement of Judas. In that way, they could receive an objective answer to their prayer (v. 24). At times the Lord's people have asked Him to use such means to help them discern His will. At times He provided objective means to do so. The Urim and Thummim (Ex. 30:29-30; Num. 27:21) were used this way. Gideon used a fleece (Judg. 6:37-40). The spoken words of prophets were sought (1 Kgs. 22:13-22).

The need to know the will of God is no less important today than then. Sometimes we seek His will revealed through the common voice of prayerful people in a church vote. We ask Him for specifics in answer to our prayers. His will is objectively revealed in the written Word of God in both commands and principles (1 Thess. 4:3). In every way we seek to live as Jesus taught in prayer, "Thy will be done in earth, as it is in heaven" (Mt. 6:10).

E. The Filling of the Holy Spirit (2:1-13)

1. The miraculous event (2:1-4)

1   And when the day of Pentecost was fully come, they were all with one accord in one place.
2   And suddenly there came a sound from heaven as of a rushing mighty wind, and it filled all the house where they were sitting.
3   And there appeared unto them cloven tongues like as of fire, and it sat upon each of them.
4   And they were all filled with the Holy Ghost, and began to speak with other tongues, as the Spirit gave them utterance.

The Feast of Pentecost was one of three pilgrimage festivals commanded to be kept annually in Israel (Ex. 23:14-17; 34:22). It was also known as "Feast of Weeks" and "Day of Firstfruits" (Lev. 23:16; Deut. 16:10). On that day the "firstfruits of wheat harvest" (Ex. 34:22) were presented to the Lord. The festival occurred fifty days (Greek *pentecostes*, "fiftieth") after Passover with ceremonial rituals marking the occasion. All work was to cease, signifying it as "an holy convocation" or "solemn assembly" (Lev. 23:15-21). It was regarded as one of the most popular pilgrim festivals, partly due to improved weather conditions from the time of Passover (Polhill, *Acts* 97). Its popularity would, in part, explain why there were so many present in Jerusalem (v. 5). However, the disciples of the Lord Jesus were there in response to a different command.

Fitzmyer (234-235) makes the case from the Qumran scrolls (Temple Scroll, cave 11) that there had developed three

41

pentecost celebrations in Judaism that occurred at different times. A "Feast of Weeks," a "Feast of New Wine," and a "Feast of New Oil." He relates this "day of Pentecost" (2:1) as the "Feast of New Wine" since the allusion is made in verse 13 to "new wine." However, the timing of Luke's accounts in both the Gospel (Lk. 22:1) and Acts 2, following the forty-day appearances of Jesus (Acts 1:3), makes clear that this is not correct. The Qumran community may have, indeed, celebrated three pentecosts, but this "Day of Pentecost" is the one originally commanded to be kept fifty days after Passover.

Only Luke records in detail what took place on that historic, watershed moment in the church's history. Interestingly, the Feast of Pentecost is mentioned only two other times in the N. T. (Acts 20:16; 1 Cor. 16:8) and then only as a scheduling reference by Paul. Bock (95-96) states that in some traditions of Judaism it was believed that on this day significant things had taken place. This somewhat vague sentiment, however, does not seem to be Luke's point of reference. More likely, he is thinking about the command of Christ for the disciples to "wait for the promise of the Father" (Lk. 24: 49; Acts 1:4). They might have anticipated it, but Jesus did not say it would come to fulfillment on the Day of Pentecost. Sometimes the significance of an event is not fully realized until we have had time to analyze it and understand what resulted (Sproul 41).

The significance of the day may be seen in the nature of the celebration and the purpose of the Great Commission. The celebration of the first fruits of the grain harvest is an appropriate analogy to the spiritual nature of the gospel in the harvest of souls; Jesus said the fields are white unto harvest (Jn. 4:35-38).

Though some argue that the Day of Pentecost had not arrived yet (Knowling 71), the phrase "when the Day of Pentecost was fully come" indicates (v. 1) that it had. Peter, in fact, specifies that it was "the third hour of the day" (v. 15), i.e., around nine o'clock. The ritual ceremonies of the day were already under way (Greek *sumplerousthai*, being fulfilled). Those ceremonies would take on a totally different significance for the Christian community before the day was over.

Though we cannot say for certain, there is no real reason to believe the "one place," "the house" (v. 2), where they were gathered is different from the "upper room" (1:13). Bruce agrees (*Acts* 50). It appears, also, that at some point they did move from the upper room, perhaps to the court area of the Temple in the process of expressing the gift of tongues (Ger 37-38).

The phrase "all with one accord" is not exactly the same as 1:14. Here it probably means "all together" and is something of a tautology (Robertson, *Acts* 20). The idea is that all one hundred and twenty of the disciples were present. They had been waiting, watching, and praying with the same heart for at least ten days since the ascension. The command of Christ to wait, the scope of His Commission to them ("the uttermost part of the earth"), and the power necessary for the task ("ye shall receive power") made all other casual life events pale in comparison. No one left to pursue other interests.

What began as a day of routine ceremony and celebration quickly turned into an overwhelming visitation of God. The Holy Spirit began moving around them and in them in three audible, visual, and verbal manifestations. When men waited before the Lord in prayerful obedience, God visited with redemptive purpose.

The first manifestation was "a sound from heaven as of a rushing mighty wind." The indication is that there was no actual blowing wind, just the sound heard by all in the house (Barnes 20; Lenski 58; Robertson, *Acts* 20). Without an actual wind, the sound alone must have been compelling.

The second manifestation was the appearance of "cloven tongues like as of fire." First sound, then sight. The word translated "cloven" (Greek *diamerizomai*) suggests that there was the appearance of a single pillar of fire that parted into smaller "tongues" of fire, which sat upon (the heads?) of each of them (Robertson, *Acts* 21, Knowling 72). The appearance of a pillar of fire is reminder of the same that led Israel in the wilderness (Ex. 13:21). It was a visible manifestation of God's presence. This manifestation must have been incredibly fascinating, if not outright scary (Heb. 12:21).

Wind and fire have been manifestations of the presence of God on multiple occasions (Ex. 3:2, 13:21, 14:21, 19:18-19; Deut. 5:4; Isa. 66:15; Ezek. 37:9-14; Jn. 3:6-8). On the Day of Pentecost these are representations of the presence of God in confirming fulfillment of the words of Christ (Bock 97; Polhill, *Acts* 97-98; Fitzmyer 238; Bruce, *Acts* 50-51). The manifestations themselves are indeed intriguing, but not the point. The presence of the Living God Himself, who comes in redemptive purpose, is greater than all these (Mt. 12:6).

The third manifestation ("third miracle," Robertson, *Acts* 22) of the Holy Spirit was that "they... began to speak with other tongues, as the Spirit gave them utterance" (v. 4). Sound, sight, then the unique verbalization of the "wonderful works of God" (v. 11). In addressing this third manifestation, the statement that they were all filled with the Holy Spirit should be noted.

There is an unmistakable connection with the prophecy of John the Baptist and the words of Christ regarding the baptism of the Holy Spirit and the "promise of the Father" (Lk. 3:16; Acts 1:4-5). Furthermore, that the initial outpouring of the Holy Spirit on the Day of Pentecost is the fulfillment of both statements is also clear (Bruce, *Acts* 51). To be sure, however, this event signals more than just a fulfillment of past prophecies. It is the beginning of a new era of relationship with God as the Holy Spirit who works intimately with His people. This relationship continues in the lives of all believers individually and the church collectively today (1 Cor. 3:16; 6:19-20).

Luke began using the phrase "filled with the Holy Ghost" initially of John the Baptist (Lk. 1:15), Elizabeth (Lk. 1:41), and Zachariah (Lk. 1:67). In the Book of Acts, the phrase itself is used eight times. The Pentecost filling of the disciples is first (2:4). Peter is "filled with the Holy Ghost" as he addresses the Jewish leaders (4:8). The assembled church is "filled with the Holy Ghost" as they pray (4:31). Those who are to serve the need of the widows are to be "filled with the Holy Ghost" (6:3). Stephen was "full of the Holy Ghost" (7:55) in testimony and spiritual insight. Newly converted Saul of Tarsus is to be "filled with the Holy Ghost" (9:17). The apostle Paul speaks the judgment of blindness on Elymas the sorcerer after being "filled with the Holy Ghost" (13:9). The new believers at Iconium are "filled with joy and the Holy Ghost" (13:52). The usage of the phrase in Acts underscores the proclamation of the gospel and empowerment for ministry (Bock 99).

Using different terms and applications, the ongoing work or ministry of the Holy Spirit is associated with an ever widening circle of believers. He is the enabler of prophecy in "the last days" (2:17-19). He is given as a gift, upon salvation, to all who obey the Lord (2:38-39; 5:32). He is the offended judge of hypocrisy (5:3). He directs in soul-winning and missions encounters (8:29; 16:6-10). He leads them in counsel to reconcile fellowship between Jewish and Gentile believers (15:28). He appoints leadership in the local church (20:28). The Holy Spirit is the Divine Author behind the human author of the Scriptures (28:25). The Holy Spirit's work is one of the dominant themes of the Book of Acts. His invisible hand should be noted, honored, and implored by all believers and churches today as well.

The Holy Spirit enabled the assembled disciples of Jesus to "speak with other tongues." The same manifestation occurs three times in the Book of Acts (Acts 2:4-12; 10:44-46; 19:6), all using the same word for "tongues" (Greek *glossa*). Modern discussion about speaking in tongues, and the larger theme of the gifts of the Holy Spirit, is the subject of much disagreement. In light of that discussion, and in an effort to interpret the text rightly, I will discuss several questions that arise about this particular manifestation.

One, the ability to "speak with other tongues" is miraculously given to the disciples, but what kind of language is spoken? For a number of reasons it seems clear that the manifestation of tongues on the Day of Pentecost was the miraculous enablement of the disciples to speak in human, foreign languages (Bock 99; Robertson, *Acts* 21; Polhill, *Acts* 99; Lenski 61; Picirilli, *Corinthians* 195).

The interpretative statements in Acts 2:6, 8, and 11 by those who heard the disciples speaking clarifies they heard them speak in their *own* native "tongues": that is, the languages they learned from their birth. There was no miracle involved in hearing what was said. The language of their birth certainly would not have been an ecstatic or heavenly language. Therefore, even the unbelievers present at the time knew what the languages were and what was being said.

When the audience heard the disciples speak in such an unusual way (2:6, 8), they used a different word for "language, tongue" (Greek *dialektos*), which can only mean human language (Thayer 139, Polhill, *Acts* 99). Further, the natural contextual reading of the event makes it hard to interpret the speaking of the disciples in anything but human languages (Barnes 22; Polhill, *Acts* 100). Any other interpretation of the gift in this text seems contrived.

In Acts 2:3, the same word is used of "tongues of fire" but these are, obviously, not **any** kinds of language, human or otherwise. In 1 Corinthians 13:1 the word is used of "tongues of angels." Though this phrase is often interpreted to mean something other than human language, one notes that without exception in the Scriptures, when it is recorded that angels speak, they speak in human language.

A second question would be, is this a gift of speaking or hearing? Luke states, "they...began to *speak* with other tongues" (v. 4). The tense of the verb translated "to speak" (Greek present) makes clear that the disciples were audibly speaking (Thayer 368). They were in fact enabled by the Holy Spirit to *speak* in human, foreign languages which were unknown to them previously (Lenski 61).

The hearing (vv. 6, 8, 11) of the words spoken, by the unsaved crowd, was simply the natural listening process (Polhill, *Acts* 99, 100). Therefore, the gift of "tongues" on the Day of Pentecost is one of speaking, not hearing.

Third, what was the theological intention of speaking in "tongues" on the Day of Pentecost? Begin with the fact that the disciples are in Jerusalem at the command of Jesus (Lk. 24:49; Acts 1:4). Further, they are promised the power necessary to accomplish the scope of the Great Commission (Acts 1:8). That naturally involves the languages of all the people groups in such a mission. On the Day of Pentecost, there are representatives from "every nation under heaven" (Acts 2:5). This phrase will be addressed a little later, but there are enough languages represented that the universal thrust of the gospel is unmistakable (Fitzmyer 239).

It must be remembered that in these early days of Christianity, the disciples were nearly all Jewish. Their provincial mindset had been so ingrained in them about the exclusiveness of their cultural faith and practices that it would take special acts of God to shake them from this mindset (Acts 10:9-43). Sometimes even good people need a spiritual jolt to awaken them to God's truth.

The timing of the event, the people present, the commands of Christ to His disciples, their maturing perspective of God's intention for all nations—all these point to the conclusion that the intended purpose of the gift of tongues on the Day of Pentecost was directly tied to the scope of the Great Commission. The Lord is so concerned about the redemption of all people with the gospel of Christ, that He miraculously enabled His disciples to proclaim the "wonderful works of God" (2:11) in representative languages. In effect, the Great Commission was personalized in each one.

One should also note that God is the Author/Creator of various human languages (Gen. 11:1-9). The Lord so moved upon the minds of men at the tower of Babel event that language comprehension and communication was altered. Whatever may be the complex historical development of language skills since, it should come as no surprise that God can miraculously enable men to speak in human foreign languages.

While some interpret this event as a "reversal of Babel" to return humanity to a common language (Davies, JTS 228-231, as quoted in Polhill, *Acts* 105), that interpretation precludes the gift of tongues as an ecstatic language that serves as the basis of common fellowship. Such is not the interpretation proposed here, nor is it the point being made. There were **many** languages spoken on Pentecost, not one. Furthermore, common fellowship among believers is not a matter of the language spoken but their common experience of salvation in Jesus Christ. That theme is clearly developed as the church is established (2:44-45; 4:34-37), extending even into Heaven itself (Rev. 7:9-10).

The phrase, "as the Spirit gave them utterance" conveys the idea that the disciples were enabled selectively ("one after another" Robertson, *Acts* 22) by the Holy Spirit to speak. Some argue that only the apostles were thus enabled (Ger 37-38) and not all the disciples. But that seems to be too restrictive (Bock 98; Bruce, *Acts* 56). The word translated "utterance" (Greek *apophthengomai*) is very rare (Robertson, *Acts* 22; Longenecker 63), occurring only three times in the N. T., all in Acts (2:4, 14; 26:25). It carries the idea of eager, impassioned speech. All contexts of its usage in Acts are of speech that is clearly understood.

One can picture the disciples assembled together in a protracted prayer meeting. Their attention is galvanized by the sudden sound of a powerful wind and the appearance of a pillar of fire hovering over them. It divides into smaller tongues of fire and comes to rest over each one. First this one, then that one begins to speak excitedly in dialects and languages of other nations proclaiming the great things God has done! The "promise of the Father," the "baptism of the Holy Spirit," is being fulfilled.

Fourth, and perhaps most challenging, is the question, "Is the "gift of tongues" normative in the life of believers and His church today?" The answer to that question lies within a larger question, "To what extent are other events, experiences, and methodologies in the Book of Acts normative for believers today?"

There is a sense in which all of the events in Acts are *theologically* normative, in that they inform us of the character and work of God to fulfill His promises and accomplish His purposes. This is seen in the regular and consistent appeals made by the disciples to the O. T. Messianic Scriptures as final authority. In essence, the God of the O. T. is at work fulfilling what He has promised.

But, in another sense, it is evident that *some* of the events, experiences, and methodologies in the Book of Acts are *ecclesiologically* unique, initiatory, and transitional from the event to final principle and practice. That concept should come as no surprise since much of the N. T. era was transitional. In the Gospel accounts, redemptive history is shifting from the prophetic and preparatory of the O. T. through Israel to the fulfillment of those prophecies and the culture of the Church in the N. T.

For example, the ministry of John the Baptist was in fulfillment of O. T. prophecy (Mt 17:10-13), therefore, preparatory and transitional (Jn. 3:30). So, too, the sacrificial observances of the followers of Christ would gradually cease as they realized their ultimate fulfillment in Christ Himself (Mt. 26:26-29; Hebrews; Crabtree 438-439). Jesus came to the "lost sheep of the house of Israel" (Mt. 15:24), but sent His disciples to every nation (Mt. 28:18-20).

Other transitional structures of the Book of Acts would include the office of the apostles and the associated "signs of an apostle" (2 Cor. 12:12). Though some use the title *apostle* today, that should not be taken in the same sense of the twelve apostles in the Book of Acts. If for no other reason, none of the original apostles are alive!

Furthermore, it would be a mistake to think that *every* time the church gathered for prayer, they could expect to hear the sound of wind and see cloven tongues of fire appear (2:1-4). The work of the Holy Spirit in Acts is imparted to believers by the laying on of hands of the apostles (8:17), yet He comes to possess all believers without any apostolic assistance as the gospel rapidly expands to places the apostles do not go (Rom. 8:9). Followers of Jesus Christ are called "disciples" (1:15; 6:1, 7, etc.), but some are said to be "disciples" who had little knowledge of Jesus Christ (Acts 19:1-7). After this event the term only refers to believers in Christ.

The early disciples in Jerusalem sold their possessions and placed the money in a common treasury for distribution (Acts 4:34-35). But this was not taught as the required practice of all believers or churches. None should expect the shaking of the building where folks gather for prayer (4:31). God certainly can but does not visit immediate judgment as He did with Ananias and Sapphira (5:1-10). The Angel of the Lord can but does not always miraculously come to deliver imprisoned believers (5:17-20; 12:3-17). Other examples could be used, but it must be concluded that *some* of the events, experiences, and methodologies of the Book of Acts were, indeed, transitional.

Some, however, are models meant to be followed by the Church until Jesus comes again. For example, the indwelling and empowering of the Holy Spirit in the bold proclamation of the gospel is certainly a model for all believers (1:8; 4:33; 5:29; 6:10; 13:52; 24:29; Rom. 8:1-27). Compassionate, monetary efforts to relieve suffering are to characterize Christians in demonstrating the love of God (11:27-30; 1 Jn. 3:17-18). The missiology of the apostle Paul and his helpers is certainly both the model and the method for church planting (Acts 13—20). The gospel's salvific con-

ditions and universal application are fully and permanently defined at the time of the Jerusalem Council (Acts 15). Its truth may be proclaimed to all nations uniformly and precisely as the written Word of God states. There is no need to have another Jerusalem Council every time some group or individual adds (heretically) other conditions to the gospel's plan of salvation.

Which events are transitional, and which are ongoing models will remain, to a certain extent, issues of discussion. However, the authority for determining such is the final, written Word of God. When the truths of Christianity were set down in Scripture and the canon of the N. T. was completed, Christian beliefs and practices were once-for-all defined. The events of the Book of Acts, itself fully inspired and inerrant, are interpreted through the lens of the rest of the Scriptures to reveal the permanent principles and appropriate practices of Christian life.

It should be noted that during the time-frame of the Book of Acts, some of the Scriptures were being written. First Corinthians, with its expanded explanation of spiritual gifts, and in particular the gift of tongues (12:1—14:40), was written during Paul's third missionary journey (Picirilli, *Corinthians* 2—3). Paul's reference to his personal experience (1 Cor. 14:18) must be understood in light of his apostolic position and his multi-linguistic audiences where he proclaimed the gospel.

Revelatory gifts were a necessary part of the early church experience. The apostles, along with their selective assistants (i.e., Luke, Mark) were used to record the revealed and inspired Word of God. With the writing of the last book of the N. T., however, revelatory gifts would of necessity cease in that regard. I am aware that some argue for continuing revelation, but that raises all sorts of questions and issues regarding the completion and authority of written revelation. Such views of continuing revelation must be utterly rejected.

Lastly, this miraculous manifestation of tongues on the Day of Pentecost sets the precedent for the N. T. gift. It is duplicated with Cornelius (Acts 10:45-46; 11:15) and with the newly enlightened disciples at Ephesus (Acts 19:6). It is possible the Samaritans spoke with tongues (8:15-17), but that is not specifically stated. I take it that all other situations where the gift of tongues is expressed in the N. T. are to be interpreted in light of its initial manifestation on the Day of Pentecost (Picirilli, *Corinthians* 195; Lightfoot 89). That being the case, it would appear that in Acts 2:1-13, we have the public expression of the gift of tongues that demonstrates its Great Commission purpose. In 1 Corinthians 14:1-40 we have the personal experience of the gift of tongues and the definition of its parameters: same gift, different dimensions.

The question is often asked, "Can't God do as He pleases when the same need arises?" Certainly He can and does do as He pleases, but He pleases to act according to His written Word, never in contradiction to it.

2. The wider audience responds (2:5-13)

**5 And there were dwelling at Jerusalem Jews, devout men, out of every nation under heaven.
6 Now when this was noised abroad, the multitude came together, and were confounded, because that every man heard them speak in his own language.
7 And they were all amazed and marvelled, saying one to another, Behold, are not all these which speak Galilaeans?
8 And how hear we every man in our own tongue, wherein we were born?
9 Parthians, and Medes, and Elamites, and dwellers in Mesopotamia, and in Judaea, and Cappadocia, in Pontus, and Asia,
10 Phrygia, and Pamphylia, in Egypt, and in the parts of Libya about Cyrene, and strangers of Rome, Jews and proselytes.
11 Cretes and Arabians, we do hear them speak in our tongues the wonderful works of God.
12 And they were all amazed, and were in doubt, saying one to another, What meaneth this?
13 Others mocking said, These men are full of new wine.**

At some point the experience of the disciples overflowed the confines of the upper room. Perhaps they moved into a courtyard of the Temple (Marshall 70), where a large crowd would have assembled for the ceremonial observances of Pentecost. It was here that the theological intention of the miraculous gift of tongues was immediately realized. In Jerusalem, there were Jewish residents, temporary festival dwellers, and proselytes from "every nation under heaven" (Polhill, *Acts* 101; Robertson, *Acts* 23). Luke's use of hyperbole here is obvious (Fitzmyer 272). Fifteen nations and regions within the parameters of the Roman Empire are represented, certainly enough to warrant Luke's hyperbole. Some object to the inclusion of the word "Jews" in the text (v. 5), but the manuscript evidence is strongly in its favor (Longenecker 68; Meyer 55).

Though Luke mentions "proselytes" (v. 10), they would not constitute the majority of those present. Even then, these proselytes would be in Jerusalem to worship as "Jews." The Jewishness of the early days of the Church is unmistakable. The wider scope of reaching Gentiles expands in chapters ten and eleven, but its preview is seen on the Day of Pentecost. The providential hand of God, as seen in the multilingual audience, is clearly evident in using this as the time to initiate the worldwide design of the gospel.

The "noise" (v. 6) that attracted the attention of the crowd could have included the sound of the wind (v. 2), but it certainly involved the expression of the gift of tongues (Robertson, *Acts* 23). One hundred and twenty Spirit-filled believers speaking loudly, orderly in recognition of the Lord's wonderful works (v. 11), was enough to get anyone's attention.

Some confusion arose over what was being heard and seen as expressed in three questions. First, who it was speaking, i.e. how could "Galilaeans" speak in these various languages (v. 7)? As with Peter's dialect the night he betrayed Jesus (Mt. 26:73), perhaps the inflections and tones of the disciples as they spoke identified them as Galileans (Lenski 65). Their pejorative meaning is that they did not believe Galileans had such diverse linguistic ability (Bock 102)—an opinion that would be expressed again later (4:13).

Second, how were they able to do this (v. 8)? It is obvious that they were, indeed, speaking in other languages, but by what means could they do such a

thing? Not knowing the spiritual cause, some mockingly associated the effects with intoxication (v. 13). Unsaved folks almost always look for a naturalistic explanation of supernatural work.

Third, what did this mean (v. 12)? Though some in the audience were perplexed about what they saw and heard, they did want an explanation. These questions, mingled with mockery and incredulity, become the bridge Peter used to address the spiritual reality behind the event.

Summary
(2:1-13)

The arrival of the Day of Pentecost found the followers of Jesus gathered in prayerful anticipation. While others who assembled in the Temple courtyard were engaged in the routine of festival ceremonies, God the Holy Spirit came suddenly upon the disciples. His presence was manifested in the sound of wind, the sight of fire, and the enabling of the disciples to speak in other languages. As they spilled forth from the upper room into the Temple court area, their testimony became so compelling that it arrested the attention of the large, multilingual crowd. The curiosity of the crowd over the actions of the disciples provided the perfect opportunity for explanation of the experience and proclamation of the gospel of Jesus Christ. It was a setting where the providential hand of God is clearly seen, both in the timing and in the audience present.

Application: Teaching and Preaching the Passage

Exegetical Outline of the Text: 1. The Assembly of the Disciples (2:1). 2. The

Arrival of the Holy Spirit (2:2-3). 3. The Audience of those Who Heard (2:5-13).

In teaching this passage, one might consider the O. T. background to the Feast of Pentecost. This would include the purpose for the festival, its timing, and the command for Israel to gather in celebration. God wants His people to be celebratory in gratitude for His provision for our needs.

Some of the various "nations" listed in 2:8-11 are reached with the gospel as the witness of the church expands in the Book of Acts. One might trace on a map of that time period the gospel's progress to those areas, especially through the missionary journeys of Paul. The intention is to observe the actual implementation of the Great Commission.

The phrase "filled with the Holy Spirit" (v. 4) is used frequently in the Book of Acts. Because the Holy Spirit continues His work today, an excellent study is to trace this phrase and usage in Acts (see previous commentary). This could easily lead to several studies of His person and work in other texts as well.

The audience for the first proclamation of the gospel was diverse and curious about the actions of the disciples. Audiences vary in time, place, and reasons for their curiosity about the lives and beliefs of Christians and local churches. Opportunities for witnessing often arise from the questions asked from family, friends, neighbors, and co-workers. These are great times to share with them, but of course that means being prepared to do so.

In light of the modern discussion about the gifts of the Holy Spirit, an excellent study would be to explore the N. T. teaching about the subject. (See the bibliography for references.)

F. Peter's First Sermon (2:14-36)

1. Appeal to the prophesy of Joel: "this is that" (2:14-21)

14 But Peter, standing up with the eleven, lifted up his voice, and said unto them, Ye men of Judaea, and all ye that dwell at Jerusalem, be this known unto you, and hearken to my words:
15 For these are not drunken, as ye suppose, seeing it is *but* **the third hour of the day.**
16 But this is that which is spoken by the prophet Joel;
17 And it shall come to pass in the last days, saith God, I will pour out my Spirit upon all flesh: and your sons and your daughters shall prophesy, and your young men shall see visions, and your old men shall dream dreams:
18 And on my servants and on my handmaidens I will pour out in those days of my Spirit; and they shall prophesy:
19 And I will shew wonders in heaven above, and signs in the earth beneath; blood, and fire, and vapour of smoke:
20 The sun shall be turned into darkness, and the moon into blood, before that great and notable day of the Lord come:
21 And it shall come to pass, *that* **whosoever shall call on the name of the Lord shall be saved.**

As questions were raised about what the disciples were doing, a perfect opportunity presented itself for explanation. Peter's response becomes the first of many apologetic responses in Acts, where the Scriptures are interpreted to explain the experiences of the disciples and their witness to the resurrection of Jesus Christ. The O. T. was viewed as authoritative for faith and practice (Shires 26). Only when the writings of N. T. revelation began to be circulated were the O. T. Scriptures supplemented.

It is significant that Peter is the one who speaks. He has already demonstrated his leadership privately in the replacement of Judas Iscariot (1:15-26). Now he speaks publically for the disciples (v. 14). In contrast to his reticence to be identified with Jesus during His trial and crucifixion (Mt. 26:56-58), now he boldly proclaims Him to the very crowd who shouted for Jesus' crucifixion only a few weeks prior. His body language ("standing up"), the elevation of his voice (he "lifted up his voice"), and his call to listen ("hearken to my words") indicate one who is bold and confident in what he is saying (Robertson, *Acts* 25). Here is further confirmation of Peter's restoration from troubled denial to triumphant declaration. It is Peter who becomes the chief spokesman for the disciples in the early chapters of Acts. God's mercy, grace, and forgiveness overcome the past and re-order one's life for the future.

Peter's message targets two main truths: the explanation of why the disciples were acting as they were (vv. 16-21), and the declaration that Jesus of Nazareth had been raised from the dead (vv. 22-36). Peter confirms both truths by appealing to the authority of the Scriptures, citing both the O. T. Messianic prophesies from Joel and selected Messianic Psalms.

A number of commentators raise questions about Luke's recording of what Peter said (Fitzmyer 105-106; Polhill, *Acts* 45; Bock 21). Were these his actual words? It is clear that he said other things (v. 40), so the fact that Luke does not record *all* he said in this sermon is stated. How did Luke find out what Peter said since he wasn't there? While such questions are valid, they are sufficiently answered when one considers Luke's diligence in research (see the Introduction, "Source Material for Luke"). His insistence on "eyewitnesses" (Lk. 1:2), his own presence beginning at Acts 16:10 ("we") for the Pauline messages, his access to those who preached the messages (with the exception of Stephen) and those who heard them, coupled with the superintendence of the Holy Spirit in the process, provide ample justification for insisting that all the sermons in Acts are reconstructed sufficiently to give accuracy to their content. Stott's summary is that they are a reliable digest of each address (69). The same is true for the Gospel accounts of the messages and statements of the Lord Jesus. While we cannot be certain of *who* Luke's sources were, we can be confident that *what* was recorded is sufficiently accurate.

Peter begins with a thinly-veiled, humorous (Polhill, *Acts* 108) correction in verse 15. He answers that the mocking accusation, that the disciples were drunk (v. 13) with new wine, is ridiculous since it was only "the third hour" (9:00 a.m.) of the day. Typically, Jews of that day would not eat or drink anything until after the third hour (Barnes 30). Peter's reference assumes that all in his audience would agree.

Peter immediately ties the Pentecost manifestation of the Holy Spirit to biblical prophecy, quoting Joel 2:28-32. He declares, "this is that..." (v. 16). But in what sense is *this* (the disciples' speaking in other tongues) the same as *that* (what the prophet Joel wrote)? Some may take Peter's usage of Joel as being merely analogous: namely, there are coincidental parallels, but that is all. However, the parallels are not merely coincidental. More appropriately, Peter sees the Joel prophecy as predictive (Ger 44-45, Fitzmyer 252). While the crowd was not yet aware of the historic significance of what was happening, Peter's intent is to make them aware that the prophecy was being fulfilled before their eyes. It should be recognized that at the heart of Peter's message is the concept that O. T. prophecies demanded some kind of fulfillment (Shires 31).

The Joel prophecy contains several notable applications that are fresh in the minds of the disciples. For example, the ministry of the Holy Spirit is pervasive as He is "poured out upon all flesh." This certainly includes all Jews, but extends to other nationalities as well as to those of different gender and age. There is little doubt that Peter sees the expanse of the prophecy (Allen 98). The prophecy states that God will enable those in right relationship with Him ("my servants... my handmaidens") with revelatory abilities ("prophesy...visions...dreams," v. 17). New revelation was required for the new age of the Messiah.

Further, there is a time dimension in the phrases "the last days" (v. 17) and "the day of the Lord" (v. 20). The manifestation of the Holy Spirit on the Day of Pentecost, coupled with the completed work of redemption through Christ, ushers in the final era of this present world. This theme of the end times will be developed in great detail in the rest of the N. T. The biblical perspective of time and space is that there will be a definitive end of this present material world and universe, culminating in God's judgment of all (2 Pet. 3:7-13; 1 Cor. 15:23-28; Rev. 20:11-15).

The physical phenomena of "blood, fire, vapour of smoke...the sun shall be turned to darkness... and the moon into blood" (vv. 19-20) have been challenges for commentators for many years (Polhill, *Acts* 109). There is no question as to the association with "the Day of Yahweh" (Allen 101), but the eschatological development is debatable. Amillennialists usually see these as figurative expressions of the spiritual dimension of this present time period that began with the life, death, and resurrection of Christ and ends in the future with His triumphant Second Coming (Stott 73). Premillennialists usually see these as literal descriptions of events occurring during the Great Tribulation just prior to the Second Coming of Christ (Longenecker 72). Whichever eschatological scheme one chooses, it is the unanimous belief of the N. T. writers that the "last days" begins with the first coming of Christ and ends with His Second Coming (Stott 73).

The ultimate intention of Peter is to declare the resurrection of Jesus Christ. Joel 2:32 (Acts 2:21) ties the outpouring of the Holy Spirit to redemption. In every way, it fits the theological parameters of the gospel. It is universal in scope ("whosoever shall call"), personal in relationship ("the name of the Lord"), and intentional in purpose ("shall be saved"). This is not only the prophetic scheme of Joel, it is the transitional statement Peter needs.

2. Jesus of Nazareth, the resurrected Christ (2:22-36)

a. His approval by God (2:22-24)

**22 Ye men of Israel, hear these words; Jesus of Nazareth, a man approved of God among you by miracles and wonders and signs, which God did by him in the midst of you, as ye yourselves also know:
23 Him, being delivered by the determinate counsel and foreknowledge of God, ye have taken, and by wicked hands have crucified and slain:
24 Whom God hath raised up, having loosed the pains of death: because it was not possible that he should be holden of it.**

Boldly, Peter makes the assertion that Jesus of Nazareth (cf. 10:38) is the fulfillment of all unfulfilled Messianic prophecies, that the whole scheme of redemption through the Messiah has reached its climax in the person and work of Jesus the Christ (Shires 31). Peter's first assertion is that Jesus of Nazareth was divinely approved by God (v. 22). The evidences of His divine attestation (Bock 119) are seen, first, in the two-fold description of His works as "miracles, and wonders and signs" (v. 22). "Miracles" (Greek *dunamis*) literally are works of power or mighty works. The compound phrase "wonders and signs" (Greek *teras* and *semeion*) is used to depict a signal that draws attention and should be observed (Thayer 573). This same phrase will be associated with the apostles and become a signature of apostolic authenticity (Acts 2:43; 2 Cor. 12:12).

Though some of Jesus' contemporaries had challenged the source of His power (Mt. 12:24), others, like Nicodemus (Jn. 3:2), concluded rightly that the works Jesus did were of God. Some of those works would have still been fresh in the minds of those who lived in the area. How could they forget the resurrection of Lazarus, which had taken place a short time ago and just over the hill at Bethany (Jn. 11:1-46)? It is certainly possible that Lazarus was still living and numbered with the disciples in Jerusalem on the Day of Pentecost.

In verse 23, Peter attributes the death of Jesus to three elements: divine purpose ("determinate counsel"; Greek *horismene boule*), the foreknowledge of God (Greek *prognosis*), and the actions of wicked men. Peter's statement is the perfect theological paradox of divine sovereignty and human free will (Polhill, *Acts* 112, Marshall 75). The death of Christ involved both the hand of God and the hands of men. The blended elements of God's sovereign ability and man's activity form a truth that is part and parcel of biblical theology. God is sovereign and acts as He pleases. God has chosen in His pleasure and ordained that men have free will to act of their own accord (Forlines, *Quest* 325-335). Such is the theological blend of culpability in the death of Jesus Christ.

This leads to the second and most important approval of Jesus of Nazareth. God not only performed miraculous works by the hands of Jesus (v. 22), He also raised Him up from the dead (v. 24)! Here is the first public proclamation of the resurrection of Jesus Christ to an audience of unbelievers (Robertson, *Acts* 29). Peter combines the word "pains" (Greek *odin*), which means the pains of childbirth (Thayer 679), with the statement that it was not possible for Jesus to be held by death. Life came from death; the idea is that death could not hold back the resurrection of Christ in the same way a mother cannot hold back childbirth (Bock 122).

b. Confirmation from Psalm 16:8-11 (2:25-31)

25 For David speaketh concerning him, I foresaw the Lord always before my face, for he is on my right hand, that I should not be moved:
26 Therefore did my heart rejoice, and my tongue was glad; moreover also my flesh shall rest in hope:
27 Because thou wilt not leave my soul in hell, neither wilt thou suffer thine Holy One to see corruption.
28 Thou hast made known to me the ways of life; thou shalt make me full of joy with thy countenance.
29 Men *and* brethren, let me freely speak unto you of the patriarch David, that he is both dead and buried, and his sepulchre is with us unto this day.
30 Therefore being a prophet, and knowing that God had sworn with an oath to him, that of the fruit of his loins, according to the flesh, he would raise up Christ to sit on his throne;
31 He seeing this before spake of the resurrection of Christ, that his soul was not left in hell, neither his flesh did see corruption.

Peter now uses Psalm 16:8-11 as predictive of the Messiah and of the fact that the Messiah would not be bound by death (Bock 126, Polhill, *Acts* 114). His interpretive argument goes like this. David's rejoicing in the Psalm was over the presence of God and hope beyond death (vv. 25-26). But he must have been speaking of someone other than himself when he said that God would not abandon his soul to hell or his flesh to corruption (v. 27). The reason David was not referring to himself is the fact that David had long since been dead and his tomb was in Jerusalem (v. 29). Therefore, he must have been speaking with prophetic foresight and referring to the Messiah who was to be his descendant (v. 30). The words about removing his soul from hell and preventing his body from corruption were therefore predictive of the resurrection of the Messiah (v. 31).

Some use this text as an integral part of a theology of the afterlife (Lenski 89-92). The view is that during the time Jesus' body lay in the grave, His soul descended into hell (1 Pet. 3:18-20) where He proclaimed His power over death, hell, and Satan. (For a summary survey, see Picirilli, "1 Peter" 179-183). The Apostles' Creed states, "His soul descended into hell." Be that as it may, Peter's intent is not to show what was happening between the death of Christ and His resurrection. He is using the Scriptures to show that the resurrection was an integral part of the Messianic promise.

Peter's apologetic appeal to the O. T. as final authority is common to nearly all the sermons of the Book of Acts. Indeed, it is an essential part of N. T. Christianity that Jesus Christ is the Messiah predicted in all O. T. references. For Peter, as with all N. T. writers, when the Scriptures speak, God speaks. It is Peter's intent to converge the Messianic elements of the O. T. with a literal application to Jesus of Nazareth as the Messiah.

c. Proclamation of Jesus of Nazareth as Lord and Christ (2:32-36)

**32 This Jesus hath God raised up, whereof we all are witnesses.
33 Therefore being by the right hand of God exalted, and having received of the Father the promise of the Holy Ghost, he hath shed forth this, which ye now see and hear.
34 For David is not ascended into the heavens: but he saith himself, The LORD said unto my Lord, Sit thou on my right hand,
35 Until I make thy foes thy footstool.
36 Therefore let all the house of Israel know assuredly, that God hath made that same Jesus, whom ye have crucified, both Lord and Christ.**

The central truth of Peter's message is summarized in verse 32. The Messianic claims of the Psalms he has quoted are fulfilled in "this Jesus," "Jesus of Nazareth" (v. 22), the One who had just been crucified a few weeks prior (v. 23). But Peter makes the startling declaration that God raised Him from the dead. Fitzmyer (256) states that the crucified Jesus of Nazareth has become the risen Lord. Furthermore, they are all eye-witnesses of that fact: that is, not of the resurrection event itself, but the living, resurrected Jesus. Peter uses the same word for witnesses (Greek *marturos*) that Jesus used in 1:8. The testimony of Peter as an eye witness of the living Christ is compelling. It is the core truth

of the Christian message. If Jesus is the risen and living Messiah, where is He now? Peter declares (v. 33) that He has been exalted into Heaven and to the "right hand of God." As further evidence of His exaltation, His hearers are witnessing the manifestation of the Holy Spirit in the disciples. Note the Trinitarian reference in the persons and work of redemption (Bock 130-133).

How does Peter know that Christ has been exalted to the right hand of God? Again, he turns to the Scriptures to prove the point, quoting Psalm 110:1. He witnessed the ascension of Christ into the sky (Acts 1:9-10), but the Scriptures define His destination.

The exaltation of the Messiah to the right hand of God is indicative of several things. It is a position of favor, of power, and of intercession. Furthermore, there is a subtle hint in verse 35 that His present position is temporary. The work of the Messiah does not conclude until all foes are subdued. Following that, He will rule as King of Kings and Lord of Lords (Rev. 19:16).

The conclusion of Peter's message (v. 36) is both pointed and provocative. It is pointed in that he lays the charge of Israel's role in crucifying the Messiah squarely on his hearers' shoulders. Their role in His crucifixion was an act of ignorance and unbelief (Lk. 23:34; Jn. 1:11). Peter's conclusion is provocative in terms of identifying who Jesus of Nazareth is. He is "Lord" and "Christ," Christological titles (Fitzmyer 260) signifying Him as equal to O. T. Yahweh and the long-awaited Messiah. This is what is meant in God's exaltation of Him in the resurrection.

Peter's message is not a "rags to riches" story of some poor, relatively unknown man from Nazareth who came out on top. Instead, it is the working out of God's plan of redemption in the person of the Messiah, whose story has been written in the prophetic messages of the O. T. for centuries. It is the fulfillment of God's redemptive plan from Genesis 3:15 forward. This is the signal message of Christianity. The advent of the Messianic age required explanation. Peter provides the inspired insight necessary in proclaiming that Jesus of Nazareth is the long-awaited Messiah of O. T. prophecy as evidenced ultimately by His resurrection from the dead.

Summary
(2:14-36)

The first recorded sermon in the Book of Acts is by the apostle Peter. Occasioned by the need to explain the unusual expressions of the disciples in speaking other languages, it becomes the precedent-setting model and message of the followers of Jesus Christ. Its themes are repeated in each sermon in Acts where the gospel is proclaimed to Jews.

Peter uses the O. T. Scriptures as proof of the manifestation of the Holy Spirit. Further, he draws upon two Messianic Psalms to show that resurrection from the dead was an essential element of the Messiah's confirmation. Not only was Jesus resurrected from the dead, but He was exalted to the right hand of God, a position of glory reserved only for deity. The application of these Scriptural proofs to Jesus of Nazareth and the eye-witness experience of His death and resurrection form the central core of beliefs of the newly-born church of Jesus Christ. This message is one of the great theological declarations of the N. T.

Application: Teaching and Preaching the Passage

Exegetical Outline of the Text: 1. Call for Attention (2:14-15). 2. Confirmation 1: "This is That," Spoken by the Prophet Joel (2:16-24). 3. Confirmation 2: "For David Speaketh," a Confirmation by David (2:25-31). 4. Conclusion: Jesus of Nazareth Was Raised Up and is Lord and Christ (2:32-36).

Peter's sermon is a model of the gospel message in Acts. It is built on the authority of the O. T. Scriptures and specific prophecies regarding the Messiah. These are fulfilled in Jesus of Nazareth in His life and resurrection. Using the outline above one can reference the prophecies and Peter's intention in using O. T. references.

Also, the sermon contains the core of the gospel message that can be summarized in a simple outline: 1. The Prophecies of the Messiah (Joel and David). 2. The Person of the Messiah (Jesus of Nazareth). 3. The Proof of the Messiah (the resurrection).

While Peter's message to the crowd about what was happening is clear and decisive, it should be noted that the means of communication is important as well. Preaching is the primary method endorsed by the Lord in the communication of His truth (1 Cor. 1:17-24; 2:1-5). Verbal proclamation of studied biblical truths that have personally impacted the proclaimer's life carry authority and have great influence.

G. Response to Peter's Message (2:37-41)

37 Now when they heard *this,* **they were pricked in their heart, and said unto Peter and to the rest**

of the apostles, Men *and* brethren, what shall we do?

38 Then Peter said unto them, Repent, and be baptized every one of you in the name of Jesus Christ for the remission of sins, and ye shall receive the gift of the Holy Ghost.

39 For the promise is unto you, and to your children, and to all that are afar off, *even* as many as the LORD our God shall call.

40 And with many other words did he testify and exhort, saying, Save yourselves from this untoward generation.

41 Then they that gladly received his word were baptized: and the same day there were added *unto them* about three thousand souls.

The response to Peter's message was nothing less than astonishing, especially when the circumstances are considered. Many in this same crowd of people had been hostile to Jesus and His followers. To these very same people Peter claimed fulfillment of centuries-old biblical prophecy in the manifestation of the Holy Spirit. Furthermore, he declared that Jesus of Nazareth was the Messiah and charged them with wickedness in His crucifixion that had taken place just a few weeks prior.

At this point, the climax of Peter's message is that God has raised this same Jesus from the dead, and the disciples are eyewitnesses of His resurrection—incredible, albeit all true, assertions. The crowd is captivated. Their collective reasoning is something like, "If Jesus of Nazareth was, indeed, the long-awaited Messiah, and they had crucified Him, what hope was left for them?" (Bruce, *Acts* 69).

Their question reflects something deeper. Peter's message was not only convincing but also convicting. This is noted by Luke's use of the phrase, "they were pricked in their heart." The word "pricked" (Greek *katanussomai*, to pierce, to sting sharply) reveals this deeper work. Here is evidence of the power of the Holy Spirit (Acts 1:8) working in the hearts and minds of those who heard the gospel for the first time. Though people are not always as open and expressive as these were, we can be sure that the Holy Spirit always accompanies the proclamation of the gospel (Jn. 16:8-11).

Perhaps what Peter does not say should be noted. He does not call for correction in the miscarriage of justice about the false accusations that led to the crucifixion of Jesus. Nor does he appeal for religious tolerance of Jesus' followers. As timely as these may seem, Peter understands that there is a much larger issue at stake: calling people to a right relationship with God as provided through Jesus Christ. At this point, all the injustices and prejudices against Jesus and His followers faded into trivial, background details that worked together to accomplish a much greater goal. Jesus died and rose again to redeem men from their sins and bring them into right relationship with God.

Peter's answer to their question, therefore, is decisive (v. 38). Taken directly from the teaching and commands of Christ, he calls them to repentance (Mk. 1:15; Lk. 24:47) and baptism (Mt. 28:19) with the promises of forgiveness of sins (Lk. 24:47, Jn. 20:23) and receiving the gift of the Holy Spirit. While this is not intended to be formulaic, Peter is clear as to what is required to become a follower of the

Messiah, Jesus Christ. Indeed, this was Peter's own discipleship journey as the gospel accounts well document.

The requirements Peter presents are significant and will become the core message of the church: how to gain remission of sins and become a Christ-follower. (It will be challenged later in relation to Gentile requirements; see Acts 11:1-3; 15:1-2). He begins with repentance (Greek *metanoeo*, to change one's mind). Repentance is a pervasive biblical concept that has always been included in a right relationship with God (2 Chron. 7:14; Ps. 51; etc.). This concept involves a complete change of mind that leads to a life reformation (Fitzmyer 265). It was central to the message of John the Baptist in preparation for the coming of the Messiah (Mt. 3:2). It was central to the preaching of Jesus when He began His ministry (Mk. 1:15). Its inclusion now by Peter is but a continuation of that same message. In this context, repentance certainly would include a change of mind about the person of Jesus of Nazareth and His resurrection. He must be understood as the Messiah who provides remission of sins.

Next, Peter includes baptism (Greek *baptize*, to immerse, submerge), but with the qualifier "in the name of Jesus Christ." While baptism was not a new or foreign concept to Jews, it was usually reserved for Gentile proselytes. However, John the Baptist called for Jews to be baptized after repentance in heart-preparation for the coming of the Messiah (Mt. 3:6, 11). Jesus even submitted to John's baptism in confirmation of John's message and endorsement of his ministry, not because Jesus needed to repent of anything (Crabtree 54). Both John the Baptist and Jesus presented models of baptism that were much dif-ferent from the ritual baptism of prose-lytes.

Further, Jesus called for baptism of those who would become His followers (Jn. 4:1-2). Very rarely did that involve anyone who was not Jewish (Mt. 15:24). Apparently, only the apostles actually performed the ritual on those who became Christ-followers. In this case, baptism is certainly identified with Jesus, not just for proselytes to Judaism.

Following His resurrection, Jesus commanded that those who would become His disciples, upon hearing the gospel, were to be baptized (Mt. 28:19-20; Mk. 16:16), using the Trinitarian name as identification. His command in the Great Commission is consistent with His practice. Though none of the baptismal scenes in Acts include the actual statement of the Trinitarian name, that fact does not mean they did not baptize as Jesus had instructed them, in the name of the Father, Son, and Holy Spirit. The name of Jesus Christ is what makes Christian baptism unique. Plus, the name of Jesus Christ is essentially identified with the Father and the Holy Spirit (Robertson, *Acts* 35). Therefore, Peter's inclusion of baptism is not surprising.

The use of the name of Jesus Christ (and the Trinity) in baptism is not merely part of a liturgical formula but rather confessional of the person of Christ. As Peter has declared, Jesus of Nazareth is the Messiah and has been raised from the dead to the right hand of God. Confessing Him as Lord (Rom. 10:9-10) is part of authentic repentance and faith. When one is baptized in the name of Jesus Christ, "he is committed to and identified with Jesus" (Longenecker 79).

The purpose of baptism is tied to "the remission of sins," but in what sense? There are endless discussions on the usage and meaning of the preposition translated "for" (Greek *eis*). (For an excellent summary see Robertson, *Acts* 35-36). While some see baptism as instrumental in gaining remission of sins and the means of joining the fellowship of believers (Fitzmyer 265), it is a mistake to do so. Bruce (*Acts* 70) and Ger (53) rightly state that it is against the whole genius of biblical religion to believe that any ritual has any value except as it reflects the work of grace within. Peter himself will clarify this very point later when he states that baptism is not about "putting away the filth of the flesh" (i.e., remission of sins), "but the answer of a good conscience toward God" (1 Pet. 3:21).

It is also evident that all believers in the Book of Acts were baptized as soon as possible after their coming to faith (Acts 8:12, 36-38; 9:18; 16:33). One simply cannot separate authentic saving faith in Jesus Christ from being identified with Him by Christian baptism. It should be noted that baptism is for those who understand its meaning. Understanding may be related to age, culture, and circumstances.

Peter also includes the reception of the Holy Spirit Himself (Greek genitive of identification) as a "gift." The Holy Spirit's manifestation earlier had led to Peter's interpretation of the event and his message about the resurrection of Christ. It should be pointed out that such interest in the Holy Spirit as part of becoming a Christ-follower will be integral in many of the accounts in Acts (e.g. 4:31; 5:3; 8:14-20, 29; 10:44-47; 12:2; 15:28; 16:6-10; 19:1-6). But the gift of the Spirit is more than a spiritual experience. He comes to indwell the life of the person who embraces Jesus

Christ as Savior with all the benefits that affords (Rom. 8:1ff). God living in us: what a gift!

In verse 39, Peter turns to the scope of such an incredible promise. Drawing upon concepts from Isaiah 54:13, 57:19, and Joel 2:28, he makes generational and international applications. Apparently, Peter understands to some extent what Jesus meant about extending the gospel to all people. The diversity of the crowd to whom he is preaching is reflected here. His personal growth in this truth will be documented later (Acts 10).

The phrase, "as many as the Lord our God shall call" is taken from Joel 2:32. It is a fitting conclusion to Peter's answer. This is a succinct statement of a spiritual work of God in the heart that accompanies the proclamation of the gospel (Mt. 22:14; Jn. 6:44; 16:8-12). The gospel is sufficient for all ("many") but efficient only for those who respond ("shall call") in saving faith (Forlines, *Romans* 239-240; *Quest* 378).

While Peter has answered the question posed in verse 37, he is not finished (v. 40). Luke does not record all he said but does include one final quote. The phrase "save yourselves" (Greek *sozo*, aorist passive) is better understood as "be saved." God does the saving. The phrase "untoward generation" has the idea of "twisted, crooked" (Robertson, *Acts* 37). Peter probably means this in the same sense of the believing remnant of Israel (those who are saved) as differentiated from the majority (those who are crooked) who reject the message of the Messiah (Bruce, *Acts* 72). The apostle Paul will later expand on this very concept (Rom. 11:5-6).

It has been estimated that Jerusalem would swell to as many as 200,000 people during feast times (Bock 146). The interaction of the disciples with the crowd on the Day of Pentecost in the Temple court area and Peter's message would have been witnessed by a very large number of people. The result was that an estimated three thousand responded to Peter's call to repent, to be saved, and to follow in baptism. Furthermore, that took place "the same day," i.e. the Day of Pentecost. This is not the conversion of a mass of people as a group, but the sum total of individuals who personally chose to accept the truth of Peter's message and believe in Jesus of Nazareth as the risen Messiah. While we may be awed by the number of people who were saved in one setting, on one day, it should be noted that God desired all to be saved, not just three thousand.

It could be argued that there should have been a greater number to respond. After all these Jews were well-schooled in Messianic theology. Perhaps, but Peter's is not a call for political or social commitments. Nor would these be considered "low hanging fruit," easily persuaded and ready to respond. Quite the contrary. All things considered, the number who responded and followed in believer's baptism is incredible.

The logistics of accommodating such a number for baptism would not have been overwhelming. There were at least twelve apostles who were experienced in the process (Jn. 4:1-2) and several pools of water available (Gower 200-201). One can picture the apostles leading groups to the various pools of water, exhorting them briefly, then immersing each one, thus signifying their new faith in the resurrected Jesus Christ.

Apparently, the number was important enough to them that they reported it. Numbers are important to Luke, especially the numbering of believers. From one hundred and twenty gathered in the upper room (Acts 1:15), to three thousand, one hundred and twenty, the witness of the disciples proved effective immediately.

H. Early Community Life of the Church (2:42-47)

42 And they continued stedfastly in the apostles' doctrine and fellowship, and in breaking of bread, and in prayers.
43 And fear came upon every soul: and many wonders and signs were done by the apostles.
44 And all that believed were together, and had all things common;
45 And sold their possessions and goods, and parted them to all *men*, as every man had need.
46 And they, continuing daily with one accord in the temple, and breaking bread from house to house, did eat their meat with gladness and singleness of heart,
47 Praising God, and having favour with all the people. And the Lord added to the church daily such as should be saved.

The Book of Acts answers the question, "What happened to the first followers of Jesus Christ?" The same question is appropriate now for those who responded to Peter's preaching. Even a casual reading of verses 42-47 shows a transformation in lifestyle and commitment. What may seem to be an idyllic representation is not, however, rooted in a new religious ritual, emotionalism, or idyllic sentimentality (Fitzmyer 268;

Bock 155). The relationship of community among the early believers has well-defined truths that give substance to their newly-placed faith. Verse 42 summarizes the basis for such a transformation.

First, the new believers were instructed in "the apostles' doctrine." The apostles acted in obedience to the Lord Jesus (Mt. 28:19) to teach His commandments. These would include all Jesus Himself had taught the apostles over the three and one-half years of their yoke of discipleship with Him. One can picture the apostles privately gathering to discuss what to teach the new converts. It should be remembered that they depended on the work of the Holy Spirit to help them recall the teaching of Christ (Jn. 14:26; 16:13-15). When they had decided what to teach, they could have easily broken off into twelve study groups led by an apostle to convey that day's "curriculum." This would have been a great time for Matthew, Peter (Mark), and John to begin cataloguing material for their Gospels.

Next, the element of "fellowship" (Greek koinonia, to partner, share common interests) is included. This would have included becoming personally acquainted with the apostles and one another. It would have involved discussions regarding O. T. Messianic texts and their fulfillment in Jesus Christ. There would have been lively question and answer sessions with the apostles. Eating meals together and the first celebrations of the Lord's Supper—with the interpretation Jesus had given—would have been sacred and blessed. The Passover ritual would never be the same. No longer would its symbolism be stuck in the historic events of the Exodus from Egypt. The wider significance of the body and blood of the Messiah applied in salvific truths would become far more personal.

Fellowship is sometimes best understood as having people to partner with in sharing life issues; this is one of the deepest needs of human life. Based on the teachings of Christ (Mt. 11:28-30, etc.) the early believers learned to bear one another's burdens (Gal. 6:2). How do people manage life, who don't have such resources for life's issues? They don't do very well.

The third dimension of the relationship was "breaking of bread." What exactly Luke means has been debated by many. Is this a common meal (cf. Acts 20:11; 27:35), taken together in table fellowship that overflows with the joy of worship and instruction, or is he referring specifically to the celebration of the Lord's Supper? It might very well have been both (Polhill, Acts 119). Sometimes the breaking of bread together might have been just the blessing and sacredness (Longenecker 86) of eating a meal together. But, as the conversation turned to Christ and His truth, the Lord's Supper would naturally follow. God's care for the physical needs of people is a truism of the Scriptures especially noted in Jesus' instruction to pray, "Give us this day our daily bread" (Mt. 6:11).

Lastly, the early believers were noted for "prayers." The church was born during a time of extended prayer (1:14), and they continued to pray as they gathered. Prayer expresses the core belief that life on earth cannot be lived as it should without Heaven's assistance. It assumes that God Himself can and does work in response to the prayers of His people. Therefore, prayer is to be pervasive in all situations, needs, and plans, as well as times when wisdom and guidance are needed. Community praying as well as private prayers are integral to Christian life and community.

Verse 43 inserts a sense of "fear" (Greek *phobos*) in the community life of the church. The word indicates a reverential awe for the sacredness of God's work among them (Fitzmyer 271) at the dawning of the new age of the Messiah. Such fear is connected with the miraculous works of the apostles defined as "wonders and signs"—the same words that had characterized the works of the Lord Jesus (v. 22). The expression is used in Acts as a type of code or shorthand for the work of the Holy Spirit through the apostles (Polhill, *Paul* 114.) The confirming Hand of God upon the message and ministry of the apostles is evident (Bruce, *Acts* 73-74).

A sense of unity and common bonds dominated the relationship (v. 44). Note that they are characterized as they who "believed," showing the essentialness of faith as the core condition of the relationship. As the gospel spread to other places and people groups, this became the basic term used to define the condition for becoming a follower of Christ (3:16; 4:4; 5:14; 6:7; 15:7).

There are many and varied opinions about the exact meaning and practice of the early church regarding the sharing of possessions. Some take it to be an early form of communalism (Marshall, *Acts* 5, 84; Bruce, *Acts* 74). Others believe they retained private ownership but were willing to sell possessions and share according to the need—which might be called "common-ism" (Fitzmyer 272; Robertson, *Acts* 39; Ger 57). This latter view seems best, particularly as indicated by the phrase "as every man had need." When the need arose, peo-ple who owned property or other possessions were willing to sell and give to meet the need. Without doubt, the sense of community and mutual support, in selfless acts of sharing, was a dominant expression of their faith. It was so strong that it continued among the believers at Jerusalem (4:34-37; 6:1-2). None of the other churches in Acts are recorded as having the same practice. Though not specifically taught as a practice to be established in all churches, such selfless giving was a beautiful model of the heart of authentic faith and compassion for the needs of others (1 Jn. 3:16-18). Communism, no! Communalism, no! Compassion, yes!

One may ask where the disciples got the idea of shared needs and community supply. The Qumran community of the Essenes and their communal lifestyle has been suggested as a possible source. However, with them, the sharing of material goods was required, not voluntary (Josephus, *Antiquities* XVIII.I.5). Greek idealism has been suggested as another possibility, but this is a stretch; if for no other reason than being Greek, the Jews among the early believers would have rejected it. The best source seems to be the practice of the Lord Jesus with the apostles during His earthly ministry. If it worked for them, then why not for the church (Bock 153)?

The Temple continued to be a central location for worship, teaching, and prayer (v. 46). Since most of these believers and all of the apostles were Jews, and since Jesus frequented the Temple areas to teach, it would continue as a place of worship and teaching for the apostles. Its court areas, particularly Solomon's porch (Gower 350), would have accommodated the crowds who gathered. The apostles went daily to teach and preach to the believers as well as to all who would come for temple ceremonies.

Their interaction also extended to personal homes in times of table fellowship. All was done with a pervasive spirit of glad and generous ("singleness") hearts that expressed praises to God (v. 47). In their hearts was joy and on their lips was praise. The result of such excellent social graces and authentic spirituality was a public sense of "favor" (respect) for the Christian community. Their fervor for the Lord resulted in favor with the people—at least for the time being. The growing popularity of the message of Jesus as the Messiah would soon enough chafe the consciences of the religious leadership in Jerusalem.

An additional result of their community life was the daily conversion of others who observed the fellowship of the believers and heard the gospel. Note that here is the first mention of the word *church* (Greek *ecclesia*) in Acts. Identification moves from the general term, "all that believed" (v. 44), to the consolidated term "church" (v. 47). Though the term "ecclesia" had other references and applications, it would become a key identification term in the N. T. for all believers in general (the "universal church") and of local groups of believers in particular (the "local church").

So concludes one of the most significant chapters in Acts as well as the history of Christianity. This is the first of seven "progress reports" (Ger 57) Luke gives in Acts (2:47; 6:7; 9:31; 12:24; 16:5; 19:20; 28:30-31). In modern terms, to use a sports analogy, it was an awesome "Opening Day."

Summary
(Acts 2:37-47)

The response to Peter's message was confirming of the Lord's promise for power in the proclamation of the gospel. Luke's statement is that "they were pricked in their heart" (v. 37). The word *pricked* is not the same as translated in 9:5 as *pricks*. The Holy Spirit powerfully works in the hearts and minds of people to convince them of their need of Christ. We are not always aware of this in the lives of those who need Christ and hear the gospel. People are often very accomplished at masking how they feel and what they are thinking. But we must never forget that the Holy Spirit attends the proclamation of the gospel in every heart. We should be encouraged to continue our prayers and witness even when it seems to us we are getting nowhere.

But the community life of those who savingly believed was also confirming of the quality of life that characterizes a follower of Jesus Christ. The church's "Opening Day" indicated that the Lord continued to work through the disciples and blessed their efforts to proclaim His truth. The summary characteristics of the early church become the desired model for all churches.

Application: Teaching and Preaching the Passage

Exegetical Outline of the Text: 1. The Request About Saving Faith: "What shall we do?" (2:37-40). 2. The Response of Saving Faith: "Then they that gladly received his word were baptized" (2:41). 3. The Results of Saving Faith: "And they continued stedfastly" (2:42-47).

63

This text is especially relevant to showing the desired response to the gospel message. Its proclamation should be followed by an expected response. To be sure not everyone who hears it will be saved, but those who are should follow the Lord in believer's baptism and continue in those essential elements of Christian life listed in the text. Of course, these make for an excellent study and presentation and can be presented individually when teaching or preaching. See the commentary above for the breakdown of each one.

Contained in verses 41-47 is the first summary model of the spiritual elements that every Bible-believing local church should strive to emulate. These should be present and simultaneous. Here is the biblical core for ecclesiology. It is a profitable study to understand each one and find specific local applications. Neither are there substitutes for these. I take it that these elements provide the model God wants for His church. In every age and generation there seems to be a proliferation of superficial substitutes for these powerful, life-changing beliefs and practices.

In contrast, there have been some notable, misguided efforts to isolate believers. Historically, communalism has always failed, as illustrated by the Shakers and others who adopted false doctrines that dictated their religious fervor. The Monastic Period represented a different brand of isolation. Any substituting of something else for what is described in this text is wrong. Here is the model to follow. Local churches that follow this model are powerful influences in their communities.

The conclusion of the model is that people were saved every day. Such ought to be the goal of every local church. Some local churches, in fact, do have a powerful witness and see people saved often in their own communities. In many communities, it is the combined efforts of local churches that need to be taken into account. If we were able to count the ones saved in any given community (as Luke was able at the time) there would be many. This applies also to the combined missions efforts of churches. Missionaries have been sent throughout the world to carry the gospel to "the uttermost part of the earth." There are folks saved through missions' efforts every day. Every day, somewhere, the gospel is being presented and people are being saved. That is one reason there will one day be "a great multitude which no man could number, of all nations, and kindreds, and people, and tongues (who) stood before the Lamb, clothed with white robes, and palms in their hands; and cried with a loud voice, saying, Salvation to our God which sitteth upon the throne, and unto the Lamb" (Rev. 7:9-10).

It should always be remembered that we are not called to keep roll of who is saved (except as it relates to our local needs). It is God who writes the names in the Book of Life (Rev. 20:12, 15).

III. THE CHURCH'S WITNESS IN JERUSALEM (3:1—8:1a)

A. Healing of the Lame Beggar (3:1-11)

1 Now Peter and John went up together into the temple at the hour of prayer, *being* the ninth *hour*.
2 And a certain man lame from his mother's womb was carried, whom they laid daily at the gate of

the temple which called Beautiful, to ask alms of them that entered into the temple;

3 Who seeing Peter and John about to go into the temple asked an alms.

4 And Peter, fastening his eyes upon him with John, said, Look on us.

5 And he gave heed unto them, expecting to receive something of them.

6 Then Peter said, Silver and gold have I none; but such as I have give I thee: In the name of Jesus Christ of Nazareth rise up and walk.

7 And he took him by the right hand, and lifted *him* up: and immediately his feet and ankle bones received strength.

8 And he leaping up stood, and walked, and entered with them into the temple, walking, and leaping, and praising God.

9 And all the people saw him walking and praising God:

10 And they knew that it was he which sat for alms at the Beautiful gate of the temple: and they were filled with wonder and amazement at that which had happened unto him.

11 And as the lame man which was healed held Peter and John, all the people ran together unto them in the porch that is called Solomon's, greatly wondering.

The Temple and its courts continued to be a convenient meeting place for the early church for teaching and worship. Peter and John go there together for evening prayers (v. 1). However, the encounter with the lame beggar along the way leads to much more than the miraculous healing that took place. Big doors often turn on small hinges.

Luke's description of the physical condition, routine, and reputation of the beggar is essential to the entire story as well as to appreciating the extent of the healing (3:10; 4:14, 22). In addition to his congenital condition, the man had to be assisted daily by family and friends to a specific place by the gate called Beautiful (vv. 9-10). One has to admire the loyalty of his supporters. The place and opportunity to receive alms were well chosen. Giving alms to the poor and needy was considered an act of compassion that merited favor with God, especially in connection with temple ceremonies (Bock 160; Polhill, *Acts* 126). There would have been a lot of people passing his way for the daily ceremonies of Temple worship.

There were two daily sacrifices—burnt offerings—in temple ceremonies, and three times set for prayer (Ps. 55:17; Dan. 6:10). The first sacrifice and time of prayer was at the third hour of the day (9:00 a.m.), the second at the ninth hour. Prayers were also offered at sunset (Longenecker 89). This healing occurred during the time of the evening sacrifice and prayer, "the ninth hour," 3:00 p.m. (Harrison 69).

The place of the healing was in the vicinity of the temple gate called *Beautiful* (vv. 2, 10). Josephus speaks of ten gates in the temple structure of that day (*Antiquities* XV.XI.3; *Wars* V.V.3). There is much disagreement as to which one was called *Beautiful*, but three are possibilities. Some believe this was the Nicanor Gate (Stott 90; Bruce, *Acts* 77; Polhill, *Acts* 127), so named in honor of the donor and the events that took place in delivering it to the Temple to be mounted. It is described as being elaborately decorated (Longenecker 90). It was located close to the Temple itself, leading from the Court of Women. According to Josephus (*Wars*, V.V.3), it was some seventy-five feet high, covered with Corinthian bronze, had huge double doors, and "far exceeded in value those gates that were plated with silver and set in gold." The description is apt to the name, but still it would have taken great effort to carry the lame man to this location up several flights of steps, across the Court of Women, and with the ceremonies of the priests possibly intruding.

Ger (60-61) and Fitzmyer (278) hold that it was the Shushan Gate, known now as the Eastern or Golden Gate, located on the eastern entrance to the outer Temple area from the Kidron Valley. It provided access through Solomon's portico into the Court of the Gentiles. The lame man's condition required assistance by others (v. 2), and access to this gate would have been difficult, though not impossible, because of the roughness of the terrain.

The third possibility is that there was another gate, known then as the gate *Beautiful*, and that its precise location was lost when the Temple was destroyed in A.D. 70 by the Romans. Though most commentators today favor the Nicanor Gate, we cannot be exactly certain which one it was. The destruction of the Temple by the Romans was total. Keener (II:1048), concluding his discussion, agrees with this assessment.

It is certainly possible that Peter and John had seen the lame beggar before, since all involved in the incident went daily to the Temple. However, routine often clouds perception. This afternoon encounter would be different as the beg-

gar spoke directly to them (v. 3) to ask "an alms" (money or goods given to the poor).

Peter responds to the man's inquiry, calling for his undivided attention. Tragedy often becomes opportunity. As the man looks expectantly (v. 5), Peter's statement to him is full of meaning and intention. He does not promise to check with the church's benevolence efforts (2:44-45) and return with an offering. Indeed, Peter himself has no money to give but is in possession of something far more valuable. It is a form of an "alms" that would exceed any the man had ever received. With the special giftedness of apostolic authority (2:43) from Christ, Peter calls for the man to "rise up and walk" (Greek *peripateo*, present imperative), meaning to walk continually. Peter's phrase, "in the name of Jesus Christ of Nazareth," is not an incantation, but the citing of the authority by which the miraculous deed must be accomplished. Peter commanded the man to be healed (Keener II:1063). To reassure and assist, he then reaches out his hand to the lame man (v. 7a) and literally pulls him to his feet (Robertson, *Acts* 42). Peter's action demonstrates his confidence in complete healing.

Luke details (v. 7) the healing by saying that "his feet and ankle bones received strength" (Greek aorist passive *estereothesan*, from *stereos*, to make firm, solid), literally meaning "were strengthened." The healing was instantaneous. Such details would be of interest to a medical doctor (Morgan 97; Walker 98; Schnabel 196). Emaciated leg muscles, deformed feet that dangled at the end of brittle ankles, suddenly spring to life! He feels in his body what he has never felt before! No wonder he needs a little assistance to stand! He has never stood on his own in his entire life. But it didn't take him long to learn!

Verses 8-9 describe the jubilant actions of a radically changed man. The verbs used indicate initial, physical response and continuous activity topped off with shouts of praise to God. And why not? He received more than money, or even what money could buy. The gift literally changed his life and the lives of those who had assisted him for so long. One can easily picture the man known as the "lame beggar who sat at the gate Beautiful" now running, leaping, and shouting praises to God in ways he has never before been able to do. Perhaps Peter and John followed behind in sacred bemusement, marveling at God's display of mercy.

Is this not what the message of Christ does? It heals what sin has crippled, overcomes disability, and sets people on their feet. "Lame humanity is the Church's opportunity" (Morgan 102). Nor was the healing done in private. At that time of day there would have been a significant crowd of worshipers and priests who witnessed what happened. His indecorous behavior, combined with his shouts of praise, echoed against the walls and gates of the Temple area. All knew the man's identity and were astonished (v. 10). They only needed definition of how and why this had taken place, and Peter would not be hesitant to explain it all.

Verse 11 serves to make transition from the healing to the explanation that Peter will offer. The exuberant actions of the lame man who was healed move them to the court area of Solomon's portico where his emotions become calmer and his shouts more subdued. A crowd gathers with a heightened sense of curiosity to know more of what has taken place. Kent (40) suggests they might have desired further miraculous displays, but none are indicated. Note that the man who was healed "held" (Greek *krateo*, to cling) to Peter and John, perhaps in gratitude to his benefactors and perhaps in reverential fear of the unexpected, mysterious, radical change that had taken place in his body. Miraculous events deserve wise analysis. That is what follows.

Summary
(3:1-11)

Two elements of ministry by the early church are represented by the healing of the lame beggar at the Beautiful Gate: the daily temple teaching and the miraculous deeds of the apostles that would often accompany the proclamation of the gospel (Acts 2:43, 46). There might have been similar events previously, but this one is the first recorded and is accompanied with exceptional publicity (Bruce, *Acts* 77). The healing is not the subterfuge of something staged for publicity. It is the exercise of the unique power of God via the apostles upon a well-known case of congenital, physical disability. None, not even those who later condemned the apostles (4:7, 16), could deny its reality. But as notable as the miracle was, the ultimate purpose of God's display of power was in confirmation of the apostles as His witnesses for the proclamation of the gospel of Jesus Christ. The story does not end with the man's healing.

Application: Teaching and Preaching the Passage

Exegetical Outline of the Text: 1. The Tragedy They Encountered—"lame from his mother's womb" (3:1-2). 2. The Transformation That Ensued—"walking, and leaping, and praising God" (3:3-8). 3. The Testimony to Be Explained—"all the people ran together...greatly wondering" (3:9-11).

The Temple itself was an incredible architectural structure (Mt. 24:1). So many events occurred in and around its precincts during the early years of the church. A great study would include some history of its construction, its design, and its extended court areas. One should remember that it was patterned after the O. T. tabernacle in the wilderness. In fact, the O. T. wilderness tabernacle was a scale model. All of its components represented some element of redemption. Models may be used to show these components and their relationship to redemption in Christ. Though quite detailed, the daily ceremonies of Temple worship might be researched from Exodus and Leviticus in order to give context for the activities that went on.

The healing of the lame man is representative on many levels. Lameness comes in many forms: physically, mentally, emotionally, relationally, and spiritually. There is a sense in which, like Peter and John, "lame" folks are present wherever we go. Historically, the church has led the way in mercy ministries to address the lameness of humanity in providing hospitals, educational institutions, shelters for the homeless, addiction recovery, orphanages, and a thousand more provisions for restoration. Churches and pastors should work hand in hand with these ministries, for lameness is our business.

Peter and John were not able to give money to meet the man's request. They did have something that was far better.

Healing and spiritual forgiveness provided far more than a few coins could ever provide. While wisely helping people materially was and is part of the compassionate responsibility of the church, the greatest help ever given is the healing that comes with saving faith in Jesus Christ. Mercy ministries should never confuse this priority nor cloud its meaning with psychobabble or nebulous spiritual talk. Sometimes ministries that began with the powerful message of the gospel, combined with compassionate help, have gotten off track. Biblical truth makes us free (Jn. 8:32).

The miracle left the on-lookers wondering how this happened (v. 11). Changed lives need definition and explanation. These are witnessing opportunities for those who are changed. That this was Paul's witness defense is clear from the fact that the story of his change by Christ is recorded three times in Acts. Peter used the occasion to proclaim the gospel as the real reason for the change in the man. In this way, Peter is shifting the focus from the miracle to the miracle-worker, Jesus Christ.

There is a story sometimes told of a conversation that took place centuries later regarding the healing of the lame beggar. Sproul (76-77) associates it with St. Thomas Aquinas and Pope Innocent II, while Barnhouse (35-36) associates it with two unnamed Catholic cardinals. The essence of the conversation—whoever the two men—is that one said, "No longer do we (the Catholic Church) say, 'Silver and gold have I none.'" To this the response was, "Yes, but neither can we say, 'In the name of Jesus Christ, rise up and walk.'" Material prestige often supplants spiritual power.

B. Peter's Second Sermon (3:12-26)

12 And when Peter saw *it*, he answered unto the people, Ye men of Israel, why marvel ye at this? Or why look ye so earnestly on us, as though by our own power or holiness we had made this man to walk?
13 The God of Abraham, and of Isaac, and of Jacob, the God of our fathers, hath glorified his Son Jesus; whom ye delivered up, and denied him in the presence of Pilate, when he was determined to let *him* go.
14 By he denied the Holy One and the Just, and desired a murderer to be granted unto you;
15 And killed the Prince of life, whom God hath raised from the dead; whereof we are witnesses.
16 And his name through faith in his name hath made this man strong, whom ye see and know: yea, the faith which is by him hath given him this perfect soundness in the presence of you all.
17 And now, brethren, I wot that through ignorance ye did *it*, as *did* also your rulers.
18 But those things, which God before had shewed by the mouth of all his prophets, that Christ should suffer, he hath so fulfilled.
19 Repent ye therefore, and be converted, that your sins may be blotted out, when the times of refreshing shall come from the presence of the Lord;
20 And he shall send Jesus Christ, which before was preached unto you:

21 Whom the heaven must receive until the times of restitution of all things, which God hath spoken by the mouth of all his holy prophets since the world began.
22 For Moses truly said unto the fathers, A prophet shall the Lord your God raise up unto you of your brethren, like unto me; him shall ye hear in all things whatsoever he shall say unto you.
23 And it shall come to pass, *that* every soul, which will not hear that prophet, shall be destroyed from among the people.
24 Yea, and all the prophets from Samuel and those that follow after, as many as have spoken, have likewise foretold of these days.
25 Ye are the children of the prophets, and of the covenant which God made with our fathers, saying unto Abraham, And in thy seed shall all the kindreds of the earth be blessed.
26 Unto you first God, having raised up his Son Jesus, sent him to bless you, in turning away every one of you from his iniquities.

Peter is quick to seize the opportunity, as he did on the Day of Pentecost, and gives his explanation about the lame man's healing (the "Colonnade Sermon," Longenecker 91). He is especially interested in presenting its larger significance. There are a few variations, but his message carries the same elements as his sermon at Pentecost (Dodd 21-22). First, regarding the power to heal the lame man, he redirects the attention of the crowd away from the apostles themselves (v. 12). Then he explains that the larger significance of the healing is that God has used this situation to glorify Jesus as the Son of God. Nearly all commentators remark that "Son" should be "Servant" (Bruce, *Acts* 80; Stott 92; Robertson, *Acts* 43). The Suffering Servant image from the Isaiah passages (Isa. 52:13—53:12 and others) was very well known among the O. T. prophecies of the Messiah. However, *Son* is certainly a reasonable translation of the original word (Greek *pais*) that can mean *child, servant,* or *slave.* Peter uses the same term twice (vv. 13, 26).

The most important truth Peter declares is that the same Jesus who healed the lame man was put to death but has been raised from the dead. And the apostles are witnesses to the fact (v. 15). This is the essence of apostolic preaching in Acts as well as the central, unique truth of Christianity (1 Cor. 15:14-17). Furthermore, it is through faith in the name of the resurrected Jesus that the lame man was made strong (v. 7). Peter even describes his healing as "this perfect soundness"— meaning perfect in all its parts, complete, whole (Robertson, *Acts* 44).

Whose faith secured the lame man's healing? Was it that of the apostles or that of the lame man himself? Harrison (74) makes the case that it had to be the lame man's faith. Others appeal to the faith of the apostles on the man's behalf (Lenski 138; Barnes 64). Both conditions may be found in the Scriptures (Mk. 2:5; Acts 14:9). While the phrasing is clear that faith is instrumental in the healing, whose faith (in this particular situation) is not clear (Fitzmyer 286). Most likely, there was faith from both. Certainly, Peter expressed faith as he commands "in the name of Jesus Christ of Nazareth" (v. 6) for the man to walk. The healed man responded in faith by

getting up as Peter assisted him (v. 7). Apostolic giftedness in invoking the name of Jesus Christ that sparked something in the heart of the lame man resulted in his healing (Keener II:1063).

Although "wonders and signs" (2:43) were initially performed by the apostles, this is the first miracle to be recorded. As such it is part of the confirming apologetic of special miracles that accompanied the proclamation of the gospel in the Acts narrative as promised by the Lord Jesus (Mk. 16:17-20). But, perhaps the main point of the miracle is not so much the possessor of faith in this instance but the person of faith's focus, i.e., in the name of Jesus Christ. The main intent of Peter's message is that if Jesus has power over death, He certainly has power to heal physical illness and restore health.

As previously stated, some of the incidents in the Book of Acts reveal a transitional period in the church's history. The time of the apostles and their giftedness to perform miracles as they did is one of those incidents. However, it should be noted that, in His sovereign wisdom, God *sometimes* chooses to heal physical infirmity in this life. Hence, we are to pray for the healing of the sick (Jas. 5:13-18). It is part of life and part of the ministry of the local church to minister to the sick (Mt. 25:36). Many genuine healings are well documented. Furthermore, the Scriptures clearly teach that one day all believers will be healed in every way, physically, spiritually, and emotionally (1 Cor. 15:42-43, 51-58; Rev. 21:4-5). But God does not always heal sickness in this life. Sometimes He chooses to heal by taking believers to Heaven (Ps. 116:15).

The contemporary clamor of the "Word of Faith" movement (one of many terms, including "health and wealth"; "name it and claim it," etc.) has cast a shadow over authentic, intercessory biblical faith, prayer, and support of those who are truly sick. The claim that it is God's will to heal all sickness in this life is not only a problem of misinterpreting the Scriptures, it is woefully misguided. Too often, biblical truths are spun to accommodate someone's personal agenda. In the wake of such purveyors of false claims of healing lie thousands of hurt and discouraged people who sincerely believed they would be healed but were not. Pastors and local churches often encounter folks who became embittered over such false claims and begin to look with skepticism on any authentic ministry of compassion for their needs.

Second, Peter boldly accuses the crowd (vv. 14-15) and the Jerusalem rulers (v. 17) of complicity (Bruce, *Acts* 82) in the killing of "the Prince of life" (vv.14-15; cf. 2:23). He even refers to Pilate's determination to release Jesus and their clamoring for the murderer, Barabbas (Crabtree 459-460), to be released in Jesus' place (Mt. 27:11-26)—a paradoxical situation if there ever was one! This is Peter's second pointed accusation (2:23) of guilt in the death of Jesus Christ.

It may be difficult to equate the actions of the rulers of Israel against Jesus as having been done in "ignorance." They were well aware of the life and ministry of Jesus of Nazareth. They had bribed (Judas Iscariot) and threatened (Pilate) to secure His arrest and condemnation. However, Jesus Himself interpreted their actions as being done, ultimately, in ignorance as He prayed for their forgiveness (Lk. 23:34). The apostle Paul confirms the same in 1 Corinthians 2:8 in referring to the leaders who crucified Jesus as well as to his own choices prior to saving faith in Christ (1 Tim. 1:13). All were well schooled in the theology of Judaism but still blind to God's truth (Mt. 23:1-33). It is possible for a person to be intellectually informed but spiritually unenlightened. Profane actions often arise from profound ignorance.

Four times Peter references the prophets (vv. 18, 21, 24). He asserts in verse 18 that God used them to speak His truth in their descriptions of the person and work of Messiah. He refers to the Suffering Servant prophecies (Ps. 22, 69; Isa. 52:13—53:12) and that Jesus Christ has fulfilled them in His crucifixion and death.

Third, Peter's call to repentance (v. 19) deserves some detailed consideration. He calls them to repentance (compare 2:38) that their sins may be forgiven. The word translated "be converted" (Greek *epistrepho*, aorist imperative) may be understood as "turn again" and is seen as reinforcing repentance. He assures them that doing this will result in sins being "blotted out" (Greek *exaleipho*, erased, wiped out). The metaphor is that of washing off that which was written on papyri (Bock 175), thus a cleansing that leaves no trace (cf. Ps. 51:9). Furthermore, this will result in seasons of "refreshing" (Greek *anapsucho*, to cool or refresh) from the very "presence of the Lord" who sends sunshine and pleasant breezes (Lenski 142) upon His people. This is quite a contrast to the dry heat and arid spirituality of Pharisaical legalism. There is no mention of baptism this time, as in 2:38. God does the forgiving and cleansing if we do the repenting. (See Barnhouse 38 for the interesting, Dispensationalist viewpoint that Peter was offering the Kingdom to the Jews at this point.)

Peter continued (vv. 20-21) by proclaiming the future dimension of the Messiah's work, His second coming (Ger 65; Bock 175). This aspect of the return of Jesus Christ was a recent reminder (1:11) as well as an ancient prophecy. The phrase "since the world began" literally means "from of old, ages past" (Greek *ap' aionos*). One may refer to texts such as Genesis 3:15; Isaiah 11, 25, 35; Jeremiah 31; Joel 2; Zechariah 12—15. The final judgment and ultimate restoration of all things is an integral part of biblical theology. It is intertwined in Messianic prophecy. Jesus is not only the One who forgives our sins, He is also the Savior of mankind and final Judge.

Fourth, Peter (vv. 22-26) appeals to the O. T. prophets as authoritative, and whose united testimonies (Stott 94) confirm his message. Specifically, he quotes fragments of Deuteronomy 18:15, 18-19. Peter's knowledge of the O. T. prophets and their Messianic message is very commendable. In effect, he is affirming all the prophets as contributing to the Messianic message and that Jesus is the Messiah of whom they spoke. The continuity is unmistakable (Longenecker 94). Note, too, that Peter names Moses as the author of the Pentateuch, the consistent N. T. testimony of the authorship of Deuteronomy. In his first message, in chapter two, he focused mainly on the Messianic message of the Psalms and specifically referred to Davidic authorship. Here he specifically refers to Mosaic authorship of the Pentateuch. No greater O. T. writers could be referenced than these two.

The person and work of the Messiah is of such paramount importance that to trifle with these great truths or neglect to hear Him is fatal (v. 23). To make this point, Peter summarizes a number of warning texts, all from the Pentateuch, regarding the gravity of such truth (Gen. 17:14; Ex. 31:14; Lev. 7:20, 23:29; Num. 9:13). There is a stark contrast between the warning and the way in which Jesus was treated by the very ones Peter is now addressing. Only repentance and forgiveness resolve such guilt.

The Samuel prophecy (v. 24) is a little more obscure since there are no specific Messianic prophecies uttered by him. However, the prophecy is in relation to the anointing of David as King of Israel and the Messianic dimension of the Davidic Covenant of 2 Samuel 7:4-17 (Bruce, *Acts* 87).

Peter concludes (vv. 24-26) with a positive affirmation of Israel's covenant relationship with God and His promise of blessing (Gen. 12:1-3). One key part of that blessing is that Jesus the Messiah and Son (Servant) of God (v. 13) was sent to Israel first. They are first in line (Rom. 1:16). The initial relationship blessing lies in the resurrected Jesus who forgives sin. A different word for *sin* is used in verse 26 (Greek *poneria*), meaning evil deeds or wickedness. The word in verse 19 (Greek *harmartia*) means sins, offenses. Perhaps these are used interchangeably, but what a blessing to know that when God forgives, all our sins are "blotted out"!

In consideration of the entire scene, Luke's record of the healing of the lame beggar is perfectly analogous to the impact of sin upon human life and the healing that results in saving faith in the risen Savior, Jesus Christ. The same person who heals the lame forgives the sin.

Summary
(3:12-26)

Peter uses the occasion of the healing of the (formerly) lame man who sat at the Gate Beautiful as a reference point to proclaim the gospel. The actions of the healed man got the attention of those present, who wondered how this was possible. In essence, Peter has a greater message for them than an explanation of the man's healing. In essence he shifts attention from the miracle to the miracle-worker.

Although there are some variations, Peter's second sermon echoes the same themes as his first one on the Day of Pentecost. He uses a notable event that had captured the attention of the crowd to address the larger significance of what was intended. The healing of the lame beggar at the Beautiful Gate was an expression of the power of the risen Christ who also forgives sin. This Christ is the Messiah of whom all the O. T. prophets spoke. His name is Jesus. He was maliciously crucified, only a few months previously, at their own hands. But He was raised from the dead! He now offers forgiveness to all who repent. This grave truth is so important that to reject it is fatal. It is now offered first to Israel as descendants of Abraham and recipients of God's covenant blessings.

Application: Teaching and Preaching the Passage

Exegetical Outline of the Text: 1. The Rejection of Christ (3:12-15a). 2. The Resurrection of Christ (3:15b-19). 3. The Return of Christ (3:20-26).

Peter was very bold in assigning responsibility for the death of the Messiah to those who were watching the sanctified antics of the healed man. While there was a particular guilt they bore, about His crucifixion, in a much deeper sense we all, as sinners, bear responsibility for the death of Christ (Rom. 5:6-8).

The fact that Luke gives a lot of space for this story is significant. The man himself is representative of spiritual truths. The healing of the lame man represents what sin does *to* us and what Christ does *for* us. Just as the lame man was crippled from birth and sat outside the Temple itself, so sin cripples us and leaves us outside the fellowship of the Lord. The healing of the lame man represents what Christ can do for us in restoring us spiritually. Restoration begins with repentance (3:19) and opens the windows of heaven for countless times of spiritual refreshing. These come from the presence of God Himself. The message of the gospel involves the return of Jesus Christ, as well (vv. 20-21). To be prepared and ready for His return, we must have received forgiveness of sins. Just as Israel is the covenant people of God (v. 25), so God makes all who trust Christ a part of His covenant people (Gal. 3:23-29; Eph. 2:11-22).

The gospel of Christ was presented many times to the Jews on many occasions. It never varied. Peter was very bold in his call for repentance and faith in Christ. Boldness is not rudeness though sometimes it is interpreted as such. We must be wise and considerate, but we should never tire of opportunities to witness to the power of Christ. A person who does not listen today may listen well tomorrow. This becomes the principle for teaching and preaching about wisdom combined with courage in witnessing. There are situations that seem to tender a person's heart. Addressing these and using discernment and graciousness make for excellent messages.

Though the healing of the lame man could not be denied (4:14), not everyone appreciated it as they should. It led to trouble for the apostles. The devil hates it when people's lives are changed, and the gospel is proclaimed. Every believer and every Bible-believing church that faithfully witnesses and sees people's lives changed can expect opposition in some form by the devil. He wants to shut the mouths of the Lord's people. This is one of his strategies and goals. This spiritual opposition is essential for believers to understand and prepare for. This principle is an excellent basis for teaching and preaching about spiritual warfare.

C. Peter and John on Trial Before the Sanhedrin (4:1-22)

1. The arrest of Peter and John (4:1-4)

1 And as they spake unto the people, the priests, and the captain of the temple, and the Sadducees, came upon them,
2 Being grieved that they taught the people, and preached through Jesus the resurrection of the dead.
3 And they laid hands on them, and put *them* in hold unto the next day: for it was now eventide.
4 Howbeit many of them which heard the word believed; and the number of the men was about five thousand.

If the healing of the lame beggar ended with Peter's explanation, all would be well. However, as miraculous and undeniable as it was, not everyone welcomed the miracle, and especially Peter's explanation. The demonstrative expressions of the man who was healed and the sizable crowd that gathered in curiosity alerted the Temple security along with high ranking members of the Sanhedrin. Thus, Peter and John were thrust into a confrontation with Jewish leaders. It was the first of many such confrontations, each becoming more threatening, and even deadly, as time passed.

As Peter and John speak to the people (v. 1), they are accosted by Temple authorities: namely, "the priests...the captain of the Temple...the Sadducees." Each deserves definition since they will be part of the ongoing Acts narrative. The "priests" (some manuscripts say "chief priests"; Acts 5:24; Fitzmyer 297; Walker 114) are those who were on call in the ceremonial observances of Temple worship for that day. Josephus estimated that there might have been over twenty thousand priests at that time (*Apion* II.8). These were arranged into twenty-four orders or courses (1 Chron. 24:1-19) and served as scheduled (Lk. 1:5-9). As such there would have been several hundred priests on call any given week (Ger 70). The commotion caused by the healing of the lame beggar may have interrupted the ceremonial proceedings and engendered some irritation on the priests' part, thus their presence. Rigid, religious ritual is often offended by authentic worship.

"The captain of the temple" was the chief security officer of the temple police, but he was more than just hired security. He was a member of the high priestly family and second in command (Bock 186). He was charged with keeping the peace and to squelch any uprisings that Roman authorities would frown upon. One must mention the distinct probability that some of these very people, perhaps this very captain of the Temple, were involved in the arrest of Jesus in the Garden of Gethsemane not many weeks prior (Mt. 26:47-51; Mk. 14:43-47; Lk. 22:52; Jn. 18:3, 12). He was responsible for all the Temple affairs (Schnabel 233), and a great affair had just taken place in the Temple precincts. He knew nothing about it and had not given permission for it to occur.

The "Sadducees" were one of the two main religious sects of the N. T. that played a major role in the religious and political backdrop of the time. While the Pharisees were the ones Jesus engaged the most, it was the Sadducees who were mainly instrumental in Jesus' arrest, trial, and death sentence from Pilate (Mt. 26—27; Jn. 18). They, especially, tried to squelch the testimony of the resurrection of Christ (Mt. 28:11-15). Although there is no surviving written evidence about much of their background and theology (Bruce, *Acts* 90), according to tradition they traced their origins back to Zadok, whom Solomon appointed as priest (1 Kgs. 2:26-27, 35). This name is often pronounced *Saddouk*, meaning "righteousness" (Bock 186; Picirilli, *Paul* 24) and evolved into our English term "Sadducee." However, this lineage and history is much disputed (Polhill, *Acts* 139-140). Though the historical background of the Sadducees is somewhat obscure (EDT 965-966), it is clear that they consisted mainly of well-to-do aristocrats. They became the ruling political and religious elite of the N. T. era (Fitzmyer 298;

Bock 196), exercising oversight of Temple observances and the High Court (the Sanhedrin), and worked to insure a peaceful relationship with the Romans at any cost (Polhill, *Acts* 139).

From their ranks came the High Priest, the most powerful religious and political figure among the Jews. Three High Priests are named in the Book of Acts: Annas, Caiaphas, and Ananias (23:2). Annas occupied the position A.D. 6-15, and continued to carry the title afterwards. Eventually, he was succeeded by his son-in-law Caiaphas, who held the office A.D. 18-36 (Lenski 157). Ananias received the appointment to High Priest from Herod of Chalcis, the younger brother of Herod Agrippa I, and served A.D. 47-58 (Bruce, *Acts* 425). The office of the High Priest was never the friend of either the Lord Jesus or any of His followers.

According to Josephus (*Antiquities* VIII.I.4; VIII.X.6), the Sadducees restricted their Scriptural authority to the Pentateuch, but adopted a limited supernaturalism in interpretation. One key belief was the denial of the immortality of the soul (Josephus, *Wars* II.VIII.14). Because of their rationalistic approach (Edersheim III:316), the Sadducees were known, among other things, for "denying the resurrection" (Acts 23:8). This is the issue that engendered most of the religious animosity between them and the Lord Jesus (Mt. 22:23-32). Interestingly, when the Sadducees confronted Jesus with a hypothetical question in an effort to stump Him, He responded by appealing to the authority of Exodus 3:6 as evidence of life after death (Crabtree 372). This issue would be central in all the confrontations with the followers of Christ in Acts as well (5:17-28; 6:12; 23:8). This was the issue in Peter's preaching that offended them most (4:2).

Further, the Sadducees saw Judaism as being religiously temple centered (EDT 966). This, too, would become a major point of offense because of Stephen's witness (7:44-54; see commentary).

Fearful of political upheaval and military suppression from the Romans, as well as resenting Peter's proclamation of the resurrection of Jesus, the Temple authorities arrested Peter and John, incarcerating them at the end of that day to await trial (v. 3). But the Word of God is not bound! Many who witnessed the healing of the lame beggar and had heard Peter's proclamation of Jesus as the prophesied and resurrected Messiah savingly believed in Christ (v.4). Note the usage of the term *believed*: this will be consistently used in Acts, not only as the key condition for saving faith in Christ, but also to distinguish those who have become disciples.

Most all writers agree that the number Luke gives of five thousand is the total number of men, excluding women, who were disciples, not the number converted on this one occasion (Robertson, *Acts* 50; Bock 188; Lenski 155). Polhill (*Acts* 90) argues that the number could include the women, too. One must remember that there were salvation decisions every day since Pentecost (2:47). Whether the women were included or not, there was a sizeable number of believers in Jerusalem. Note Luke's progression of numbering from one hundred and twenty (1:15), to three thousand (2:41), to five thousand (4:4), to the number of disciples multiplying (6:1, 7), to numbering in the thousands (21:20). Even if the population of Jerusalem was as many as 250,000, as

some assert (Marshall, *Acts* 98-99), the number of early believers was significant. Apparently, Luke desired to show a quantitative response to the gospel message. What he saw as a measure of success, however, was regarded as a threat by those who opposed the message of the gospel (5:28; 17:6).

2. The arraignment before the Sanhedrin (4:5-7)

5 And it came to pass on the morrow, that their rulers, and elders, and scribes,
6 And Annas the high priest, and Caiaphas, and John, and Alexander, and as many as were of the kindred of the high priest, were gathered together at Jerusalem.
7 And when they had set them in the midst, they asked, By what power, or by what name, have ye done this?

The listing in verses 5-6 of the three leadership groups makes it clear that this was an official assembly of the Jewish high court. The *rulers* mentioned were the priestly representatives on the council. The *elders* were respected leaders who were wealthy and influential members of the Jewish upper class. Teachers and interpreters of the Law would be the *scribes*, most likely including the Pharisaic element of the council (Polhill, *Acts* 141).

The Sanhedrin ("the council," v. 15) numbered seventy men (Num. 11:16-17) plus the High Priest (Fitzmyer 299; Harrision 81). This group of men held the highest position of power politically, economically, and religiously in Jerusalem. In the time of the N. T., they held great power over the issues they adjudicated (Edersheim I:97). Though the extent of their power regarding capital offenses is somewhat unclear, they had succeeded in getting the Lord Jesus condemned to death. What is clear is that they would assert such power and influence against His followers as the Acts narrative continues (5:17, 24; 6:12). The arraignment of Peter and John before them and their reciprocal responses sets the precedent for the relationship between the Jewish leadership and the early church. It was a relationship of intimidation, threats, and torturous deaths from the Council, but of joyful submission from the church.

Annas and Caiaphas are well known, but one point of clarification is needed. Luke refers to Annas as "the high priest" when, in fact, his son-in-law, Caiaphas, *technically* held the office. At issue is the simple fact that though Caiaphas held the office, Annas was the power behind the office, making him the high priest in effect. Luke is referring to the actual state of affairs.

John and Alexander are not so well known. Some have speculated that John was probably Jonathan, son of Annas (Fitzmyer 299-300; Polhill, *Acts* 142; Schnabel 236) who succeeded Caiaphas as High Priest in A.D. 36-37. No record of Alexander exists except here, but of interest is the fact that he has a Greek name and sits on the Jewish High Court. Apparently, he was known well enough at the time, by Luke's source of information, to be listed by name. Luke also references "kindred of the high priest." These are probably extended family who occupy prominent administrative positions in Temple worship, more than likely all being Sadducees (Marshall, *Acts* 99). The nepotism

should be obvious but is of no consequence.

Someone not listed here, but possibly present and worth the reference at this point, was Saul of Tarsus (7:58; 22:5; 26:10). More about his association with the Sanhedrin will be said later. Perhaps he was Luke's source for some of the information about this event, including the name of Alexander.

There is a divine irony in the whole scene as it unfolds. In this very position, before this very Council, Jesus had stood just weeks prior. The initial trial of Jesus was probably a preliminary hearing (Picirilli, *Mark* 409) following His nighttime arrest in the Garden of Gethsemane. It had taken place in the palace of the High Priest (Mt. 27:58). The actual trial (Crabtree, *Matthew* 455) had probably moved to the official Council chamber close to the Temple (Picirilli, *Mark* 409). While Jesus was standing before the Council in the palace of Caiaphas, Peter was watching from a distance (Mt. 26:58; Lk. 22:54). Now he himself stands in the same spot before the very men who condemned Jesus to die (Lenski 158).

This is not to say that all who sat on the Sanhedrin agreed with the death sentence of Jesus, nor that all would agree to silence the apostles. Joseph of Arimathaea (Lk. 23:50, 51) and Nicodemus, for example, would have been exceptions. One has to wonder if they were still on the Council, and if they were whether they spoke up for the apostles. However, Luke does not tell us of any dissenting votes in this instance.

Assembled then were the highest officials in Judaism at the time to decide what to do with Peter and John, and by implication, the people and teaching they represented. It would be negligent not to reference the larger picture represented here. Christianity itself goes on trial, and, theologically, the Lord Jesus Himself (Acts 9:5)—again! Furthermore, we know there is an unseen, spiritual battle being waged (Eph. 6:12). The stakes could not be higher.

The question posed to Peter and John by the Council exposed the officials' problem with the authority or source for the miracle (v.7). The Sanhedrin was responsible for the Temple ceremonies and teachings, so in one sense theirs was a fair question of accountability. But accountability is always qualified by authority, and authority is always evidenced by its fruits (Mt. 7:15-20; Lk. 7:35). The Council demanded to know the source of their authority for their actions and teaching. This raises the question, had they not been aware of what had been going on in the Temple courts the past several weeks? Or is this merely rhetorical to gain a confession and an official connection with Jesus of Nazareth whom they had convicted and condemned? That was a matter of record.

Nor is this the first time this question has been asked. It is the same question posed to Jesus previously in a very similar context (Lk. 20:2). It is inconceivable that these men are basically clueless and uninformed of the growing numbers of the followers of Jesus.

Ironically, and with a twist of sarcasm, just as the Sanhedrin had not sanctioned the ministry and miracles of Jesus, neither had they given permission to the apostles for miraculous healings and teachings about Jesus of Nazareth. Though there had been previous miracles and regular teaching of the Temple attendants (2:43, 46), this latest miracle, though undeniable, was too

demonstrative and public to be overlooked. They especially resented the explanation offered by Peter (3:16). Now, officially, they confront Peter and John, perhaps expecting them to cower before them in submission—and if not to face more serious consequences.

But why was there such a conflict to start with? Why the show of force against the followers of Jesus? There may be many factors involved in the answer, but two stand out as significant enough to call a meeting of the Sanhedrin. These reasons would remain the basis for confrontation in the coming days as well. First, there was a theological conflict. The Sadducees had an embedded, restrictive theology limited to the Pentateuch, at least their interpretation of it. Their theology did not allow for *any kind* of resurrection, much less a resurrected Messiah. Interestingly, when they had confronted Jesus with a contrived question about the resurrection (Mk. 12:18-27; Lk. 20:27-38), Jesus answered them from the Pentateuch!

They absolutely did not believe that Jesus of Nazareth was the Messiah. His affirmation that He was the Messiah constituted blasphemy in their minds. To them, this alone was sufficient cause to condemn Jesus to death (Mt. 27:63-66). Plus, they had done all they could to squelch any talk of His resurrection. Since they were responsible for the Temple and its teachings, they were compelled to put a stop to the use of the Temple courts as a platform for the apostles (2:46; 3:18), whose teachings proclaimed Jesus of Nazareth as the Messiah; and they had just worked so intensely to have Him crucified. It was a matter of theological integrity. However grandiose their claims of spiritual responsibility, they were empty and superficial.

On the other hand, the apostles believed all that the O. T. prophets had predicted concerning the coming of the Messiah and His resurrection over death as the confirming act of His identity. Furthermore, they believed that Jesus of Nazareth was the long-predicted Messiah and they had personally witnessed His resurrection. The Temple was a perfect setting to proclaim these truths about Jesus Christ, so the apostles took advantage of the setting.

But this was more than just a matter of differing theological viewpoints to be shown tolerance and equanimity. Entitled leaders are often the most intolerant and vindictive, especially those who are in powerful positions. As history has shown, corrupted theology often corrupts relationships and engenders vicious conflict. Here is the precedent-setting event that marks such a conflict with the church. The apostle Paul would later characterize this as "the offense of the cross" (Gal. 5:11).

Second, the Sadducees had a political agenda with the Romans and occupied a prestigious position that was perceived to be at risk. They had succeeded in getting Pilate to acquiesce to capital punishment for Jesus on the grounds that He was a threat to Roman sovereignty (Picirilli, *Mark* 410). Even one of Jesus' apostles (Simon, Lk. 6:15) was a Zealot. Jerusalem was a political powder-keg with a lit fuse. Therefore, to them, the followers of Jesus would pose the same threat. The growing number of disciples invited suspicion of a possible uprising (as contrived as this was) and might bring Roman intervention. The previous decision of the Sanhedrin about Jesus was a matter of record (Stott 96).

On the other hand, the apostles had no political agenda but were boldly telling what they had learned and witnessed in the resurrection of Jesus. Their interest was in the Kingdom of God. We can be sure the irony of the whole event was not lost on Peter and John.

3. The answers to the charges (4:8-22)

a. Response from Peter and John (4:8-12)

**8   Then Peter, filled with the Holy Ghost, said unto them, Ye rulers of the people, and elders of Israel,
9   If we this day be examined of the good deed done to the impotent man, by what means he is made whole;
10 Be it known unto you all, and to all the people of Israel, that by the name of Jesus Christ of Nazareth, whom ye crucified, whom God raised from the dead, *even* by him doth this man stand here before you whole.
11 This is the stone which is set at nought of you builders, which is become the head of the corner.
12 Neither is there salvation in any other: for there is none other name under heaven given among men, whereby we must be saved.**

Jesus had told the disciples they would face such situations (Lk. 12:11-12; Mt. 10:16-20). Ultimately, the same conflict the Sanhedrin had with Jesus continues with His disciples. Peter's boldness (v. 8) is evidence of the Holy Spirit's fullness, at that very instant giving him the appropriate response to the inquiry. If he is intimidated by the situation, it certainly does not show. Though he and John had been arrested and incarcerated overnight, he begins his answer to the charges with courteous deference shown to the Council in their respective positions of leadership.

In the question posed by the Council (v. 7), *this* is a generalization that refers to the healing of the lame man. Peter quickly clarifies the healing as complete ("whole") and personifies it by pointing to the man ("this man," v. 10) who is now standing beside them. He is not an impersonal object lesson but a recipient of God's mercy. But Peter wants to make it clear that the healing of the lame man cannot be separated from the person of Jesus Christ (Bock 192). And it was by the authority of this "name" that they had acted in the miraculous healing. Peter's point is: if God can raise Jesus from the dead, then He has power to make men whole. Nor does Peter mince any words about the manner of Jesus' death. Again he lays the charge of crucifixion at their feet (v. 10). If there had been any doubt as to the connection of Peter and John to Jesus, then that doubt has been dispelled (Prov. 28:1)!

References to Messianic prophecy in the O. T. (v. 11) are central to the defense of the apostles regarding Jesus as the Messiah. Here Peter quotes Psalm 118:22 using the "stone" as a Christological motif. This reference may not, in its context, appear to be Messianic (Kaiser 100), but Peter's use of it is more than a seemingly isolated quote. Indeed, this is the very same reference Jesus had made when He stood before some of these very same men who had asked the very same question (Mt. 21:42; Mk. 12:10-11; Lk, 20:17). Jesus' meaning was clear, as was Peter's. The "builders" refers to Israel's leaders,

before whom Peter stands, as did Jesus. The "stone" is Jesus, the Messiah. Their rejection of Jesus as Messiah is analogous to the rejection of the "stone" considered to be unfit for use (Jn. 1:11). But that very "stone," via the resurrection of Jesus Christ, has become the centerpiece of the whole building. The building motif is later repeated by Peter (1 Pet. 2:4-8) and expanded upon by the apostle Paul (1 Cor. 3:9-17; Eph. 2:20-22).

However, Peter's message does not end with accusation. Using the threefold refrain of salvation, from Psalm 118 (Leupold 819), he quickly moves to the very heart and essence of the message of the gospel (v. 12). The one rejected has become the one who receives. Jesus saves! Here is the first usage of *salvation* (Greek *soteria*, from the verb *sozo*, to deliver, rescue, save) in the preaching of the gospel. Whether Luke is intentionally using word-play on the meaning of the name of Jesus ("Jehovah saves," Mt. 1:21) and salvation is unclear (Fitzmyer 302). The connection is true, nevertheless. Deliverance and rescue from sin is what Christ exclusively does, and it is imperative that men be saved (Harrison 84).

The concept of universality in salvation is also intended here, since salvation in the name of Jesus Christ is for all men (Fitzmyer 302). This theme will be expanded upon as the Acts narrative develops and the proclamation of the gospel extends to the Gentiles.

With this, Peter completes his explanation of the healing of the lame beggar. He was healed by the "name" of the one who was crucified, rose again, and now saves from sin.

b. Response from the Sanhedrin (4:13-22)

13 Now when they saw the boldness of Peter and John, and perceived that they were unlearned and ignorant men, they marvelled; and they took knowledge of them, that they had been with Jesus.
14 And beholding the man which was healed standing with them, they could say nothing against it.
15 But when they had commanded them to go aside out of the council, they conferred among themselves,
16 Saying, What shall we do to these men? for that indeed a notable miracle hath been done by them *is* manifest to all them that dwell in Jerusalem; and we cannot deny *it*.
17 But that it spread no further among the people, let us straitly threaten them, that they speak henceforth to no man in this name.
18 And they called them, and commanded them not to speak at all nor teach in the name of Jesus.
19 But Peter and John answered and said unto them, Whether it be right in the sight of God to hearken unto you more than unto God, judge ye.
20 For we cannot but speak the things which we have seen and heard.
21 So when they had further threatened them, they let them go, finding nothing how they might punish them, because of the people: for all *men* glorified God for that which was done.
22 For the man was above forty years old, on whom this miracle of healing was shewed.

The members of the Sanhedrin find themselves in a predicament. They do not like, nor will they tolerate, the continued preaching and teaching in the name of Jesus as the risen Christ. However, standing before them is an undeniable miracle performed in that very name. Furthermore, since Peter and John are obviously untrained commoners in theological matters, how can they possibly teach anyone anything? Two words are used to characterize them (Greek *agrammatos*, unlettered; *idios*, devoid of special learning), both of which are not complimentary. Their complete disagreement about the resurrection, the use of the Scriptures, perhaps even their provincial, Galilean accent, renders the apostles unfit for sanction. What they are sure of is that these men are linked with Jesus, who was Himself a "commoner" too. The criticism of their lack of formal training may not have been a compliment from the Council, but to the apostles, association with Jesus was a compliment.

The irony of the situation cannot be dismissed (Polhill, *Acts* 145). Peter and John, the "unlearned and ignorant," have spoken with boldness and insight. The learned and well-instructed members of the Sanhedrin are reduced to silence (v. 14). The only thing left to do is discuss it privately (v. 15) and figure something out. Given enough time and bias, anything can be rationalized away.

How did Luke know of the content of the private discussions (vv. 16-17)? Clearly, someone who was there passed the information to him. Saul of Tarsus and Gamaliel are the two most likely insiders (Stott 98; Longenecker 102). Nicodemus and Joseph of Arimathea (Bock 197) are, also, suggested. Bruce (*Acts* 95) leans toward a summation by

Luke. What is perfectly clear is that they could not deny the miracle or the sentiment of the people about it (v. 21). They were, also, just as committed to once-and-for-all halting the spread of the dreaded "name" of Jesus.

What they did not address is of great significance as well. Nowhere did they try to dispel the belief of the resurrection of Jesus (Bruce, *Acts* 96). But that was one of the most offensive issues in this whole matter (v. 2) and one of the reasons for calling a meeting of the High Court! If they could produce His body, or by some other means refute the resurrection, then all this would go away. They would never have a more opportune time than this, but they did not attempt it. The reason is obvious. They could not refute the resurrection! The fact of the resurrection was greater than their bias against it. So, they attacked the men instead. When some people don't like the message, they attack the messengers.

They concluded that threats in the form of a "restraining order" (Kent 47) were the way to achieve the silencing of these men (v. 17) from speaking to anyone using "this name." This would certainly prohibit their continued use of the Temple courts as their classrooms and pulpits. The resistance of the Council, even to the apostles' saying the name of Jesus, is obvious. But neither did they want the name used in any other way, including being invoked for another miracle (3:16; 4:10). They wanted to stop the entire movement.

When Peter and John are returned to the Council (v. 18), they are given the official mandate. They are ordered to completely refrain from public proclamation and teaching in the name of Jesus "in toto." The order of the Council

carried the weight of the law and was enforceable by any means necessary (Walker 127). Nothing could be clearer: stop or else!

If the Council believed Peter and John would meekly submit, they were in for a surprise. The bravado of the Sanhedrin paled in comparison to the boldness of the apostles (vv. 19-20). Brilliantly, almost defiantly, Peter and John faced their own dilemma now, although it is not nearly as vague as the dilemma of the Council. Obey the Council or obey God? What would the Council do if they faced the same alternatives—which, in fact, they did? The answer should be obvious. The apostles would follow their consciences, reinforced with the reality of what they had seen and heard regarding Jesus. They would obey God regardless of the threats and actions the Council would take.

We see demonstrated here one of the great apologetics of the resurrection of Jesus Christ as well as the narrative genius of Luke. The apostles were willing to put their very lives on the line because they could not, nor would they, deny the reality of the resurrection. In a sense, they had everything to gain as well as everything to lose if they chose to obey the orders of the Council. This was not just religious passion, or fanaticism, or political defiance, but fact-based faith. Here is the heart of Christianity. Faith rooted in reality and borne by the unflinching testimony of eye-witnesses.

Not getting the response they had hoped for from the apostles, the Sanhedrin reaffirmed their threats (v. 21). Such would have included the legal and social consequences of disobedience (Bock, 199). But that is all they did at this time. Again, they were faced with a dilemma. There was really no basis for punishment. The healing of the lame beggar was an act of God and publicly known, for which God was being glorified at large. The apostles were released from custody.

Almost as a footnote to the event, Luke inserts the age of the man who was healed (v. 22) as being over forty. This fact was apparently well known. The miracle (Greek *semeion*, a sign) would have been just as significant if the man had been half that age, but the longevity of his condition (3:2) highlights its drama.

Summary
(Acts 4:1-22)

The ecstatic joy of the lame beggar, the curiosity of the crowd that gathered in the Temple court, and the explanation of Peter attracted the attention of the Temple security and officials of the High Court. They did not approve of what they were seeing and hearing. They moved quickly to arrest Peter and John, dispersing the crowd so things could return to normal. But there was a "new normal" coming. Things would never be the same again.

This chapter records the beginning of confrontations between the church and Jewish leaders, confrontations that will lead to intense and deadly persecution of the disciples. Christianity goes on trial, in this text, before the highest court and the most powerful leaders in Judaism. The mettle of the apostles will be tested in all forms. On the side of the apostles is the undeniable evidence of the lame beggar who was completely healed. Coupled with their reasoned appeal to O. T. Messianic prophecy and their boldness as eyewitnesses of the resurrected Jesus of Nazareth, they bear

unflinching testimony in the face of real and measured threats. Jesus had told them they would face this very sort of situation in following Him (Mt. 10:16-20; Lk. 12:11-12). Now, they experience the challenge of their convictions and the Holy Spirit's fullness in the face of intimidation.

The nature and intent of the Jewish Sanhedrin of that era is also revealed in this text. Though responsible for the spiritual leadership of Israel, they show they have other agendas. Fresh in their minds is the trial, arraignment before Pilate, and crucifixion of Jesus. Attempts to silence rumors of His resurrection have been futile, and now, standing before them, is miraculous testimony of His resurrection power. Their arguments against the apostles are reduced to silence. Their motives are to protect themselves. Their methods are intimidation and threats. These are real enough, but they are hardly worthy of men in such high positions and with such great responsibilities.

Application: Teaching and Preaching the Passage

Exegetical Outline of the Text: 1. The Detaining of Peter and John (4:1-4). 2. The Demand of the High Court (4:6-7). 3. The Defense of Peter (4:8-12). 4. The Dilemma of the High Court (4:13-18). 5. The Decision of Peter and John (4:19-22).

Although there is no direct reference to Satan in this action (that will come!), note the beginning of the ways he attacked the church. His first attempt is to intimidate the church. Unsaved and power-hungry people are often the tools of the devil against the Lord's people. Next will come imitation (5:1-11), then infiltration (20:30). These can be traced in a series of lessons or messages. The strategies of Satan are many and still used today.

Also, this text suggests studies in apologetic responses to challenges to faith in Christ, as the apostles demonstrate. The trial motif occurs many times in the Acts record and certainly offers insights about how the Lord's people should respond with readiness in spiritual dependence (Lk. 12:11-12) and biblical truth (1 Pet. 3:15). This would certainly entail analysis of how Peter and John responded to the high court in courage and boldness.

D. The Report to the Church (4:23-31)

23 And being let go, they went to their own company, and reported all that the chief priests and elders had said unto them.
24 And when they heard that, they lifted up their voice to God with one accord, and said, Lord, thou *art* God, which hast made heaven, and earth, and the sea, and all that are in them is:
25 Who by the mouth of thy servant David hast said, Why did the heathen rage, and the people imagine vain things?
26 The kings of the earth stood up, and the rulers were gathered together against the Lord, and against his Christ.
27 For of a truth against thy holy child Jesus, whom thou hast anointed, both Herod, and Pontius Pilate, with the Gentiles, and the people of Israel, were gathered together,

28 For to do whatsoever thy hand and thy counsel determined before to be done.
29 And now, Lord, behold their threatenings: and grant unto thy servants, that with all boldness they may speak thy word,
30 By stretching forth thine hand to heal; and that signs and wonders may be done by the name of thy holy child Jesus.
31 And when they had prayed, the place was shaken where they were assembled together; and they were all filled with the Holy Ghost, and they spake the word of God with boldness.

The works of the Lord through His servants deserve to be recounted. Burdens and concerns need to be shared. Most of all, believers need to bind their hearts together and pray. The events of the last twenty-four hours had been dramatic. A routine trip to the Temple for prayer had led to an encounter with a congenitally lame beggar who had been completely healed. The dramatic healing had afforded another opportunity to proclaim the gospel to a large audience, and hundreds had been saved upon hearing Peter's message. But the apostles were accosted and arrested by the Temple guard, imprisoned overnight, and placed on trial before the Sanhedrin. Though there were no charges of legal violations, they were ordered to be silent regarding the name of Jesus. Yet, in the face of threats and intimidation, Peter and John had given unflinching testimony of the person and resurrection of Jesus Christ. Yes, an ordinary time for prayer at the Temple had exploded into an extraordinary turn of events. Such was the report

(v. 23) given by Peter and John (and the formerly lame beggar?) to their eagerly waiting friends. The text makes clear that these were their *own* (Greek *idios*) people; in a way, that had not quite been the case when they were before the Sanhedrin. To be sure, the other apostles were present for this report, but no doubt there was a large number of others as well.

As was their practice (1:14; 2:46), in unified prayer (v. 24) the disciples lifted up their "voice." Most likely one person articulated (Marshall, *Acts* 105) the sentiment of the entire group. Luke records their petition, beginning with their recognition of the Lord (Greek *despotes*, from which our English word "despot" is derived, but without negative connotation; Bock 204) as the one of absolute authority. Further, they acknowledge Him as the Sovereign God, the Creator of all things. In contrast to their recent appearance in a high court before the authorities of the land, the Lord is Creator of all things and the absolute sovereign ruler of all. His court exceeds all others.

The beginning of the prayer (v. 25) includes a reference to Psalm 2:1-2. It is entirely appropriate to the situation. The titles of opposition from the Psalm are specifically named (v. 27), so there is no doubt that the disciples fixed culpability for the death of Jesus on these men and groups. Herod Antipas (Jones 181) and Pontius Pilate are the "Kings," "rulers," and "Gentiles" in the psalm. The Sanhedrin and the fickle crowd who called for Barabbas instead of Jesus are the "people of Israel." It cannot be clearer that all these alike have come in concert against "the Lord and against His Christ" (v. 26). The disciples are wise in discerning that the ultimate tar-

get of these trials is the Lord Himself (Kaiser 97). But, as His "witnesses" (1:8; 4:20), they catch the brunt of the attack.

Twice (vv. 27, 30) the disciples make reference to "thy holy child, Jesus" (Greek *pais*, child, son, servant). The KJV translation preserves the theme of sonship from Psalm 2:7, 12, but the word may also be understood as "servant" (Bock 207; Bruce, *Acts* 99).

For the second time (v. 28; 2:23), the disciples acknowledge both the divine ordering of, and human culpability for, the events of the crucifixion of Christ. As Marshall (*Acts* 106) observes, "The thought is of God's mighty hand which carried out what his will ordained, and this will include not only the plotting of his enemies, which he allowed, but also their frustration and defeat."

The appeal in the prayer is two-fold. First, they asked for boldness in proclaiming God's Word. Interestingly, they did not pray for intervention to stop the threats of attempted intimidation or for legal assistance. But they did desire to be faithful in their calling. Their prayer indicated that they embraced the very real possibility of ongoing suffering at the hands of the enemies of God. Indeed, that had been the case for centuries. The demand of the authorities was for their silence (v. 18). The prayer of the disciples was that they might be bold in speaking. They had no intention of obeying anyone but the Lord. Obviously, they made the right choice.

Second, they asked for continued, confirming, works of power performed by the Lord's hand in the name of Jesus (3:16; 4:10). By such works, opportunities would arise to proclaim the message of the gospel, just as had the healing of the lame beggar. Their focus was clearly

85

on the message of the gospel, to which these special works would be testimonial.

No sooner had they finished the prayer (v. 31) when the very building shook as from an earthquake (16:26). This was Heaven's physical response, representing that they would shake the world spiritually. This response is reminiscent of the dramatic manifestations of the presence of God (Ex. 19:16-20; Ps. 18:7-9). This is, of course, the very case as God the Holy Spirit fills the disciples with fresh power for ministry. Consequently, they proclaim the word of God boldly. Spiritual fullness will always be displayed in courageous boldness.

There is no reason to interpret this event as simply a different account of Pentecost (Polhill, *Acts* 150). The two events are far different in circumstances and time. However, the promise of God's presence and power, which is involved in both events, is the same.

E. The Church Continues Community Life (4:32-37)

32 And the multitude of them that believed were of one heart and of one soul: neither said any of *them* that ought of the things which he possessed was his own; but they had all things common.

33 And with great power gave the apostles witness of the resurrection of the Lord Jesus: and great grace was upon them all.

34 Neither was there any among them that lacked: for as many as were possessors of lands or houses sold them, and brought the prices of the things that were sold,

35 And laid *them* down at the apostles' feet: and distribution was made unto every man according as he had need.

36 And Joses, who by the apostles was surnamed Barnabas, (which is, being interpreted, The son of consolation,) a Levite, *and* of the country of Cyprus,

37 Having land, sold *it*, and brought the money, and laid *it* at the apostles' feet.

The church is not deterred from its community life because of the orders from the Council. It continues its shared faith and mutual support (v. 32), expressed in voluntary provision for the material needs of the believers. So strong is this sense of community that personal ownership is outweighed by the needs of others. The summary is virtually the same as in 2:44-47.

Added to that is fresh power and grace (v. 33), furnished to the apostles in testimony of the resurrection of the Christ. *Power* was the promise of Jesus in 1:8, and this is manifested in their witness to others. "Great *grace*" speaks of God's provisions and blessings upon them personally. Both are evidential answers to their prayer and selfless giving. Little is more Christ-like than these.

This sense of community was widespread enough that some organization was required (vv. 34-35). The apostles initially became the ones who accounted for receiving and distributing the material generosity of the believers. Luke does not detail how they went about the process, but the results were sufficiency ("neither was there any among them that lacked") and deference ("distribution...unto every man according as he had need").

In this context of shared community life, a key leader in the Book of Acts is introduced (vv. 36-37). Though his given name is "Joses" ("Joseph"), he is never referred to again in Acts by that name. Three things involved in his identity are stated. One, his gift of encouragement characterizes his life so much that he is called and known as "Barnabas," apparently meaning "son of consolation."

The etymology of his nickname and its stated meaning are somewhat unclear. The Aramaic *bar* is certainly patronymic and means "son of," but "son of" whom or what? Neither Greek, Aramaic, or Hebrew suggest that *nabas* means "consolation." More likely, there is a play on words, as is common with nicknames, to get *nabi* (Hebrew for "prophet"), and a key function of a prophet is to encourage (Bock 216-217). Combined with his generosity and gift of encouraging others, he is given the name "Barnabas, son of consolation" (Greek *paraklesis*, comfort, encouragement). He is obviously well-served by that name.

Two, he is a *Levite*. Not all Levites were priests but all certainly had Temple privileges. Originally, Levites were not to own property in Israel (Num. 18:20; Deut. 10:9). Perhaps the property of Barnabas was located elsewhere. Regardless, he sells the land, possibly farmland (Greek *agros*, whence our *agri*-culture), and donates the proceeds to the church. There were many others who did the same, but Barnabas is identified to commend his heart of leadership that will soon emerge.

Three, he is a native of Cyprus, an island in the Mediterranean some sixty miles off the coast of Syria. Known for its rich farm land and large Jewish population, Cyprus will be a significant place of ministry later in the narrative.

Summary
(4:23-37)

Peter and John quickly return from the court of the High Council to the eagerly awaiting disciples. After reporting the details of their arrest and trial, the disciples immediately turn to the Lord in unified prayer. For sure, the Lord has witnessed all that has gone on, but prayer invokes the presence of God for help at such times. Appealing to the Scriptures with Messianic insight, they realize that their encounter is part of what has been prophesied. Their appeal is more for power and faithfulness through the difficulty instead of deliverance from it. God confirms His approval of their courage with a literal shaking of the house where they are assembled. The attempt at intimidation by the Council is rebuffed by the boldness and continued witness of the disciples.

Nor is their fellowship with one another adversely affected. If there ever was a group with compelling reasons to quit, the early disciples had them. However, the reality of the resurrection of Christ, biblical prophecies being fulfilled before them, and the incredible experience of personal saving faith in Jesus, exceeds the threats of intimidation. With grace and generosity they continue their idyllic community life, serving as needs arise. From this context of prayer, bold witness, and generous giving Barnabas is introduced to the Acts narrative. His leadership will be invaluable for years to come.

Application: Teaching and Preaching the Passage

Exegetical Outline of the Text: 1. The Report to the Church (4:23). 2. The

Requests of the Church (4:24-30). 3. The Response to Prayer (4:31-33). 4. The Resources of the Church (4:34-37).

Instead of being silenced and fearful of the threats against them, Peter and John were quick to report what had happened. This text highlights the sharing of burdens, especially during attacks on the Lord's people. The first response was to give the problem to the Lord. Believers and churches need to pray and to know how to pray in times of trouble. Prayer is the basis for shared burdens but also for spiritual boldness. This text lends itself to studies on prayer in times of persecution and spiritual attack. Note, also, the confirming work of the Holy Spirit in response to their prayers. How He works and confirms today would be an excellent study.

The church has come under attack from the very beginning. The period of the Roman persecution is an infamous part of church history. However, as bad as that was, it pales in comparison with what has happened since then. The twentieth century alone saw more believers martyred for the cause of Christ than all the previous centuries combined. There are underground churches in various countries in the world today. There are governments that oppress and imprison believers. One only has to become aware of the persecuted church to know how pervasive persecution still is. A part of every church should be its remembrance of the persecuted churches in countries where Christianity is not tolerated. Persecution is part of the devil's strategy to shut the mouths of believers and close the witness of the gospel. The devil does not want "lame" people healed by the power of God. Neither does he want bold witnesses to continue for Christ. This, too, presents

an opportunity for pastors, Sunday School teachers, and Christian workers to be informed and to inform their churches of the persecuted church and pray for them regularly.

The sharing of needs and assets by believers would be a great analysis. Knowing what the early church actually did would clarify and give basis for procedures. Not only did the early believers have courage and boldness in witnessing (c. 33), they demonstrated great community service with their personal sacrifices. Usually every church is faced with how to meet the material needs of people in their local communities in ministries of compassion. There are different strategies for different needs. This text presents a basis for teaching and discussion about how to minister compassionately and wisely as good stewards of our resources. God blesses us to bless others. Being a blessing does not mean enabling sinful dependencies or naïve giveaways. However, it is difficult sometimes to know the difference when trying to minister to people. We should do well and not be weary in well-doing (Gal. 6:9). All giving should be done with prayer for the providential guidance of God. One never knows when "bread cast upon the waters" (Eccl.11:1) will be found or how many days later it will return. It is for sure that this area of ministry should be carefully studied in the Scriptures and the best means developed.

F. The Deceit of Ananias and Sapphira (5:1-11)

1 But a certain man named Ananias, with Sapphira his wife, sold a possession,

2 And kept back *part* of the price, his wife also being privy to *it*, and brought a certain part, and laid *it* at the apostles' feet.

3 But Peter said, Ananias, why hath Satan filled thine heart to lie to the Holy Ghost, and to keep back *part* of the price of the land?

4 Whiles it remained, was it not thine own? and after it was sold, was it not in thine own power? why hast thou conceived this thing in thine heart? thou has not lied unto men, but unto God.

5 And Ananias hearing these words fell down, and gave up the ghost: and great fear came on all them that heard these things.

6 And the young men arose, wound him up, and carried *him* out, and buried *him*.

7 And it was about the space of three hours after, when his wife, not knowing what was done, came in.

8 And Peter answered unto her, Tell me whether ye sold the land for so much? And she said, Yea, for so much.

9 Then Peter said unto her, How is it that ye have agreed together to tempt the Spirit of the Lord? behold, the feet of them which have buried thy husband *are* at the door, and shall carry thee out.

10 Then fell she down straightway at his feet, and yielded up the ghost: and the young men came in, and found her dead, and, carrying *her* forth, buried *her* by her husband.

11 And great fear came upon all the church, and upon as many as heard these things.

If we assume there were never any problems that arose within the church in the Acts record, we would be sadly mistaken. As honorable and generous as was Barnabas (4:36-37), Ananias and Sapphira proved to be the opposite. In keeping with the practice of the voluntary sharing of needs and assets, this husband and wife sold a piece of property and gave part of the proceeds for distribution. The act of giving (v. 3) appears, on the surface, to be simple enough, but there are very serious undertones. Involved was a sin so serious that God immediately sent death as a judgment upon them. But exactly what was the sin and why was it judged so quickly and severely? Marshall (*Acts* 110) proposes that their lie was "an attempt to gain credit for greater personal sacrifice than they actually made." Stott agrees (109-110). Bock (225) suggests it was an "attempt to deceive God." All this was true—and perhaps more.

By implication, it appears they had openly committed the total amount of the sale (Polhill, *Acts* 156; Bruce, *Acts* 105) to the Lord's work. That being the case, the commitment would have identified the gift as devoted to the Lord. However, they agreed together privately (v. 9) to keep a portion of the money for themselves. When they gave their offering (v. 2), it would have been counted for accuracy of records and distribution. Peter's discernment of the situation, however, went beyond the simple total of the money given. He was supernaturally directed to confront them about the truth (Keener II:1190), exposing the sin specifically as lying to the Holy Spirit (v. 3). He also discerned the hand of Satan in the whole situation (vv. 3-4).

Discernment often accompanies leadership responsibility.

In summary, their decision was tantamount to embezzlement of that which was devoted to the Lord, a flagrant act of hypocrisy (Morgan 148; Fitzmyer 323). Further, it gave a foothold to Satan, allowing an opportunity to muddle the fellowship of the believers. Embezzlement and hypocrisy are both lies, just in different forms. In this instance, because of the intention of the offering, the lie was not only to men, but to the Holy Spirit.

The confrontation of Ananias and Sapphira may be considered harsh, given Peter's own experience (Lk. 22:31-34). But his personal experience has taught him the evil of Satan's influence and how serious the devastation of spiritual hypocrisy is.

Up to this event, Luke has taken pains to show the authenticity of those who were followers of Christ (2:44-47; 4:34-37). Ananias and Sapphira are examples of those who would corrupt faith. Superficial imitation is the nature of hypocrisy (Barnes 92). It perverts that which is genuine. Jesus' harshest words of condemnation were about the sin of hypocrisy (Mt. 23:1-33). It is the very essence of lying, and God hates lying.

Incredibly, Ananias died (Greek *ekpsuxo*, to breathe out, expire) on the spot. It was an instantaneous death that shocked those who heard of it (v. 5). His body was attended to for burial, post haste (v. 6). There was no memorial service scheduled. Even his wife was not made aware of what happened until later (v. 7). Who the "young men" are is not clear, except that they attended to the details of burial as directed by the apostles and were strong enough for the task (Walker 144). Robertson (*Acts* 60)

suggests the quick burial was for sanitary and ceremonial purposes. While for those reasons burials in those days might have been somewhat hasty in comparison to modern procedures, they were not *that* hasty! This was a divinely-inflicted death (Marshall, *Acts* 111). Removing the body of Ananias must have been awkward as well as necessary.

We are not told why there was a delay, but three hours later (v. 7) Sapphira came before the apostles, probably assuming her husband was there or had been there with the gift. By this time, Peter had considered that she might have been a willing party to the whole, sordid affair. It is not part of the record if Peter informed her of the death of Ananias when she first arrived. But Peter was compelled to know more. Upon being questioned (v. 8), she had the same answer as her husband. Without mincing any words, Peter charged her with complicity and announced her judgment to be the same as her husband's (v. 9). Indeed, she died on the spot as well! The same young men attended to her burial, placing her beside her husband (v. 10). Both died ignominiously.

One of the results of this unusual event is that a second shock wave of fear rippled through the church and community (v. 11). Whatever else resulted, it was clear that the things of God are not to be trifled with. As Marshal (*Acts* 110-111) observes, "It is certainly true that the story introduces us to a different world of thought from that of today. It is a world in which sin is taken seriously."

The whole incident is reminiscent of the sin of Achan (Josh. 7:1-26). In fact, in verse 2, Luke uses the very same word (Greek *nosphizo*, to keep back, defraud, purloin, rob) for this sin as the Septuagint does of Achan's sin (Josh. 7:1).

Nor is this the last time Luke records divine visitation of immediate judgment. Herod Agrippa I suffers and dies at God's judgment hand (12:20-23). Elymas the sorcerer is smitten with temporary blindness (13:8-11). Even the earthquake that freed Paul and Silas from prison at Philippi may have been a type of judgment for the unjust treatment they received (16:25-26).

Furthermore, the situation has other parallels involving the immediate death/judgment of God. Going all the way back to the Garden of Eden, the blissful surroundings and relationships of Adam and Eve were convoluted by the influence of Satan, sinful choices, and death (Gen 3:17). The slaying of Nadab and Abihu (Lev. 10:1-3), the rebellion of Korah (Num. 16), and others are in nature the very same. Sin corrupts authenticity and fellowship with God.

While some suggest the severity of the incident raises some troublesome questions (Polhill, *Acts* 155), these are incidental to what actually happened. The very same questions may be asked of other similar death/judgment events recorded in Scripture. However, interpretive sentiments may often cloud historical reality. Therefore, it is essential to understand the event in its context and those parallel situations where the same swift justice occurs. Three conclusions are consistent in all of these. One, sometimes God judges some sinful actions immediately (1 Tim. 2:24-25). Sometimes He does not, but His judgment will come (2 Cor. 5:10). Since we do not know all God knows about any given situation, we are not in any posi-

tion to insist that He treat all situations the same. Second, these events illustrate that what is devoted to God has sacred significance (Eccl. 5:4-5). Third, God's toleration of sin is not His approval or apathy about it: "Though the mills of God grind slowly, yet they grind exceeding small; though with patience He stands waiting, with exactness grinds He all" (Friedrich von Logau).

Whether Ananias and Sapphira were authentic believers is not stated in the account. It seems they were. Can authentic believers commit such sin and suffer immediate death/judgment? Apparently so (Picirilli, *Corinthians* 171). Whether this kind of sin that resulted in immediate death/judgment is the same as the "sin unto death" as in 1 John 5:16-17 is a valid discussion (Marberry and Shaw 95-98). It is certainly within the scope of discussion that there is "*a* sin unto death" that is differentiated from "*the* sin unto death" (Marshall, *Epistles of John* 245-251). Either way, if sin is to be taken as seriously as God intends, then the eternal consequences of sin must be considered.

G. Further Signs and Wonders by the Apostles (5:12-16)

12 And by the hands of the apostles were many signs and wonders wrought among the people; (and they were all with one accord in Solomon's porch.
13 And of the rest durst no man join himself to them: but the people magnified them.
14 And believers were the more added to the Lord, multitudes both of men and women).
15 Insomuch that they brought forth the sick into the streets, and

laid *them* on beds and couches, that at the least the shadow of Peter passing by might overshadow some of them.
16 There came also a multitude *out* of the cities round about unto Jerusalem, bringing sick folks, and them which were vexed with unclean spirits: and they were healed every one.

The ministry of miraculous deeds by the apostles (v. 12) was not diminished by the visitation of divine judgment on Ananias and Sapphira. If anything, the continued miraculous works testified of God's blessings. It also galvanized the disciples with a sense of fresh unity. They continued their public ministry of teaching and preaching, using Solomon's porch (portico) as one of their pulpit areas (3:11), even though they had been issued a legal, restraining order from the Sanhedrin to cease and desist (4:18).

An interesting contrast arose, as indicated by the two groups implied in verses 13-14. On the one hand, some refused to be associated with the apostles, perhaps in fear that the fate of Ananias and Sapphira might befall them. In effect, the immediate death/judgment frightened off those who were not totally committed (Bruce, *Acts* 109). On the other hand, multitudes of both men and women responded in authentic faith. What alarmed some appealed to others (Stott 113). The same sun that hardens the clay softens the butter. As part of Luke's intention to show the growth of the church, he now moves from numbering the disciples to the more general term of "multitudes" since the numbers now are so much larger. There is simply no way to place an

actual count on this term. That may be the intention.

Reminiscent of the healing ministry of the Lord Jesus (Mt. 4:23; 9:35; Lk. 6:19), the apostles ministered to all who came to them (vv. 15-16). Peter, especially, was used to bring healing even when his shadow passed over people as they lay in wait for him to walk by. Bock (232) references the concept of that time as believing that one's shadow was an extension of that person. We remember that at least one person believed that just touching the hem of Jesus' garment would bring healing (Mt. 9:20-21).

Word spread to the surrounding areas bringing the sick, afflicted, and demon-oppressed to be healed and delivered. In the phrase "vexed by unclean spirits," vexed (Greek *ochleomai*) means to be agitated, troubled, or tormented. The reluctance of some to associate with the church (v. 13) receded into the background. People who suffer pain and desperation will seek relief where they can find it. All were healed without exception, apparently unconditionally. Perhaps this accounts for multitudes (v. 14) coming to spiritual healing by saving faith in Christ as well as to physical healing.

Also, note that Luke distinguishes between those who have physical illness and those who are spiritually oppressed by "unclean spirits." The biblical record in Acts and elsewhere shows the toll taken on human lives by the devil's direct influence—a reality all too common in cultures where there is little Christian influence.

Later, the apostle Paul (19:12) used cloths as extended instruments of healing. These are unique, apostolic gifts (2 Cor. 12:12) that confirmed the gospel message of the risen Christ. This ministry also confirmed the promise of the Lord Jesus about the performance of "greater works" through their ministries (Jn. 14:12).

It is here that the attractiveness of God's benefits and blessings upon His people accounts for a positive response from those in need. The response reminds one of the Queen of Sheba's visit to Solomon, having heard of God's blessings upon him and Israel (1 Kgs. 10:1-9). Such blessings are indicative of the mercy and kindness of the Lord exhibited in this world; they point to His eternal blessings in Heaven.

Although there are excellent writings available that analyze them, a word should be said here of today's "faith healers" imitating the same by offering "specially anointed" prayer cloths and shawls that promise physical healing and deliverance when applied. Oh, that such were true! Who among the Lord's people does not groan and weep over the sick, demon-oppressed, and dying? What local church of authentic believers does not have a long prayer list of family and friends who are sick and over whom they pray? Come, go with me to the children's wing of any hospital, especially of those with terminal illnesses, and weep and pray for the Lord to send healing to little bodies impacted by disease. What pastor has not presided over the funerals of folks who died of disease, wept as he sought to comfort the families, and longed for the day when there will be no more funerals to conduct?

The Acts record does *not* show that apostolic gifts continue today in the same fashion and methodologies. Instead, it reveals that there was a short period of time when the Lord Himself gifted the apostles to demonstrate His compassion and mercy that will culminate in final, eternal healing at His return (Rev. 21:1-4). The Lord is concerned with both the spiritual and physical dimensions of human life. The Bible addresses His plan (Rom. 8; 1 Cor. 15) for the total restoration of life as He intended. The miracles of the Acts narrative are promissory notes of that time when the Lord Jesus returns to fulfill those promises.

Summary
(5:1-16)

Following the example of Barnabas (4:36-37), Ananias and Sapphira decided to donate the sale of some land they owned to the common treasury of the church. But theirs was a gift tainted with spiritual and selfish subterfuge. Before the day was over, both suffered the consequences of a really bad decision that merited the death/judgment of God. They would be hastily and without ceremony buried beside one another in testimony that the things of God should not be trifled with.

The upside of such a difficult situation was that a strong message was sent regarding authenticity in worship and honesty in giving. Neither did it quench the ministry but gave definition to its integrity. The results included miraculous manifestations of God's hand of blessing, people's lives being blessed, and many folks saved.

Application: Teaching and
Preaching the Passage

Exegetical Outline of the Text: 1. The Deception of Ananias and Sapphira (5:1-2). 2. The Discernment of Peter (5:3-9). 3. The Death/Judgment That

Resulted (5:10). 4. The Display of the Lord's Power (5:11-16).

This section lends itself to a number of studies regarding the need for authenticity in the practice of saving faith and worship of God. Biblical examples of the immediate judgment of God could be studied including Adam and Eve (Gen. 3); Moses and Aaron/Miriam (Num. 12); Nadab and Abihu (Lev. 10). This study should be tempered with the admonition Jesus gave to the apostles over calling down fire from heaven (Lk. 9:51-56). The impact of sin on a person's private life as well as its influence in the fellowship of believers is especially clear in this text.

Lessons and messages could be developed to deal with the role of church leaders in addressing the problem of sinful actions in the local church. This can be expanded to consider the area of church discipline in its various contexts and needs. The relational fellowship of believers in a local church and the spiritual authenticity of that fellowship can be impacted by certain sinful actions. That has been the history of all relationships with a thrice-holy God (Gen. 3:1-12; Ex. 32:1-33; Josh. 7:1-26; Isa. 6:1-7). When sin happens it is not only wise but essential to address it as the Scriptures direct. Careful attention should be given to the principles and procedures given in such texts as Matthew 5:21-26; 18:1-35; 1 Corinthians 5:1-13; and Galatians 6:1-3.

The authority of the Scriptures is paramount in church discipline; however, in today's litigious society, the pastor and leadership of a local church will be wise to make sure its main organizational documents are legally proper and insurance coverage adequate and explicit. Although the legal documentation is necessary, there is never a substitute for prayer and patience in the restoration of erring believers. None of us are apostles today. While there should be a reverential fear never to taint the work of God, black marks do occur. Regardless how difficult, it is spiritually necessary that we not only confront sinful actions but also seek restoration of the offenders when they occur.

The spiritual dimension of Satan's influence would also be a significant study. His strategy here is that of imitation. Undermining the church from within, by feigned faith, seriously deceives.

This text provides a good basis for considering the principles and practices of good stewardship in the local church. Pastors should lead churches in wise and ethical development of giving to churches. There are many guidelines for accountability and confidentiality that are necessary. Church budgets and careful reports should be part of the stewardship practices of churches. Corrective measures should be taken where they are absent.

It seems that Ananias and Sapphira wanted, selfishly, to be acclaimed like Barnabas for their giving. While the example of others is a proper spiritual motivation (2 Cor. 8:1-4), what others give is never the measure. Nor is acclaim to be the reward (Mt. 6:1-4). The Scriptures carefully teach us about our responsibilities as stewards of our possessions. This makes for excellent studies and messages to facilitate growth.

H. All the Apostles Arrested and Arraigned Before the Sanhedrin (5:17-42)

1. Arrested by the Sanhedrin, released by the angel of the Lord (5:17-26)

17 Then the high priest rose up, and all they that were with him, (which is the sect of the Sadducees,) and were filled with indignation
18 And laid their hands on the apostles, and put them in the common prison.
19 But the angel of the Lord by night opened the prison doors, and brought them forth, and said,
20 Go, stand and speak in the temple to the people all the words of this life.
21 And when they heard *that* they entered into the temple early in the morning, and taught. But the high priest came, and they that were with him, and called the council together, and all the senate of the children of Israel, and sent to the prison to have them brought.
22 But when the officers came, and found them not in the prison, they returned, and told,
23 Saying, The prison truly found we shut with all safety, and the keepers standing without before the doors: but when we had opened, we found no man within.
24 Now when the high priest and the captain of the temple and the chief priests heard these things, they doubted of them whereunto this would grow.
25 Then came one and told them, saying, Behold the men whom ye put in prison are standing in the temple, and teaching the people.
26 Then went the captain with the officers, and brought them without violence: for they feared the people, lest they should have been stoned.

It should come as no surprise that the coming and going of so many people, in and around Jerusalem and the Temple courts, caught the attention of Temple security and the Sanhedrin. The disciples made no attempts to be secretive about their teaching the people or the miraculous things that frequently happened. Motivated by jealousy ("indignation" is Greek *zelos*, anger, envy, zeal), the high priest and the Sadducees, who controlled the Council, had all the apostles (vv. 18, 29) arrested and placed in a common holding prison under heavy guard (v. 23).

One cannot help wondering what prompted their jealousy and why they reacted as they did. After all, there was a regular stream of folks coming to town sick, oppressed by demons, and with various physical impairments, who walked away carrying their beds of affliction and in their right minds. More than likely, Temple attendance and offerings were up due to the changed lives of those who trusted in Jesus as the Messiah. Furthermore, a general spirit of good will and peace prevailed (2:47a; 4:32; 5:13). Marshall (*Acts* 117) defends the legitimacy of the Acts record as to the size and influence of the early church. Its rapid expansion drew the attention of the Sanhedrin.

But not everyone rejoices over success. The Judaean culture was an "honor-shame society" (Keener II:1206-1207) where success could breed envy.

Indeed, this same response occurred later (14:2; 17:5). Such is a problem of the human heart, no matter where or when it occurs. No greater contrast can be found than in these chapters that show the positive impact of the gospel and the negative response of the Sanhedrin.

God intervened by sending "the angel of the Lord" to execute a miraculous and secretive deliverance of the apostles from prison (vv. 19-20). Instead of becoming fugitives from the law and fleeing for their lives, the angel commanded them to return to the Temple area and continue with their open-air teaching and preaching. Unless one denies the existence of angels and their interaction with people, there are no compelling reasons to argue that the angel (Greek *angelos*, messenger) was actually a human agent who might have been one of the prison guards (Bruce, *Acts* 110; Stott 114). Another similar instance occurs later in Acts 12:1-10, when Peter is imprisoned with the intent to actually slay him, not just silence him. These are not just narrative motifs of miraculous escapes to enhance the story (Keener II:2012; Bock 238-239) but actual events. There were twelve men who could, and perhaps did, provide testimony to Luke of what happened. It is clear that in the initial days of Christianity, the Lord intervened in miraculous ways to protect the apostles that they might continue to proclaim the gospel. As church history records, all but one of the apostles would eventually die for the cause of Christ. For now, however, God preserved their lives to accomplish His purpose.

In obedience to the directive of the angel of the Lord, the apostles did as instructed, returning immediately to the Temple area to teach and preach (v. 21a). That they did so "early in the morning" (Greek *orthros*, the dawn) is typical of the life routines of that time (Keener II:2013). Business was often begun at 6:00 a.m. The Temple doors would be opened to accommodate early worshipers. The apostles were there as usual but out of unusual circumstances. Some in the audience might have witnessed their arrest the previous day and would wonder how they managed to get back to the Temple so quickly. Their story of the angel's intervention and instruction would further embolden the apostles as well as gain more sympathetic support, a sympathy that would help the apostles later when they were re-arrested (v. 26).

Luke is deliberate in emphasizing that all the officials assembled to determine what to do with the apostles (v. 21b). Though some see these as two different groups, the phrase, "the council ... and all the senate" (Greek *gerousia*, council of elders) is most likely an expression called a hendiadys (identifying one entity by two words) that is used for emphasis and definition. In other words, all the members of the Sanhedrin were present (Marshall, *Acts* 118; Fitzmyer 335; Bock 240; Walker 153). With all in place they sent for the apostles to be arraigned for trial.

The ironic humor (Morgan 159; Ger 87; Fitzmyer 336) of what happens next is not lost in Luke's telling of the story (vv. 22-25). Officers were sent (v. 22) to escort the apostles from custody where they had been placed the night before. Returning to the Council empty-handed, they reported that the prison doors were shut and locked, the security guards at their posts, but the prisoners were not there (v. 23)! There was no explanation for the disappearance of the apostles. It stunned and baffled them!

These powerful men had done their best to secure the apostles (just as these same officials had done with the tomb of Jesus), but were unsuccessful and completely without rational explanation. Also, the Sadducees did not even believe in the existence of angels, much less their intervention in the affairs of men. Perhaps it was time for a reality check!

The captain of the Temple would bear responsibility for the escape and suffer loss of standing before the Council. But even more troubling was how to explain the situation and the potential outcome (v. 24). They realized quickly that the standing of the apostles would be enhanced in the eyes of the people. They were not wrong in that assessment.

As if on cue, someone came to tell them that the men who had been imprisoned were not far away (v. 25). They were, in fact, in the Temple, publicly teaching the people. While that might have brought some relief to the security officials, it did nothing to deter the second arrest and arraignment of the apostles (v. 26). It did, however, alter the manner of treatment. The sentiment of the crowd listening to the apostles was clearly in their favor. With deference shown out of fear of being stoned by the crowd, the Council had the apostles arrested without the rough treatment usually unleashed on escapees by the Temple guard (Keener II:1215). Apparently, the apostles did not resist arrest. Perhaps remembering the example of Christ, His instructions (Mt. 10:17-20; Mk. 13:9-11), and His submission to the hands of these same authorities, they submitted as well.

2. Arraigned before the Sanhedrin (5:27-40)

a. The testimony of the apostles (5:27-32)

27 And when they had brought them, they set *them* before the council: and the high priest asked them,
28 Saying, Did not we straitly command you that ye should not teach in this name? and, behold, ye have filled Jerusalem with your doctrine, and intend to bring this man's blood upon us.
29 Then Peter and the *other* apostles answered and said, We ought to obey God rather than men.
30 The God of our fathers raised up Jesus, whom ye slew and hanged on a tree.
31 Him hath God exalted with his right hand *to be* a Prince and a Saviour, for to give repentance to Israel, and forgiveness of sins.
32 And we are his witnesses of these things; and *so is* also the Holy Ghost, whom God hath given to them that obey him.

When all parties were finally in place before the entire Council, the high priest began his interrogation. What is not addressed in the initial charges against the apostles is how they had escaped (v. 28). Perhaps out of embarrassment over the escape, perhaps in a show of force, perhaps in total denial of the ultimate authority of the Living God being displayed before their eyes, the high priest was more interested in the violation of the previous gag order (4:17-18). With words chosen carefully, he obviously avoids using the name of Jesus (Polhill,

Acts 168). Rather than silencing them with the gag order, they had spread their teachings throughout Jerusalem. Furthermore, they charged the apostles with trying to impose blood-guilt on the Council (Deut. 19:10; 21:8-9).

This last charge is compelling. Indeed, this very Council *had* condemned Jesus to death and called for the release of Barabbas over Jesus (Mt. 27:15-23), even over the objections of Pilate. Nor had the apostles previously hesitated to herald the guilt of the Council in the death of Jesus (2:23; 3:13-15; 4:10-11). It appears that this note had finally got home to them (v. 33). Of course they did not accept its validity, but they were offended that they would be accused of such. Their reaction would not be repentance of the sin.

With all the apostles standing before the Sanhedrin, Peter again becomes the spokesman for the group. Persecution is often the opportunity for witness (Fitzmyer 336). Succinctly, he responds with a statement of allegiance to the authority of God that is higher than allegiance to the authority of men (v. 29). This echoes his previous response (4:19). Throughout church history, the same truth has been the rally cry of the Lord's people when persecution has come.

Furthermore, Peter's bold testimony (vv. 30-32) includes the basic truths of the gospel to the most elite group in all of Israel. He offers the same message as before without omitting even the accusation of guilt in the crucifixion of Jesus. Of note is Peter's assertion of being Jesus' "witnesses" (1:8; 2:32; 3:15; 4:20) and the confirming witness of the Holy Spirit. Keener (II:1217) observes that Peter's boldness may be motivated by a twist of terms: namely, that the

charge of blood-guilt on those who slew the Lord Jesus would also apply to the apostles as the Lord's witnesses if they did not proclaim what they had seen (Ez. 33:7-9).

b. The reasoning of Gamaliel (5:33-40)

**33 When they heard *that*, they were cut *to the heart*, and took counsel to slay them.
34 Then stood there up one in the council, a Pharisee, named Gamaliel, a doctor of the law, had in reputation among all the people, and commanded to put the apostles forth a little space;
35 And said unto them, Ye men of Israel, take heed to yourselves what ye intend to do as touching these men.
36 For before these days rose up Theudas, boasting himself to be somebody; to whom a number of men, about four hundred, joined themselves: who was slain; and all, as many as obeyed him, were scattered, and brought to nought.
37 After this man rose up Judas of Galilee in the days of the taxing, and drew away much people after him: he also perished; and all, *even* as many as obeyed him, were dispersed.
38 And now I say unto you, Refrain from these men, and let them alone: for if this counsel or this work be of men, it will come to nought:
39 But if it be of God, ye cannot overthrow it; lest haply ye be found even to fight against God.
40 And to him they agreed: and when they had called the apostles,**

and beaten *them*, they commanded that they should not speak in the name of Jesus, and let them go.

The response (v. 33) to Peter's message is one of outrage. That they were "cut to the heart" (Greek *diaprio*) means being cut in two, thus having intense anger or rage (compare 7:54). What Peter said was to them a clear expression of contempt of court (Longenecker 117; Bock 248), so serious it merited death. Never mind the fact that they technically did not have the legal authority to impose capital punishment (Longenecker 117), they could find a way around that just as they had done with Jesus, the man in question. Peter's assertion of the resurrection of Jesus added insult to injury since the majority Sadducees on the Council vehemently denied such. All things considered, their intentions to kill the apostles were clear.

When it appeared the verdict was in, there arose a Council member (v. 34) whose voice was respected enough to change the outcome. His was a cool head in the midst of heated emotions. Five characteristics are given of Gamaliel in Acts. He was a member of the Sanhedrin. He was a Pharisee. He was a teacher ("doctor") of the law. He was of high and distinguished reputation among the people. He was the apostle Paul's mentor (22:3). We also know that he was a student of the liberal, rabbinical teacher Hillel. Bock (249) comments, "He is a voice of mature, wise reason among the apostles' opponents."

After the apostles were dismissed from the immediate presence of the Council, Gamaliel warned the Council about their intention to kill the apostles (v. 35). Perhaps he knew of the enormous popularity of these men and saw

their deaths as extremely difficult to deal with (Polhill, *Acts* 171). Furthermore, he made a bold appeal to withdraw the charges and release them from custody (v. 38). His reasoning was two-fold. If the movement led by the apostles was merely another religious or political uprising born from the passion of men, given a little time, it would likely fail on its own. But, if it was of God, the Council would appear to be fighting God in the matter. They certainly would not want such a perception.

In his first argument, Gamaliel based his appeal on two examples of other revolutionaries, Theudas (v. 36) and Judas of Galilee (v. 37). These men led rebellions in the time of "the taxing" (Geldenhuys 105), which occurred in A.D. 6-7. Both men and their causes stirred up the people but were short-lived. These examples present a historical challenge that some commentators use to question Luke's chronological accuracy (Barrett, *Acts* 80; Haenchen 257; Keener II:1234). Fitzmyer regards the issue as "problematic" (340).

Some who question the accuracy of Gamaliel's speech, or of Luke's record of it, think that Acts was written too late for Luke, as a companion of Paul, to have written it. They accept Josephus as being historically correct (*Antiquities* XX.V.1) and believe the author of Acts used Josephus for his information, constructing Gamaliel's speech in that light. In fact, according to Josephus, Judas's rebellion occurred in A.D. 6-7 and Theudas's rebellion some ten years later. Thus Gamaliel's "speech" is not accurate, and the author of Acts is to blame for the error. Furthermore, for the author to put this (incorrect) information in Gamaliel's mouth is anachronistic: he could not possibly have known this since

Josephus's *Antiquities* was not published until a few years before A.D. 100. What is the solution to these concerns?

According to Polhill (*Acts* 172), the answer lies in three possibilities. One, Josephus was in error about Theudas and the time of his insurrection. Lenski (233) makes the point that studies have shown that he could be guilty of some glaring errors and contradictions (Keener II:1231; Marshall, *Acts* 122). However, when all the evidence is considered, this doesn't appear to be the case.

Two, Luke (or the unknown author of Acts) was in error. Some argue that he had gotten his information about the two rebellions from Josephus and confused it. This cannot be the case if, as we believe, Luke was the author of Acts, since Josephus was not published until about A.D. 93. Longenecker (119) aptly states, "But the arguments for Luke's dependence on Josephus have been fairly well demolished." Given the historical accuracy of Luke throughout his work, the superintendence of the Holy Spirit in the writing, and the best dates for composition (see Introduction), Luke was not the one in error.

Three, both Josephus and Gamaliel, as recorded by Luke, were correct but referring to two different men named Theudas (Marshall, *Acts* 122; Polhill, *Acts* 172; Longenecker 119; Stott 118). Josephus records the fact that there were "ten thousand other disorders" that arose shortly after the death of Herod the Great that fit the scenario posed by Gamaliel (*Antiquities* XVII.X.4). The name "Theudas" was common enough and might even have been a Greek nickname (Polhill, *Acts* 173) to identify one of the many leaders of such insurrections. That being the case, Gamaliel's examples would be well

known to the Council. This is the best solution to the issue.

A word should be said about historical accuracy in light of the doctrine of plenary, verbal inspiration of the Scriptures. Longenecker (117) is correct in stating, "How we react to the discrepancy will depend on our basic presuppositions." One of those presuppositions is the superintendence of the Holy Spirit in guiding Luke, the author of Acts, to record accurately and without error the words and events of the composition. It is a presupposition just as viable as others. The idea is that the Bible is inspired in the whole and in every part (Forlines, *Quest* 47). Furthermore, as Warfield (113) states, the Bible is inspired "in all its elements alike, things discoverable by reason as well as mysteries, matters of *history* [emphasis added] and science as well as of faith and practice, words as well as thoughts." Therefore, the presupposition of the accuracy of Luke's account is valid. As shown, there are no compelling reasons to deny his accuracy.

Now to Gamaliel's second line of reasoning (vv. 38-39). His counsel not to kill the apostles, drop the charges, and release them has a spiritual element as well. In essence, he is saying that if what the apostles are about is merely a religious movement born of men, it will die of itself and be forgotten. However, if this movement is born of God, it will be futile to oppose it since to do so will be to fight against God. To this, the Council agrees (v. 40a).

It should be noted that while the wisdom of Gamaliel appeased the hot blood of the Council at the time, he was only partially correct. While all that is born of God will endure eternally, historically some movements born of the passion of men's flesh politically and religiously have also survived the test of time (Sproul 122).

Not to appear weak or deterred in their actions against the apostles, though they did not sentence them to death (v. 40), the Council summarily had them beaten (Greek *dero*, to flog, scourge, flay). This punishment was administered with the victim in a kneeling position, upper torso bared. The one administering the flogging used a triple strap of leather and gave thirty-nine lashes (2 Cor. 11:24). Men were known to have died from the ordeal (Polhill, *Acts* 174). These twelve men were stripped and flogged openly. One can picture the apostles as they were dragged back before the Council, bruised, bleeding, and berated; then, being ordered to be silent in teaching in the name of Jesus, they were released.

3. The continuing witness of the apostles (5:41-42)

41 And they departed from the presence of the council, rejoicing that they were counted worthy to suffer shame for his name.
42 And daily in the temple, and in every house, they ceased not to teach and preach Jesus Christ.

Dismissed again, with the same order to cease and desist, the apostles would have assisted one another to a place of refuge and some degree of medical assistance. Though suffering physically from being beaten, they rejoiced (v. 41) in being identified with the sufferings of Christ (Phil. 3:10). The sacred irony is that the apostles were in solidarity (Keener II 1242) with the "Suffering Servant" (Isa. 53:3-5) dimension of the

Messiah in divine payment for the sins of humanity. That they had been chosen to teach and preach the greatest of all messages for the greatest of all persons was the greatest of all privileges, and the basis for rejoicing, not regret.

Apparently, there was little or no break in the strategy of the apostles to continue their ministry (v. 42). They returned to publicly teaching and preaching in the name of Jesus Christ in the very Temple area where they had just been arrested. Plus, they carried their efforts to the private homes of the citizens of Jerusalem. "We ought to obey God, rather than men" (5:29) was more than a mission statement. It was the heartfelt conviction upon which they were willing to risk their lives.

Summary
(5:17-42)

This time, all the apostles are arrested for their continued ministry in the name of Jesus. When they were imprisoned together overnight, scheduled to be arraigned before the entire Sanhedrin, the Lord sent an angel to deliver them from the prison. This was effected in such a fashion that even those guarding the doors where they were incarcerated were unaware of what happened. The apostles were instructed not to flee but to return to teaching in the Temple area.

Much to the chagrin of the Council, when they were summoned to appear, the apostles were not there and no explanation for their absence could be offered. However, they were soon discovered in plain sight, re-arrested without incident, and arraigned before the Council. Emboldened, perhaps by the miraculous deliverance, Peter's answer to the questioning of the high priest was straightforward and clear: "We ought to obey God rather than men" (v. 29).

Incensed to the point of intending to kill all the apostles, the Council moved to do so when one of their own, Gamaliel, appealed for a different approach. He reasoned that if the movement led by the apostles was born of men, it would be short-lived. He cited two known examples of men who led insurrections that ended quickly. On the other hand, if indeed the movement was born of God, the Council could not prevail against it. Either way, his counsel was to release the apostles, not kill them.

The Council bowed to this reasoning, but in a show of force flogged the apostles to make their point. The apostles left the Council beaten and bloody but rejoicing in their solidarity with the sufferings of Christ. As soon as they were able they returned to teaching and preaching openly in the name of Jesus Christ, again in the very Temple area where they had been arrested!

Application: Teaching and Preaching the Passage

Exegetical Outline of the Text: 1. The Arrest of the Apostles (5:17-18). 2. The Deliverance by the Angel of the Lord (5:19-20). 3. The Arraignment of the Apostles Before the Council (5:21-33). 4. The Counsel of Gamaliel (5:34-39). 5. The Determination of the Apostles (5:40-42).

This passage suggests a number of themes that can be developed for teaching and preaching. For example, using examples throughout the Scriptures, like Joseph or Daniel, lessons and messages can show how believers should respond when their faith is on trial.

The role of angels in the lives of believers merits study, especially when and how they act. This blends into a study of miraculous deliverances in biblical history, and treating them needs to be balanced with the providential actions of God in permitting persecution. God does not always miraculously deliver His people from imprisonment; therefore, the whole scope of this truth needs to be studied.

How the apostles responded in the face of all that happened to them is very instructive. They obeyed the angel's direction to return to the Temple and not flee. They did not alter their message nor acquiesce to the Council's demands even when they faced death. They rejoiced over being beaten instead of reacting in anger against God.

Of note is Gamaliel's advice to the Council. Was this really wisdom or being non-committal? In developing this study, one could evaluate what was wise about his advice and what was not. Ultimately, the gospel of Christ requires life commitment, not a wait-and-see attitude.

Gamaliel's reference to Judas of Galilee and Theudas and the questions raised about their historicity (see comments above) challenges us to address the importance of our doctrine of inspiration of the Scriptures? One might address any number of historical references (in Acts) and reinforce faith in the inerrancy of the Scriptures.

I. Further Organization of the Community Life of the Church (6:1-7)

1 And in those days, when the number of the disciples was multiplied, there arose a murmuring of the Grecians against the Hebrews,

because their widows were neglected in the daily ministration.
2 Then the twelve called the multitude of the disciples *unto them*, and said, It is not reason that we should leave the word of God, and serve tables.
3 Wherefore, brethren, look ye out among you seven men of honest report, full of the Holy Ghost and wisdom, whom we may appoint over this business.
4 But we will give ourselves continually to prayer, and to the ministry of the word.
5 And the saying pleased the whole multitude: and they chose Stephen, a man full of faith and of the Holy Ghost, and Philip, and Prochorus, and Nicanor, and Timon, and Parmenas, and Nicolas a proselyte of Antioch:
6 Whom they set before the apostles: and when they had prayed, they laid their hands on them.
7 And the word of God increased; and the number of the disciples multiplied in Jerusalem greatly; and a great company of the priests were obedient to the faith.

The number of the disciples grew rapidly: literally, the number "was multiplying" (Greek *plethuno*, present participle). With this growth came human needs and the challenge of how to minister to them (Barnhouse 57). The early church in Acts was compassionate and sacrificial in caring for the needs of the disciples and the community (2:45; 4:34-35; 5:16). One of those situations involved the daily food distribution for widows. Widows were a disadvantaged group in any circumstance since the basic resources for survival were diminished with the passing of the husband. In the Scriptures, they were the special focus for compassionate care (Deut. 14:29; 24:17; 1 Tim. 5:9-16; Jas. 1:27). The church in Acts was very active, apparently, in caring for widows; but the demand became greater than the supply, at least in the distribution of the supply. Compassionate efforts can often reveal larger issues. An otherwise noble and necessary ministry resulted in the accusation that some were being neglected (v. 1).

The accusation came from within the fellowship of believers, specifically "the Grecians against the Hebrews" (v. 1). Some commentators (Longenecker 126; Hughes 94) interpret the accusation as a case of outright prejudice that stemmed from a clash of cultures. Stott (120) sees the situation as a strategy of Satan to distract the apostles from their priority. Sometimes it is difficult to distinguish between the time demands of ministry and the spiritual significance of distraction. Others (Stott 120; Bruce, *Acts* 120; Polhill, *Acts* 179) see it as a functional problem due to limited manpower, not a deliberate neglect. Given the sense of community, the sacrificial sharing of needs and assets, the example of compassion provided by the apostles, and the fact that with few exceptions all the believers in Jerusalem were Jews, this was more likely a case of functional limitation, not social prejudice.

It appears that the apostles were the ones who oversaw the ministry since they were responsible for the distribution of funds (4:35). That being the case, as the demands grew, they would have limited availability for the time and effort required. However, the problem commanded their attention and needed a lasting, workable solution. Critics should be listened to, but solutions should come from leadership.

Three terms used here are significant and need to be defined; they will be referenced later: *Grecians*, *Hebrews*, and *proselytes* (6:5; 9:29; 11:20; 13:43). These terms provide insight as to the make-up of the church in Jerusalem. Most commentators agree that the distinction between *Grecians* (Greek *Hellenistes*) and *Hebrews* (Greek *Hebraios*) is mainly a linguistic one, with some minor cultural differences (Polhill, *Acts* 178, 179; Fitzmyer 347; Bruce, *Acts* 120; Hughes 94). Succinctly stated, "The distinction between them turned on the different relation of the original nationality to Judaism" (Meyer 123). A *proselyte* would be a Gentile convert to Judaism—or, later, to Christianity (Fitzmyer 243; TDNT VI:727-744).

With the exception of some Gentile proselytes, all the believers in Jerusalem were Jews. Greek-speaking Jews, *Grecians*, would be Diaspora Jews from various cities and immigrants to Jerusalem. Though Greek would be their common language, it does not mean they were not well-versed in Hebrew nor unfamiliar with Jewish customs and practices (Longenecker 123-124). Their lifestyles would have inculcated some Greco-Roman tastes, but they were thoroughly Jewish.

Hebrew-speaking Jews, *Hebrews*, would be native to Judaea and all Jewish customs. There are some exceptions. Paul, for example, called himself "an Hebrew of the Hebrews" (Phil. 3:5) though he was born in Tarsus of Cilicia (22:3), where Greek would have been the common language. Evidently Hebrew was the language in his home.

Other than the visitors in Jerusalem on the Day of Pentecost (2:10), Nicolas of Antioch (6:5) was the only proselyte to be named among the believers in Jerusalem. Of course, Antioch will become a key center of Christianity later (11:19-26).

With deliberate response (v. 2) the apostles ("the twelve," used only here in Acts) called for an assembly of the believers to initiate a solution to the complaint. The solution needed to be two-fold. The apostles needed to keep their priorities and qualified men should be appointed to oversee the need. The apostles were clear that their focus should be prayer and teaching the Word of God (vv. 2, 4). There was much to pray about and the teachings of Christ, especially, needed to be taught to His followers. The apostles were the only ones who were sufficiently qualified to do that. It should be noted that the apostles did not arbitrarily hand down the decision, but did offer specific guidelines about what should be done.

From among the multitude of the disciples, the believers were to select seven men (v. 3) who were distinguished as spiritual and wise. They needed to be personally filled with the Holy Spirit, since they would need the Spirit's leadership in assessing spiritual needs, especially for witnessing. They needed wisdom for proper administration of funds and for equitable distribution. The assumption is that the disciples would collectively know who these were and agree to their appointment (v. 3). The fact that they were to be presented to the apostles for confirmation (vv. 3, 7) shows solidarity in agreement with all involved. The process shows that the apostles were confident in the corporate decision of the body of Christ.

It should come as no surprise that all the men chosen were Grecians (v. 5), as indicated by their Greek names. From the area of need came the solution (Bock 257). The list begins with Stephen and Philip. These two men would lead in larger initiatives that emerged as the church expanded its witness beyond Jerusalem. The other five men are not mentioned again in the N. T. but certainly are significant in their roles as indicated by the results of their work (v. 7).

The incident and the solution provide a bridge for the role of Stephen (vv. 8-10), and of Philip in expanding the mission of the church into Samaria. Furthermore, this serves, through Stephen's martyrdom, as a bridge to the ministry of the apostle Paul to the Gentile world. It will be the Greek-speaking Jews who are instrumental in initially expanding the scope of the gospel's proclamation beyond Jerusalem and Judaea (Polhill, *Acts* 176-177; Bock 256).

The decision was a consensus approval (v. 5a) that had profound effects. The ministry of the Word of God increased in influence and effect (Barrett, *Acts* 89) since the apostles were no longer distracted (v. 7a). Multitudes turned to Christ in saving faith, including a large number of priests (v. 7b). One could pray that all church decisions were as smooth and productive!

It is especially significant that a large number of priests turned to Christ. The usage of the phrase "obedient to the faith" (v. 7) shows the nature of authentic, saving faith in Christ (Jas. 2:17-18). Obedience and faith are not exclusive to each other. One is not authentic without the other (Picirilli, *Discipleship* 114).

The priests' intimate knowledge of the Temple itself, of Temple worship ceremonies, and of the O. T. teachings of Messiah would make them prime candidates for evangelism. Their conversions validated even further the apostles' teaching of Jesus Christ as both High Priest and eternal sacrifice.

Summary
(6:1-7)

The church in Jerusalem was not only aggressive in evangelism but compassionate in ministering to people. Apparently, the sharing of needs and assets (4:34-35) included the care and feeding of widows, who would have limited means for subsistence. The apostles were responsible for the distribution, but the sheer number of those in need placed a demand on them that was greater than they could meet on a daily basis. This gave rise to a complaint of neglect from within the fellowship; the distribution seemed to favor one group over another.

The apostles moved quickly and decisively to resolve the issue, placing the responsibility on the body of believers to select qualified, additional help. The proposal was met with much approval by both the body of believers and the apostles, and seven men were selected to oversee the ministry of food distribution. This had the effects of maintaining the priorities of the apostles as well as resolving the complaint. Ultimately, the church was strengthened and the work of witnessing was propelled forward in teaching the Word of God and outreach to the unsaved. Specifically, a large number of priests were saved.

Included in the list of the seven men who were given oversight of food distribution to widows were Stephen and Philip. This incident gave rise to the expanding witness of the church to Samaria via these Greek-speaking, Spirit-filled men. The appointment gave them a platform for ministry that resulted in powerful witness and, sadly, the death of Stephen as the first martyr for Christ in the Book of Acts.

Application: Teaching and Preaching the Passage

Exegetical Outline of the Text: 1. The Complaint of Neglect (6:1). 2. The Discernment of the Apostles (6:2-4). 3. The Appointment of Capable Men (6:5-7).

Perhaps an obvious theme to be discussed is the process of addressing problems that arise within the fellowship of a local church (or any organization for that matter). Discussion could include the principles that gave rise to the problem, how they resolved it, and the results.

It is premature in the developmental organization of the church to conclude that these seven men were the first "deacons." However, they certainly model the heart and purpose needed for the office. This could provide the backdrop for study and discussion on the leadership offices of the N. T. church, qualifications for such, and contemporary applications.

The effort by the early church to feed widows reflects the example of Christ (Mt. 14:15-21; Mk. 6:35-44; Lk. 9:12-17; Jn. 6:5-13). Jesus also said He was the Bread of Life (Jn. 6:35). This passage in Acts can spark an excellent study of the church ministering to all human needs. Later, the apostle Paul gave specific instructions about the church's responsibilities toward widows (1 Tim. 5:1-16). One can connect the intention of the second greatest command (Mt. 22:39) as well. History reveals that the greatest efforts of compassion and healing in medicine, hospitals, care for the elderly and children, etc., originate from Christ's commands, example, and the model of the church.

J. The Witness of Stephen (6:8—8:1a)

1. Stephen's ministry (6:8-10)

8   And Stephen, full of faith and power, did great wonders and miracles among the people.
9   Then there arose certain of the synagogue, which is called *the synagogue* of the Libertines, and Cyrenians, and Alexandrians, and of them of Cilicia and of Asia, disputing with Stephen.
10 And they were not able to resist the wisdom and the spirit by which he spake.

The extensive narrative about Stephen signals a major transition from Jerusalem and the leadership of the apostles to Samaria and beyond, while introducing the leadership of other men.

In particular, it reveals the specific points of differences between Christianity's view of redemptive history and Judaism. Stephen is a key apologetic witness via his life and ministry, as well as by his sermon before the Sanhedrin. His sermon, the longest recorded in Acts, is not only his defense against the charges, it also defines the transition message of the gospel (Lightfoot 116-117).

Apparently, Stephen's appointment put him in position for an extended ministry beyond caring for widows. One open door often leads to others. His life and work were attested by the Holy Spirit's power (v. 8), confirming the choice of the disciples in recommending him (v. 5). Up till now only the apostles were noted for "wonders and miracles" (2:43; 5:12), but Stephen is used in this way as well.

Within Jerusalem there were several synagogues as well as the Temple (Fitzmyer 356-357; Robertson, *Acts* 75; Bruce, *Acts* 124). Though somewhat historically obscure as to origin, the synagogue as a place of assembly for teaching and prayer probably arose during the period of the Babylonian exile (EDT 1061-1062). In Jerusalem, these became gathering places for various groups with similar language and interests (Marshall, *Acts* 129), particularly if they were Hellenistic. Being "Grecian" himself, Stephen would have gone to these where he proclaimed the gospel of Christ.

Though some argue that verse 9 lists possibly five synagogues in which Stephen preached (Robertson, *Acts* 75; Fitzymyer 357; Meyer 129), others (Bruce, *Acts* 125; Ger 96; Stott 126) are probably more correct in identifying only one, known as the "synagogue of Libertines"—literally, of *Freedmen*. It was known as such because former Roman slaves or children of former slaves from Cyrene, Alexandria, Cilicia, and Asia attended. Further, it was there that those with Roman citizenship could identify with others of the same standing.

The naming of Cilicia should be noted since that was the home of Saul of Tarsus (22:3). His Hellenistic background and Roman citizenship (22:28) readily identified him with this synagogue, even though it is not absolutely certain he attended there, and he was not a Freedman. It is certainly possible, even likely, that a young Saul of Tarsus (7:58) was in the thick of the debates with Stephen (Robertson, *Acts* 76; Keener II:1310). The fact that Saul, with all his training under Gamaliel and personal brilliance, could not outwit Stephen might have given rise to his hostility and opposition. It does not appear coincidental that Saul was among those present at the stoning of Stephen (7:58).

In his recorded message before the Sanhedrin, Stephen addressed the specific subjects of the debate, in the form of charges of "blasphemy." The main point of contention would have been that Jesus of Nazareth was the Messiah predicted in the O. T. (Bruce, *Acts* 125). The teaching and witness of the apostles, their explanations of O. T. Messianic truths, and the empowering and enlightening of the Holy Spirit would have been the source and power for Stephen's arguments. The result was that the Sanhedrin simply could not stand against the truths Stephen presented (v. 10). This is yet another example of testing and blessing under these circumstances as predicted by the Lord Jesus (Lk. 21:15).

2. Stephen's arrest (6:11-15)

**11 Then they suborned men, which said, We have heard him speak blasphemous words against Moses, and *against* God.
12 And they stirred up the people, and the elders, and the scribes, and came upon *him*, and caught**

him, and brought *him* to the council,
13 And set up false witnesses, which said, This man ceaseth not to speak blasphemous words against this holy place, and the law:
14 For we have heard him say, that this Jesus of Nazareth shall destroy this place, and shall change the customs which Moses delivered us.
15 And all that sat in the council, looking stedfastly on him, saw his face as it had been the face of an angel.

Thwarted by their inability to outwit and silence Stephen, the officials secured witnesses against him. That they *suborned* them (Greek *hupoballo*) means that they were the secret instigators of the witnesses' so-called testimony. The idea is that they probably bribed them and told them what to say. There was a two-fold charge of blasphemy (v. 11): speaking blasphemy against Moses and against God. This successfully incited the emotions of the people and the leaders of the synagogue ("elders and scribes") enough to bring formal charges against him. The result was that Stephen was arrested and brought before the Sanhedrin (vv. 11-12). Sadly, some who don't like the message attack the messenger.

In a scene reminiscent of the trial of Jesus (Mt. 26:59-66; Mk. 14:57-64), Stephen is arraigned before the Council (vv. 13-14). This time the charges are restated more specifically. He is guilty of blasphemy against the Temple (God Himself) and against the Law (Moses), by which they mean that he has advocated destruction of the Temple and

desecration of the Law. Nothing was more sacred in the minds of the Jews (Stott 128). But in what sense could these charges be even remotely true? In the minds of his accusers, the teaching of Jesus about His resurrection (Mt. 26:61) was tantamount to an act of terrorism against the structure of the Temple and therefore an act of blasphemy against God. The same with the Messianic fulfillments of the Law and Moses. This linking will be the basis for continuing conflict in the future as well as here. The Book of Hebrews answers all these concerns (Outlaw 10).

These are essentially the same charges as those brought against Jesus. In effect, not only is Stephen on trial, but Jesus is, too—again! Indeed, the core message of the gospel is on trial before the religious elite of Israel. In fact, counting the trial of Christ, this makes four times the high court of Israel has considered the truths of the gospel (4:5-21; 5:17-40), rejecting it all four times (Jn. 1:11). Polhill (*Acts* 186) states, appropriately, that ultimately the Sanhedrin is actually on trial.

With the charges leveled against him, all attention was directed toward Stephen (v. 15). In such a setting, lesser men would fold, but instead of seeing a look of fear they saw his face transfigured to be angel-like. What, exactly, does the face of an angel look like, to make this comparison? Some (Stott 129; Keener II:1326; Meyer 131) interpret this as his face shining, externally aglow, making an allusion to Moses before the burning bush and later reflecting God's glory after coming down from Mount Sinai (Ex. 3:2-6; 24:29). Others see it as the look of serenity, courage, confidence, the look of clarity in one's eyes (Bock 274; Bruce, *Acts* 128).

Clearly, the Holy Spirit is resting upon Stephen with favor and power in such proportion that it is evident in his face.

3. The message of Stephen to the Sanhedrin (7:1-53)

a. The time of Abraham and the Patriarchs (7:1-8)

1 Then said the high priest, Are these things so?
2 And he said, Men, brethren, and fathers, hearken; The God of glory appeared unto our father Abraham, when he was in Mesopotamia, before he dwelt in Charran,
3 And said unto him, Get thee out of thy country, and from thy kindred, and come into the land which I shall shew thee.
4 Then came he out of the land of the Chaldaeans, and dwelt in Charran: and from thence, when his father was dead, he removed him into this land, wherein ye now dwell.
5 And he gave him none inheritance in it, no, not so *much* as to set his foot on; yet he promised that he would give it to him for a possession, and to his seed after him, when *as yet* he had no child.
6 And God spake on this wise, That his seed should sojourn in a strange land; and that they should bring them into bondage, and entreat *them* evil four hundred years.
7 And the nation to whom they shall be in bondage will I judge, said God: and after that shall they come forth, and serve me in this place.
8 And he gave him the covenant of circumcision: and so *Abraham begat* Isaac, and circumcised him the eighth day; and Isaac begat Jacob; and Jacob *begat* the twelve patriarchs.

Stephen's message to the Sanhedrin has been both criticized and applauded by commentators. The criticisms range from outright denial that these were the actual words of Stephen to the seeming lack of coherence in what he said (Fitzmyer 364-365; Keener II:1338-1340; Barrett, *Acts* 97; Marshall, *Acts* 132; Haenchen 286-289). This latter criticism may be due, in part, to a lack of understanding of Stephen's recorded sermon and underestimating his debate abilities (6:10). These views make Stephen's message a construct of Luke's that he gathered from sources other than those citing the words of Stephen himself. This way, the message represents a later view of redemptive history inserted into the story. In an ironic twist, these writers are literarily "stoning" Stephen again!

Others applaud the sophistication of Stephen's message and the careful recording by Luke as an essential apologetic of the gospel (Polhill, *Acts* 187-188; Stott 129-130; Longenecker 133-134; Bruce, *Acts* 130-132; Lightfoot 126-136; Sproul 132; Meyer 135-136). This view is the accurate one. There are simply no compelling evidences that show the message of Stephen has any other source than Stephen himself, as remembered by Paul or some other(s) present, and that Luke accurately records what he said. Lightfoot (133) states, "In sum, the arguments against the genuineness of the speech entirely failed."

Furthermore, a careful analysis of Stephen's message reveals a sophisticated interpretation of redemptive history (Sproul 132). What may appear to be an impromptu speech is hardly that. It is the very essence of Stephen's previous arguments (6:10, 13, 14) in the synagogues. There is no doubt the Council knew the facts of Israel's history as well as Stephen. But they had failed to interpret those events through the lens of redemptive theology. This was Stephen's expertise that stumped those who opposed him.

In summary, Stephen selected four eras of Israel's history from which to draw the truths that he proposed: the time of Abraham and the Patriarchs (vv. 2-8); the time of Joseph (vv. 9-16); the time of Moses (vv. 19-44); and the time of David and Solomon (vv. 45-50). From these time periods, he argued, it was clear that God was with His covenant people no matter where they were, especially before they inherited the promised land. Also, the Law was always looking forward to the Messiah, never an end to itself. Moses himself prophesied of the Messiah, whom Israel was to hear. Finally, no building constructed by men could ever be sufficient to restrict the presence and worship of the living God.

In effect, Stephen accuses them of creating three "sacred cows" (Hughes 10). Those "sacred cows" were the land, the Law, and the Temple. First, by vesting so much spiritual significance to the land itself, they had diminished the truth that God cannot be confined to any particular time or place. His promise of a land to inherit, made to Abraham, was secondary to knowing God's presence in all places.

Second, they claimed to honor Moses, the lawgiver, and had placed their trust in the ceremonies of the Law to save them instead of in what the ceremonies represented. In fact, historically, Israel had been spiritually fickle with both Moses and the Law. Hence, Moses prophesied of one who was greater than both Moses and the Law itself.

The third "sacred cow" was the Temple. It began as a portable worship structure in the wilderness wanderings and evolved into Solomon's Temple and subsequent versions. An imposing structure, yes, but, as Stephen would argue, it was merely a "Temple made with hands" (v. 48) compared to the fact that Heaven was the throne of God and the entire earth His footstool (v. 49). How can this great God be confined to a building? And so why attach so much value to it that one could be charged with blasphemy for putting it in proper perspective?

Furthermore, present Israel represented by the leaders of the Council, like their forefathers, continued in the same pattern of missing these great truths and rejecting God's prophets and leaders. Israel's past was their present (v. 51). Ultimately, they even rejected and murdered the long-awaited Messiah Himself, Jesus of Nazareth, the "Just One." Just as they had rejected the prophets in the past, they were rejecting the Lord's prophets of the present day, the apostles and Stephen himself. Their sins were, in effect, a total repudiation of the very essence of Israel's covenant identity and purpose. It was a sin of national proportion.

It should be noted that these criticisms of "sacred cows," addressed in summary by Stephen, would be expanded on in great detail later in the writings of the apostle Paul (Romans and Galatians, especially), in the Book of Hebrews, and in other N. T. writings. Ironically, Saul of Tarsus, prior to his conversion, would have argued vehemently against Stephen about these very same issues. After his conversion to Christ, as the apostle Paul, he would argue for them.

The high priest, probably still Caiaphas, gave Stephen permission (v. 1) to speak to the charges leveled at him. With permission given, he presented a credible defense against the charges, ultimately laying the true guilt at the feet of the Council before whom he stood.

The first era Stephen targets was the time of the Patriarchs (vv. 2-8). It should be noted that he speaks with deference and respect (v. 2) to those present as his Jewish "brothers" and to the Council members as "fathers." One can be bold without being rude. He immediately refers to the call of Abraham (Gen. 12:1), by the "God of glory," to leave his country and family to follow God's leading. Stephen places the initial call of Abraham in Chaldean Ur (Gen. 11:27, 28) and names it as "Mesopotamia." While usage of that term usually did not include Ur of the Chaldees (Bruce, *Acts* 133; Keener ll:1355), they are identified together in the Septuagint (the "standard" Greek translation of the O. T.) in Genesis 27:43. Most commentators agree that Stephen's use of the Septuagint is apparent.

There should be no problem with Stephen's stating that the initial call of Abraham took place in Chaldean Ur instead of Canaan. It is certainly possible that the wording in Genesis 12:1— "Now the LORD had said"—represented an affirming call (Marshall, *Acts* 135)

of the one journey from Ur to Canaan (Gen. 15:7; Neh. 9:7). The larger point from the beginning of Stephen's message is that the "God of glory" spoke (and does speak) where and when necessary.

Abraham's obedience led him to the land of Canaan. Here God promised him an inheritance of the entire region as far as his eyes could see (Gen. 13:14-17). But Abraham himself did not inherit any of it, not even the size of a foot print (Greek *bema podos*, literally "a step of a foot"). His purchase of a burial site for Sarah (Gen. 23) was not a gift from God. Furthermore, he was promised descendants as numerous as the stars in the heavens (Gen. 15:5-6) to occupy it, even though he was childless at the time (v. 5).

Abraham was informed (vv. 6-7) that the future was both bright and bleak. There would indeed be a multitude of heirs, but they would dwell in a foreign land in cruel bondage for four hundred years before they would inherit the land as promised. They would be delivered and the nation responsible for their slavery would be punished for their unjust treatment of them. In this way, Stephen summarizes Israel's time in Egypt and the judgments of the Exodus, making again the point of God's presence and blessings that extend beyond the borders of Canaan.

Here is a good place to address questions about numbers in the Book of Acts. Exodus 12:40 says the time of Israel's sojourn in Egypt was four hundred and thirty years, while Stephen says it was four hundred. Which is correct? Without doubt Luke has been careful and intentional in recording several numbers in his narrative, beginning in 1:3 with the forty days of appearances by Jesus to the apostles. The numbers of the disciples are carefully stated as one hundred and twenty (1:15), three thousand (2:41), and five thousand (4:4). In later situations, Luke will give other numbers regarding the event he is recording. Why is this something important to consider?

The answer is that considering the accuracy of the numbers is important to our view of the plenary, verbal inspiration of the Scriptures and their inerrancy. While the issue is too broad for all the "apparent" discrepancies of the Scriptures to be addressed in this commentary, the accurate use of numbers in Acts is appropriate to address. The simple answer about the numbers in Acts is that they are all accurate, including what Luke says about the number of years Israel spent in Egyptian bondage. Here's the reason for saying this.

It is clear that Luke is speaking in *summary* terms when he uses some of the numbers he does—the number of disciples, for example. In other cases, his intention is to be more *precise*, as when he indicates the number of men who came to see Peter at Joppa (10:19); the twelve disciples at Ephesus (19:7); Paul's Roman escort to Caesarea (23:23), and so on. The difference is the intention of "accuracy versus precision" (Forlines, *Quest* 58). This is normal interpretation of such uses. Thus, the number of years Stephen used about the period of cruel slavery is accurate for a summary, while the precise number is recorded in Exodus 12:40.

The sealing of the Abrahamic covenant was circumcision (Gen. 17:9-14), a simple surgical procedure showing God's connection to life (v. 8). That covenant sign was confirmed through Isaac, Jacob, and the twelve sons ("patriarchs")

that grew into the twelve tribes of Israel. God established a covenant people before they inherited the place to live. From the very beginning God's focus was on His covenant people.

b. The time of Joseph (7:9-16)

9　And the patriarchs, moved with envy, sold Joseph into Egypt: but God was with him,
10 And delivered him out of all his afflictions, and gave him favour and wisdom in the sight of Pharaoh king of Egypt; and he made him governor over Egypt and all his house.
11 Now there came a dearth over all the land of Egypt and Chanaan, and great affliction: and our fathers found no sustenance.
12 But when Jacob heard that there was corn in Egypt, he sent out our fathers first.
13 And at the second *time* Joseph was made known to his brethren; and Joseph's kindred was made know unto Pharaoh.
14 Then sent Joseph, and called his father Jacob to *him*, and all his kindred, threescore and fifteen souls.
15 So Jacob went down into Egypt, and died, he, and our fathers,
16 And were carried over into Sychem, and laid in the sepulchre that Abraham bought for a sum of money of the sons of Emmor *the father* of Sychem.

Stephen moved quickly to selected material about Joseph, contrasting the actions of his brothers with God's favor and blessing on him (vv. 9-10). While God's favor upon Joseph took him from slave to "Governor over Egypt," his brothers ("our fathers," v. 11) suffered drought, famine, and destitution. Interestingly, Stephen used the phrase "our fathers" some ten times (vv. 2, 11, 12, 15, 19, 38, 39, 44, 45), showing common ancestral connection with the events. But when he made his point about the sin involved (v. 51) he referred to them as "your fathers." The not-so-subtle shift of emphasis was not lost on the Council (v. 54).

Stephen drew attention to the two occasions when the brothers of Joseph were sent by Jacob to Egypt to purchase food and grain (vv. 12-14). They were not aware that the stored provisions in Egypt were because of the wisdom and favor of God upon Joseph (Gen. 41), whom they presumed was dead. Not until the second visit did Joseph reveal his identity to them (v. 13). Christological comparisons to Joseph are frequently made (Keener II:1368; Bock 268; Polhill, Acts 192) making the two visits of the brothers significant. In the first visit, like Christ, Joseph was not recognized (Jn. 1:11) by his own kin. It was during the second visit that Joseph revealed who he was. In like manner, it will be at the Second Coming of Christ that all will bow before Him and acknowledge Him as Lord (Phil. 2:9-11).

The famine and provision became the occasion that God providentially used to move the family of Jacob (v. 14) from Canaan to Egypt, just as had been predicted to Abraham. For every one time we become aware of God's providential work, there are a thousand of which we are not aware.

The question of numbers arises here again, since the Hebrew text (Gen. 46:27; Ex. 1:5) says seventy and the Septuagint, which Stephen was quoting, says seventy-five "souls" (Greek psuche, a human being) who came into Egypt. Evidently the Septuagint arrived at this number without counting Jacob himself or Joseph, who was already in Egypt (Ex. 1:5), and by adding to the sixty-six people who came with Jacob into Egypt (Gen. 46:26) nine sons for Joseph rather than two (Gen. 46:27). But, after all, there is a discrepancy between the Massoretic Hebrew text, which states there were seventy (Deut. 10:22) and that Joseph had two sons, and the Septuagint, which says seventy-five and nine sons. Most commentators recognize this as a discrepancy (Lightfoot 109-110; Bock 288; Lenski 270; Meyer 144) but do not see it as a problem that demands reconciliation. Stott (133) comments that the discrepancy is probably due to whether Joseph's sons were included in the total.

The Septuagint is frequently used in the N. T., particularly by the apostles and in the writings of Luke. There is much discussion as to its origin, accuracy, and trustworthiness (ESV footnote, The Septuagint 2601-2603). However, the use of it by Luke, at least, qualifies it to be cited in the inspired writings of the N. T.

Further investigation sheds light on the Septuagint number used by Stephen. It is clear that more children were born to Joseph than just Manasseh and Ephraim (Gen. 48:6). Also, the grandsons of Joseph may be included in the number (Gen. 50:23). Thus, beginning with the sixty-six people who came with Jacob (Gen 46:26), add Jacob, Joseph and his two sons (Gen. 46:27), and the number is seventy. Then add the others to be born to Joseph (Gen. 48:6), including his grandsons (Gen. 50:23). The total number of seventy-five places

(v. 14) the entire covenant family, including all the family of Joseph, in Egypt. It does not appear that Stephen, or the Council, had any questions about the accuracy of the Septuagint and accepted that number confidently (Keener II:1369).

Stephen asserts that Jacob and his sons died in Egypt (v. 15), and all were buried in Canaan (v. 16). However, there are questions raised about this detail as told by Stephen. First, the O. T. does not record the burial of the sons of Jacob in Canaan. But popular Jewish tradition (Josephus, *Antiquities.* II.VIII.2) in Stephen's time says they were. This is probably his point of reference (Marshall, *Acts* 138-139; Bock 288) and would have been acknowledged as accurate by the Council.

The second detail in question regards the two patriarchal burial places in Canaan. According to Genesis 23:17-20, Abraham bought the cave of Machpelah close to Hebron from Ephron the Hittite, not from Hamor as Stephen seems to say. The second burial site was near Shechem, which Jacob bought from the children of Hamor (Gen. 33:18-20). According to Genesis 50:12-13, Jacob was buried in the cave of Machpelah, not Shechem as Stephen seems to say. Joseph was buried at Shechem (Josh. 24:32).

Commentators vary greatly in addressing this apparent discrepancy. Some state that Stephen was simply mistaken (Meyer 145; Fitzmyer 374; Haenchen 280). Robertson (*Acts* 84) believes the matter is cleared up if "Jacob" is inserted in the place of "Abraham" and the problem is a copyist's error. But there is no manuscript evidence to support this. Several see the issue as Stephen conflating or telescoping the two burial records into one for the sake of summary (Bock 289; Polhill, *Acts* 193; Bruce, *Acts* 137; Stott 134; Walker 190). Some see the use of the name of "Abraham" as a patriarchal representative (ESV footnote, 2093-2094) for all his descendants, including Jacob. Bock (289) argues that Abraham might very well have previously purchased the site since he had been there long before Jacob (Gen. 12:6-7). Later, Jacob re-purchased the site in the original name of Abraham as Isaac had to do with the wells of water previously dug by his father (Gen. 26:15-33). This doesn't seem likely, either, since it would mean that Stephen, speaking with theological inspiration, was giving "new revelation" about an old story. If this was claimed there would have been an immediate reaction by the Council, who knew the history and traditions as well as Stephen.

Because of his intimate knowledge of the O. T., and the fact that this is not the first time he had argued these very points (6:10-14), it can be ruled out that Stephen simply made a mistake. Given the fact that Stephen had previously used the same method regarding the call of Abraham (vv. 2-3), it appears the best interpretation may be that he conflated the burial accounts and traditions. Therefore, it is best to keep to the main point being made, i.e., both Abraham and Jacob made provision for burials of all the patriarchs in the land of Canaan as an expression of faith that God would keep His Word.

c. The time of Moses (7:17-43)

(1) The first forty years (7:17-22)

17 But when the time of the promise drew nigh, which God had

sworn to Abraham, the people
grew and multiplied in Egypt,
18 Till another king arose, which
knew not Joseph.
19 The same dealt subtilly with
our kindred, and evil entreated our
fathers, so that they cast out their
young children, to the end they
might not live.
20 In which time Moses was born,
and was exceeding fair, and nourished up in his father's house three
months:
21 And when he was cast out,
Pharaoh's daughter took him up,
and nourished him for her own
son.
22 And Moses was learned in all
the wisdom of the Egyptians, and
was mighty in words and in deeds.

Moses lived to be one hundred and
twenty years old (Deut. 34:7). Rabbinical
tradition has his life marked into three
distinct time segments of forty years
each. Stephen's longest comments are
for Moses, distinguishing each of the
segments and the events that defined
him. The first forty years (vv. 17-22) are
marked as the time for the fulfillment of
God's promise to Abraham (Gen. 15:13)
upon the sizeable population of his
descendants (v. 17). Because of the
power and favor of the God who works
His will, a childless couple now has
descendants "as the dust of the earth"
(Gen. 13:16).

The legacy of Joseph was eventually
lost as the years passed (v. 18). If he was
remembered at all, it hardly mattered
since the political agenda of Pharaoh
outweighed any previous arrangements
(v. 19). Perhaps the thriving population
of Israel intimidated the Pharaoh to the
point he felt threatened (Ex. 1: 9-10)

and forced the entire nation of Israel
into cruel slavery. Along with that came
government-ordered infanticide as parents were forced to abandon their children ("cast out"), leaving them to die of
exposure (Ex. 1:15-22). Despotism has
little morality and even less mercy. It is
hard to imagine the despair this engendered. Plus, it was a direct assault (ultimately by Satan) on the covenant promise of fruitfulness in descendants.

Stephen's accurate summary of the
suffering of Israel in Egypt is punctuated
with the birth story of Moses (vv. 20-21).
Out of despair came hope. Again, the
providence of God was highlighted as
Moses was not only spared from death
but was adopted by Pharaoh's daughter
and reared as her own child! Josephus
(*Antiquities* II.IX, 6-7) describes Moses
as "having understanding superior to
others his age, unusual beauty in appearance, tall, polite, of divine form, and
ability." Pharaoh's daughter presented
him as worthy of being the heir of the
throne. In addition, she engaged Moses'
own parents to nurture him in the early
years. The providential irony of the
story is compelling. Who but God could
arrange such a thing (Rom. 8:28)?

The education and exploits of Moses
marked his maturity to manhood (v. 22).
His training equipped him with leadership skills on a national level that were
demonstrated early in his life by
"mighty...deeds." Such was the providential influence on his life that prepared him for the development and
defining of the nation of Israel.

Interestingly, Stephen describes
Moses as "mighty in words," though
Moses himself claimed to be "slow of
speech" (Ex. 4:10). This may be his
personal assessment or an expression of
humility (Bock 291). Polhill (*Acts* 195)

references the possibility that he was unskillful in writing. Moses may very well have been confident and skillful in the courts of men, but before the living God he was awkward and uncomfortable. Who would not be! However, aside from the assistance of Aaron (Ex. 4:14-16), it was Moses who spoke so eloquently and penned the first five books of Scripture.

Stephen is asserting that Moses was prepared for leadership by the Egyptians who were bent on Israel's enslavement. According to His promise, the Lord began delivering His people by raising up a deliverer first. However, Stephen's intention is not to show just the preparation of Moses, but his initial rejection by the very people he was prepared to deliver. Stephen is intentionally using the facts to portray the larger point he makes of the rejection of Jesus as the Messiah.

(2) The second forty years (7:23-29)

**23 And when he was full forty years old, it came into his heart to visit his brethren the children of Israel.
24 And seeing one *of them* suffer wrong, he defended *him*, and avenged him that was oppressed, and smote the Egyptian:
25 For he supposed his brethren would have understood how that God by his hand would deliver them: but they understood not.
26 And the next day he shewed himself unto them as they strove, and would have set them at one again, saying, Sirs, ye are brethren; why do ye wrong one to another?**

**27 But he that did his neighbor wrong thrust him away, saying, Who made thee a ruler and a judge over us?
28 Wilt thou kill me, as thou diddest the Egyptian yesterday?
29 Then fled Moses at this saying, and was a stranger in the land of Madian, where he begat two sons.**

Stephen moved to the second forty-year period in Moses' life. Apparently, the nurturing he received from his biological parents included instruction in their covenant history. At the age of forty, he arrived at the conclusion that he was God's appointed deliverer of Israel (v. 25). There is no particular O. T. reference that confirms that Moses was forty when this event took place. But as Keener (III:1389-1390) asserts it is an age approximation that is consistent with other forty-year time frames, as well as a natural division of what is known of other age references in Moses' life (Ex. 7:7; Deut. 31:2).

The belief that he was God's appointed deliverer motivated Moses to visit his people to establish himself in that capacity (v. 23). Seeing the cruel treatment of an Israelite at the hand of an Egyptian taskmaster, Moses intervened, killing the Egyptian and hiding his body (Ex. 2:12). For Moses, this act was more than a mere intervention in cruel treatment; he believed the action would be understood as evidence of where his sympathies lay and of his intention to deliver Israel from Egyptian bondage. However, that was not the Israelites' perception (v. 25).

When he returned the next day, Moses encountered two Israelites fighting. As he intervened, appealing to their kinship, one retorted that Moses was not in any position (v. 27) to say anything given his previous actions, which were much more serious than merely fighting (v. 28). This response was a clear rejection of Moses, and he took it as such (v. 29).

Stephen's brilliance is seen again as he subtly inserts, for the second time, the theme of rejection of one who was prepared to lead Israel (v. 9). Many see this as an intentional allusion to the rejection of Jesus (Bock 293; Bruce, *Acts* 139-140; Lenski 279). That point will not be so subtle in Stephen's conclusion (v. 52).

"Then fled Moses" (v. 29). Stephen omits that the slaying of the Egyptian taskmaster became public information known even to Pharaoh who sought to kill Moses as a result (Ex. 2:15). His former status had been revoked, he had been rejected by his own people, and then he became a fugitive. Stephen concludes this period of Moses' life with a very brief summary of the place to which he fled (Midian), where he married and had two sons (Ex. 2:15-22; 4:20). God's timing is not always perceived immediately, nor was the training Moses received in Pharaoh's court sufficient. Lenski (279) aptly states, "Moses needed not only the forty years of Egyptian schooling but forty more of desert schooling in order to make him the man God wanted." This sets the stage for the third forty-year period of his life.

(3) The third forty years (7:30-43)

30 And when forty years were expired, there appeared to him in the wilderness of mount Sina an angel of the Lord in a flame of fire in a bush.

31 When Moses saw *it,* **he wondered at the sight: and as he drew near to behold** *it,* **the voice of the LORD came unto him,**

32 *Saying,* **I** *am* **the God of thy fathers, the God of Abraham, and the God of Isaac, and the God of Jacob. Then Moses trembled, and durst not behold.**

33 Then said the Lord to him, Put off they shoes from thy feet: for the place where thou standest is holy ground.

34 I have seen, I have seen the affliction of my people which is in Egypt, and I have heard their groaning, and am come down to deliver them. And now come, I will send thee into Egypt.

35 This Moses whom they refused, saying, Who made thee a ruler and a judge? the same did God send *to be* **a ruler and a deliverer by the hand of the angel which appeared to him in the bush.**

36 He brought them out, after that he had shewed wonders and signs in the land of Egypt, and in the Red sea, and in the wilderness forty years.

37 This is that Moses, which said unto the children of Israel, A prophet shall the Lord your God raise up unto you of your brethren, like unto me; him shall ye hear.

38 This is he, that was in the church in the wilderness with the angel which spake to him in the mount Sina, and *with* **our fathers: who received the lively oracles to give unto us:**

39 To whom our fathers would not obey, but thrust *him* **from them, and in their hearts turned back again into Egypt,**

40 Saying unto Aaron, Make us gods to go before us: for *as for* this Moses, which brought us out of the land of Egypt, we wot not what is become of him.
41 And they made a calf in those days, and offered sacrifice unto the idol, and rejoiced in the works of their own hands.
42 Then God turned, and gave them up to worship the host of heaven; as it is written in the book of the prophets, O ye house of Israel, have ye offered to me slain beasts and sacrifices *by the space of* forty years in the wilderness?
43 Yes, ye took up the tabernacle of Moloch, and the star of your god Remphan, figures which ye made to worship them: and I will carry you away beyond Babylon.

The next forty-year segment of Moses' life began with his encounter with the living God who appeared in the burning bush (vv. 30-35; Ex. 3:1-6). Though a few differentiate between "an angel" and the Lord Himself (Keener II:1397), the context and the personal identification statements (v. 32) make it clear that this is an encounter with the Lord Himself (Lenski 280; Robertson, *Acts* 89; Bock 294).

Stephen concludes the scene with God's call and commissioning of Moses: "I will send thee into Egypt" (vv. 34-35). The very one they had rejected was the one the Lord chose. God is merciful and gives second opportunities. Stephen's intention is clear. As with Joseph (v. 9), so with Moses, and ultimately with Jesus.

In a succinct statement (v. 36), Stephen summarizes the entire Exodus event, the crossing of the Red Sea, the giving of the Law at Mount Sinai, almost the entirety of the books of Exodus, Leviticus, and Numbers, together with the forty-year wandering in the wilderness! Obviously, he has something else in mind.

"This is that Moses" (vv. 37-43). Stephen makes three points regarding Moses, the Law, and Israel's history of idolatry. The first (vv. 37-38) is that even though Moses was God's man in leadership and the instrument for Israel's establishment as a nation, he spoke prophetically (Deut. 18:15, 18) of a future prophet like himself, but greater. This prophet would be the Messiah (Kaiser 60). The greatness of Moses pales in comparison to the infinite greatness of the Messiah.

Stephen's second point (vv. 39-41) is that although Moses was significant in his calling, his leadership, and his instrumentality in mediating the Law, Israel was fickle about following him and obeying the Law of God. In short order, they repudiated the leadership of Moses and demanded of Aaron that he should give them gods they could see (Ex. 32). In an ultimate irony, while Moses was alone atop Mt. Sinai communing with the living God and receiving His Law, the rest of Israel was cavorting in idolatry at the foot of the mountain! Moses had gotten Israel out of Egypt but getting Egypt out of Israel was another challenge altogether. One cannot miss the intentional corrective Stephen gives regarding the charges against him of "blasphemous words against Moses" (6:11). One can almost hear him say, "And you said I blasphemed Moses!"

Stephen's third point, and the most poignant of all, draws on the prophet Amos (5:25-27) in commentary on Israel's ignominious history of idolatry.

While there are some differences of interpretation as to the particular construction of Amos' statement (Polhill, *Acts* 143-145), the point Stephen clearly makes is that from the very beginning of the nation, idolatry had plagued the nation's spiritual conscience. The forty-year wilderness wandering (v. 42) served as a precursor to the long history of Israel's idolatry that resulted in the Babylonian captivity (v. 43).

d. The time of David and Solomon (7:44-50)

44 Our fathers had the tabernacle of witness in the wilderness, as he had appointed, speaking unto Moses, that he should make it according to the fashion that he had seen.
45 Which also our fathers that came after brought in with Jesus into the possession of the Gentiles, whom God drave out before the face of our fathers, unto the days of David;
46 Who found favour before God, and desired to find a tabernacle for the God of Jacob.
47 But Solomon built him an house.
48 Howbeit the most High dwelleth not in temples made with hands; as saith the prophet,
49 Heaven *is* my throne, and earth *is* my footstool: what house will ye build me? Saith the Lord: or what *is* the place of my rest?
50 Hath not my hand made all these things?

One can sense the emotion of the whole scene intensify as Stephen builds his case. Up to now, he has made it clear: as seen in His dealings with Abraham, God is everywhere present and speaks when He pleases. He is not confined to any one place. As in the cases of Joseph and Moses, Israel has rejected some of its greatest leaders who were chosen and sent by the Lord. As in the wilderness, Israel has a checkered history of idolatry.

Having countered the charge of "blasphemous words against Moses" (6:11), Stephen turned to the charge of "blasphemous words against this holy place" (6:13). He referenced the "tabernacle (tent) of witness in the wilderness" (v. 44) as a continual reminder of God's presence among them. It was no ordinary tent but one constructed after the pattern shown to Moses (Ex. 25:40; Heb. 8:1-5). That pattern represented Heaven itself. His point was that though God is everywhere present, as seen in the lives of those previously referenced, He chose a uniquely-constructed tent to represent His presence among His people. With those words Stephen was showing respect and reverence for the "tent of testimony."

The "tabernacle of witness" was brought into the promised land under Joshua's leadership. (The Hebrew name is translated *Jesus* in our KJV (compare Heb. 4:8), which is the same as the name *Joshua* in Greek.) With the tabernacle as testimony of God's presence among them, incredible victories were wrought by Israel as they advanced through the land (Josh. 3, 6). Their victories were not because of the tent but because of whom it represented. God was with them.

The "tabernacle of witness" remained as the visible representation of God's presence until the time of David (vv. 45-46). David brought it to Jerusalem where he established a permanent locale for it on Mount Zion. He desired to ultimately replace it with a permanent building. However, at the prophet Nathan's counsel, the best he could do was assemble the materials for it (1 Chron. 28:9—29:5).

It was Solomon's task to build the Temple (v. 47). In one short statement Stephen summarized what took Solomon years to construct and, later, centuries to rebuild after it was destroyed in the Babylonian invasion. But Stephen's point is the same as the statement Solomon made (2 Chron. 6:18) at the dedication of the Temple (vv. 48-50). The almighty, living God cannot be confined to a building made by the hands of men when He Himself has made all of heaven and earth (Isa. 66:1-2). The Temple was not a house for God, but only to be a place of worship for Israel. It was to be a place of prayer (Mt. 21:12-13; Lk. 19:45-46), not a place where God Himself, or worship of God, could be confined. This is exactly the truth the Lord Jesus made when He cleansed the Temple. It was also His point in refocusing attention from the physical building of the Temple to His resurrected body (Mt. 26:61; Mk. 14:57-58). Stephen is echoing that same truth here, and to the very same ones who rejected it when Jesus was accused.

There is a clear connection between the phrase "made with hands" and the golden calf (v. 41), and the Temple constructed by Solomon (v. 48). Stephen's charge is that the Temple had been made into something never intended. It had become a "house for God" instead of a place of worship for Israel. When a particular object, or even a particular place that is hand-made, becomes a substitute for God Himself, that is idola-

try (Polhill, *Acts* 203), a violation of the Second Commandment (Ex. 20:4-6). Even the Temple itself could become an idol. In this way Stephen answers the charge of speaking "blasphemous words against this holy place" (6:13). It is not Stephen who has blasphemed, but they! Again, the charge is not lost on the Council.

Stephen has masterfully used the authority of the Scriptures to make his case. It is a powerful moment. He has defended his position as well as exposed their sins.

e. Stephen's pointed application (7:51-53)

51 Ye stiffnecked and uncircumcised in heart and ears, ye do always resist the Holy Ghost: as your fathers *did*, so *do* ye. 52 Which of the prophets have not your fathers persecuted? And they have slain them which shewed before of the coming of the Just One; of whom ye have been now the betrayers and murderers: 53 Who have received the law by the disposition of angels, and have not kept *it*.

Stephen has not finished. In case they missed the point, which they did not, he indicts them with numerous sins against the truths he has been presenting. First, their attitudes are sinful (v. 51). Stephen uses three terms only found here in the N. T. They are "stiffnecked" (Greek *sklerotrachelos*) which means, literally, unable to turn one's head, stubborn (Ex. 33:3-5). They are "uncircumcised in heart and ears," meaning they are covenantally unfaithful. Circumcision was the sign of God's covenant with them, but it involved more than just the physical action (Lev. 26:41; Jer. 4:4). It began as a matter of the heart. "They do always resist the Holy Ghost"; the tense in the original (Greek present) suggests continual opposition or resistance. They continually resisted and opposed the work of the Holy Spirit (Bock 304-305).

Second, Stephen accuses them of sinful actions (v. 52). The not-so-subtle shift of the phrase "our fathers" (vv. 19, 38-39, 44) to "your fathers" should be noted. Stephen's previous personal identification with the history of Israel now shifts to their sinful actions in imitating the sins of the past. In doing so, he levels the most serious of all the charges against them. Just as their fathers had rejected and murdered the prophets (2 Chron. 36:16), even the very ones who prophesied of the coming Messiah (v. 52), so had they. But, even greater than that, they had betrayed and murdered "the Just One" (the Messiah), too! Although they had received the Law via angelic mediation (Gal. 3:19) they had not obeyed it. Again, they are the ones who were guilty, not Stephen.

Response to truth indicates personal character. The audience at Pentecost, who heard some of the same truths, especially about the death of the Messiah, were "pricked in their heart" (2:37) and repented. The response of the Council was not so positive.

4. The martyrdom of Stephen (7:54—8:1a)

a. Stephen's vision of Jesus (7:54-56)

**54 When they heard these things, they were cut to the heart, and they gnashed on him with *their* teeth.
55 But he, being full of the Holy Ghost, looked up stedfastly into heaven, and saw the glory of God, and Jesus standing on the right hand of God,
56 And said, Behold, I see the heavens opened, and the Son of man standing on the right hand of God.**

The response of the Sanhedrin to Stephen's message is compelling in several ways. Peter's message to this same Council had also "cut to the heart" (5:33), evoking death emotions then, as well. Here the Council is so infuriated they grind or gnash (Greek *bruxo*) their teeth at him in anger (Job 16:9). In effect, they snap their jaws open and shut in animal-like behavior (Stott 141), making a loud noise. They are livid with religious indignation.

In the face of such anger, however, Stephen remained calm. Luke records that he was "full of the Holy Ghost" (v. 55). The Holy Spirt in Stephen enabled him to face certain death with dignity and grace. In that moment, Stephen caught a brief glimpse of Heaven at full attention. He saw "Jesus standing at the right hand of God." Here is the only occasion of the Lord Jesus "standing" at the right hand of God, not "seated" (2:34).

There is considerable discussion about the significance of Jesus' "standing" rather than being "seated" (Bock 311-312). While much in these views is commendable, it seems to me the best idea is that of Jesus, the ultimate and righteous Judge, was standing in vindication of His witness, Stephen. The

Council condemned him, but the Lord of Heaven commended him.

The parallels between the trial of Jesus and Stephen are numerous (Stott 142; Keener II:1430). Both stood before this very Council. Both were charged with blasphemy. Both announced the Son of Man at the right hand of God. Both were condemned to die. Both were slain outside the city. Both verbalized some of the same thoughts regarding forgiveness and receiving their spirits. Stephen's death is significant in many ways, not the least of which is this parallel.

b. Stephen is stoned to death (7:57—8:1a)

57 And they cried out with a loud voice, and stopped their ears, and ran upon him with one accord,
58 And cast *him* out of the city, and stoned *him*: and the witnesses laid down their clothes at a young man's feet, whose name was Saul.
59 And they stoned Stephen, calling upon *God*, and saying, Lord Jesus, receive my spirit.
60 And he kneeled down, and cried with a loud voice, Lord, lay not this sin to their charge. And when he had said this, he fell asleep.
8:1a And Saul was consenting unto his death.

At the announcement of the vision of Jesus, emotions reached fever pitch, religious fervor overruled reason, and the crowd became a "lynch" mob (vv. 57-60). They descended on Stephen and dragged him out of the city where they stoned him to death. He is described as falling "asleep." Bruce (*Acts* 160) states that it is "an unexpectedly peaceful description for so brutal a death."

There is some discussion (Bock 314; Bruce, *Acts* 159; Keener II:1431-1435) as to the execution of Stephen without Roman approval (Jn. 18:31). It is certain that the Council believed they had "Biblical authority" (Lev. 24:14-16, etc.) to do so (Fitzmyer 393; Wenham 310-313). The case with Jesus was much too public for them to risk Roman disapproval. It is possible the Council had special permission for some executions (Marshall, *Acts* 148). Also, it may have been a mob action not sanctioned by the Sanhedrin (Lenski 307-308). Bruce (*Acts* 148) seems more correct in that it was a "legal" execution authorized and witnessed by the Sanhedrin but carried out by the crowd-turned-mob. It was not the first or last time the Romans turned a blind eye to such actions (Josephus, *Antiquities* XX.IX.1).

Almost incidentally, Saul of Tarsus is introduced (v. 58) as being present and approving (8:1a) of Stephen's death. There is some debate over his role in the matter. His presence may be connected with the previous debates with Stephen in the synagogues (6:9), where he was probably heavily engaged. The message of Stephen recorded in 7:2-53 would not have been the first time he had heard it. It is possible to associate Saul with the actions of the Sanhedrin but probably too much to assume he was an actual member. Picirilli (*Paul*, 31) states that he "may well have been an official observer, appointed by the Sanhedrin." Saul's opposition escalated into a personal vendetta in the coming months (8:3; 9:1-2) as he tried to eradicate the church. However, in his mind, he never escaped the scene of Stephen's death (22:20).

So ends the witness of Stephen in the narrative. He died as did the Lord Jesus. His message defined the teachings of Jesus and the apostles in contrast to the prevailing view of Judaism at that time. By the time of the N. T., Judaism had deteriorated into a shadow of its original meaning and become cultic. What was gloriously and prophetically fulfilling, for Stephen and the church, was blasphemy to the views of Judaism held by the leadership of the Council. The two views could not be more different.

Summary
(6:8—8:1a)

The witness of Stephen is one of the most compelling stories in the Book of Acts. It presents a man of brilliance, courage, and unflinching faith even in the face of certain death. He was Christianity's first martyr. His message is the longest one recorded in Acts and is the watershed message that shows the difference between Christianity's interpretation of redemptive history and Judaism's interpretation.

The apostolic message of the gospel fully embraced the truths of the O. T.— its Law, its customs, and its Messianic prophecies. These were all viewed as preparatory until the actual coming of the Messiah. Once the Messiah, Jesus of Nazareth, had come, all these were viewed as being fulfilled. A new order of worship would be inaugurated, replacing the customs and sacrifices of Temple worship. The Temple itself would no longer be central to worship (Bruce, *Acts* 127-128). The teachings of Christ were to become the focus of the Lord's people.

Tradition sometimes dies hard. This is especially true when traditions themselves have become "the truths" they once reflected. Jewish culture, and to a certain extent Jewish identity, had been defined by these traditions for centuries. Furthermore, the longer the traditions had endured, the more difficult it was to bring the focus back to the truth they reflected. Thus, the conflict between the Judaism of the N. T. era and Christianity.

The narrative of Stephen also reveals the hostility of those in Israel's leadership who refused to accept the fact of the resurrection of Jesus of Nazareth. Their intent was to silence those who were eyewitnesses to His living presence.

Stephen is shown to have the favor of God in serving and witnessing (6:8). He is an extremely effective apologist (6:10) whose truths cannot be denied, only circumvented by false accusations (6:11-14). When brought before the high Council (6:12ff), he does not flinch or falter but offers a clear testimony of the same truths he has been presenting in the synagogues. With brilliant analysis and insights into the history of Israel from the O. T., he argued his points. He proved the presence of the living God in all places and times. He showed the appointment of key leaders by the Lord for His covenant people. He emphasized the fickleness of Israel over those leaders and the Law as they chose to worship idols and reject their leaders. They even made the Temple itself into something never intended, thus making it an idol. Ultimately, they rejected the Messiah Himself, betraying and murdering Him. The result was that the sins of the fathers were still evident in the leaders of Israel. They were the ones guilty of blasphemy, not Stephen. This was the absolute truth, but they would not accept it. With grace and dignity, being full of the Holy Spirit, Stephen died at the hands of a mob blinded with religious fanaticism.

Stephen's death was not the result of the suicidal efforts of a radical extremist. It was the result of the radical extremism of the audience who rejected the truth. How many people are there who have so little to live for because they have nothing worth dying for? Authentic Christianity in its N. T. form is of such profound truth it is worth dying for (Lk. 14:26, et.al.). If Stephen died for Christ with such grace and dignity, surely we can live for Him in the same manner.

Application: Teaching and Preaching the Passage

Exegetical Outline of the Text: 1. Stephen the Man (6:8-15). 2. Stephen the Messenger (7:1-53). 3. Stephen the Martyr (7:54-60).

This text offers multiple themes for teaching and preaching, not the least of which is the very text itself. For example, from 6:8-10 the need to become informed enough to offer "an answer" (1 Pet. 3:15-16) about the faith and practices of Christianity is paramount. The area of apologetics is certainly in focus in the witness of Stephen.

An excellent study is to compare the trials of the Lord Jesus and Stephen. What are the charges, the response, and the significance of each? What are the contemporary applications of this?

It is very enlightening to understand Stephen's interpretation of the four O. T. eras he used to make his defense. This is especially true in understanding how he arrived at the conclusions he did in 7:51-53. In particular, it would be insightful to analyze why the court reacted so angrily to his interpretations.

As Christianity's first true martyr, Stephen offers an example of Jesus' statements about sacrificial faith in Luke 14:26-35.

IV. THE CHURCH'S WITNESS IN JUDAEA AND SAMARIA (8:1b-40)

A. Persecution and Dispersion Throughout Judaea and Samaria (8:1b-4)

1b And at that time there was a great persecution against the church which was at Jerusalem; and they were all scattered abroad throughout the regions of Judaea and Samaria, except the apostles.
2 And devout men carried Stephen *to his burial*, and made great lamentation over him.
3 As for Saul, he made havock of the church, entering into every house, and haling men and women committed *them* to prison.
4 Therefore they that were scattered abroad went every where preaching the word.

The brutal death of Stephen was followed rapidly (Greek literally, "in that day") by intense and widespread persecution in Jerusalem. What began as rebuke and warning (4:31) had led to flogging (5:40), then to killing (7:59), all with the intention to intimidate and stop the movement. But the wind intended to stifle the fire only fanned the flames. In fleeing the persecution (v. 1b), believers did not abandon their faith or message. The regions of Judaea and Samaria became both haven and opportunity as believers proclaimed the word (v. 4) wherever they went.

Some commentators (Polhill, *Acts* 211; Bock 318-319; Bruce, *Acts* 162-163) see the persecution directed mostly against the Hellenistic believers and not so much against the Hebrew believers (see comments on 6:1). The reasoning is that Hebrew believers would not have taken as firm a stand regarding the Law and the Temple and, therefore, would have avoided the direct onslaught. Stephen (a Hellenist) had proclaimed the message of the living God who was not confined to the land of Judaea or to cultic interpretations of the Law and the Temple. The gospel of Jesus Christ was initially for the Jews, but never to be restricted by nationalistic prejudice. However, the idea that one group of believers was less committed than the other raises the issue of a divided message within the church. There is no textual indication of that whatsoever at that time. Later (15:1-2), a faction arose regarding Gentile compliance, but that was much later and in very different circumstances. Further, the text says "they were all scattered abroad." Keener (II:1467-1469) is right arguing that while the Hellenists might have been targeted, the persecution certainly was not confined to them. In the face of opposition, the apostles remained in Jerusalem, perhaps going "underground." Their continued presence ensured stability and continuity. Luke does not say that they escaped persecution, just that they chose to stay in Jerusalem. Their favor with the people (5:13) might have afforded them some degree of protection.

It is possible that the Jerusalem church had limited its witness with regard to the scope of Acts 1:8, so persecution was the Lord's way (providentially) of forcing them to broaden their efforts (Keener II:1485-1486). With all that was happening in Jerusalem to disciple new believers, minister to needs, and deal with the impact of persecution, it is hard to conclude that the church was guilty of disobedience: delay, perhaps, but probably not disobedience. It is apparent, however, that the Lord used persecution to extend their witness (Walker 212; Harrison 130).

Luke adds a note of closure about the death of Stephen (v. 2). In what may appear to be a misplaced reference, he inserts the respectful burial and mourning of Stephen by "devout men" in contrast to the delirious fervor of the mob who stoned him. Further, it shows the connection of his death with the ensuing persecution (Polhill, *Acts* 210; Bock 317). The reference is not misplaced.

Whatever his official role might have been at the stoning of Stephen (7:58), Saul led the charge against the church (v. 3). He became "persecution personified" (Polhill, *Acts* 212). With the intent to eliminate them altogether, Saul attacked the church like a wild animal. That he *made havock* (Greek *lumaino*) of the church indicates his attempt to ravage or violently maltreat. Saul pursued believers in "every house" in Jerusalem (Heb. 10:32-34), literally dragging ("haling") both men and women to prison. Women were not usually subjected to the same level of treatment as men, but Saul's vendetta showed little mercy (22:4; 26:10-11). To do so means he had the legal authority necessary (9:1-2; 26:10). The one bested by Stephen in the synagogue debates now thought he would ultimately prove who really wins. Perhaps he should have listened to Gamaliel (5:39).

B. The Witness of Philip (8:5-40)

1. Initial ministry in Samaria (8:5-8)

5 Then Philip went down to the city of Samaria, and preached Christ unto them.
6 And the people with one accord gave heed unto those things which Philip spake, hearing and seeing the miracles which he did.
7 For unclean spirits, crying with loud voice, came out of many that were possessed *with them*: and many taken with palsies, and that were lame, were healed.
8 And there was great joy in that city.

Acts 8:1b-4 is intentionally transitional in the narrative as the mantle of witness is transferred from Stephen to Philip. The ministry of Stephen was significant in his apologetic for the gospel in the synagogues and before the Sanhedrin. The ministry of Philip is significant as he pioneers the work of the gospel in Samaria (v. 5) and initiates its extension to the "uttermost part of the earth" by leading the Ethiopian to Christ. Neither of these men is an apostle. As Hellenists they would be more open to the cultural differences beyond the borders of Israel, both geographically and religiously. They also represent the extension of leadership beyond the apostles as the gospel transitions from Jews to Gentiles, from Jerusalem to the world.

In all likelihood, Philip knew the history of Jesus with Samaritans (Jn. 4; Lk. 10:30-37; 17:11-19). It had not been that long ago that Jesus Himself had gone there with all the providential

plans such a trip implied. Even though Jesus had restricted the apostles initially from going to Samaria (Mt. 10:5-6), that destination would certainly have been included in His larger mission of redemption (Jn. 10:16), since He specifically included them in the Great Commission. It may even be that the "woman at the well" was still faithful and was included among those who heard Philip. Some knew of Jesus, but not everyone had heard, and they knew little, if any, about His resurrection. With that as backdrop, and because of Samaria's specific inclusion in the scope of the Great Commission (1:8), it is not coincidental that Philip chose this area. His choice proved to be very fruitful.

But Samaria was more than just the next geographical step in the proclamation of the gospel. It occupied a special place in the history of Israel. However, Samaria also had a long history of political and spiritual intrigue. At one time, an integral part of covenant Israel, the ten tribes of Israel had broken from Judah after Solomon's death (1 Kgs. 12). Under the idolatrous leadership of all its kings, Samaria fell into moral and spiritual decadence. They forfeited their covenant privileges (2 Kgs. 17:18-23), and the city of Samaria eventually fell to the Assyrians in 722 B.C. (2 Kgs. 17). Many of the people who were left intermarried with the Canaanite tribes around them and with the Assyrian occupational settlers. Of course, there were some, a remnant, who retained their Jewish ethnicity in spite of this.

The checkered history of Samaria was rife with spiritual collusion with idolatry that resulted initially in a hybrid form of Yahweh worship (2 Kgs. 17:29-41). They had established an alternative place of worship on Mt. Gerizim (Bruce,

Acts 164) and held a form of Messianic hope based on Deuteronomy 18:15-19. Jesus encountered these views with the Samaritan woman (Jn. 4:20, 25). Regarded as neither Jewish nor Gentile, Samaritans were viewed by the Jews as something of an anomaly (Jn. 4:9), to be avoided if at all possible (TDNT VII:91-94).

There is some question as to where exactly Philip went in going to "the city of Samaria" (v. 5). Textual readings favor the definite article "the," noting a specific city. Samaria at the time was a region, but, obviously, Philip went to a particular city in the region (vv. 8-9). Some suggest it was the city of Gitta, traditionally the hometown of Simon the Magician (Bruce, *Acts* 165). Lightfoot (143-144) and Bock (325) offer that it was probably Shechem. The ancient city of Samaria had been rebuilt by Herod the Great and re-named "Sebaste"; it also came to be known as "Samaria" according to its O. T. name (Bruce, *Acts* 165; Barnes 138). It was the only major city in the region (Keener II:1494) and seems to me to be the most likely place Philip went.

Like Stephen (6:8), Philip was filled with the Holy Spirit and favored with special miracles attending and confirming his ministry (v. 6). Generational sins had resulted in the consequences of widespread cultural and spiritual chaos, perpetuated by religious charlatans like Simon the sorcerer (v. 9). Beneath the surface (v. 7) lay a sordid mix of demonism, brokenness, oppression, and sickness—the very picture of hopelessness and despair. The power of the gospel, however, delivered them from all these physical and spiritual maladies. For a short time, the Lord demonstrated His eternal plan for humanity's cure

(Rev. 21:4). Ultimately, the gospel of Christ brings healing to both soul and body. The impact of the gospel resulted in a city with a changed disposition, from despair to joy (v. 8). The sins of the fathers had separated them from the covenant promises of Israel. The gospel of Jesus Christ, proclaimed by Philip, was reuniting them (Eph. 2:11-22). The profound truth of becoming a "new creature" in Christ (2 Cor. 5:17) brings cultural, as well as personal, redemption. History shows that where the gospel of Jesus Christ and biblical truth are honored, cultures enjoy the benefits of Christian enlightenment.

2. The conversion of Simon the sorcerer (8:9-25)

9 But there was a certain man, called Simon, which beforetime in the same city used sorcery, and bewitched the people of Samaria, giving out that himself was some great one:
10 To whom they all gave heed, from the least to the greatest, saying, This man is the great power of God.
11 And to him they had regard, because that of long time he had bewitched them with sorceries.
12 But when they believed Philip preaching the things concerning the kingdom of God, and the name of Jesus Christ, they were baptized, both men and women.
13 Then Simon himself believed also: and when he was baptized, he continued with Philip, and wondered, beholding the miracles and signs which were done.
14 Now when the apostles which were at Jerusalem heard that

Samaria had received the word of God, they sent unto them Peter and John:

15 Who, when they were come down, prayed for them, that they might receive the Holy Ghost:

16 (For as yet he was fallen upon none of them: only they were baptized in the name of the Lord Jesus.)

17 Then laid they *their* hands on them, and they received the Holy Ghost.

18 And when Simon saw that through laying on of the apostles' hands the Holy Ghost was given, he offered them money,

19 Saying, Give me also this power, that on whomsoever I lay hands, he may receive the Holy Ghost.

20 But Peter said unto him, Thy money perish with thee, because thou hast thought that the gift of God may be purchased with money.

21 Thou has neither part nor lot in this matter: for thy heart is not right in the sight of God.

22 Repent therefore of this thy wickedness, and pray God, if perhaps the thought of thine heart may be forgiven thee.

23 For I perceive that thou art in the gall of bitterness, and *in the* bond of iniquity.

24 Then answered Simon, and said, Pray ye to the LORD for me, that none of these things which ye have spoken come upon me.

25 And they, when they had testified and preached the word of the Lord, returned to Jerusalem, and preached the gospel in many villages of the Samaritans.

It is the pattern of Luke's record in Acts to highlight the conversion of at least one well-known figure in many of the places where the gospel is proclaimed (9:1-19; 10:1-48; 13:12; 16:14-15; 25-34). That conversion is representative of the contrast between the gospel and all sorts of circumstances, situations, and religious beliefs. In Samaria, that representative person is Simon the sorcerer. The issue of whether Simon became a genuine believer is addressed below, but his story is significant to the Samaritan revival.

Philip's ministry defined Christianity in contrast to the shadowy world of sorcery. (For an extended survey on "Magic and Magicians" see Keener II:1500-1507.) As the gospel penetrated the wider Roman world, sorcery on every level, from the pretentious to the real, was encountered (13:8-11; 16:16-18; 19:13-19). Already Philip had encountered "unclean spirits" (v. 7) among the general population of Samaria, but with Simon he encountered the one who epitomized the craft (TDNT IV:358-359).

Several details are given in the description of Simon (vv. 9-11). He had a long history of sorcery and was very well-known, with clients of all classes ("least to the greatest"). He had gained the reputation, at least in his own mind, of being of great importance ("some great one"). Some even revered him as "the great power of God." With a large following ("to whom they all gave heed"), he and his magic were deeply entrenched in the spiritual psyche of the people ("of a long time he had bewitched them").

But Philip was full of the Holy Spirit (6:3) and his preaching, attended by physical healings and deliverance from demonic possessions (v. 6), convinced many of the Samaritans that their faith in Simon the sorcerer and his ways had been misplaced. In significant numbers (vv. 8, 14), both men and women (v. 12) turned to Jesus Christ in saving faith and followed with believer's baptism "in the name of Jesus Christ" (v. 12). This does not mean that Philip didn't use the Trinitarian formula commanded by the Lord Jesus (Mt. 28:19) for baptism. Rather, it means Christian baptism—baptism by the authority of Jesus—as opposed to other ritual baptisms and washings (Fitzmyer 400).

In dramatic testimony, Luke adds that "Simon himself believed...was baptized...continued with Philip" (v. 13). It appears that an incredible victory was scored for the gospel of Christ and the ministry of Philip. However, to say the least, commentators are divided about whether Simon had actually become a genuine believer. Some argue against the genuineness of his faith (Bruce, *Acts* 167; Stott 149; Hughes 113; Longenecker 154; Barnes 140), pointing to his fascination with the miraculous side of Philip's ministry as the motivation for his profession. In this view, he saw in Philip a more powerful means of manipulation and wanted in on the action. His was a profession of faith rooted in the outward manifestations of the miraculous.

This view is compounded by the writings of patristic fathers Justin Martyr (c. 150), Irenaeus (c. 180), and Tertullian (c. 197). All addressed "Simon, a Samaritan," and other incidentals that fit the Acts' record of him. Reportedly Simon became an early teacher of Gnosticism and other misdeeds, rendering his "conversion" suspicious. The early testimony of the patristic fathers is not easily dismissed, although there is

much to question whether the Simon of Acts 8 is the same person they described. Some propose that the name "Simon" was later co-opted by Gnostics in an attempt to root their movement in the N. T. (Polhill, *Acts* 216).

If Simon's "conversion" is not authentic, then the purpose of the account would be to show the real possibility of appearing to have saving faith but not really possessing it, a matter of *professing* but not *possessing*. Calvin (I:233) suggested that Simon was somewhere between faith and pretense.

On the other hand, some see his conversion as genuine (Barrett, *Acts* 119-120; Fitzmyer 405). There is nothing to suggest that Philip preached anything less (vv. 5, 12) than the same call to repentance, saving faith in Jesus Christ, and believer's baptism that was issued by Peter on the Day of Pentecost ("One Lord, one faith, one baptism, one God and Father of all," Eph. 4:5-6). It should be noted that the terminology for the conversion of the Samaritans is the same as previously stated of others, i.e., they believed, were baptized, and continued (2:41; 4:4; 5:14; 6:7). The same is also said of Simon the sorcerer, "Simon himself believed...was baptized... continued with Philip" (v. 13).

The question of authenticity arises because of Simon's response when seeing the bestowal of the Holy Spirit on the Samaritan believers by the apostles, Peter and John, who came to confirm the word of the Samaritan revival (vv. 14-17). There is no mention of the special gifts being manifested as on the Day of Pentecost, but apparently some manifestations did occur that both confirmed the conversion of the Samaritans to the apostles and impressed Simon. One can speculate about his motives, but Simon mistakenly assumed that the power of the Holy Spirit could be bargained for and offered to pay (vv. 18-19) what was necessary for him to obtain it (the origin of our English term "simony").

Peter minced no words in rebuking him and his offer (v. 20). Contrary to Simon's thinking, the "gift of God" is neither given nor received based on monetary arrangements. Furthermore, he judged that Simon's heart was not right with God, that he needed to repent of the wicked offer, and that he—at least in this sin—was bound in bitterness and iniquity (vv. 21-23). These are strong words, indeed, but are they indicative of Simon's lack of authentic faith in Christ as Savior, as some commentators conclude? Or, on the other hand, is this indicative of lesser need, the need to repent of "spiritual baggage" from his previous lifestyle?

Simon's response to Peter (v. 24) is revealing, too. Nothing in the wording expresses anger and rebellion, but humility and personal concern. He specifically asks for personal prayer "to the Lord" and for deliverance from the very condemnation that his misguided request has engendered from Peter. Metzger (314) suggests that Simon weeps as he expresses remorse and repentance.

The testimony of the Ephesians who "believed" (19:18-19) has parallels to this experience. They had been saved out of demonism and sorcery but had clung to some of their previous magic arts in both practice and literature. The demonstration of spiritual power over evil (19:13-17), as with Philip (8:7), convinced them of the Lord's superior power, and they openly confessed their sins, burning their fetishes and books. Hardly any commentator questions the authenticity of their faith.

One should never interpret the Scriptures through the lens of personal experience, even though personal experience often confirms the Scriptures. Pastors, missionaries, and those who labor in ministry with people who have been saved out of cultic religions or enslaving sinful lifestyles know the challenges of discipleship presented by folks who bring the "baggage" of such with them into their newfound faith in Christ. There are many "Simons." But their "baggage" does not mean their faith in Christ is not real. What is "real" is the challenge of mortifying the deeds of the flesh in all its forms (Col. 3:5-11).

In my opinion, then, the testimony of Simon the (previous) sorcerer would be that of a genuine believer who must deal with some deeds (in this case demonism) from his old life. Simon represents something more than just his own personal struggle with his old lifestyle and the new one as a believer in Christ. He represents the ongoing battle between the flesh, with its multi-formed entrenchments in human life, and the Holy Spirit, who delivers and renews one who has been saved (Gal. 5:16-25; Col. 3:1-11).

Indeed, in a larger sense, Simon also represents the Samaritans, whose history from the very beginning of their separation from the covenant promises to Israel involved idolatry and demonism (1 Kgs. 12:28). The indwelling power of the Holy Spirit, inherent with saving faith in Jesus Christ, reveals the oppressive work and lifestyle of consorting with idols and demons (1 Jn. 4:4). As with individuals, so with an entire city (v. 8). Simon's conversion is a precursor of things to come as the gospel message confronts the entrenched strongholds of

Satan in a pagan world as the rest of Acts will record.

News of the Samaritan revival soon reached Jerusalem, getting the full attention of the apostles. Samaria was the next geographical phase of the Great Commission (1:8), so it seems appropriate that the apostles would inspect the work. As the "founding fathers" of Christianity, and having been charged with apostolic responsibility, with "keys to the kingdom of God" (Crabtree 282-283; Morris 848-850), their interest is understandable. Peter and John were sent to establish solidarity and fellowship with the Samaritan believers.

Upon arrival, Peter and John discovered a "missing element." They discerned that the Samaritans had not received the Holy Spirit (v. 15), for "he was fallen on none of them" (v. 16). They gathered the believers together and laid their hands on them and "they received the Holy Ghost" (v. 17). This was what led Simon to the very serious error of thinking he might purchase the power of the Holy Spirit; and this led in turn to his stern rebuke.

While stated simply enough, the bestowing of the Holy Spirit upon the Samaritans via the laying on of the hands of the apostles, subsequent to salvation, raises even larger questions than whether Simon's conversion was authentic. A quick survey of commentators reveals a wide variety of interpretations about this text (Stott 150-159; Keener I:1522-1527). Marshall (*Acts* 157) proposes that "this is the most extraordinary statement in Acts."

Bock (331) asserts that the Acts record confirms that the work of the Holy Spirit is, to us, like the wind and something of mystery in origin, direction, and purpose (Jn. 3:8). That does not mean His work is whimsical and chaotic, but sovereign.

From this text, many Pentecostals and Charismatics (like Douglas Oss, in Grudem 239-244), Roman Catholics (Fitzmyer 406), and other groups advocating a second experience of the Holy Spirit after conversion (Keener I:1522) have argued their insistence on what is called a "second work of grace." The definition of that subsequent work varies greatly from tradition to tradition.

Others see this as a unique, Acts-only pattern of confirmation (like Richard Gaffin, in Grudem 37-41) in the advancement of the gospel in relation to the command of Christ to preach the gospel to all nations (1:8). They do not regard this text as teaching a subsequent-to-salvation, necessary experience with the Holy Spirit as normative for believers (Stott 158; Marshall, *Acts* 158).

This latter view is to be preferred, and for several reasons. Peter's initial proclamation of the gospel included the promise of receiving the Holy Spirit upon personal, saving faith in Jesus Christ (2:38-39). That statement defined the normative salvation experience (Keener I:1523). There is no indication that Philip's preaching to the Samaritans was anything less than all previous presentations of the gospel.

As the gospel advanced, according to 1:8, to new geographical and spiritual demographics, an initial, confirming work of the Spirit was manifested: Jerusalem (2:38-41); Judaea/Samaria (8:5-17); the world of Gentiles (10:45). Indeed, some commentators refer to each of these as something of a mini "Pentecost" (Bruce, *Acts* 170; Polhill, *Acts* 218). Apostolic confirmation accompanies these advances. In each successive advance of the gospel, at least one apostle is "on site" when the initial work begins. With the presence of an apostle, there occurs the outpouring of the Holy Spirit described as "falling on them" (8:16; 10:44) or "came on them" (19:6).

The advance of the gospel from Judaea to Samaria was a historical event (Meyer 170; Bruce, *Acts* 170; Polhill, *Acts* 218) that needed and received apostolic confirmation. The Samaritan believers presented something of an even more unique situation than that of the Gentiles. The history of Samaria resulted in their being considered neither Jew nor Gentile (Stott 157; Longenecker 155). Therefore, the advancement of the gospel into Samaria and the delay in the reception of the Holy Spirit until apostolic confirmation had the significance of re-incorporating them into the community of Jerusalem Christians (Marshall, *Acts* 157), and becoming partakers of the covenant promises of Israel (Bruce, *Acts* 170) through Jesus Christ (Eph. 2:11-22). This unique manifestation of the Holy Spirit via apostolic confirmation conveyed the truth that the sins of centuries of alienation from those covenant promises had now been forgiven. Thus, the pattern of the Holy Spirit's work in these special manifestations is in the initiation of the gospel's advance according to Acts 1:8.

While the writings of the apostle Paul (particularly Romans) would not occur for a few years yet, in relation to the time of the Samaritan revival, there are no reasons to conclude that Paul's pneumatology was any different from Luke's. The same Holy Spirit inspired both authors when they wrote respectively. Paul is clear that authentic faith in Christ includes the personal possession of the Holy Spirit (Rom. 8:9). In fact, to argue for a difference between Luke and Paul is to propose possible contradictions in the biblical record. The gospel of Jesus Christ that brought salvation to those in Jerusalem and Samaria was the gospel that Saul of Tarsus heard and began to proclaim and write about.

Therefore, the normative experience of authentic faith in Christ includes the personal reception of the Holy Spirit when one savingly believes. It was the sovereign work of the Spirit in Acts to manifest His presence uniquely in the initial advances of the gospel according to Acts 1:8.

This interpretation of Act 8:15-18 does not exclude the enabling and equipping ministry of the Holy Spirit in the giving of spiritual gifts (Eph. 4:7-12), in providential guidance (Acts 8:26; 16:6-7, etc.), in spiritual growth (Gal. 5:22-24), and so on. Indeed, each day, each new ministry opportunity, each new personal challenge requires fresh and continual fullness of the Holy Spirit in the believer's life (Eph. 5:18). We do not simply need a "second work of the Spirit" in our lives, we need unnumbered and continual works of the Spirit within us.

The situation raises the question what actually happened to confirm to the apostles that the Samaritans had indeed received the Holy Spirit. The text notes the action of the laying on of hands by the apostles and the receiving of the Holy Spirit (v. 17), and that Simon visually "saw" (v. 18) the manifestation. The text does not say directly but clearly implies that something visual (and audible?) took place. Some (Bruce, *Acts* 169; Bock 332; Polhill, *Acts* 218; Meyer 171; Barnes 142) conclude that it was most likely the same "glossolalia" that was manifested on the Day of Pentecost (see commentary on 2:1-12), in the household of Cornelius (10:44-47; 11:15-17), and in the Ephesian disciples of John (19:5-6). All three instances carried a visible and audible manifestation to those who witnessed the events. If "glossolalia" was the manifestation of the Holy Spirit in Samaria, its purpose would have been the confirmation of the intention of the gospel for all nations.

Others (Marshall, *Acts* 158; Earle 353) are reluctant to conclude that "glossolalia" was the manifestation, since Luke does not state this specifically. There might have been overwhelming joy rather than charismatic gifts.

It is risky to reach a specific conclusion when the Scriptures are silent. The only obvious conclusion is that "the Scriptures are silent" on this. While it may seem the Samaritans experienced the manifestation of tongues, given the circumstances as commented above, it is best to accept the silence of the Scriptures about it. Whatever the manifestation was, the apostles were satisfied with the result.

Peter and John extended their stay with the Samaritans (v. 25) long enough to add their words of teaching that came from the Lord Jesus. These men had literally sat at the feet of Jesus for over three years. Their eyewitness accounts of His resurrection and His teachings would have been invaluable in making disciples of the Samaritan believers. The apostles' return trip to Jerusalem included intentional evangelism in many of the villages along the way. One cannot help speculating that perhaps they re-visited Jacob's well near Sychar, the village

where the Samaritan woman had testified so effectively of her encounter with Jesus (Jn. 4:4ff).

The work of Peter and John, apostles who were thoroughly Jewish, among the Samaritan villages is a further endorsement of the Samaritan revival and a historic re-establishment of relationships with an entire group of people who had once been regarded as outcasts (Jn. 4:9). The personal growth of Peter and John in doing this is noteworthy. Peter, of course, will soon be spiritually stretched even more (10:28). The gospel of Jesus Christ targets all people, including the messengers, regardless of their ethnicity and history (Gal. 3:28). Indeed, the message of the gospel is that one's history does not have to define one's future.

Therefore, verse 25 should be seen as more than just a summary statement charting the movements of two of the apostles. Rather, it is an itinerary of endorsement of apostolic affirmation of the Lord, extending the gospel of Christ to a people who once were estranged from the covenant promises of God to Israel. These very people are shown forgiveness and restorative grace into the family of God. A historic event indeed!

3. The conversion of the Ethiopian eunuch (8:26-40)

26 And the angel of the Lord spake unto Philip, saying, Arise, and go toward the south unto the way that goeth down from Jerusalem unto Gaza, which is desert.
27 And he arose and went: and, behold, a man of Ethiopia, an eunuch of great authority under Candace queen of the Ethiopians,

133

who had the charge of all her treasure, and had come to Jerusalem for to worship,

28 Was returning, and sitting in his chariot read Esaias the prophet.

29 Then the Spirit said unto Philip, Go near, and join thyself to this chariot.

30 And Philip ran thither to *him*, and heard him read the prophet Esaias, and said, Understandest thou what thou readest?

31 And he said, How can I, except some man should guide me? And he desired Philip that he would come up and sit with him.

32 The place of the scripture which he read was this, He was led as a sheep to the slaughter; and like a lamb dumb before his shearer, so opened he not his mouth:

33 In his humiliation his judgment was taken away: and who shall declare his generation? for his life is taken from the earth.

34 And the eunuch answered Philip, and said, I pray thee, of whom speaketh the prophet this? of himself, or of some other man?

35 The Philip opened his mouth, and began at the same scripture, and preached unto him Jesus.

36 And as they went on *their* way, they came unto a certain water: and the eunuch said, See, *here is* water, what doth hinder me to be baptized?

37 And Philip said, If thou believest with all thine heart, thou mayest. And he answered and said, I believe that Jesus Christ is the Son of God.

38 And he commanded the chariot to stand still: and they went down both into the water, both Philip and the eunuch; and he baptized him.

39 And when they were come up out of the water, the Spirit of the Lord caught away Philip, that the eunuch saw him no more: and he went on his way rejoicing.

40 But Philip was found at Azotus: and passing through he preached in all the cities, till he came to Caesarea.

With the return of the apostles to Jerusalem, Luke continues with the ministry of Philip, who demonstrates, again, that he is a Spirit-filled believer (6:3). From the very fruitful work in Samaria, he was divinely directed to travel south on a particular road leading from Jerusalem to Gaza (v. 26), which lay some sixty miles from Jerusalem. Philip would, of course, have to know which road to take or else he would have missed the opportunity. The phrase "Arise and go" (both Greek imperatives) implies that he is to begin his trip without tarrying. So he is told where to go and to get started quickly. The details of the rest of the story will reveal a specific time, place, person, and purpose for the planned encounter.

A quick reference on any map of that time period will show that Gaza is many miles away from Samaria and fairly remote. It was the southernmost of the five strongholds of the ancient Philistine kingdom. In fact, it was the last oasis in southwestern Palestine before entering the desert area in route to Egypt and the African continent. The word "desert" may refer to either the road or the city, perhaps both since it aptly describes the area (Keener I:1548-1549). Later references to "water" (vv. 36, 38) highlight the arid conditions.

There were two possible roads to Gaza. The most likely one for Philip would be the road due south of Jerusalem, then westerly toward the city. Though the phrase "toward the south" was sometimes used to mean "noon" or "midday," it is probably used in a directional sense here (Polhill, *Acts* 223). Either way, the *timing* of the encounter is crucial. If Philip had been late, he would have missed the eunuch as he proceeded on his way south.

Though some identify the supernatural beings in the story as the same (Stott 159; Marshall, *Acts* 161) there may be a distinction between the "angel of the Lord" here and "the Spirit" in verses 29 and 39. Both work in concert (Lk. 1:26-35). It is clear, also, that the Lord is guiding and preparing throughout the entire event. In fact, the providence of God is an unmistakable theme woven into the Acts narrative.

Luke's detailed description of the encounter (vv. 27-28) is significant and needs some clarification. "Ethiopia" is not the modern day country by that name but most likely the ancient Nubian kingdom, Meroe and Napata being its two main cities (Bruce, *Acts* 174; Polhill, *Acts* 223). The eunuch was a man of authority being in charge of the treasury of the Queen. There is some question as to whether he was actually a black, African man or a dispersion Jew (Stott 160), though most hold that he was not Jewish. Most see him as a Gentile, God-fearing man (like Cornelius in ch. 10), but because of his physical status as a eunuch (Deut. 23:1) he would not be considered a full convert to Judaism. He would have access to the Court of the Gentiles in the Temple area, but not into the Temple itself.

The reason for any question about his nationality is his journey to Jerusalem to worship and his interest in the Isaiah text. Both are indicative of Jewish interests. But that would also be true of one who was as spiritually interested as he. "Candace" (pronounced "Kan-dak-e") is actually a dynastic title, not a proper name. At any rate, this man was a high-ranking government official whose faith in the God of Israel and interest in the Messianic, Servant Song of Isaiah rendered him a prime candidate to hear the gospel of the Messiah, Jesus Christ. Regardless of his physical status as a eunuch, and limited access to the Temple according to the O. T. Law, the gospel of Christ would provide him full access to the throne of God as a born-again child of God.

At some point on the road to Gaza, Philip met up with the eunuch (vv. 28-29), who was sitting in his chariot and reading aloud (v. 30) from the book of Isaiah. Reading ancient manuscripts was almost always done aloud since the lettering was crowded and difficult (Bruce, *Acts* 175; Polhill, *Acts* 224; Cadbury, *Acts* 18)—which I can confirm from personal experience. The Holy Spirit directed Philip to join the man at his chariot, whereupon the exchange began with Philip asking him if he understood what he was reading. His question implied both personal interest and ability to answer. At this point, the reason for the Lord's directing him to remote Gaza must have been clear to Philip.

The Ethiopian's question to Philip reveals a man who is intelligent and informed. Though charged with great government responsibility, he has deep spiritual concerns. All men do, regardless of the veneers. Furthermore, it reveals a man of remarkable modesty and honesty, not one, as Calvin (I:246) comments, who is "swollen headed in confidence." Though he occupies a powerful position, he asks for help in understanding.

The text of interest is from the Septuagint version of the Servant Song of Isaiah 52:13—53:12, in particular the part of the suffering Servant (53:7-8). "Who is the person of the prophecy?" is his question (v. 34). While most traditional Jewish interpretations relate this to the nation of Israel, the parallels to Jesus are undeniable (Oswalt 397).

Philip could not have been more delighted with the opportunity to explain exactly who the person of the prophecy was and the rest of its implications (v. 35). The phrase "preached unto him Jesus" means that Philip showed how that text was fulfilled in the person, ministry, death, and resurrection of Jesus of Nazareth. This is the gospel of Christ. He is the fulfillment of this and all other O. T. Messianic prophecies and types. His life, from incarnation to resurrection and ascension, was Scripturally prophesied and approved by God, including His vicarious suffering for sin.

Neither is it coincidental that the Isaiah text is the one of interest. No other O. T. Messianic prophecy is more apropos than this one (Oswalt 397). Bruce (*Acts* 176) suggests that even Isaiah himself was not aware of some things meant in his prophecy. However, there is no question that, in retrospect, all matched perfectly the sufferings of Jesus. In fact, Jesus had used this very text (Picirilli, *Mark* 296) in reference to Himself (Mk. 10:45; Lk. 22:37). The apostles, and those whom they taught, would have focused on this text and

truths about Jesus as part of their teachings.

We can be sure that Philip had answered this very question before in other venues. It is also central to the apologetics of apostolic preaching in the synagogues. There has always been Scriptural authority for the message of the gospel. From the very beginning the apostles appealed to the Scriptures in the proclamation of the gospel of Christ (2:16-21, for example).

This particular witness event, involving Philip, is fluid in movement (as are most witness events), as the men (perhaps in caravan) continue the journey southward. Philip's explanation of the Isaiah text proves to answer the eunuch's question sufficiently, so, coming to a place where there is sufficient water, the eunuch asks about personal baptism (v. 36). Apparently, Philip had also included baptism as part of his answer, referring to Jesus' command (Mt. 28:19-20; 2:38, 41; 8:12) and thus sparking the inquiry. The eunuch would have been familiar with proselyte baptism; indeed, Keener (II:1567) suggests that he might very well have been so baptized since exceptions to the original rule were sometimes made for those of wealth or high standing (as he was). Regardless, believer's baptism is totally different in meaning and intent. It should be noted that, in the Book of Acts, believer's baptism was administered soon after there was a clear profession of saving faith.

The eunuch's question (v. 37), what would hinder him from being baptized, gives rise to Philip's response that personal, saving faith in Christ is necessary, and this is followed by the affirmation of the eunuch. The Western text (and the KJV) includes this exchange as part of Luke's account. Many commentators assert that it was a later addition to emphasize that Philip would not have baptized the eunuch without a confession of saving faith (Robertson, *Acts* 111; Metzger 315; Bruce, *Acts* 178). There is no reason to believe that Philip would not have clarified the meaning of believer's baptism before the actual ceremony itself. Having said that, here is the first interpretative statement in Acts about the intent of baptism. It is a sacred, ceremonial ritual meant to express authentic, saving faith from the heart (Rom. 10:9-10).

Halting the chariot, both Philip and the Ethiopian waded ("went down") into the pool of water. The scene is arresting. On the surface, in matters of appearance, here is a Jewish man and a black Ethiopian standing in a pool of water in ceremonial procession. Beneath the surface, in matters of the heart, all racial and religious barriers are erased. Saving faith in Jesus Christ forgives all sins and immerses the believer fully into the family of God. No longer is he a religious proselyte confined to the outer court of a man-made Temple in Jerusalem. Now he has direct access to the throne of God in Heaven!

One can argue that the means of baptism was not important, that sprinkling or pouring is as acceptable as immersion. However, if sprinkling was sufficient, they would have been carrying enough drinking water for that method. Stopping at a pool of water for the purpose of baptism would have been unnecessary. The Greek word is *baptize*, meaning "immersion" (Thayer 94), which is the consistent N. T. pattern (Polhill, *Acts* 226). That is not to say that the method is more important than the meaning. It isn't. But for those who believe the N. T. teaches baptism by immersion, this text certainly supports it as indicated in verses 38-39. Both going into and coming up from the water certainly imply immersion (Bock 345; Knowling 227). Stott (162) goes too far in stating that if going down into the water meant baptism, then since both of them went down into the water that would mean that both were immersed. Philip must go down into the water to baptize (immerse) the Ethiopian.

A few writers (Keener I:1591-1592; Bock 345) try to identify the possible pools of water that might have been used for the baptism. Since the exact location of the event is unknown, these are, at best, guesses. The place is not as important as the purpose.

As compelling as is the beginning of this witness event (v. 26), so is the completion. As the two men emerge from the baptismal waters (v. 39), Philip is miraculously "caught away" (Greek *harpazo*, to seize, snatch away). While some are reluctant to see in this a miraculous removal of Philip (Keener I:1594; Stott 162: Morgan 218), the word is forceful and the means not without precedent (2 Kgs. 2:11-16; 1 Thess. 4:17). Philip is, indeed, miraculously "snatched away" (Meyer 177) from the event. We can only speculate why the Lord did that. The eunuch is left alone but continues his journey back to Ethiopia with the joy of the Lord in his heart (8:8).

The question where the Lord took Philip is answered with the statement "Philip was found" in Azotus, ancient Ashdod, some few miles north of Gaza. From here he began proclaiming the gospel of Christ in the cities of the coast, making his way to Caesarea. Luke completes this account of Philip's ministry but will re-introduce him later (21:8-14) as an "evangelist."

One cannot help asking what happened to the Ethiopian. He is never mentioned again in the Scriptures, but he is not forgotten. Irenaeus (*Heresies*, 3:12.8) states that he became a missionary to his own people. Another tradition states that he was martyred (Keener I:1595). While these may be merely traditions that seek to fill in the gaps, they are close enough to the time period to lend at least some credibility to the possibility of his influence upon returning home. A man of such intelligence, humility, and spiritual interest, coming to Christ in such unusual circumstances, surely told the story to others, along with the reasons for his new-found faith. The design of God's providential guidance always includes others who need the same truth.

In the progression of the Acts narrative, why is Philip so directed to the Ethiopian, since the majority of Acts records the witness to the Gentiles via Peter and Paul? Polhill (*Acts* 222) observes that Ethiopia was considered to be the "ends of the earth" by Greeks and Romans of that day. Though Peter initiated a different direction of witness to Gentiles (15:7) and Paul continued it (Gal. 2:7-9), it was Philip whom the Lord used as the early bridge. Keener (I:1534) defines the conversion of the Ethiopian eunuch as a proleptic fulfillment of Acts 1:8. The two accounts of Gentile opportunity, involving Philip and Peter, should not be viewed as competing accounts indicating who should get credit, but as the providential timing of the Lord to get the message of the gospel to "all nations" (Mt. 28:19) by all witnesses. The Lord used prepared servants to minister to prepared hearts at the prepared time.

Summary
(8:1b-40)

The ministry of Philip records a significant and historical advancement of the gospel into Samaria and beyond. While all who are saved are equally significant in the eyes of the Lord, it is the pattern of Luke to select certain ones as representative of that witness situation. He chooses two men to illustrate Philip's historical witness, all in accord with Luke's intentional design for his writing of Acts (1:8). What was lost in the identity of the Samaritans in their history of spiritual intrigue was regained in Christ. Joy (v. 8) replaced despair. The conversion of Simon the sorcerer represents both the power of the gospel over the fallen culture of Samaria and the life of a misguided individual. The advancement of the gospel into this region is confirmed by the unique manifestation of the Holy Spirit and apostolic fellowship and solidarity with the Samaritans. The growth of discipleship requires clarification and repentance of spiritual "baggage," as represented in Peter's rebuke of Simon as he thought the power of the Holy Spirit could be purchased.

As a precursor to extending the gospel to the "uttermost parts of the earth," Philip is providentially directed from the Samaritan revival to remote Gaza. Here he encounters an Ethiopian eunuch, a man of significant position in the Nubian government, a proselyte to Judaism, whose heart has been prepared by the Lord for Philip's witness. The eunuch embraces the gospel, is baptized, and returns to Ethiopia. One tradition has him becoming an eager witness for Christ. The Ethiopian is the representative conversion account that shows the gospel of Christ is timeless and universal in its provision for redemption for all people.

Unlike Stephen, who died for his witness, Philip continued his witness in many coastal towns and villages, eventually settling in Caesarea. God's will was different for these two gifted men.

Application: Teaching and Preaching the Passage

Exegetical Outline of the Text: 1. The Persecution of Saul of Tarsus (8:1b-4). 2. The Proclamation of the Gospel to the Samaritans by Philip (8:5-13). 3. The Confirmation of the Apostles (8:14-25). 4. The Conversion of the Ethiopian Eunuch (8:26-40).

In addition to this exegetical outline, I suggest an expository outline for preaching or teaching on the subject, "The Providence of God in the Witness of the Gospel." (These same principles can be traced throughout Acts, especially in the next two chapters with the Ananias/Saul exchange and the Peter/Cornelius witness.) 1. *God is preparing me for what others need to hear*, as seen in the preparation for Philip in Samaria, the preparation of Ananias for Saul, and the preparation of Peter to witness to Cornelius. 2. *God is preparing others for what I need to share*, as seen in the Ethiopian's interest in Isaiah, the encounter of Saul with Jesus, and the appearance of the Angel of the Lord to Cornelius. 3. *I must be willing to adjust my schedule to follow the Lord's leading*, as seen in the fact that Philip "arose and went" (8:27), as did Ananias (9:17) and Peter (10:23). 4.

The Lord's timing is essential, as seen in Philip's meeting the eunuch at a certain time in a certain place, in Ananias' being prepared as Saul comes to Damascus, and in Peter's preparation as the servants of Cornelius are on their way. 5. *One person's life opens the door for others*, as seen in the return of the Ethiopian to his country, the ministry of Saul/Paul, and the salvation of the entire household of Cornelius. 6. *No one is beyond the grace of God*, as seen in Simon the sorcerer, the Ethiopian Eunuch, Saul of Tarsus, and Cornelius the soldier. 7. *God can use anyone in His work*, as seen in the fact that Philip was not an apostle and that Ananias is only referred to again by Paul.

By now the pattern of Luke's narrative, showing the progression of the gospel, is clear (1:8). This can be traced in succeeding chapters. A good study is to show key figures and events that take place in each segment. The same is true in individual lives. There is always a pattern of growth and development. It is challenging to chart that pattern over the course of one's life, no matter how long the person has been saved.

Another great study is to examine the background of Samaria in the O. T. and the intentional ministry of Jesus when He went there (Jn. 4). All of that preceded the ministry of Philip before he went to Samaria with the gospel. Jesus gave the principle of sowing and reaping (Jn. 4:36-38). Philip actually reaped where Jesus had already sown. Some ministries are sowing ministries while others reap. Most ministries must do some of both. There are spiritual truths to be learned from the analogy of sowing and reaping (Gal. 6:7-9). These can be developed into several lessons and messages.

Philip was a man described as "full of faith and the Holy Spirit" (6:5). Of significant interest would be a study of the N. T. teaching on the Holy Spirit in the life of the believer. This would include such key texts as John 14-16, Romans 8, Galatians 5, and others. There are many messages and lessons on the person, work, and ministry of the Holy Spirit that encourage, strengthen, and empower the believer when biblically understood.

A good lesson from this text involves the principles of soul winning and personal witnessing. Those include the following: 1. Be open to the Holy Spirit's leading. 2. Be willing to go where directed. 3. Be prepared to witness to anyone to whom the Lord leads you. 4. Be respectful and speak with deference. 5. Learn the right questions to ask. 6. Use the Scriptures. 7. Counsel new believers to follow the Lord in believer's baptism.

Simon the sorcerer presents a lesson about how confusion can arise when a person is not grounded in biblical truth. Sometimes a wise and bold pastor, in similarity to Peter's candid response, can bring correction and repentance. It is the responsibility of those in leadership to do such correcting.

V. THE CHURCH'S WITNESS "TO THE UTTERMOST PART OF THE EARTH" (9:1—21:17)

A. The Conversion of Saul of Tarsus (9:1-31)

1. Saul encounters the living Christ (9:1-9)

1 And Saul, yet breathing out threatenings and slaughter against the disciples of the Lord, went unto the high priest,

2 And desired of him letters to Damascus to the synagogues, that if he found any of this way, whether they were men or women, he might bring them bound unto Jerusalem.

3 And as he journeyed, he came near Damascus: and suddenly there shined round about him a light from heaven:

4 And he fell to the earth, and heard a voice saying unto him, Saul, Saul, why persecutest thou me?

5 And he said, Who art thou, Lord? And the Lord said, I am Jesus whom thou persecutest: *it is* **hard for thee to kick against the pricks.**

6 And he trembling and astonished said, Lord, what wilt thou have me to do? And the Lord *said* **unto him, Arise, and go into the city, and it shall be told thee what thou must do.**

7 And the men which journeyed with him stood speechless, hearing a voice, but seeing no man.

8 And Saul arose from the earth; and when his eyes were opened, he saw no man: but they led him by the hand, and brought *him* **into Damascus.**

9 And he was three days without sight, and neither did eat nor drink.

The conversion of the Ethiopian eunuch (8:26-40) was a precursor to the next phase of the expansion of the witness of the church to "the uttermost part of the earth" (1:8). As one reads the progression of Acts, there is no mistaking the pivotal events that transition to each successive expansion. Three conversion stories defining the expansion of the gospel witness are recorded back-to-back: the Ethiopian eunuch, the conversion of Saul of Tarsus, and the Roman Centurion, Cornelius. These are not randomly inserted into the narrative. Further, there is the unmistakable providential guidance of the Lord in these events.

Some writers (Keener II:1598) suggest that Luke "struggles" with arranging his material. However, Luke writes in hindsight. His insertion of Saul's conversion at this point in his narrative is intentional and preparatory. The expansion of the church's witness into "all the world" includes the conversion and equipping of the apostle to the Gentiles.

Most conservative commentators are in agreement that Saul of Tarsus was converted A.D. 33-34 (Bruce, *Paul* 475; Picirilli, *Paul* 52; Bock 31). How this corresponds with Philip's ministry (ch. 8), Peter's western Judaean ministry (9:32-43), and his witness to Cornelius (ch. 10) is uncertain, but it fits that general time frame. Given the intensity of Saul's pursuit of believers (8:1-4; 9:1) and his own testimony of pressing the persecution to "strange cities" (26:11), his campaign of terror probably was simultaneous to the Samaritan witness. The conclusion that the churches were able to "rest" following his conversion covers the areas of Judaea, Samaria, and Galilee (9:31) where the witness of the church had expanded.

Again, one cannot miss the irony of the conversion of Saul. The church's witness in obedience to the command of the Lord Jesus came to be championed by the one who was its worst enemy. Christ changes the direction of one's life as well as one's eternal destiny. When the early reports about Saul becoming a disciple of the Lord were heard, probably no one foresaw his role in fulfilling the Great Commission. We are reminded again that "God hath chosen...the things that are not to bring to nought the things that are" (1 Cor. 1:28).

Luke begins the story of Saul's conversion by referencing his campaign of terror (v. 1). Saul was not content with his efforts to put a stop to the witness of the disciples in Jerusalem. Emboldened by the death of Stephen, he became obsessed with trying to eradicate them wherever they were. The phrase *breathing out* (Greek *empneo*, used only here in the N. T.) *threatenings and slaughter* (v. 1) carries the idea of an obsessed man who lived and breathed to imprison and slay anyone who professed that Jesus was the Messiah (Robertson, *Acts* 113). Paul himself characterized this time of his life as "being exceedingly mad against them" (6:11). As a descendant of the tribe of Benjamin (Phil. 3:5), he fulfilled, at least in part, the patriarchal prophesy of Jacob (Gen. 49:27), "Benjamin shall ravin as a wolf."

Obtaining legal permission from the high priest, who shared Saul's sentiments, he pressed the campaign targeting the believers in distant Damascus. There is some disagreement as to the exact legal authorization of the "letters" he obtained (v. 2). Some (Bock 355; Fitzmyer 423) propose they are letters of extradition with Roman authorization via the Sanhedrin. Others (Polhill, *Acts* 233; Keener II:1625) suggest they are letters of introduction from the high priest to the synagogues at Damascus calling for discipline and expulsion of any who were disciples. Either way, the intent was the same. Saul was given authority to arrest and return to Jerusalem for trial any and all ("men or women") who were followers of Christ (26:12). Furthermore, if they did not recant their "blasphemy," the same as Stephen's offense (26:11), they were put to death.

The phrase "this way," and its variations, is used in verse 2 and several times in Acts (16:17; 18:25-26; 19:9, 23; 24:14, 22) as the early identification of believers. Probably derived from Jesus' statement in John 14:6, and perhaps Matthew 7:13-14, it reflected the belief that the gospel of Christ was the way of salvation and access to God.

Why Damascus? In view of the dispersion of the believers from Jerusalem following the death of Stephen, and Saul's door-to-door campaign (8:1-4), he probably believed he had been somewhat successful enough to go farther. Damascus lay some 140 miles northeast of Jerusalem and had a large population of Jews and several synagogues. Josephus (*Wars*, II.XX.1) records an occasion when ten thousand Jews of Damascus were slaughtered "in one hour's time." This implies a large Jewish population in the city. With written authority from the high priest, the synagogues of Damascus would provide support for Saul's efforts. It was the logical choice to go there.

The trip to Damascus would normally take a week, depending on conditions of travel. There were others who were in the group (22:9; 26:13), but no specific identification is given as to who they were and for what purpose they were with Saul. They might have been members of the Temple guard, appointed to protect him, or even other like-minded

zealots who went with him to verify and satisfy their own agendas (Keener II:1639).

Normally, travel would have been suspended during midday because of the heat and need for rest, but that is the time when the encounter with Christ occurred (26:13). The group was certainly getting close to Damascus (v. 3) and might have been pressing to get to the city before the Sabbath began at sundown on a Friday, hence their travel at noon.

To say that what happened next was totally unexpected is a gross understatement! One needs to compare the three testimonies in Acts (9:1-9; 22:4-11; 26:11-18) to get the full picture (Picirilli, *Paul* 42) of what exactly happened on the Damascus Road. Here is a summary.

- *The people on the mission*—Saul of Tarsus and unspecified company (9:7; 22:9; 26:13).
- *The purpose of the mission*—search out, find, arrest, and return to Jerusalem for trial those who followed "this way" (9:2; 22:5; 26:11, 12).
- *The time of the encounter*—midday, noon (22:6; 26:13).
- *The place of the encounter*—on the road, near Damascus (9:3; 22:6; 26:12).
- Specifics of the encounter itself:
  —A sudden, blinding light from heaven, spotlighting the entire group (9:3; 22:6; 26:13),
  —All falling to the ground (9:4; 22:7; 26:14),
  —A voice speaking in Hebrew (9:4; 22:7; 26:14),
  —A verbal exchange between "the voice" (Jesus) and Saul (9:4-6; 22:7-8, 10; 26:14-18),

142

—The response of the companions (9:7; 22:9),

—Saul blinded by the light, led into Damascus by his companions (9:8; 22:11).

There are two specifics that need clarification for the purpose of the integrity of the narrative. These have been discussed many times by commentators. First is the question about the hearing of the voice from Heaven. The account in 9:7 says they heard a voice but saw no one, whereas 22:9 says they heard not the voice. In response, the issue is probably not a matter of whether the others understood Hebrew or not (26:14). If, indeed, they were either Temple guard or like-minded zealots of Saul, they would have known the language. On the other hand, it is possible the group heard audibly *the sound* of the voice but did not distinguish *what* was being said (Jn. 12:29). There could be several reasons for that. The *voice* heard is not quite the same in the two accounts (Greek genitive case in 9:7 and accusative in 22:9), and perhaps this could explain the apparent difference—though some disagree (see Bruce, *Acts* 184-185; Picirilli, *Paul*, 44; Polhill, *Acts* 235; Marshall, *Acts* 355). A similar possibility involves *whose* voice was heard; perhaps the companions were only able to distinguish Saul's voice in the exchange, but not the voice of Jesus. Saul was the one being addressed, so the directed voice from Heaven might not have been understood.

Furthermore, the emotional impact of the encounter could easily account for the difference in perception. The shock of the sudden appearance of a light brighter than the sun, then being knocked to the ground like the arresting mob in the Garden of Gethsemane in the presence of Jesus, the Great I AM (Jn. 18:5-6), could have addled their senses momentarily. Anyone who has been in a traumatic situation knows how normal perception may be suspended momentarily; and this was definitely a traumatic situation. The difference in the story, then, is not one of contradiction in the accounts, but of understanding the minor variations.

The second concern in the accounts is the issue of whether the companions fell to the ground (26:14) or remained standing (9:7). Some see this as a contradiction (Haenchen 235; Meyer 186-187). However, to say the least, one must give credit to Luke that he would be aware of the details in the accounts since he recorded the testimony three times! The natural response of those who were knocked to the ground would be to get back up quickly, and stand where they would observe the prostrate Saul in conversation with someone they could not see! Thus they "stood speechless" after getting up. Understanding people's natural tendencies helps account for the details. One has to have an alternative agenda to find contradiction here.

The exchange between Saul and the Lord Jesus on the Damascus Road is most compelling. With minor variations, probably due to different circumstances for the telling, the three accounts relate the specifics of what was said. This is no nebulous, transcendental mind experience of a mystic subjectively interpreting a private event. It is, rather, a very public theophany of the living Christ (Myer 184; Robertson, *Acts* 118). Later, as the apostle Paul, he would affirm that he saw the living Christ (1 Cor. 9:1; 15:8; Gal. 1:16). The specifics of that exchange include the following.

- *A direct question to Saul*, from "a voice" out of the light: "Saul, Saul, why persecutest thou me?"
- *A direct question from Saul*, about identity: "Who art thou, Lord?"
- *A direct response of identification*: "I am Jesus whom thou persecutest."
- *A statement of assessment from Jesus*, directly to Saul: "It is hard for thee to kick against the pricks."
- *A question from Saul*, asking for instruction: "Lord, what wilt thou have me do?"
- *A specific answer from Jesus*: "Arise, and go into the city."

The exchange was initiated with a confrontational, direct question to Saul, whose name was spoken twice in emphasis. The charge was concerning the mission Saul had maddeningly pursued, persecuting the followers of Christ. It was not just the disciples themselves who felt the pains of persecution; the Lord Himself felt them. This statement reveals the undivided unity the Lord has with His followers as the body of Christ (Eph. 4:15-16). To persecute them is to persecute Him.

In two of the three accounts, the phrase "It is hard for thee to kick against the pricks" is included. (For discussion of its place in the text of the accounts, see Robertson, *Acts* 116, 448; Metzger 318). The saying was an agricultural proverb using the analogy of a sharpened stick used to prod or goad an animal into action. If the animal resisted ("kick against the pricks"), it would be painful. So it was with Saul as he recalled this particular statement from Jesus, apparently admitting that there had been "pricks" of some kind and he had "kicked" against them. (See Stott

171-172, for suggestions as to what those "pricks" might have been.) People under conviction often react adversely rather than respond positively.

Four times (vv. 5-6) the term "Lord" is used (Greek *kurios*, master, sovereign). Saul might have spoken it first in respect, but after identification, he speaks it reverently. His submission is indicated by his desire to know what to do next. The transformation did not take long. One cannot encounter the living Christ and ever be the same again.

Saul was directed to go into Damascus where he would receive further instructions. The brightness of the heavenly light had physically blinded him, so he had to be led by the others. Eventually, they made their way to the house of Judas on "the street called Straight" (v.11). It is likely that Judas was the original host to whom letters of introduction would have been directed. In that case, they had a previously arranged destination in the city. The intention would have been to take care of Saul and his group while they did their dirty work in Damascus (Keener II:1642). However, all that had changed! Saul spent the next three days physically blind and spiritually fasting (v. 9). The encounter with the living Christ was so traumatic that it called for total self-inspection and prayerful repentance (v. 11, "he prayeth").

The situation in which Saul finds himself deserves some analysis (Tenney 244-245). Through the years, some have tried to explain the radical and sudden change in Saul in different ways. Suggestions range from physical maladies like epilepsy, to overwhelming guilt over his treatment of believers, to total rejection of apocalyptic Pharisaism (Picirilli, *Paul*, 46-47; Polhill, *Acts* 239-

240). Polhill probably captures the spiritual reality of what happened by asserting that "a totally different man emerged from that vision of the risen Lord; and that is conversion."

To say the least, Saul is at a crossroads in his life. He is in unfamiliar surroundings, having just encountered the person of the living God, having been physically blinded by the light, being totally dependent on others, and now having to re-examine nearly everything he has been taught and believed. The mission of his life recently has been to oppose and eradicate the notion that Jesus was the Messiah and had been raised from the dead. He has been obsessed with eliminating all who followed such an idea. Now, he himself has experienced firsthand the Living presence of the very one he denied.

It would not be an understatement to say that his state of mind was full of confusion. No wonder he spent the time fasting and praying. No wonder he would need even more time to get it all sorted out (Gal. 1:15-18). The road to Damascus took him to an entirely different "place." Only the question remained, "What now?"

2. Ananias sent to help Saul (9:10-19a)

**10 And there was a certain disciple at Damascus, named Ananias, and to him said the Lord in a vision, Ananias. And he said, *Behold, I am here,* Lord.
11 And the Lord *said* unto him, Arise, and go into the street which is called Straight, and enquire in the house of Judas for *one* called Saul, of Tarsus: for, behold, he prayeth,**

**12 And hath seen in a vision a man named Ananias coming in, and putting *his* hand on him, that he might receive his sight.
13 Then Ananias answered, Lord, I have heard by many of this man, how much evil he hath done to thy saints at Jerusalem:
14 And here he hath authority from the chief priests to bind all that call on thy name.
15 But the Lord said unto him, Go thy way: for he is a chosen vessel unto me, to bear my name before the Gentiles, and kings, and the children of Israel:
16 For I will shew him how great things he must suffer for my name's sake.
17 And Ananias went his way, and entered into the house; and putting his hands on him said, Brother Saul, the Lord, *even* Jesus, that appeared unto thee in the way as thou camest, hath sent me, that thou mightest receive thy sight, and be filled with the Holy Ghost.
18 And immediately there fell from his eyes as it had been scales: and he received his sight forthwith, and arose, and was baptized.
19a And when he received meat, he was strengthened.**

Not only was the Lord working providentially in the life of Saul of Tarsus, drawing him (Jn. 6:44) to saving faith, He was working in the life of Ananias to provide confirming counsel. God does the saving, but often we do the counseling. That is part of being a "witness" (1:8). Appearing in a vision to Ananias (v. 10), the Lord directly instructed him about his role in assisting Saul. That there were two visions in this story, to

Saul and Ananias respectively, emphasizes God's confirming activity in both lives (Gen. 41:32) regarding the same event (Bock 360). The response of Ananias to the vision was one of surrender, "I am here, Lord."

Supernatural visions were an integral part of the work of the Holy Spirit (2:17) in communicating with believers in the Acts record (7:55-56; 9:3-6, 10-12; 10:3-6, 10-17; 16:9-10). It is a dimension of the work of the Holy Spirit when needed. The completion of the biblical record minimizes that need since God has given us His full, written counsel. However, the Holy Spirit works as He wills when He sovereignly determines, but always in confirmation of the written Scriptures.

The instructions to Ananias were very specific (v. 11). He was to go to a certain house on a certain street and ask for a certain person. The street ("Straight") where Saul was staying is still there today as the main east-west thoroughfare in the old city of Damascus. It was so named at the time because it was an exception to the narrow twisting and turning of most avenues in the ancient city. It is called Darb al-Mustaqim today. There is also a traditional location of the house of Judas marked on its western end (Bruce, *Acts* 186). Bock sees the name of the street as ironic to the situation, as well (360-361). The Lord is setting things "straight" on a street name "Straight."

Saul was said to be praying, awaiting the arrival of Ananias as he was instructed in the vision (v. 12). This vision might have been subsequent to the one on the road to Damascus, occurring while Saul was in prayer. Lenski aptly states, "The raging lion has been changed into a bleating lamb" (361). Both Saul and

Ananias were informed by the Lord about what was expected from the life of Saul.

Perhaps it should come as no surprise that Ananias ingenuously balked (vv. 13-14) at being sent to counsel the one who had terrorized believers in Jerusalem. Saul's reputation and mission to Damascus had preceded him. We are not told exactly how Ananias knew the detail how Saul had obtained authority from the high priest for his campaign, but there would have been plenty of time and travel from Jerusalem to inform believers about it.

Verses 15-16 record the divine mission of Saul's life as told to Ananias. He was a "chosen vessel" to carry the witness of the gospel. The three groups identified as "Gentiles, kings, and the children of Israel" are something of a preview of the apostle Paul's life-mission as fulfilled in the rest of his story in Acts (Marshall, *Acts* 171-172). The Gentile witness would be recorded in his missionary journeys (chs. 13—21:17). His witness before "kings" would be recorded in his imprisonment and appeal to Caesar (21:26—28:16). His witness before "the children of Israel" (Rom. 1:16) would be his continual appeals in the synagogues of the cities where he traveled, culminating in his meeting with the Jews in Rome (28:17-29). His ministry would directly reflect the mission of Acts 1:8 and the intent to communicate the gospel of Christ to all people everywhere, regardless of their nationality, language, or position in life.

None of these dimensions of witness were to be without suffering. Later, Paul himself would record some of these trials of suffering (2 Cor. 4:8-12; 6:4-10; 11:23-27). The witness of Christ is never promised to be without difficulty, sacrifice, and sometimes great suffering for His sake. The world does not view authentic Christianity as merely an equal alternative point of view. It is seen as a threat to be eradicated (Jn. 15:18-20, 16:33).

There are no compelling reasons to conclude that there is yet another "contradiction" in the conversion story of Saul (Haenchen 325-328) by placing the divine plan for his life as being spoken only to Ananias and not to Saul (26:14-19). Why not to both? The only difference is when Luke chose to write that part in his own narrative.

Informing Saul of what the Lord had told him about His life-plan for him must have been personally encouraging to Ananias as well as informative to Saul. Ananias went from balking at the Lord's instruction to making his way obediently (v. 17) to the house of Judas. Here he greeted Saul with contact, "putting his hands on him," and words of acceptance: "Brother Saul." Furthermore, he confirmed that he had been sent to be instrumental in the restoration of his eyesight and the inauguration of a new relationship with the Lord: namely, being filled with the Holy Spirit. Paul's expanded testimony in 22:12-16 includes a summary of Ananias' statement to him and instruction to be baptized.

The exchange between Ananias and Saul culminated with the healing of Saul's blindness and his baptism (vv. 18-19a). A scale-like substance, perhaps burn scabs from the intensity and heat of the Shekinah Light, fell from his eyelids and eyesight was restored immediately. It should be noted that Ananias was not an apostle, nor one chosen for the kind of ministry the apostles were to have (6:5-6). His role was to confirm

Saul's conversion, assure him of his healing, and baptize him. He did not supply nor supplant the message given directly to Saul (Gal. 1:12). The Lord uses anyone and everyone whose hearts are open to His leadership. The three days of fasting concluded with some much-needed food (v. 19a) and initial confirmation of Saul's spiritual transformation.

There is some question as to where exactly Saul was saved. Was it on the road to Damascus, when he submitted to Jesus and called Him *Lord* (1 Cor. 12:3)? Or in the house of Judas when Ananias instructed him to be baptized and call on the name of the Lord? That God can instantly transform a person's life is clear enough. He does that when that individual's faith is sufficiently focused on the living Christ. Both the Lord Jesus (Lk. 7:50; 18:42) and Paul (Rom. 10:9-10; 1 Cor. 12:3) link saving faith with the personal acknowledgement of Jesus as Lord. Be that as it may, perhaps Picirilli (*Paul* 46) is correct in observing, "We are probably trying too hard to formalize God's ways when we press such issues."

3. Saul preaches in Damascus (9:19b-25)

19b Then was Saul certain days with the disciples which were at Damascus.
20 And straightway he preached Christ in the synagogues, that he is the Son of God.
21 But all that heard *him* were amazed, and said; Is not this he that destroyed them which called on this name in Jerusalem, and came hither for that intent, that he

might bring them bound unto the chief priests?
22 But Saul increased the more in strength, and confounded the Jews which dwelt at Damascus, proving that this is very Christ.
23 And after that many days were fulfilled, the Jews took counsel to kill him:
24 But their laying await was known of Saul. And they watched the gates day and night to kill him.
25 Then the disciples took him by night, and let *him* down by the wall in a basket.

The next step in Saul's new life (v. 19b) is interaction with the disciples in Damascus for "certain days." This phrase is indefinite (Greek *tis*, several, some, certain). We could only hope that Luke had been more specific, defining exactly when and how long his interaction was with the disciples at Damascus. Note two other indefinite time references in this context, *straightway* (v. 20) and *many days* (v. 23). Later, Paul inserts that, following his encounter with Christ, he "immediately" left for Arabia (Gal. 1:17). Expressions like *straightway* don't give us specific information.

There are numerous other questions about those early days and years of Saul's life following his conversion. Where and when exactly did he go into Arabia (How immediate is "immediately")? What was his purpose for going into Arabia? How soon did he travel back to Jerusalem? Did Barnabas have a private meeting with Saul prior to his arrival in Jerusalem? There are others.

Numerous writers have addressed the apparent "discrepancies" between Luke's account and Paul's account (Bruce, *Acts* 194-195; Picirilli, *Paul* 52-56; Ogg, 31-35; Polhill, *Acts* 239-240; Bock 363-364). While there are certainly challenges to piecing the details together, that does not mean there are contradictions in the different accounts in the Acts record and Paul's record. What it does mean is that there are different intentions on the part of Luke and Paul, respectively, in their accounts. That Luke omits certain details is not a matter of either ignorance of them (as Lightfoot proposes, 152) or an inaccurate accounting, but intent. One would assume his personal relationship with Paul and access to the details from Paul himself would discount the idea that he was ignorant of the details. It should be noted, also, that there are other times in the Acts record that Luke chooses to record the bigger picture of the event without details that Paul supplies in his epistles (2 Cor. 11:24-26).

Notably, the three years spent in Arabia (Gal. 1:17-18), wherever he went and why, are important for the entire chronological sequence of events. Some place the time in Arabia between the sentences here in verse 19. Some allow for an initial few days with the disciples in Damascus and place the time in Arabia between verses 21 and 22, while others place the time between verses 22 and 23, and yet others between verses 25 and 26 (Picirilli, *Paul*, 52; ESV 2246, footnote). Bruce (*Acts* 190) does not see any problem with Saul spending a few days with the disciples in Damascus before going to Arabia. Neither do I. It seems logical that he would spend some time initially with the disciples in Damascus. This would verify the testimony of Ananias, who would surely have shared his story, alleviate any concerns that Saul might be arrested, and introduce Saul to their fellowship.

As for the question of where in Arabia he went and for what purpose, there are no concrete statements either in Acts or Paul's letters. Technically, "Arabia" extended from just east of Damascus all the way to the Red Sea. Morgan (240) has him going to Mt. Sinai, the place where the Law was given, so he could meditate and clarify his beliefs. Keener (II:1676-1683) cites numerous sources suggesting he traveled extensively in Arabia preaching in the synagogues—which generated such hostility that it followed him back to Damascus (2 Cor. 11:32-33). Perhaps there were both meditation and preaching. It certainly would have been a time to solidify his thoughts as well as begin proclaiming what he had discovered (Marberry 21-22).

The theme of Saul's preaching in the synagogues of Damascus (v. 20) was that Jesus is "the Son of God" (13:33). Though this is the only time in Acts where this phrase is used, it would come to define a significant part of Paul's theology (Gal. 1:16; Rom. 1:1-4). "Son of God" was both a Messianic term and a title indicating Deity (Forlines, *Quest* 83; EDT 1034).

Saul's preaching was electrifying to those who heard him (v. 21). The persecutor against the followers of Jesus was now the proclaimer that Jesus was the Son of God! All, including those who were not followers of Christ, were astonished at the change in his life. His mission was completely reversed!

I would place the time in Arabia (Gal. 1:17-18) between verses 21 and 22 and interpret the phrase "Saul increased the more in strength" (v. 22) to be a result of his extended time alone with the

Lord. This would also allow for his statement in Galatians 1:17 that he "returned *again* unto Damascus." His preaching in the synagogues of Damascus and confounding the Jewish opposition was reminiscent of his own experience hearing Stephen (6:9-10). Perhaps using some of the same arguments Stephen used, he proved that Jesus is the Christ. His apologetic included his own life change (2 Cor. 5:17).

Choosing to stay in Damascus for "many days" (v. 23), his preaching has the same effect as Stephen's had. Plans are made to kill Saul, probably using the same charges of blasphemy and the same means as he had originally employed in preparing his attack against the disciples at Damascus. Note that the term "Jews," as a group distinct from believers, is used here for the first time in Acts.

The plot to kill him, however, is discovered (v. 24), even as the gates of the city are watched continually for his appearance. The disciples came to his assistance, secreting him at a remote part of the city wall, and lowering him to the ground in a basket for his escape. The event is recalled by Paul later (2 Cor. 11:32-33) with other details added. He adds that the governor (Greek *ethnarch*) of Damascus, under the Nabatean king, Aretas (9 B.C—A.D. 40. Cadbury, *Acts in History* 19-21), was a part of the plot against him. Some suggest that Saul had riled those in Arabia during his time there and that animosity followed him in his return to Damascus (Keener II:1679-1683; Polhill, *Acts* 242). Further, collusion between powerful Jewish leaders and political leaders was common (as seen in the trial of Jesus), so it should not be surprising that the same sort of thing happened in

Damascus, and for the same reasons. It is not clear that Paul means his reference to this in 2 Corinthians to suggest a time of humiliation (Polhill, *Acts* 242). It seems rather that he counted it as an honor that he would suffer for the cause of Christ (Phil. 3:10).

Of significant interest is the chronology of the Book of Acts and the year of Saul's conversion (see Introduction). Writers vary in their conclusions (Picirilli, *Paul* 52; Fitzmyer 433; Ogg 30; ESV 2100, footnote; Harnack, *Acts* 2-48), but it seems that A.D. 33-34 is very likely. That means the impact of the early believers as recorded in the first eight chapters of Acts took place in approximately one year. Incredible!

4. Saul comes to Jerusalem as a Christ-follower (9:26-31)

**26 And when Saul was come to Jerusalem, he assayed to join himself to the disciples: but they were all afraid of him, and believed not that he was a disciple.
27 But Barnabas took him, and brought *him* to the apostles, and declared unto them how he had seen the Lord in the way, and that he had spoken to him, and how he had preached boldly at Damascus in the name of Jesus.
28 And he was with them coming in and going out of Jerusalem.
29 And he spake boldly in the name of the Lord Jesus, and disputed against the Grecians: but they went about to slay him.
30 *Which* when the brethren knew, they brought him down to Caesarea, and sent him forth to Tarsus.
31 Then had the churches rest throughout all Judaea and Galilee and Samaria, and were edified; and walking in fear of the Lord, and in the comfort of the Holy Ghost, were multiplied.**

Although it has been at least three years since Saul left Jerusalem (Gal. 1:18) on his campaign to Damascus, and his life has been completely changed, he has not overcome his previous reputation as one who persecuted believers door to door in Jerusalem (8:3). His attempt to join with the disciples was met with skepticism and fear (v. 26). They simply did not believe him. It is also possible they thought this might have been a different tactic to get inside information, an agent provocateur (Bruce, *Acts* 193). It's easy to understand the suspicion of the disciples.

Barnabas, however, was of a different opinion (v. 27). If, indeed, Saul had been saved, what a testimony that would be! Implied is a personal meeting with Saul ("Barnabas took him"), probably to verify the rumors of his conversion and to get personally acquainted. Exactly when that private meeting took place is not indicated here but such a meeting could easily fit in the entire scheme of the account. Barnabas gained an audience with the apostles where he vouched for Saul. The precise wording of the summary testimony could be that Saul himself told his story, referencing the encounter on the Damascus Road and his bold preaching "in the name of Jesus" in the synagogues of Damascus. Barnabas proved as encouraging in his support as he was generous in his giving (4:36-37). Would that we all were more like him!

Luke's summary of this trip to Jerusalem does not include some details that are recorded later. Among those are the Temple vision (22:17-21), Saul's fifteen-day, private visit with Peter, that James was the only other person Saul saw while he was there, and that he was basically unrecognized in the churches of Judaea (Gal. 1:18-19). This statement could mean that he was unknown as a believer among the churches. Presumably, his prior campaign of terrorism would have rendered him well-known by name, but not necessarily by face. That Luke chooses not to include that information here is a matter of the author's selecting material and condensing the information for the intent of the story at this point in writing, not a factual discrepancy.

In Jerusalem, Saul picked up where Stephen had left off (v. 29), presenting the case for Christ to the Grecians, probably in the same synagogues (6:9-10). His efforts met with the same response, too! They began the process to kill Saul just as they had Stephen. Again, the irony is obvious. The very one who had led the fight against Stephen is now the one who is being targeted for the same reasons. When the plot was discovered by the other disciples, they determined to preserve Saul's life by sending him to his home in Tarsus (v. 30). That would, perhaps, cool down the situation for everyone as well as preserve Saul's life.

Verse 31 is a summary of this incredible turn of events that resulted with the conversion of Saul of Tarsus. What began as a campaign against the churches (8:1b-4) that scattered the believers and challenged their very lives, has changed completely, bringing rest and respite to the churches.

We are also informed that there were churches in Galilee by this time. Galilee would be included in the Judaean stage of witness. It should come as no surprise that there were believers and churches in Jesus' home area, where he had begun His ministry and appeared after His resurrection (Mt. 28:16-17; Jn. 21:1-22).

Summary
(9:1-31)

There are some events that are truly historic and pivotal, none more than the conversion of Saul of Tarsus. Not only was the life of one man changed, but history itself hinged on the role he would play in the development of Christianity (Polhill, *Acts* 231). Much of the history of the Europe and Western civilization as we know it derives its values and life philosophy from his writings. Studies of his life and writings are second only to the life and teachings of the Lord Jesus.

No one pursued the church with persecution and torment as did Saul of Tarsus. With legal authority to arrest and imprison men and women he pressed the issue to include the cities and towns all the way to Damascus. But God had a different plan for him. In a special manifestation of the risen Christ to him on the road to Damascus, Saul's life was changed forever and the church relieved of the pressure.

The reputation of Saul was such that it was difficult at first to accept the authenticity of his conversion. Two men were instrumental in the initial affirmation of his faith, Ananias and Barnabas. However, as he began to openly and convincingly tell of his encounter with Christ and confront the Jews in the synagogues with the truth of the gospel, he was met with stiff opposition. It became so intense that his life was threatened in Damascus where he had to be ferried away secretly at night to avoid arrest. When he arrived in Jerusalem he was met with the same skepticism until Barnabas was willing to risk his companionship and support.

Once he was accepted into the fellowship of the apostles and the church at Jerusalem, he began to persuade the Jews in the synagogues just as Stephen had done. This soon enough wore thin with many, who determined that he should be killed and his voice silenced. Wisely, Saul was sent away to his home area of Tarsus in order for things to cool down and his life to be spared. That began a period of silence in his life. It was not long before Barnabas would seek him out to help him with the growing ministry at Antioch of Syria (11:25-26).

Application: Preaching and Teaching the Passage

Exegetical Outline of the Text: 1. Saul's Intention for the Believers (9:1-2). 2. Saul's Encounter with the Risen Christ (9:3-9). 3. Saul's Encouragement From Ananias (9:10-18). 4. Saul's Proclamation of Christ in the Synagogues of Damascus (9:19-25), 5. Saul's Ministry in Jerusalem (9:26-29). 6. Saul sent to Tarsus (9:30-31).

The big question in this text is, "What can be learned of the conversion of Saul of Tarsus?" That is appropriate since he said his life was a pattern for others (1 Tim. 1:16). Among the lessons to be learned would be the *ironies* of the story. Some of those could be listed as: 1. The one who was the church's worst enemy became an apostle to the Gentiles, bearing witness to the very truth he once considered blasphemy. 2. The place where he intended to arrest

believers was the place he began his witness for Christ. 3. One of the very persons he would have arrested for being a believer is the one who gives counsel and assurance of his new-found faith. 4. Saul goes from being the one who came to persecute to being the one who is persecuted and has to escape for his life. 5. The greatest irony, perhaps, is the revolutionary change that occurs in a person's life when he savingly believes in Christ.

Another good lesson or message can be developed around the role of Ananias in Saul's conversion. It would include addressing the personal struggles one may have in spiritual counsel, especially about the intimidation Ananias felt when having to face a person of the stature of Saul. Such a study certainly should include the need for personal surrender to follow the Lord's leading. It also includes the fact that we never know who just may be under conviction and in need of our words of direction.

One might study the various names given to believers in the Book of Acts including: "those of this way," "disciples," "saints," "brothers," "Christians," and "witnesses." Each one conveys a distinct feature of those who are Christ-followers.

B. Peter's Ministry in Western Judaea (9:32-43)

1. The healing of Aeneas (9:32-35)

32 And it came to pass, as Peter passed throughout all *quarters*, he came down also to the saints which dwelt at Lydda.
33 And there he found a certain man named, which had kept his

bed eight years, and was sick of the palsy.
34 And Peter said unto him, Aeneas, Jesus Christ maketh thee whole: arise, and make thy bed. And he arose immediately.
35 And all that dwelt at Lydda and Saron saw him, and turned to the Lord.

With Saul safely removed from the scene at Jerusalem, Peter continued his witness, traveling throughout the Judaean area (v. 31). The conversion of Saul of Tarsus and the cessation of his campaign of persecution would be great relief to them. Plus, there were other areas that needed to hear the gospel. Eventually, he made his way to the town of Lydda, some thirty miles northwest of Jerusalem, where he encountered a man named Aeneas (v. 33). We are not told whether he was a believer or not. As usual, Luke the physician gives details of the man's physical condition. He is a paralytic and has been confined to his bed (Greek *krabattos*, a one-man bed or pallet; Mk. 2:4, 9) for eight years. Peter pronounces healing, calling his name first and then using the name of Jesus Christ (3:6). This is not a formulaic chant but rather an apostle being used of God as an instrument of healing.

Peter also instructed him to make his bed, a somewhat ambiguous though interesting addition. In the original, the command is simply "make ready for yourself." The verb *make ready* (Greek *stronnumi*) means, literally, to spread or furnish or prepare; it can mean, for example, to make preparations for eating. To dine, healthy, on the bed that represented eight years of sickness would be an expression of healing and

celebration. Here, however, it probably means simply to fold up his mat and walk with it, reminiscent of a similar situation with Jesus (Mk. 2:11). That he is to do this *for himself* (Greek dative case) emphasizes the contrast between doing it himself and his prior circumstances when others had to do it for him. I make this point knowing the joy of those who are finally able to do for themselves after extended illness. It is a time of celebration that often includes a meal.

The effects were immediate. Aeneas arose from his bed and walked (v. 34)! Furthermore, the healing testified to the saving grace of God. People who resided in Lydda and other villages on the coastal plain of Sharon ("Saron") turned to the Lord in saving faith. Implied, of course, is the fact that Peter would have further defined who Jesus Christ was and His power to heal and save. The *all* (v. 35) may simply provide a general summary of the whole population in those parts, but it could possibly mean that every person who lived in that area, capable of saving faith, turned to the Lord. History testifies to such a thing in other places. In any event, the healing of Aeneas proved to be a powerful testimony of both physical and spiritual healing. People who lived in the surrounding areas "saw him and turned to the Lord" (v. 35).

Such miracles in the first generation of Christianity were evidences affirming the authenticity of the gospel (Bock 157). In a similar way that miracles were an affirmation of Jesus as "approved of God" (2:22), so were the early apostles (2 Cor. 12:12) and some disciples (6:8; 8:6; 1 Cor. 12:28) so empowered.

2. The raising of Tabitha (Dorcas) from the dead (9:36-43)

36 Now there was at Joppa a certain disciple named Tabitha, which by interpretation is called Dorcas: this woman was full of good works and almsdeeds which she did.
37 And it came to pass in those days, that she was sick, and died: whom when they had washed, they laid *her* in an upper chamber.
38 And forasmuch as Lydda was nigh to Joppa, and the disciples had heard that Peter was there, they sent unto him two men, desiring *him* that he would not delay to come to them.
39 Then Peter arose and went with them. When he was come, they brought him into the upper chamber: and all the widows stood by him weeping, and shewing the coats and garments which Dorcas made, while she was with them.
40 But Peter put them all forth, and kneeled down, and prayed; and turning *him* to the body said, Tabitha, arise. And she opened her eyes: and when she saw Peter, she sat up.
41 And he gave her *his* hand, and lifted her up, and when he had called the saints and widows, presented her alive.
42 And it was known throughout all Joppa; and many believed in the Lord.
43 And it came to pass, that he tarried many days in Joppa with one Simon a tanner.

Joppa was one of the main port cities of Judaea and lay some ten to twelve miles northwest of Lydda. One of Joppa's prominent and well-beloved disciples was Tabitha (Dorcas), whose works and deeds of service were widely known. Here is Luke's only use in Acts of the feminine form of the word "disciple." (Other uses are masculine but certainly include both genders.) It appears here probably as a way to honor both her faith in Christ and her good deeds. Luke adds the Greek equivalent, *Dorcas*, to Tabitha's Aramaic name; both mean "gazelle" in English (v. 36). She was known by both names, depending on the language of those who knew her. Usually such deeds reflect a radiant life that attracts and embraces folks of all walks of life. Tragically, she died after suffering some sort of sickness (v. 37). Faith and good works do not insure against calamity in this life. However, her death served as the setting for another miraculous healing that testified to the saving grace of Christ.

Upon her death, her body was prepared ("washed") and a place designated ("an upper chamber") for a time of mourning (v. 37). But the news of the healing of Aeneas at the hands of Peter gave the disciples at Joppa the hope of another possible miracle. They sent two men to request that Peter come to Joppa for that purpose. Furthermore, the Lord had providential intentions for leading Peter to Joppa.

When Peter arrived in Joppa, he was shown where the body lay (v. 39). Many were there, not only to mourn but also to give testimony of her kindness, displaying to Peter the garments Dorcas made for their comfort. The compassionate deeds of godly people are like comforting garments that we wear in testimony of their lives even after they have passed.

The scene (vv. 40-41) is reminiscent of the same type of occurrence with Jesus in the raising of the daughter of Jairus (Mk. 5:35-43; Lk. 8:49-56). The obvious parallel shows the continuing work of the Lord Jesus through his disciples (1:1). Since Peter was present when Jesus raised the daughter of Jairus from the dead, perhaps he chose a similar approach in this situation. (After all, there are no procedural manuals on what to do when asked for such a miracle.) We are not informed of just what he prayed, but the prayer preceded a bold act of faith to speak to the dead body. In words almost identical to those Jesus used, Peter commanded her, by name, to arise. And she did! Taking her by the hand, he assisted her to her feet. Then she was presented *alive* to those who had come to mourn her death. A funeral turned to a festivity.

Healing the sick was incredible enough, but resuscitation of the dead was an even more compelling evidence of the power of God. Theologically, the raising of Tabitha, like the son of the widow of Nain, the daughter of Jairus, and Lazarus, was not a resurrection, but the temporary restoration of life (Polhill, *Acts* 248). It demonstrated that God Himself has the ultimate power over death (Heb. 2:14-15).

The miracle, which it was indeed, was a "sign" (Mk. 16:15-18) that affirmed the message of the gospel of Jesus Christ (Stott 182-184). The most important event that happened at Joppa was not the raising of Dorcas from the dead but the fact that "many believed in the Lord" (v. 42). The gospel that changes lives and gives hope of eternal life is an even greater miracle than the temporary restoration of life in N. T. events like this. If one lives his present life free of sickness but dies without Christ as Savior, the consequences of going to hell are eternal. However, even if one's present life is marked by illness, but he dies with Christ in his heart, the reward of Heaven and the promise of eternal health far outweigh the pain (Rom. 8:18). The miracles of healing and even restoration to life are temporary, albeit important enough to those who experience them; but getting saved has eternal promises. Nor does God choose to perform such miracles on everyone in this life. But the promise of redemption is for *all* who savingly trust Christ.

Following the raising of Dorcas, Peter chose to remain in Joppa for a while. With all the recent conversions, there was great opportunity for teaching and discipling them. Peter's host was one "Simon," whose trade was that of a "tanner" (v. 43). This trade would be considered "unclean" by Pharisees, but Peter was not a Pharisee. He had claimed some degree of dietary purity (10:14), but where he was staying reveals that he was not as strict as some. The occupation of Simon might be a relevant "object lesson" the Lord would soon use for the vision of unclean animals shown to Peter (10:9-16), to prepare him for the open door of witness to people considered "unclean."

The testimony of Dorcas, as one who blessed people with her good works, represents the intended effects of living in the way taught by the Lord Jesus (Mt. 5:16). Whether personal good works or the collective efforts of churches, the ultimate goal is to glorify God and turn people to the gospel of Jesus Christ. Throughout history the church has led the efforts to assuage injustice, bring healing and health, feed the hungry, clothe the naked, defend the helpless, etc. All civilized societies live in the overflow of the Dorcas efforts of believers. Rightly understood, these efforts impact culture by ministering to genuine human needs of all kinds (Wolters 131).

Summary
(9:32-43)

Luke transitions away from the narrative of the conversion of Saul of Tarsus by returning to the ministry of Simon Peter, preparation for his witness to Cornelius the Roman centurion. Cornelius represents the opening of the door for the church's European witness to Gentiles. Although Saul will become the apostle to the Gentiles (Gal. 2:9), the responsibility to carry the gospel to "the uttermost part of the earth" (1:8) was everyone's command and task. Peter would be the apostle who did that first (15:7). Luke selects two key miraculous events in Peter's ministry that put him in the vicinity of Cornelius. These miracles attest to Peter's instrumentality in affirmation of the gospel as well as to his leadership as an apostle.

Application: Preaching and Teaching the Passage

Exegetical Outline of the Text: 1. Peter's Ministry at Lydda—the healing of Aeneas (9:32-35). 2. Peter's Ministry at Joppa—the raising of Tabitha (9:36-43).

The two miracles in this text involve the apostle Peter. Although the account has prepared to shift to Saul of Tarsus, Peter's role continues. His ministry in Western Judaea is preparatory for the next big event in his life and the witness of the gospel to Gentiles. A good lesson

from this would involve how God prepares us for future ministry with others. Just as the areas of Lydda and Joppa expanded Peter's horizons, so God wants our horizons expanded as well.

"Dorcas Day" in some churches is based on the event recorded here. It makes for a great study to explore the biblical teaching of "good works"—as to motive, intent, and goals in the actions of the church. One must always balance motive with the message.

The healing of Dorcas (Tabitha) parallels a similar work of Jesus in raising the daughter of Jairus (Lk. 8:41-56). These two events can be compared in showing the similarities and purpose of their healings.

The N. T. records numerous instances when the Lord demonstrated His power over sickness and death. These make a good study, treating the people and situations, as well as the ultimate promise that one day the Lord will remove all sickness and death (Rev. 21:4-5).

C. The Conversion of Cornelius the Roman Centurion (10:1—11:18)

1. The vision of Cornelius (10:1-8)

1 There was a certain man in Caesarea called Cornelius, a centurion of the band called the Italian *band,*
2 A devout *man,* **and one that feared God with all his house, which gave much alms to the people, and prayed to God always.**
3 He saw in a vision evidently about the ninth hour of the day an angel of God coming in to him, and saying unto him, Cornelius.

4   And when he looked on him, he was afraid, and said, What is it, Lord? And he said unto him, Thy prayers and thine alms are come up for a memorial before God.
5   And now send men to Joppa, and call for *one* Simon, whose surname is Peter:
6   He lodgeth with one Simon a tanner, whose house is by the sea side: he shall tell thee what thou oughtest to do.
7   And when the angel which spake unto Cornelius was departed, he called two of his household servants, and a devout soldier of them that waited on him continually;
8   And when he had declared all these things unto them, he sent them to Joppa.

If the conversion of the Ethiopian eunuch (8:26-40) was the bridge to the church's witness to the Gentiles, the conversion of Cornelius is the open door. His is more than just another conversion story. It is an historic event signaling the expansion of the witness of the church to the "uttermost part of the earth" (1:8). It is also the pivotal event that was intended to end religious isolationism and unite all believers into the body of Christ (Eph. 2:11-22). There are many reasons it is the longest conversion narrative in Acts, showing the importance the writer places on it (Polhill, *Acts* 250).

First, consider the leadership of Peter in the event. Contextually, one should begin this study with Peter's Western Judaean ministry (9:32-43) that carried him away from Jerusalem and put him in the vicinity of Cornelius. His stay at Joppa was not coincidental. "The steps

[and stops] of a good man are ordered of the Lord" (Ps. 37:23). When he returned to Jerusalem to account for his interaction with Gentiles, he rightly attributed the entire episode to the work of God (11:17). A later summary is given (15:7-9) that reinforces his role. Peter's leadership again emerges in this next stage of witness as it has in each preceding one (Mt. 16:18-19).

Second, both Cornelius and Peter experienced complementary visions preparing them according to their respective needs. The Lord has never opposed Gentile conversions, but some of His people have. As with the preparation of Philip to witness to the Ethiopian eunuch (8:26), the visions of Saul and Ananias (9:3-6, 10-16), so the Lord initiated the timing of the witness to the Gentiles with preparatory visions granted to the principals in the story. One cannot miss the providential leading of God and the obedience of faithful men.

Third, food and fellowship traditions had become a means of isolation (11:1-3). The practices that had developed over the years were not O. T. directives but religious traditions that became barriers to outreach. It is amazing how minor traditions can evolve into major teachings (Mt. 15:1-9). Jesus sought to correct this traditional way of thinking. The Great Commission (1:8) necessitated overcoming personal biases to interact with and proclaim the gospel to the Gentiles who were considered unclean. The vision to Peter confronted him with his personal biases. As the default leader of the apostles, Peter was the one chosen to lead the way. He became the catalyst for the necessary change. Thankfully, he got the point (10:34). However, certain traditions die hard sometimes; Peter vacillated on this later

(Gal. 2:11-18). In effect, there are two "conversions" in the story, Peter's as well as Cornelius' (Stott 186). If one considers the response of the leaders of the church in Jerusalem (11:18), there were three.

Fourth, and perhaps the most challenging, is the theological issue of the salvation standing of some particular people and the groups they represent in the time frame of Acts. This is particularly relevant in considering the account of the conversion of Cornelius since he is first mentioned specifically as a "God-fearer" (v. 2): that is, "one who feared God."

At issue is this question: What does salvation specifically mean for a person who fit in this category of being a "God-fearer"? As Leroy Forlines (*Quest* 389) states, "If some of the Jews were saved by faith before the coming of Jesus, it follows that some of the Gentile proselytes and God-fearers were also saved by faith. I think any serious study of Acts must keep this observation in mind." What Forlines proposes is that O. T. believers (whether Jew or Gentile) knew enough of the character of God, the necessity for righteousness, and the promise of the Messiah that they savingly "believed" (Gen. 15:6) according to the light of revelation they had at the time. In effect, they exercised saving faith in *anticipation* of the redemptive work of the Messiah according to those promises and as symbolized in the sacrifices and offerings of the O. T. dispensation (Forlines, *Romans* 102-109). There were many alive and active during the ministry of the Lord Jesus and the time frame of the Acts record.

In that sense, saving faith today is *retrospective* in that we look back historically on the completed work of the Messiah. Faith has always been the condition for personal salvation (Gal. 3:6-7). The issue in this regard is the object of faith, whether the *promises* of the Messiah who would come or the *Person* of the Messiah who did come.

Forlines (*Quest* 388-390) asserts that, in the time of the Gospels and the Book of Acts, there were many who were O. T. saints and were therefore already "saved," but their faith needed "updating." When informed about the Messiah, they readily put their faith in Him, thus, completing or fulfilling their faith. At that particular time, saving faith for some would have included a dimension of updating, completing, or refocusing. The point is well taken, but the following observations must be considered.

An analysis of the Gospels and the Book of Acts, reveals that people were not all on the same level of enlightenment. There is not room for a fuller treatment here, but for the sake of making this point, the people fall into the following broad categories: (1) faithful Jews (O. T. saints), (2) religious Jews (ethnically), (3) proselytes, and (4) God-fearers (Sproul 181). I would add that Acts also includes, as yet another category, those Gentiles who had never heard of the Jewish Messianic promises and so were not persons of faith. These are illustrated by the Gentiles whom Paul reached on his missionary journeys.

The first group, faithful Jews/O. T. saints, I would define as those Jews who had genuine faith in the Messianic promises of the O. T. I think it can be reasonably concluded that at the time of the ministry of Jesus Himself, there were many in this category, awaiting the coming of the Messiah. This would include, for example, both parents of Jesus, as well as Simeon and Anna (Lk. 2:25-38).

Beginning with the preparatory ministry of John the Baptist (Mt. 3:1-2; Lk. 3:1-17; Acts 13:24-25), the general public was made aware of the soon coming Messiah. When those who were already faithful Jews/O. T. saints heard Jesus, they readily put their faith in *Him* because they were already "believers." The Lord Jesus became the object of their faith as the fulfillment of the Messianic promises. The same can be said of Jesus' apostles as represented by Andrew, Philip, Nathaniel, and Simon Peter since we have their stories (Jn. 1:35-51). All these would represent the remnant prophecies of the O. T. (Isa. 46:3; Joel 2:32; Rom. 11:5), which generationally extended to the time of Christ. In this regard, when they became personally acquainted with Jesus, they "updated" or re-focused their faith to Him. Jesus' encounter with the Samaritan woman at Jacob's well reveals that there was a remnant knowledge of the Messiah even among the Samaritans (4:25-26, 42). Many responded with faith in Him (4:39-42).

I think this analysis would account, in part anyway, for the early "success" of the Lord Jesus as people heard Him and responded with "updated" faith. It also accounts for some of the success of the gospel among the Jews and Samaritans in the first eight chapters of the Book of Acts. There were thousands who responded to the Spirit-empowered proclamation from the apostles that the Messiah had come. Some would have seen and heard Jesus themselves. Upon hearing the testimony of the apostles that Jesus was the Messiah and the validation of His resurrection they re-focused their faith to Him.

In the second category were those who were ethnically Jews and religious, who were antagonistic to Christ and His followers. These were the religious elite, including most of the Pharisees and perhaps all of the Sadducees. They had political and religious self-interests that superseded O. T. Messianic promises and provided filters through which they reinterpreted those promises. Hence their conflicts with Jesus. They had no interest in the claim that Jesus of Nazareth was the Messiah. Some, however, like Saul of Tarsus, did come to saving faith in Christ.

Next, in the third category, were the proselytes (TDNT VI:730-744). These were Gentiles who had come to faith in the God of Israel (2:10). Jewish traditions provided different standings and different degrees of Temple access for proselytes depending on their degree of commitment and personal situations. Nicolas of Antioch (6:5) was a proselyte and one of those chosen to assist the apostles in the serving of widows. He would be one in this category who, like some of the faithful Jews, "updated" or re-focused his faith to the person of Christ.

Finally, in the fourth category, were the God-fearers (10:2; 13:16, 26, 43; 17:4, 17): Gentiles, like Cornelius, who might be afforded some synagogue access but very limited Temple access. These were not necessarily proselytes (Polhill, *Acts* 252), but being defined as such shows that these, also, had a higher degree of enlightenment about the God of Israel (TDNT IX:212-214). It is not clear that God-fearers knew the promises of the Messiah. That would depend on the extent of their exposure to, and teaching in, the O. T.

From the witness in Antioch of Syria (11:19-26) through the rest of the Acts narrative, the largest group to receive the gospel message were the Gentiles who had probably never heard of the Jewish Messiah. Though Paul always went first to the synagogues, inevitably he turned to the Gentiles with the gospel. The Gentiles who believed the gospel, unless they were already Jewish proselytes, did so without the amount of biblical enlightenment afforded to others. Their saving faith was equally valid.

Where does Cornelius fit in this consideration? It is clear that Cornelius was very sincere and engaged in his faith-practices, even to the point that they were memorialized before the Lord (10:4). It is not recorded, however, to what extent his faith was defined by the promise of the Messiah. We are told that when Peter reported his visit to Cornelius, he added the detail that the angel of the Lord said he needed to be "saved" (11:14). It appears, then, that Cornelius was not a Gentile "O. T. saint" but a sincere, religious man who believed in the God of Israel and needed to hear the gospel of Jesus Christ so he could be saved. The manner in which he and Peter were providentially directed by the Lord to a circumstance in which he could hear the gospel also shows that those who fit this "category" needed the rest of the story about the Messiah in order to be saved.

Up to this point in Acts there have been conversion examples that cover the salvation standing of those in the previous categories. This gives rise to a question: At what point in time and in the scheme of redemption did the O. T. "arrangement" cease to be sufficient and the necessity of the N. T. focus of faith begin? That issue is certainly involved in understanding the Book of Acts. Luke's inspired account records the beginning of the church's obedience to the Great Commission, which requires a present faith in the gospel of Christ. This, in turn, implies the shift in "arrangement" that would cover the time frame of Acts—as indicated by the stories of Apollos and the Ephesian disciples (18:24—19:7).

Historically, the whole scheme of redemption was implemented over a long period of time. From the fall of man and his judgment, the Lord has promised a redeemer for fallen humanity (Gen. 3:15). Centuries passed before He chose Abraham as the progenitor of a covenant people. Centuries more passed before He would first model redemption via a sacrificial system and ultimately produce the Messiah, Jesus Christ. Until the time of His first coming, people were saved by their faith in the promise of a redeemer. The Scriptures record the faith of some during these times: people like Noah, Melchizedek, Naaman the Syrian, and others. The point here is that, unless one wants to consider Genesis 3:15 as the starting date, there is no particular time given when the O. T. "arrangement" began, but it is clear that it did.

With all due respect to strict dispensationalists, I do not regard biblical history to be as divided as their view calls for. However, a specific distinction of revelatory eras is given in Luke 16:16 between the time of "the law and the prophets" and "the kingdom of God" with the ministry of John the Baptist as the hinge. By "revelatory eras" I mean the plan or scheme of progressive revelation by which God administers His will for this world (EDT 321). I find very appealing the analogy of N. T. Wright (*Perspective*

170-172), who treats the Bible as a metanarrative in a five-act play.

That being said, from the very beginning of the proclamation of the gospel in Acts (2:14-40), it appears that the presupposition was that men must *presently* and *personally* believe in Jesus Christ in order to be saved (3:12-26; 4:12; 5:31). The question asked by those who heard Peter on the Day of Pentecost was, "What must we do to be saved"? Peter gave them a specific answer (2:38-40). Their submission to believer's baptism indicates that they had come to a personal faith in the person of Jesus as the Messiah.

I believe this also means the time of Christ's life on earth, as recorded in the Gospels, was a time of transition from the O. T. era to the N. T. era (Mk. 1:15; Lk. 16:16). I would regard the time as one of *fulfillment*, based on Matthew 5:17-18 (Moo 347). With respect to traditional dispensationalists (like J. N. Darby, C. I. Scofield, James M. Gray, and others), I am not proposing the particular framework they have outlined, although, as dispensationalist Wayne Strickland rightly states, "There are compelling reasons to understand a basic discontinuity between Old and New Testaments" (Moo 262). I take it that the Book of Acts defines this discontinuity with specific conversion stories covering these categories of enlightenment.

There are numerous other such transitions recorded in the Acts narrative. Of necessity, with the new dispensation of the Messiah—that is, the "church age"— and its redemptive provision for people of all nations, came a new faith culture. Preeminent among these transitional elements is further N. T. revelation. Others include the establishing of the church, universal and local; the shift in worship from the Temple in Jerusalem to each believer as the "Temple of the Lord" (1 Cor. 6:19) and to the local church-gathering of believers as the place for corporate worship. There were also new leadership positions, as seen in the offices of the apostles, pastors, and deacons. This would include the expansion of the covenant promises of God to include all believers, Jews and Gentiles (Gal. 3:7-14). There were major changes in table fellowship. Certainly, an expanded ministry of the Holy Spirit in the lives of believers was initiated (Jn. 16:13-14). Other transitions may be noted but these serve to make the point.

My conclusions about the transitions in the Book of Acts, then, are these. First, while it is impossible for us to pinpoint just exactly when the O. T. "arrangement" ceased, it did (Lk. 16:16). I would, therefore, regard the Book of Acts as the record of the *termination* of the dispensation of "the law and the prophets," a time that allowed for transitional phases. For example, the updating of the faith of Apollos and the Ephesian disciples, who knew only the baptism of John the Baptist (18:25; 19:1-7), would signal the termination time for those who responded to his preparatory ministry. Some consider these to be Christians already and are uncertain as to what exactly they needed with further instruction (Bruce, *Acts* 358; Polhill, *Acts* 396). Whatever else that may mean, at least they needed "updating" in their faith.

Second, our theological understanding of the concept of being "saved" must include the object of saving faith (Forlines, *Arminianism* 254-257). One has to believe in the person of Jesus Christ in order to be saved. He cannot have authentic, saving faith in anything less (Picirilli, *Grace* 171). While there was a time when genuine faith in the *promise* of the Messiah was acceptable, that time passed. Saving faith had to be updated or re-focused to the *person* of the Messiah. As it relates to the Acts record, this would necessitate the transitional element that some were "updating" their faith. Theologically, then, the concept of saving faith or belief, in the Book of Acts, must include both those who had previously been saved according to the O. T. "arrangement" and those who were not. In either case, it is absolutely clear that saving faith must be focused on the person of the resurrected Messiah, Jesus Christ.

Third, if indeed Acts is the termination of the O. T. "arrangement," there would not be any modern day "O. T. saints." The Jews in Rome who believed when they heard Paul's gospel instruction, as Acts closes, would be the last of the "O. T. saints" whose faith needed updating. There may be similar circumstances, of course, but no actual "O. T. saints," Jewish or Gentile, who continued to be such after the conclusion of Acts (see further commentary on Apollos and the Ephesian Disciples in the discussion of 18:24—19:7).

Fourth, and perhaps ultimately, we need to remember that redemption and all the necessary provisions for it are entirely given by the grace of God (Ps. 3:8; Jn. 2:9). That He sets time boundaries, i.e., "dispensations," should come as no surprise (Rom. 11:5, 25; Acts 17:30-31), but we would be wise not to be too specific about the boundaries. We are just challenged to chart their courses in the Scriptures.

It is understood that there are other discussions implied, especially along the lines of missiology. Those must be reserved for other contexts. The mission of the early church as recorded in Acts was to proclaim the gospel with the understanding that all men everywhere needed to hear its truth and presently, personally be saved by faith.

It should be noted, also, that of the numerous writers and commentators on Acts and related themes consulted, there is almost no discussion about this transitional shift or the re-focusing of faith from the promise of the Messiah to the person of the Messiah. Most, if not all, appear to assume that all who needed to hear the gospel in Acts, no matter the level of their existing enlightenment, needed to be saved. Little regard seems to be given to there being "O. T. saints" whose faith needed updating. Bock (592) comes closest, in commenting on Apollos, when he states that Apollos is a figure caught up in transition and needs to be brought up to date. His faith was incomplete. Bock (599) offers the same view of the Ephesian disciples (Acts 19:1-7) whose faith needed "finishing." Keener appropriately states (I:438, 439) "Luke-Acts seeks to continue the Biblical story by pivoting it, albeit in a way predicted and prefigured earlier in the story...Without denigrating the foundational story of Israel, Luke-Acts redirects the focus from heritage to mission."

Another concern expressed by some writers is the issue of sources for Luke's account of the conversion of Cornelius (Haenchen 355-363; Keener II:1731-1732). The extensive details are interpreted by some to be contrived and redacted to fit Luke's intentions. However, this view is extreme and imposed (Marshall, *Acts* 182). There is nothing that would have prevented

Luke's personal interviews with both Cornelius and Peter about the incident. In fact, if Luke and Acts are taken together (and they should be, see Introduction) then the source material is drawn directly from "eyewitnesses" (Lk. 1:2). Unless one has an alternative agenda that proves the contrary, it is unnecessary to propose that Luke was anything but truthful and factual in the account.

Returning to the text, the setting of the narrative about the conversion of Cornelius is the seaport city of Caesarea (v. 1). Formerly known as "Strato's Tower," it was built to prominence by Herod the Great and its name changed to honor Caesar (Jones 90-91). As such it became a Roman provincial capital and necessitated the presence of a military garrison. There were no legions in Judaea (Marshall, *Acts* 183) but auxiliary units were. This explains why Cornelius was there.

A number of details about Cornelius are given (vv. 1-2), beginning with his military affiliation. A Roman legion consisted of six thousand men commanded by a *Legatus legionis* (a general). A legion was divided into ten cohorts of six hundred men each and commanded by a tribune (21:31, "Claudius Lysias"). A cohort was further divided into six centuries of one hundred men in each century, commanded by a centurion (EHB 507). As a rule there would be fifty-nine centurions in a legion with the ranking centurion in command of the first two centuries (Fitzmyer 449). Cornelius was a centurion connected with a cohort named "The Italian band" or "The Italian Cohort," so-called because they all originated in Italy. Some writers further identify this particular cohort as an auxiliary unit of archers (Keener II:1737;

Polhill, *Acts* 251). In his position, Cornelius would have been well paid and well positioned in society.

Integral to the account (v. 2) is the fact that Cornelius was "devout" (Greek *eusebes*, pious) and a "God-fearer," literally, "one fearing God." This term was used of Gentiles who had come to believe in the God of Israel but had limited access to synagogue and Temple participation (13:16, 26, 43; 17:4, 17). Most writers distinguish between a "proselyte" and a "God-fearer." No details are given about his spiritual journey but Romans were notoriously polytheistic. By implication, something or someone had influenced him away from the Roman gods to embrace the Lord God of Israel, at least as far as he understood at the time. Furthermore, he has led "all his house" to that point of faith. A Roman household not only included immediate family but all who might be slaves as well (Keener II:1745). His influence can be seen by the others he gathered to hear Peter (v. 24). As a man noted for his good deeds and prayer, he had lived what he professed.

The "ninth hour of the day" (3:00 p.m.) was a traditional time of Jewish prayer (Dan. 6:10), coinciding with the afternoon burnt offering. As Cornelius goes about the routines of his faith (v. 3), the "angel of the Lord" spoke to him (v. 2), calling his name. Never trivialize the routines of the disciplines of faith. Does God hear the prayers of unsaved folks? God hears everything. He answers those prayers according to His sovereign will, but we can expect that the prayers of one who is seeking the Lord has first been prompted by the Holy Spirit (Ps. 65:2; Jn. 16:7-11).

It must be asked, in what sense were the prayers and alms-deeds of Cornelius accepted as a *memorial* (Greek *mnemoskunon*, a memorial offering) before God (v. 4)? The language is that of sacrificial offering (Ex. 17:14; Lev. 2:9). However, it is not to be understood as sufficient for redemption but for further enlightenment (Bock 387). In this sense, Cornelius can be understood as a "seeker" after the Lord who has some spiritual light but needs more. And in this sense, God responds by giving him more light.

The light that is given to Cornelius is in the form of instruction to find a certain messenger, Simon Peter (v. 5), who will tell him what he needs to know. The angel includes the place where he may be found (v. 6). Though not recorded here, later Peter will add that Cornelius would be told what he needed to know in order to be saved (11:14). His spiritual interest is piqued but not satisfied until Peter arrives several days later (v. 33). In one regard, the angel could have simply told Cornelius about the Lord Jesus since angels attended every facet of the gospel story, but God has ordained that men be His instruments in proclaiming that truth (2 Cor. 1:21).

As a man of duty and command, Cornelius immediately obeyed the directions of the heavenly messenger by sharing his experience with two servants and a loyal soldier who also was "devout." That Cornelius shared his experience with these men suggests a common spiritual relationship. These three were charged with the task of going to Joppa to find Simon Peter and escort him back to Caesarea (vv. 7-8).

2. The vision of Peter (10:9-16)

9 On the morrow, as they went on their journey, and drew nigh unto the city, Peter went up upon the housetop to pray about the sixth hour:
10 And he became very hungry, and would have eaten: but while they made ready, he fell into a trance,
11 And saw heaven opened, and a certain vessel descending unto him, as it had been a great sheet knit at the four corners, and let down to the earth:
12 Wherein were all manner of fourfooted beasts of the earth, and wild beasts, and creeping things, and fowls of the air.
13 And there came a voice to him, Rise, Peter; kill, and eat.
14 But Peter said, Not so, Lord; for I have never eaten any thing that is common or unclean.
15 And the voice *spake* unto him again the second time, What God hath cleansed, *that* call not thou common.
16 This was done thrice: and the vessel was received up again into heaven.

Joppa was some thirty miles south of Caesarea and a full day's journey. Apparently, the three men selected to represent Cornelius immediately set out on their trip to find Peter. The day following they approached the city of Joppa about noon ("the sixth hour"). In the meantime, Peter had gone to the rooftop of Simon's house to pray (v. 9). The rooftops in the architecture of houses at that time accommodated many activities for its dwellers, not the least of which was its setting for personal prayer. A simple act in the course of the day would prove to be life changing for Peter personally and historic in the whole scheme of the gospel.

Generally, meals were served mid-morning and late afternoon, but that does not prevent one from getting hungry at other times. The word translated "very hungry" (Greek *prospeinos*) is used only here in the N. T. and is only found elsewhere in a medical reference outside the N. T. (Moulton and Milligan 550; Bock 388). Its usage, along with the phrase "knit at the four corners" (v. 11) which specifically was used of bandages, lends support to the proposal that Luke was a doctor.

While waiting for a noon-day snack (v. 11), Peter fell into a "trance" (Greek *ekstasis*). Taken with the word "vision" (Greek *horama*) in verse 17, this mental-spiritual state of mind was a means of God communicating directly with someone (11:5; 16:9; 22:17). Peter's interaction in the process shows that he was not "out of control" but thoughtful and able to communicate (Bock 388-389). It should be obvious that the vision coincided with Peter's hunger. God is able to use any particular need we have to teach us what we need to know.

The vision entailed a large sheet, perhaps in the form of a ship's sail or sheet of linen, that was tied at the four corners and contained all sorts of animals, including fowls and reptiles (vv. 11-12). According to O. T. dietary laws, some were clean, but even then would have to be ritually cleansed before eating. Others were unclean and ordinarily off limits, to Jews, for food.

The command to Peter to kill, prepare, and eat to satisfy his hunger (v. 13) and his reply (v. 14) indicates that, at first, Peter simply did not understand the vision—which is not surprising. This was complicated in his mind by the interpre-

tation that was given to him (v. 15). There is no doubt that Peter thought he had been obedient to the Lord and His dietary laws (Lev. 20:25-26), hence his negative reply to the command. It is commonly said that one cannot properly say, "Not so" and "Lord" in the same sentence and claim to have a heart of submission. True, but Peter is expressing the food traditions of hundreds of years as well as his life-long personal practice. In one fell swoop, all that is now challenged. Obedience to new truth is often hesitant.

That being the case, this was not the first time Peter had heard food laws addressed. Jesus had already spoken to the deeper issues involved (Mk. 7:14-23), but apparently Peter had not made the association. Like planted seed, truth must have time to take root and grow. However, the Lord was persistent in this particular time of teaching. Peter's position as an apostle, his personal grasp of the larger truths intended, and the soon coming mission to the house of Cornelius all converge with the vision. Therefore, the vision was repeated three times (v. 16) to reinforce the importance of the truth intended, as well as to overcome Peter's probable reticence. Peter's spiritual needs were often addressed in "three's": his three-fold denial, his three-fold restoration, now the thrice-repeated vision. This is one reason why he is often portrayed as impetuous. But some of the Lord's greatest truths were revealed through this unique man (Mt. 16:16-17; Acts 2:14-36).

With respect to the larger intended meaning of the vision regarding people, many writers agree that this vision also intended to change the food laws and traditions—which had major social implications (Bock 390; Polhill, *Acts*

255-256; Marshall, *Acts* 186). Food laws symbolized religious and social separation of Jews from Gentiles. Often times the food of Gentiles had previously been offered to idols, rendering it off limits for Jews (an issue dealt with extensively by Paul; see 1 Cor. 8:1—11:1). Even meats that were considered clean might not have been properly prepared, thus rendering them unclean (Bock 389-390). On that basis, Peter could go to the house of Cornelius and then answer with a clear conscience those who challenged him about it (10:34; 11:2-3). Later, the issue of table fellowship will be addressed (15:20-29), but as a matter of cultural deference.

3. Peter's witness to the household of Cornelius (10:17-48)

a. Peter meets the representatives of Cornelius (10:17-23a)

17 Now while Peter doubted in himself what this vision which he had seen should mean, behold, the men which were sent from Cornelius had made enquiry for Simon's house, and stood before the gate.
18 And called, and asked whether Simon, which was surnamed Peter, were lodged there.
19 While Peter thought on the vision, the Spirit said unto him, Behold, three men seek thee.
20 Arise therefore, and get thee down, and go with them, doubting nothing: for I have sent them.
21 Then Peter went down to the men which were sent unto him from Cornelius; and said, Behold, I am he whom ye seek: what is the cause wherefore ye are come?

22 And they said, Cornelius the centurion, a just man, and one that feareth God, and of good report among all the nation of the Jews, was warned from God by an holy angel to send for thee into his house, and to hear words of thee.
23a Then called he them in, and lodged *them.*

There was much to consider. The vision had given Peter considerable food for thought (v. 17). As he tarried on the roof he "doubted" (Greek *diaporeo*) in himself; that is, he was perplexed, utterly at a loss over the meaning of the vision. At that very time the men sent by Cornelius arrived at the house gate, inquiring for him (v. 18). The Holy Spirit interrupted Peter's thoughts by directly speaking to him (vv. 19-20). He informed Peter of the men's presence and instructed him to meet them and go with them. Some manuscripts read "two men" instead of "three," but "three" is best and is confirmed by 10:7 and 11:11 (Metzger 328). The men had actually been sent on mission by the Holy Spirit.

The hand of God is very evident in the details of the whole scenario, not the least of which is the timing of the men's arrival at the house of Simon the tanner while Peter was trying to figure out just what the vision meant. Even the instructions issued by Cornelius to the men is to be understood as the means of the Holy Spirit's sending ("I have sent them"). Sometimes ordinary instructions have an extraordinary source.

One can imagine the piqued interest of both parties as they met at the gate of Simon's house (v. 21). Peter's question about their purpose for seeking him had to be spiced with more than just curiosity. After all, he was still perplexed about the vision and there were Gentiles wanting to talk with him. But Peter was a man of spiritual integrity. By then he knew enough and had seen enough to follow the Lord's direction, even when he did not necessarily understand all that was taking place. Understanding often accompanies obedience.

The response of Cornelius' committee to Peter (v. 22) conveyed three things: the spiritual devotion of Cornelius, the visit of the angel of God to him, and the request for Peter to come to the house of Cornelius with whatever message he needed to share. Their wording reflects not just their carefully prepared report but also their spiritual interest. They also wanted to know what Peter knew.

The next step may seem incidental but it is hugely important (v. 23a). Gentiles were invited to enter a Jewish house where an apostle was staying, and remain for the night! That, of course, meant all that would be necessitated by the hospitality including eating a meal. The open door of hospitality was significant, but small, in comparison to the open door of the gospel to the rest of humanity. The conversations that night must have been arresting!

b. Exchange between Peter and Cornelius in Caesarea (10:23b-33)

23b And on the morrow Peter went away with them, and certain brethren from Joppa accompanied him.
24 And the morrow after they entered Caesarea. And Cornelius waited for them, and had called together his kinsmen and near friends.
25 And as Peter was coming in, Cornelius met him, and fell down at his feet, and worshipped *him.*
26 But Peter took him up, saying, Stand up; I myself also am a man.
27 And as he talked with him, he went in, and found many that were come together.
28 And he said unto them, Ye know how that it is an unlawful thing for a man that is a Jew to keep company, or come unto one of another nation; but God hath shewed me that I should not call any man common or unclean.
29 Therefore came I *unto you* without gainsaying, as soon as I was sent for: I ask therefore for what intent ye have sent for me?
30 And Cornelius said, Four days ago I was fasting until this hour; and at the ninth hour I prayed in my house, and, behold, a man stood before me in bright clothing,
31 And said, Cornelius, thy prayer is heard, and thine alms are had in remembrance in the sight of God.
32 Send therefore to Joppa, and call hither Simon, whose surname is Peter; he is lodged in the house of *one* Simon a tanner by the sea side: who, when he cometh, shall speak unto thee.
33 Immediately therefore I sent to thee; and thou has well done that thou art come. Now therefore are we all here present before God, to hear all things that are commanded thee of God.

Though this even might not have seemed so significant at the time, never has there been a more important group on a more important mission than these ten men (10:19; 11:12). The Committee of Five, appointed on June 11, 1776, by the Continental Congress to draft a declaration of independence from British authority, acted in the founding of a nation that would impact history. Even more significantly, this group of ten men acted on behalf of Heaven to open the door for the gospel to the Gentiles, thus impacting eternity. Their journey to Caesarea included an overnight stay (vv. 23b-24) making for a turnaround time of four days (v. 30).

Awaiting their arrival, Cornelius had gathered family and close friends (v. 24b) to hear what Peter had to say. Implied is their respect for Cornelius and some degree of personal interest as well. Peter's message would, indeed, apply and impact all who heard his truth (v. 44).

It would have been surprising to see the powerful centurion as he fell at Peter's feet and "worshipped" him (v. 25). The word so translated (Greek *proskuneo*) was probably meant as an acceptable action of respect and homage, not of deity worship (Robertson, *Acts* 140; Polhill, *Acts* 258). For a normally haughty, powerful, Roman military leader to fall at the feet of a common Jewish man shows an inner change of attitude. For a Jewish man to be in that position shows the same. Regardless how Cornelius meant his expression, Peter did not want any misunderstandings of his status. Assisting him to arise (v. 26), he assured Cornelius and those observing that he was merely a man, not deity or even a heavenly messenger (compare 14:13-18). He did bear a heavenly message, however.

As they entered the house proper (v. 27), polite conversation quickly turned more substantive. A large number of people waited expectantly to hear what this Jewish man had to say to them that was so important. Peter began with a statement (vv. 28-29) of something he had just learned that occasioned his coming to the house of Cornelius, though he did not tell them of his vision experience. Assuming they knew the Jewish tradition that prohibited social interaction with Gentiles, he declared God had taught him that he should no longer judge any person to be "common or unclean"; both terms refer to ceremonial uncleanness. He had made the connection between the Lord's declaration in his vision (v. 15) and its intention about all people. That in itself was an incredible admission since social and religious customs are among the most binding in relationships. On that basis Peter had consented to come to Caesarea without hesitation ("gainsaying"), but he did not yet fully understand the significance of the vision. And for that reason he asked what they wanted with him (v. 29).

Verses 30-33 contain the reply of Cornelius, reiterating the details of his own vision (vv. 3-6). He concludes with his obedience to the directions given to him and a compliment to Peter for his coming. The reply makes the purpose of the visit clear: God has directed them privately that they may meet publicly in this setting. Therefore, their meeting must be very important. Having said that, neither does Cornelius know just exactly what they needed to hear from Peter. But Peter does know what they needed to know. And they are all ready to listen. One could not hope for a more receptive audience.

c. Peter's message to the household of Cornelius (10:34-43)

34 Then Peter opened *his* mouth, and said, Of a truth I perceive that God is no respecter of persons:
35 But in every nation he that feareth him, and worketh righteousness, is accepted with him.
36 The word which *God* sent unto the children of Israel, preaching peace by Jesus Christ: (he is Lord of all:)
37 That word, *I say,* ye know, which was published throughout all Judaea, and began from Galilee, after the baptism which John preached;
38 How God anointed Jesus of Nazareth with the Holy Ghost and with power: who went about doing good, and healing all that were oppressed of the devil, for God was with him.
39 And we are witnesses of all things which he did both in the land of the Jews, and in Jerusalem; whom they slew and hanged on a tree:
40 Him God raised up the third day, and shewed him openly;
41 Not to all the people, but unto witnesses chosen before God, *even* to us, who did eat and drink with him after he rose from the dead.
42 And he commanded us to preach unto the people, and to testify that it is he which was ordained of God *to be* the Judge of the quick and dead.
43 To him give all the prophets witness, that through his name whosoever believeth in him shall receive remission of sins.

What Peter knows that Cornelius needs to know begins with Peter putting the final piece of the puzzle together about the ultimate meaning of his vision in Joppa (vv. 34-35). That vision was not about dietary adjustments or even about removing barriers to social interaction with people (v. 28). The vision was about the fact that "God is no respecter of persons" and the implications of that truth with regard to the gospel of Christ. That truth is now pivotal in the whole scheme of redemptive history and should be explored.

The word translated "respecter of persons" (Greek *prosopolemptes*) is a compound word used only here in the N. T., literally meaning to lift up or receive a face. This idiomatic expression means that God does not judge anyone on the basis of what the face represents, including the person's status or ethnic background. Succinctly, God does not discriminate or show partiality. But this does not mean that God has recently changed in His character or person. He has always been loving and gracious, making provision for "the stranger" (Ex. 12:48, 49; Lev. 16:29; 19:33-34; Isa. 56:3-7), and commanding His people to love others as He does (Mt. 22:39). And He is immutable (Heb. 13:8). Of course, this does not mean God has had a change in attitude, but it does mean a change is required of His people in order to extend the gospel "to the uttermost part of the earth" (1:8). The old barriers must come down. No one is any longer to be judged as "common or unclean." It appears that Peter (and all those who previously thought the same way) had for all these years missed the ultimate point about laws and traditions. These were meant to be distinctive features to identify the Jews. They were not about the character of God or the value He placed on people. Peter has now come to understand a greater truth about the Lord and about himself.

It must be asked in what sense is fearing the Lord and working righteousness acceptable to God (v. 35)? What is the reward to which Peter alludes? Clearly, Peter does not mean that fearing God and doing righteousness earn forgiveness of sin or justification from sin. If this were the case there would be no need to know more and there would have been no purpose for Peter's visit. Rather, Peter means the acceptability of people regardless of race or rank (Stott 198-199; Bock 396). This acceptability is not earned by doing righteousness, but it is the reward of faith, albeit incomplete faith, and it leads to being given the privilege to learn more—light that was insufficient for salvation but sufficient for further light (Polhill, *Acts* 261).

Peter then proceeds to share the gospel of Jesus Christ, the "kerygma" (the basic gospel message) he initiated on the Day of Pentecost. The basics are the same, but there are a few notable additions. Among them is the fact that Cornelius was already aware of the public ministry of Jesus ("that word....you know," v. 37). Interestingly, this reveals that Jesus was the topic of public information and discussion. That really should not come as a surprise given the widespread scrutiny He received from both religious and political leaders (26:26).

Peter makes four summary statements (vv. 38-43). First, he speaks of the public ministry of Jesus of Nazareth (vv. 38-39a), a ministry empowered by the Holy Spirit (Lk. 4:14) and evidenced by deeds of mercy and overcoming evil. The phrase "went about doing good"

speaks of one engaged in deeds that benefit society (Bock 397-398). We would call this kind of person a "public servant" and vote to give him or her honor and recognition. Ironically, Jesus was deemed a threat and condemned to die. Peter himself witnessed these deeds.

Next, he speaks of Jesus' death and resurrection (vv. 39b-40). His death is characterized as being "hanged on a tree," an allusion to Deuteronomy 21:22-23 (Gal. 3:13). The O. T. statement saw its fullest application in the cross of Christ. But the "curse" of being crucified was overcome by His resurrection from the dead as a direct action of God.

Third, Peter asserts that the resurrected Christ was openly seen but not by the general public. Those who were privileged to be His witnesses (v. 41) shared meals and times of interaction with Him during His post-resurrection days (1:3). They were "commanded" (a term Cornelius would certainly understand) to preach and teach (v. 42) that this Jesus was "ordained of God" as to be the final Judge of all people, the "quick" (living) and the dead.

Finally, Peter references the authority of the O. T. prophets whose Messianic promises preceded and prepared people for this very time and person. Further, he ties all the previous vision truths, which both he and Cornelius have learned, to the message he has just delivered. He does this with an all-inclusive appeal: "Whosoever believeth in him shall receive remission of sins" (v. 43). As Stott (191) asserts, "Jesus is Lord of all (v. 36), Judge of all (v. 42) and Savior of all (v. 43)."

At this point, Peter has told Cornelius and his household guests what they needed to know in fulfillment of the directives given to both himself and Cornelius. The message did not fall on deaf ears as the next part of the story unfolds.

d. The Holy Spirit falls on the household of Cornelius (10:44-48)

44 While Peter yet spake these words, the Holy Ghost fell on all them which heard the word.
45 And they of the circumcision which believed were astonished, as many as came with Peter, because that on the Gentiles also was poured out the gift of the Holy Ghost.
46 For they heard them speak with tongues, and magnify God. Then answered Peter,
47 Can any man forbid water, that these should not be baptized, which have received the Holy Ghost as well as we?
48 And he commanded them to be baptized in the name of the Lord. Then prayed they him to tarry certain days.

There was an immediate reaction to the culminating truth of Peter's message that "whosoever believeth in him shall receive remission of sins" (v. 43). As Peter was speaking, the Holy Spirit "fell on them which heard the word" (v. 44): namely, the Gentiles in the household of Cornelius. They began to manifest the presence of the Holy Spirit with the gift of tongues (v. 46). This signals the final stage of witness "to the uttermost part of the earth" (1:8), just as the previous stages were so evidenced (2:1-11; 8:17). What happened in Cornelius' house is often termed "the Gentile Pentecost"

(Bruce, *Acts* 216; Bock 400; Polhill, *Acts* 264).

Perhaps Peter himself was not surprised at the response, but the believing Jews ("they of the circumcision which believed") who came with him from Joppa certainly were (v. 45). They had not yet reached full understanding of the visions shared by both Peter and Cornelius. While it is possible that these men were not present at Pentecost, they certainly knew of the ministry of the Holy Spirit. The undeniable evidence of God's work was manifested before them audibly and visibly.

To confirm even further the salvation response of these Gentiles, Peter asked, somewhat rhetorically, if anyone could offer any reasons why they should not be baptized (v. 47). The wording is similar to the request of the Ethiopian eunuch in 8:36 where the same root word (Greek *koluo*) is translated "hinder" and "forbid." The idea is that the same faith in the same gospel should not "hinder" anyone from being baptized, particularly these Gentiles who have now become fellow believers. Perhaps, Peter sensed some reticence on the part of his companions to accept what they were seeing. Believer's baptism would certainly help to confirm to them the reality of the saving faith of Cornelius and his household. Furthermore, Peter made it clear that the experience of the Gentiles in the reception of the Holy Spirit was the same as theirs. With that he directed them to be baptized (v. 48). Bock (401) rightly observes the activity of the Trinity in the story. God the Father directs. The Son is the Savior. The Holy Spirit confirms.

This part of the narrative concludes with Peter staying with Cornelius for several days (v. 48). Luke does not say how long. Apparently, it was long enough to necessitate table fellowship and instruction in discipleship for the new converts. This gave time for whatever social awkwardness there might have been to begin dissipation in the newly discovered truth of the fellowship of all believers in Christ. While this might not have been difficult for Peter, who was prepared for it by direct vision from God, it was for those back in Jerusalem who heard about it.

4. Peter's testimony of the conversion of the household of Cornelius (11:1-18)

a. Contention with Peter at Jerusalem (11:1-3)

1 And the apostles and brethren that were in Judaea heard that the Gentiles had also received the word of God.
2 And when Peter was come up to Jerusalem, they that were of the circumcision contended with him,
3 Saying, Thou wentest in to men uncircumcised, and didst eat with them.

Peter's visit with Cornelius was soon known back in Jerusalem and became major news (v. 1). It was rightly reported that the door of the gospel ("the word of God") had opened among the Gentiles and they had received it. This was nothing short of revolutionary to the cause of Christ, but it was troubling to some. In any group of believers there are different levels of faith and maturity.

It is entirely appropriate that the rest of the apostles be apprised of Peter's experience with Cornelius. After all,

being entrusted with the responsibility for leadership in the early years of the church, they needed to know what he knew. He was not summoned to Jerusalem but when he does returned he was confronted by those "of the circumcision." Some interpreters distinguish these as a strict, extremist group of believers who held views different from those of the apostles and larger assembly (Polhill, *Acts* 266). The phrase, however, could relate to every person of traditional Jewish birth (Stott 194). Even if this was a minority group, they raised a legitimate question. As yet, all the believers at Jerusalem, regardless of their standing, were not aware of Peter's vision and its truth. What might have been verbalized by a few was probably in the minds of the rest. It is also ironic that the apostles as a group were facing their own situation involving interaction with "sinners" just as did Jesus (Lk. 5:27-32; 15:1-2). They needed them to become more Christ-like.

But the meeting with Peter involved more than just a question of courtesy. Nor did his position as a leading apostle place his actions above questioning. He was confronted over eating with Gentiles. Interestingly, nothing is said about his proclamation of the gospel to those Gentiles, or about the manifestation of the Holy Spirit, or about baptizing them as they responded in saving faith. We may find it hard to understand the gravity of their thinking, but their thinking was the filter through which everything must pass, and which prioritized everything for them (Keener II:1818-1821). This may be the same group who later proposed that Gentiles had to be circumcised in order to be saved (15:1) but that is not clear. The charge of eating with Gentiles and breaking table traditions was exactly where the Lord had met Peter in the vision of the great sheet (10:11-16). That experience was Peter's answer to the charge.

b. Peter's testimony and the glorious agreement (11:4-18)

4 But Peter rehearsed *the matter* **from the beginning, and expounded** *it* **by order unto them, saying,**
5 I was in the city of Joppa praying: and in a trance I saw a vision, A certain vessel descend, as it had been a great sheet, let down from heaven by four corners; and it came even to me:
6 Upon the which when I had fastened mine eyes, I considered, and saw fourfooted beasts of the earth, and wild beasts, and creeping things, and fowls of the air.
7 And I heard a voice saying unto me, Arise, Peter; slay and eat.
8 But I said, Not so, Lord: for nothing common or unclean hath at any time entered into my mouth.
9 But the voice answered me again from heaven, What God hath cleansed, *that* **call not thou common.**
10 And this was done three times: and all were drawn up again into heaven.
11 And, behold, immediately there were three men already come unto the house where I was, sent from Caesarea unto me.
12 And the Spirit bade me go with them, nothing doubting. Moreover these six brethren accompanied me, and we entered the man's house:

13 And he shewed us how he had seen an angel in his house, which stood and said unto him, Send men to Joppa, and call for Simon, whose surname is Peter;
14 Who shall tell thee words, whereby thou and all thy house shall be saved.
15 And as I began to speak, the Holy Ghost fell on them, as on us at the beginning.
16 Then remembered I the word of the Lord, how that he said, John indeed baptized with water; but ye shall be baptized with the Holy Ghost.
17 Forasmuch then as God gave them the like gift as *he did* **unto us, who believed on the Lord Jesus Christ; what was I, that I could withstand God?**
18 When they heard these things, they held their peace, and glorified God, saying, Then hath God also to the Gentiles granted repentance unto life.

Peter repeats in extensive detail the vision given him while in Joppa (vv. 4-12). In doing so, he attributes the truth he learned and the directive to go with the men from Caesarea to the work of the Holy Spirit. It was a heavenly mission on which he was sent. The repetition emphasizes the importance of the event (and perhaps an admission of his own perplexity at the time). An added detail is that there were six believers (v. 12) who accompanied Peter from Joppa, in addition to the three from Cornelius. Apparently, these six men now stood with Peter in verification of his explanation ("these six men").

In verses 13-14, Peter summarizes the parallel vision of Cornelius. An added detail, however, provides more of the content of what the angel of the Lord had said to Cornelius. While Cornelius wasn't told the content of the words Peter would say, the purpose of those words was that he and his household might be saved.

Peter leaves no doubt (v. 15) that the manifestation of the Holy Spirit on the household of Cornelius was the same as what they had experienced on the Day of Pentecost: the same person of the Godhead and the same manifestation of tongues (see discussion on ch. 2). Peter sees in this (v. 17) that the Gentiles who have the same faith as they, in the same Savior as they, who possess the same Holy Spirit as they, are not to be regarded as "common or unclean" but as brothers in Christ. The promise (v. 16) of the Holy Spirit's manifestation as told by John (Mt. 3:11; Lk. 3:16) applies to Gentile believers as well as to them. Further, this was entirely the work of God Himself. That being the case, to refuse to obey the clear leading of the Lord would be tantamount to opposing God (v. 17).

Whatever the objections in the beginning, those who were opposed to Peter's visit to Cornelius are now completely silenced (v. 18). To their credit, they acknowledged the truth of Peter's testimony and agreed with his conclusion. Gentiles are now "granted repentance unto life." The changing of their minds represents the third "conversion" in the story. More importantly, it is clear that the Lord has directed in opening the door to the final stage where the gospel is to be proclaimed: namely, to "the uttermost part of the earth."

Summary
(10:1—11:18)

In the most extensive and detailed conversion story in Acts, Luke records the opening of the door of witness to the rest of the world beyond Judaea and Samaria. In complementary visions, the Lord prepared the hearts of a Roman centurion, Cornelius, and a Jewish apostle, Simon Peter, for their encounter. Two different worlds converged providentially for the purpose of communicating that the gospel of Jesus Christ is intended for all people everywhere. There had to be divine intervention and guidance for that to take place. To the credit of both Cornelius and Peter, they were obedient to God's leadership and instrumental in this next stage of witness.

The Lord directly intervened with both Cornelius and Peter. With Cornelius, it was in reward and promise of more to know. With Peter, it was in personal preparation to move beyond his religious exclusivism as the gospel required. When necessary and expedient to His plans, God interacts with people in this world to affirm His control and activity in the affairs of humanity. Of course, the Holy Spirit led in that process to record accurately the events, but the narrative describes how those men were re-telling what happened to them.

When word of the conversion of Cornelius and the role Peter played in it got back to the believers in Jerusalem, some were not ready to accept this new development. The "circumcision party" were less open to accepting Gentiles since the implications meant a change in their understanding of Jewish practices. They demanded an explanation from

Peter. Of course, Peter gladly re-told the story, including the visionary experience he had that prepared him for what he needed to do. His summary (11:17) was that the Gentiles were given the same gift of salvation and the same indwelling of the Holy Spirit that they had been given.

In what must be telling evidence of grace and spiritual growth, the "circumcision party" accepted Peter's story, concluding that what had happened was the work of God.

Application: Teaching and Preaching the Passage

Exegetical Outline of the Text: 1. The Vision of Cornelius (10:1-8). 2. The Vision of Peter (10:9-18). 3. The Messengers Arrive for Peter (10:19-23). 4. The Meeting with Cornelius (10:24-33). 5. Peter's Message to the Household of Cornelius (10:34-43). 6. The Conversion of Cornelius and His Household (10:44-48). 7. The Report Given to the Believers in Jerusalem (11:1-18).

There are many lessons and messages contained in this historic event. One area is how God takes the initiative in meeting with people. This can be traced in Acts right from the beginning, from the appearances of Jesus to the apostles to the Lord's appearance to Paul on the ship to Rome to reassure him.

One of the most obvious lessons is the difficulty of dealing with entrenched traditions that have taken a life of their own, as seen from Peter's vision. This is especially applicable in the lives of those who are called to ministry. Even the patience of the Lord in repeating the vision to Peter three times shows we sometimes struggle with growth even as

God is patient with our personal life-issues. This would extend to the way the report was received by those back in Jerusalem when they heard of Peter's involvement with Gentiles.

For a little more in-depth study one can examine the messages of Peter to find the common truths of the gospel and how he communicated them to different audiences.

D. The Establishing of the Church at Antioch (11:19-30)

1. Many at Antioch converted upon hearing the gospel (11:19-21)

19 Now they which were scattered abroad upon the persecution that arose about Stephen travelled as far as Phenice, and Cyprus, and Antioch, preaching the word to none but the Jews only.
20 And some of them were men of Cyprus and Cyrene, which, when they were come to Antioch, spake unto the Grecians, preaching the LORD Jesus.
21 And the hand of the Lord was with them: and a great number believed, and turned to the Lord.

Following the story of the conversion of Cornelius, Luke returns to the impact of the persecution of Stephen (8:1) upon the church. Instead of stopping the witness of the disciples it had rippling effects in sending the gospel out farther. Luke's purpose is to record the witness of the church to "the uttermost part of the earth." The Lord used persecution as one means to achieve that end (Rom. 8:28).

The timing of this expansion of the church's witness into Antioch, in relation to the conversion of Cornelius, is not clear. The account appears in the narrative following the conversion of Cornelius, but this advancement in witness is linked to persecution, not to visions. We simply do not know if the open door to the Gentiles, as represented in Cornelius' conversion, was known by those who were scattered by the persecution (v. 19). Regardless of motivation and circumstances, the result was the same. Perhaps Luke presents the information about Antioch as confirmation of the open door to the Gentiles but by others who were just as obedient to the Acts 1:8 command.

The initial witness of those who fled the persecution in Judaea was, at first, "unto the Jews only" (v. 19). But reluctance would be overcome by obedience as they gained opportunity. Their witness extended to the cities of the coastal plain area of Phoenicia (modern Lebanon) and to the island of Cyprus, which was some sixty miles off the Syrian coast.

Because of the role Antioch will come to play, some background on the city shows its strategic importance for the advancement of the gospel (Polhill, *Acts* 268-269; Keener II:1834-1838). Founded about 300 B.C. by Seleucus I Nicator and named for his famous father, Antiochus, one of the leading generals of Alexander the Great, it grew to be the third largest city in the Roman Empire. Its population was over half a million people and was a center of Greek culture in the region. It lay some fifteen miles up the Orantes River from the Mediterranean coast and was furnished with a major harbor. In 23 B.C. the Romans organized the coastal area into the province of Syria, with Antioch being the seat of government and culture. It was also granted the status of being a "free city," allowing for independent government. Herod the Great invested heavily in the city, adding to its beauty and appeal. However, it was also known for its rampant immorality, much of which centered on the worship practices of the ancient fertility goddesses of the Greeks (Daphne) and the Assyrians (Astarte). There was a large Jewish population, estimated at between twenty-five and fifty thousand. Its strategic location, travel convenience, moderate climate, and large Jewish population made it appealing for the witness of the gospel.

One key factor in this expansion of the gospel is who the leading witnesses were *not*. There was no apostle leading the way or involved in this endeavor. Paul would come later (v. 26). Furthermore, the witnesses are unnamed (v. 20). Some were from the island of Cyprus, the home of Barnabas (4:36). Cyrene was on the north coast of Africa and the home of Lucius, named later as a leader in the church (13:1). These unnamed men were bold witnesses for Christ and were rewarded with great response. The authority of their witness was the Spirit-empowered gospel they preached ("preaching the Lord Jesus"). Sometimes the only applause needed is for the gospel itself!

Of note are questions about those who received their witness: namely, "the Grecians" (v. 20). Are these Greek-speaking Jews (see 6:1) or Gentiles? There is much scholarly debate on the manuscript evidence of the exact term (Picirilli, *Paul* 61; Fitzmyer 476; Lenski 449; Robertson, *Acts* 156), but most writers agree that they at least *included*

Gentiles—for two reasons. First, some argue that the term "Grecians" (Greek *Hellenistes*; 6:1; 9:29) can refer to those who are culturally Greek but may or may not be of a different nationality. The contextual usage must decide its meaning (Metzger 340; Stott 202; Lightfoot 159-160).

Second, the contrasting expression in verse 20, "and some...spake unto the Grecians," as compared to the previous witness to "Jews only" (v. 19), indicates a different audience. If they were Greek-speaking Jews, there would be no need for such a contrast (Polhill, *Acts* 270-271; Robertson, *Acts* 156; Bock 414; Keener II:1842; Barnes 183-184). Therefore, in this view, these must be Gentiles.

I would add that it was the intention of Luke to show the expanding witness of the church to Gentiles; therefore, this usage of *Grecians* in the context of Antioch would certainly seem to favor Gentiles as well as Greek-speaking Jews. There really is no need to restrict the usage of the term. Both Jewish and Gentile believers are present in the church later. Here, then, was the first church that demonstrated the fellowship of all believers, Jewish and Gentile, as they worshiped, ate, and ministered together.

If Cornelius represented the opening of the door of the gospel to the Gentiles (10:34; 11:12) as an extension of the witness of the church at Jerusalem, the Gentile witness gave birth to the church at Antioch. It later became the headquarters for the Pauline missionary efforts that included Jews but focused on Gentiles (Acts 18:4; Rom. 1:16).

The efforts of the persecution-driven witnesses were confirmed by the "hand of the Lord" (v. 21) in favor upon them.

Biblically, the phrase carries the idea that God Himself approved and blessed the effort (Ex. 9:3; Isa. 59:1; Lk. 1:66). In this case, Luke does not record a specific number of people who were saved, but that "a great number believed." If, indeed, many of these were Gentiles who were not previously aware of the Messianic promises of the O. T., then it is most compelling that they "turned to the Lord" from idolatry and the lifestyle that attended it. They received a Spirit-empowered witness that had been refined in the fire of persecution (8:4). Their faithful efforts, the blessing of God upon them, and the impact among those who had probably never heard these truths, give hope and confidence for all similar efforts today.

2. The Jerusalem church sends Barnabas to confirm (11:22-26)

22 Then tidings of these things came unto the ears of the church which was at Jerusalem: and they sent forth Barnabas, that he should go as far as Antioch.
23 Who, when he came, and had seen the grace of God, was glad, and exhorted them all, that with purpose of heart they would cleave unto the Lord.
24 For he was a good man, and full of the Holy Ghost and of faith: and much people was added unto the Lord.
25 Then departed Barnabas to Tarsus, for to seek Saul:
26 And when he had found him, he brought him to Antioch. And it came to pass, that a whole year they assembled themselves with the church, and taught much peo-

ple. And the disciples were called Christians first in Antioch.

The Jerusalem church was the "mother church" and rightly so. Most of the apostles remained there and were the direct link to the Lord Jesus. It was incumbent on them to insure the integrity of the ministry as it expanded, so when they heard the news, literally the "word" (Greek *logos*) of the revival in the Syrian province, they sought a firsthand report. If, indeed, the converts in Antioch were predominantly Gentile, there would have been some needed confirmations of the work. Being separate does not mean being unaccountable.

Barnabas had become a respected, seasoned leader and was chosen to represent the Jerusalem church in confirming the work in the cities of the Syrian province as far as Antioch (v. 22). He was not a lesser authority, since he represented the interests of the Jerusalem church. But he was one who was well-suited for the purpose, being from Cyprus and fluent in Greek (4:36). Plus, he was the "son of consolation," a bridge-builder, one who could discern as well as encourage. He was the perfect selection for the situation.

Nor was his visit disappointing (v. 23). There is no record of what he was to look for when he went to Antioch, but when he arrived he was thrilled with what he saw. Evidenced in the lives of the people was "the grace of God" (v. 23) that made him "glad." God's grace is the basis for a glad heart, especially when seen in the lives of others. Apparently, Barnabas was not as much concerned about the traditions of social interaction as some of his brethren (11:2-3). The impact of the gospel was more important. As a result, he encouraged them (as was his nature; 4:36; 9:27) with a very pertinent message. He counseled them to have purpose of heart and "cleave unto the Lord." This construction (Greek present infinitive of *prosmeno*) literally means "to keep on abiding" or "remaining loyal." Heart-purposed continuation is the essential nature of saving faith. Both were very appropriate in the pagan culture of Antioch—and anywhere else, for that matter.

In what may be a personal note by Luke (v. 24), the character of Barnabas is summarized in three ways: he was "a good man...full of the Holy Spirit...and faith." His relational skills grew out of a Spirit-filled life that was evidenced by a walk of faith as he was willing to extend a helping hand to those who needed it, including the Gentiles at Antioch, Saul of Tarsus (9:27), and John Mark (15:37, 39). It should come as no surprise that the growth of the Antioch church was enhanced by this good and godly man. Would that we were determined to be more like him!

Then Barnabas remembered Saul (v. 25). The situation, the need, the timing was suited for himself and another with a similar heart. By now Saul was surely ready for this area of ministry. God prepares a place for a prepared man. Apparently, Saul was mobile in the Tarsus area (v. 26), for it took a while to locate him ("when he found him"). Saul's mobility was probably because of his ministry that carried him throughout the area (Gal. 1:23; Acts 15:41). Apparently, Saul had been neither silent nor inactive after being sent away from Judaea (9:29-30). His boldness and fervor, evidenced in Damascus and

Jerusalem following his conversion, carried over into his home area of Tarsus.

There is some question about the time interval between Saul's being sent away to Tarsus and Barnabas' bringing him to Antioch. Opinions vary from six years (Ogg 36; Picirilli, *Paul* 53) to ten years (Polhill, *Acts* 272). Such discussion helps with the chronology of Paul's life as well as with the Acts narrative itself. Regardless how long the time away was, it was not time wasted.

Barnabas and Saul labored together for a year in Antioch, identifying with and teaching the new believers (v. 26). Writers disagree on the date of that year, ranging from A.D. 43 (Ramsay, *Traveller* 45) to 45 (Ogg 36). The differences are based on when the Antioch church actually sent the famine-relief offering (vv. 29-30), to help their brethren in Judaea, via Barnabas and Saul. My opinion is that the year A.D. 43 seems best.

It was at Antioch that the term *Christian* was coined, by those who were not believers, to identify the believers. Polhill (*Paul* 73), however, believes that the name might have been developed by the disciples themselves. The term is a Latinized Greek word and means a "Christ follower." But it is a term where part of one's identity is shaped by the one followed. Opinions vary as to the exact intent of the term. Some think it was a derisive label from opponents of the new movement (Keener II:1847; Marshall, *Acts* 203; Picirilli, Paul 63). Others believe it was merely a jocular term used to distinguish the believers from Judaism as an emerging group of their own (Bock 416; Meyer 223; Stott 205; Bruce, *Acts* 228). It may be impossible to determine the exact motive for the usage of the term, but apparently at the time of the writing of Acts by Luke it was being used more and more, hence his reference to its origin. Used only three times in the N. T. (Acts 26:28; 1 Pet. 4:16), it did not become the main term of recognition until the close of the first century and into the second century. Ignatius was the first to use it of other believers (Bock 416; Polhill, *Acts* 273; Bruce, *Acts* 228). Our central usage of it today (although it has become somewhat tarnished over the years) is long removed from the original. It appears that the Acts believers themselves (or perhaps Luke) preferred to identify themselves as "disciples" or "those of the way" (19:9, 23; 22:4, 14, 22).

3. The beginning of the famine relief offering (11:27-30)

**27 And in these days came prophets from Jerusalem unto Antioch.
28 And there stood up one of them named Agabus, and signified by the Spirit that there should be great dearth throughout all the world: which came to pass in the days of Claudius Caesar.
29 Then the disciples, every man according to his ability, determined to send relief unto the brethren which dwelt in Judaea;
30 Which also they did, and sent it to the elders by the hands of Barnabas and Saul.**

As the church at Antioch grew, recognition by the Jerusalem church continued as prophets visited to minister. With the introduction of Agabus (v. 28) comes recognition of the office and function of the N. T. prophet among the churches. These are noted elsewhere in

Acts (13:1; 21:10-11) and the N. T. (1 Cor. 12:28; 14:1-40). Similar to the O. T. prophet, these gave forth inspired speech to communicate the will of God. The content of their messages ranged from proclamation of the gospel to predicting the future (TDNT VI:818). In this setting, Agabus gave a dire prediction of "great dearth" (Greek *limos*, famine) that was soon to grip the entire Roman Empire: that is, "all the world" (v. 28). Luke adds that it, indeed, came to pass during the reign of Claudius Caesar who ruled from A.D. 41-54. His reign was marked by a series of famines in various places, specifically in Judaea from A.D. 46-48 (Josephus, *Antiquities* III. XV. 3; Polhill, *Acts* 275; Keener II:1856-1858).

There is no need to date the famine predicted by Agabus prior to the beginning of the *reign* of Claudius since Luke is writing in retrospect. In hindsight, he is confirming that the famine did take place during the reign of Claudius. There may have been an even earlier localized famine in A.D. 42-43 in Judaea, but the one predicted by Agabus was later.

A few writers (Metzger 344-345; Bruce, *Acts* 229) make reference to a variant reading of the text as the first "we" passage in Acts (16:10) making verse 28 read "in these days when *we* were come together." This is partially based on the tradition that Antioch was the home of Luke, with some identifying him as the "Lucius of Cyrene" in 13:1. However, the best textual evidences make this improbable (Bruce, *Acts* 260; Keener II:1987).

The prediction was, no doubt, informative and preparatory. God does not always inform us ahead of time of tragedies that are coming, nor should we expect Him to do so. Of interest is the question of the time of the prediction. Had Agabus already made this announcement to the church at Jerusalem before coming to Antioch? Or was this a new revelation given after he arrived at Antioch? The text is not clear regarding the time, but the response was clear and immediate. The Antioch church determined to provide some monetary assistance (v. 29). Noted for its generosity (4:32-35; 6:1), even the Jerusalem church would be stretched thin when the famine occurred. The decision to send relief appears to be the natural expression of compassion that a church should have. The principle of giving according to individual ability is stated and becomes the ongoing principle Paul expands upon later (1 Cor. 16:2; 2 Cor. 9:6-7). Perhaps even more telling is the fact that a predominantly Gentile church is reaching out in support of a Jewish church. Authentic faith draws no lines of fleshly prejudice.

Barnabas and Saul were chosen as the bearers of the offering (v. 30) and perhaps even the news of the coming famine (if Agabus had not told about the coming famine in Jerusalem). Though Barnabas had been in Jerusalem for some time before coming to Antioch, it had been several years since Saul was there. Opinions vary as to the date of the famine relief mission to Jerusalem. Picirilli (*Paul* 52) places it as early as A.D. 44 thus in *preparation* for the famine and prior to the death of Herod (12:1-19). Others place the offering later, between A.D. 45 and 46 (Bruce, *Acts* 244; Ramsay, *Traveller* 51) at the early stages of the famine and after the death of Herod (12:23). If the earlier date of A.D. 44 is correct this would put them in Jerusalem at a crucial time, not only for the relief offering but involving the events of the next chapter as well. Any of these dates will technically work as long as they do not conflict with the first missionary journey.

More difficult is answering the question whether this is Paul's second visit to Jerusalem or perhaps a third, depending on when Galatians was written (Gal. 2:1-10). Some argue the famine relief visit recorded here is the same as Galatians 2:1-10, making this his second visit (Ramsay, *Traveller* 57; Marshall, *Acts* 205). Others disagree (Keener II:1861-1862; Polhill, *Acts* 275; Marberry 25). The question is not easily answered since views of the chronology of his life vary (Ogg 43-54; Polhill, *Paul* 79). Perhaps the most important factor to consider here is the expression of mercy by the Antioch church and their trusting the integrity of Barnabas and Saul with the relief offering.

Summary
(11:19-30)

The conversion of Cornelius and its implications for the Jerusalem church is validated by the witness of those who fled the persecution led by Saul of Tarsus. Traveling north to the coastal areas of the Syrian province and the island of Cyprus, they expanded their witness to Gentiles and not just Jews. God honored the efforts and multitudes turned to the Lord.

It was in the large city of Antioch that their witness met with great success, so much that the news reached back to Jerusalem. Barnabas was sent to verify. When he arrived he was overjoyed at what he found, lending wise counsel and encouragement. The number and needs of these believers required more than what Barnabas alone could provide. Remembering Saul, he went to Tarsus to find him and bring him back to assist in the work. Out of that ministry experience, they become a close and effective team for years to come. It is no coincidence that the believers were called "Christ followers" first at Antioch.

The Antioch church would become the next sending church for the expansion of the gospel "to the uttermost part of the earth." It was from Antioch that Paul, Barnabas, and Silas launched their missionary journeys. The Antioch church initiated the famine relief offering that models mercy ministries for all churches. The Jerusalem church had modeled these, too, but with the uniqueness of the Antioch church comes validation that such is desired of all churches.

Application: Teaching and Preaching the Passage

Exegetical Outline of the Text: 1. The Extension of the Gospel to Antioch (11:19-22). 2. The Establishing of the Believers at Antioch (11:20-26). 3. The Ministry of Support for the Churches in Judaea (11:27-30).

In the Acts narrative, there are two great churches that demonstrated the balance needed for healthy Christianity. The Jerusalem church was noted for evangelistic zeal, mercy ministry, and doctrinal clarification (15:1-30). The Antioch church was noted for its strong base of teachers and prophets, mercy ministry, and missionary zeal (13—14). Healthy churches (and individual believers) need these elements: doctrinal integrity, compassionate ministry, and evangelistic zeal. This is the model for believers and churches to imitate today.

Some writers (Robertson, *Acts* 156) state that the church at Antioch supplanted the Jerusalem church as the center of witness. I do not believe that is the case. Rather, the witness of the church in Jerusalem was duplicated and expanded by the Antioch church. The Acts narrative covers the Jerusalem church in basically the first twelve chapters. The focus then shifts to Antioch as the sending church for the Pauline ministry, which occupies the next twelve chapters.

The theme of persecution in Acts is part of the story of the extension of the gospel "to the uttermost part of the earth." A great study is why believers were persecuted, how they responded, and how this applies today. In the world at large, Christians are mercilessly persecuted in some areas. Even in America, we face a growing intolerance of biblical truth and Christian testimony. A really good, on-going study is how this happens today, showing specific areas and people who are targeted for persecution.

Barnabas presents a good role model to emulate, and so for teaching and preaching. There are five elements about his life (vv. 24-25) that are pertinent: His character ("he was a good man"), his spiritual empowerment ("full of the Holy Spirit"), his trust in the Lord ("full...of faith"), his fruit ("much people was added unto the Lord"), and his partnering ("Then departed Barnabas...to seek Saul"). These are easily alliterated if desired.

Another key truth to teach or preach regards the name *Christian* and its origin with the Antioch church. Why is this the case? What does it mean? How should it apply today?

The mercy ministry of the church at Antioch, to send relief for the famine, provides a basis for study in determining needs and how to fund them ("every man according to his ability," v. 29). There are ten principles developed in relation to this in 2 Corinthians 8—9 for supplemental study.

E. Herod Targets the Church for Persecution (12:1-25)

1. James is killed, and Peter is imprisoned (12:1-19)

a. The killing of James by Herod (12:1-2)

1   Now about that time Herod the king stretched forth *his* hands to vex certain of the church.
2   And he killed James the brother of John with the sword.

There are six members of the Herod family referenced in the N. T.: Herod the Great (birth and early life of Christ); Herod Archelaus (Mt. 2:22); Herod Philip (Lk. 3:1); Herod Antipas (Mt. 13:32; Lk. 23:6-11); Herod Agrippa I (Acts 12:1-23); Herod Agrippa II (Acts 25:13—26:32). (For expansion of these see EHB 540; Jones; Gundry, *A Survey of the New Testament* 12-13.) With the exception of Philip, with whom there is no direct exchange, all of them are either murderous or antagonistic toward Christ and/or His followers. The story here is a case in point and a study of political favors being curried at the expense of blood. The entire narrative is of the utmost gravity. We weep over the murder of the apostle James. We smile at the comic irony of Peter's release. We see divine justice with the ignominious death of Herod.

With the famine relief offering being taken for those in Judaea and entrusted for delivery to Barnabas and Saul, the Acts narrative shifts back to Jerusalem and returns to the theme of persecution (11:19). The somewhat ideal ministry of the church at Antioch was not the norm for all churches. Satan's method of intimidation to stifle the witness of believers was still very much in process.

Luke's words, "about that time" (v. 1), connect the timing of the relief offering to the persecution events of 12:1-23 though there are cracks left as to the exact timing. There are four specific references in these two chapters that hold the keys of the timing: the famine (11:28), the reign of Claudius Caesar (11:28), the Passover (12:4), and the death of Herod (12:23). The reign of Claudius is known to be from A.D. 41-54. That provides the larger chronological setting. The Judaean famine is usually dated A.D. 46-48. Herod died in A.D. 44 after the Passover when Peter was imprisoned, though we don't know how much time passed between these two events. This Passover could have been as early as A.D. 43 or the Passover prior to Herod's death in A.D. 44 (Josephus, *Antiquities* XIX. VIII. 2; Keener II:1867; Picirilli, *Paul* 64; Bock 424; Polhill, *Acts* 284). Given this chronology, the time of Herod's persecution in Jerusalem appears to be perhaps as early as A.D. 43 or, more likely, early 44. Either date coincides with the growth of the church in Antioch.

This would also put the visit of Barnabas and Saul to Jerusalem, with the famine relief offering, in early A.D. 44. On the surface, this may seem too early for Agabus' prediction of a famine.

This is a reasonable possibility, however, if their visit included reporting the prediction of Agabus about a famine to come, since this was given at Antioch and might not have been at Jerusalem. Ramsay (*Traveller* 69) objects to such an early visit, stating that this would not have been "a natural or a useful procedure." However, isn't it "natural and useful" if the believers in Judaea were unaware of the coming calamity for those who knew about it to tell them ahead of time and make an effort to help? Regardless, and whatever the case, the action of the church in Antioch, in sending Paul and Barnabas in response to Agabus' prophecy, was a great show of support and solidarity.

Furthermore, the Lord's timing is always perfect and providential. As Picirilli (*Paul* 64) suggests, it may be that Barnabas and Saul arrived in Jerusalem during the brief time between Peter's escape and Herod's death. If so, it would be just like the Lord to send Barnabas and Saul to give comfort by bringing "good news from a far country" (Prov. 25:25).

The Herod in this story (v. 1) is Agrippa I, whose personal history tied him to Rome and friendship with Roman emperors, from Tiberius to Claudius (Bruce, *Acts* 232-233). By A.D. 41 Herod had been appointed "king" over the regions of southern Syria, Galilee, Peraea, and Judaea. Somewhat popular among the Jewish elite, he did what was politically expedient to keep their approval, including collusion with them to silence the witness of the church in Jerusalem.

Apparently, the Jewish leadership grew tired of tolerating the apostles and the followers of Christ and pressed their agenda politically. The religious trials initiated by the Sanhedrin had not stopped the movement, so perhaps their thinking was that political power would. They had succeeded in gaining political support for the death of the Lord Jesus, so maybe that would work for His followers, who were becoming quite popular in Jerusalem. Implied in the action of killing James and intending to kill Peter was raw political power to curry favor (v. 3), as the capricious Herod targeted the church intending to do harm ("vex," Greek *kakoo,* to cause evil, oppress). Of course, there were spiritual forces at work as well (Eph. 6:12). Herod first singled out the apostle James, whom he ruthlessly and mercilessly killed "with the sword" (v. 2). Keener (II:1872-1873) points out that Herod probably was implementing the method of execution he learned from the Romans while he was a student there. It was quick, efficient, and sent a chilling message of power and authority.

The apostle James was the brother of the apostle John, one of the sons of Zebedee (Mk. 10:35), to be distinguished from James the less (Mk. 15:44) and James the Lord's brother who wrote the book that bears his name. Jesus had predicted his suffering (Mk. 10:39). James was the first apostle to be martyred.

b. Peter is imprisoned by Herod but released by the angel of the Lord (12:3-19)

**3   And because he saw it pleased the Jews, he proceeded further to take Peter also. (Then were the days of unleavened bread.)
4   And when he had apprehended him, he put *him* in prison, and delivered *him* to four quaternions of soldiers to keep him; intending after Easter to bring him forth to the people.
5   Peter therefore was kept in prison: but prayer was made without ceasing of the church unto God for him.
6   And when Herod would have brought him forth, the same night Peter was sleeping between two soldiers, bound with two chains: and the keepers before the door kept the prison.
7   And, behold, the angel of the Lord came upon *him*, and a light shined in the prison: and he smote Peter on the side, and raised him up, saying, Arise up quickly. And his chains fell off from *his* hands.
8   And the angel said unto him, Gird thyself, and bind on thy sandals. And so he did. And he saith unto him, Cast thy garment about thee, and follow me.
9   And he went out, and followed him; and wist not that it was true which was done by the angel: but thought he saw a vision.
10 When they were past the first and the second ward, they came unto the iron gate that leadeth unto the city; which opened to them of his own accord: and they went out, and passed on through one street; and forthwith the angel departed from him.
11 And when Peter was come to himself, he said, Now I know of a surety, that the LORD hath sent his angel, and hath delivered me out of the hand of Herod, and *from* all the expectation of the people of the Jews.
12 And when he had considered *the thing*, he came to the house of**

Mary the mother of John, whose surname is Mark; where many were gathered together praying.

13 And as Peter knocked at the door of the gate, a damsel came to hearken, named Rhoda.

14 And when she knew Peter's voice, she opened not the gate for gladness, but ran in, and told how Peter stood before the gate.

15 And they said unto her, Thou art mad. But she constantly affirmed that it was even so. Then said they, It is his angel.

16 But Peter continued knocking: and when they had opened *the door,* and saw him, they were astonished.

17 But he, beckoning unto them with the hand to hold their peace, declared unto them how the Lord had brought him out of the prison. And he said, God shew these things unto James, and to the brethren. And he departed, and went into another place.

18 Now as soon as it was day, there was no small stir among the soldiers, what was become of Peter.

19 And when Herod had sought for him, and found him not, he examined the keepers, and commanded that *they* should be put to death. And he went down from Judaea to Caesarea, and *there* abode.

The killing of James was met with the approval (v. 3) of the Jews (the Sanhedrin?), so Herod imprisoned Peter with the same intention. Lenski (470) alludes to an intent by Herod to duplicate the trial of Jesus. The circumstances were, indeed, very similar. That trial would have been well-known and part of the lore of the Herod family—not exactly a desirable heritage! In yet another bit of irony, he delayed action until after the Passover season (v. 4). Why kill an innocent man during a religious festival?

The KJV translates the Greek word *pascha* as *Easter* in verse 4. This translation dates back to William Tyndale's translation (1525) and Miles Coverdale's translation (1535) and was kept in the KJV translation later (1611). The word simply means *Passover*, but came to be called *Easter* by Anglo-Saxon Christians who celebrated the resurrection of Christ—which, of course, occurred at the Passover season (Barnes 190).

Significantly, while Peter was imprisoned, the church was engaged in continual, intercessory prayer (v. 5). The Jerusalem church had thousands of believers scattered all over the city. As indicated later (v. 12), believers were gathered in various homes to pray for Peter and, no doubt, for the Lord's intervention in the persecution. The targeting of the church's leaders portended more and worse to come unless the Lord should stop it.

Herod made Peter's imprisonment as secure as humanly possible (vv. 4, 6), perhaps being told of a previous "escape" (5:17-20). The heavy security included four squads of four guards each ("four quaternions"), who changed every three hours to insure alertness. Two were chained directly to Peter (v. 6) while two stood watch at the door. In spite of all this, Peter slept soundly!

We are not told exactly how many days Peter was imprisoned, but the night before his trial is the focus of the text. Suddenly, the angel of the Lord appeared in the cell where he was, his appearance lighting the room. It may be that the soldiers were asleep, too, or had fainted at the appearance of the heavenly deliverer (Mt. 28:2-4). Whatever the case, they are rendered inactive. Almost comically, Peter was sleeping so soundly that he had to be struck by the angel to awaken him. As he stumbled to his feet, the shackles fell from his wrists, but he had to be told to put his shoes on and get his coat (v. 8)! As he was led out of the prison cell, he thought he was dreaming (v. 9). The angel of the Lord escorted Peter completely out of the prison with the iron gates opening before them like the automatic doors at a grocery store! Once they were safe enough, the angel departed, his mission completed (v. 10). Finally, Peter came fully awake, realizing what the Lord had just done in delivering him from a sure and certain death at the hands of Herod and his sympathizers (v. 11).

It should be noted that some writers regard the story as merely a Lukan construct or legend (Meyer 231; Haenchen 387-390) mingled with enough history to be somewhat believable. Their view is that Peter's escape, if he was imprisoned at all, was entirely an "inside job" and written in this fashion as a literary foil to overshadow the killing of James. Such a view discounts both the supernatural intervention of the almighty God in the affairs of men as it pleases Him and the inspirational integrity of the written account.

From the side street where he finally awakened to where he was, Peter made his way to the familiar house of Mary and John Mark (v. 12), where folks were gathered in prayer. The narrative introduces John Mark, who will play a significant role later in the life of Paul. When Peter knocked at the outer gate of the courtyard to get the attention of

those within, a young girl named Rhoda (meaning "rose") responded (v. 13). Some writers hold that Rhoda was a servant/slave girl (Keener II:1905; Polhill, *Acts* 282; Ger 177) while others take it that she simply was a daughter of folks gathered for prayer (Lenski 478) because she is named. Either one is possible, but it is clear she was familiar with Peter because she recognized his voice (v. 14). She was so overjoyed to hear his voice that she forgot to open the gate to let Peter in.

Rhoda's report that Peter was at the gate was not believed by those who were praying for that very thing (v. 15). Again, the irony is not lost. Even her insistence was re-interpreted to mean that his "angel" stood there, not Peter himself. Here is evidence of the belief in "guardian" angels (Ps. 91:11; Heb. 1:14) who may be the spiritual counterparts of those to whom they minister (Harrision 193; Keener II: 1946-1948). However, God had sent an angel to deliver Peter from death, not to report it.

Peter's persistent knocking (v. 16) finally gained his entrance to the completely astonished group who were gathered to pray. One can imagine the outburst of emotion and barrage of questions that greeted him (v. 17). Reassuring them by telling the story of his miraculous deliverance, he instructed them to report it to James (the Lord's brother and probably the senior pastor of the Jerusalem church) and the "brethren" (other leaders and apostles) who needed to know and were probably engaged in similar prayer meetings all over Jerusalem.

It is likely that Peter leaves the house as soon as he can to safeguard the others. Where he goes is left to speculation;

the text seems intentionally vague, stating he "went into another place" (v. 17). It is too soon in his life to go to Rome (Fitzmyer 489). Antioch is possible (Bock 429), since he does appear there (Gal.2:11). Later he is back in Jerusalem (15:7), at least temporarily. If he was regarded as a fugitive after Herod's death, he might have become an itinerant apostle, ministering here and there to avoid arrest.

Of note are the details of the entire episode. These could have only come from those who were there at the time and later told Luke, probably smiling while they repeated it. Luke would have personally known Peter and John Mark. He might even have interviewed Rhoda for her input. To be sure, the Holy Spirit guided him in gathering and writing his information (Lk. 1:2).

The story does not end with Peter's deliverance. Not until daylight was Peter's escape discovered. The guards who were charged with Peter's keeping were completely baffled over what happened (v. 18) and where he was. It is implied that they searched "high and low" for him but to no avail. When Herod heard of his disappearance, he made inquiry, then had the guards put to death (v. 19). Such was in keeping with Roman law and practice. Perhaps frustrated and with other political situations on his agenda (v. 20), he left for the more favorable climate of the sea coast town of Caesarea.

It would be a mistake to conclude that God always delivers His people in such miraculous ways if we have enough faith and engage in continuous prayer meetings. Remember that James had just been executed (vv. 1-2). There was no miraculous deliverance for him as for Peter. He was as much in the will of God

as Peter. Only the Lord knows who, how, and why some are delivered from death while others are not (Heb. 11:32-40). Nor should we presume that all is decreed and previously determined, so that prayer and other intercessory means are meaningless. It is a truism often repeated, "We should work as if everything depended on us, but pray as if everything depended on God." Both are appropriate.

2. The death of Herod (12:20-23)

20 And Herod was highly displeased with them of Tyre and Sidon: but they came with one accord to him, and, having made Blastus the king's chamberlain their friend, desired peace; because their country was nourished by the king's *country*.
21 And upon a set day Herod, arrayed in royal apparel, sat upon his throne, and made an oration unto them.
22 And the people gave a shout, *saying, It is* the voice of a god, and not a man.
23 And immediately the angel of the Lord smote him, because he gave not God the glory: and he was eaten of worms, and gave up the ghost.

The leaders of the coastal cities of Tyre and Sidon (v. 20) had agitated Herod. The verb translated "was highly displeased" (Greek *thumomaxeo*) means to be very angry, enraged, infuriated. This had resulted in economic sanctions being imposed. It did not take long to force reconciliation (Bock 430-431). Little is known of *Blastus*, except that he was Herod's personal servant, his "chamberlain" (Greek *koiton*, bed-chamber), one who controlled access to the king something like a "chief of staff," and was able to negotiate peace in this issue. Herod's political agenda, however, was short-lived.

The city in which Herod died was Caesarea. The occasion of celebration and pomp (v. 21), in which Herod was acclaimed, is unnamed but might have been the emperor's birthday. If so, it would have been August, A.D. 44. Josephus provides a close parallel to Luke's account of the event (*Antiquities* XIX.VIII. 2), describing in detail Herod's apparel and the adulation of the audience. Neither writer gives the content of the speech, but the fawning crowd proclaimed Herod a "god" (v. 22).

Luke states that Herod was "immediately" struck by the angel of the Lord (v. 23) because he arrogantly accepted the acclaim that should have been reserved only for God (Isa. 42:8). The phrase "eaten of [by] worms" appears to be the literal case as verified by Josephus who described it as "pain in his belly" (*Antiquities* XIX.VIII.2) and possible rotting flesh (Robertson, *Acts* 176). Herod lingered only five days before dying.

One cannot miss the sense of justice with which this incident of persecution of the church closes. Did this send a message to the Jewish leaders back at Jerusalem bent on silencing the church? Perhaps, but the animosity lingered and would arise again later when Paul was apprehended in Jerusalem (22:30ff). If anything was learned about Herod's death by successive leaders, it does not show. People often misinterpret what God does (Jn. 12:28-29).

It would be a mistake to conclude that God always immediately judges arro-gance in evil kings and rulers, as He did with men like Herod or Nebuchadnezzar (Dan. 4:30-33). But He does and will judge ultimately (Phil. 2:10-11; 1 Tim. 5:24). The death of Herod is a grue-some reminder of the fact that God, on occasion, judges the actions of men in this life.

3. The church continues in minis-try (12:24-25)

24 But the word of God grew and multiplied.
25 And Barnabas and Saul returned from Jerusalem, when they had fulfilled *their* ministry, and took with them John, whose surname was Mark.

Whatever the contents of the words of Herod and the words of acclamation by the crowd, these are in contrast to the growth and influence of God's Word (v. 1). The intended stifling of the wit-ness of the church only fueled its fire. That witness was victorious over direct assault by religious, political, and spiri-tual powers (Isa. 55:9-11). Luke's sum-mary is both conclusive and transitional.

Barnabas and Saul, also, completed their mission by delivering the famine relief offering for distribution to the church at Jerusalem (v. 25). They returned to Antioch with John Mark, perhaps in preparation for their first extended witness in what we call the first missionary journey. *John* was his Jewish name (13:5, 13) and *Mark* his Roman name (12:25; 15:39). Thus Luke refers to the beginning of Mark's spiritual apprenticeship. The N. T. only partially chronicles his growth, but ultimately, he will be used as a writer of the Gospel account that bears his name.

There is a textual and syntactical issue in verse 25 addressed by some writers (Metzger 350-352; Bock 434-435) over whether the text should read "returned from Jerusalem" or "returned to Jerusalem." The best solution ties the phrase to the mission of Barnabas and Saul in delivering the famine relief offering as the KJV translation does (Fitzmyer 493; Haenchen 387). The verse makes no sense any other way.

In this way, Luke summarizes the narrative of the Jerusalem church. The remainder of Acts transitions to the leading role of the Antioch church in extending the witness of the gospel "to the uttermost part of the earth."

Summary
(12:1-25)

Chapter twelve turns our attention from the Antioch church back to the Jerusalem church. It also records yet another attempt to persecute the church, this time from a political source. Up till now, persecution has been religiously motivated and initiated by the Sanhedrin. For whatever reasons, Herod Agrippa I becomes involved. James, the brother of John, is killed, becoming the second martyr for Christ in the Acts narrative. Peter is the intended third, and is imprisoned to await his fate at the hands of the capricious king.

However, the Lord intervenes as the church unceasingly prays for help from Heaven. With irony woven into the story, Peter is miraculously delivered from maximum security right under the noses of the guards who fail to lift a finger to prevent his escape. Even the prison doors and gates open without human assistance.

Peter's appearance at the house of Mary was met initially with unbelief that soon turned to joy at his explanation of deliverance. But his stay at her house quickly ended as he became a fugitive from injustice, leaving for an unnamed place. He does not appear again in Acts until chapter fifteen.

Herod's vicious actions are not left unrequited by the Judge of all men. The narrative records a few details leading to Herod's miserable death, including his arrogant acceptance of adulation as a "god." With secular history (Josephus) verifying the Lukan account, the integrity of the entire story is further confirmed.

Chapter twelve is both conclusive and transitional. It concludes the focus of Acts on the Jerusalem church and transitions focus to the Antioch church. Both are models of what a N. T. church should be. Also, focus shifts from the ministry and leadership of Peter to that of Paul. The rest of Acts will chronicle his life and ministry until his imprisonment in Rome.

Application: Teaching and Preaching the Passage

Exegetical Outline of the Text: 1. The Death of James at the Hand of Herod (12:1-2). 2. The Deliverance of Peter by the Hand of the Lord (12:3-19). 3. The Death of Herod by the Hand of the Lord (12:20-23). 4. The Growth of the Word (12:24-25).

The various members of the Herod family who are mentioned in Acts are identified in the commentary above. A profitable study would be to trace these to show how and why political leaders often oppose the gospel. This easily leads to discussion on present applications and response.

Certainly the theme of prayer is central to this chapter. The study of prayer in Acts is very instructive. The church was born in a prayer meeting and is characterized by prayer in all situations. The words of 12:5 present a good three point lesson: 1. The Problem, "Peter was kept in prison." 2. The Petition, "but prayer was made." 3. The Persistency, "without ceasing." 4. The Person, "unto God for him."

The ministry of angels is an important element of this chapter, as with other situations in Acts. How and when they worked is a very good study.

The death of Herod by the death-judgment of God is a key part of this text. This could easily be the basis for addressing the ultimate accountability of leaders to the Lord. Furthermore, Herod's attempt to destroy the church was not the first or last time political leaders have attacked the church. It isn't coincidental that the chapter concludes with the note of triumph of the church and the Word of God in spite of the actions of evil men.

F. The First Missionary Journey (13:1—14:28)

1. The call and commissioning of Barnabas and Saul (13:1-3)

**1 Now there were in the church that was at Antioch certain prophets and teachers; as Barnabas, and Simeon that was called Niger, and Lucius of Cyrene, and Manaen, which had been brought up with Herod the tetrarch, and Saul.
2 As they ministered to the Lord, and fasted, the Holy Ghost said,**
**Separate me Barnabas and Saul for the work whereunto I have called them.
3 And when they had fasted and prayed, and laid *their* hands on them, they sent *them* away.**

Chapter 13 opens a new era in the progress of the Acts narrative as well as a new dimension to the witness of the church. It is sometimes referred to as "Acts, Vol. II." Some review is helpful at this point. Approximately twelve years have passed since the ascension of the resurrected Christ (1:9-11) and from the Day of Pentecost (2:1-41) until the first missionary journey begins.

Remarkable progress has been made in obedience to the command to carry the gospel to the "uttermost part of the earth." As shown in the recorded messages of Peter, Jesus of Nazareth was the long-awaited Messiah of all O. T. prophecy as verified by His God-approved life (2:22) and bodily resurrection (2:24). Thousands in Jerusalem and Judaea responded to the Spirit-empowered proclamation of the gospel. A new fellowship called "the church" (2:47) has been born, consisting of those who savingly believe in the resurrected Jesus Christ.

The fellowship of the early church was noted for its spiritual power to minister to hurting people (4:33; 5:15-16) and for its generosity in caring for their needs (4:34-35). There was a regular traffic of hurting, oppressed, and sick people who stumbled or were carried through the streets of Jerusalem to the apostles. The Lord attested His truth through them with physical miracles. The greatest miracle, however, was the healing of sin-sick souls. These broken people left healed and happy.

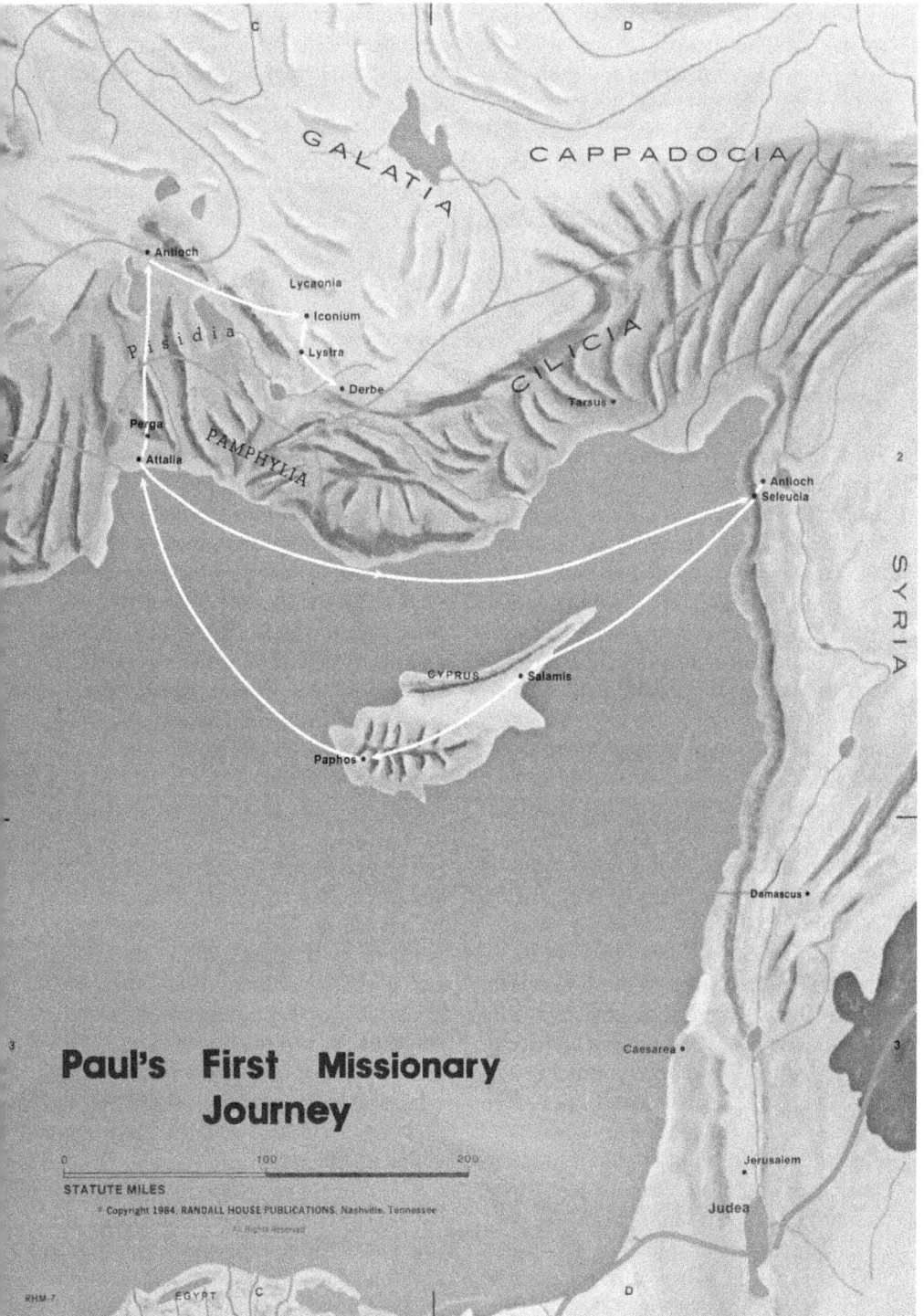

Paul's First Missionary Journey

STATUTE MILES

0   100   200

Not everyone rejoiced over the "Good News" of the gospel, however. The popularity of the disciples and their message of the risen Messiah was met with jealousy as Jewish religious leadership attempted to stifle the growing movement by arresting, threatening, and beating the apostles (chs. 4-5). This only added fuel to the flame as believers responded with a well-articulated defense (4:4-12; 5:29-32) and a continuing, courageous witness.

Stephen argued fervently in the synagogues (probably with the unconverted Saul of Tarsus) and before the Sanhedrin for a Messianic, redemptive history that began with Abraham (7:2ff) and was fulfilled with the coming of "the Just One" (7:52). His pointed truth regarding the rejection of this very theological perspective was characteristic of the Jewish fathers as well as the very Jewish leaders before whom he stood (7:51-53). That was one reason they were guilty of murdering the Messiah. Just as the fathers had killed the prophets who proclaimed these truths in generations past (7:52), the current generation killed Stephen, too (7:59-60).

His death opened the flood gates of persecution against the church, led by Saul of Tarsus (8:1-3). Instead of stopping the witness of the disciples, however, the hostility caused them to scatter across Judaea and Samaria (8:4-13), proclaiming the Word of God with boldness. Multitudes more responded in saving faith as the Lord moved upon their hearts—as He had done in Jerusalem. Philip was the evangelist whom the Lord used to open the door of witness to the Samaritans and the Ethiopian eunuch.

The conversion of Saul of Tarsus (9:1-19) was a historic turning point in the witness of the gospel. Of all people, he might have been the most unlikely candidate to become a Christian, at least in our fleshly way of thinking. His conversion provides a key apologetic for the life-changing impact of the truth of the resurrection of Jesus Christ. He soon began his own ministry, using the same truths he once argued against (9:20). Saul, too, was targeted for persecution (9:23-25), even as he had targeted others prior to his conversion. When things got too hot to handle over his impassioned preaching, the believers sent Saul to Tarsus for things to cool down (9:29-30).

The conversion of the Roman centurion, Cornelius, as well as the "conversion" of Simon Peter (10:34-35) and of some in the Jerusalem church (11:18), marked the opening of the door for the witness of the gospel "unto the uttermost part of the earth." Believers traveled to the Syrian province north of Judaea, proclaiming the gospel first to the Jews in the synagogues of the towns (11:19). Some made their way to the large city of Syrian Antioch, where multitudes of Jews and Gentiles turned to the Lord (11:21).

The apostles and leaders in Jerusalem sent Barnabas to confirm the news of the revival at Antioch. Barnabas found things to be as reported and decided to stay a while to help. With the needs greater than he could serve, he went to get Saul to assist him (11:26). The Antioch church was strongly established and became the sending church for the missionary journeys and the next major center of ministry.

The Jerusalem church, meanwhile, was targeted again for persecution, this time politically, by the capricious Herod Agrippa I (12:1-28). Focusing attention on the key leaders, he had the apostle

James killed and Peter imprisoned for the same purpose. The Lord intervened in delivering Peter from certain death and visited death-judgment upon Herod (12:23). Though there was weeping over the death of James, there was rejoicing over the deliverance of Peter. His role of leadership did not cease, but he did grow somewhat more silent as a fugitive from the injustice of Herod's attempt to kill him. The notable history of the Jerusalem church is marked with victory over political persecution. Thus, the focus of the Acts narrative transitions to the church at Antioch.

Our comments return, now, to the text. With the completion of the mission to deliver the famine-relief offering, Barnabas and Saul returned to Antioch (12:25). This setting now becomes the focus of the Acts narrative as Luke shifts to a new place and protocol for witness and ministry. The church at Antioch is the new place from which to carry the gospel to the rest of the world outside of Judaea. The protocol is that the witness and ministry respond to a Spirit-led intentionality that becomes more and more Gentile oriented.

All three missionary journeys began at Antioch and the first two ended there. The missionaries targeted large cities from which an entire region might be evangelized. They always began with "the Jew first" (Rom. 1:16), usually in the synagogues. When the witness to the Jews became hostile, they turned to the Gentiles. In the end, the churches established were predominantly Gentile.

Furthermore, the focus of apostolic leadership shifts from Peter to Barnabas to Saul of Tarsus, whose Roman name, Paul, is used from 13:9 forward. He will lead in defining missions while his inspired writings, that form the major corpus of the N. T., occur during his three missionary journeys and imprisonment in Rome.

All that preceded, in preparing believers to accept the Lord's worldwide intention for the gospel (chs. 10-11), has now matured into a universal mindset that embraces the possibility that all men everywhere may be saved. Therefore, when the Holy Spirit called men to this work, the church at Antioch had no reservations (11:1-18).

The leadership of the Antioch church was as notable in its spiritual focus as it was cosmopolitan in its make-up. Five men are listed as leaders (v. 1). We know about Barnabas and Saul already, but the other three are significant as well. One of these is "Simeon that was called Niger." *Simeon* was a common Jewish name. *Niger* (Latin for "black") is more likely a nickname, based on a dark complexion to distinguish him from other by the same name. Writers disagree on exactly what is meant and where he was from. Some suggest he might be the Simeon who carried the cross of Christ (Mt. 27:32). Others offer that he could be a descendant of proselytes from North Africa, perhaps an African who took a Jewish name (Robertson, *Acts* 177; Keener II:1984-1987; Bruce, *Paul* 148).

Lucius of Cyrene was thought, by some early church fathers, to be the Luke who wrote the Gospel and Acts. But there is little actual evidence for that (Polhill, *Acts* 259; Bruce, *Acts* 245). For one, the names are different enough to distinguish them: Luke (Greek *Loukas*) and Lucius (Greek *Loukios*). More likely, Lucius of Cyrene was one of the pioneers of the Antioch witness (11:20).

Manaen (from the Hebrew *Menahem*), on the other hand, is further identified as having "been brought up with Herod the tetrarch." This was Herod Antipas, whom Jesus referred to as "that fox" (Lk. 13:32). This means that Manaen was Jewish, not a blood relative of Herod, but something of a "foster brother" who knew intimately the people and lifestyle of the royal family. It was a common practice by elites of those days to engage social peers for their children. These were sometimes extended family members, other children needing the same social interaction, or even trusted slaves. Manaen was probably Luke's source for some of the details contained in the Gospel of Luke (8:3; 13:32; 23:7-12). This was no small matter since he would have been highly educated and provided high social standing (Keener II:1988-1990).

How these men with such different backgrounds came to be Christians is not part of the record but would be fascinating to know. As was the case with the apostles themselves, who were radically different, the common bond was Jesus Christ. What is most significant about the Antioch leaders is not their social standing but their spiritual leadership. They were "prophets and teachers" of the Word of God. They were influential men in society, but mostly men with spiritual vision who provided the support needed for the coming missionary journeys. Recognition of them in the inspired record stamps their leadership role in the historical significance of this great N. T. church. Everything rises and falls on leadership. The Antioch church was blessed with strong, visionary leadership.

The atmosphere of the Antioch church (v. 2) is described as one of ministering to the Lord, fasting, and hearing the voice of the Holy Spirit. Such a description indicates hearts of dedication, service, and openness to the Lord— and shouldn't these characterize every church? In that atmosphere, the Holy Spirit called for Barnabas and Saul to be "set aside" (Greek *aphorizo*, to separate from the rest) for a specific *work*. This word signified the mission, from its beginning to its conclusion (14:26). Apparently, they knew what was meant as they prepared for extensive travel. As with every new stage of witness in Acts, the Holy Spirit initiated the effort by leading those prepared for it.

One can imagine the extensive planning that must have taken place as these men prayerfully mapped out where they were going, how to get there, whom to take with them, and what they would do when they got there. It was intentional, prayerful, and in full dependence on the Holy Spirit's leadership. There is no reason to believe anything less than this went into the preparations for "the work" (Greek *to ergon*, always with the article; 13:2; 14:26; 15:38).

In solidarity with Barnabas and Saul, the church spent time fasting and praying over them (v. 3). A great calling requires great consecration. Ceremonially, they "laid their hands on them," representing their agreement that the Lord had laid His hands of favor on these men as well. Barnabas and Saul not only represented the Antioch church but the very gospel itself. This is the basis for our modern commissioning services for those with similar calling.

Two different words are used for the missionaries' *sending*. In verse 3, "sent them away" (Greek *apoluo*) means to loose or release from a tie. In verse 4, "being sent forth" (Greek *ekpempo*) means to send away. Each indicates a specific action by a specific sender. Used together, the church partnered with the Holy Spirit in releasing Barnabas and Saul from the ministry at the Antioch church to the calling and sending by the Holy Spirit to "the work."

The question of financial support is integral to the journey, though only implied. Based on Philippians 4:15, Robertson (*Acts* 178) surmises that the Antioch church did not make any financial contribution to the effort. Keener (II:1998) believes the opposite, that *sent* (v. 3) implies support. It could be that Barnabas and Saul were able to finance the trip themselves. Barnabas appears to have been financially secure (4:36-37), and that might also have been the case with Saul. Later, Paul would supplement his income using the craft of his trade (18:3), but that was not the case on the first missionary journey. Given the leadership of the church, its visionary witness, and the later teaching of the apostle Paul on giving (1 Cor. 9:6-11; Phil. 4:15-17), one would assume the financial support of the church for the journey.

2. Witness on the island of Cyprus (13:4-12)

a. First witness, in the synagogues (13:4-5)

4 So they, being sent forth by the Holy Ghost, departed unto Seleucia; and from thence they sailed to Cyprus.
5 And when they were at Salamis, they preached the word of God in the synagogues of the Jews: and they had also John to *their* minister.

The itinerary of the journey was carefully recorded by Luke, and we can see some of the reasons for where the missionary team chose to go. Seleucia was about fifteen miles west of Antioch at the mouth of the Orantes River as it emptied into the Mediterranean Sea. It was a significant port for commerce and travel. From there they boarded a ship to the island of Cyprus located just sixty miles off the Syrian coast.

Opinions vary about the dates for the first missionary journey. They are usually figured in relation to the date of the Judaean famine and the famine relief offering taken to Jerusalem by Barnabas and Saul (see the commentary above). Picirilli (*Paul* 52) dates the first missionary journey from A.D. 45 to 46. Ramsay (*Traveller* 128) dates it from March, A.D. 47, to July/August, A.D. 49. Others suggest A.D. 46-50, taking anywhere from two to five years (Ogg 65; Bock 31; Fitzmyer 495; Bruce, *Paul* 475). Since there are no specific time references given during the journey, estimates of the amount of time needed for the events listed must be based on other considerations, like distances between cities, average travel time, reasonable time allowed between Sabbaths (since they went to the synagogues first), and means of travel. A fair estimate of these factors suggests that this first journey required from a year to eighteen months. If they left in the spring of either A.D. 45 or 46, when the sailing season began, they could have returned to Antioch by the fall of either A.D. 47 or 48, before the sailing season was over (27:9-12).

The island of Cyprus is the third largest island in the Mediterranean Sea. It is one hundred and forty miles long and sixty miles wide. Cyprus had a long history of settlement by different people groups but had been under Roman jurisdiction since the middle of the first century B.C. It was noted for its rugged beauty and dry climate as well as its production of copper and wood (Bock 442; Bruce, *Acts* 246-247). It was strategically located along the sea routes from Egypt to all points north and from the Syrian coast to all points west.

Why Cyprus? For one, it was the home of Barnabas (4:36), who would have known the area well enough to make travel easier. Second, there were believers from Cyprus (11:19) who had helped pioneer the work at Antioch. These would be contact sources and might have already opened the door of witness for them. Plus, Cyprus was well populated with both Jews and Gentiles who needed to hear the gospel (Bock 442).

Salamis was the port city on the east coast of the island and the center of commerce (Ramsay, *Traveller* 71-72; Keener II:1998-2001). It, also, had a Jewish population large enough for at least two synagogues. As was the method in every place possible, the first witness was in the synagogues (17:2; Rom. 1:16). There is no record of how these responded to the witness of the gospel.

Almost incidentally, Luke references John Mark as accompanying them. Some writers allude to the reference of "minister" as intentional playing down of Mark's role. The word translated *minister* (Greek *huperetes*) literally means "under rower" and originally referred to a galley-slave who manned the oars. Paul referred to himself with this term (1 Cor. 4:1), therefore, it is not a term of denigration but represents an attitude of service. Opinions vary regarding Mark's role with Barnabas and Saul. Some

interpreters even suggest that Mark had not been called as were Barnabas and Saul and should not have gone. But it should be noted that later Paul took others with him to assist in the work (16:1-3; 20:4) who are not listed as being "called."

Also, John Mark's role may have been to provide a first-generation eyewitness link to Jesus (Mk. 14:51-52) prior to His resurrection. This would have been significant to Jews especially. In that regard, Mark would have been an invaluable help. However, his later abandonment of the work (Ramsay, *Traveller* 71; Robertson, *John Mark* 55) became a major point of contention between Barnabas and Paul (15:36-40). More will be said about him later, but we should not be surprised at his presence or critical of him at this point.

b. The conversion of Sergius Paulus (13:6-12)

6 And when they had gone through the isle unto Paphos, they found a certain sorcerer, a false prophet, a Jew, whose name *was* Barjesus:
7 Which was with the deputy of the country, Sergius Paulus, a prudent man; who called for Barnabas and Saul, and desired to hear the word of God.
8 But Elymas the sorcerer (for so is his name by interpretation) withstood them, seeking to turn away the deputy from the faith.
9 Then Saul, (who also *is called* Paul,) filled with the Holy Ghost, set his eyes on him,
10 And said, O full of all subtilty and all mischief, *thou* child of the devil, *thou* enemy of all righteous-

ness, wilt thou not cease to pervert the right ways of the Lord?

11 And now, behold, the hand of the Lord *is* upon thee, and thou shalt be blind, not seeing the sun for a season. And immediately there fell on him a mist and a darkness; and he went about seeking some to lead him by the hand.

12 Then the deputy, when he saw what was done, believed, being astonished at the doctrine of the Lord.

As was his style of writing, Luke often summarized events without providing much detail. Such is the case with the east to west tour of Cyprus (v. 6) from Salamis to Paphos; he gives no information about what might have happened in between. Most writers assume the team traveled along the major, Roman road that traversed the island from east to west. Along the route were many villages and towns that could provide both opportunities to proclaim the gospel as well as necessary accommodations. It was a journey of some ninety miles and would have taken several days. Metzger (354) and Haenchen (397), however, offer that the wording, mostly from silence, suggests they sailed from Salamis along the southern coast of the island to Paphos. Whichever the case, it appears to be Luke's main intention to record the conversion of a significant individual, the Roman proconsul ("governor") of the island, Sergius Paulus.

History did not preserve all the names of all the proconsuls who served on Cyprus (Keener II:2014-2015). However, the family of one Sergius Paulus was well-known. The family connection is clear. Keener (II:2015) suggests that there is a family connection

even with Pisidian Antioch, to which the team traveled following Cyprus and Perga (v. 14). They might have gone there with recommendations from the governor of Cyprus. If so, we could credit the providence of God for such an opportunity—one reason Luke is careful to record his conversion.

Great accomplishments are often preceded by great obstacles. Such was the case in getting the gospel to the Roman governor. Though we are not told how he learned of the preaching of the missionary team, he knew enough to extend them an invitation to hear "the word of God" (v. 7). It is certainly possible, perhaps likely, that he wanted to make sure these men represented no public threat. There were plenty of political agitators whose business was to keep things stirred up (Bruce, *Paul* 162). One gathers that their ministry might have created enough of a stir in the synagogues for it to be reported to him. His prudence is noted in that he desired to hear the missionaries himself. At this point, he might or might not have had great spiritual interest, but that interest grew into full saving faith when he did hear and see the power of the gospel.

The audience with the proconsul turned out to include more than an articulate presentation of their faith. They had to deal with the opposition of Satan. This came in the form of a court sorcerer who openly opposed them. Luke refers to him as "Elymas the sorcerer" (Greek *magos*, magi, magician). The etymology of the name *Elymas* is not clear. "Barjesus" (son of Joshua) most likely was his personal name. "Elymas" may be an intentional play on Semitic words that he used to add a mysterious tone to his resumé.

Apparently, he had become successful enough to adopt such a name openly as his career moniker. His position of influence as the court magician should not be surprising since Roman officials commonly sought esoteric counsel and often surrounded themselves with their own oracles. Some regarded Jews as particularly good at the magic arts, with a corrupted association of the power of Moses over the Egyptian magicians as an example (Keener II:2009). This represented, of course, a misapprehension of the power of God versus Satan, as well as ignorance of biblical commands against dabbling in such practices (Deut. 18:9-12).

The position of Elymas was, no doubt, a very lucrative one and afforded him and his family a luxurious lifestyle. That was all threatened by the missionaries who proclaimed a different message and different source of faith. Their spiritual power and insight exposed him as the charlatan he was. That he was a charlatan does not mean there was no real spiritual power at work. Apparently, Paul saw the hand of Satan at work (5:3) through him. One can see a parallel between the confrontation of Moses with Pharaoh's court magicians over who really is God (Ex. 7:10-22).

In the course of Acts, Luke is careful to identify those who have evil, satanic relationships and oppose the gospel. This is especially the case with Jews who abandoned the biblical commands against all forms of sorcery (Deut. 18:9-12). It should be remembered that Philip encountered "unclean spirits" in Samaria (8:7) and a famous and influential sorcerer in Simon the Samaritan (8:9-10). Paul will deal powerfully with this at Ephesus (19:12-19). As great and good as the gospel of Christ is, to the opposite end of the spectrum is the influence of Satan. We should not be surprised that Acts records these incidents of opposition but should be reminded of the spiritual warfare that rages behind the scenes (Eph. 6:10-12).

When Elymas openly withstood Barnabas and Saul, trying to divert attention away from their apologetic for faith ("the faith" v. 8), Saul took the lead in confronting him. At this point, Luke shifts from the name "Saul" (his Jewish name) to "Paul" (his Roman name), which will be used for the rest of Acts. This name would be more convenient in the predominantly Roman world where they were circulating. It should be noted that Saul did not change his name to Paul. He always had those names as both a Jew and a man of the Graeco-Roman world (Robertson, *Acts* 181). Bruce (*Acts* 25, 249) asserts that, as a Roman citizen, he would have actually had three Roman names, a *praenomen* (Latin for first name), a *nomen* (Latin for family name), and a *cognomen* (Latin for nickname). *Paulus* (Paul) was his cognomen. His Jewish name, Saul, called a *signum*, would make four. Two of those Roman names have not been preserved. There is little doubt that when he went into the synagogues he used his Jewish name. The different usages are more related to cultural context than to theological intention.

With a penetrating gaze and energized by the Holy Spirit (v. 9), Paul minced no words in characterizing Elymas as a "child of the devil" (v. 10) who baited (Greek *dolos*), deceived, and perverted the "right ways of the Lord." The position and influence of Elymas was everything that was wrong with an apostate Judaism that had turned from the Lord to Satan. Note the emphatic, triple use of "all" in "all subtilty," "all mischief," "all righteousness." There followed an immediate, temporary, judgment (v. 11) of blindness that came upon Elymas that rendered him helpless to walk about on his own. This is the third judgment miracle in Acts (5:1-11; 12:20-23). Some situations called for strong, confrontational words. However, these must be at the direction of the Holy Spirit, not from our flesh.

The miracle judgment, combined with the teaching about the Lord (v. 12), convinced the Roman proconsul of the validity of the gospel. This was often the case in Acts (3:2-18; 5:14; 8:6-7), as it was in the life of Christ. Some may question whether the proconsul was actually saved when he "believed," but in Acts this is characteristic of those who turn to Christ in saving faith. Of all that might have happened on Cyprus (of which Luke mentions very little), the conversion of the Roman governor is certainly the highlight. If, indeed, he was the only spiritual fruit of this leg of the journey, it was certainly worth the effort.

3. John Mark abandons the work (13:13)

13 Now when Paul and his company loosed from Paphos, they came to Perga in Pamphylia: and John departing from them returned to Jerusalem.

This verse needs singular consideration. Three significant things are recorded. First, Luke posits Paul in the leadership and ownership of the work with Barnabas and John Mark referred to as "his company." That is not to exclude the leadership role of Barnabas

entirely, but it does indicate the leading role Paul assumes from here on.

Second, the next leg of the journey takes them from the island of Cyprus just over one hundred miles north to the province of Pamphylia in southeastern Asia Minor. They would have landed at the coastal port of Attalia (14:25), then traveled about eight miles up the Cestrus river to the city of Perga. The river itself probably could not accommodate the sea craft, but they might have boarded a smaller craft for the trip upriver. Or they could have walked.

As with Cyprus, why would they go here? One suggestion is based on the possible personal recommendation of Sergius Paulus to family and friends in government with whom he was familiar (Keener II:2017). The more likely case (Ramsay, *Traveller* 91-92) is that this area was a part of the "silent years" of Paul's ministry (9:30). He would have been familiar with the area and was not that far from his home in Tarsus. It is doubtful the itinerary was not planned.

Third, when they reached Perga, John Mark left the team and returned to Jerusalem. Suggestions abound as to the reasons for his departure. Those include that he left because of the toughness of the work, the emerging leadership of Paul over Barnabas, a change in strategy with which he disagreed, or the strangeness of Gentile lifestyle (Robertson, *John Mark*, 55-67; Polhill, *Acts* 296-297). It could have been none of these—or possibly all of these since such decisions are seldom of singular motivation. Whatever the reasons, his departure would have put more pressure on the others and did result in later tensions between Barnabas and Paul (15:37-40). Interestingly, Luke uses a verb cognate to this one for "depart" when he describes Paul's and Barnabas' "departing" from one another over John Mark later (15:39). Separation is sometimes necessary but never easy.

4. Witness in Antioch of Pisidia (13:14-52)

a. Paul's first recorded sermon to Jews (13:14-41)

(1) The setting (13:14-15)

14 But when they departed from Perga, they came to Antioch in Pisidia, and went into the synagogue on the sabbath day, and sat down.
15 And after the reading of the law and the prophets the rulers of the synagogue sent unto them, saying, Ye men *and* brethren, if ye have any word of exhortation for the people, say on.

Without elaboration Luke simply states that Paul and Barnabas left Perga and traveled to Antioch of Pisidia (v. 14). This Antioch was only one of sixteen cities named after the famed Hellenistic ruler, Antiochus the Great—each one identified by its location. Even though Antioch actually lay just across the border in Phrygia, it is identified as "Pisidian Antioch." It was the leading city of the region and, like Paul's home of Tarsus, was a Roman colony-city, operating autonomously and exempt from certain taxes (Ramsay, *Cities* 249-251). Furthermore, and more to the point of their mission, it had a large Jewish population. Antioch lay some one hundred miles north of Perga across the rugged and hostile Taurus Mountains. The area was noted for bandits and

inhospitable terrain (2 Cor. 11:26-27). Even the Romans had trouble keeping the peace here! (Polhill, *Acts* 297). It was no simple trek, though Luke's record mentions nothing of the hardships they must have endured getting there. Many are not aware of the herculean efforts of self-sacrifice exerted by faithful and dedicated Christian laborers, but the Lord does and will reward accordingly.

As was their intention (Rom. 1:16), Paul and Barnabas first went to the Jews by attending the synagogue on the Sabbath. The synagogues of the N. T. era were centers of Jewish cultural life. They were not just places for corporate worship but for education, social gatherings, judicial process, and even some forms of entertainment (Edersheim III:433-450). If one was going to reach the Jews in any given town, it would be necessary to go to the synagogue.

A typical synagogue order of service included prayers and the reading of selected O. T. texts as directed by the senior rabbi. It would have been customary to invite visiting rabbis to speak at some point during the service. Of course, this offered Paul and Barnabas the perfect opportunity to proclaim the message of the gospel. As seen in his message that follows, the N. T. gospel of Christ is the fulfillment of some of the very texts that might have been read that Sabbath day.

(2) The sermon (13:16-41)

(a) God's favor in choosing Israel (13:16-25)

16 Then Paul stood up, and beckoning with *his* hand said, Men of

Israel, and ye that fear God, give audience.

17 The God of this people of Israel chose our fathers, and exalted the people when they dwelt as strangers in the land of Egypt, and with an high arm brought he them out of it.

18 And about the time of forty years suffered he their manners in the wilderness.

19 And when he had destroyed seven nations in the land of Chanaan, he divided their land to them by lot.

20 And after that he gave *unto them* judges about the space of four hundred and fifty years, until Samuel the prophet.

21 And afterward they desired a king: and God gave unto them Saul the son of Cis, a man of the tribe of Benjamin, by the space of forty years.

22 And when he had removed him, he raised up unto them David to be their king; to whom also he gave testimony, and said, I have found David the *son* of Jesse, a man after mine own heart, which shall fulfill all my will.

23 Of this man's seed hath God according to *his* promise raised unto Israel a Saviour, Jesus:

24 When John had first preached before his coming the baptism of repentance to all the people of Israel.

25 And as John fulfilled his course, he said, Whom think ye that I am? I am not *he*. But, behold, there cometh one after me, whose shoes of *his* feet I am not worthy to loose.

Just as Peter's first message on the Day of Pentecost was rooted in the authority of O. T. Messianic references, so Paul's first message to the Jews continues with the same basic thematic approach (Dodd 17-24). No doubt, one of Luke's reasons for carefully recording the messages by different witnesses is to show the consistency of the gospel message in every setting.

Something of Paul's personality and style of communication is seen in how he speaks. Note that he stands and uses hand gestures (v. 16). His body language conveys the idea of one who is confident in speaking. He also speaks directly to those present with the repetition of "men of Israel," "men and brethren" (vv. 16, 26, 38). Twice (vv. 16, 26) Paul refers to the God-fearers ("ye that fear God"). (See comments above on Acts 10 and the conversion of Cornelius.)

Paul's message has three main components. The first (vv. 16-25) concerns God's favor in choosing Israel as the people of His witness who would ultimately herald the promise of the Redeemer-Messiah. Beginning with the call of the patriarchal fathers, he quickly compresses centuries of other events by carefully selecting the path of those events that led to the promise of the Messiah and its fulfillment. Note the repetition of God's initiative of interaction with O. T. Israel in phrases like, "God...chose" (v. 17); "brought he them out" (v. 17); "he divided" (v. 19); "He gave" (vv. 20-21); "He raised up... David" (v. 22). This culminates with the Messiah, Jesus, being "raised unto Israel" (v. 23), and "raised him from the dead" (v. 30). One cannot miss the divine initiative in providing Israel as a people for witness (Isa. 43:10, 12; 44:8) and in the ultimate provision of redemption through the Lord Jesus Christ.

One factor of the messages in Acts is confirming them with other details given regarding the times and incidents to which the speakers refer. There are a couple of these in Paul's message. His number of "seven nations" (v. 19) being conquered by Israel in Canaan verifies the number given in Deuteronomy 7:1.

His time reference of "four hundred and fifty years" (v. 20), however, is more difficult to interpret. The time seems to refer to the length of the period of the Judges. However, there are some textual and exegetical considerations (Metzger 358-359) regarding the point of reference. Most writers agree that Paul is not indicating the length of time for the judges, but the length of time preceding the judges that includes the Egyptian bondage (four hundred years), the wilderness wandering (forty years), then ten years dividing of the land (Bock 452; Lenski 519-520; Lightfoot 177; Marshall, *Acts* 223; Stott 223; Barnes 205-206).

Further, if the time of "four hundred and fifty years" refers to the period of the Judges, it makes it difficult to reconcile with the time reference of 1 Kings 7:1. It is best, exegetically, to take the phrase "and after that" to refer to the beginning of the period of the Judges (Robertson, *Acts* 188).

As for the time period of the judges, I begin by taking the early date of 1446 B.C. as the time of the Exodus. Then Jephthah's reference to "three hundred years" (Judg. 11:26) is to the occupation of Canaan previous to his time. Add to this the length of the reigns of the judges in the book itself, and the period of the judges is between 350 and 400 years (ESV Study Bible 33).

After referencing Saul (Paul's namesake and from the same tribe of Benjamin) as Israel's first king (v. 21), Paul proceeded to the Davidic kingdom and his Messianic emphasis (vv. 22-23; 34-36). The phrase used to describe David as "a man after mine own heart" needs attention. What exactly is meant? The phrase is used in contrast to Saul who began his rule with great promise and potential (1 Sam. 10:1, 6, 9, 26), but quickly moved from following the will of God to his own will (1 Sam. 13:9-14; 15:22-26). During those days Samuel rebuked Saul for his rule of self-will (1 Sam. 13:13-14), and the phrase was first used as the primary qualification for the king of Israel. The words certainly do not mean that God was looking for a man who did not sin but for a man who would put the will of God above his own self-will (Acts 13:22). David was that man early on in his life and operated by the principle for most of it. We know that later he fell into fleshly sins of self-will, but Paul's summary is not intended as a critique of his entire life. His point was that in this characteristic of being a man after the heart of God, David modeled it for most of his life, and prophetically wrote of the ultimate one who would perfectly express the will of God (v. 23), Jesus, the Savior of Israel. The Davidic promises of the Messiah are central to the preaching of the gospel to Jews (2:25-27; 7:45).

The inclusion of the ministry of John the Baptist, who is referenced eight times in Acts, is somewhat surprising and raises the question why Paul would use him in speaking to the Jews in Pisidian Antioch. Apparently, even they knew by now of the life and ministry of John, enough for Paul to make the reference. Is it possible that Paul was one who personally critiqued the ministry of John (Mt. 3:7-12; Jn. 1:24-27)? Now, in retrospect, he interprets John's ministry as transitional from the O. T. era of promise to the age of Messianic fulfillment (Bock 453-454; Polhill, *Acts* 301). More likely, Paul had learned from the apostles, and possibly from the Lord Jesus Himself (Gal. 1:1-12) to include the ministry of John in the Messianic era, and rightly so. His was a preparatory ministry that culminated with the public announcement of Jesus as the "Lamb of God" who would baptize with the Holy Spirit (Jn. 1:29-34). Although Herod thought he had silenced the voice of John when he had him killed (Mt. 14:1-12), the truth John proclaimed was not silenced (Mt. 11:7-15; Lk. 7:26-28).

(b) God's promise of the Messiah fulfilled in Jesus (13:26-37)

26 Men *and* brethren, children of the stock of Abraham, and whosoever among you feareth God, to you is the word of this salvation sent.
27 For they that dwell at Jerusalem, and their rulers, because they knew him not, nor yet the voices of the prophets which are read every sabbath day, they have fulfilled *them* in condemning *him*.
28 And though they found no cause of death *in him*, yet desired they Pilate that he should be slain.
29 And when they had fulfilled all that was written of him, they took *him* down from the tree, and laid *him* in a sepulchre.
30 But God raised him from the dead:

31 And he was seen many days of them which came up with him from Galilee to Jerusalem, who are his witnesses unto the people.
32 And we declare unto you glad tidings, how that the promise which was made unto the fathers,
33 God hath fulfilled the same unto us their children, in that he hath raised up Jesus again; as it is also written in the secondp, Thou art my Son, this day have I begotten thee.
34 And as concerning that he raised him up from the dead, *now* no more to return to corruption, he said on this wise, I will give you the sure mercies of David.
35 Wherefore he saith also in another *psalm*, Thou shalt not suffer thine Holy One to see corruption.
36 For David, after he had served his own generation by the will of God, fell on sleep, and was laid unto his fathers, and saw corruption:
37 But he, whom God raised again, saw no corruption.

The second component of Paul's message (vv. 26-37) announced that the promised and long-awaited Messiah had, indeed, come. But, instead of being recognized and received with open arms, as would be expected after such a long history of God's favor and promises, the rulers of Israel did not recognize Him as the Messiah. They did not know Him (1 Cor. 2:7-8) or acknowledge the authority of the O. T. prophets whose writings are read every Sabbath day in the synagogues (v. 27). Instead, they falsely accused Him before Pontius Pilate (v. 28) and put Him to death on

203

the cross ("the tree"), laying His body in a tomb. However, God raised Him from the dead (v. 30)! This is the unique message of the gospel. It is this last sentence that changed everything, including the life of Paul himself.

Paul used two types of evidences to confirm the resurrection of Christ from the dead. The first evidence was the testimony of the witnesses (v. 31) who interacted with Him for "many days." The gospel records of the appearances of Jesus are here confirmed by the apostle as key, eye-witness evidences (1 Cor. 15:6-8).

The second type of evidence, which is particularly testimonial to the authority of the O. T. Scriptures, is "the promise which was made unto the fathers" (vv. 32-37): that is, the O. T. Messianic promises. Paul used two references from the Psalms (vv. 33, 35) and one from Isaiah 55:3 (v. 34). Psalm 2:7 establishes the Trinitarian relationship of Jesus with the Father as His "Son." Psalm 16:10 points to the resurrection as fulfilling the promise of avoiding the corruption (decaying) of His flesh (2:27). David, the author of the Psalm, did not avoid that, of course. After serving the Lord during his time, he died, and his body decayed like everyone else's. It was the one about whom he prophesied who did avoid the decay of the flesh in death via His resurrection.

But what of the Isaiah 55:3 reference and giving "the sure mercies of David"? The historical setting of the Isaiah text relates the renewal of an eternal covenant with Israel, should they respond to the Lord's gracious invitation (Isa. 55:1-2) to return to spiritual favor. Securing such an eternal covenant requires the conquering of death, for death is terminal. Paul ingeniously ties these promises

together in the resurrection of the Lord Jesus as the "Son" (Ps. 2:7), descendant of David who fulfilled the Davidic covenant in securing his "mercies" (Isa. 55:3), and whose flesh did not "see corruption" (Ps. 16:10). Here, again, the message of the apostles provided a Christian interpretative construct for O. T. Messianic promises (Shires 30).

(c) Paul's appeal and warning (13:38-41)

38 Be it known unto you therefore, men _and_ brethren, that through this man is preached unto you the forgiveness of sins:
39 And by him all that believe are justified from all things, from which ye could not be justified by the law of Moses.
40 Beware therefore, lest that come upon you, which is spoken of in the prophets;
41 Behold, ye despisers, and wonder, and perish: for I work a work in your days, a work which ye shall in no wise believe, though a man declare it unto you.

The third component of Paul's message (vv. 38-41) is an appeal to repentance and faith in the Messiah, coupled with a stern warning about rejection. Of note is his appeal to "all that believe"—literally, all who "are believing" (Greek present participle) as the basis for being "justified" (v. 39) before the Lord. Here is the first mention of the concept of justification (Greek _dikaioo_) in connection with the gospel message. In this usage, it carries the meaning of liberation from guilt (TDNT II:218). One is declared to be set free from the guilt of sin and righteous before God. (For an interesting and informative discussion of Paul's concept of "justification" see Wright, *Really Said* 117-133; and Wright, *Justification*). This is something the O. T. Law of Moses could not do. Its intention was to indict, to reveal the sinful guilt of humanity. The Law was very good at that. Paul was especially self-aware of this effect (Rom. 7:7-13). For Paul to address the limitation of the Law, in that it could not liberate us from the guilt it imposed, was not to destroy the Law but to show its character and purpose. The gospel of Christ supplied by grace what the Law could not do (Rom. 7:24—8:4). However, this dimension of the gospel was probably not well received by the Jews. These Pauline concepts are developed in detail in Romans and Galatians. The appeal to "all that believe" would have been especially poignant for the Gentile "God-fearers" (v. 16) in Paul's audience.

The apostle used Habakkuk 1:5 as a warning of rejection (vv. 40-41) that targeted all who heard but particularly the Jews. Paul's purpose in the quote was the same as Habakkuk's. Great truth is not to be trifled with. After all, the fulfillment of Messianic promises given over hundreds of years and now fulfilled in the person of Jesus Christ are of eternal consequence!

One can easily see the common denominators of the recorded sermons in Acts that are preached to Jews. Those include a link to the history of Israel showing God's favor on them as His covenant people, the tracing of key Messianic promises that were fulfilled in Jesus of Nazareth, the offer of forgiveness of sins to all who repent and believe in Him, and a warning against rejection.

b. Gentile opportunity, Jewish opposition (13:42-52)

42 And when the Jews were gone out of the synagogue, the Gentiles besought that these words might be preached to them the next sabbath.
43 Now when the congregation was broken up, many of the Jews and religious proselytes followed Paul and Barnabas: who, speaking to them, persuaded them to continue in the grace of God.
44 And the next sabbath day came almost the whole city together to hear the word of God.
45 But when the Jews saw the multitudes, they were filled with envy, and spake against those things which were spoken by Paul, contradicting and blaspheming.
46 Then Paul and Barnabas waxed bold, and said, It was necessary that the word of God should first have been spoken to you: but seeing ye put it from you, and judge yourselves unworthy of everlasting life, lo, we turn to the Gentiles.
47 For so hath the Lord commanded us, *saying*, I have set thee to be a light of the Gentiles, that thou shouldest be for salvation unto the ends of the earth.
48 And when the Gentiles heard this, they were glad, and glorified the word of the Lord: and as many as were ordained to eternal life believed.
49 And the word of the Lord was published throughout all the region.
50 But the Jews stirred up the devout and honorable women, and the chief men of the city, and

raised persecution against Paul and Barnabas, and expelled them out of their coasts.

51 But they shook off the dust of their feet against them, and came unto Iconium.

52 And the disciples were filled with joy, and with the Holy Ghost.

Paul's message received a mixed response (as does all preaching of the gospel). When the service concluded, and the congregation was leaving (vv. 42-43), some remained behind. Notably there were many Jews, but also Gentile proselytes who wanted to hear more and urged Paul and Barnabas to stay and speak the next Sabbath day. For identifying the "God-fearers" and the "religious proselytes" see the commentary on chapter ten.

The message and the messengers caused quite a stir as word of what had been proclaimed by Paul spread like wildfire throughout the entire city. The widespread talk resulted in a large crowd that gathered to hear what would be said. Why would the preaching of Paul garner such interest? For one, the idea of one rising from the dead with multiple eye-witnesses would spark curiosity even from among the pagans. Also, while there were many Jews in Antioch, there were many more Gentiles. The excitement of the Gentile "God-fearers" was contagious as they had heard that they were included in God's plan of redemption (v. 39). They turned out *en masse* to listen (v. 44).

Luke defines the message of Paul and Barnabas as "the word of God" (v. 44). It should be noted that the message of the gospel is, theologically, just that, God's Word (1 Cor. 14:37; 1 Thess. 2:13). The truths of the gospel of Christ

are the revelation of God. No other voices or writings outside the biblical canon qualify as the Word of God.

As was the case too often, many of the Jews did not receive or even express tolerance for the proclamation of the gospel. The popular response of the Gentiles fostered envy and open, hostile retaliation against Paul and Barnabas (v. 45). But in what sense were they envious? Perhaps the Jews saw that their process of gaining proselytes was being overshadowed (Mt. 23:15); in that case they resented the response of the Gentiles to Paul's preaching. More likely, however, they resisted the inclusion of Gentile in the message of forgiveness of sins (vv. 39, 43). Paul's message of the fulfillment of all the O. T. Messianic promises in Jesus Christ, coupled with its inclusion of Gentiles, proved to be too much to accept. The problem was not the "newness" of this message so much as the limited interpretation given for so many centuries by the Jews to those O. T. promises. That view of things had resulted in an exclusive mindset (Bock 462; Polhill, *Acts* 307). Such a mentality of exclusiveness cannot be biblically justified.

True to his warning (vv. 40-41), Paul and Barnabas boldly condemned the envious response of the Jews as self-judgment against the promise of eternal life. Rejection by them was a closed door of opportunity but an open door to others (vv. 46-47). They turned their attention to the Gentiles who were eager to hear. God never closes one door without opening another.

The concept of everlasting or eternal life is mentioned only here in Acts (vv. 46, 48) in connection with the gospel message. Of course, this was a key component of the gospel of Jesus Christ (Jn.

3:16). Faith in the Messiah, Jesus Christ, results in forgiveness of sins: that is, being "justified from all things" (v. 39). Justification brings the promise of eternal life (TDNT II:866-870). Justification is a major Pauline theological concept (Rom. 3:24—5:21; Gal. 2:16—3:29), one he developed extensively in his letters.

Apparently, the confrontation with the Jews and their rejection was public enough to be heard and publicized by the sizeable Gentile audience who clamored to hear Paul and Barnabas. They rejoiced that they were included (v. 48a) among those privileged to hear the Word of God.

With regard to the interpretation of verse 48 there is much disagreement, arising over the clause "as many as were ordained to eternal life believed." The order of the phrase in the Greek places "believed" before "ordained." Often the arrangement of terms suggests emphasis. While that is certainly important, interpreting this clause also involves the context as well as the translation of the word "ordained." First, I want to offer that "ordained" is not the best translation here.

The Greek word translated "ordained" (Greek tetagmenoi) is a perfect passive participle and is taken from a military term meaning "to appoint, arrange, position, or assign." The construction here (in Greek, pluperfect) can appropriately be rendered (smoothing it out a little for translation) "as many as had been appointed to eternal life." Robertson (Acts 200) agrees that "appointed" (as rendered in both the NASB and ESV) is a better translation than "ordained." Brian Abasciano ("Acts 13:48") argues strongly for the translation "were disposed" (rather than

"ordained" or "appointed") in order to preserve the ambiguity of the Greek text and avoid an intentional theological bias in translation. His appeal for an unbiased translation is well-noted since this text is often cited as an "unqualified... statement of absolute predestination" (Barrett, Acts 208). While we should let the Scriptures determine our theology, we should not let our theology determine the wording of the Scriptures.

Contextually, whatever else Luke means, it is clear that Gentiles were now included in the plan of redemption. The response of Gentiles in Antioch of Pisidia parallels the response of Gentiles in Antioch of Syria. At Antioch of Pisidia, Gentile inclusion in the message of the gospel is directly tied to the Jewish rejection of that gospel (v. 46). Gentile inclusion confirms all previous truths of inclusiveness and means that all people everywhere who hear the gospel may be saved.

Second, the question of how these "were appointed to eternal life" is not addressed in the text except in reference to their faith ("believed"). The following presents a brief summary of the two main schools of thought regarding this.

Calvinists (Bock 464-465; Stott 227; Bruce, Acts 267) hold that it confirms the teaching of sovereign election in the choice of people who are saved by the "sovereign good pleasure of God" (Berkhof 115). John Calvin (I:393) states, "For this particular ordaining can only be understood of the eternal purpose of God...for He does not choose us after we have believed; but He seals His adoption, which was hidden, by the gift of faith in our hearts." Calvinists therefore hold that some in Antioch had been elected to be saved by sovereign decree in eternity past and now they acted in faith as decreed. I am intentionally summarizing. This view would interpret the phrase to say, "as many (individuals among the Gentiles and Jews) as were ordained (that is, were decreed by sovereign choice to be among the elect) to eternal life believed (in personal confirmation of their sovereign election)."

On the other hand, Arminians holds that this phrase is not confirmation of a sovereign election of individuals but records the progress of redemptive history with the inclusion of Gentiles. Neither does the phrase, when rightly interpreted, remove the means of personal faith in Christ as necessary for salvation. As Robertson (*Acts* 200) comments, "There is no evidence that Luke had in mind an *absolutum decretum* of personal salvation. Paul had shown that God's plan extended to and included Gentiles." Meyer (264) and Knowling (300) concur with this assessment.

Picirilli (*Free Will* 115-116) agrees as well. After showing the contextual inclusion of Gentiles, he explains that the Greek verb translated "ordained" can be understood as either middle or passive voice, and he believes it is middle usage (Knowling 300 concurs). He states,

"Even in the English language a passive voice verb can be used with such a 'middle' sense, having no reference at all to some agent other than oneself. Thus we say, for example, 'I am disposed' to do something or other, or 'I am inclined' to act in a certain way, and we do not mean that someone else has disposed or inclined us...There is no convincing reason, then, to think that Acts 13:48 means that God had already ordained or appointed to eternal life those who were saved by faith in Antioch."

In his discussion, Picirilli also points out that the words are intended, in the context, to be seen as the opposite of those who "judged themselves" to be "unworthy of everlasting life" in verse 46.

This view would interpret the clause to mean, "as many (among all Gentiles who are now included in the plan of redemption) as were ordained (put themselves in position) for eternal life (personally) believed." I believe this provides a better understanding of the phrase and especially satisfies the contextual reference to Gentiles.

A more specific development of this second line of interpretation is that these are the Gentile "God-fearers" who were O. T. saints (see the commentary on chapter ten) and re-focused their faith on the person of Jesus Christ. Leroy Forlines (*Arminianism* 165) states,

"I think what the verse is telling us is that all of those who had been saved prior to their hearing the New Testament gospel subsequently believed when they heard the gospel being presented by Paul and Barnabas. At the moment of their salvation in the past, they were appointed to eternal life. When they heard about the redemptive work of Jesus the Messiah, they believed and became New Testament believers."

Marshall (*Acts* 231) agrees that this is a distinct possibility.

This view would interpret the clause to mean, "as many (of the Gentile God-fearers who had previously been saved according to the O. T. promise of Messiah) as were appointed (at the time of their recent faith decision) to eternal life (personally) believed (now re-focused their faith on the person of Jesus Christ as the Messiah)."

While this concept presented by Forlines is, indeed, valid for some in the Acts narrative as previously discussed, I am of the opinion that, in this situation, it limits the receptor audience too much and too narrowly defines what "believed" means. The receptor audience in verse 48 is "the Gentiles," not just the "God-fearers." I assume there were Jews, too, who were saved (v. 43). Furthermore, the word "believed" is commonly used in Acts of initial saving faith (4:4, 32; 8:12-13, 37; 9:42; 11:21; 16:31), not just previous saving faith as per the O. T. arrangement. There is no qualification here that this "belief" is limited to one dimension of saving faith (see previous discussion in chapter ten).

Picirilli deals with this in regard to Peter's statement at the Jerusalem council in 15:7-9. It is the very same theological issue about saving faith. The very same group of people is in focus when he addresses this concept (*Grace* 171-172). He states, "Peter spoke, the Gentiles heard, they believed... and God gave them the Holy Spirit... '(thus) purifying their hearts by faith.'" On that occasion, both Peter and Paul testified of Gentile inclusion. Certainly, Paul's point of reference at the Jerusalem Council would have included the Gentiles at Antioch of Pisidia (the Jerusalem Council *followed* the first missionary journey).

I am of the opinion that God did, indeed, ordain or appoint *something* in the salvation process, just not individuals. What was ordained was the *means and scope* of receiving eternal life. The *means* that was ordained was personal, saving faith. The *scope* was "the uttermost part of the earth" (1:8), i.e., Jews and Gentiles. Therefore, Acts 13:48 confirms in Paul's ministry what was

previously initiated in Peter's with Cornelius (10:1ff) and even earlier with Philip and the Ethiopian eunuch (8:26-39). All men everywhere are saved by the same gospel and by the same means. Furthermore, this summary, I believe, better complements the whole theological construct of saving faith. (To which I add, *Hallelujah!*)

As a result of such widespread response in Antioch to the message of Paul and Barnabas, the whole surrounding region (v. 49) buzzed with their message. The "word of the Lord" was the main topic of discussion. But the excitement proved to be a two-edged sword. While many were glad to hear its truth, Jewish opposition worked to expel Paul and Barnabas from the city (v. 50). One group the unbelieving Jews managed to influence were the "devout and honorable women." As the word "devout" indicates, these were religious proselytes to Judaism of high standing. We are not told who the "chief men of the city" were, but they must have been city officials with whom the women and Jews had influence. Thus, the intolerance of some elite against the message of the gospel resulted in outright persecution, and Paul and Barnabas were officially escorted out of the area.

In an act reminiscent of Jesus' command (Mt. 10:15; Mk. 6:11; Lk. 9:5), Paul and Barnabas expressed their regrets over this injustice by intentionally wiping the dust from their feet on the outskirts of the city. The act applied to those who chose to reject the message of the gospel and expel them from the city. It was not directed to the believers who remained. The believers, in contrast, were blessed with fullness of joy and the Holy Spirit (v. 52); the tense of the verb (Greek imperfect) suggests that they kept on being filled.

Paul and Barnabas set their sights on the city of Iconium some ninety miles southeast (v. 51). The rejection and persecution of one group in one place did not deter them from their mission. Sometimes character and dedication are measured by what it takes to stop a person from obedience to God's will.

Summary
(13:1-52)

The first missionary journey is a major development in the life of the church. It represents an intentional witness to Gentiles, on the part of those who were specifically called by the Holy Spirit and affirmed by a local church. Until now the witness of believers was somewhat spontaneous as they sought refuge from persecution. The essence of authentic missions arises from the heart of faithful followers of Christ wherever they are. Organized mission's efforts only build upon this.

The calling of the Spirit occurred in the atmosphere of worship and ministry in the Antioch church. That church itself owed its existence to the faithful witness efforts of believers who had fled the persecution of the church in Judaea (11:19-21). In yet another sense of irony so often characteristic of the Acts record, the very one who had been the key source of persecution (Saul of Tarsus) was now one of the missionaries called to carry the gospel!

With John Mark as their helper, Barnabas and Saul began "the work" to which they had been called by traveling to the Island of Cyprus, the home of Barnabas. Their efforts become public enough that the Roman governor sched-

uled an audience with them. Although confronted by an apostate Jew who had become a sorcerer and counselor to the governor, their witness was believed by the governor. The conversion of Sergius Paulus marks a somewhat common response to the gospel by those in civic leadership. It was here that Saul of Tarsus took on the identity of Paul the apostle.

The realities of the work impacted John Mark quickly, and he abandoned the team in Perga and went home to Jerusalem. It was a discouraging blow to them but did not halt their efforts. With what can only be described as disciplined resilience, Barnabas and Paul pressed on to other cities. In Antioch of Pisidia, Paul preached his first recorded message in the synagogue. It was met with mixed response. But the entire city was stirred, and many Jews and Gentiles responded in saving faith to the gospel.

However, many of the Jews so opposed their work that they succeeded in getting people in high positions to join with them in forcing Paul and Barnabas to leave the city. Luke concludes their work in Antioch of Pisidia with a footnote about the joy-filled and Spirit-filled believers they left behind as they moved to the next city for witness.

Application: Teaching and Preaching the Passage

Exegetical Outline of the Text: 1. The Calling of Barnabas and Saul (13:1-3). 2. The Confrontation With Elymas the Sorcerer (13:4-11). 3. The Conversion of Sergius Paulus (13:12). 4. The Continuation of the Journey (13:13-14). 5. The Message of Paul at Antioch of Pisidia (13:15-41).

6. The Response to Paul's Message (13:42-49). 7. The Rejection of the Missionaries (13:50-52).

The church at Antioch of Syria deserves study for many reasons. It became the second leading church in the Acts narrative. It may be noted for its cosmopolitan make-up, its atmosphere of worship and ministry, and its on-going missionary efforts to extend the gospel witness to all the world. It was this church that Paul considered his "headquarters" and to which he gave account for the first two missionary journeys.

The confrontation with Elymas and the conversion of Sergius Paulus go hand in hand. The devil does not want the gospel to succeed and has his workers stationed at strategic places for attempts to deter efforts to win others. This principle of Satan's strategies can be traced right through the Book of Acts. Previously, we saw him at work with *intimidation* (4:18), then *imitation* (5:1-11). Here his strategy is *intervention*.

John Mark's departure was, no doubt, discouraging to the team, and yet they did not quit the work. As is often the case in ministry there are those who "turn back." Some are lost to the ministry and even Christian life. But some are restored, as with John Mark. While someone's quitting is discouraging, we must keep our focus on the Lord and serve Him faithfully.

The first recorded message of Paul had mixed results. There were many who were saved but many who rejected its truth. There were enough influential people to succeed in getting Barnabas and Paul run out of town. Even the best and greatest of Christian laborers are sometimes unappreciated and rejected.

But they left behind many, too, who were saved and Spirit-filled believers.

5. Witness in Iconium (14:1-7)

**1 And it came to pass in Iconium, that they went both together into the synagogue of the Jews, and so spake, that a great multitude both of the Jews and also of the Greeks believed.
2 But the unbelieving Jews stirred up the Gentiles, and made their minds evil affected against the brethren.
3 Long time therefore abode they speaking boldly in the Lord, which gave testimony unto the word of his grace, and granted signs and wonders to be done by their hands.
4 But the multitude of the city was divided: and part held with the Jews, and part with the apostles.
5 And when there was an assault made both of the Gentiles, and also of the Jews with their rulers, to use *them* despitefully, and to stone them,
6 They were ware of *it*, and fled unto Lystra and Derbe, cities of Lycaonia, and unto the region that lieth round about:
7 And there they preached the gospel.**

Iconium (modern Konya) was the next largest and most important city to occupy their attention. It was about ninety miles southeast of Antioch and, though associated with Phrygia, it geographically lay on the western edge of Lycaonia. Situated in a mountainous setting, somewhat isolated, but at the convergence of several Roman roads, it offered a significant agricultural economy (Keener II:2110-2112; Ramsay, *Cities* 317). Though it was probably not yet a Roman colony, it was a city of considerable cosmopolitan blend. Its sizeable population and Jewish synagogue were the main reasons for Paul and Barnabas to go there. If they walked the distance, it would have taken them four to five days through the rugged, steep terrain to get there, even though there was a decent Roman road, the Via Sebaste. Though rough and crude by today's standards, inns existed but were unreliably secure. Hospitable accommodations would have been scarce. One can appreciate Paul's summary of his journeys in 2 Corinthians 11:26-27; that description would certainly have included this trip.

When they arrived, they found a positive response to the gospel in the synagogue with many Jews and Greeks coming to saving faith in Christ (v. 1). Though Luke uses the phrase "Jews and...Greeks" only here in Acts, he is probably referencing the Gentile "God-fearers" (13:16, 26), since they are associated with the synagogue witness.

As in Antioch, however, there were those who rejected the message of the gospel (v. 2), particularly some Jewish leaders. They were not content with mere verbal disagreement but influenced local Gentile leaders and embittered them ("made their minds evil affected") against Paul and Barnabas. The basis of their accusations is not recorded but had to be sufficient to convince the city officials that Paul and Barnabas somehow presented a threat to the peace. Nothing could have been farther from the truth, but prejudice and bias thrive on false accusations. A pattern of response can be seen in that some accepted the message of the gospel and some rejected it.

Those who rejected it initiated persecution.

Though we wish Luke were more definitive about how long was a "long time" (v. 3) they stayed in Iconium, the length of time was not his focus. The mission of proclaiming the gospel was. Paul and Barnabas remained in spite of the persecution. Their ministry was graced with boldness in preaching, teaching, and "signs and wonders" that attested to its veracity (2:43; 4:29-30; 5:12; 6:8; 8:6). The number of believers would have given them some security and purpose to remain and disciple them. They were a good team in this ministry (11:25-26).

Hostile intentions against them, however, fueled division within the city at large (vv. 4-5). Sides were chosen with some for and some against Paul and Barnabas. Ultimately, this was an issue of choosing sides about the message they preached, but bias personifies differences rather than discusses principles. Here and in verse 14 are the only two times the term *apostles* (Greek *apostolos*, one sent, a messenger) refers to both Paul and Barnabas. Normally it was used in a more restricted sense of the inner circle chosen by Jesus; namely, "the Twelve" (Jn. 20:24; Acts 6:2; 1 Cor. 15:5). Its use here is in the broader sense of the term. Apparently, Paul regarded Barnabas as his equal in ministry (1 Cor. 9:6; Gal. 2:9). However, while he strongly stated his own apostleship, he never made the case officially for Barnabas. Luke's usage here, using "apostles" of them both, may be in reference to their being sent by the call of the Holy Spirit and the commissioning of the Antioch church (13:3-4). Some regard the missionary call today to be associated with this broader sense of "apostle."

Support from the city's leaders was enlisted and plans were made (probably not legally) to stone Paul and Barnabas. But they became aware of the plot (v. 6) and left town before it could be perpetrated on them. They fled to the cities of Lystra and Derbe, deeper in the region of Lycaonia. At the time these cities were surrounded by small villages that did not constitute being called "cities," hence, Luke refers to this area as "the region that lieth round about."

Lystra was some eighteen miles southwest of Iconium and Derbe another sixty miles from there. These were not particularly significant cities with large populations and were culturally regional in language and religion, as Paul and Barnabas would soon see (vv. 11-13). The Romans regarded them as isolated and illiterate. Ramsay (Cities 408) describes the area as a "quiet backwater." Stott (229-230) suggests it was not so much a target city for evangelism as much as a place of refuge for the missionaries, withdrawing from the animosity and intended stoning in Iconium. Be that as it may, Paul and Barnabas found opportunity to preach the gospel there as they had in other places (v. 7).

6. Witness at Lystra and Derbe (14:8-21a)

a. Healing of the lame man (14:8-10)

8 And there sat a certain man at Lystra, impotent in his feet, being a cripple from his mother's womb, who never had walked:
9 The same heard Paul speak: who stedfastly beholding him, and perceiving that he had faith to be healed,
10 Said with a loud voice, Stand upright on thy feet. And he leaped and walked.

One cannot miss the parallels between this incident and a similar one earlier, involving Peter (3:2-11). In both cases, the miraculous healing drew a lot of attention and provided a witness opportunity. The difference, here, is that Paul and Barnabas were proclaimed as gods and frantically sought to correct such a misinterpretation.

Though we are not told the exact setting of the healing, it might have occurred at the city gates. That was a place of social interaction and the place where the sacrifice was attempted (v. 13). No mention is made of a synagogue in Lystra, although there might have been one. Wherever the event took place, Paul was able to speak openly (v. 9) and others were there to witness the miracle. Public oratory was common in Greek culture (Keener II:2132-2136), so Paul's speaking to those around was not out of the ordinary. However, what he said was very much out of the ordinary. That Paul preached the gospel (v. 7) determined the content of what he said.

The congenitally lame man caught Paul's attention (v. 9), who discerned a spark of faith in him sufficient for healing. Paul's apostolic discernment is certainly understandable, but where did this man's faith originate? Most likely he was a pagan who had very little, if any, knowledge of biblical truth. In most all healing miracles in the N. T., the element of faith can be seen in some capacity. No doubt his physical condition and hope for relief contributed, but such hope might have been sparked by the gospel of the Great Physician, the Lord Jesus, as preached by Paul. Faith does not have to be "big" in order to be effective. The size of a mustard seed will do nicely (Mt. 17:20). That truth shot as an arrow into his heart and gave him some sense of hope for his needs, both spiritual and physical. With what must be regarded as bold, almost brash confidence, Paul spoke loudly for the man, who had never walked in his entire life, to "stand upright on his feet." And he did!

Here is yet another instance of the medical insights of Luke as a physician (Ramsay, *Luke* 56-59). How is it that a man who had never walked, whose legs must have been undeveloped and muscles atrophied, and whose bodily movements and mental capacities had totally adapted to immobility, was suddenly able to leap up and walk? The extremity of the case provides proof of the miraculous. Only God could do such a thing! The same, of course, is true of the spiritual healing of a sin-emaciated heart. Only God can forgive and heal such a heart. I am, of course, taking the incident to be literally as Luke recorded it, a true and factual event. One dimension of the apologetic of the gospel is the premise that if Jesus literally and bodily rose from the grave, He certainly can perform the miraculous as He deems it necessary.

b. Barnabas and Paul proclaimed as gods (14:11-18)

11 And when the people saw what Paul had done, they lifted up their voices, saying in the speech of Lycaonia, The gods are come down to us in the likeness of men.

12 And they called Barnabas, Jupiter; and Paul, Mercurius, because he was the chief speaker.
13 Then the priest of Jupiter, which was before their city, brought oxen and garlands unto the gates, and would have done sacrifice with the people.
14 *Which* when the apostles, Barnabas and Paul, heard *of*, they rent their clothes, and ran in among the people, crying out,
15 And saying, Sirs, why do ye these things? We also are men of like passions with you, and preach unto you that ye should turn from these vanities unto the living God, which made heaven, and earth, and the sea, all things that are therein:
16 Who in times past suffered all nations to walk in their own ways.
17 Nevertheless he left not himself without witness, in that he did good, and gave us rain from heaven, and fruitful seasons, filling our hearts with food and gladness.
18 And with these sayings scarce restrained they the people, that they had not done sacrifice unto them.

The healing of the lame man resulted in a response from the people that was totally different from what Paul intended. No doubt, he wanted it to be a testimony of God's grace and confirmation of the gospel. The people, however, proceeded to proclaim, in their local dialect, that Paul and Barnabas were gods who had come from above to visit them (v. 11). An ancient local legend written by the Latin poet, Ovid, tells of a previous visit to the area by the gods Jupiter and Mercury. The Greek equivalents were Zeus and Hermes, as in the Greek text here, but translated by the names of the equivalent Roman gods. According to the legend, the gods visited the area and sought for hospitality among the people but were rejected. An older, impoverished couple, Philemon and Baucis, however, provided for them and were generously rewarded. A flood was sent upon the others, devastating the area and killing those who rejected them. The people must have learned their lesson for they built a temple to Jupiter at the entrance of the city (v. 13). Now they mistakenly thought they would celebrate the re-appearance of the two gods. They did not want to repeat the previous mistake. Such is the mindset of idolatry and the persistence of legends. (It should be noted that Haenchen, 432-433, denies the factualness of the healing told in Acts; Marshall, *Acts* 237, repudiates Haenchen's proposal.)

According to the Roman system, the Lystrans were calling Barnabas *Jupiter* (father of all the Romans gods), probably because he was older and perhaps more regal in appearance. They called Paul, *Mercury*, because he was the chief speaker (Marshall, *Acts* 236-237; Keener II:2146-2150).

With all the pomp and circumstance occasioned by a personal visit from the gods, the pagan priest to Jupiter paraded garland-strewn oxen to the gates of the city for sacrifice (v. 13). However, when Paul and Barnabas learned of it, they tore their garments in an expression of revulsion and ran among the people shouting to stop the procedure (v. 14). The opportunity and audience are notable. Not only is the man who was healed there, but the Jupiter priest, the city officials, and the followers of the

Jupiter cult are also there. The missionaries' explanation quickly followed, telling why this was unacceptable. The situation dictated the content of the explanation. The message, although a brief one, represents the summary truths needed in addressing idolatry.

The brief explanation (vv. 15-17) given by Paul and Barnabas (assuming Paul was the spokesman), is three-fold. First, they are mere mortal men as everyone else, not gods in human form. Second, they do represent the true, living God who is the Creator of the entire material world and all that it contains. This great God provides for the needs of all people in supplying seasonal rain and harvests that nourish and provide for the general happiness and well-being of society. Third, the Creator God has tolerated the misguided practices of idolatry and now desires that people turn from the emptiness of idols to know Him.

Even with the impassioned speech and explanation, the missionaries were barely able to prevent the sacrifice from being made (v. 18). No doubt the situation included additional interactions and even more explanation, but Luke does not expand on what he has recorded. The intervention against the sacrifice was probably offensive to the Jupiter priest and his followers. This may be used against Paul later.

c. Jews from Antioch and Iconium stir opposition (14:19-21a)

19 And there came thither *certain* Jews from Antioch and Iconium, who persuaded the people, and, having stoned Paul, drew *him* out of the city, supposing he had been dead.

20 Howbeit, as the disciples stood round about him, he rose up, and came into the city: and the next day he departed with Barnabas to Derbe.
21a And when they had preached the gospel to that city, and had taught many...

Although Lystra was over one hundred miles from Antioch in Pisidia, and Iconium was nearly twenty miles away, the distance did not deter the previous opposition from pursuing Barnabas and Paul there. The irony that some were incensed against the followers of Christ and pursued them to prevent the proclamation of the gospel should not be lost (8:3; 9:1-2). The implication is that there was no synagogue in Lystra, since Jews from Antioch and Iconium had to come and join with any Jews in Lystra (who are not mentioned) to persuade the city leaders to perpetrate injury to Paul (Polhill, *Acts* 278; Marshall, *Acts* 239). It may very well be that the missionaries' recent rejection of the sacrifice left some of the leaders, especially the influential Jupiter priest, somewhat offended, chagrined, and embarrassed. After all, their very livelihood and function was brought into question; so was their interpretation of the healing of the lame man in light of the local legend. It would not have taken much to get them to agree to deal with the missionaries.

In what, indeed, must have been a case of strange bedfellows, Jews (even unsaved ones), who abhorred idolatry, joined with idolaters against the Christians. They succeeded in preferring charges that resulted in Paul being stoned (v. 19) and his body dragged from the city. The fact that the stoning took place inside the city limits shows

the hostile emotions that erupted in the impetuous act. The grim irony, too, of this reversal of fortunes is not lost in the account. One immediately remembers Stephen (7:57-60). The stoning of Paul is not regarded as repayment or retribution for his earlier sins but reveals some of the same extreme bias generated by religious fanaticism. Nothing is said about why Barnabas was spared.

Apparently, the disciples thought Paul was dead and gathered around his body to take it away for burial (v. 20). One cannot help wondering if Timothy was one of those (16:1). But as they pondered the situation, "supposing" he was dead, Paul arose. One can almost hear exclamations of praise and thanksgiving! Did he literally die from the stoning and was he raised from the dead? Marshall indicates so (*Acts* 239-240). But others are not sure (Lenski 583; Picirilli, *Paul* 74-75; Polhill, *Acts* 317). Keener (II:2177) records others who were stoned but survived. Stoning did not always result in death. Regardless, Paul was so severely wounded that he appeared dead. Either way, there is a miraculous dimension to the event. Either he was miraculously spared from death by stoning or he was raised from the dead after being stoned. Paul later referred to the incident (2 Cor. 11:25; 2 Tim. 3:11) and to the scars he bore from it and other abuses (Gal. 6:17).

After Paul arose from the ground, he and Barnabas, returned to the city from which he had just been dragged. Perhaps they went to the home of Timothy to be treated for his wounds and given food and rest. The next day they departed to go to the city of Derbe, some sixty miles southeast of Lystra. It would take them at least three days to get there, depending on Paul's state of health.

In short, summary fashion, Luke records that they stayed long enough to preach the gospel in Derbe and teach the disciples they made (v. 21a). There is no mention of opposition here. This is the easternmost witness of the missionaries on this journey. Geographically, it would have been easier for them to continue in this direction, traveling through the Cilician Gates, a narrow pass through the Taurus Mountains. It would have been some one hundred and fifty miles to Paul's home town of Tarsus. From there, they could travel on to Antioch of Syria. However, they did not do that, believing there was some unfinished work yet to do among the churches and believers made along the way. Their sense of commitment to the work was greater than their sense of personal convenience.

7. Paul and Barnabas return to Antioch (14:21b-28)

21b they returned again to Lystra, and *to* Iconium, and Antioch,
22 Confirming the souls of the disciples, *and* exhorting them to continue in the faith, and that we must through much tribulation enter into the kingdom of God.
23 And when they had ordained them elders in every church, and had prayed with fasting, they commended them to the Lord, on whom they believed.
24 And after they had passed throughout Pisidia, they came to Pamphylia.
25 And when they had preached the word in Perga, they went down to Attalia:
26 And thence sailed to Antioch, from whence they had been recom-
mended to the grace of God for the work which they fulfilled.
27 And when they were come, and had gathered the church together, they rehearsed all that God had one with them, and how he had opened the door of faith unto the Gentiles.
28 And there they abode long time with the disciples.

In what must be regarded as choices of great commitment and courage, Paul and Barnabas returned to the cities where they had met with both great success and incredible opposition. The needs of the disciples won to Christ were greater than their sense of security. There is little doubt they were risking life and limb to do so. They ministered in three ways (vv. 22-23). First, they "confirmed the souls" of the disciples: that is, they strengthened them in the faith. This would have included instructions about living the Christian life in the power of the Holy Spirit and by the commandments of Christ (Jn. 16:1-33). Second, they exhorted them to faithfulness in spite of hardships and trials. The "kingdom of God" was worth all the sacrifices needed to attain it. Paul and Barnabas had modeled such faithfulness, having borne the brunt of persecution. Many of these converts came from pagan backgrounds and suffered rejection from friends and family. They needed all the encouragement they could get (Lk. 14:25-35). Third, they established leadership, ordaining *elders* (Greek *presbuteros*, elders, pastor) in the local church assemblies. The pastoral role of these men would be essential for the continuation of the work begun by the missionaries. The need is no different today. Pastors and local churches are essential for healthy Christian life. In each situation, they gave time to prayer and fasting in commending the believers of that area to the Lord's keeping (v. 23). Who in Christian ministry has not done the same when moving to other fields of service?

Paul and Barnabas retraced their steps through each area (vv. 24-25), including the rugged mountain paths and crude roads of Pisidia that made for harsh travel conditions. As they moved on into the coastal plains of Pamphylia, travel would have been somewhat easier. Then they came to Perga, from which John Mark had left the team (13:13). Perhaps the trauma of that event had left them unsettled enough to move on, before, without preaching the gospel there. This time, however, they did just exactly that.

Completing their ministry there, they made for the coast and the town of Attalia, where they boarded a ship ("they sailed" v. 26) for Syria. They would have arrived at the seaport town of Seleucia at the mouth of the Orantes River (13:4), then made their way up to Antioch. In Antioch they had announced their calling and partnered with the church for the work. Now they returned to give a report of the journey. Poignantly, Luke states, "the work which they fulfilled."

In what must have been a great assembly to welcome and celebrate the work of Paul and Barnabas, the Antioch church gathered (v. 27) to hear their report. The men gave a full accounting of what had transpired as they "rehearsed all," the good and the not so good. The greatest conclusion was in confirmation that "God had opened the door of faith unto the Gentiles"—a theologically and historically pregnant phrase regarding both their calling and the entire scope of the Great Commission (1:8). Their steps of faith confirmed the Lord's direction and favor.

The first missionary journey ended as it had begun, with Paul and Barnabas fellowshiping and ministering in the Antioch church (13:1). There was more, much more, to come.

Summary
(14:1-28)

From Antioch of Pisidia, Paul and Barnabas travel a well-known Roman road to populous cities. Their strategy of ministry is to begin in the synagogue ("to the Jew first," Rom. 1:16) then move outwardly to the Gentiles. Often their work is affirmed by miraculous signs of healing that bring blessing to people who would otherwise have lived in physical infirmity the rest of their lives. But their work is also met with vicious opposition, and they are forced to flee to other cities. Such was the case with their continued travels on this missionary journey.

At Lystra a man congenitally lame is miraculously healed. Paul and Barnabas are hailed as gods and are barely able to clarify just who they really are before being worshiped with sacrifices. This probably does not set well with the local shamans, as Jews from Antioch and Iconium press their efforts to kill Paul and succeed in getting him stoned. He recovers and is able to resume the work with Barnabas, moving on to Derbe.

They return through the cities where they had ministered, establishing and encouraging the believers and organizing them into local churches with appointed leaders. Apparently, they believe they have completed this journey, so they return to Antioch of Syria to report on the work. The main conclusion was that God had "opened the door of faith unto the Gentiles."

Application: Teaching and Preaching the Passage

Exegetical Outline of the Text: 1. The Witness at Iconium (14:1-5). 2. The Witness at Lystra (14:6-20a). 3. The Witness at Derbe (14:20b-21a). 4. Retracing Their Steps to Perga (14:21b-25). 5. Return to Antioch of Syria to Report (14:26-28).

A pattern of ministry and response soon emerged as Paul and Barnabas continued the journey. Their faithful proclamation of the gospel was met with the positive response of salvation decisions and the negative response of persecution. Persecution arose no matter how greatly people's lives were blessed and changed, sometimes by miraculous healings. Such is still the response to the gospel. Some people accept, some reject. Those who labor in ministry must always keep their focus on being faithful and being grateful for those who respond in faith.

With the healing of the lame man at Lystra came notoriety for Paul and Barnabas. They were barely able to deflect the well-intended adulation heaped upon them. There are great lessons to learn about not letting the successes of ministry inflate one's ego. The glory and honor always belong to the Lord.

Paul was stoned at Lystra. Even the greatest of God's servants are often treated wrongly. But God was not through with him yet and raised him up for greater works to come. The rough treatment imposed in one place may be replaced with blessing and success in another. All who serve faithfully will receive some "scars" along the way.

One of the great blessings of ministry is sharing the stories of what God has done in one's life and ministry. When Paul and Barnabas returned to Antioch of Syria, they gave a full report concluding that God had opened the door of faith for the Gentiles. What rejoicing and confirmation that must have brought! Local churches are encouraged when those they send to the mission field or in ministry return to report on the open doors they have entered because of the partnership they share.

G. The Council at Jerusalem (15:1-35)

Some informative details about chapter fifteen give helpful perspective. In the progress of Acts, this chapter stands at the very center of the book, as it develops Luke's intent to show the obedience of the church to the command of Jesus in Acts 1:8. Fitzmyer (538) observes that there is even a similar number of words (in the English translation) in each half. Luke's genius in writing is again revealed in his selective treatment of key events, leading figures, and conversions that trace the witness of the church in obedience to the command of Christ is Acts 1:8. These receive proportionate treatment.

Though there are transitional events and leading characters, the first half of the book focuses on the church in Jerusalem and the witness to "Jerusalem, Judaea, and Samaria." The apostle Peter provides the senior leadership and figures prominently in opening the door of witness to the Gentiles. The second half of Acts transitions to the Syrian

Antioch church's witness to "the uttermost part of the earth" through the leadership of the apostle Paul, Barnabas, and Silas. They are careful to continue the witness to the Jews, but their ministry is primarily to the Gentiles, partly due to the Jewish rejection of the gospel.

There is much disagreement among writers over the timing and purpose of the Jerusalem Council (15:1-29). Given the previous conversion accounts and confirmations of the Samaritans (8:5-25), Cornelius (10:1—11:18), the Gentile converts at Syrian Antioch (11:19-26), and extensive Gentile conversions on the first missionary journey (13:1—14:28), the teaching that it was necessary for the Gentiles to be circumcised might seem unbelievable. However, enough time had passed for serious reflection and it appears there were some theological "loose ends," at least in the minds of some. Keener observes (III:2228) that it was one thing to allow for the conversion of Cornelius, but only as an exception and not the rule. The developing Gentile witness and the long-standing practices of Judaism, therefore, logically generated the issue raised by the Judaizers who came to Antioch. There were also those in the Jerusalem church who were "Pharisees which believed," who agreed with the teaching (v. 5). For a while, at least, it was a matter of division among brethren. Their argument had merit, though fraught with error. Picirilli (*Paul* 90) is correct in saying, "Their error can be better understood when we see it from their perspective."

Their thinking lay along the lines of how to interpret Judaism now in light of the fulfillment reached in the gospel of Christ. If Gentiles were equally welcome to saving grace via personal faith, what were the implications of some key components of the covenant relationship with Israel established in the O. T.—of circumcision, in particular? After all, it was the covenant sign of God's approval that dated all the way back to Abraham (Gen. 17:9-14). It was to be "an everlasting covenant" that established acceptance and approval. Was this centuries-old covenantal sign to be disregarded now? Was God's covenant law to be ignored by Gentile converts? Many did not believe so and insisted on its practice, believing it to be essential to personal salvation. However, such a view necessitated a reinterpretation of the very nature of saving faith (Gal. 2:16; Rom. 4:1-25), particularly the doctrine of justification (13:39)—which was of significant interest to Paul. Circumcision constituted human effort, a "work" that negated the singular condition of saving faith. In essence, the very gospel itself was at stake.

Integral to the whole issue, too, was the process of proselyting that had been the norm for centuries. In effect, a Gentile proselyte became a Jew in all the ceremonial practices necessary. With the expansion of the gospel to the Gentiles, however, a new norm was introduced. The process of becoming a proselyte was no longer necessary. Paul and Barnabas proclaimed the same gospel to both Gentiles and Jews and established churches for the discipleship and fellowship of both groups in the respective cities of their travels. They made no mention of Gentiles adopting Jewish ceremonial practices, nor did they suggest that the Jews surrender their Jewishness for the sake of the Gentiles. In fact, they opposed both. Hence the basis for the controversy addressed in chapter fifteen, which records the watershed event intended to settle these issues. There was much contention over the entire issue. If one holds to an idealistic view of the church in the Book of Acts, this event should correct that thinking.

As for the timing of the meeting, one is challenged to harmonize the chronology of the council at Jerusalem with the overview of Paul's visits to Jerusalem in Galatians 2:1-21. While there are multiple views as to how the Galatians account fits with Acts, here I am only addressing how the Jerusalem Council fits with Galatians. (The famine-relief visit has been addressed previously; see commentary on 11:27-30.) The various views fall along two lines of thinking with multiple variations of each, including the time of the writing of Galatians and its target audience. (One of the best summaries of these views is by Keener III:2195-2206.)

One view is that Acts 15 corresponds with Galatians 2:1-10 (Polhill, *Acts* 321-322; Fitzmyer 539-540; Robertson *Acts* 221; Marberry and Shaw 25). The affinity of themes, even with the questions it raises, makes this a distinct possibility.

A second view is that Galatians 2:1-10 was a more private meeting that preceded the Council in Acts 15, and that the latter is not described in Galatians. (In that case, the visit referred to in Galatians 2 might have been the same as the visit to take relief for the famine; see the commentary above on that passage. Or it might have been a visit not mentioned in Acts at all. Stott (242) takes the latter view and thinks the visit of Peter to Antioch, described in Galatians 2:11-16, was the same as what Acts 15:1 describes, when "certain

men" (including Peter) had gone there and taught the necessity of circumcision, thus leading to the Jerusalem Council. In that case, by the time of the Council, Peter had learned his lesson! (But this becomes more a matter of interpreting Galatians than of interpreting Acts; for more information consult commentaries on Galatians.) As Picirilli asserts (*Paul*, 151-153), the scenarios presented by both constructs are certainly possible.

I am not in agreement with Barrett (*Acts* 226) and Haenchen (458) that the event of Acts 15 is "an imaginative reconstruction" by Luke. Nor do I agree that the events of the famine-relief visit and the Jerusalem Council are conflated into one, as some suggest.

The Jerusalem Council settled the question of authentic conversion regardless of ethnicity and sought to establish some parameters for fellowship when the situation so required. That applied particularly to the N. T. era of church fellowship between Jews and Gentiles. The principles, of course, extend to similar situations today (cf. Rom. 14:1—15:12; 1 Cor. 8:1—11:1).

1. The controversy (15:1-5)

**1   And certain men which came down from Judaea taught the brethren, *and said*, Except ye be circumcised after the manner of Moses, ye cannot be saved.
2   When therefore Paul and Barnabas had no small dissension and disputation with them, they determined that Paul and Barnabas, and certain other of them, should go up to Jerusalem unto the apostles and elders about this question.
3   And being brought on their way by the church, they passed through**

Phenice and Samaria, declaring the conversion of the Gentiles: and they caused great joy unto all the brethren.
4 And when they were come to Jerusalem, they were received of the church, and *of* the apostles and elders, and they declared all things that God had done with them.
5 But there rose up certain of the sect of the Pharisees which believed, saying, That it was needful to circumcise them, and to command *them* to keep the law of Moses.

The arrival of men in Antioch from Judaea generated the first great theological controversy within the fellowship of the church. Their exact identity and credentials are not clear. Assuming they would have been accepted as believers (v. 5), it is possible that they presented themselves as spokesman for James (Gal. 2:12); therefore they would have been afforded opportunities to speak. But they brought with them a theological agenda that quickly exploded in a heated exchange with the leading teachers and missionaries, Paul and Barnabas. There is no question that Paul regarded them and their teaching as "false brothers" (Gal. 2:4) who preached a false gospel (Gal. 1:6-9).

The response to their teaching was nothing short of confrontational (v. 2). Men and women of peace do not like controversy but sometimes it cannot be avoided. There are some issues that are worth the effort. In effect, what was at stake was the gospel itself. The ramifications included all places and people where it would be proclaimed. It would mean serious adjustment in theology

and methodology for mission if, indeed, Paul and Barnabas had been wrong. On the other hand, if these visitors were in error, which they were, they would need to be silenced.

Apparently, the controversy did not end quickly, even with the arguments presented by Paul and Barnabas. The extended and somewhat heated discussion lends credence to the position held by the Judaizers and their (supposed) claim of support from the Jerusalem church. In the effort to clarify, the Antioch church selected a representative committee to journey to Jerusalem to address the issue with the apostles and other church leaders. It is not necessarily the case that the Jerusalem church constituted the supreme authority, but the other apostles were there, with whom there would need to be collaboration and solidarity. If indeed the Judaizers had claimed to be emissaries of James (v. 24), that would need clarifying as well. The committee consisted of Paul, Barnabas, and other unnamed men who accompanied them. One wonders if the Judaizers returned to Jerusalem with them as well.

The journey from Syrian Antioch to Jerusalem was some two hundred and fifty miles and might have taken a month. Along the route were churches previously reported about in Acts (11:19); they now served as places to stop for hospitality as well as to report the expanding mission and reception of the gospel. The reports brought much rejoicing (v. 3). Who doesn't rejoice over the expansion of the gospel and people being saved!

Upon arrival at Jerusalem, they were welcomed and received by the church and its leaders (v. 4). All who needed to be there were there. The first part of the visit occasioned an extended report of the work the Lord had enabled Paul and Barnabas to do. One can imagine the blessings of hearing of the progress of the gospel and rehearsing the incredible events of their missionary journey. Was John Mark present?

The report of the missionary journey and the conversion of the Gentiles opened the door for the controversy that occasioned the trip to Jerusalem. This time, the assertion that circumcision was, indeed, necessary for Gentile converts was raised by some who were believing Pharisees (v. 5) who were also part of the Jerusalem church. It should come as no surprise that many Pharisees had come to Christ. Paul himself had been a Pharisee (Phil. 3:5). The sect believed in the promise of the Messiah, life after death, the resurrection of the body (Acts 23:7-8), and the authority of the Scriptures (Polhill, *Acts* 324-325). While these views prepared them well enough for the gospel, their strict adherence to ceremonial practices blurred the lines of acceptance and fellowship with Gentile converts (11:1-3).

2. The consideration of the controversy (15:6-12)

**6 And the apostles and elders came together for to consider of this matter.
7 And when there had been much disputing, Peter rose up, and said unto them, Men *and* brethren, ye know how that a good while ago God made choice among us, that the Gentiles by my mouth should hear the word of the gospel, and believe.
8 And God, which knoweth the hearts, bare them witness, giving them the Holy Ghost, even as *he did* unto us;
9 And put no difference between us and them, purifying their hearts by faith.
10 Now therefore why tempt ye God, to put a yoke upon the neck of the disciples, which neither our fathers nor we were able to bear?
11 But we believe that through the grace of the LORD Jesus Christ we shall be saved, even as they.
12 Then all the multitude kept silence, and gave audience to Barnabas and Paul, declaring what miracles and wonders God had wrought among the Gentiles by them.**

The elements of the controversy were clear. Some believed the Gentile converts needed to be circumcised in order to be saved. The others did not believe that circumcision, or any other ceremonial practice, was necessary for anyone, Jews or Gentiles, to be saved. With that the apostles and other leaders of the church held a "formal inquiry" over the issue (v. 6). This does not mean that they went into a private setting or "executive session." Verses 12 and 22 indicate an open meeting for all who would attend with plenty of time given for each side to argue their case (v. 7).

The controversy and the manner of addressing it, as recorded here, sets a good precedent for dealing with a doctrinal concern. The passionate, yet orderly, presentation of each side in an open forum with the oversight of leaders is a good model for needed debate. The history of the church shows that theological debate is often necessary, but many times it has been under less than civil circumstances. One has only to reference the Protestant Reformation for examples. In these cases, the lack of civility on the part of some has overshadowed the importance of the truths being argued. (For further background, see Philip Schaff.)

Peter was the first of the apostles to respond (vv. 7-11). This is interesting in that the last reference to Peter was that he had left Jerusalem (12:17) to go into hiding. Obviously, he had returned to Jerusalem with some sense of purpose and security, although he might technically have been, still, be a fugitive from injustice (Ogg 79-83). Peter rightly referenced God's use of himself in the initial proclamation of the gospel to Gentiles in the case of Cornelius (ch. 10). That had happened some ten years previously. A lot had taken place since, but the truth of the gospel had not changed. Peter summarized what he learned from the vision given him (10:9-16). Particularly, he had come to understand that God saw the hearts of all men, both Gentiles and Jews (vv. 8-9). He understood that by faith, and faith alone, God purifies the hearts of all men from sin. The manifestation of the gift of the Holy Spirit to Gentiles when they were converted confirmed the same as His manifestation to Jews.

Peter's phrase, "no difference between us and them" (v. 9), is very revealing. Note the four-fold usage of "us-them, we-they" (vv. 8-11). The intention was to show similarity of purpose in a diversity of people. This meant precisely that no ceremonial practices, like circumcision, were needed to accomplish saving faith. That is further confirmed with Peter's assessment of the ceremonial practices of the law as a "yoke upon the neck" (v. 10) that was oppressive and impossible to bear, even by the Jews.

Peter's theological summary (v. 11) is almost confessional in wording. Jews and Gentiles alike are saved by the grace of the Lord Jesus Christ and personal faith in Him. (Hallelujah!) Given the significance of Peter's message before the church, it is interesting that some writers, like Ridderbos, do not include it in their listings. It certainly qualifies.

Here is the last appearance of Peter in the Acts record, though certainly not in other records of church history. It is fitting that his final words are recorded and that they serve to confirm and secure the same message of the gospel he proclaimed on the Day of Pentecost. There is no doubt that Peter had grown since then to understand more fully what Jesus meant by His command to be His witnesses "unto the uttermost part of the earth" (1:8). Now the entire church was grappling with that very command and its implications for theology and relationships.

The testimony of Paul and Barnabas (v. 12) not only coincided with Peter's but added miraculous events as confirming evidence of God's work through them in reaching the Gentiles. The combined testimonies served to inform the multitude of believers of the validity of their work in proclaiming the gospel to the Gentiles. Their message never included the necessity of circumcision or any other Jewish practices.

3. The counsel of James (15:13-21)

13 And after they had held their peace, James answered, saying, Men *and* brethren, hearken unto me:

14 Simeon hath declared how God at the first did visit the Gentiles, to take out of them a people for his name.
15 And to this agree the words of the prophets; as it is written,
16 After this I will return, and will build again the tabernacle of David, which is fallen down; and I will build again the runs thereof, and I will set it up:
17 That the residue of men might seek after the Lord, and all the Gentiles, upon whom my name is called, saith the Lord, who doeth all these things.
18 Known unto God are all his works from the beginning of the world.
19 Wherefore my sentence is, that we trouble not them, which from among the Gentiles are turned to God:
20 But that we write unto them, that they abstain from pollutions of idols, and *from* fornication, and *from* things strangled, and *from* blood.
21 For Moses of old time hath in every city them that preach him, being read in the synagogues every sabbath day.

One can easily picture the scene: the gathered believers hearing and evaluating the arguments of both sides in the controversy. It was a truly *decisive* moment in the history of the church. Following the testimony of Paul and Barnabas (v. 12), in confirmation of Peter's words, there was a silence of anticipation (v. 13) that permeated the scene. It is as if all were asking, "Now what?" At this moment James arises and offers a fitting conclusion and a proposed solution. Two questions arise. First, who is James that his opinion would be so highly valued? Second, what exactly does he propose that meets with the approval of so many?

As for the first, James is the same as referenced first in 12:17 and again in 21:18. He was the half-brother of Jesus to whom Jesus specifically appeared (1 Cor. 15:7) following His resurrection. Paul refers to him as an "apostle...the Lord's brother" (Gal. 1:19) and one of the "pillars" of the church (Gal. 2:9). While we are not sure how all of Jesus' siblings (Mt. 12:46-47; 13:55-56) responded to Him, we know that James not only became a believer but also distinguished himself as the senior leader of the Jerusalem church. He was also the author of the epistle in his name (Paul Harrison 1-4). That James was held in such high regard by the people was evidenced later by the shock of the people when the high priest, Ananus II, had him stoned in A.D. 62. Some attributed the Roman destruction of Jerusalem in A.D. 70, in part, to this atrocity (Josephus, *Antiquities* XX. IX. 1). Keener observes (III:2241) that in an honor-shame culture, offering a public resolution to a problem was risky business for a speaker unless he was a person who was respected, and his proposal was noteworthy. Such was the case with James. When he arose to speak, people listened.

After making connection to Peter's testimony, he confirmed its veracity by referencing the authority of the Scriptures. That James did not connect to the testimony of Paul and Barnabas is seen by some as intentional (Marshall, Acts 251). However, they are referenced in the official letter (vv. 25-26). Since Peter was the one whom God chose to initiate the proclamation of the gospel to the Gentiles, and the one most familiar to the Jerusalem church, it seems wise for James to begin by citing Peter. But that would be a matter of wisdom in making the initial connection, not in judgment on the men themselves.

Referencing Amos 9:11-12, James used this prophecy as the biblical basis for his proposal. The authority of the Scriptures was paramount to the Jews, and rightly so. But the wisdom of James is also clearly seen with his choice of the Amos prophecy on which to base his remarks. The prophecy references both Israel ("the tabernacle of David") and the Gentiles ("all the heathen which are called by my name"). That is the exact situation being addressed. First, James referenced God's promise to restore "the tabernacle of David" (v. 16). Here the dispersed nation of Israel is described as a "tabernacle" that had fallen and lay in ruins. As such, God promises to set up again and restore Israel. James sees the work of the Messiah as the fulfillment of that prophecy. Indeed, in Christ, redeemed Israel finds its purpose as the witness to give testimony to the world (Isa. 2:1-5; 43:10). The reference of Amos' prophecy to the Jews present must have been most encouraging and confirming. But the Amos text was not just cited for its situational relevance. What they were witnessing was the actual fulfillment of the prophecy.

Second, James submits that God is establishing for Himself a people from among the nations (Shires 83). This, too, is accomplished by the Messiah, whose name is called upon for salvation (v. 17). Right before their eyes they are seeing the fulfillment of the Amos prophecy, with the conversion of the Gentiles as "the heathen which are called by my name." That speaks to the very situation that occasioned the meeting. This must have been very encouraging and confirming to Paul and Barnabas and any Gentile believers present. I assume some from Antioch were Gentile believers.

It is interesting that James exclusively used the Greek O. T. (Septuagint) instead of the Hebrew in establishing the biblical authority for his comments (Lightfoot 197-198). Perhaps his intention was to appeal to Greek-speaking Jews as well as to make his point about the inclusion of the Gentiles. While there might have been the perception that James was sympathetic with the view of the Judaizers, he was not. There are subtle differences between the Hebrew text and the Greek text of the O. T. However, the key point regarding Gentile inclusion as those "upon whom my name is called" is the same in both. Inspiration is preserved in both the Hebrew and the Greek O. T., thus the use of either is consistent with the authority of the Scriptures.

With what appears to be a reference to Isaiah 45:21, James concludes his biblical support for the ongoing activity of God in this world. Although the fulfillment of the prophecy was contemporary to them, the fact that God works among nations is nothing new. God continues to work among His people and the nations of the world to redeem a people for Himself. The point James was making was that what they were witnessing was the work of the Lord.

With that said, James offered his judgment ("sentence," Greek *krino*, I judge, give my opinion) regarding the controversy (v. 19). Such a great problem required an equally great solution and James was the person whose judgment was trusted. His first conclusion was that the Gentiles who savingly believed in Christ should not be saddled with the ceremonial practices of the Law, circumcision in particular. There was no need to complicate their faith with ceremonial "trouble."

Second, this did not, however, resolve the question of how to facilitate fellowship between Jews and Gentiles. It was no problem for Gentiles to omit the practice of ceremonial traditions which they had never followed; but for Jews, who were defined by those very practices, to omit them would have been very complicated. Though Gentiles would not be compelled to observe circumcision, that did not mean the Jews must abandon some of their own cultural practices, or that Gentiles should be disrespectful of Jewish traditions. The church had corrected the theological issue of salvation by grace through faith for everyone (v. 11), but the relational issue remained. There would be barriers to overcome and concessions to be made if believers on both sides were to fellowship together. The proposal of James spoke to this concern. He enumerates four specific areas Gentile believers were asked to respect for the purpose of fellowship.

Even though, at the time, the four-fold proposal was clearly understood and accepted without challenge (vv. 22, 25, 31), what exactly James meant by what he proposed is the subject of much discussion by various interpreters since. As most observe, there are textual questions that developed over the years regarding the precise wording preserved (Metzger 379-381; Marshall, Acts 254-255; Polhill, Acts 331-332; Robertson Acts 232-233). Some manuscripts include an additional, interpretative neg-

ative Golden Rule regarding "blood." Still other manuscripts reduce the proposal to three matters, and some to two. That being said, there are no compelling textual reasons to discount the authenticity of the proposal as it appears in the KJV (Metzger 382; Fitzmyer 556).

When taken together with the actual wording of the letter (vv. 20, 29), the four-fold proposal is that the Gentile believers should abstain from: 1. food offered to idols, 2. blood, 3. things strangled, and 4. fornication (Wenham 244-261). Some (Bock 505-506; Marshall, Acts 243; Picirilli, Paul 93) regard these as a mixture of ceremonial food practices ("food offered to idols"; "things strangled") and moral principles ("blood" or bloodshed (murder); "fornication"). Others see these as moral principles: "idolatry, fornication, murder" (Robertson, Acts 232). A third view (Stott 247-248) is to regard all four as being ceremonial with "fornication" limited to eating food offered to idols. Whatever the specific nature of the four, the categories were defined enough to provided parameters for fellowship between Jewish and Gentile believers. At the time, those involved seemed to understand these clearly.

I believe the larger question is why James made these specific proposals? Where did they come from? Were they simply derived from his observations and personal experience? No, I believe they were rooted in a specific biblical scenario that, again, related to their then-present situation. Leviticus 17–18 addresses all of these and includes the "stranger (Gentile) that sojourneth among you" (Lev. 18:26). It was a text that specifically addressed both ceremonial and moral practices for the fellowship of Jews and Gentiles. As such, the text would be regarded as representative summaries of other ceremonial practices and moral principles. Specifically, Leviticus 17:7-9 speaks to "food offered to idols"; Leviticus 17:10-12 speaks to "blood," not as murder but as part of one's food preparations; Leviticus 17:13-14 speaks to "things strangled," with the blood remaining in the flesh in food preparation; and Leviticus 18:6-23 speaks to "fornication." This section of Leviticus was called "the Holiness Code" and would have been well-known and understood by the Jews (Wenham 239-261). Again, the wisdom (and genius) of James is clearly seen in the biblical basis of his proposal and in its relevance to the situation.

James concluded with the statement that "Moses" (the O. T.) was preached and studied every week wherever there were synagogues (v. 21). The O. T. basis for his remarks was available for Jewish believers everywhere to know for themselves. As such, I don't regard his concluding remarks as "puzzling" (Marshall, *Acts* 254) but confirming of the basis for his proposal. Furthermore, this new understanding of the fulfilled Scriptures does not negate the continuing study and proclamation of other O. T. truths. Jewish culture as such would not be discounted or threatened by Gentile inclusion (Keener III:2279).

4. The conclusion that was reached (15:22-29)

22 Then pleased it the apostles and elders with the whole church, to send chosen men of their own company to Antioch with Paul and Barnabas; *namely*, Judas surnamed Barsabas and Silas, chief men among the brethren:

23 And they wrote *letters* by them after this manner; The apostles and elders and brethren *send* greeting unto the brethren which are of the Gentiles in Antioch and Syria and Cilicia:
24 Forasmuch as we have heard, that certain which went out from us have troubled you with words, subverting your souls, saying, *Ye must* be circumcised, and keep the law: to whom we gave no *such* commandment:
25 It seemed good unto us, being assembled with one accord, to send chosen men unto you with our beloved Barnabas and Paul,
26 Men that have hazarded their lives for the name of our Lord Jesus Christ.
27 We have sent therefore Judas and Silas, who shall also tell *you* the same things by mouth.
28 For it seemed good to the Holy Ghost, and to us, to lay upon you no greater burden than these necessary things;
29 That ye abstain from meats offered to idols, and from blood, and from things strangled, and from fornication: from which if ye keep yourselves, ye shall do well. Fare ye well.

It was essential that the conclusions of the Jerusalem Council be made known as soon as possible, not only at Antioch where the controversy began, but also in all churches where the same issues would be raised. It would have been at least a couple of months since the controversy began and the journey to Jerusalem was undertaken. Approximately another month would pass for the return trip.

Unanimously, the wisdom of James was accepted and efforts were set in motion to communicate those conclusions (v. 22). The first step was the selection of respected men to return to Antioch with Paul and Barnabas to convey the results. Two men were chosen. Judas Barsabas is not otherwise named in the record but may have been related to Joseph Barsabas of 1:23. Evidenced by his name, he was a Hebrew (6:1). Silas (short for the Latin *Silvanus*) was a "Grecian" (6:1) and a Roman citizen (16:37) and would soon distinguish himself further on the second missionary journey with Paul. These men were regarded as "chief (leading) men among the brethren." The character of the men matched the responsibility given them. They bore the official letter and served as official spokesmen.

Of note is the fact that the letter is essentially copied word for word by Luke in his account. This means that, in all likelihood, he would have had a copy in front of him as he wrote Acts. That there were copies of the letter in circulation should come as no surprise. Luke might very well have had access to a copy as he accompanied Paul and Silas on the second missionary journey (16:4). It would have been included in their ministry documents to convey to Jewish and Gentile believers as they opened new churches where the two groups would face the same questions. I disagree with Haenchen (460) that Luke composed the letter on his own. The word-for-word accuracy and the style of writing suggest that Luke copied, rather than constructed, it.

The significance of the letter and the need to disperse it among the churches required copies to be made. The style of the letter was decidedly that of a formal Greco-Roman letter (Polhill, Acts 334), listing the senders, a formal greeting, contents, and a concluding and equally formal ending. Perhaps this was chosen to show deference to Gentile believers. The letter was addressed specifically to the Gentiles in churches at Antioch, Syria, and Cilicia (v. 23): namely, those churches that would have been established in relation to the first missionary journey. Of course, it would be relevant to all situations in new churches where table fellowship between Jewish and Gentile believers had to be determined.

Except for the prohibition against fornication, the decrees regarding dietary restrictions would have been mostly temporary—or, at least, relevant only in situations where applicable. The rest of the N. T. shows consistent prohibition against sexual sins (1 Cor. 7:2; 1 Thess. 4:3). History shows, however, that by the end of the first century, there were fewer and fewer Jewish believers and the parameters of fellowship set by the Jerusalem Council all but ceased to be relevant. That does not mean the principles of brotherly deference detailed in 1 Corinthians 8:1—11:1 are no longer applicable (Sproul 275-276; Stott 255-257).

The content of the letter was threefold. First, they denied any connection with those who initiated the controversy and claimed to represent the apostles and elders in Jerusalem (v. 24). Second, they commended Paul, Barnabas, and the men chosen to confirm by word of mouth the agreement reached at the Council (vv. 25-27). Third, they set forth the decision of the Council in partnership with the Holy Spirit (v. 28) that no additional practices were necessary for Gentile conversion. However, they did propose as "necessary"—but not commanded—the four abstentions listed as important for Gentile well-doing. In context, the spirit required to abstain from these practices for the sake of fellowship was one of maturity and wisdom. They would, indeed, "do well" to observe them for the purpose intended. These proposals were subsequently referred to as "decrees" (Greek *dogmata*, authoritative opinions) in 16:4, meaning they were strongly urged upon those addressed in them.

5. Conferring with the church at Antioch (15:30-35)

30 So when they were dismissed, they came to Antioch: and when they had gathered the multitude together, they delivered the epistle:
31 *Which* when they had read, they rejoiced for the consolation.
32 And Judas and Silas, being prophets also themselves, exhorted the brethren with many words, and confirmed *them.*
33 And after they had tarried *there* a space, they were let go in peace from the brethren unto the apostles.
34 Notwithstanding it pleased Silas to abide there still.
35 Paul also and Barnabas continued in Antioch, teaching and preaching the word of the Lord, with many others also.

Until the reading of the letter from the Jerusalem Council when Paul and Barnabas returned to Antioch, there had not been a more anticipated meeting in the young history of the church. Neither had there been an occasion for more rejoicing when the Christians at

Antioch learned of the wise conclusions reached. The personal testimonies of Judas Barsabas and Silas served to confirm all that was related. The two men added their own words of encouragement (v. 32).

The atmosphere of the Antioch church was apparently compelling and comforting, so much that all remained for a while. When believers worship and fellowship in Spirit-filled unity, they tend to linger (Ps. 133). The ministry of Judas and Silas extended beyond the confirming testimony of the letter as they ministered to the church. However, the time did come to conclude that part of the work, since the issue was settled (vv. 32-33). Judas chose to return to Jerusalem, but Silas chose to remain in Antioch with Paul and Barnabas (v. 35). His decision would prove to be providential.

Summary
(15:1-35)

Acts 15 is a key chapter in the progression of the mission of the church as well as the theological issue faced. The first missionary journey and the openness of Gentiles to the gospel galvanized the concerns of Jewish believers about the traditions of keeping the Law, especially the signature of the Abrahamic covenant, circumcision. It was one thing to accept Cornelius and his household, but quite another to completely open the gates to all Gentiles. The theological truths of the gospel needed clarification.

There is much scholarly debate as to the harmony of Acts 15 and Galatians 2. The various scenarios of the diverse possibilities are all compelling. The main concerns are not so much the interpretation of the events but seeking to harmonize them in the chronological constructs of the time period.

It is significant that the issue was initiated at the church at Antioch where the Gentile mission of the church was in full development. The peaceful and progressive atmosphere of the church was interrupted by teachers from Judaea, with seemingly authentic credentials, who began to teach that Gentile converts must do more than believe in Christ in order to be saved. They taught that Gentiles must continue in the practice of becoming proselytes and submit to circumcision. This resulted in serious confrontation with Paul and Barnabas over the issue. The Antioch church wisely chose to send men to Jerusalem to clarify the situation.

The assembly in Jerusalem was attended by all the apostles and elders. The forum for discussion was open to both sides to present their arguments, although only the testimonies of those who evangelized the Gentiles is recorded. After the testimony of Paul, Barnabas, and Peter was heard, the conclusion was confirmed that all men are saved equally by the same condition: the grace of God coupled with personal, saving faith (15:9-11). It was a theologically decisive moment.

However, there remained another issue: how to effect positive fellowship between Jewish and Gentile believers whose cultural lifestyles were very different. Speaking to this issue, the senior pastor of the Jerusalem church, James, offered his analysis and gave recommendations. The result was a unanimous recommendation of four specific fellowship practices based on Leviticus 17—18. James' conclusion and proposal were both wise in inclusiveness and ingenious in biblical basis. Later,

Paul would address the key principles of application as questions arose in implementation (1 Cor. 8:1—11:1).

A committee of men was chosen to convey the results of the Council's decisions to all the churches. An official letter was adopted to accompany the men. Luke has preserved that letter, word for word. Upon returning to Antioch, and probably stopping by the churches along the route, Paul and Barnabas and the two delegates delivered the decision; it was met with approval and relief. Thus the resolution of the first major theological controversy of the church. Of course, over the course of church history that would not be the last controversy.

Application: Teaching and Preaching the Text

Exegetical Outline of the Text: 1. A Dispute Arises in Antioch (15:1-2). 2. Delegates Are Sent to Jerusalem (15:3-4). 3. Division Occurs With Some (15:5). 4. Deliberation of the Issue (15:6-21). 5. The Decision Is Made (15:22-29). 6. The Decrees That Were Delivered (15:30-35).

Christianity has never been without its theological controversies. One may think the unity of believers means that no one disagrees. However, unity is more often the result of deliberate choices made after even more deliberate debate. This was especially true in the first three hundred years of the church. The great theological councils produced the studied decisions of leaders to clarify doctrinal issues. The Jerusalem Council foreshadowed all these as they sought to figure out not only the sufficiency of the gospel for the salvation of all men but the parameters of fellowship when cultures clash. This chapter provides an excellent model for such discussions. Included are the elements of controversy, debate, clarification of the issue, and the wisdom necessary to reach an acceptable conclusion.

The decrees that were recommended to be observed between Jews and Gentiles over table fellowship were expanded upon by Paul in Romans and 1 Corinthians. The principles he gave are still very appropriate for today. Actually, several lessons and messages could be developed to explain these principles.

H. The Second Missionary Journey (15:36—18:22)

1. Division and separation of Paul and Barnabas (15:36-41)

36 And some days after Paul said unto Barnabas, Let us go again and visit our brethren in every city where we have preached the word of the LORD, *and see* how they do. 37 And Barnabas determined to take with them John, whose surname was Mark. 38 But Paul thought not good to take him with them, who departed from them from Pamphylia, and went not with them to the work. 39 And the contention was so sharp between them, that they departed asunder one from the other: and so Barnabas took Mark, and sailed unto Cyprus; 40 And Paul chose Silas, and departed, being recommended by the brethren unto the grace of God. 41 And he went through Syria and Cilicia, confirming the churches.

With the resolution of the "circumcision controversy" and the ministry at Antioch resumed, Paul proposed to Barnabas that they return to those cities and churches of the first missionary journey. His intention was a spiritual follow-up to check on their status ("see how they do"). Christian life and church ministry are never static. Spiritual health check-ups are as important as physical health check-ups. A dispute between Paul and Barnabas, however, clouded the picture and did not find a resolution as unifying as did the "circumcision controversy."

Barnabas was apparently in agreement with Paul about the mission but insisted ("determined") on taking John Mark with them again. Why? He had proven unreliable on the first journey (13:13) and Paul had not forgotten it (v. 38). It was entirely like Barnabas to give someone another chance. He was, after all, the encourager (4:36); the one who risked endorsing Paul himself (9:26-28); the one sent to confirm the ministry at Antioch (11:22-24); the faithful ministry partner (13:2—14:28; 15:25-26); and now was willing to give John Mark a second chance. He was acting consistently with his character and testimony. In his view, the worker was as important at the work itself.

On the other hand, Paul was not so inclined toward John Mark. His reasoning was probably that if he abandoned them one time, he would more likely do it again (Robertson, *John Mark* 83-87). In Paul's mind, the work was too important to depend on one who had "put his hand to the plow and looked back." It is also possible that the tensions over the vacillation of Barnabas on table fellowship at Antioch (Gal. 2:13) still lay just beneath the surface (Marshall, *Acts*

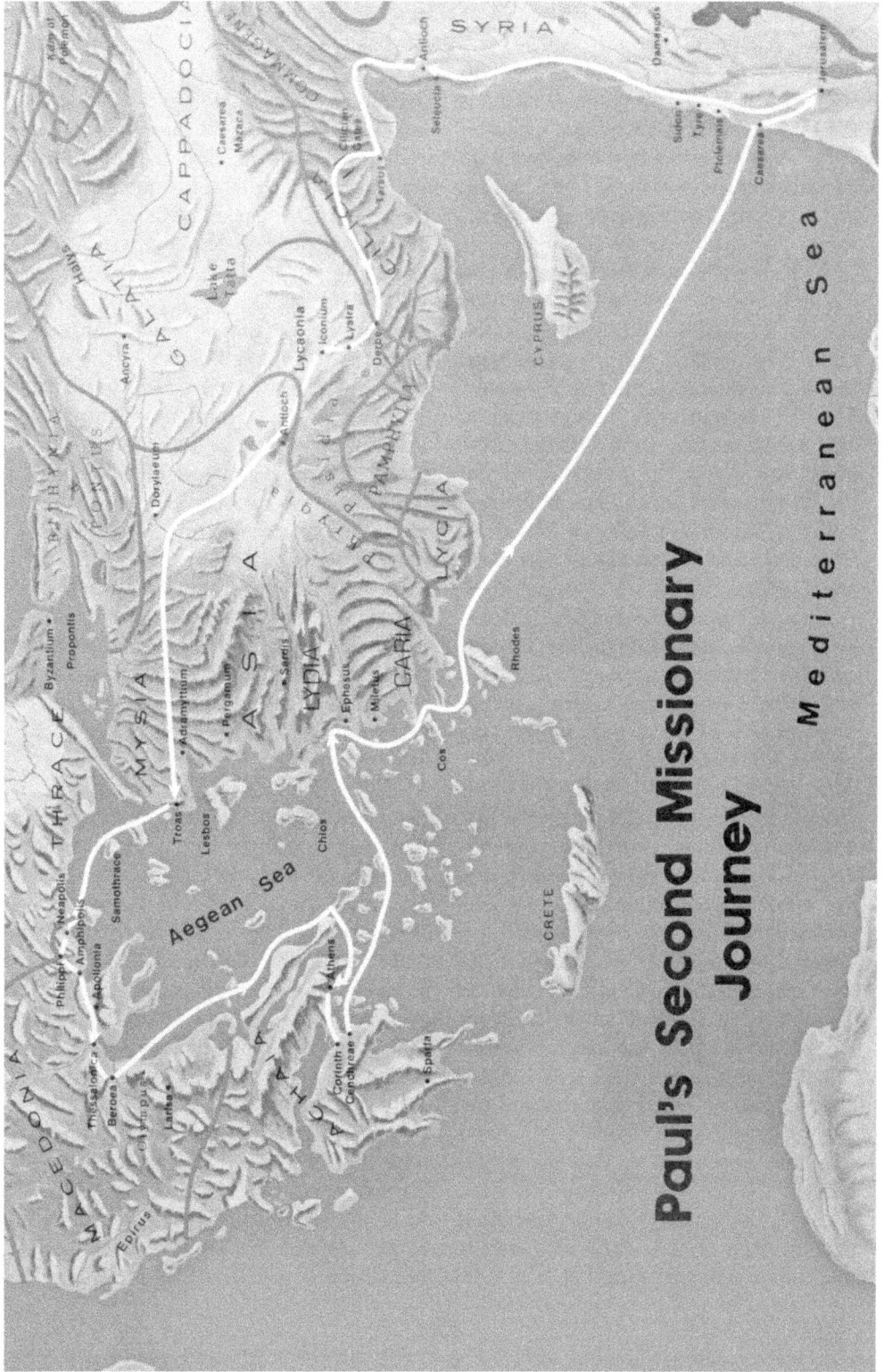

Paul's Second Missionary Journey

247; Picirilli, *Paul* 94; Bruce, *Acts* 302). Fitzmyer, however, disagrees (572). The time implied in verses 35-36 is ample for the events of Galatians 2:11-14 to have taken place, including Peter's visit to Antioch, the influence on Barnabas, the visit of those from Judaea, and the confrontation over table fellowship.

As insistent as was Barnabas on taking John Mark, so Paul was equally against it. Neither acquiesced to the other. When opposing views are believed to be convictions, conflict is inevitable. The resolution for them was to separate into two teams and go in different directions. Apparently, they agreed on that much. Barnabas took John Mark and sailed to Cyprus. Paul was joined by Silas and went overland through Syria and Cilicia (v. 41).

Though the answer is not so obvious, one cannot help asking the obvious question, "Who was right?" Perhaps both were. Perhaps it all depends on the point of view. Out of the conflict, two missionary teams of good and godly men developed. The Island of Cyprus was the first area evangelized on the first missionary journey and those churches needed a follow-up visit. The effort was not secondary or misguided. It seems obvious that both parties agreed on where they would go.

Furthermore, Barnabas focused on the man. Paul focused on the mission. Fortunately we have the inspired record of both efforts. John Mark was, indeed, restored, wrote a Gospel account of the life of Christ (Picirilli, *Mark* 10-11), and was later considered by Paul as "profitable to me for the ministry" (2 Tim. 4:11). Barnabas was also complimented later by Paul (1 Cor. 9:6). Friendships may often suffer bruising but heal with time and grace. The second missionary journey was even more successful than the first, and Silas proved to be a faithful partner to Paul. The focus of the rest of Luke's account is on the ministry of Paul. That is not to disparage any others, but was merely his intention in showing the expansion of the witness of the gospel through Paul's (and Luke's) efforts.

A word should be said about the authenticity of the account. Already Luke has shown his honesty in presenting some of the "rough spots" in ministry: Ananias and Sapphira, Simon the magician, the reaction to the conversion of Cornelius, the contention of Paul and Barnabas with the Judaizers. Nor does he soften his words in reporting the dispute between Paul and Barnabas. Their friendship ran deep but the temporary division ran deeper. It must be remembered that Luke probably knew all the parties involved on a personal basis. Yet his commitment to an honest accounting of the events is paramount (Lightfoot 208-209; Keener III:2299).

That there were other churches in Syria is no surprise (11:19-21), but what of those in Cilicia? When were these established? It's certainly possible that the Syrian Antioch church was aggressively evangelistic and had extended their witness into Cilicia. But there is a more likely scenario. As previously alluded to in chapter nine, when Paul was sent home to Tarsus because things in Jerusalem were just too hot to handle, in all likelihood he was neither silent nor still during those years. The length of time for his stay in Tarsus before Barnabas enlisted his help at Syrian Antioch (11: 24-26) was probably between six to ten years (Picirilli, *Paul* 60; Bruce, *Paul* 126-128). Most likely, it was during those "silent years" that some of the experiences recorded in 2 Corinthians 11:24-27 took place. Most of these are not included in the Acts record. Implied in the difficulties and sufferings he experienced are encounters in the synagogues as he preached the gospel, being expelled, then tortured and abused for the sake of the gospel. Also implied, there were some who responded to the gospel and churches established. Now, Paul and Silas visited these churches in order to strengthen them in the faith.

This missionary journey would take them far beyond the cities and provinces visited during the first journey and would take longer. Estimates are that the second missionary journey took from three to four years (Picirilli *Paul* 97; Bruce, *Paul* 475; Ogg 200). The time frame for this was probably A.D. 48-51.

2. Return to Lystra and Derbe: Timothy joins the team (16:1-5)

1 Then came he to Derbe and Lystra: and, behold, a certain disciple was there, named Timotheus, the son of a certain woman, which was a Jewess, and believed; but his father *was* a Greek:
2 Which was well reported of by the brethren that were at Lystra and Iconium.
3 Him would Paul have to go forth with him; and took and circumcised him because of the Jews which were in those quarters: for they knew all that his father was a Greek.
4 And as they went through the cities, they delivered them the decrees for to keep, that were
ordained of the apostles and elders which were at Jerusalem.
5 And so were the churches established in the faith, and increased in number daily.

Returning to the cities of Lystra and Derbe required Paul and Silas to cross the rugged Taurus Mountains along a rough-cut wagon road through a narrow passage called "the Cilician Gates" (Ramsay, *Cities* 114-115). Travel itself in such difficult areas reveals the resilience of these men whom we must admire for their determination. Lesser men would have turned back. Furthermore, the very fact that Paul is returning to the place he was stoned and left for dead (14:19-20) speaks to his personal courage and trust in the Lord's providential oversight of his life. The fruit, however, was worth the effort. In addition to helping the churches along the way, the enlistment of Timothy of Lystra is a signal accomplishment, not only to be their helper but one who will prove to be the capable protégé of the apostle Paul.

Timothy is noted as being a believer and the son of a mixed marriage (v. 1). That is not a racist issue (as the current political correctness insists) but a religious-cultural issue significant for that time. His mother, Eunice (2 Tim. 1:5) was a Jewish Christian and his father a Greek. We are not told whether his father was a Christian. The omission of this detail, when the faith of Timothy's mother and grandmother are stated, implies, though not conclusively, that his father was not a believer. Timothy and his family were of significant reputation among the believers at Lystra and Iconium (v. 2).

Paul persuaded Timothy to join them in their work (v. 3). This implies both an affinity of relationship with Paul and Silas and Timothy's own desire for ministry service. In order to circumvent criticism and limitations in reaching out to Jews, Paul had Timothy circumcised according to his Jewish heritage. That he did this is interesting, given the background of the "circumcision controversy" they had just resolved (ch. 15) and the leading role Paul had played in it. This is further complicated when one reads Galatians 2:3 and the victory he claimed when Titus, who was Greek, was not compelled to be circumcised. How does one harmonize these?

Before addressing this, let me say that I do not agree with Barrett (*Acts* 245) or Haenchen (481-482) that Luke has contrived the incident. Of the many reasons for disagreeing with these scholars, not the least is the fact that Luke knew personally the parties involved and could easily get the facts directly from them.

As to the circumcision of Timothy, first, there is a cultural issue. Titus was a Greek and Timothy was mixed Jewish and Greek. Paul was not against his Jewish cultural heritage, but desired that Timothy honor his heritage and identify with those he intended to reach with the gospel—to the extent he could without mixing the legalistic mindset of some into the situation (Gal. 3:1-5). This is exactly the principle Paul expresses in 1 Corinthians 9:19-22.

Second, the circumcision of Timothy was not a theological issue or redemptive necessity; it was not required in order to be saved (15:9-11; Gal. 2:16). Timothy was already a disciple (v. 1); therefore, his circumcision honored his Jewish heritage but mostly circumvented

unnecessary barriers to his testimony among Jews. Hence the phrase, "because of the Jews" (v. 3). It would have been a barrier in the synagogues where the team first proclaimed the gospel in each city. As Bruce (*Acts* 304) observes, it was a "minor surgical operation carried out for a practical purpose—his greater usefulness in the ministry of the gospel." In effect, everyone who enters the ministry must consider any and all areas of personal growth to reach all people no matter their cultural identities. Cultural identification for the sake of the gospel is not the same as embracing a false gospel in the process (Bock 521-522; Bruce, *Acts* 304; Polhill, *Acts* 342-343); nor is it the same as placing oneself in any positions of moral compromise.

In keeping with their commission to report the conclusions reached at the Jerusalem Council, Paul and Silas communicated the "decrees" to the churches (v. 4). The effect was the strengthening of the churches in bridging the gap of fellowship between Jews and Gentiles, securing their faith even further, and seeing them successful in reaching others with the gospel (v. 5).

Summary
(15:36—16:5)

The idea of returning to the churches established on the first missionary journey was wise on several levels. The personal interests of Paul and Barnabas in those efforts and with those people would be satisfied, and they would fulfill the need to encourage and strengthen the believers. As modeled in Antioch of Syria (11:22-26), new believers needed instruction and encouragement. But the idea was clouded by a serious disagreement over taking John Mark with them. The perspectives of Paul and Barnabas on John Mark were so different that they divided over it.

Their division did not end the mission but multiplied the efforts. Barnabas and John Mark went to Cyprus. Paul chose Silas as his new partner in mission and began the trek overland to check on the churches. In a passing detail so indicative of Luke, we learn there were churches in Cilicia that had not been included by name in the previous narrative. That is pervasively true. We will never know this side of eternity all the people and places the gospel has impacted.

Returning to the same cities where Paul had previously been rejected and stoned, the team enlisted the assistance of Timothy. In a balance of what circumcision meant and didn't mean, Paul prepared Timothy so he would not be hindered in reaching different groups (1 Cor. 9:20-23).

Keeping their commitment to convey the decisions of the Jerusalem Council, they faithfully conveyed them to the churches to advance the fellowship of Jewish and Gentile believers. The effect was that the churches were established in spiritual health and outreach.

Application: Teaching and Preaching the Passage

Exegetical Outline of the Text: 1. The Proposal They Made (15:36). 2. The Problem That Arose (15:37-39). 3. The Partnerships That Resulted (15:40—16:3).4. The Progress of the Work (16:4-5).

The disagreement and separation of Paul and Barnabas over their different perspectives on John Mark illustrates a frequent occurrence among believers throughout church history. Friendships, churches, and ministries have divided over differing views on their mission and ministers. Sometimes those divisions have been as contentious as the one in this text. While it may be argued that division should never occur, in reality it does. If men as great as Paul and Barnabas are susceptible to division so are the rest of us. But, like them, we should not let the division defeat us from our calling and commitment in ministry. Also, like them, we must never close the book on our relationships but allow for restoration. One area of teaching and preaching this text could be to address the causes and consequences of divisions among believers. Both causes and consequences are varied.

Historically, in the broadest definition of the term, Christianity has long since been divided into at least three major groups: Catholics, Orthodox, and Protestants. There are any number of sub-divisions under each. Historical perspective is essential in our understanding of where we live today. This text provides a real life example to analyze.

The division had its silver linings. John Mark and Barnabas went to Cyprus to minister among the churches there. Both men were commended later by Paul (1 Cor. 9:6; 2 Tim. 4:11). Silas became a very faithful and capable ministry partner for Paul. His name was forever etched in the annals of church history and sacred Scripture. The work of witness was multiplied. Teaching or preaching this text might address the "silver linings" or providential mercies of God that turn trouble into triumph.

In returning to the places where he suffered greatly for the cause of Christ, Paul showed courage and determination. While at Lystra, Timothy was enlisted and steps were taken to prepare him for ministry. Yet another approach to the truths of this text is the example of Paul in facing previous times and places of hurt. All of us have had them. It is a great text for teaching the necessity of facing our hurts. Another great truth to consider is the necessity of preparing oneself for ministry. A little pain now (as illustrated by the "circumcision") may equip one for great service later. There are many applications for this truth.

3. The call to Macedonia (16:6-10)

6 Now when they had gone throughout Phrygia and the region of Galatia, and were forbidden of the Holy Ghost to preach the word in Asia,
7 After they were come to Mysia, they assayed to go into Bithynia: but the Spirit suffered them not.
8 And they passing by Mysia came down to Troas.
9 And a vision appeared to Paul in the night; There stood a man of Macedonia, and prayed him, saying, Come over into Macedonia, and help us.
10 And after he had seen the vision, immediately we endeavoured to go into Macedonia, assuredly gathering that the Lord had called us for to preach the gospel unto them.

What Luke means by the regions of "Phrygia and Galatia" is not clear to us. Some writers understand he means these as the ethnic territories of the north (Fitzmyer 578; Barrett, *Acts* 246-247; Polhill, *Acts* 345). Others under-

stand "Galatia," at least, as the official name of the Roman province and so view Luke as meaning the southern areas (Bruce, *Acts* 353-354; Marshall, *Acts* 261-262; Bock 526-527). Citing textual evidence, Keener (III:2324-2325) understands the phrase as "the Phrygian and Galatian region," thus meaning a southerly route.

What is clear is the intention of the team to carry the gospel farther into Asia (v. 6). Stemming from what was apparently prophetic revelation from the Holy Spirit, they were re-directed twice: once, away from ministry in "Asia" (their apparent intention), then from "Bithynia" (vv. 6-7). That the Holy Spirit so directs is part of His ministry (8:26, 29; 9:10-16; 10:19; 20:23; 21:10-11). He certainly made His will clear enough that their journey was adjusted accordingly. Neither did they conclude that they were to cease the journey. Instead, they headed straight west through Mysia to the coastal town of Troas near the ancient remains of Troy some twenty-five miles to the north. While it is clear that their strategy of witness was to go where the most people were, the particular place was a matter of discerning the leading of the Holy Spirit. In every Christian life and ministry there needs to be a "Troas," a time and place for determining the will of God.

At Troas, two significant things happened. One, Paul had a night vision of a Macedonian man bidding him to come to Macedonia. There was no doubt as to the meaning of the vision (v. 10). Ramsay (*Traveller* 202-204) opines that the man in the vision was an acquaintance of Paul's, perhaps Luke, else he would not have known that the man in the vision was a Macedonian. Yet another suggestion (Keener III:2343; Polhill, *Acts* 346) is that he was a representation of Alexander the Great who was from Macedonia and who sought to conquer the world. In this case, the vision would be symbolic of Paul seeking to "conquer" the world with the gospel of Christ as per the command of Christ to go "to the uttermost part of the earth" (1:8). Cultural differences of language, dress, even physical features would have been clear to them. Though we are not told exactly how Paul knew he was a Macedonian so it is probably best to interpret him as representative of all those, men and women, who needed the message of the gospel of Christ. Names and faces would soon enough fulfill the visionary representative as the team reached Macedonia and began to win folks to Christ. This clarified the direction in which they should go to carry the gospel witness.

Second, here is the first of the "we" texts in Acts ("*we* endeavored to go to Macedonia"). Scholars have debated the meaning of the use of "we." Some think it was merely a literary device used by Luke, some that it refers to some fictional person, and others that this is the first personal reference to Luke (Keener III:250-274). As early as Irenaeus (210-211), many interpreters have regarded Luke as the companion of Paul and author of Acts, using "we" when he was personally involved. This is also my view (see Introduction). Marshall (*Acts* 45) concludes, "In fact the tradition in favor of Luke's authorship of the Gospel and Acts is as good as that for any other of the Gospel writers." That being the case, up until now, Luke is mostly recording the eyewitness reports of others; but from this point on he himself will be one of the eyewitnesses. This is

the first of many "we" texts in the rest of the Acts narrative.

Though the tradition of the Western text (11:28) and Irenaeus (3.11.1-4) associates Luke with Antioch of Syria, there is no reason he should not be connected with Troas. If, indeed, he was a ship's doctor (Ramsay, *Luke* 35-38), his travels could have carried him to the port city of Troas where he providentially met up with and joined Paul, Silas, and Timothy for the next stage of the journey.

4. Witness in Philippi (16:11-40)

a. The conversion of Lydia (16:11-15)

**11 Therefore loosing from Troas, we came with a straight course to Samothracia, and the next *day* to Neapolis;
12 And from thence to Philippi, which is the chief city of that part of Macedonia, *and* a colony: and we were in that city abiding certain days.
13 And on the sabbath we went out of the city by a river side, where prayer was wont to be made; and we sat down, and spake unto the women which resorted *thither.*
14 And a certain woman named Lydia, a seller of purple, of the city of Thyatira, which worshipped God, heard *us*: whose heart the Lord opened, that she attended unto the things which were spoken of Paul.
15 And when she was baptized, and her household, she besought us, saying, If ye have judged me to be faithful to the Lord, come into**

my house, and abide *there*. And she constrained us.

Obedience should follow leadership. That is exactly what the team did as they secured ship's passage to Macedonia. It is interesting to note that, though Paul was the only one to have seen the vision, all were convinced of the Lord's leading. They concluded together that "the Lord had called *us*." Indicated is trust in Paul's leadership and his spiritual integrity. The Lord uses godly men and women in leadership to direct entire ministries in service to Him.

It is historically significant that the direction of witness was westerly. With this move, the door of the gospel to Europe was opened prior to its advance northward (which would come many years later). Eventually, the witness of the gospel would penetrate all the way to Spain and the British Isles. We in America can trace part of our spiritual heritage to this very act of obedience to the leadership of the Holy Spirit by the missionary team. Big doors turn on small hinges.

There are a number of sailing references in the record of Paul's travels, as indicated by the term "loosing" (Greek *anago*), which was often used to mean to "set sail" or "put to sea." It is clear that Luke knew well the means and methods of sea travel in his day. The names of the places stated are stops along the route where cargo and passengers would be exchanged. With favorable winds they made the journey to the port city of Neapolis in just two days (v. 11). It was another ten miles inland to the city of Philippi via the Roman road, the *Via Egnatia*, the main road east and west across Macedonia.

Paul and his team would travel this road often.

Philippi was an ancient city, renamed after Philip of Macedon, father of Alexander the Great, when he conquered it in the fourth century B.C. It was noted for its copper and gold mining thus making it a very desirable resource for men such as Philip in his quest for power. Later, it played a significant role in Roman history, being granted the status of "a colony" (v. 12) with special privileges afforded to them (Polhill, *Acts* 347-348; Keener III:2380-2383). It is also termed the "chief city of that part of Macedonia" by Luke. The interests of the missionary team are that it is well-populated with folks who need to hear the gospel. Thus, they settle in, find lodging, and await the Lord's providential leading to "the man of Macedonia" (v. 9)—whoever that would be.

As was his method, Paul would seek to find a synagogue to begin the proclamation of the gospel (Rom. 1:16). However, apparently, there was not a synagogue in Philippi. It took ten Jewish heads of family to formally establish a synagogue (Edersheim 430-440). This did not prevent their observing the Sabbath, so they found a place of worship and prayer along the riverside, probably the Gangites River that lay a little more than a mile west of the city (Bock 533). This was the closest thing to a synagogue available (v. 13). Only women are mentioned as having assembled there. Given the status of Paul as a rabbi, he would have been afforded the opportunity to speak. What he said proved to be a spiritually-defining moment for the witness of Christ in Philippi and for those who heard him.

Lydia is specifically named with some details identifying her. Her home city was Thyatira (Rev. 2:18-29), a town in provincial Asia Minor which had once also been known as "Lydia." Stott (263) suggests that "Lydia" may be her business or trade name ("the Lydian lady"), not her personal name. She is also identified as a salesperson for purple-dyed, fine cloth usually afforded by the rich (Lk. 16:19) and royalty (Jn. 19:2, 5), and for which her home area was famous and prosperous. The process of producing the purple dye, making the fine cloth, and dyeing it was stigmatized because of its smell and materials used (Keener III:2398-2403). But Lydia was a "seller" not a producer, and as a "seller" she would not have been so stigmatized. She was not necessarily as wealthy as those who purchased her cloth, but would have been somewhat successful in the business. This is indicated, also, by her hosting the team in her own house (v. 15), which must have been large enough to accommodate her household and the team.

The marital status of Lydia is often addressed by writers who suggest that she was a widow or single as indicated by her business, owning her own house, and the lack of any reference to her husband (Marshall, *Acts* 268; Stott 263-264; Robertson *Acts* 252). Roman and Greek society of that time certainly allowed for women in such positions without attaching a moral stigma. There is little doubt Lydia enjoyed an enhanced social status in Philippi. There is no indication in any early writings that she became the wife of the apostle Paul (Haenchen 494). The reference to a "true yoke-fellow" (Phil. 4:3) could hardly be construed as a veiled reference to Lydia as Paul's wife since the expression is masculine!

While there was no synagogue in Philippi, there was one in Thyatira, the original home of Lydia. Most likely it was there she had come to embrace Judaism and would be considered a "God-fearer" (10:2). It appears that those in her "household" (like those in Cornelius' household) were also God-fearers. Paul's message of the gospel of the Messiah would have been taken from O. T. Messianic prophecies and applied to the Lord Jesus. Lydia (like the Ethiopian eunuch) would have been familiar with some of those prophecies. It is highly unlikely that she knew of Jesus of Nazareth and His resurrection until Paul's messages.

Not only did Lydia respond in faith to the gospel, so did those of her household (v. 15). They soon followed the Lord in believer's baptism. Though this is the first reference to an entire household responding in saving faith, it is reminiscent of Cornelius (10:2, 24, 48). The same will soon take place with the household of the jailer (16:31-34). As Polhill (*Acts* 350) alludes, there is no reason to think that Luke assumed, on the basis of Lydia's faith and baptism alone, that this included the others in her household. As the Acts narrative and the rest of the N. T. shows, saving faith is a personal matter. One may certainly be influenced by the faith of another, but one must have personal saving faith in order to be saved (Rom. 10:9-10). The saving faith of one person in a family may very well open the door of influence to others.

While baptism is representative of the physical resurrection of the Lord Jesus and the spiritual resurrection of the believer inwardly, its practice for those who were saved, in the Acts record, was as soon as possible. There is no question that baptism was meant as a serious expression of initial saving faith (2:38).

The hospitality extended to Paul and the missionary team was not only an act of gracious generosity but a personal expression of Lydia's faith ("if ye have judged me to be faithful"). Her desire to share her material things is, also, reminiscent of earlier believers (4:34-37; 1 Cor. 9:14). Indications are that her house also became the hub for believers there, in the establishment of a church in Philippi (16:40; Phil. 1:1, 15).

b. Deliverance of the spirit-possessed damsel (16:16-18)

16 And it came to pass, as we went to prayer, a certain damsel possessed with a spirit of divination met us, which brought her masters much gain by soothsaying: 17 The same followed Paul and us, and cried, saying, These men are the servants of the most high God, which shew unto us the way of salvation.
18 And this did she many days. But Paul, being grieved, turned and said to the spirit, I command thee in the name of Jesus Christ to come out of her. And he came out the same hour.

While returning to the place of prayer for worship (v. 13), they encountered a young girl ("damsel") who was possessed with "a spirit of soothsaying" (v. 16), the only use of the term in the N. T. The Greek text words it, literally, as a "spirit of the Python," the Python being the serpent or dragon thought to guard the famous Oracle at Delphi. Often the practice in Roman and Greek culture utilized young, beautiful girls or older,

emaciated women in the manner of Homer's "Circe." This girl in Philippi was a slave girl who was used and abused for profit and pleasure by her masters. Roman and Greek culture was not only permeated with the practice of soothsaying, belief in it was so powerful that Roman and Greek leaders depended on oracles for everything from political plans to military battles. One of the most famous of these was the Oracle at Delphi in central Greece. In some instances, as with this young girl, the python snake represented the god Apollo who was believed to have the ability to predict the future. The slave girl with such a spirit was a virtual money machine for her owners (Bock 536-537; Keener III:2422-2456).

Reminiscent of the encounters of Jesus with demon possessed persons (Lk. 4:33-37; Mk. 3:10-12), the damsel followed Paul and the rest of the team (v. 17) crying loudly for all to hear that the missionaries were servants of the "Most High God which show unto us the way of salvation." In those days, there were many who claimed to be special emissaries of the gods and "saviors" of society; in one sense, then, her proclamation was nothing new. However, few Gentiles would be familiar with the biblical intent of the phrases "Most High God...the way of salvation." One can rightly ask, "What was the real source of her information?" Was it merely a dramatic show to appeal for business or the expression of the spirit world openly confessing the person and purpose of the gospel? One could argue either way, but, again, the incident is reminiscent of Jesus' encounter with the Gadarene demoniac and the demons who cried loudly through him (Mt. 8:28-34). This is not the first (5:17) or last time (19:13-16) Acts records encounters with demon-possessed people.

At first, the intrusive behavior of the girl was tolerated but it persisted over several days as the team traveled about (v. 18). Finally, Paul grew impatient and grieved by the distraction and commanded the evil spirit to leave the girl. Even truth spoken by unclean lips can send forth an uncertain sound. As Morgan (385) says, "We are to refuse the patronage of hell when it attempts to tell the truth about our Christ." The effect was immediate ("that very hour"). The evil spirit departed and the girl was transformed (Mk. 5:15).

What Paul said to cast out the demon is recorded. It should be noted that he spoke "to the spirit" indicating an entity separate from the girl. He "commanded" the spirit "in the name of Jesus Christ." It was an authoritative declaration invoking the authority of the Messianic Jesus over the spirit world. Furthermore, he commanded the spirit "to come out of her," thus delivering her from possession and control. She had only been a tool of manipulation. Missionaries and those who carry the gospel to similar cultures today testify of similar encounters and experiences.

c. Imprisonment of Paul and Silas (16:19-40)

(1) Arrested on false charges (16:19-24)

19 And when her masters saw that the hope of their gains was gone, they caught Paul and Silas, and drew *them* into the marketplace unto the rulers,
20 And brought them to the magistrates, saying, These men, being Jews, do exceedingly trouble our city,
21 And teach customs, which are not lawful for us to receive, neither to observe, being Romans.
22 And the multitude rose up together against them: and the magistrates rent off their clothes, and commanded to beat *them*.
23 And when they had laid many stripes upon them, they cast *them* into prison, charging the jailor to keep them safely:
24 Who, having received such a charge, thrust them into the inner prison, and made their feet fast in the stocks.

While we are not told all that happened to the girl, apparently she did lose the ability of prediction (v. 19). She was delivered from at least one kind of slavery, spiritual slavery. Such is the power of the gospel's truth (Jn. 8:32) and such is the intent of Christianity: deliverance and transformation. Wicked men enslave; Christ delivers. Wicked men deform, but Christ transforms. Lydia and now the young girl represent the dignity and honor due women, which are found in Christ. As is characteristic of Luke, women are honored and find fresh meaning and purpose by faith in Christ.

With her transformation, her masters lost a means of profit and prompted the arrest of Paul and Silas (v. 19). Even when fraud is exposed, it seldom goes quietly. However, in that culture, where spiritualism was widely practiced along with slavery, their business trade was fully sanctioned and found legal support. Furthermore, there were more serious matters implied by their actions. Paul and Silas were unceremoniously dragged to the city's marketplace where the city's magistrates presided over public matters. Apparently, Luke and Timothy were not arrested, perhaps not being with Paul and Silas at the time. The city magistrates were men usually appointed by Roman authority, bearing the position of a *duumvir* or *praetor*. They were charged especially to maintain public order and were answerable directly to the Emperor of Rome (Keener III:2468-2469). This is the reason they acted as they did, both in the treatment of Paul and Silas initially, and later in their fearful apology (16:38-39).

Why Paul and Silas did not immediately appeal to their rights as Roman citizens is uncertain and the stuff of scholarly debate. It is likely they were not shown any fairness or due process, but often in courts of that day those on trial shouted above their accusers (23:1-6). It is entirely possible they were muzzled by the threatening mob and had to silently endure what was to come. While the procedural requirements of modern courts were not available to them, they did have their rights as citizens, but these were totally suppressed. There must have been mitigating circumstances that kept them silent about this until later. The timing of their appeal (vv. 37) proved to be effective and might have been the most important consideration to make (Keener III:2480).

Paul and Silas were first labeled as "Jews" (v. 20), which apparently carried a negative characterization in Philippi. (Perhaps this is one reason there was no synagogue there). Then they were charged as trouble-makers who meddled in the affairs of others with unlawful religious practices (v. 21), i.e. illegal proselytization. While this was not exactly illegal then, the fact that the privileged Roman citizens of Philippi pressed the issue to the rulers and charged Paul and Silas with public disorder served only to heighten the emotion of the situation. It stirred up others ("the multitude"), who joined in the melee and threatened a breach of peace. The magistrates did not bother to inquire any further, and summarily had Paul and Silas stripped and beaten with rods (compare 2 Cor. 11:25). This was usually administered by men known as *lictors*, who thrashed their victims with a cane or stick. It was a lesser punishment than scourging (Jn. 19:1), but it was nonetheless very painful and wounding (16:33).

Adding insult to injury, the magistrates had Paul and Silas imprisoned (vv. 22-23) and charged the jailer to put them in maximum security. He did so, putting them in the inner cell and securing them in the stocks (v. 24). Stocks were commonly made of wood with holes for the legs and chained to the wall in a manner that would cause incredible discomfort and pain. It was not the jailer's business to attend to their comfort but to follow orders. The text indicates he did his job well. As Bruce (*Acts* 315) states this did not "include the milk of human kindness."

(2) The conversion of the jailer and his household (16:25-34)

25 And at midnight Paul and Silas prayed, and sang praises unto God: and the prisoners heard them. 26 And suddenly there was a great earthquake, so that the foundations of the prison were shaken: and immediately all the doors were opened, and every one's bands were loosed.

27 And the keeper of the prison awaking out of his sleep, and seeing the prison doors open, he drew out his sword, and would have killed himself, supposing that the prisoners had been fled.
28 But Paul cried with a loud voice, saying, Do thyself no harm: for we are all here.
29 Then he called for a light, and sprang in, and came trembling, and fell down before Paul and Silas,
30 And brought them out, and said, Sirs, what must I do to be saved?
31 And they said, Believe on the Lord Jesus Christ, and thou shalt be saved, and thy house.
32 And they spake unto him the word of the Lord, and to all that were in his house.
33 And he took them the same hour of the night, and washed *their* stripes; and was baptized, he and all his, straightway.
34 And when he had brought them into his house, he set meat before them, and rejoiced, believing in God with all his house.

The incident of the miraculous deliverance of Paul and Silas along with the conversion of the Philippian jailer and his household are somewhat typical of Luke's record and typical of what the Lord does on certain occasions. It had happened before (12:3-19), why not again? Haenchen (500-501) does not disappoint us with his skepticism and denial of the validity of the incident. However, if we assume the providential acts of God in the affairs of His witnesses, there is nothing He cannot do, and this includes the Holy Spirit's super-

intendence of Luke as he recorded the event.

The "accommodations" afforded Paul and Silas were not exactly conducive for a praise and worship service. But as Tertullian (Bock 540) observed, "The legs feel nothing in the stocks when the heart is in heaven." Instead of seething in bitterness over the injustice of their condition, they used it as an occasion to rejoice (5:41). They might have been bound, but the Word of God was not! So would Paul say later in his letter to the Philippians when he suffered the same in Rome (Phil. 1:12-18). The effect was that all within earshot heard their prayers and songs of praise (v. 25). The prison had failed to imprison their hearts or silence their voices. Such is the testimony of multitudes of the Lord's servants over the years, including John Bunyan, Madame Guyon, Adoniram Judson, Richard Wurmbrand, and others.

This area of Macedonia was known for its frequency of earthquakes, but the timing of this one was more than coincidental. It literally shook the prison to its foundations, opening the cell doors and loosing the chains from the walls that secured the stocks (v. 26). All who were imprisoned could have escaped but did not.

In what must have been details gotten later from the jailer himself, Luke records his reaction when he awakened from sleep and saw the cell doors flung open (v. 27). How else would Luke have known he was sleeping and what he thought when he awakened? Given the steps taken to secure the prisoners, he might very well have assigned the oversight of the prisoners to his helpers and taken a nap. Apparently, there had been no contingent arrangements for the possibility of an earthquake that night. Keener (III:2498-2507) addresses the concept of suicide in a shame culture, but the situation may be more than shame that motivated the jailer to pull his sword. He had been charged to secure the prisoners (vv. 23-24) and their escape would cost him not only his job but his life as well (12:19). If his motivation was shame, better he do it in private than suffer public humiliation.

Seeing the jailer's desperation (v. 28) Paul yelled out to him in such a manner that it prevented carrying out his suicidal intention. The jailer's conclusion was wrong. All the prisoners were still there. Though Paul and Silas had been treated unjustly, in part by this very man, there were larger issues to consider. To have concurred with the jailer's suicide would be a betrayal of several principles taught by the Lord Jesus, including "turning the other cheek" (Mt. 5:38-39). Mercy and graciousness always trump vengeance. Why the others did not flee would be speculation; perhaps they were as impressed with the reaction of Paul and Silas as was the jailer and wanted to know more, too.

From the darkness of the inner prison, Paul called for the jailer to bring a light (usually a torch or brazier) and see for himself (v. 29). The jailer responded quickly, leaping into the cell where the men were, and fell down before Paul and Silas in a position of subservience, perhaps even worship. His actions were those of one who is overwhelmed by what has transpired. It is clear that he connected the earthquake and its effects in the jail to Paul and Silas. Paul had rejected such an expression of personal deification before at Lystra (14:8-18) and quickly clarified the situation in the exchange that followed.

After leading Paul and Silas from the remoteness of the inner prison, the jailer blurted out a question that encapsulated the whole scene (v. 30). The question, and Paul's answer (v. 31), represents the human heart overwhelmed by the unexplainable or the miraculous. But some clarification was needed. Two particular terms are significant to consider in the question. First is his use of "Sirs" (Greek *kurioi*, lords). Though it was a term of courtesy often used in general greetings (Greek vocative), its use here definitely indicates a change of mind regarding Paul and Silas. In what is probably a play on words, Paul responded for him to believe on "*the Lord (kurios) Jesus Christ*" (emphasis added), deflecting attention from them to the Lord about whom they had been singing.

The second term is the jailer's use of "saved" (Greek *sozo*). Bruce (*Acts* 317) speculates that his concern was more emotional and temporal than spiritual. Others (Polhill, *Acts* 355; Keener III:2510; Bock 541; Lenski 680) see his question as legitimately spiritual in nature, stemming from his connection with the proclamation of the demon-possessed girl (v. 17), the content of the worshipful prayers and songs, and the earthquake. I may add that the Holy Spirit would have accompanied the truths contained in these so his heart was opened. He might not have known and understood all he needed to know yet, but it was a good start. His inquiry represents the same question posed previously in Acts about the same spiritual need (2:37-39; 10:33; 11:14). We may not know exactly why he asked the question, but it seems more likely that it was asked in the full religious sense indicated.

Paul's response is as "classic" as the jailer's question (v. 31). Whatever the jailer might have intended, it is clear that Paul and Silas channeled the attention from themselves to the true Lord. Personal salvation cannot be phrased any simpler than "Believe on the Lord Jesus Christ and thou shalt be saved." The addition of "thy house" shows Paul's larger perspective. Thus, the question and response have echoed through church history, asked by men and women whose hearts were exposed to the ultimate need of humanity: to be saved (Rev. 20:15).

With the inclusion of the jailer's household in Paul's response, at some point they entered the picture (v. 32). The poignant question and answer about salvation needed further definition so the entire household heard the gospel and responds in saving faith. This response of an entire household to the gospel is thematic to Acts (10:2, 24, 33; 16:1-3, 15; 21:8-9). There is no element of proxy faith in the story; salvation is a personal matter in Acts as well as in the rest of the N. T. (Rom. 10:9-13).

Though it was well past midnight (v. 25), the newly-converted jailer administered first aid to the wounded backs of Paul and Silas. Their bloody stripes would have dried and caked, leaving them hurting and miserable. Prisons were notorious for their squalor, including the total absence of human hygiene, insects, and rat infestation. Perhaps this detail of washing their wounds indicates Luke's medical interest as well as his concern for their comfort.

The saving faith of the jailer and his household is confirmed by the fact that they are baptized (v. 32). This action itself would have been done in a public

area where sufficient water was available. There are two "washings" here: the washing of the wounded backs of the missionaries (v. 23) and the washing away of the sins of the jailer and his household symbolized by baptism (v. 33). Again, there is little delay in administering baptism though it seems an inconvenience to do so at that time, under those circumstances. They would not have had to travel all the way to the Gangites River (v. 13), for there were public fountains available nearby.

One assumes that the other prisoners were re-secured in the jail, but Paul and Silas were allowed to leave the premises even though the jailer had been charged to make their incarceration sure (v. 23). The public baptism, though late at night, was risky, but taking them into his house, which was probably close by, if not adjacent to the jail, was very risky. The provision of food (v. 34) brought some respite from hunger after a long day of deprivation. The new-found faith of the jailer and his family was "food" (Jn. 4:32) for them, as they experienced the rejoicing that always accompanies personal redemption.

(3) Humiliation of the city leaders (16:35-40)

35 And when it was day, the magistrates sent the serjeants, saying, Let those men go.
36 And the keeper of the prison told this saying to Paul, The magistrates have sent to let you go: now therefore depart, and go in peace.
37 But Paul said unto them, They have beaten us openly uncondemned, being Romans, and have cast us into prison; and now do

they thrust us out privily? nay, verily; but let them come themselves and fetch us out.

38 And the serjeants told these words unto the magistrates: and they feared, when they heard that they were Romans.

39 And they came and besought them, and brought *them* out, and desired *them* to depart out of the city.

40 And they went out of the prison, and entered into *the house* of Lydia: and when they had seen the brethren, they comforted them, and departed.

The concluding exchange reveals that at some point Paul and Silas had returned to the jail. It seems appropriate that they did so to avoid charges to the jailer as well as to "tie up a loose end" of legalities. When the time came the next day to finalize actions against Paul and Silas, it was determined they should be released and "run out of town." The term "serjeants" (Greek *rhabdouchoi*, the bearers of the rods) means these were lictors, in all likelihood the men who had beaten them the previous day. These were the local police who enforced the law on behalf of the magistrates.

The news of their release conveyed to them by the newly-saved keeper of the prison (v. 36) was not exactly met with enthusiasm by Paul and Silas. There is little doubt the authorities expected them to slink out of town licking their wounds and having learned their lesson. But there was a "little detail" that had been totally suppressed in the entire matter. That detail was the fact that both Paul and Silas were Roman citizens (v. 37). The injustices perpetrated on them were not only inju-

rious to them physically but were serious violations of the rights of Roman citizens. That became the leverage the missionaries used to bring some justice into the picture for themselves and possibly for believers in Philippi in the future.

Roman citizens were afforded at least four specific rights. They could not be condemned or punished without a fair trial. They could not be scourged. They could appeal personal legal situations directly to the emperor. They were exempt from certain taxes (Cadbury, *Acts* 65-82; Picirilli, *Paul* 13). While local officials skirted citizenship rights often enough, it was nonetheless a serious offense for which there could be serious consequences. This is implied in the reaction (v. 38) of the city officials when they learned of the citizenship status of Paul and Silas.

Upon hearing this, the officials themselves took a trip to the jail and, this time, courteously saw to their release (v. 39). This might have been a bitter pill for the city's elite to swallow, but it was a necessary one. Some translate "they besought" (Greek *parekalesan*) as "they apologized" (ESV, RSV, NLT). While that may be overstated, their appeal nonetheless had the effect of an apology as they repeatedly begged (Greek present tense) Paul and Silas to leave. As Roman citizens they could not be expelled from the city, but neither could they be guaranteed protection.

The question arises as to the timing of their appeal about their rights as Roman citizens. Why did they wait until now to let that be known? Why did they not announce that in the beginning? Polhill (*Acts* 358) offers that Paul had been "huffy" in demanding restitution. But, there are several reasons that was not the case, not the least of which was the high-handed way they were treated initially, apparently suppressing any attempts to speak. Mobs are hardly known for their decorum and respect for individual rights to speak. It was not the first time, nor would it be the last, when Paul's rights would be totally ignored. Further, it was clear that the reputation of believers in Philippi needed some degree of correction. They had done nothing wrong and the record needed to be cleared. Most important, the future relationship of believers in the town hinged somewhat on this challenge.

It should be remembered that Acts is a historical record of the times. Roman law was the supreme law of the land. As much as Augustus Caesar's *Pax Romana* (the peace of Rome) was in effect, the warfare of spiritual higher powers was neither abated nor diminished. In spite of the rights of Roman citizens even, Christians suffered at the very hands of those sworn to uphold the law. Such is the battle waged "not against flesh and blood" (Eph. 6:12; 2 Cor. 10:3). In light of that, we have both a model and a theology for balancing a citizen's rights and suffering for the cause of Christ. In the providential guidance of God in the governments of this world, the civil rights of citizens—which provide for the common good—are necessary for a peaceful and orderly society. But even the best of governments are often ruled or influenced by men with wicked hearts. Christianity has both prospered and suffered ill at the hands of the governments of this fallen world.

Summary
(16:6-40)

There should be little doubt that the missions team prayerfully planned to go to the most populated cities and towns. However, the Lord's providential guidance defined their strategy. Obeying the Holy Spirit's leadership, they decided to wait for specific directions. They did not have long to wait as the Lord directed them with a vision given to Paul in the night. Instruction by vision is one means of communication the Lord used a number of times in the Acts record.

Upon arrival in Philippi, one of the most populous cities of Macedonia, they discovered there was no synagogue but did meet with a group of women who went to the riverside for prayer on the Sabbath. Lydia and her household soon became Christ-followers as well as hosts for the missionary team. She was the first to personalize "the man of Macedonia" in Paul's earlier vision.

The spiritual deliverance of a young demon-possessed woman led to the arrest, physical beating, and imprisonment of Paul and Silas. However, their faithful witness through the abuse and the miraculous timing of the earthquake resulted in the open heart of the jailer and an open door to his family. All were saved that very night as further confirmations of the "man of Macedonia" of the vision.

When the city officials decided the next day to wash their hands of the incident with Paul and Silas by expelling them from the city, they were shocked to find out they were the ones who were law-breakers. Both Paul and Silas were Roman citizens whose rights had been violated. The magistrates' treatment of them could have serious consequences. In a case of city officials truly "eating crow," they personally appealed to Paul and Silas to leave the city peacefully. The whole situation presents a study in how believers are sometimes mistreated for the cause of Christ and the timing of appeals to civil rights.

Application: Teaching and Preaching the Passage

Exegetical Outline of the Text: 1. The Direction They Needed (16:6-12). 2. The Conversion of Lydia and her Household (16:13-15). 3. The Deliverance of the Demon-possessed Girl (16:16-18). 4. The Arrest and Abuse of Paul and Silas (16:19-24). 5. The Conversion of the Jailer and His Household (16:25-34). 6. The Apology of the City Officials (16:35-40).

This text highlights several important factors regarding Christian life. It clearly shows the need for knowing the will of God as to time and place for ministry. When it was clear to the team where they were *not* supposed to go, they decided to wait on the Lord to know where they *were* to go. This is an excellent text from which to teach and preach about following the Holy Spirit's leadership and how to know it. While visions are rarely used today, since the Scriptures have been completed, I think the main idea is that if one has an open heart or is wanting to know God's direction, the Lord can certainly communicate His will to us. The means of doing so are usually these: 1. the principles of the written Word of God; 2. the counsel of godly men and women; 3. the wisdom of discernment and life experience; 4. the inner witness of the Holy Spirit.

The vision assured them of the direction they needed to follow but not the specific people they were to meet. As they did the things they normally would do they met people in the process. These became the personifications of the "man of Macedonia" in the vision.

So it is with our lives. The routines of life are usually the means for meeting people who need the Lord. It takes a heart of discernment and a sense of priorities to share the gospel with them when it is appropriate.

The account of the imprisonment of Paul and Silas presents many truths to teach and preach. Certainly included would be how believers should respond to being mistreated for the cause of Christ. Also, that in every situation there are people who need the Lord. God can take a bad situation and turn it into something incredible. "Imprisonments" do not always involve jail facilities.

The fact that Paul and Silas appealed to the authorities regarding their rights shows the appropriateness of doing so when required and allowed. Suppressive governments may or may not respect the laws of the land. There is a duality in the event: suffering for the cause of Christ and the appeal to citizen's rights. This has often been abused historically as the Lord's people have been hated and despised by evil people.

5. Witness in Thessalonica (17:1-9)

1 Now when they had passed through Amphipolis and Apollonia, they came to Thessalonica, where was a synagogue of the Jews:
2 And Paul, as his manner was, went in unto them, and three sabbath days reasoned with them out of the scriptures,
3 Opening and alleging, that Christ must needs have suffered, and risen again from the dead; and that this Jesus, whom I preach unto you, is Christ.

4 And some of them believed, and consorted with Paul and Silas; and of the devout Greeks a great multitude, and of the chief women not a few.
5 But the Jews which believed not, moved with envy, took unto them certain lewd fellows of the baser sort, and gathered a company, and set all the city on an uproar, and assaulted the house of Jason, and sought to bring them out to the people.
6 And when they found them not, they drew Jason and certain brethren unto the rulers of the city, crying, These that have turned the world upside down are come hither also;
7 Whom Jason hath received: and these all do contrary to the decrees of Caesar, saying there is another king, *one* Jesus.
8 And the troubled the people and the rulers of the city, when they heard these things.
9 And when they had taken security of Jason, and of the other, they let them go.

Traveling southwest on the *Via Egnatia*, the team passed through the cities of Amphipolis, some thirty-three miles away, and Apollonia, another twenty-seven miles (Keener III:2535-2536). Both cities were strategic and substantial cities in themselves. Each lay a day's journey apart. Luke does not mention any evangelistic efforts in either of these. It seems the intention was to put some distance behind them from Philippi and get to Thessalonica, still some thirty-five miles further from Apollonia.

Thessalonica (modern Salonica) was a significant city in many ways, as it still is today. It was the chief port city of Macedonia, a Roman "free city" with a very sizable population of some sixty thousand. More important, there was a synagogue in Thessalonica.

Of note also is the use of "they" instead of "we" (v. 1). Obviously, Luke remained in Philippi. Apparently, he does not rejoin the team until the third missionary journey when they returned through Philippi (20:6).

In keeping with his commitment to proclaim the gospel to "the Jew first" (Rom. 1:16), Paul began his witness in the synagogue and continued for three Sabbaths. Whether these were consecutive Sabbaths is not stated, but that seems likely, given the dialogue generated initially by Paul's preaching. However, that does not indicate that the length of their stay in Thessalonica was only three weeks. Indications from 1 Thessalonians are that Paul and his two companions stayed longer. Even so, their stay was abbreviated by civil and religious pressures (Bruce, *Paul* 224; Picirilli, *Paul* 114; Robertson, *Acts* 269-270).

How Paul made his case to the synagogue Jews is instructive. He "reasoned with them out of the Scriptures, opening and alleging" (vv. 2-3). His method was somewhat syllogistic. He asserted that the Scriptures predicted the suffering of the Messiah and His subsequent resurrection from death caused by His suffering. His conclusion was that Jesus of Nazareth did just that and is, therefore, the Messiah. Paul's personal encounter with the risen Lord and his three-year spiritual retreat in Arabia would have certainly been included in his testimony.

Paul based his argument on the authority of the Scriptures: namely, the O. T. Messianic prophecies. This was the same basis of appeal that Jesus Himself used (Lk. 24:25-27) as well as the very same content. (Did Luke inform Paul of this post resurrection event?) For Jews, the Scriptures were the ultimate authority of God. The same should be true for Christians. As Calvin (II:92) states, "If there is a discussion about human affairs, then human reasons may have their place, but in the teaching of the faith, the authority of God alone ought to be sovereign, and we ought to be dependent upon it." All Jews would be familiar with the Messianic prophecies, even unbelieving Jews (Mt. 2:4-6). The disputed issue was whether Jesus of Nazareth was the promised Messiah.

The results of the proclamation of the gospel were mixed. On one hand many of the Greek God-fearers ("devout Greeks") and "chief women" savingly believed (v. 4). There is no way to define by number how many "a great multitude" was, or the number of "chief women" characterized by "not a few." Luke has long since quit giving specific numbers of converts. It is clear, however, that the number was large.

Some regard the "chief women" as wives of prominent city leaders (Marshall, Acts 277; Metzger 401; Bock 551). Others think the reference is to women of high rank (Robertson, Acts 269). Either way, they were women of high social standing. Macedonian women enjoyed much more freedom than in many other areas. We are not told exactly how these women heard the gospel, but it might have been as an overflow from the synagogue proclamations. It is typical of Luke to include the response of women to the gospel. It

should not be inferred that only those of higher social standing responded to the gospel. The Thessalonian epistles indicate otherwise (1 Thess. 4:11-12; 2 Thess. 3:6-12).

On the other hand, many of the Jews reacted against Paul (vv. 5-8) so vehemently that they secured the "muscle" of hired thugs and went about to totally disrupt things. Their motive was "envy" (v. 5). Perhaps they saw the conversion of some of Thessalonica's leading citizens as threats to their own positions of influence. Or perhaps they disagreed with the Messianic fulfillment message of Paul so strongly they reacted in anger and jealousy. This had happened before (6:9-14).

The translation "certain lewd fellows of the baser sort" can be understood as "certain evil men who were market-loungers." These were men who hung idly around the market place looking for trouble and who could stir it up as well. All cities have their troublemakers. These men began a riot in the city, resulting in widespread unrest and rumored treasonous beliefs. Apparently, Paul and the team had been staying at the house of "Jason" (Greek alternative for "Joshua"), who appears to have been a convert. His house was targeted and when it was discovered that the missionaries were not there, Jason himself was assaulted. Mob mentality always finds a victim.

Jason and a few unnamed brothers (v. 6) are literally dragged before the city leaders where three charges are pressed upon them (16:19-22). First, the charges begin with the accusation of disrupting the civil peace. The phrase "turned the world upside down" can be understood as "set the habitable world in confusion" or "caused trouble everywhere," specifically meaning the Roman world and Rome's political order. The charge is stated in hyperbole since it's intended to be a political charge. Second, Jason is accused of harboring those who are responsible (v. 7a). This would make him complicit in the whole affair.

Third, the specific accusation that was charged with political overtones was the charge of sedition: namely, that the new believers were proclaiming a rival to the ruling power of Caesar, Claudius at the time (v. 7b). Again, this was the very essence of the charges brought against Jesus (Jn. 19:11-15; Lk. 23:1-2), although it is doubtful the city officials knew anything about Jesus of Nazareth. Though Thessalonica was a free city with authority to conduct its own civil affairs, they were still under the thumb of Rome. If word got out that they were tolerating political rivals to Caesar, serious consequences would result.

The situation raises the question where this charge came from? It is the first time in the Acts record that this kind of charge is named, though it might certainly have been part of the charges at Philippi. Luke does not record the initial proclamation of the gospel as having a theme of rivalry (vv. 2-3). But given the eschatological nature of the Thessalonian epistles (1 Thess. 4:13—5:11; 2 Thess. 2:1-12) and the fact that Paul had taught these truths when he was there (2 Thess. 2:5), someone looking for an excuse could easily twist the message of the Second Coming of Christ to mean a present political rivalry with Caesar. Of course, these were trumped-up charges, but lies have always been at the root of false accusations against authentic Christianity. Until now

opposition against believers has been mostly religious in nature and seen as a rivalry with Judaism. This charge shifts the focus of the accusations to political opposition, although it was instigated by the Jews of Thessalonica.

While they meant these to be negative accusations with political overtones, there is an ironic sense in which they were compliments, just as were the accusations against Jesus. Christianity does proclaim Christ as King of Kings and Lord of Lords. His kingdom is not of this world (Jn. 18:36)—at least not yet! Eschatologically, He will ultimately rule and reign and we will reign with Him (Rev. 20:4). Further, there is a sense in which Christianity is revolutionary. It does "turn the world upside down." Individual "worlds" and even whole societies are revolutionized by the gospel that brings moral and spiritual order to chaos and destitution. Missionary history is filled with incredible stories of the revolutionary impact of the gospel on men, women, and entire cultures and societies that were mired in moral chaos. In that sense, authentic Christianity is a rival to the corrupt systems of this world (2 Thess. 1:7-10). But those promises are entirely administered by the Sovereign God in His time. Believers are commanded to be model citizens in the cultures of this world (Matt. 5:13-16; 1 Tim. 2:1-2; 1 Pet. 3:8-16).

The effects of the charges raised sufficient alarms to spark a loud outcry, from some, to the city rulers. Luke's usage of the term "politarchs" for the "rulers" is entirely accurate for that time (v. 6). The accusations could have resulted in severe punishment, but the city rulers did not overreact as did those at Philippi (16:22-23). They did order

Jason and those arrested with him to put up "bail money" ("security," v. 9) to guarantee the peace, including, perhaps, that the missionary team would leave town. Upon compliance, the men were released. Unless he is the "Jason" referred to in Romans 16:21, this is the last time the biblical record mentions him, but he is certainly not lost to biblical history.

It is an ironic and discourteous pattern that the men who brought the message of good news and peace with God were often run out of town. Their witness at Thessalonica was one of triumph and trial. Such is the response of the unconverted heart to spiritual truth. Such is the response of self-serving political powers to the Kingdom of God. The success of the witness in Thessalonica can be better measured by the epistles (Morgan 403). Believers had "turned to God from idols" (1 Thess. 1:9), became the hub of "sounding out" the gospel of Christ to the entire region (1 Thess. 1:8), and served as "examples" of authentic Christianity to others (1 Thess. 1:7). Though Paul and Silas had to leave Thessalonica, they left behind the eternal fruit of their labors (1 Thess. 2:19-20).

6. Witness in Berea (17:10-15)

10 And the brethren immediately sent away Paul and Silas by night unto Berea: who coming *thither* went into the synagogue of the Jews.
11 These were more noble than those in Thessalonica, in that they received the word with all readiness of mind, and searched the scriptures daily, whether those things were so.
12 Therefore many of them believed; also of honourable women which were Greeks, and of men, not a few.
13 But when the Jews of Thessalonica had knowledge that the word of God was preached of Paul at Berea, they came thither also, and stirred up the people.
14 And then immediately the brethren sent away Paul to go as it were to the sea: but Silas and Timotheus abode there still.
15 And they that conducted Paul brought him unto Athens: and receiving a commandment unto Silas and Timotheus for to come to him with all speed, they departed.

The situation in Thessalonica had become too dangerous for Paul and Silas so they left under the cover of darkness (v. 10). (Apparently Timothy was able to remain.) Instead of continuing to travel the main road, the *Via Egnatia* (which extended to Rome), they turned more inland, southwesterly, to the city of Berea (modern Veroia), some fifty miles away. It might have taken three days walking, especially if they were nursing wounds from previous encounters. Berea itself was a significant city in the region with some history of importance (Keener III:2561-2562).

Upon arrival they entered the synagogue, as was Paul's strategy of witness wherever he went. All synagogue witnessing had seen both positive and negative responses (Matt. 13:3-23). The negative responses, however, did not deter them from the task. The response of the Bereans was a breath of fresh air as Luke reports their openness to the message of the gospel. Luke describes them as *more noble* than those of

Thessalonica. This word (Greek *eugenesteros*) originally meant "of high birth, well-born" but came to mean "open minded, tolerant" (Thayer 257). With eagerness they heard the message of the gospel and made diligent, daily examinations of the claims of Paul and Silas, measured by the authority of the Scriptures (v. 11). It should be remembered that the authority of the Scriptures was paramount to the Jews—as it should be. It should also be remembered that the message of the gospel is firmly rooted in the Messianic promises of the O. T. In essence, the Bereans laid the claims of the gospel alongside the claims of the Scriptures for verification. The result was that "many of them believed" (v. 12), as would be expected.

Among the new converts were prominent women as well as Jews and Greeks (v. 4). Some of these were probably "God-fearers," as in other settings. Again, a specific number is not recorded but Luke states that there were many ("not a few"). Times of testing are often rewarded with times of refreshing. Nothing refreshes those who minister more than seeing folks respond in saving faith.

News of the reception of the gospel in Berea reached back to the agitators in Thessalonica soon enough (v. 13). Not content to leave well enough alone, they made their way to Berea to continue the opposition. Before long they succeeded in raising another mob ("stirred up," from Greek *saleuo*, to shake or disturb) against the missionaries (Bock 556). The devil never rests. The situation shows the level of influence exerted by powerful, influential people. They were able to generate significant opposition not just from the local Jews but the Gentile populace as well ("the people," v. 13).

The opposition was strong enough to warrant the departure of Paul. Some Bereans accompanied him, with the approval of the believers (v. 14). Silas and Timothy (who had apparently come from Thessalonica) remained in Berea, at least for a while longer. That Paul went to Athens is clear. How he got there is not so clear. The wording is "to go as it were to the sea" (v. 14). Some manuscripts actually read that he went by sea (Metzger 403; Polhill, *Acts* 364). However, the wording could also mean that this was a diversionary tactic to avoid those who were after his head. In that case, he only traveled toward the sea but then turned south on the coastal road. It was just over two hundred miles south to Athens. At any rate, he was accompanied to Athens, from which he sent his unnamed companions back to Berea with the message that Silas and Timothy should join him there posthaste (v. 15).

From 1 Thessalonians 3:1-2 we know that Silas and Timothy did, indeed, join Paul in Athens as soon as they could get there. However, he sent them to other places of ministry and he remained alone. Timothy was dispatched back to Thessalonica and Silas to an unnamed city. There is no need to even suggest a contradiction in the accounts; what appears to be a difference between Acts and 1 Thessalonians is easily explained (Haenchen 513; Polhill, *Acts* 364; Bruce, *Acts* 328).

7. Witness in Athens (17:16-34)

a. In the synagogue and market (17:16-17)

16 Now while Paul waited for them at Athens, his spirit was stirred in

**him, when he saw the city wholly given to idolatry.
17 Therefore disputed he in the synagogue with the Jews, and with the devout persons, and in the market daily with them that met with him.**

Athens, Greece, was the cultural and philosophical center of the Roman Empire, although in Paul's time it was a mere shadow of its former glory days. The "Golden Age of Athens" occurred in the fourth and fifth centuries B.C. and involved such notable figures as Socrates, Hippocrates, Herodutus, and Thucydides—to name a few. However, its architectural, intellectual, and cultural influence remained. It was still a formidable city in the Empire (Schnabel 722). Even today the city is admirable for its philosophical and cultural influences. What may be admired today as incredible works of architecture and art—apart from the idolatrous nature originally intended—were viewed entirely differently in the N. T. world. To an extent these "artistic" artifacts should always be understood by Christians as representing idolatry. Biblically, the Greek culture represents "the world's wisdom" that challenged and rejected the knowledge of God (1 Cor. 1:21-24). It is, therefore, very significant that the apostle Paul not only went to the synagogue and agora (market-place) in Athens but also was providentially given an opportunity to proclaim the gospel of Jesus Christ to the Areopagus, which represented the "wisdom of the world."

That Paul was waiting for Silas and Timothy at Athens (v. 16) does not necessarily mean he had not intended to go there to proclaim the gospel. It certainly fit his evangelistic strategy. Their support would have been significant in the arenas of debate he was about to enter. But the apostle's spirit was "stirred" (Greek *paroxuno*, provoke to anger) at the pervasive idolatry of the city (Bruce, *Acts* 329). Idolatry was nothing new to Paul, having been exposed to it all his life; but he had been rigorously taught the first two commandments of the Decalogue (Ex. 20:2-5; Deut. 5:6-9) and all they meant. Plus, he had personally encountered the living Christ who revealed the utter futility and emptiness of idolatry. It is therefore easy to understand Paul's emotional reaction.

Paul began his proclamation of the gospel in the synagogue (v. 17), as was his usual first choice. Here he "disputed" (Greek *dialegomai*, suggesting dialogue)—that is, he engaged in reasoned argument—with the Jews and God-fearers ("devout persons"). This method allowed for questions and discussion as well as proclamation. He would have used the same approach as he did previously (17:2-3, 11) showing that Jesus of Nazareth fulfilled the O. T. Messianic promises.

Paul also carried the gospel to the Greek population in general, engaging people in conversation in the agora or "market." Keener (III:2576) reports that Athens had a Roman agora as well as a Greek agora. The Greek agora in Athens was not only a place for selling and buying goods but used as a forum for philosophical debate (Schnabel 723-724; Bruce, *Acts* 329-330). It was lined with idols and pillars, many of which depicted the moral decadence of the gods they worshiped. Though offensive to Paul spiritually, the place and its art suited him perfectly, providing him opportunity to proclaim the gospel; as he went there each day there were people who needed the gospel. Sometimes one has to narrow his focus away from the environment to the spiritual needs of the person.

b. Challenged by the Epicureans and Stoics (17:18-21)

18 Then certain philosophers of the Epicureans, and of the Stoics, encountered him. And some said, What will this babbler say? other some, He seemeth to be a setter forth of strange gods: because he preached unto them Jesus, and the resurrection.
19 And they took him, and brought him unto Areopagus, saying, May we know what this new doctrine, whereof thou speakest, is?
20 For thou bringest certain strange things to our ears: we would know therefore what these things mean.
21 (For all the Athenians and strangers which were there spent their time in nothing else, but either to tell, or to hear some new thing.)

Paul's vigorous and engaging proclamation of the gospel soon caught the attention of two of Athens' most prominent philosophical cults, the Epicureans and Stoics (v. 18). That in itself is somewhat surprising since there were many who vied for the attention of the public. The Epicureans developed from the philosophy of Epicurus (341-270 B.C.) whose beliefs and lifestyle were summarized by one Diogenes Laertius, "Nothing to fear in God; Nothing to feel in death; Pleasure can be attained; Pain can be endured" (Bock 561). They did not deny the existence of the gods but believed they took no interest in the affairs of men. They denied any kind of life after death. There were some extreme examples of indulgences among the Epicureans but most tried to strike some sort of balance between indulgence and moderation. They sought to experience just the right amount of pleasure in food, drink, sexual experience, etc. (Sproul 308). In effect, they were the hedonists of that day. Our contemporary term "Epicurean Delight," which describes a gourmet feast that appeases physical appetites, derives from this.

The Stoics were somewhat the opposite. Their cult arose at the same time as the Epicureans and claimed Zeno, a Cypriot (340-265 B.C.), as their founder. They were named "Stoics" after the colonnade (Greek *stoa*) in the agora where Zeno taught his followers (Bruce, *Acts* 330). Stoicism taught the preeminence of human rationality, self-sufficiency, living with a high sense of duty and morality, and held to a polytheistic view, embracing the gods as directly involved in the affairs of men. They did believe in a supreme "God" whose identity was obscure and pantheistic. (An excellent excursus on these two groups can be found in Keener III:2584-2595.)

As different as these groups were they did agree on one thing, that Paul was a "babbler" (Greek *spermologos*, a seed picker) who proclaimed "strange gods." They regarded him as one who gathered crumbs of thought from here and there, like a flitting bird, trying to piece them together in some sort of philosophical combination. In their intellectual arrogance they mocked him because he proclaimed "Jesus and the resurrection" (v. 18), both of which were in total contradiction to their own views. But they were correct in their charge.

That was exactly what he proclaimed. The proclamation of "Jesus" would include the deity of His person as well as His incarnation in the person of Jesus of Nazareth. The "resurrection" would include His humanity, suffering, death, and resurrection from the dead. Paul's theology and philosophy pre-dated the Epicureans and Stoics by a thousand years (Ex. 20:1-17).

The Areopagus was both the title of the court of men and the place where they met. *Ares* was the Greek god of war; *pagus* means hill (v. 19). It was also called "Mars hill" (v. 22) because "Mars" was the corresponding Roman god of war. The court itself had been a venerable institution for a long time, made up of some one hundred of its leading citizens who were of wealth and high social status (Keener III:2600-2601). Their authority was far-reaching. Stott (282) refers to this court as "the supreme council of Athens." Keener (III:2602) regards it as the "ruling council of Athens...the highest administrative body and court in the town." Their authority certainly included regulation of religious ideas that appeared to cause disruption in the city.

Whether Luke intended it or not, there are parallels between the trial of Socrates and the hearing granted to the apostle Paul before this same court (Polhill, *Acts* 368). Socrates was accused of corrupting the youth of Athens by presenting strange gods, too. Now Paul is accused of corrupting the minds of citizens by doing the same thing. The parallels end there, of course. In the providential guidance of God, the apostle Paul appears often before city councils, rulers, and kings (9:15).

The charge that warranted Paul's appearance before the Areopagus was simply that he was proclaiming things they did not believe and had not encountered previously (v. 20). The phrase translated "they took him and brought him unto Areopagus" is ambiguous enough that it can mean either a formal arrest and hearing or merely an informal inquiry (Ramsay, *Traveller* 247). Either is possible but it seems more likely that this was a request to satisfy curiosity rather than a legal charge. This is probably indicated by Luke's aside regarding the insatiable appetite of the Athenians for novel ideas and discussion (v. 21).

Whatever the nature of the inquiry, the opportunity presented itself for Paul to proclaim "some new thing," at least to the Areopagites. Of course, what Paul believed and said was not new to biblical history and theology. Ingeniously, he blended the "old" and the "new" together to present the gospel of the God of the Bible to those who sat listening. What an opportunity!

c. Paul's message to the Areopagus (17:22-31)

22 Then Paul stood in the midst of Mars' hill, and said, Ye men of Athens, I perceive that in all things ye are too superstitious.
23 For as I passed by, and beheld your devotions, I found an altar with this inscription, To The Unknown God. Whom therefore ye ignorantly worship, him declare I unto you.
24 God that made the world and all things therein, seeing that he is Lord of heaven and earth, dwelleth not in temples made with hands;
25 Neither is worshipped with men's hands, as though he needed

any thing, seeing he giveth to all life, and breath, and all things;
26 And hath made of one blood all nations of men for to dwell on all the face of the earth, and hath determined the times before appointed, and the bounds of their habitation;
27 That they should seek the LORD, if haply they might feel after him, and find him, though he be not far from every one of us:
28 For in him we live, and move, and have our being; as certain also of your own poets have said, For we are also his offspring.
29 Forasmuch then as we are the offspring of God, we ought not to think that the Godhead is like unto gold, or silver, or stone, graven by art and man's device.
30 And the times of this ignorance God winked at; but now commandeth all men every where to repent:
31 Because he hath appointed a day, in the which he will judge the world in righteousness by *that* man whom he hath ordained; *whereof* he hath given assurance unto all *men*, in that he hath raised him from the dead.

Of all the sermons and speeches in Acts, this one has received as much scrutiny as any, perhaps more. Polhill (*Acts* 369) states that no text in Acts has received more scholarly attention than this one. Setting aside the comments of those who regard the entire episode with skepticism (Haenchen 527-528), most interpreters conclude that Paul's message to the Areopagus is nothing short of brilliant. It certainly fits the apologetic theme of Acts expressed in the recorded speeches. As such, it is a masterful blend of defense and proclamation, of courteous deference and apostolic authority, of Greek philosophy and biblical truth.

Paul's position is described as he "stood in the midst of Mars' hill" (v. 22). The setting of the court itself was about half way up the hill of the Acropolis where the men of the court seated themselves to hear the accused. Paul was positioned in the middle of the assembly where he began by making a specific point of contact by referencing the religious zeal of the Athenians. The word translated "too superstitious" (Greek *deisidaimonesteros*) can be taken, technically, either in a good sense (to mean being very devoted) or in a bad sense (meaning fearful superstition). It seems Paul purposely chose this word (under the leadership of the Holy Spirit) for its ambiguity. To the Greeks it could appear to be somewhat complimentary. To Paul, who was already angry over their idolatry (v. 16), it may have meant something uncomplimentary. Because it colors Paul's entire message, it is highly unlikely that he is being condescending. Rather, he is showing courteous deference to the court and getting directly to the point (24:2-3; 26:2-3). Robertson (*Acts* 285) is correct in saying, "It seems unlikely that Paul should give this audience a slap in the face at the very start."

Paul's reference point is an idol's altar with the inscription "TO THE UNKNOWN GOD" (v. 23). There were many altars in and around Athens with a similar inscription. The Greeks of Athens were particularly concerned not to omit any god they might have missed (Marshall, *Acts* 286). But Paul does not mean the Greeks were actually worshipers of the true God. He is not confirming the authenticity of either their idol or

259

their intent. He is merely using this as a segue to proclaim to them the truth about the God who was alluded to in ignorance by their altar. Neither the irony of the situation nor the genius of Paul should be missed, for here we have a "seed picker" (v. 18) enlightening those who claimed to be the most enlightened people on the planet. Paul does not begin his speech with references to the enlightened intellect of the Greeks or to a summary of their philosophical positions—though he could have done so. Rather, he goes to the heart of the whole matter. Life and all that makes up life ultimately begins with God; hence his choice of "religion" as the main point to consider. His message is a declaration of five premises about this "Unknown God."

First, Paul declares God as the Creator of the material universe (v. 24). This premise is very different from either the Epicurean view of the chance existence of the universe or the Stoic view of pantheism. (Both of these have modern counterparts.) Paul further asserts that as Creator, it is ludicrous to think this great God, who is greater than the material world itself, needs man-made shrines or temples in which to dwell. It should be remembered that Paul said this against the backdrop of the Acropolis, known for its temples to the gods. Throughout history there have been multitudes of "structures" (architecturally and philosophically) that have been erected based on false assumptions. There are a multitude of "Acropolises."

Second, Paul declares God as the sustainer of all He has created (v. 25). He exists independently of men ("as though He needed anything"). He is the source of "all life," physical functions ("breath"), and "all things" that are needed to sustain life. This also contradicted both the Epicureans who believed the gods had abandoned all and the Stoics who believed all things that needed sustaining were gods. The same notions are part of modern secularism.

Third, Paul declares God as the overseer or ruler of humanity (vv. 26-27). Instead of "one blood," some manuscripts have "one man," and some commentators (Bock 566; Stott 285; Robertson, *Acts* 287; Polhill, *Acts* 374; Lenski 728) follow this and insist that it is a reference to Adam. Either way, the idea is the unity of the human race from a common origin. This contradicted both the Greeks' and Jews' sense of their exclusiveness (Col. 3:11).

Furthermore, as ruler of the nations, God oversees the rise and fall as well as the geographical boundaries of each. Paul mingles both the interplay of sovereign control of the affairs of governments as well as human free will (Job 12:23). As free, men choose their course; but God ultimately rules. Paul asserts that God intervenes in the affairs of men for the purpose that they may acknowledge His existence and seek after Him. His interventions show that He certainly is not indifferently removed from human affairs. He is present everywhere and available to "every one of us."

Fourth, Paul declares God as the giver of all life (vv. 28-29). Again, Paul will point out the vanity of idolatry (v. 29), but he does so by showing that the God he has defined, not the gods made by the efforts of men, is the origin of all life. He does so with two quotations from Greek philosophers (Stott 286; Bruce, *Acts* 338). (Polhill *Acts* 375 and Bock 568 say there is only one philosopher quoted.) While Christians and Jews present would have viewed the Scriptures as authoritative, the Greeks would have regarded them as meaningless. Hence, to quote the Greek philosophers is to appeal to authorities the Greeks acknowledged. However, Paul is, in effect, turning the philosophy of the Greeks against them. The first quote is "for in him we live, and move, and have our being" from the sixth century B.C. poet, Epimenides of Cnossos in Crete (Stott 286; Polhill, *Acts* 375). Note the three verbs used that depict God's immanence with humanity: life, movement, existence (Sproul 314-317). Paul would quote from the same philosopher later in commentary on the character of the Cretans (Titus 1:1-13).

The second quote, "For we are also his offspring" is from the third century B.C. Stoic philosopher Aratus, who was from Paul's native region of Cilicia. Paul's point of reference is entirely different, however, from that of Aratus since Aratus was referring to Zeus, not Yahweh.

Given that, the quote makes the point. All humanity derives existence from a source greater than ourselves, as these Greek philosophers understood. That being the case, it is misguided to think such a God can be fashioned by hand, even with the most expensive materials ("gold, silver, stone") and most sophisticated designs ("art and man's device"). The same truth is certainly foundational to Christianity (Gen. 1:1-28; Jn. 1:1-4; Col. 1:16-17). Since "all truth is God's truth" (Thomas Aquinas), it was only reasonable for Paul to cite these Greek writers to make his point. Again, Paul was merely confirming the authenticity of the truth, not of the

entirety of the writings of the Greek poets.

Fifth, Paul declared God to be the ultimate judge of all (vv. 30-31). On this point, he became very candid and intentional as he returned to the issue of "ignorance" (vv. 23, 30). The concept of final judgment of the world was new to Greeks (Bruce, *Acts* 340-341). But the concept of culpability and judgment for one's actions was very familiar to his hearers. His argument was that in the writings of the Greeks themselves they showed a degree of understanding about the dependence of humanity on the origin of life beyond themselves. However, the Athenians chose to define "God" by the works of their own hands, thus acts of ignorance. Further, God has "winked at" (Greek *huperorao*), overlooked, such actions until now (14:16). In essence, God has tolerated, not condoned the sins of humanity, for His own sovereign reasons until the present time. Now He commands that men repent of such actions of ignorance and rejection. They are culpable for all they do. Note that the reference is universal: to "all men everywhere."

The reasons for the termination of God's tolerance are three. One, there is a fixed day of final judgment set for the entire world. Although this concept is entirely biblical, it logically fits the progression of knowledge and responsibility for one's actions. Two, it will be done in righteousness. God the creator, the sustainer, the ruler, the giver of life, the final judge, is both absolutely righteous and judges righteously. Third, the judge who will execute such a final judgment has been ordained (or appointed) for that role and is identified as the one who was raised from the dead: Jesus Himself. His resurrection evidences His right to judge.

Here is the culmination and definition of Paul's answer to the charge that he "preached unto them Jesus and the resurrection" (v. 18). He did exactly that, showing the logic of what he preached and why.

d. Response to Paul's message (17:32-34)

32 And when they heard of the resurrection of the dead, some mocked: and others said, We will hear thee again of this *matter.*
33 So Paul departed from among them.
34 Howbeit certain men clave unto him, and believed: among the which was Dionysius the Areopagite, and a woman named Damaris, and others with them.

Paul's culminating reference to the resurrection brought verbal mockery and jeering (Greek *chleuazo*, jeer, jest, scoff). The NASB translation, "began to sneer," expresses it well. This was probably from the flippant Epicureans (v. 32). The others, though probably just as skeptical, were at least more polite, suggesting the possibility of another hearing. With that, Paul left the court of the Areopagus, having presented a clear apologetic for the Christian faith (1 Pet. 3:14-16).

One may think such a radical and different "philosophy" would be met with total indifference. But some men did respond in saving faith, one being Dionysius who was himself one of the court of the Areopagus. That alone was a great victory. Eusebius (Bruce, *Acts* 343, footnote) reports that he became the first bishop of Athens and died a martyr. Another was a woman named Damaris (v. 34) who was probably one of many bystanders listening to Paul's presentation. While we would love to know more, Luke does not give us more. That he shows honor to women in his writings is significant in itself. However, Ramsay (*Traveller* 252) opines that she was a well-educated foreigner, not an Athenian. Robertson (*Acts* 293) adds that she was probably an aristocrat. Since Luke had stayed in Philippi his information about those who responded in saving faith would have come from Paul himself.

Some (Ramsay, *Traveller* 252; Bruce *Acts* 344) have concluded that Paul was frustrated and disappointed by the response at Athens. There are no recorded baptisms and the family of Stephanas of Corinth is referred to later as the "firstfruits of Achaia" (1 Cor. 16:15). However, Stott (288-290) adequately diffuses these opinions. Even if only one person had responded in saving faith to Christ, that would have been worth all the effort; but there were many. Paul's later inspired analysis of "worldly wisdom" served to show its total inadequacy and highlighted the profoundness of the gospel (1 Cor. 1-2).

Summary (17:1-34)

Luke records the route of travel as the missionary team traveled southwest from Philippi through Macedonia. Arriving in Thessalonica they immediately began their witness in the synagogue. They were able to present the gospel in that setting for three weeks where they, as usual, found a mixed response. Particularly they reached a large number of proselytes ("devout Greeks") and leading women of the city.

Soon enough, however, they were targeted by envious and angry Jews who hired thugs to harass them and incite a riot in the city. The charge against them was couched in political terms of proclaiming a rival king to Caesar. This raised the suspicions of the city leaders enough for them to pursue further actions. Paul and Silas were sent away to relieve some the pressure put on the new believers.

The witness at Berea was a breath of fresh air. It was the ideal situation as the Bereans studied the Scriptures for themselves and embraced the truths of the gospel. However, the Thessalonian Jews came and stirred up trouble. For the second time (vv. 10, 14) Paul was sent away, leaving Silas this time to strengthen the believers.

Paul's ministry at Athens is historical. Appearing before one of the highest courts of the Greeks, Paul's recorded message shows how Christianity stacks up against the philosophy of the world. He clearly and brilliantly answers the essential life questions of origin, purpose, design, and destination. While many mock Paul's proclamation of the resurrection, a few respond in faith including one of the Areopagites.

Application: Teaching and Preaching the Passage

Exegetical Outline of the Text: 1. Reception by Some, Rejection by Others in Thessalonica (17:1-9). 2. Reception by Some, Rejection by Others in Berea (17:10-15). 3. Reasoning With the Philosophers and the Areopagus in Athens (17:16-34).

The repetition of reception by some and rejection by others was typical wherever Paul went and is a lesson in

itself. This provides perspective on ministry and especially evangelism. It is a testimony of growth and stability when those who minister and believers in general continue to serve and witness faithfully after some reject their efforts to win them to Christ. Paul and Silas moved on to other places. So, too, today in ministry.

Especially significant is Paul's message to the Areopagus. It deserves analysis and application to the empty philosophies of this world. Paul's courage, genius, and refusal to be intimidated in the face of high-sounding rhetoric serve as an example of the fact that biblical truth presents a reasonable apologetic for the big issues of life. There are many "Athens" situations today. This text makes an excellent study for giving a Christian response to the world's philosophies.

8. Witness in Corinth (18:1-17)

a. Joining with Aquila and Priscilla (18:1-3)

1 After these things Paul departed from Athens, and came to Corinth;
2 And found a certain Jew named Aquila, born in Pontus, lately come from Italy, with his wife Priscilla; (because that Claudius had commanded all Jews to depart from Rome:) and came unto them.
3 And because he was of the same craft, he abode with them, and wrought: for by their occupation they were tentmakers.

Corinth lay some forty miles southwest of Athens on the isthmus that connected the main Grecian peninsula to the Peloponnesus of Greece. It was situated so it had access to two harbors east and west. The isthmus itself was only three and a half miles wide, so the westerly harbor at Lechaeum was connected to the easterly harbor at Cenchrea by a slipway for smaller vessels that were hauled overland between the two: thus effectively connecting the Adriatic Sea on the western side to the Aegean on the eastern side. Corinth was consequently one of the great commercial centers of the Mediterranean world (Barrett, *Essays* 2-3; Stott 293-294).

Historically, Corinth had been leveled to the ground in 146 B.C. by the Romans when the city led a civil rebellion against Rome. Julius Caesar rebuilt it in 44 B.C. into a remarkably beautiful city. There were no buildings more than one hundred years old. It featured multiple cultures, trade goods, languages, and sport. The Isthmian games (somewhat parallel to our Olympic games) were held there every two years (1 Cor. 9:24-27). It boasted the Temple of Aphrodite, which perched some 1900 feet on a prominent hill called the "Acrocorinth" that overlooked the city. Along with the Temple came all the licentious practices associated with it. Corinth was the "sin city" of the Greco-Roman world. Robertson (*Acts* 294) states that "to Corinthianize" had become an idiom for immorality (Stott 295-296).

Corinth's population of approximately two hundred thousand made it one of the largest cities in the empire. Its world-class trade economy made it an attractive area for the intellectual, the wealthy, and the cultured. It even exceeded Athens in political prestige. It also held a significant Jewish population and a large synagogue. It should come as no surprise that the apostle Paul chose to go there.

Upon arrival in Corinth, Paul became acquainted with the married couple, Aquila and Priscilla (v. 2). Aquila was a Jew from Pontus. Priscilla, formal name "Prisca" (2 Tim. 4:19), might well have been a woman of means and high social status, perhaps affiliated with a noble Roman family, *gens Prisca* (Bruce, *Acts* 348). They shared a number of things in common with Paul, one of which was the same trade (v. 3). The skilled craft they shared was tentmaking, which required manual labor. Paul would have learned the trade as part of his Jewish upbringing (Polhill, *Acts* 383). Bruce (*Paul* 250-251) suggests that Aquila and Priscilla were fairly wealthy and might have had branch businesses in Rome, Corinth, and Ephesus; if so, that allowed them to move easily to these cities as needed (18:18, 26; Rom. 16:4).

It appears that when Paul arrived in Corinth he needed to work to raise some money for his needs. In finding a job suited to his personal trade, he also found close friends. Is that not often the same everywhere? This providential meeting developed into a blessed ministry relationship (18:18, 26; Rom. 16:3; 1 Cor. 16:19).

Aquila and Priscilla were in Corinth due to the imperial proclamation of Claudius Caesar expelling all Jews from Rome (v. 2). Fortunately, the edict of Claudius is one of the most attested events of that day, having taken place in A.D. 49-50. The Roman historian Seutonius records that the expulsion was occasioned by constant disturbances among the Jews "at the instigation of one Chrestus" (Lightfoot 237-238). While the name "Chrestus" was common enough, many commentators agree that this form is a slight corruption of the name "Christus," Latin for Christ (Stott 298; Bock 577; Bruce, *Acts* 347; Polhill, *Acts* 383). If this was indeed the case, it means that Christianity had already made its way to Rome (2:10). We already know from Paul's experiences that tensions and disturbances arose among the Jews over the proclamation of Jesus of Nazareth as the Christ. It would come as no surprise if that were the case in Rome, too (Keener III:2697-2711). Whether or not Aquila and Priscilla were Roman citizens is debatable. If they were they would not have been subject to the expulsion edict. However, they might have chosen to leave Rome voluntarily, especially if they were believers.

The date of the expulsion edict helps us with the chronology of Acts, especially the time of Paul's ministry in Corinth. It firmly fixes his labors there as A.D. 50 to 52.

Whether Aquila and Priscilla were already Christians prior to meeting Paul is a matter of speculation, though most commentators agree they were. All Jews in Rome had been expelled, not just Christians. It is clear, however, that if they were not believers already, they soon became believers and close companions of the Apostle, living and laboring together in their craft and ministry.

b. Witness to the Jews (18:4-11)

**4   And he reasoned in the synagogue every sabbath, and persuaded the Jews and the Greeks.
5   And when Silas and Timotheus were come from Macedonia, Paul was pressed in the spirit, and testified to the Jews *that* Jesus *was* Christ.**

**6   And when they opposed themselves, and blasphemed, he shook *his* raiment, and said unto them, Your blood *be* upon your own heads; I *am* clean: from henceforth I will go unto the Gentiles.
7   And he departed thence, and entered into a certain *man's* house, named Justus, *one* that worshipped God, whose house joined hard to the synagogue.
8   And Crispus, the chief ruler of the synagogue, believed on the Lord with all his house; and many of the Corinthians hearing believed, and were baptized.
9   Then spake the Lord to Paul in the night by a vision, Be not afraid, but speak, and hold not thy peace:
10 For I am with thee, and no man shall set on thee to hurt thee: for I have much people in this city.
11 And he continued *there* a year and six months, teaching the word of God among them.**

Every Sabbath day found Paul in the synagogue "reasoning and persuading"—literally "dialoging and convincing"—all who would hear of the gospel of Christ (v. 4), both Jews and Greeks who were "God-fearers." The arrival of Silas and Timothy from Macedonia (see previous comments on 17:14-15) was both comforting and supportive (v. 5). Apparently, they brought with them enough funds, sent from other churches, that allowed Paul to quit his "day job" and return to full-time ministry (v. 5). Where some manuscripts have "was pressed/constrained in [his] *spirit*," others have "was pressed/constrained in [the] *word*." Either way, the idea is that Paul devoted himself completely to the ministry of the word (NASB). Certainly

Paul was not above manual labor and chose to do that when necessary (1 Cor. 9:6-18). But it was best if he was able to teach and preach the Word full time. The whole picture suggests to us that Paul was a driven man. Most great leaders are.

Eventually, Paul's opportunity in the synagogue ended as enough resistance was mounted to thwart his effort. Opposition Jews became hostile and blasphemous to the point Paul demonstrably "shook his raiment" (Mt. 10:14) in a gesture of exasperation (Ramsay, *Traveller* 256). Announcing a disclaimer of responsibility ("I am clean") to the Jews, since he had faithfully borne witness to them, he candidly announced his focus on the Gentiles (v. 6). His reference to "your blood be upon your own heads" is one of judgmental responsibility for one's personal choices (Ez. 3:17-21; Mt. 27:25). This does not mean, however, that he altogether forgot about the Jews.

Paul moved the place of his evangelistic efforts from the somewhat public setting of the synagogue to the private home of a Gentile God-fearer name "Justus," whose home was situated adjacent to the synagogue (v. 7). This may have appeared to be an act of defiance, but more likely was simply at the offer of the host as well as an expression of continuing concern for the Jews. Some writers (Roberston, *Acts* 297; Polhill, *Acts* 385; Bruce, *Paul* 251) identify Justus as "Gaius Titius Justus" (1 Cor. 1:14; Rom. 16:23), a Roman citizen and member of a prominent family of potters in Corinth; some Greek manuscripts have "Titius Justus" here. In most every city, there were prominent people who responded to the gospel.

The continuing efforts to win the Jews resulted in the conversion of Crispus, the senior ruler of the synagogue (v. 8) and his entire household (16:15, 32-34). His was a prominent position, coordinating the religious, administrative, and political affairs of the Jewish community in Corinth (Schnabel 760). Furthermore, there were many other Corinthians who heard the gospel, savingly believed, and were baptized.

In a spiritual epiphany (vv. 9-10), the Lord appeared to Paul in reassurance. The vision has five parts to it: one, for Paul not to be afraid; two, for him to speak boldly; three, a promise of the Lord's comforting presence and enabling; four, that Paul would be protected during times of trial (not *from* but *during* trial); five, that many would come to Christ. This is the second of four recorded visions in Acts that Paul experienced (16:9-10; 23:11; 27:23-24). One was for direction; the other three gave words of encouragement and promise.

Regarding this last dimension of the vision, the Lord says, "I have much people in this city" (v. 10). Calvinists point to the phrase to support the idea that in the city were many who were among God's elect, and had their names written in the Book of Life, but who had not yet heard the gospel and been converted (Calvin II:136; Meyer 350). Even Robertson (*Acts* 299) states, "There is the problem for every preacher and pastor, how to win the elect to Christ." However, the phrase is better interpreted as attesting to the foreknowledge of God of those who would be saved by the bold proclamation of the gospel as Marshall (*Acts* 296) asserts. Picirilli (*Paul* 111) adds, "Both Calvinists and Arminians readily acknowledge that

God has lovingly identified as His own, from eternity, those who put faith in Him." Indeed, there was much fruit in Paul's ministry at Corinth. With this reassurance, Paul remained in Corinth for another eighteen months. The time could be reckoned either from the beginning of his labors in Corinth or from the vision. Either way, it was Paul's longest stay in any city, so far, for ministry on his missionary journeys—at least as far as Acts indicates.

c. Trial before Gallio (18:12-17)

12 And when Gallio was the deputy of Achaia, the Jews made insurrection with one accord against Paul, and brought him to the judgment seat,
13 Saying, This *fellow* persuadeth men to worship God contrary to the law.
14 And when Paul was now about to open *his* mouth, Gallio said unto the Jews, If it were a matter of wrong or wicked lewdness, O *ye* Jews, reason would that I should bear with you:
15 But if it be a question of words and names, and *of* your law, look ye to *it*; for I will be no judge of such *matters*.
16 And he drave them from the judgment seat.
17 Then all the Greeks took Sosthenes, the chief ruler of the synagogue, and beat *him* before the judgment seat. And Gallio cared for none of those things.

The vision's promise of God's protection was soon fulfilled. The appointment of a new Roman proconsul to Achaia, Gallio, was viewed by the opposition

Jews as the time to press for the expulsion of Paul from Corinth. Gallio was the son of Seneca the Elder and had strong ties to Rome, so there was reason for the Jews to think they might use this to their advantage (Bock 580; Keener III:2763). The very situation that had gotten the Jews expelled from Rome (v. 2) over "Chrestus" (see comments above), might just be the leverage to get rid of Paul, who preached "Christ." If that was the Jews' reasoning, they thought that the same civil disturbances caused in Rome were possible in Corinth. It would therefore be wise for the new proconsul to move swiftly to prevent this from happening.

In a unity of evil intentions, they hauled the apostle before Gallio's judgment seat (Greek *bema*) to press their cause (v. 12). The charge was one of illegal religious practices (v. 13). It is clear that they wanted Gallio to declare Paul's beliefs altogether as *religo illicita* (Latin for an illegal religion). Perhaps they had heard of local city governments (Thessalonica, for example) moving to silence Paul's voice.

The response of Gallio was immediate and clear. He fully knew about the edict of Claudius but was wise enough to see through the thinly-veiled charge. Apparently, he knew enough of the whole matter to cut the hearing short without allowing Paul to present his side (v. 14). With judicial clarity, he separated the issue into Rome's concerns with civil violations ("a matter of wrong or wicked lewdness") and the Jews' concern with religious differences ("words, names, and of your law"). He would not be used to make judgments when no civil laws had been violated. And with that he dismissed them from the judgment seat (v. 16). The incident shows that Gallio did not perceive any civil threats from Christians in Corinth.

This did not prevent hostility, however, against one "Sosthenes, the chief ruler of the synagogue" (v. 17), who probably succeeded Crispus in that position (v. 8). If he was the same as person as in 1 Corinthians 1:1, then he too had become a believer and was the target of the Jews' hostility (Bock 582; Polhill, *Acts* 389). However, it is possible that Sosthenes was actually Paul's accuser and the aggression shown was an act of frustration that he was not able to get Paul censored. That he was beaten by Greeks may reveal an act of anti-Semitism (Marshall, *Acts* 289-299; Fitzmyer 630-631). Whichever the case, Gallio turned a blind eye to the whole scene.

The scene is indicative of the two political and religious powers that Christians faced in the Acts time frame. At this point, they faced mostly hostile and unbelieving Jewish opposition to the gospel. At times influential Jews succeeded in bringing civil pressure to bear on believers, but that was confined to local situations. Gallio's ambivalence represented the present Roman tolerance of Christianity. Roman hostility did not begin until Nero's edict in A.D. 64. According to the vision's promise of protection, Paul was spared physical harm in this instance.

9. Paul returns to Antioch in Syria (18:18-22)

18 And Paul *after this* tarried *there* yet a good while, and then took his leave of the brethren, and sailed thence into Syria, and with him Priscilla and Aquila; having shorn *his* head in Cenchrea: for he had a vow.

19 And he came to Ephesus, and left them there: but he himself entered into the synagogue, and reasoned with the Jews.
20 When they desired *him* to tarry longer time with them, he consented not;
21 But bade them farewell, saying, I must by all means keep this feast that cometh in Jerusalem: but I will return again unto you, if God will. And he sailed from Ephesus.
22 And when he had landed at Caesarea, and gone up, and saluted the church, he went down to Antioch.

The favorable ruling by Gallio cleared the way for a continuing ministry at Corinth. Paul stayed "a good while"—literally, "many days," which could either be a part of the eighteen months (v. 11) or in addition to them. But he labored with a sense of timing, for he desired to observe a certain feast (Passover?) at Jerusalem and to report to the home church at Antioch of Syria (v. 21).

When the time came to begin his journey, Priscilla and Aquila accompanied him with intentions of going to Ephesus (see comments earlier on vv. 1-3). Luke does not specifically tell whether Silas and Timothy traveled with him, as Picirilli (*Paul* 113) proposes. At the eastern port of Cenchrea, Paul took a vow and cut his hair in relation to a vow, perhaps connected to his plan to observe the feast in Jerusalem. What exactly the vow was is the subject of much discussion. Some argue that it was a temporary Nazarite vow (Num. 6:1-21) that would have to be concluded with a sacrifice in Jerusalem (Picirilli, *Paul* 113; Marshall, *Acts* 300; Fitzmyer 634). That Paul would observe a Nazarite vow would not be a contradiction of Christian teachings but an expression of his own Jewishness (1 Cor. 9:19-22). Others assert that it could have been another type of vow, including an expression of gratitude or appeal for traveling mercies (Robertson, *Acts* 303-304; Bock 585-586; Bruce, *Acts* 355).

Ephesus was the capital of the province of Asia and a very significant city in the Empire. More about its culture and significance will be detailed later, but it would become a very important hub of Christianity in just a few years. It was a stopover for Paul on his way back to Jerusalem and Antioch, but Aquila and Priscilla stayed there when he moved on. Apparently, they owned a house in Ephesus (1 Cor. 16:19) in which they began a church.

As was his conviction and strategy (Rom. 1:16), Paul went to the synagogue to initiate his witness there (v. 19). Here he "reasoned" (17:2; 18:4; 20:25) with the Jews regarding the gospel of Christ. His efforts were met with some degree of acceptance, and they desired further discussion. However, Paul's commitments and the timing of things would not permit. His mention of going to Jerusalem would fit the scenario of a Nazarite vow and of Passover being the feast. Since sailing the Mediterranean was seasonal, because of weather and Passover coming in early April of that year (Bock 587), timing was of the essence. With a promise to return, God willing, he sailed from Ephesus (v. 21).

The stopover in Ephesus was preparatory for a later ministry. With Aquila and Priscilla there and an initial, favorable response from the synagogue witness, the groundwork was laid for the future.

In typical fashion Luke summarized Paul's arrival at Caesarea, and (apparently) his trip to Jerusalem to observe the Passover and complete his vow (Keener III:2794-2795). Ordinarily, Paul could have traveled by ship directly to Seleucia (and so Antioch). Apparently, he sailed for Caesarea, instead, in order to fulfill his intention to go to Jerusalem (v. 21). That he "went up" from Caesarea almost certainly means that he went up to Jerusalem, which was of higher elevation than Caesarea; that would not have been the case for going to Antioch.

After the Jerusalem visit, he then took his long journey (about 350 miles) to Antioch of Syria (v. 22). One can only imagine the reception he received from believers and church leaders at each place along the way and in Antioch. I am sure Paul was glad to inform each one about the Lord's blessings and the extension of the witness of the gospel, and that his reports were met with rejoicing.

Summary
(18:1-22)

Paul had only been in Athens a few weeks before he moved on to Corinth, another strategic city in Achaia. There are significant events that took place there. First, in yet another providential act of God, he met and labored with Aquila and Priscilla in his trade as a tentmaker. They had been expelled by the edict of Claudius, the Emperor of Rome, in A.D. 49-50. They would also become life-long fellow-laborers in the gospel.

Next, there were some successes in reaching Jews, particularly two of the chief rulers of the synagogue, Crispus and Sosthenes. Paul moved his witness from the synagogue to the house of

Justus, whose house was next door to the synagogue. He is the last named "God-fearer" in the Acts record. Turning to the Gentiles, Paul had yet another vision reassuring him of much fruit in the city. He remained there for a year and a half.

The attempted legal proceedings before the newly-appointed "deputy" (proconsul) of Achaia, Gallio, was not successful. Rome's ambivalence toward Christianity was underscored again. (Of course, this all changed in a few years under Nero.)

Paul's next city of choice was Ephesus. This time he took Aquila and Priscilla with him, planning to leave them in Ephesus in preparation for his return. He spent a short time there, witnessing in the synagogue, before leaving to fulfill his vow in Jerusalem and report to the home church in Antioch.

Application: Teaching and Preaching the Passage

Exegetical Outline of the Text: 1. Partnership Formed With Aquila and Priscilla (18:1-3). 2. Proclamation of the Gospel to Jews and Gentiles (18:4-8). 3. Reassuring Vision From the Lord (18:9-11). 4. Accusation Before Gallio, the Roman Proconsul (18:12-17). 5. Return to Jerusalem and Antioch (18:18-22).

The providential meeting with Aquila and Priscilla was, no doubt, a great encouragement to Paul as well as a means for him to labor in meeting his material needs. Silas and Timothy did not arrive until later, so the fellowship with the husband and wife must have been a great blessing to him personally. Christian life, and especially ministry life, is so often blessed and encouraged by the friends and partners made along the way.

Yet again, the pattern of acceptance and rejection was evidenced in Corinth as the Jews responded to Paul's witness in the synagogue. And, yet again, we see the faithfulness of Paul not to quit, but to find an alternative place of ministry in the house of Justus. There were significant conversions and the Lord reassured Paul that his labors there would be fruitful.

Legal proceedings involving churches and ministers are always difficult and require unusual wisdom and skill. Ours is a litigious society where people often target churches out of religious animosity and/or for material gain. Fortunately the Lord has raised up Christian legal teams to assist churches and ministers. This text provides an excellent basis to teach and discuss the key issues this arise, including the need for important church documents and legal papers.

The conclusion of the second missionary journey was not abrupt or final. With plans for the future, Paul laid the groundwork for the next step in ministry by taking Aquila and Priscilla to Ephesus and personally getting acquainted with those in the synagogue. He would return soon for an incredible ministry there. There is wisdom in strategic ministry planning. There should always be a vision for the future.

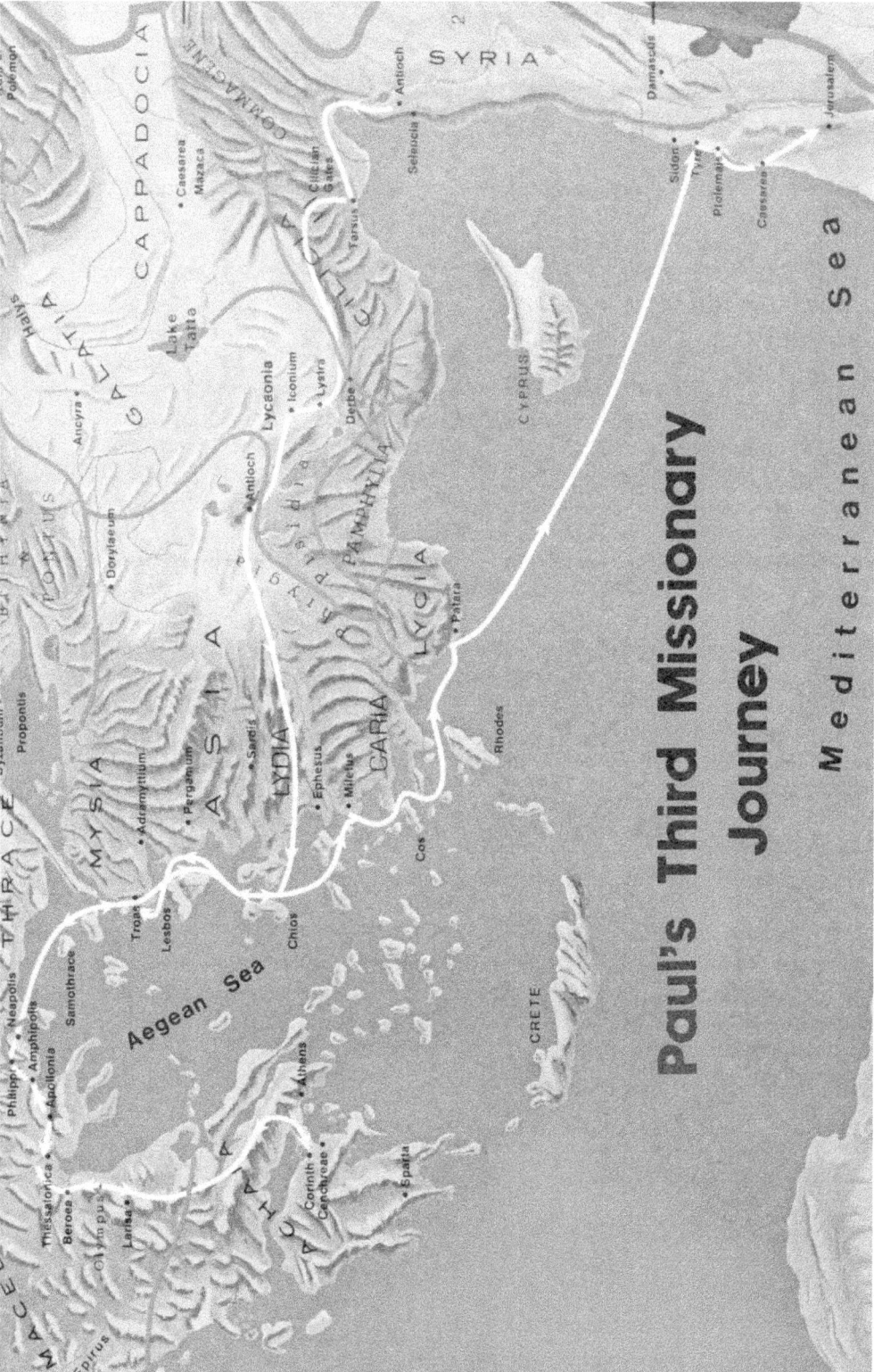

Paul's Third Missionary Journey

I. The Third Missionary Journey (18:23—21:16)

1. Strengthening the churches (18:23)

23 And after he had spent some time *there*, he departed, and went over *all* the country of Galatia and Phrygia in order, strengthening all the disciples.

Even though Paul was at the beloved church at Antioch, his heart was with the disciples in the churches established on the missionary journeys. After spending as much time there as he felt sufficient to reconnect, he left. This time it appears he began the journey alone since no others are listed as accompanying him. Going overland through the Cilician Gates (see comments earlier), no easy trek in itself, he made his way to those cities where churches had been established. Here he would have taught them, answered their questions, settled disputes, ordained pastors, enjoyed their fellowship, and challenged them to faithfulness. These and any other concerns would have been involved in the spiritual strengthening of believers and local churches.

In typical summary fashion, Luke reduced a fifteen-hundred-mile journey to one statement. We could wish he had been more detailed sometimes. There were churches in the cities along that route that he must have visited. Paul might simply have chosen to report to Luke later that nothing really was worth reporting. While it isn't exactly clear which region of Galatia and Phrygia is meant, it seems more likely that it was the same as on the previous journey (16:6). His intention was not so much

evangelism but to strengthen those who were already believers. Of course, this does not mean he neglected to proclaim the gospel when the opportunity presented itself.

2. Witness in Ephesus (18:24—19:41)

a. Apollos (18:24-28)

24 And a certain Jew named Apollos, born at Alexandria, an eloquent man, *and* mighty in the scriptures, came to Ephesus. 25 This man was instructed in the way of the Lord; and being fervent in the spirit, he spake and taught diligently the things of the Lord, knowing only the baptism of John. 26 And he began to speak boldly in the synagogue: whom when Aquila and Priscilla had heard, they took him unto *them*, and expounded unto him the way of God more perfectly. 27 And when he was disposed to pass into Achaia, the brethren wrote, exhorting the disciples to receive him: who, when he was come, helped them much which had believed through grace: 28 For he mightily convinced the Jews, *and that* publicly, shewing by the scriptures that Jesus was Christ.

Having left Aquila and Priscilla at Ephesus, as he was concluding the second missionary journey (18:18), Paul clearly intended to return and establish the work there. His return to Ephesus is prefaced by two events: the appearance of Apollos (18:24-28) before he arrived and the encounter with twelve Ephesian disciples after he arrived (19:1-7). Luke skillfully places these encounters back to back because of their common concern: the limitations of the baptism of John the Baptist. It is significant that even in the absence of Paul himself, his co-laborers Aquila and Priscilla instructed Apollos in what he needed to know. In doing so, they demonstrated theological solidarity with Paul when he addressed the same concerns with the disciples at Ephesus.

Before he arrived Luke records a cameo appearance of an emerging leader. Apollos appeared at Ephesus as suddenly and dramatically as John the Baptist did in the Judaean wilderness, and with a similar response (Mt. 3:1-2; Jn. 1:19-21). We are not told why he was in Ephesus since he was from Alexandria in Egypt. Bruce (*Acts* 358) suggests he was a traveling merchant. As a Jew, he would have visited the synagogue and used the opportunity to speak of his faith. He was a powerful and convincing witness. What is known about him is factually stated in the text. Schnabel (784-785) lists eight characteristics.

But there are questions about him that have generated much debate. For example, what is meant by the phrase that he was "instructed in the way of the Lord"? Most commentators are willing to concede this meant he was an authentic believer in Jesus. The question remains, however, what was the extent of his knowledge about Jesus? The baptism of John included references to the person of Jesus (Jn. 1:29-37) and His redemptive role ("the Lamb of God"), but these truths were anticipatory, not in fulfillment (Mt. 1:7-8).

There were Jews from Egypt in Jerusalem who heard Peter's message on Pentecost (2:10) and probably carried the core message of the gospel back to Egypt. It is generally conceded that Christianity had made its way to Alexandria early (Bruce, *Acts* 359; Schnabel 784). It is possible that Apollos had gotten what he knew from one of these but his knowledge was lacking in some detail.

That being the case, what was lacking? What exactly did Aquila and Priscilla have to teach him that brought him up to date? There are numerous suggestions. Schnabel (785-786) suggests that he needed instruction about "the significance of repentance and immersion in relation to Jesus." Keener (III:2806) points to his knowing "only John's baptism...unaware of the greater Spirit baptism." Marshall (*Acts* 304) states "we can presume that he was instructed in the distinctive Pauline doctrines." Meyer (357-358) is firm in stating "that he knew nothing of a distinctively Christian baptism." Picirilli (*Paul* 126) summarizes "We could wish we knew exactly what he did and did not know."

In my view—although it is not altogether different from that of other interpreters—it is contextually significant that there are two, back-to-back situations involving the same concern: namely, the inadequacy of the baptism of John (18:25; 19:3). In context, each of these informs the other. Both parties involved needed updating, although they were apparently not on the same level of understanding. The two central elements of John's baptism that needed updating were: one, the attending presence of the Holy Spirit in the life of a believer and, secondly, the focus of faith on the person of Jesus as the Christ who had been raised from the dead. Obviously, neither the resurrection of

Jesus nor the N. T. coming of the Holy Spirit had occurred when John preached and baptized.

To understand Apollos, and to a certain extent the Ephesian disciples, then, we need to understand the extent of their connection with John the Baptist (Mt. 11:7-15). Apollos had been "instructed in the way of the Lord... knowing only the baptism of John" (18:25). Some of the same terminology is used of John (Mt. 3:3; Isa. 40:3). John himself needed "updating" about Jesus as well (Mt. 11:1-6). John also had disciples who fully embraced his message and followed him (Mt. 11:2; Jn. 1:35-37). Encountering Jesus, they soon transferred their discipleship to Jesus. I see the same scenario with Apollos. He had fully embraced the preparatory message of John and the imminent appearance of the Messiah. He might even have heard of Jesus, but it seems he did not know the rest of the story. He was, in effect, a "disciple of John," at the same level of understanding, whose faith needed to be transferred to Jesus. In the same way some of the disciples of John became disciples of Jesus, this was Apollos' need. This may very well have been the update he received from Aquila and Priscilla: namely, that Jesus was indeed the Christ as confirmed by the resurrection.

Another area which needed updating would have been regarding the Holy Spirit. The person and presence of the Holy Spirit in the life of a believer is pervasive and evidentiary in the Acts record (2:38; 8:15-17; 9:17; 10:44-45; 11:15-16; 13:52). Apollos is described as being "fervent (Greek *zeo*, boiling, burning) in the spirit" (18:25). Some see this as describing his personal zeal and enthusiasm (Lenski 772; Barnes 273;

Ger 251; Stott 302). Others (Bruce, *Acts* 363; Schnabel 785; Marshall, *Acts* 304) believe it refers to the Holy Spirit. Given the interest of Aquila and Priscilla to give Apollos further instruction, it seems that part of the instruction he needed might have been about the Holy Spirit. It was not until after he had been instructed by Aquila and Priscilla that Luke records Apollos preaching effectively, showing "by the scriptures that Jesus was Christ" (18:28).

In this sense, Apollos would be regarded as an "O. T. saint" (see previous commentary on Cornelius) with the same transitional status as John the Baptist. I concur with Bock (592) who states, "Apollos is a figure caught in transition...and thus needs to be brought up to date. His preaching is not inaccurate, merely incomplete."

We are not told that Apollos was re-baptized like Paul insisted for the Ephesian disciples (19:5). Luke simply may not have recorded the action since re-baptism under these specific circumstances apparently was not necessary as a testimony to authentic (up-dated) faith.

Taken together, then, both parties needed some of the same instruction. As Bruce (*Acts* 364) summarizes regarding these two examples, "Now that Jesus had come and accomplished his mission on earth, now that he had returned to the Father's presence and sent to his followers the promised gift of the Holy Spirit, an anticipatory baptism was no longer appropriate or adequate."

A word needs to be added regarding the theological progression of biblical redemption. Jesus had said that the O. T. era of the "law and the prophets" terminated with John the Baptist. The N. T. era of the "kingdom of God" ensued, following John (Lk. 16:16).

Here is the last reference in the N. T. to the baptism of John and its comparison with the fulfilled, redemptive work of Christ. The two situations show that the O. T. era had been brought to completion and was finally over. The "baptism of John" was transitory and no longer acceptable.

Verses 27-28 indicate that Apollos decided to continue his ministry in Achaia with the Corinthian believers. A letter endorsing his ministry was written to confirm his message and ministry. He had not been officially endorsed by the apostle Paul, but the word of Aquila and Priscilla would have gone a long way in opening the door of ministry in Corinth. That is exactly what happened, as Paul's first letter to the Corinthians confirms (1 Cor. 1:12; 3:6). Apollos' ministry was very powerful and effective, as seen in the fact that "helped them much which had believed through grace" (18:27). All references to Apollos by Paul are positive and supportive (1 Cor. 3:4-9; 16:12).

b. The Ephesian disciples and the baptism of John (19:1-7)

**1 And it came to pass, that, while Apollos was at Corinth, Paul having passed through the upper coasts came to Ephesus: and finding certain disciples,
2 He said unto them, Have ye received the Holy Ghost since ye believed? And they said unto him, We have not so much as heard whether there be any Holy Ghost.
3 And he said unto them, Unto what then were ye baptized? And they said, Unto John's baptism.
4 Then said Paul, John verily baptized with the baptism of repen-tance, saying unto the people, that they should believe on him which should come after him, that is, on Christ Jesus.
5 When they heard this, they were baptized in the name of the Lord Jesus.
6 And when Paul had laid his hands upon them, the Holy Ghost came on them; and they spake with tongues, and prophesied.
7 And all the men were about twelve.**

Paul's journey to Ephesus had been overland, through the mountainous areas of southern Galatia and Phrygia ("the upper coasts") instead of by the regular trade route of the lower Lycus and Maeander valleys (Ramsay, *Traveller* 265). It helps one greatly to follow a good map of his journeys. One can only guess why he chose the harder route, but it seems likely Paul would have sought areas to proclaim the gospel "where Christ was not named" (Rom. 15:20). Opinions vary about the date of his arrival, but it was probably in the late summer or early fall of A.D. 53-54.

The city of Ephesus was a very strategic mission location. Its harbor access to the Aegean Sea via the Cayster River placed it on the main commercial trade route east of Rome. It was also situated on the main land trade route east to west. It was the capital of the province of Asia, larger and richer even than Corinth. Its population of some two hundred and fifty thousand to three hundred thousand placed it in the top five cities of the Roman Empire at the time. The rest of the province had other great cities such as Smyrna, Pergamum, Thyatira, Sardis, Philadelphia, Laodicea—the locations of the seven churches of Revelation 2—3. These probably owed their existence to the ministry of the Apostle Paul in Ephesus.

The religious cult of the fertility goddess *Diana* (Greek *Artemis*, the name in the text; *Diana* was the corresponding Roman goddess) was based in Ephesus. The temple of Diana (Artemis) was one of the Seven Wonders of the Ancient World, four times larger than the Parthenon at Athens (and its modern replica in Nashville, Tennessee). A large part of the local economy derived from the images, shrines, and festivals involved in its cultic worship. Its celebrations involved expressions of every lust (Marshall, *Acts* 316-317; Bock 606-608). The success of the gospel witness at Ephesus and the surrounding cities must be measured against the entrenched strongholds of Satan at Ephesus—in one sense the "gates of hell" (Mt. 16:18).

When Paul arrived he would have reconnected with Aquila and Priscilla to catch up on things. They would have joyfully told him about Apollos and his present ministry at Corinth. It may be that Paul also learned about the twelve disciples from them.

Upon meeting with the Ephesian disciples (vv. 1-2), apparently something aroused Paul's suspicions to question them about their faith. (See Stott 303 and Carson 149 for a possible sequence of questions and responses.) His discussion with Aquila and Priscilla regarding Apollos might have raised questions. If Apollos needed correction, perhaps there were others with the same need. This was apparently what made Paul suspicious about the faith of these twelve disciples at Ephesus.

The question Paul posed to them needs clarifying. The Greek text literally reads, "(the) Holy Spirit did you receive having believed?"—in other words, "Did you receive the Holy Spirit when you believed (or upon believing)?" Using this text to teach that the Holy Spirit is received subsequent to salvation is totally unwarranted (Saucy 300; Stott 303-304; Forlines, *Quest* 236-238). Their response was an honest confession of ignorance about the Holy Spirit. This, in turn, led to yet another question, which Paul raised regarding their baptism. Sometimes it is necessary to clarify the content and focus of faith.

The connection of the Holy Spirit's work in the believer, represented by baptism, is an integral part of the N. T. record beginning with the baptism of Jesus (Mt. 3.16; Acts 2:38; 9:17-18; 10:47); hence the inclusion of the Holy Spirit in the baptismal formula (Crabtree 484). It is possible not to know the right theological terminology and yet be saved, but terminology did not appear to be the problem here.

The baptism of John is, again, shown to be limited in its redemptive content (v. 4). Paul rightly recalls the message of John and its intent of preparation for faith in Christ. Upon hearing that, the disciples gladly submitted to Christian baptism, which was now focused on the person of Jesus Christ (v. 5). Accompanying their baptism was a special manifestation of the Holy Spirit in tongues and prophesying (v. 6), the last of such manifestations in the Acts record. It should be noted that at each stage of the witness of the gospel (as according to Acts 1:8) this special manifestation of the Holy Spirit occurred. The terms describing speaking in tongues are the same as in previous usages, so there is no need for a different interpretation here. The gift involved the miraculous ability to speak in human foreign languages. There is a parallel between this action of Paul and that of Peter and John with the Samaritans (8:14-17). It is a decisive, historical moment of the Holy Spirit's confirmation in missionary effort. It signaled the completion of the O. T. era and the message of the "baptism of John."

The question whether these were authentic believers before Paul encountered them cannot be avoided. Opinions vary, of course, with some (Stott 304; Marshall, *Acts* 306; Polhill, *Acts* 398; Schnabel 788; Meyer 365) denying they were. Others take it they were authentic believers, but nominal at best (Bock 599; Fitzmyer 642).

It seems to me that their faith, while genuine enough, needed completing or updating, the same as that of Apollos. They are specifically called "disciples," a key term in Acts that every other time depicts authentic believers. I am not willing to change Luke's (inspired) usage for this one incident. However, as Carson (149) states "these disciples are living one dispensation earlier than the actual state of play." These two incidents at Ephesus are not therefore in juxtaposition but complementary to each other, showing a common truth: namely, the limitation of faith in connection with John's baptism but not its total emptiness. In this regard, the baptism of John was the transitional witness from the O. T. era to the N. T. era. Both Apollos and the Ephesian disciples (and all believers from that time forward) were now transferred from the O. T. era to the N. T. era with this final reference to John's baptism. I fully concur with John Stott (305) who states, "There are no Samaritans or disciples of John the Baptist left in the world today."

Luke concludes the incident (v. 7) by telling that there were twelve of these disciples. As most all commentators agree, there is no symbolic significance to the number. It is just the number of men involved. These men would most likely become the nucleus of the Ephesian church, which became the hub of evangelistic efforts to Asia Minor. Time spent to disciple and bring young believers to maturity is never wasted.

c. In the synagogue and school of Tyrannus (19:8-12)

**8 And he went into the synagogue, and spake boldly for the space of three months, disputing and persuading the things concerning the kingdom of God.
9 But when divers were hardened, and believed not, but spake evil of that way before the multitude, he departed from them, and separated the disciples, disputing daily in the school of one Tyrannus.
10 And this continued by the space of two years; so that all they which dwelt in Asia heard the word of the Lord Jesus, both Jews and Greeks.
11 And God wrought special miracles by the hands of Paul:
12 So that from his body were brought unto the sick handkerchiefs or aprons, and the diseases departed from them, and the evil spirits went out of them.**

As always Paul began his witness of the gospel in the synagogue (v. 8), using the same message and method of discussion and persuasion. In all likelihood, Apollos had preceded him there with a preparatory and effective presentation of the gospel (18:28). That may be why

Paul was able to continue his witness in the synagogue for three months. The length of time he was tolerated in the synagogue was usually much shorter.

His witness became frustrated as some hardened their hearts against the message of the gospel and began a verbal campaign of opposition to anyone who would listen (v. 9). Note the terminology used to describe the believers as being of "that way" (9:2; 18:26; 22:4). When the situation became intolerable, Paul left the synagogue, taking the believers with him, and shifting his place of ministry to the lecture hall (Greek *schole*, whence our "school") of Tyrannus (literally "tyrant"); Bruce (*Acts* 388) wonders whether this was the name his parents gave him or a nickname given by his students. Paul probably rented the facility, using it when normal business hours were suspended during the daytime, from 11:00 a.m. to 4:00 p.m. (Bruce, *Acts* 366; Robertson, *Acts* 314-315). Paul probably labored himself at his trade in the morning hours (20:34), then spent the rest of the day in ministry. If so, it speaks to his zeal and tireless efforts to teach and preach the gospel (1 Thess. 2:9; Eph. 5:16).

What is most significant is that he continued using the lecture hall for two more years, during which the entire province of Asia Minor was evangelized, reaching both Jews and Greeks. If one adds the three months already spent witnessing in the synagogue (v. 8) and his stay "for a season" (v. 22), then we get a total of some three years for his ministry at Ephesus (20:31)—a time that is accurate though not necessarily precise. There were probably several men who assisted Paul, among them Epaphras (Col. 1:7-8), who carried the gospel to the cities of the Lycus valley. It

was probably during this time that the seven churches of Revelation 2—3 were founded. Bruce (*Acts* 366) observes that this province was a stronghold of Christianity for many centuries.

As before (4:15-16; 8:6-7; 9:32-35), the Lord confirmed the message and ministry of the gospel with the manifestation of the miraculous (vv. 11-12). The "handkerchiefs and aprons" were the sweat rags and leather aprons Paul would have used in plying his trade. It should be noted that it was God who performed these "special miracles," not the strips of cloth or leather aprons. This healing authority was also part of the special giftedness of apostolic confirmation upon Paul (2 Cor. 12:12). We should always be careful and discerning of counterfeits. They were not limited to the time period of the Acts record.

d. Encounter with Jewish exorcists (19:13-20)

13 Then certain of the vagabond Jews, exorcists, took upon them to call over them which had evil spirits the name of the LORD Jesus, saying, We adjure you by Jesus whom Paul preacheth.
14 And there were seven sons of *one* Sceva, a Jew, *and* chief of the priests, which did so.
15 And the evil spirit answered and said, Jesus I know, and Paul I know; but who are ye?
16 And the man in whom the evil spirit was leaped on them, and overcame them, and prevailed against them, so that they fled out of that house naked and wounded.
17 And this was known to all the Jews and Greeks also dwelling at Ephesus; and fear fell on them all,

and the name of the Lord Jesus was magnified.

18 And many that believed came, and confessed, and shewed their deeds.

19 Many of them also which used curious arts brought their books together, and burned them before all *men*: and they counted the price of them, and found *it* fifty thousand *pieces* of silver.

20 So mightily grew the word of God and prevailed.

Ephesus had the reputation of being the center for magic arts in the Greco-Roman world. That should come as no surprise, given that the cultic worship of Diana (Artemis) was so dominant. Demonism in all its raw and real forms often abounds where idolatry is prevalent. God's display of power through the ministry of Paul aroused heightened interest on the part of some who sought to profit by the exorcising of demons. "Sharks" are not confined to the oceans. Of note are certain Jews who tried to capitalize on the situation.

Interestingly, some Jews of the N. T. world were commonly associated with exorcism, using Hebrew incantations and chemical formulas to promote their craft. Josephus (*Antiquities* VIII.II.5) reported that even Solomon developed secretive powers for expelling demons, but that seems questionable. Some commentators (Polhill, *Acts* 369; Bock 602; Bruce, *Acts* 367-368) document several books of papyri that have survived, describing the practice particularly associated with some Jews. The practice was so successful and widespread that some Jews "took their show on the road" ("vagabond": literally, "to stroll about or travel around"). Apparently, some of

these became aware of Paul's ministry and they wanted a piece of the action.

Luke takes pains to name the group as the "seven sons of Sceva" and that the father was "chief of the priests" (v. 14). It is entirely possible that this was the "business moniker" of the group, and that they had developed their name and position as "chief priest" for commercial purposes. There is no record of a Jewish High Priest by the name of "Sceva." It is possible, however, that he came from one of the families of the priests (Marshall, *Acts* 311; Polhill, *Acts* 404). It is not my view (as Haechen 565 proposes) that Luke fabricated the entire story to enhance his construct of the success of Paul over the religions of the day. One only has to know the reality of demonism and idolatry to see the authenticity of the story. Even so, there seems to be a keen sense of irony. Luke must have smiled as he wrote this part of his account.

With the appearance of Paul and the miraculous display of the power of the gospel, these men sought to expel demons from a "client" using the name of Jesus in a new incantation. As it turned out the use of Jesus' name, even in pretense, backfired on them like a novice trying to use an unfamiliar weapon. One cannot help but be reminded of a similar incident with Simon the magician (8:18-19). The demonic spirit residing in the hapless man responded in a mocking voice and with candid honesty (v. 15). He knew Jesus (Mt. 8:29-31) and the apostle Paul, but these fakes were totally unknown to him. It may be a back-door compliment to Paul that the forces of hell knew about him and trembled at his name. With abnormal strength (Mk. 5:3-4) the man physically assaulted the seven men, stripping their clothes off and wounding them as they fled in terror (v. 16).

It was not long before the incident was widely known (v. 17). It deserved to be re-told. The result was that even though the entire episode was a counterfeit attempt, the true name of Jesus as spoken by Paul was distinguished from the false. The name of Jesus was not to be trifled with. Nor should it ever be (Ex. 20:7; Phil. 2:9-11).

The incident also served to galvanize a healthy fear, not only in the general populace, but even in the lives of the believers (vv. 18-19). Apparently, some had clung to previous esoteric practices, keeping the literature associated with them, perhaps even trying to mesh the practice with Christianity. But when the authenticity of the name of Jesus was revealed and the counterfeit exposed, they "came, confessed and shewed their deeds." Involved was the burning of the books containing the incantations, formulas, symbols, magical names, talismans, and potions—all purported to have power over demons, diseases, weather, and any other situation that portended difficulties. These "books" were called "Ephesian Letters" (*Ephesia Grammatica*). There are many that have survived the ravages of time and are housed in museum collections (Bock 603-604; Bruce, *Acts* 368). When the cost of these was totaled it came to "fifty thousand pieces of silver," measured by the Greek drachma or the Roman denarius, each a day's wage, the amount was fifty thousand days' wages. One only has to figure that in terms of the modern economy to see how much money went up in smoke. Sin is expensive. But the highest price paid is not measured in monetary terms. One cheapens the gospel by trying to mesh the practices of demonism with the gospel. Theological syncretism is never approved by the Lord.

The overall result, however, was the advancement of God's Word as it prevailed in the lives of believers (v. 20). Its power and blessings were shown to be far greater than anything the devil promised. The Lord has a way of using that which is bad to accomplish good in the lives of His people when honest confession and repentance are involved.

e. Paul's intention to go to Jerusalem, then Rome (19:21-22)

21 After these things were ended, Paul purposed in the spirit, when he had passed through Macedonia and Achaia, to go to Jerusalem, saying, After I have been there, I must also see Rome.
22 So he sent into Macedonia two of them that ministered unto him, Timotheus and Erastus; but he himself stayed in Asia for a season.

As Paul sensed the completion of his work at Ephesus, he turned his attention to Rome, then Spain (Rom. 15:22-25), the most westerly outpost of civilization at the time. This marks a new stage in the record as Luke begins to shift the events of his narrative toward Rome (chs. 26—28).

Note that Paul was led by the Spirit about his plans (v. 21). His determination is reflected in his use of "must" (Greek *dei*, "it is necessary"). He feels compelled to go to Rome. Of course, this sense of drive meshes with the Lord's plans for him to bear witness before the principal political leaders of the day (9:15-16). This brief reference to the Spirit's leadership would soon become a pivotal point of discussion and decision-making, as Paul made his way to Jerusalem (20:22-23; 21:4, 11).

Paul believed he needed to check on the saints in Macedonia and Achaia before making his journey back to Jerusalem. In preparation, he sent two trusted assistants, Timothy (18:5) and Erastus (Rom. 16:23; 2 Tim. 4:20), ahead of him. Part of their responsibility was to collect the famine-relief funds for the suffering saints in Judaea (Acts 11:27-30; Rom. 15:31; 2 Cor. 8:4). Having made these arrangements, Paul remained for a short time in Ephesus. The reason for his stay (1 Cor. 16:8) was the open door of opportunity at Ephesus even with its many "adversaries." One of those adversaries is part of the next story Luke records.

f. The riot of the cult worshipers against the believers (19:23-41)

(1) The charge of Demetrius and the silversmiths (19:23-28)

23 And the same time there arose no small stir about that way.
24 For a certain *man* named Demetrius, a silversmith, which made silver shrines for Diana, brought no small gain unto the craftsmen;
25 Whom he called together with the workmen of like occupation, and said, Sirs, ye know that by this craft we have our wealth.
26 Moreover ye see and hear, that not alone at Ephesus, but almost throughout all Asia, this Paul hath persuaded and turned away much people, saying that they be no gods, which are made with hands:
27 So that not only this our craft is in danger to be set at nought; but also that the temple of the great goddess Diana should be despised, and her magnificence should be destroyed, whom all Asia and the world worshippeth.
28 And when they heard *these sayings*, they were full of wrath, and cried out, saying, Great *is* Diana of the Ephesians.

It is inherent in Christianity that believers reject idolatry and all that is associated with it. The previous incident with the magic paraphernalia sets the stage for this one. This essential Christian rejection certainly includes abandoning shrines and images to man-made gods and goddesses. The riot at Ephesus serves to highlight this necessary result. Its inclusion in the Acts narrative is part of the apologetic intent of Luke to show the power of the gospel over idolatry. The objection of Haenchen (576-579) to the historical integrity of the story has been well discounted by Marshall (*Acts* 314-317). Indeed, the story provides historical insights into the Greco-Roman world of idol worship regarding its economics, its emotional grip on the devotees, and certain civic concerns. This particular reaction might well have taken place in the spring and a week-long festival celebration called "Artemision" (Polhill, *Acts* 409; Keener III:2871-2873). Robertson (*Acts* 323) helpfully distinguishes between the Diana (Latin) cult, the Greek Artemis cult, and the local Ephesian Artemis cult (Keener III:2873-2878). Regardless, the distinctions are superficial and the effects, in either case, were the same.

People were enslaved in idolatry and the lascivious practices associated with it.

Apparently, the impact of the gospel was so widespread in Ephesus and the entire province of Asia that sales of shrines, images, and esoteric literature (vv. 18-19) took a nosedive. That would have been especially true if the incident took place during the festivity of the Artemision. Soon those who profited monetarily from idol worship reacted ("no small stir" 12:18) against the believers, labeled as those of "that way" (9:2; 18:26; 19:9; 22:4; 24:22). As Polhill (*Acts* 410) states, "The gospel is always at its most controversial when it comes into conflict with economic interests."

The reaction by the silversmiths included Paul's being singled out as the main leader (v. 26). Perhaps Paul had this incident in mind when he referred to fighting with "wild beasts at Ephesus" (1 Cor. 15:32); that may be a reference to the animal-like actions of men, not so much to being thrown to wild beasts in the arena (Picirilli, *Corinthians* 227). His Roman citizenship should have prevented him from being thrown to the literal beasts; but his rights as a Roman citizen were not always honored (14:19; 16:37-39).

It is also possible that over the course of his long ministry there, Paul was imprisoned at Ephesus (2 Cor. 11:23), but if so Luke does not include that in the Acts record. At any rate, the situation with the silversmiths soon escalated into a life-threatening one, as the speech of Demetrius (vv. 25-27) ignited the anger of the craftsmen of the same guild (Soards 102-103). While he proposed no solutions, we should at least "give the devil his due." He is correct in that Paul did persuade the people to turn from idols since his message stated there are "no gods made with hands" (v. 26). While this is exactly what Paul said to the Areopagus (17:29) there is no reason to restrict his teaching to Athens. It fit well at Ephesus, too. Demetrius would have been correct, too, in Paul's depreciation of the temple of Diana (Artemis). He would not have seen it merely for its architectural grandeur, but for its idolatrous usage (v. 27). What was overstated was the extent of the cultic practice ("the world worshippeth"). There were many other gods in the Greco-Roman world. However, such speeches are not usually known for their historical accuracy.

The speech was very successful in getting the attention of the guild and sufficiently working them into a frenzy (v. 28). Chanting repeatedly, they heralded their devotion by shouting "Great is Diana (Artemis) of the Ephesians." Every riot seems to need a catchy slogan.

(2) The frenzied mob in the theater (19:29-34)

29 And the whole city was filled with confusion: and having caught Gaius and Aristarchus, men of Macedonia, Paul's companions in travel, they rushed with one accord into the theatre.
30 And when Paul would have entered in unto the people, the disciples suffered him not.
31 And certain of the chief of Asia, which were his friends, sent unto him, desiring *him* that he would not adventure himself into the theatre.
32 Some therefore cried one thing, and some another: for the assembly was confused; and the more

part knew not wherefore they were come together.
33 And they drew Alexander out of the multitude, the Jews putting him forward. And Alexander beckoned with the hand, and would have made his defense unto the people.
34 But when they knew that he was a Jew, all with one voice about the space of two hours cried out, Great *is* Diana of the Ephesians.

The guild of the silversmiths took their cause to the streets of Ephesus, keeping up the chant. The main avenue of Ephesus, which led from the harbor to the theater, was known as the Arcadian Way. If the occasion was the spring festival of Artemision, it would have been filled with near-delirious devotees already psyched up for the occasion. Added to that was the chant of the silversmiths that only added fuel to the fire. Somehow, two of Paul's companions, Gaius and Aristarchus, were recognized and accosted as the crowd-turned-mob rushed into the open air theater at the end of the street (v. 29). It may very well be that Luke got some of the details about the incident from these two men.

The theater at Ephesus had been built into the western slope of Mt. Pion. With its seating capacity of nearly twenty-five thousand, it would have been used for any number of gatherings. This gathering, however, was a "flash mob" that moved like a flock of birds into the arena. But it was a confused crowd (v. 29), as one group chanted "Great is Diana of the Ephesians" while displaying two men on the stage. What sense did that make? But mob psychology seldom makes sense.

Paul himself was about to enter the arena (v. 30), but the disciples restrained him, no doubt fearful of what the mob might do to him once he was identified. Of note is the reference to "certain of the chief of Asia" (literally, "some of the Asiarchs"), who also warned him against a public appearance at that time (v. 31). These were wealthy, high ranking officials of great stature in each province who were chosen to promote the public image of the emperor, preside at public games and festivities, and oversee funds connected for the imperial cult (Bruce, *Acts* 376; Robertson, *Acts* 327; Keener III:2908-2909). That these were friends of Paul's speaks to his deftness of relationships with the political class and suggests that they were not hostile to Christianity. They would have also been very concerned about the legality of the flash mob and how the Romans would respond.

With wry humor, Luke reports that it was a confused mob (v. 32). The guild of the silversmiths chanted one thing while others seemed to invent their own chants. Most had no clue as to why they were there. They were just happy to be there as part of the raucous crowd on a holiday.

The appearance of Alexander the Jew only added to the confusion (v. 33). Some suggest that the Jews wanted the crowd to know they were not complicit in the attempt to impugn the integrity of the worship of Diana (Artemis). Alexander's appearance was to convey that idea (Polhill, *Acts* 412; Bruce, *Acts* 377; Fitzmyer 660). They wanted them to know there was a distinct difference between Jews and Christians. If so, it shows their own confusion or political expedience regarding idolatry. Common enemies have sometimes joined in feigned friendships to oppose Christians—as when Herod and Pilate became friends over Jesus (Lk. 23:12).

Be that as it may, the appearance of Alexander was a futile attempt to make their case, and it utterly failed to bring order to the chaos. The mob only shouted him down (v. 34), with the noise morphing into a singular chant "Great is Diana of the Ephesians." In what can only be described as the delirious emotion of the mob, they chanted over and over for two hours. Morgan (463) aptly observes, "One lie, multiplied by ten thousand voices, never becomes a truth."

(3) The town-clerk dismisses the assembly (19:35-41)

35 And when the townclerk had appeased the people, he said, Ye men of Ephesus, what man is there that knoweth not how the city of the Ephesians is a worshipper of the great goddess Diana, and of the *image* which fell down from Jupiter?
36 Seeing then that these things cannot be spoken against, ye ought to be quiet, and to do nothing rashly.
37 For ye have brought thither these men, which are neither robbers of churches, nor yet blasphemers of your goddess.
38 Wherefore if Demetrius, and the craftsmen which are with him, have a matter against any man, the law is open, and there are deputies: let them implead one another.
39 But if ye enquire any thing concerning other matters, it shall be determined in a lawful assembly.

40 For we are in danger to be called in question for this day's uproar, there being no cause whereby we may give an account of this concourse.
41 And when he had thus spoken, he dismissed the assembly.

The town-clerk (Greek *grammateus*, secretary, recorder) was the chief administrative officer of the city as well as the liaison between the city and the Roman government (Polhill, *Acts* 412; Robertson, *Acts* 330; Bruce, *Acts* 378). His position made him personally responsible for any and all civic affairs and probably the most powerful man in the city. When he finally stood before the crowd they grew quiet. His speech is exemplary in pacifying the mob. Soards (104) describes it as a "polished deliberation."

Appealing to popular opinion, he assured them that there was no real threat posed against the worldwide worship of Diana (Artemis) and the honor of the city of Ephesus was not at risk. Therefore, they needed to cease and desist from the gathering (vv. 35-36). He mentioned the "image which fell down from Jupiter (Zeus)," which was probably a reference to a meteorite and the superstition that it came from the gods (Polhill, *Acts* 413; Schnabel 809, 810). If so, it would have been an image not made by men's hands per se, and might have been a clever response to Paul's argument about "gods made with hands" (v. 26). Of course, that does not negate the fact that men assigned deity to the image and thus, in effect, made the god. But the argument worked for the town clerk.

Further, the town clerk argues that there were no substantial charges of robbery or blasphemy against Paul and his associates (v. 37). The phrase "robbers of churches" (Greek *hierosuloi*, temple thieves, plunderers) would refer to stealing images, or artifacts, or even the respect due to the temple of Diana (Artemis). If there were charges to be preferred, there was due process according to the law of the land. Demetrius and the craftsmen could use the legal process to settle any disputes they had (v. 38). Otherwise, this was an unlawful assembly and they were all in jeopardy of Roman reprisal (v. 40). The Romans were very suspicious about public gatherings and civil discord.

While it was true that Paul had not stolen any images, he had, indeed, spoken against the worship of idols. This could have been regarded as blasphemy. His teaching and the widespread response to the gospel had impacted the sale of Diana cult images. But, at this point, it seems the speech of the town clerk was politically crafted to dismiss the crowd, not to argue the finer points of the issues. It also served to show that Christianity posed no real threat to civic order. With the crowd dismissed (v. 41), Gaius and Aristarchus were free to go; more importantly, the believers of Ephesus were spared government hostilities—at least for the time being.

Summary
(18:23—19:41)

The completion of the second missionary journey was, in itself, a great accomplishment but it did not represent a work that was entirely finished. It was yet another step in fulfilling the command of Christ to bear witness (1:8) in all the world. Plus, the churches that had been established needed encourage-

ment, stability, and guidance. Therefore, Paul almost immediately launched the next missionary journey to strengthen these churches before extending the witness of the gospel to new areas.

The assistance of Aquila and Priscilla was extremely valuable to Paul, as seen by their efforts with Apollos at Ephesus. They personify the principle of "laborers together with God" (1 Cor. 3:9). Furthermore, the cases of Apollos and the Ephesian disciples show the transitional nature of redemptive history as it is being fulfilled in the N. T. They show that faith in the promise of the Messiah must be further defined by faith in the person of the Messiah.

Paul's ministry at Ephesus was long and fruitful, and there were a great number of Gentiles who turned to the Lord in saving faith. His ministry there, however, was not without its challenges. Paul's battle with demonism is expressed even with miracles attending the work. There were those who tried to counterfeit the power of the Holy Spirit, thinking that magical chants and repetition of someone's name would work for them. The very real problem of demon possession and its dangerous potential was shown by their fake efforts as the demon-possessed man physically assaulted them. This did result in exposing spiritual error, and many of the believers confessed their error and burned their cultic materials.

Perhaps the most detailed account in the N. T. of cultic fanaticism and its rejection of Christianity occurs at Ephesus. When the gospel changes lives people abandon lifestyles and beliefs that have imprisoned them for years. Sometimes this is so pervasive that it has an economic impact. The world is not very tolerant when faith reaches the pocketbook or reveals the emptiness of false religion. At Ephesus there was a show of force against the believers and especially Paul. In what may be described as a flash mob, thousands of fanatical worshipers of Diana (Artemis) joined their voices, attempting to reassure themselves with noise and to silence the voice of the Apostle Paul. Order was restored by the political authority of a city official who voiced grave concerns over the possibility of military reprisal as a result of the unauthorized gathering. The "success" of the ministry at Ephesus is shown by the fact that it was opposed in this way by the devil and his crowd.

Application: Teaching and Preaching the Passage

Exegetical Outline of the Text: 1. Confirming the Churches (18:23). 2. Completing the Faith of Apollos and the Ephesian Disciples (18:24—19:7). 3. Confirming the Ministry With Miracles (19:8-12). 4. Counterfeits (19:13-20). 5. Chaos in Ephesus (19:21-41).

The ministry at Ephesus was seriously challenged by demonism and the cultic fanaticism of idolatry. This makes for an excellent study of the principles of spiritual warfare as found in Ephesians 6:10-18. Included should be ways in which spiritual counterfeits arise and fail, as did the misguided efforts of the sons of Sceva.

Also, many of the believers at Ephesus had not abandoned their fetishes. When the sons of Sceva were exposed, it also revealed the problem of believers' trying to cling to the practices of false religion as well as lifestyle choices that are displeasing to God. They came under conviction about this and burned their cultic paraphernalia. Though those materials

had been expensive in terms of money, that was nothing compared to the cost of spiritual compromise. Trying to compartmentalize and keep lifestyle choices that displease God has always been a challenge for believers. Some learn more quickly than others. But all authentic believers must come to the place of complete surrender to the Lordship of Christ in all things. The demands of discipleship, as summarized by Jesus in Luke 14:25-35, make another excellent study that stems from this event in Acts. Robert Picirilli's *Discipleship, the Expression of Saving Faith* (see bibliography) is highly recommended as a study guide.

3. Journey to Jerusalem (20:1—21:16)

a. Paul returns to Macedonia and Achaia (20:1-5)

1 And after the uproar was ceased, Paul called unto *him* the disciples, and embraced *them*, and departed for to go into Macedonia. 2 And when he had gone over those parts, and had given them much exhortation, he came into Greece, 3 And *there* abode three months. And when the Jews laid wait for him, as he was about to sail into Syria, he purposed to return through Macedonia. 4 And there accompanied him into Asia Sopater of Berea; and of the Thessalonians, Aristarchus and Secundus; and Gaius of Derbe, and Timotheus; and of Asia, Tychicus and Trophimus. 5 These going before tarried for us at Troas.

Paul had already made plans to revisit the churches of Macedonia and Achaia before making his way to Jerusalem (19:21-22). What could have been a bad situation in the uproar caused by the silversmiths had resulted, instead, in a positive outcome. To Paul, then, this seemed like a good time to begin that trip. Writers disagree on the exact dates. Polhill (*Acts* 415), Picirilli (*Corinthians* 254), and Bock (617) agree that the date was about A.D. 55-56. Ogg (138-139) has it as A.D. 57-58. The earlier date is best. But the situation of Paul's departure from Ephesus was not without its drama. Again, Luke provides only the main events of the trip; some details can be added from 2 Corinthains 1-7 (Picirilli, *Corinthians* 252-254; Bruce, *Acts* 381).

Paul had written First Corinthians from Ephesus and probably sent it by the men named in 1 Corinthains 16:17. But Paul learned from someone (Timothy or Erastus?) that the situation in the church at Corinth was not good. Among other things, there was apparently tensions over Paul himself. So Paul made a short but painful and unsuccessful trip to Corinth to try to resolve the situation (Picirilli, *Corinthians* 254; *Paul* 142; Bruce, *Paul* 273-274). Returning to Ephesus, he wrote a "severe letter" (2 Cor. 2:3-4, 9; 7:8-9) and sent it to Corinth by Titus. He was given instructions to take the letter, assess the situation, and then return through Macedonia to meet Paul, apparently at Troas. With that plan in place, Paul left Ephesus for Macedonia. When he came to Troas, Titus did not arrive as he hoped (2 Cor. 2:12-13). Paul continued into Macedonia, ministering to the churches there, and finally encountered Titus (at Philippi?), who was able to inform him that corrections that had taken place at Corinth. With that news, Paul wrote Second Corinthians from somewhere in Macedonia (Philippi?), sending it to them via Titus and an unnamed brother (Luke? Compare 2 Cor. 8:16-18). Paul then proceeded with his plans to minister to the churches in Macedonia and Achaia, arriving in Corinth to spend the winter months there.

Luke does not tell us these details but simply informs us of Paul's Macedonian ministry and his arrival in "Greece" (Achaia). The details do not fit his purpose. Paul remained in Corinth for the winter months awaiting the arrival of spring when he could travel by ship to Syria. Voyages on the open sea did not begin until early March (Ramsay, *Traveller* 283).

While in Corinth for the three winter months, old animosities arose from the Jews (18:12-13), who plotted against him (20:3). We are not told how Paul was made aware of the plot, but it changed his travel plans. He chose to travel by land instead of sea to a safe port from which to depart and to take several companions with him (v. 4). These would provide protection as well as guard the collection for the saints in Judaea that Paul was sponsoring during this journey. Among these were representatives of the churches Paul had established on the two previous missionary journeys. These were sent ahead to Troas to await him there. Luke, of course, does not name himself, but the use of the personal "us" (v. 5) and "we" (v. 6) connect him with Paul again as they move on from Philippi.

The inclusion of several other fellow-laborers (v. 4) is significant for a number of reasons. As the work grew, so did the responsibilities and opportunities. As men and women were won to the Lord and matured in their spiritual lives, they were afforded opportunities to assist in the ministry. In all likelihood those named here were well known to Luke, as shown by his identification of them along with where they were from. Some of these are named by Paul in his epistles as trusted fellow servants. We can be sure these are not the only ones who served with him faithfully. Their inclusion here was in reference to the journey and the security needed for Paul and the offering he was taking to Jerusalem.

Paul explains a larger principle in 1 Corinthians 3:1-9. Although the situation at Corinth involved a carnal spirit, in comparing the leadership qualities of Paul, Peter, and Apollos, the larger principle remains; all are "laborers together with God" (1 Cor. 3:9). Spiritual leadership is not to be viewed as competitive but complementary. Paul certainly saw no competing interests about his leadership as seen in his personal practice of partnership with others as the Acts narrative shows. One of the great blessings of ministry is the fruit of fellowship and laborers for Christian service.

b. Paul at Troas and the restoration of Eutychus (20:6-12)

6 And we sailed away from Philippi after the days of unleavened bread, and came unto them to Troas in five days; where we abode seven days.
7 And upon the first *day* of the week, when the disciples came together to break bread, Paul preached unto them, ready to depart on the morrow; and continued his speech until midnight.

8 And there were many lights in the upper chamber, where they were gathered together.
9 And there sat in a window a certain young man named Eutychus, being fallen into a deep sleep: and as Paul was long preaching, he sunk down with sleep, and fell down from the third loft, and was taken up dead.
10 And Paul went down, and fell on him, and embracing *him* said, Trouble not yourselves; for his life is in him.
11 When he therefore was come up again, and had broken bread, and eaten, and talked a long while, even till break of day, so he departed.
12 And they brought the young man alive, and were not a little comforted.

Paul and his companions, now including Luke, would have boarded the ship at Neapolis (16:11) for their trip to Troas where they were to meet the rest of the group (v. 5). Luke does give us a time reference, in relation to the week of "unleavened bread" in connection with the Jewish Passover. Most writers place the time as the spring of A.D. 57; Ogg (140) places it as A.D. 59. It is clear that for Paul, "the clock was ticking" because he wanted to be in Jerusalem for Pentecost (v. 16). Keener (III:2961) and Ramsay (*Traveller* 294-295) calculate the time required to make the journey, indicating that they had ample time to get there as planned.

The short trip southeasterly across the Aegean Sea took five days. This was twice as long as the previous northwesterly trip (16:11), apparently because of contrary winds. Upon arrival in Troas, they rejoined their companions and stayed for seven more days, presumably waiting for their ship to leave again (Polhill, *Acts* 418). It is fortunate that the last day of their delay was the first day of the week and the time for assembled worship.

The gathering of the believers at Troas affords us insights into early church worship (vv. 7-12) as well as the miraculous restoration of the life of a young man named Eutychus (whose name means "fortunate, lucky"). There are four elements in the worship service. 1. It was on the first day of the week. There is some question about the specific meaning of the "first day of the week." If it was by Jewish reckoning it would have been Saturday night (Keener III:2967). If Luke used the Roman system, it was a Sunday night (Polhill, *Acts* 418). Either way, this is the first reference in Acts to believers gathering on the first day of the week. 2. They met together in a common gathering place. They were in a house large enough to accommodate the group, perhaps the home of their host. 3. Their worship service included preaching. Certainly there were no clocks but the opportunity to hear the apostle was not to be interrupted, no matter how long he chose to speak. 4. They broke bread. This was probably the celebration of the Lord's Supper (2:42; 1 Cor. 11:23-27) as well as a meal (v. 11).

An additional event took place at Troas that Luke must have recorded with a wry smile: the restoration of Eutychus. Even as we read the story, we cannot help being sympathetic with the "lad," perhaps between eight and fourteen years old. It was springtime, warm, and even though it was the apostle Paul preaching, the sermon was really long.

The burning torches that provided light would have consumed even more of the breathable air in a crowded room. Finding some relief in an open window, Eutychus seated himself on the sill and was soon overcome with sleep. Who among us has not witnessed this a hundred times in church services today, although it is usually in a church pew? Unfortunately, he was so sound asleep he fell from the open window to the ground three stories below. All rushed down to check on him and found that the fall was fatal. Most writers agree that he was actually dead (Polhill, *Acts* 419; Bruce, *Acts* 385; Marshall, *Acts* 326; Bock 620; Robertson, *Acts* 341; Keener III:2977). Luke, the physician, was satisfied he had died (Greek *nekros*, dead).

It was most "fortunate" for Eutychus (see above) that Paul was there, for God miraculously, using the apostle, raised the young man from the dead. The incident reminds us of Peter and Dorcas (9:36-41). This is the only instance of Paul's restoring life to someone. Polhill (*Acts* 419) observes that the incident belongs in the category of resurrection miracles. Furthermore, Passover had just taken place and Jesus arose on the first day of the week; how providentially fitting was this miracle for the believers at Troas, not to mention the young man himself. It was a story he would remember for the rest of his life—and it was recorded in the Word of God!

We have to admire those who were gathered in Troas as they seemed to cling to every minute afforded them by the presence of Paul. The restoration of Eutychus must have been without lingering effects, for he had fully recovered and everyone was greatly comforted (v. 12). With the restoration of Eutychus, they returned to eat a meal and continue with Paul's message (v. 11). He preached and visited until daylight, then departed.

c. From Troas to Miletus (20:13-16)

13 And we went before to ship, and sailed unto Assos, there intending to take in Paul: for so had he appointed, mindful himself to go afoot.
14 And when he met with us at Assos, we took him in, and came to Mitylene.
15 And we sailed thence, and came the next *day* over against Chios; and the next *day* we arrived at Samos, and tarried at Trogyllium; and the next *day* we came to Miletus.
16 For Paul had determined to sail by Ephesus, because he would not spend the time in Asia: for he hasted, if it were possible for him, to be at Jerusalem the day of Pentecost.

One must admire the resilience and drive of the apostle Paul. After speaking all night, the rest of the group embarked on a ship while Paul went afoot (v. 13). It was some twenty miles to Assos directly but the Roman road was curved, making it nearly a forty-mile trip. Opinions vary as to why Paul did not take the boat and rest. Suggestions range from his desire to visit someone on that route, to considerations for his safety. We are not told why he chose to do this. It was certainly not a time saver, for he was pressed by both his personal schedule to be in Jerusalem for Pentecost as well as the ship's next port of call.

Verses 14-16 record the progress of the ship as they made their way along the coast line. Each port of call represents a day's journey and overnight at the same port (Ramsay, *Traveller* 293-295; Polhill, *Acts* 421). The ship was a cargo ship carrying passengers and cargo for commercial purposes. Luke records an adjustment made in Paul's plans (v. 16) about his intended visit to Ephesus. With Pentecost only five weeks away, he was fearful he might be delayed if he went on to the city of Ephesus; from Miletus, therefore, he sent word for the Ephesian leaders to meet him at Miletus.

d. Paul addresses the Ephesian elders at Miletus (20:17-38)

(1) Paul's personal ministry (20:17-27)

17 And from Miletus he sent to Ephesus, and called the elders of the church.
18 And when they were come to him, he said unto them, Ye know, from the first day that I came into Asia, after what manner I have been with you at all seasons,
19 Serving the LORD with all humility of mind, and with many tears, and temptations, which befell me by the lying in wait of the Jews:
20 *And* how I kept back nothing that was profitable *unto you*, but have shewed you, and have taught you publicly, and from house to house,
21 Testifying both to the Jews, and also to the Greeks, repentance toward God, and faith toward our Lord Jesus Christ.
22 And now, behold, I go bound in the spirit unto Jerusalem, not

knowing the things that shall befall me there:

23 Save that the Holy Ghost witnesseth in every city, saying that bonds and afflictions abide me.

24 But none of these things move me, neither count I my life dear unto myself, so that I might finish my course with joy, and the ministry, which I have received of the Lord Jesus, to testify the gospel of the grace of God.

25 And now, behold, I know that ye all, among whom I have gone preaching the kingdom of God, shall see my face no more.

26 Wherefore I take you to record this day, that I *am* pure from the blood of all *men*.

27 For I have not shunned to declare unto you all the counsel of God.

Apparently, the ship would stay at Miletus for a few days, either as it was scheduled or as an accommodation for Paul. It was some thirty miles to Ephesus, a long day's journey at the time. But it would have taken some time to get the elders together, arrange transportation, and then make the return trip. It could easily have taken three days for them to get to Miletus. Their response testifies of their devotion to the apostle and their own sense of commitment to the cause of Christ. There are some men and the causes they serve worth the sacrificial efforts to hear them, the greatest of which is the cause of Christ. There was only one Apostle Paul.

Most all conservative writers agree that Acts records, here, the very message given by the apostle himself. In fact, Luke heard him deliver it (21:1). Haenchen (596-597) and Fitzmyer

(675), however, see it as yet another construct by Luke; Fitzmyer repeatedly refers to him as "the Lucan Paul." One cannot help wondering why these commentators thought that such a capable and brilliant man as Paul needed an avatar.

There are some notable features of Paul's address. First, it is the last of his missionary journey messages. Second, it is his only recorded message exclusively made to believers. Third, it contains a number of themes commonly found in his epistles (for a listing of these see Keener III:3000-3001). Fourth, it is his "legacy" speech. He does not believe he will ever see these folks again, so he is in effect bidding them farewell.

Though there is some repetition, the whole message falls into two broad categories; Polhill (*Acts* 423) sees four; Stott (324), three. First, Paul speaks of his personal life and ministry (vv. 18-27). Then he speaks to the responsibilities of the Ephesian elders, in effect shifting the mantle of leadership to their shoulders (vv. 28-35).

Paul began by reviewing his past life and service among the Ephesians (vv. 18-21). He was very transparent regarding the integrity of his personal life. He spoke of living consistently ("at all seasons," v. 18); of serving with "humility" and compassion ("many tears") during times of testing (v. 19); and of the fact that his ministry was without reserve ("I kept back nothing that was profitable to you," v. 20). Furthermore, he faithfully proclaimed the gospel to all men, "Jews and Greeks" (v. 21). These elements present a model for personal ministry for anyone. Leaders should always model what they expect in others.

Paul then moved to his future plans, again being very transparent about the uncertainty he faced (vv. 22-27). The phrase, "bound in the spirit" (v. 22) is further defined by the witness of the Holy Spirit portending trouble for him in Jerusalem (v.23). Some of the details were unclear, but he was told that "bonds and afflictions" awaited him there. These terms refer to imprisonment and antagonism from people. Paul added that the Spirit had conveyed this message repeatedly to him "in every city." The means of conveying this message could have been directly to Paul and/or through the witness of prophets—as will be illustrated later (21:10-11).

The fact that Paul felt driven to go to Jerusalem (19:21; 20:22), but was also warned of what would happen if he did, should not be viewed as contradictory. Jesus knew the same (Mt. 17:22-23), as did Peter (Jn. 20:18-19); but they were not deterred from their mission. It is rare that anyone knows what the future may hold for them. It is even rarer that when one knows trouble lies around the corner he continues on the same path. I suppose doing this depends on one's life purpose.

In Paul's response about his future trouble, he conveyed a commitment to Christ that is greater than to his own life (v. 24). This does not mean that he had a death wish but rather he saw the cause of Christ as greater. It is a dimension of Christian faith and commitment that has characterized the teachings of Christ and the testimonies of countless saints throughout history (Lk. 14:26-27; Phil. 1:20-21; 2 Tim. 4:6-8). Christ is worth living for because He is worth dying for. The most obvious passage in Paul's writings that parallels this theme in his message is his commitment to "finish my course with joy" (2 Tim. 4:7).

Paul's statement that the Ephesians would not see him again (v. 25) needs to be understood in light of the Pastoral Epistles and the possible return of Paul later (Polhill, *Acts* 426; Keener III:3023-3026). That he was released from the first imprisonment, made a fourth missionary journey, and endured a second imprisonment in Rome before his death is likely, but certainly not contradictory to his statement here. If, indeed, Paul later revisited Ephesus (1 Tim. 1:3), he was simply premature in his conclusion. And if he did not go back to Ephesus, he was correct. Either way, Paul was expressing what he thought, at the time, to be the case (Robertson, *Acts* 351). He was not without good reasons for believing and expressing this to the Ephesian elders.

One striking statement is Paul's conclusion that he was "pure from the blood of all men" (v. 26). This alludes to the watchman analogy from Ezekiel 33:1-6. It means that he has fulfilled his responsibility to "blow the trumpet" of warning about impending danger. In this case, it refers to the gospel's call to repentance and the future judgment of all men (17:30-31; Phil. 2:9-11; Eph. 1:20-22). Paul's proclaiming "all the counsel of God" to everyone (vv. 20-21) absolved him from blood-guiltiness. It is a statement worth pondering for all who preach the Word of God.

(2) Charge to the elders (20:28-35)

28 Take heed therefore unto yourselves, and to all the flock, over the which the Holy Ghost hath made you overseers, to feed the church of God, which he hath purchased with his own blood.

29 For I know this, that after my departing shall grievous wolves enter in among you, not sparing the flock.

30 Also of your own selves shall men arise, speaking perverse things, to draw away disciples after them.

31 Therefore watch, and remember, that by the space of three years I ceased not to warn every one night and day with tears.

32 And now, brethren, I commend you to God, and to the word of his grace, which is able to build you up, and to give you an inheritance among all them which are sanctified.

33 I have coveted no man's silver, or gold, or apparel.

34 Yea, ye yourselves know, that these hands have ministered unto my necessities, and to them that were with me.

35 I have shewed you all things, how that so laboring ye ought to support the weak, and to remember the words of the Lord Jesus, how he said, It is more blessed to give than to receive.

The second area the apostle addressed was the responsibilities of the Ephesian elders (vv. 28-35). Not only was Paul's life a model for ministry, theirs was to be as well. He uses two motifs to convey their responsibilities. First is that of a shepherd. This analogy is often used in the N. T., beginning with Jesus Himself as the Good Shepherd (Jn. 10:11; Heb. 13:20). Of course, the idea is that just as the shepherd cares for his flock in all that it entails, so these men should view their role with the local churches in Ephesus. He uses the terms "the flock," "to feed," and the shepherd's watchfulness, which was necessary to guard against "grievous (fierce) wolves." As shepherds they were "to feed" the flock ("the church of God"), referring to teaching the truths of the Word of God (Heb. 5:12-14; 1 Pet. 2:2-3). The particular admonition regarding wolves is "to watch" (Greek *gregoreo*, stay awake, be alert). Apparently, with all the positive characteristics of the early church in Acts, it was always a target of Satan. Infiltration was his strategy.

The second analogy is that of an overseer (Greek *episkpos*). Used five times in the N. T., this term conveys the responsibilities to guard the group, manage the affairs, and give direction to common activities (TDNT II:616). The agency of the Holy Spirit should be noted in the calling of these men to their position. The apostle Paul was the Holy Spirit's initial means of appointment, but it was a divine calling.

The phrase "the church of God, which he hath purchased with his own blood" is very intriguing, both interpretatively and theologically. Whose blood is meant? Does God have blood? What is the intent of Paul with this phrase? Some manuscripts read "the church of the Lord" while others "the church of God" as here (see Metzger, 425-427, for analysis of textual possibilities). Robertson (*Acts* 353), Metzger (427), and Meyer (391-392) agree that the reading should be "God." It is God's church because it has been purchased with the price of blood.

Theologically, since God is immaterial spirit and not flesh (Jn. 4:24), He is not a material being dependent on the same bodily functions and physical components (blood) required for human beings (Forlines, *Quest* 65; Berkhof

293

65-66). But this does not negate the deity of Christ, at once fully God (Rom. 9:5; Col. 2:9; Tit. 2:13) and fully human (Berkhof 333; Forlines, *Quest* 170) including all the bodily functions and components required by a human body (1 Tim. 2:5-6; Heb. 2:14). Later, Paul affirms the shedding of the blood of Jesus Christ as integral to ecclesiology (Rom. 3:24-25; Eph. 1:7; Col. 1:14, 20).

The phrase "purchased with his own blood" can also be read as "purchased with the blood of his own," referring to Christ as does Romans 8:31. This makes the best sense and satisfies all the theological and ecclesiological concerns (Bock 630; Marshall, *Acts* 334; Polhill, *Acts* 428; Robertson, *Acts* 352; Bruce, *Acts* 392-393; Schnabel 846-847). We should not miss the Trinitarian relationship to the church in this one verse.

It was Paul's particular concern that the elders (pastors) be on guard regarding spiritual attacks on the churches. His intent is to show the source and effects of false prophets and teachers. These would come from within the flock: "of your own selves." The result of false teaching, "speaking perverse things" (Greek *diestrammena*, twisted, perverted, distorted things), would be like the results of an attack of ravenous wolves on a flock of sheep. Such an attack would destroy them. So does false doctrine. If truth make us free (Jn. 8:32), lies enslave.

Next, Paul repeats the exhortation to be watchful (v. 31). He uses his own labors with them as their model. His was a 24/7 labor that extended for three years (19:8, 10), characterized by tearful warnings of potential dangers. Apparently, the ministry at Ephesus was continually challenged by the devil (Eph. 6:10-12), with no let-up in sight.

Paul pointed these men to God's care via His Word (v. 32) that was sufficient to sustain and reward. Pastoral leadership finds its worth and strength in the Word of God. Paul concluded by referencing again his own work to supply his material needs and support those who labored with him (vv. 33-34). He made it clear that material gain was not his motive for ministry.

Labor need not always be just to supply one's own needs but for the needs of others (Lk. 6:30, 38; 11:41; 12:33; 18:22), as confirmed by the quote from the Lord Jesus. Interestingly, this quote is not found in any of the Gospels (v. 35), but its inclusion here confirms its source. Robertson (*Acts* 357) suggests that Paul might have known Jesus personally. Paul could have easily gotten it from one of the other apostles who could have, indeed, heard Him say it. The apostles themselves would have known many sayings of Jesus and would make them part of an apostolic oral tradition. This should come as no surprise since John tells us that not everything Jesus did (or said) was written down (Jn. 21:25). This saying, the "last beatitude" (comparing the beatitudes of Mt. 5:3-11), is an appropriate summary of the entire life of the Lord Jesus, so it certainly sounds like Jesus. Given its very likely apostolic source, certainly with Paul repeating it, the quote must then be regarded as authentic. Its inclusion here adds it to the Gospel writings and records it for us as reference.

There were a number of parallel sayings in Greek literature, which leads some interpreters to suggest that it is a Christianized Greek maxim (Marshall, *Acts* 336; Polhill, *Acts* 429; Keener

III:3063-3065). However, it could easily be something original that Jesus said, now being stated for this occasion. The fact that there are any number of extra-biblical writings that claim authenticity does not mean they are inspired. These have long since been analyzed and provide study beyond the scope of this commentary.

(3) Tearful farewell (20:36-38)

36 And when he had thus spoken, he kneeled down, and prayed with them all.
37 And they all wept sore, and fell on Paul's neck, and kissed him,
38 Sorrowing most of all for the words which he spake, that they should see his face no more. And they accompanied him unto the ship.

With the completion of his message to the elders (vv. 36-38), there was a tearful time of prayer and farewells. One cannot miss the bond of fellowship and brotherly love that is evident in the scene. The words of admonition Paul gave to these men were wise counsel that would serve them in days to come, but they were immediately struck by the distinct possibility that they might never see Paul again (v. 38). It must have been a tearful farewell as they accompanied him to the ship and he embarked on the rest of his journey.

e. From Miletus to Tyre (21:1-6)

1 And it came to pass, that after we were gotten from them, and had launched, we came with a straight course unto Coos, and the day following unto Rhodes, and from thence unto Patara:
2 And finding a ship sailing over unto Phenicia, we went aboard, and set forth.
3 Now when we had discovered Cyprus, we left it on the left hand, and sailed into Syria, and landed at Tyre: for there the ship was to unlade her burden.
4 And finding disciples, we tarried there seven days: who said to Paul through the Spirit, that he should not go up to Jerusalem.
5 And when we had accomplished those days, we departed and went our way; and they all brought us on our way, with wives and children, till we were out of the city: and we kneeled down on the shore, and prayed.
6 And when we had taken our leave one of another, we took ship; and they returned home again.

The journey to Jerusalem continued with the boarding of the ship sailing east. Luke records each port of call along a coastal route indicating the vessel was one suited for short commercial trips. When they arrived at Patara they found a ship more suited for open sea travel and destined for the Syrian coast (Ramsay, *Traveller* 298-300). Luke states they "discovered Cyprus" (v. 3) meaning they "sighted" the island to their north and passed to its south. Luke's knowledge of sailing in each record of sea travel is obvious.

The ship reached its destination at the port of Tyre (v. 3) on the Syrian coast where they disembarked. Here they sought out the community of believers with whom they might not have been previously acquainted, as indicated by the phrase "finding disciples." These believers were probably the result of the dispersal of Christians from Jerusalem due to the persecution that arose over Stephen (11:19). "Coincidentally" Paul (at the time Saul of Tarsus) would have been a major contributor to that persecution. Now he seeks fellowship with those believers!

The destination was Jerusalem, but apparently, they had time for a week's stay (v. 4). It was during this layover these disciples reaffirmed the Holy Spirit's word to Paul that impending trouble lay ahead in Jerusalem. This was nothing new to either him or those who accompanied him.

As previously addressed (20:22), there is no contradiction between the revelation of the Holy Spirit regarding the coming trouble and the concerns of the Tyrian disciples who, naturally, would counsel Paul to change his plans. Paul never sought trouble and usually heeded the counsel of others to avoid it (9:30; 14:5-6; 17:10). He certainly did not have a martyr's spirit or death wish but accepted trouble as part of suffering for Christ that was to be endured with grace. Likewise, the Tyrian Christians could not be faulted for wanting him to change his plans (Marshall, *Acts* 338-339; Bruce, *Acts* 398). It should not be concluded that Paul's insistence on continuing to Jerusalem was an act of disobedience or self-will over the Lord's will. Jesus had acted in the same way that Paul acted (Mt. 26:39; Lk. 9:51).

When the day came to continue the journey, the entire community of believers in Tyre, including the extended families, accompanied them to the port (vv. 5-6). Reminiscent of the farewell to the Ephesian elders (20:36-37), there was a solemn prayer for guidance and blessing as the group knelt on the seashore. With final goodbyes said, they went their separate ways. The incident records yet another confirming message of the Holy Spirt to Paul as well as a time for bonding with this Christian community. At many of these ports of call there was a community of believers. The fellowship of the saints is always a source of encouragement for those in ministry.

f. From Tyre to Caesarea (21:7-14)

**7   And when we had finished *our* course from Tyre, we came to Ptolemais, and saluted the brethren, and abode with them one day.
8   And the next *day* we that were of Paul's company departed, and came unto Caesarea: and we entered into the house of Philip the evangelist, which was *one* of the seven; and abode with him.
9   And the same had four daughters, virgins, which did prophesy.
10 And as we tarried *there* many days, there came down from Judaea a certain prophet, named Agabus.
11 And when he was come unto us, he took Paul's girdle, and bound his own hands and feet, and said, Thus saith the Holy Ghost, So shall the Jews at Jerusalem bind the man that owneth this girdle, and shall deliver *him* into the hands of the Gentiles.
12 And when we heard these things, both we, and they of that place, besought him not to go up to Jerusalem.
13 Then Paul answered, What mean ye to weep and to break mine heart? for I am ready not to be bound only, but also to die at**

Jerusalem for the name of the Lord Jesus.
14 And when he would not be persuaded, we ceased, saying, The will of the Lord be done.

After two more days of travel, with the ship stopping at familiar ports where there were communities of believers, they arrived at Caesarea (v. 8). Here they were hosted by Philip, who had established his ministry there (8:40). He is distinguished from the apostle Philip by identifying him as one of "the seven" (6:3-6) and by the title "the evangelist." Paul would have already been acquainted with him and the community of believers at Caesarea (9:30; 18:22).

Philip had four daughters who were unmarried (v. 9) and had the gift of prophecy. Bruce (*Acts* 400) informs us that several years later, Philip and his family moved to the province of Asia where they lived out their lives in ministry and were highly esteemed, providing information about the early years of Judaean Christianity to men such as Papias. One can imagine the incredible time of fellowship that Paul and his companions had with Philip and his family, sharing their stories of serving the Lord in ministry. While here, Luke might have received first-hand information from Philip and recorded the information about his Samaritan ministry and the conversion of the Ethiopian eunuch (8:5-40).

The prophet Agabus is re-introduced to the narrative (11:27-28); he has journeyed to Caesarea with a particular word from God (vv. 10-11), just as he had when he went to Antioch. This time it was particularly for Paul. Dramatically, he used Paul's girdle, a long cloth that would have been wrapped around his waist (Wight 93-94) to bind his own feet and hands. The action indicated trouble for Paul when he went to Jerusalem. Agabus specified that the Jews would bind him and deliver him to the Gentiles (Romans). It should be noted that the prophecy did not include instructions from the Lord that Paul should *not* go to Jerusalem. A distinction should be made between the prediction and a prohibition.

All who observed the dramatic actions of Agabus, including Luke ("we"), implored Paul to change his plans and not go (v. 12). If Luke had previously believed Paul to be right in going on to Jerusalem (Stott 333), it appears that he had changed his mind. Perhaps he interpreted the prediction of Agabus to be prohibitive. However, Paul responded with the same insistence as before (v. 4). He did not interpret the prophecy as forbidding him to go, but rather that it was informing him of what would happen when he did (v. 13). He firmly believed it to be the will of God for his life and would not be dissuaded. The exchange terminated with all appealing to the will of God for him (14). The conclusion reached by Luke and the others sounds like something they might have learned from James (Jas. 4:15), who would have already written his epistle to the Judaean believers who had been scattered by the economic impact of the famine (Jas. 1:1). It should be noted that if Paul had changed his plans, the prediction of Agabus would have been false.

g. From Caesarea to Jerusalem (21:15-16)

15 And after those days we took up our carriages, and went up to Jerusalem.

16 There went with us also *certain* of the disciples of Caesarea, and brought with them one Mnason of Cyprus, an old disciple, with whom we should lodge.

The journey to Jerusalem was just under seventy miles from Caesarea. There was a large group that included Paul's company and several believers from Caesarea, including an aged disciple named Mnason from Cyprus (13:4; 15:39). Arrangements had been made for them to lodge with him since he had a house in the area of Jerusalem. Luke mentions their "carriages" (baggage) which would have been considerable. Until now it would have been transported by ship. Most likely they used pack animals to carry the load. Among the baggage would have been the offering from the Pauline churches for the Judaean believers. Given the intrigue of the many prophecies regarding this trip, for Paul and the mission of mercy with the offering, there must have been mixed emotions of anticipation and trepidation as they made this final leg of the journey. Indeed, everything would change for some over the next few years.

In this way, the third missionary journey was completed. Churches had been strengthened, new fields of witness had been reached, battles with the forces of spiritual darkness had been fought and won, and God's hand of guidance and protection had been observed. The completion of one task had opened the door to others. Paul's witness would soon take on a different tack (to use a sailing term), as he was placed in multiple situations to give witness to powerful political and religious leaders.

Summary
(20:1—21:16)

It had been Paul's plan to make the journey back to Jerusalem upon completing the work at Ephesus (19:21). His plans were to visit the churches of Macedonia and Achaia, first, to strengthen them. It was less than an ideal trip when they discovered a plot against him and he had to adjust his travel plans.

A large company of helpers joined him, including Luke (20:4-6), to insure his safety and secure the offering intended for the believers in Judaea. Arriving in Troas, Paul spoke during an all-night service, which included the miracle of a young man being raised to life. Paul demonstrated his tireless spirit as he traveled on foot to the next port of call.

At Miletus, Paul met the Ephesian elders for what he expected to be his last words and face-time with them. Among the great truths about ministry he shared, he included the fact that the Holy Spirit was warning him of what lay ahead in Jerusalem. From Miletus the team sailed to Caesarea where they reconnected with Philip, who hosted them for a few days. There the prophet Agabus confirmed that if Paul continued to Jerusalem he would be bound and imprisoned. Against the pleas of the others, Paul refused to change his plans, believing he was following the Lord's leadership even if it meant giving his life for the cause of Christ. The team arrived in Jerusalem, no doubt with mixed emotions of joy and keen anticipation of what lay ahead, given the repeated warnings of the Holy Spirit.

Application: Teaching and Preaching the Passage

An Exegetical Outline: 1. Strengthening the Churches With His Fellow-laborers (20:1-4). 2. Midnight Miracle at Troas (20:5-12). 3. The Message at Miletus to the Ephesian Elders (20:13-38). 4. Journey to Caesarea and Reconnecting With Philip (21:1-9). 5. The Agabus Prophecy and the Continued Journey (21:10-16).

There are many truths to glean from a study of the completed three missionary journeys. The following summarizes the major elements of witness and missions that made the work successful. 1. The work of the Holy Spirit. 2. Strategic places chosen for ministry. 3. Proclamation of the gospel to everyone. 4. Discipling of new converts. 5. Establishing and organizing leadership in local churches. 6. Return visits to encourage, strengthen, and establish. 7. The potential for persecution. 8. Appeal to civil rights when necessary. 9. Multiple helpers in ministry. 10. The sending agency of the local church. 11. Accountability to the local church. 12. Stewardship of funds for the ministry.

Just as Paul had fellow-laborers and companions in ministry, so do we. Several times in his epistles, Paul refers to some of these listed in 20:4 and compliments them in some way. Timothy is the most frequently named, with two epistles written to him. An excellent study is to trace the references to each of these (and others) in Paul's epistles noting the characteristics and contributions of each. A good concordance is very useful for such a study. These become brief biographies, which encourage and challenge us, and which we can emulate.

In the Acts record, one can trace four of the strategies of Satan used in attacking the church. First, he uses *intimidation*, as seen in the threats of the Sanhedrin (4:1-21; 5:11-17; 24:1-21). Second, he uses *imitation*, as seen in the incidents involving Ananias and Sapphira (5:1-10), Simon the magician (8:18-24), and the sons of Sceva (19:13-16). Third, he uses *intervention*, as seen in the confrontation by Elymas on the island of Cyprus (13:6-11). Fourth, he uses *infiltration*, as seen in Paul's warning of fierce wolves who would arise from within the church (20:29-30). These four strategies are not the only ones he has in his spiritual arsenal. These can be discussed on several levels.

We cannot help admiring the resilience and determination of the Apostle Paul. Though being warned of trouble to come he remained committed to the ministry, even if it meant his life. The cause of Christ was seen as worth living for because He was worth dying for. Such is the stuff of Christianity. God's grace has powerfully worked in the lives of believers to enable them to labor sacrificially for the furtherance of the gospel. God uniquely prepares each person for the work to which He has called them. We are not naturally as strong or determined as we should be, apart from God's grace and enabling by His Spirit. Many great Christian men and women have given testimony to this fact, and their witness has resonated through the centuries.

There are different opinions about whether Paul should have continued on to Jerusalem. Some regard the warnings as prohibitions, while others see them as preparatory. This makes an excellent study about making wise choices when the way ahead appears to hold danger.

VI. PAUL'S WITNESS BEFORE KINGS AND RULERS (21:17—28:31)

The ending of the third missionary journey, with Paul's final return to Jerusalem (18:22), marks a major change in the Acts narrative. There should be no doubt that he planned to continue with his missionary work after this visit (19:21; Rom. 15:23-25), but the prophecy of troubles that awaited him came to pass. From freely traveling to strategic cities and aggressively proclaiming the gospel in those places, his movements become dramatically reduced. He will be under arrest and on the defensive and will be transferred from one imprisonment to another: first in Jerusalem and then to Caesarea for at least two years, then to Rome where Luke concludes his narrative. But Paul's voice is not silenced. In fact, the imprisonments provide opportunities to proclaim the gospel to audiences he would not have had under "normal" circumstances. As he writes later from imprisonment in Rome (28:30-31), "The things which happened unto me have fallen out rather unto the furtherance of the gospel" (Phil. 1:12).

The change in the narrative, however, does not negate or alter Luke's intention to show the witness of the gospel to "the uttermost part of the earth" (1:8). Paul's imprisonment and journey to Rome become part of the means by which God accomplishes this ultimate design, as well as the fulfillment of His design for Paul's personal life (9:15; 22:15; 26:17-19). The devil might have tried to stop his witness with the imprisonment years, but "God meant it unto good" (Gen. 50:20).

Interestingly, only twelve days are involved from 21:17 to 23:35 (see 24:11) and probably only seventeen days to the time he gives his defense (24:1). But the rest of the narrative covers at least two more years (24:27). The time and pace might have been tedious to Paul, but Luke probably used the time to gather information for both of his volumes (Polhill, *Acts* 445; Bock 655).

Acts records six trials or defenses Paul encounters where he faced the "bonds and afflictions" about which he had been repeatedly warned. Of all his recorded speeches in Acts, there is more room given to his defense testimonies than to his missionary messages. He is not only the apostle to the Gentiles as a witness to the gospel, he is also a defender of the faith. In every situation, he defends himself. The first such defense/testimony was in Jerusalem, on the steps of the "castle" (21:34—22:21) before the mob that had just tried to kill him. The second was before the Sanhedrin in Jerusalem (23:1-10) where his life was again in jeopardy. The third trial was before the Roman procurator Felix (24:1-26) in Caesarea, where he faced off with the hired legal gun of the Sanhedrin. The fourth trial, with other private meetings implied (24:24-26), was before Felix and his wife Drusilla, still in Caesarea. The fifth trial, two years later, (25:1-12) was in Caesarea and before the newly-appointed Roman procurator Festus, where Paul appealed to be heard before Caesar. The sixth trial is still in Caesarea (26:1-30) before Festus and the Jewish king, Herod Agrippa II, together with his wife Bernice and a political entourage that accompanied them. The Acts narrative ends with Paul awaiting yet another trial before Caesar. Though his future is uncertain and his circumstances limiting, he is still in ministry (28:16, 30-31).

This section covers almost seven chapters of the narrative, fully one fourth of the entire Book of Acts (see Bock 655 for details). Except for the space given to the voyage to Rome and Paul's arrival there, all the events took place in Jerusalem and Caesarea. The trials are real enough, but the trial motif becomes the setting for the defense of the gospel in relation both to its acceptance by Jews and Gentiles and to its initial sanction by Roman political power—for a while, anyway.

Three communities of people are woven together in the trial motif. First is the community of believers, although they are not mentioned directly in any of the trial settings. Paul is their representative and Luke's presence is clearly indicated by the fact that he records the details of what happened. Other believers are not specifically identified until Paul gets close to Rome after the harrowing journey by sea (28:14-15). Did James and the other elders visit Paul? Were they even able to do so? The record does not say, but one cannot help believing they were supportive (Jas. 2:17). It is as though they are sitting silently in the balcony section of a courtroom as their chief representative answers for them all.

Second is the Jewish community, increasingly hostile as they try again and again to eliminate the apostle—who was viewed as a great threat to their way of life. There are parallels between the treatment of Jesus and Paul, with the crowd rising up against Paul as they did against Jesus (Polhill, *Acts* 444). Even their cry of "away with such a fellow" (22:22) is basically the same as what they said about Jesus (Jn. 19:15). The

appearance before the Sanhedrin and the smiting of Paul is another parallel (Mt. 26:67), as are the trials before Roman procurators (governors) and yet another Herod.

The third community present is represented by the Roman authorities, and it is ironic that they continued to be friendly and often protective (Stott 335-336). The Roman tribune, Lysias, rescued Paul from certain death twice but embellished his report (23:27) to promote his own favor. A later centurion, Julius (27:1-3), treated Paul with courtesy, although he was a political prisoner. Julius even listened to Paul's advice (27:31, 42-43). The Roman procurators were not exactly paragons of justice, as Felix actively sought to be bribed (24:26). Both he and Festus bowed to political correctness in exacting justice (24:27; 25:9) and yet, in one sense, protected Paul from the intentions of the Sanhedrin. Roman protection would change soon enough, but in the Acts record the Roman authorities wielded the political power God providentially used to provide protection for the apostle and so to facilitate the spread of the gospel (1 Tim. 2:1-4). Had they not done so Paul would have been killed outright by the mob in Jerusalem.

A. Meeting With James and the elders at Jerusalem (21:17-26)

17 And when we were come to Jerusalem, the brethren received us gladly.
18 And the *day* following Paul went in with us unto James; and all the elders were present.
19 And when he had saluted them, he declared particularly what

things God had wrought among the Gentiles by his ministry.

20 And when they heard *it*, they glorified the Lord, and said unto him, Thou seest, brother, how many thousands of Jews there are which believe; and they are all zealous of the law:

21 And they are informed of thee, that thou teachest all the Jews which are among the Gentiles to forsake Moses, saying that they ought not to circumcise *their* children, neither to walk after the customs.

22 What is it therefore? The multitude must needs come together: for they will hear that thou art come.

23 Do therefore this that we say to thee: We have four men which have a vow on them;

24 Them take, and purify thyself with them, and be at charges with them, that they may shave *their* heads: and all may know that those things, whereof they were informed concerning thee, are nothing; but *that* thou thyself also walkest orderly, and keepest the law.

25 As touching the Gentiles which believe, we have written *and* concluded that they observe no such thing, save only that they keep themselves from *things* offered to idols, and from blood, and from strangled, and from fornication.

26 Then Paul took the men, and the next day purifying himself with them entered into the Temple, to signify the accomplishment of the days of purification, until that an offering should be offered for every one of them.

It appears that none of the other apostles were in Jerusalem at the time, since James and the elders are the only leaders named in meeting with Paul (E. F. Harrison 325). Their reception of him included rejoicing over the reports of the great accomplishments in Paul's ministry among the Gentiles (vv. 17-19). Schnabel (871), in an unnecessary criticism, suggests that Luke omitted any reference to the presentation and reception of the offering that Paul and his companions brought, and that he forgot because the imprisonment of Paul overshadowed everything else. Luke did not include a lot of details, but we wish he had. We assume the Holy Spirit's inspiration of Acts; consequently, the matter of the offering was apparently deemed to be a detail not needed in the account. However, the offering was such an important part of the trip to Jerusalem that it could easily have been one reason for the glad reception of the missionary team (v. 17). Further, Paul confirms later (24:17) that he did bring the money with him; and that is part of Luke's account, after all.

With the good news of Paul's report, however, there were some reservations about trouble that could arise when others found out he was in Jerusalem (v. 20). Though the person saying this is not named, one assumes he was James (Polhill, *Acts* 446; Bock 645), since he refers to the counsel he had given at the Jerusalem conference (v. 25). Schnabel disagrees (872-873). It is clear that the advice given to Paul about his actions in Jerusalem had been considered before he arrived. That counsel took in consideration the presumptions of the believing Jews who had serious reservations and misunderstandings about what exactly Paul believed and taught regarding Jewish customs of law-keeping. It also showed that James understood Paul's position about keeping those customs, as verse 24 clearly indicates. We need to remember that Paul had shaved his head (18:18) on the second missionary journey in keeping a vow (probably the Nazarite vow) and had completed its observation in Jerusalem. I think it can be safely assumed that when Paul went up to Jerusalem at the conclusion of the second missionary journey, he would have visited with James, who would have personally witnessed Paul's practice. This demonstrated what he had previously stated about his personal commitment in keeping Jewish customs (1 Cor. 9:20-22).

James, now, candidly addresses the reality of the situation they all were facing. Even though the ones from whom James anticipated criticism were believing Jews, i.e. Christians (v. 20), they were still Jews whose cultural identity was tied to the customs of the Law and were very zealous in keeping them. In particular, they were very concerned about circumcision, the identifying sign of God's covenant with Abraham. They were under the impression that Paul was teaching other believing *Jews*, in the mixed Gentile-Jew community of Christians, that it was no longer necessary to practice circumcision (v. 21). Paul, indeed, had taught that circumcision was unnecessary for saving faith (Rom. 4:9-12; Gal. 5:6, 6:15), but there is no evidence he advised abandoning the practice among *Jews* as part of their "Jewishness." One could practice circumcision but not look upon it as a condition for salvation in Christ. In fact, he himself made sure of its practice among Jews when necessary (16:3; 1 Cor. 7:18-19).

James now advises Paul to demonstrate his Jewishness to these brothers who will observe for themselves what Paul believes and the false rumors will be put to rest (v. 24). Paul is counseled to again shave his head along with four other men (Christian Jews?) and follow the customs of the vow. His practice and association with these brothers should convince those who had questions about Paul's true position. Opinions vary about just what the vow is. Polhill (*Acts* 448-449), Schnabel (876), and Keener (III:3135-3139) agree it is the Nazarite vow. Marshall (*Acts* 345-346), Barrett (*Acts* 331-332), and Bock (647-648) do not think so but point to ceremonial purifying to enter the Temple. Either is possible, but the main point is that Paul was willing to demonstrate his own practice of the Law for the occasion.

Referencing the conclusion of the Jerusalem Council (v. 25), James makes it clear that he is still in agreement with those decrees for Gentile believers. In doing so, he differentiates between Gentile and Jewish believers and their respective practices regarding the Law. The repetition here solidifies the ongoing acceptance of that decision some years previously and shows that it was still the standard for the relationship.

The counsel of James itself was wise enough and certainly included all the necessary elements to consider. Because of that, and the fact that he had come to celebrate Pentecost (20:16), Paul took the advice given (v. 26) and began the process of purification with the four men. The rituals included entering the Temple for an offering and sacrifice to signify completion. All seemed well enough—but one can never predict how people will react in any given situation.

303

In an interesting twist, Stott (339-340) proposes that Luke is showing that some serious conflicts existed between Paul and James, that they believed different gospels and thus "two Christianities." Stott surmises that James believed in salvation by works (Jas. 2:14-26) and Paul taught salvation by grace (Eph. 2:8-9). These were two means of becoming Christians. Further, the advice by James and acceptance by Paul were due to their "conciliatory frame of mind." This view shows both a misunderstanding of James' view of saving faith (2:14-26) and a discounting of the history of these men in ministry together. Furthermore, it disregards the doctrinal conclusions previously reached at the Jerusalem Conference (15:11-19).

It should be noted that not all believing Jews were enlightened to the developing body of Christian truth, especially as written by the apostle Paul. In particular Romans, 1 Corinthians, and Galatians, which address this very issue, had been written but might not have been read and taught to them. Therefore, it is entirely likely that they had not yet merged O. T. Messianic theology with its N. T. ramifications. This may have contributed to the false assumptions by Christian Jews. Nor is this to say that Christian Jews were the ones responsible for the riot that would soon ensue. It was sparked by "the Jews of Asia" (v. 27; 24:18). I will say more about this below.

As for James, from whom we never hear again in Acts, his position and influence are established in both the Scriptures and secular history. Josephus (*Antiquities* XX.IX.1) records his death at the hands of the high priest, Ananus, at a politically opportune time after

Festus (24:27) died. His death would have been in A.D. 62 not long after Paul's imprisonments began.

B. The Riot Over Paul in the Temple (21:27-40a)

1. Paul accosted and beaten by the mob (21:27-30)

27 And when the seven days were almost ended, the Jews which were of Asia, when they saw him in the temple, stirred up all the people, and laid hands on him,
28 Crying out, Men of Israel, help: This is the man, that teacheth all *men* every where against the people, and the law, and this place: and further brought Greeks also into the temple, and hath polluted this holy place.
29 (For they had seen before with him in the city Trophimus an Ephesian, whom they supposed that Paul had brought into the temple.)
30 And all the city was moved, and the people ran together: and they took Paul, and drew him out of the temple: and forthwith the doors were shut.

Rituals of purification were required on the third and seventh days (Num. 19:12). All had gone well for the first few days of Paul's vow as, apparently, he had gone unrecognized in the crowd. But as he neared the end of his commitment, he was spotted by "the Jews of Asia" (v. 27). These Jews would have come to Jerusalem from Ephesus for the Pentecost festival, just as Paul had. They would have readily known him for he had spent at least three years there

(20:31) and disputed with them over the gospel. They might have been the very ones who forced him and the other believers from the synagogue to the nearby school of Tyrannus (19:9). Robertson (*Acts* 376) suggests that the same Alexander of the Ephesian riot (19:33), who had caused Paul such grief (2 Tim. 4:14), might have instigated this uproar in Jerusalem. While speculative, of course, there are enough similarities to make this view plausible, especially since Paul made a direct reference later to "certain Jews of Asia" (24:18).

Perhaps these Asian Jews remembered how Paul had gotten away at Ephesus, so they seized him roughly as they yelled for others to help (v. 28). "This is the man," they shouted, as they made serious accusations that were charged with enough emotion to incite a mob reaction. The accusations were two-fold. One, they claimed he taught against the Jews, the Law, and the Temple (see above for his teaching and personal practice). Marshall (*Acts* 347) comments on the irony of this accusation, given that Paul was in process of purification in order *not* to defile the Temple. It is also ironic that these accusations were similar to those Saul of Tarsus would have lodged against Stephen (6:9-14). If this accusation did not stir them up sufficiently the next one did.

The second accusation is that Paul had brought a Gentile into the Temple itself and violated all that was sacred. That this was a trumped-up charge of guilt by association meant nothing. They had seen Paul in the city, earlier, with Trophimus whom they recognized from Ephesus (v. 29), and they had jumped to the conclusion that Paul had taken him into the Temple. That charge was a total

fabrication, but truth means nothing when there are ulterior motives.

The boundaries for Gentile access to the Temple were clearly established, with warning stones placed at intervals (Polhill, *Acts* 452; Keener III:3147-3149). Though the original instructions for the Temple had not included an outer court for Gentiles (1 Kgs. 8:41-43), the access of Gentiles had become so severely restricted, by Paul's day, that breaches were regarded as life and death situations.

These charges were sufficient to incite the sizeable crowd and turn them into a mob. Paul was dragged from an inner Temple area to one of the outer courts and the gates to the Temple itself were slammed shut. This is the last reference to the Temple in the Acts narrative. Some writers (Polhill, *Acts* 453; Bock 652) see something of a symbolism in the event. Polhill asks, "Is this symbolic that with this final refusal of God's messenger the Temple was forever closed to God's purposes?"

The trouble that James had suspicioned (vv. 20-22) had come about, but probably not from those he was concerned about. The previous warnings that the Holy Spirit and others had communicated to Paul were coming to pass. Of course Luke writes in retrospect but as the events unfolded he must have been overwhelmed with the scope of what was taking place. One can imagine that Paul's companions and the Jerusalem church began praying for him just as they had done for Peter (12:5). Except for brief meetings with believers once they arrived on the Italian peninsula, there are no believers mentioned in any of the trial/defense scenes from here to the end of Acts. That does not mean there were none who had access to him, but Paul is clearly the central figure who represents Christianity on trial. When one considers the content of his defenses, and his demeanor and self-control when his life was at stake, it must be concluded that he acquitted himself well.

2. Paul rescued by the Roman guard (21:31-40a)

**31 And as they went about to kill him, tidings came unto the chief captain of the band, that all Jerusalem was in an uproar.
32 Who immediately took soldiers and centurions, and ran down unto them: and when they saw the chief captain and the soldiers, they left beating of Paul.
33 Then the chief captain came near, and took him, and commanded** *him* **to be bound with two chains; and demanded who he was, and what he had done.
34 And some cried one thing, some another, among the multitude: and when he could not know the certainty for the tumult, he commanded him to be carried into the castle.
35 And when he came upon the stairs, so it was, that he was borne of the soldiers for the violence of the people.
36 For the multitude of the people followed after, crying, Away with him.
37 And as Paul was to be led into the castle, he said unto the chief captain, May I speak unto thee? Who said, Canst thou speak Greek?
38 Art thou not that Egyptian, which before these days madest an uproar, and leddest out into the wilderness four thousand men that were murderers?
39 But Paul said, I am a man** *which am* **a Jew of Tarsus,** *a city* **in Cilicia, a citizen of no mean city: and, I beseech thee, suffer me to speak unto the people.
40a And when he had given him licence, Paul stood on the stairs, and beckoned with the hand unto the people.**

Because Jerusalem was often a political powder-keg with the fuse lit, a cohort of soldiers was stationed there. A cohort consisted of a thousand men with seven hundred and sixty infantry and two hundred and forty cavalry (23:23). A tribune (Latin *tribunus militum*) was over the cohort, with centurions under him. These were charged with keeping the peace at any cost. They were garrisoned in the "castle" (v. 34), also known as the Fortress of Antonia. This structure was built by Herod the Great for the defense of the Temple. It was located on the northwest corner of the wall that surrounded the Temple complex and overlooked the entire area. Stairs led to the Fortress directly from the court of the Gentiles (Polhill, *Acts* 453; Keener III:3161-3163; Bock 652-653).

Luke is absolutely sure the mob would have killed Paul had not the Roman soldiers rescued him (v. 31). With their vantage point in the Fortress of Antonia, the noise and commotion of the mob would have put the soldiers on alert. The beating of Paul would have been quickly spotted and men immediately dispatched. The stairs gave easy access to the area where the commotion was, so they arrived post haste and none too soon. The "chief captain" (Greek *chiliarch*, for "tribune"), Claudius

Lysias (23:26), dispatched at least two centuries of men (v. 32) and led them himself to the scene. The arrival of two hundred armed soldiers who would have been totally intolerant of any resistance quickly quelled the crowd, which immediately ceased beating Paul (v. 32). The crowd would have moved back as the soldiers formed ranks around the man being beaten. In yet another irony, the Jews for whom Paul's heart yearned (Rom. 9:1-5) rejected him and the gospel (Jn. 1:11), while Roman power protected him. That would change soon enough, however.

Securing Paul with two chains of manacles (v. 33), probably hooked to a soldier on either side, the tribune demanded explanation of who the beaten man was and what was his crime? He might as well have asked the wind, for the answers he got were worthless (v. 34). His decision was to secure Paul as a prisoner in the "castle" until he could get the story straight. More important for him, peace was restored. The prophecy of Agabus (21:11) had begun to be fulfilled.

The beating of Paul had left him weak and unable to ascend the stairs on his own strength. He might also have been encumbered by the chains if they were bound to his ankles as well. He was assisted by the soldiers up the stairs (v. 35). Seeing him being escorted away, the crowd found its voice again, hoarsely calling for Paul's death—as intended by the phrase "away with him" (v. 36). It was a motto of madness! The same was said to the Lord Jesus (Lk. 23:18).

Just as Paul was about to be taken into the "castle" (v. 37), with polite and polished Greek he requested the right to speak to the tribune. Taken somewhat aback when he heard a familiar lan-

guage, the captain responded rhetorically (it was obvious Paul could speak Greek!). With that the captain disclosed (v.38) that he thought Paul was an Egyptian rebel who had recently caused a stir (Keener III:3172-3178). Josephus alludes to this particular Egyptian revolutionary but with his usual exaggerated numbers of thirty thousand (*Wars* II.XIII.5). Lysias put the number at four thousand. Festus had put down the rebellion, but the Egyptian leader had escaped. Lysias presumed the man he had arrested was this rebel terrorist.

Paul quickly dispels the idea with a brief resumé of his background for the purpose of putting some definition on exactly who he is and is not (v. 39). He is a Jew from Tarsus of Cilicia, a city of significance ("no mean city") and a citizen of that city. (He is not referring to his Roman citizenship at this point.) With that he presses his desire to speak to the people. His answer has conveyed to Lysias that, as a Jew, he can communicate with the people, and that, with his manner, he is not there to incite a riot. Perhaps from curiosity, perhaps from courtesy, perhaps thinking it might silence and bring some order to the crowd, Lysias consents to give Paul an opportunity to speak. Waving his hand for attention, Paul positions himself to speak (v. 40a).

One can easily picture the scene. The crowd filling the Gentile court area, restrained by the Roman soldiers standing in rank, and now growing silent as Paul beckons with a hand to be heard. Paul, standing at the top of the stairs, beaten, bloody, disheveled, and looking down on the crowd, but courageously wanting to speak words of explanation and witness to those who had just tried to kill him. Two hundred Roman soldiers positioned defensively and ready to take action if necessary. Again, one has to admire and respect the resilience of the Apostle Paul. One has to revere the fact that only God could have so worked to provide such an opportunity for Paul (Rom. 8:28). Paul's testimony is that of one man but representative of Christianity and what could be for all of Israel.

C. Paul's Defense Before the Temple Mob (21:40b—22:21)

1. His appeal to be heard (21:40b—22:2)

40b And when there was made a great silence, he spake unto *them* in the Hebrew tongue saying,
1 Men, brethren, and fathers, hear ye my defence *which I make* now unto you.
2 (And when they heard that he spake in the Hebrew tongue to them, they kept the more silence: and he saith,)

The chapter break here is unfortunate, as indicated by the punctuation and shift in the narrative. The fact that not only was Paul given an opportunity to speak to the crowd, but also that they grew silent is significant. Mobs are not easily squelched. It is not necessary to suggest that Luke constructed this account, showing a hero figure rising to the occasion after being beaten within an inch of his life (Haenchen 630-631; Fitzmyer 703). Stranger things have happened throughout history. Besides, Paul was incredibly resilient (16:23-40; 20:11-13).

It was not the gesture (21:40) that silenced the crowd but the fact that Paul

was speaking in Hebrew. Some commentators believe the language was actually Aramaic, a form of Hebrew most commonly spoken in Judaea at the time. Others suggest it was actually Hebrew, the language of the O. T. (Keener III: 3191-3195). Hebrew was formally learned and used in the study of the Torah in more restricted educational settings. More likely, Paul was speaking in Aramaic since all Jews present would readily understand it. That Paul was fluent in at least three languages (Greek, Hebrew, Aramaic) speaks to his learning.

Paul uses the word "defence" (Greek *apologia*, whence our "apology" and "apologetics") to describe his testimony. In this case, the word means "to defend one's self; to make good his cause" (Thayer 65). That's exactly what Paul is doing, defending not only his personal actions but also the larger understanding of Christianity as the fulfillment of O. T. Judaism. Haenchen (631) is correct when he says (regarding Paul's defense): "Then there is no fundamental gulf between Judaism and Christianity, the continuity between the two is unbroken, and Christianity can claim to be tolerated like Judaism." In this sense, all of Paul's testimonies during the following trials are apologetics for Christianity.

2. His life before conversion to Christ (22:3-5)

3 I am verily a man *which am* a Jew, born in Tarsus, *a city* in Cilicia, yet brought up in this city at the feet of Gamaliel, *and* taught according to the perfect manner of the law of the fathers, and was zealous toward God, as ye all are this day.

4   And I persecuted this way unto the death, binding and delivering into prisons both men and women. 5   As also the high priest doth bear me witness, and all the estate of the elders: from whom also I received letters unto the brethren, and went to Damascus, to bring them which were there bound unto Jerusalem, for to be punished.

Paul does not reference his life prior to his conversion merely to provide biographical information. He intends to establish a point of reference to show the things he has in common with all those to whom he is speaking, as well as to show that the change in his life was in total contrast to his former lifestyle. In doing so we see confirmation of several details we already know about him as well as a couple of additional ones. Some of these details would have been known by some in the crowd.

Representatively, before his conversion to Christ, Paul personified Judaism. He was formally trained by one of the best instructors of the day, Gamaliel (5:34-39). He was thoroughly immersed in the study and practice of the Law just like those who were listening to him. From these sources he had learned the jaded Judaism that prevailed when John the Baptist and the Lord Jesus came along. Like the Judaism of the Pharisees and Sadducees of the N. T., he participated in every possible attempt to eradicate Jesus of Nazareth and His followers (those of "this way"). Here Paul confirms that he saw Christians as threats to Judaism and worthy of arrest, imprisonment, and death. Furthermore, he announces that he was appointed with legal authority by the high priest and high court to arrest and punish believ-

ers, and that he had pressed those efforts all the way to Damascus (v. 5). The high priest could vouch for what Paul was saying, if he would.

3. His conversion to Christ (22:6-16)

6   And it came to pass, that, as I made my journey, and was come nigh unto Damascus about noon, suddenly there shone from heaven a great light round about me. 7   And I fell unto the ground, and heard a voice saying unto me, Saul, Saul, why persecutest thou me? 8   And I answered, Who art thou, Lord? And he said unto me, I am Jesus of Nazareth, whom thou persecutest. 9   And they that were with me saw indeed the light, and were afraid; but they heard not the voice of him that spake to me. 10 And I said, What shall I do, LORD? And the Lord said unto me, Arise, and go into Damascus; and there it shall be told thee of all things which are appointed for thee to do. 11 And when I could not see for the glory of that light, being led by the hand of them that were with me, I came into Damascus. 12 And one Ananias, a devout man according to the law, having a good report of all the Jews which dwelt *there*, 13 Came unto me, and stood, and said unto me, Brother Saul, receive thy sight. And the same hour I looked up upon him. 14 And he said, The God of our fathers hath chosen thee, that thou

shouldest know his will, and see that Just One, and shouldest hear the voice of his mouth.

15 For thou shalt be his witness unto all men of what thou hast seen and heard.

16 And now why tarriest thou? arise, and be baptized, and wash away thy sins, calling on the name of the Lord.

The original version of the conversion of Saul of Tarsus (9:1-19) was told by Luke in the third person. Here, Paul uses first person language as he tells the story himself. Most of this is the same in the retelling, both here and later (26:9-18), but with some details added and/or clarified. For example, we learn that the encounter with Jesus took place "about noon" (26:13). Also, the light that appeared is differentiated from the noon day sun. It did not just shine on Paul but on the whole company (26:13); but he was the only one blinded (v. 11). Here is a reference to the unique Shekinah light of the presence of the almighty God (Ex. 3:2; 13:21-22; 2 Chron. 5:13-14). That Jesus is God in flesh is theologically accurate, but note that He referenced His humanity to Paul in identifying himself as "Jesus of Nazareth" (v. 8). As Bruce (*Acts* 416) observes, this is the only one of the three testimonies of Paul's conversion that includes this self-identification of Jesus.

Perhaps the most common question about the consistency of the three accounts relates to whether the others with Paul heard the voice from Heaven. The probable explanation is that they did hear the voice as a sound (Greek genitive in Acts 9:7) but only Paul heard it (Greek accusative in Acts 22:9) well enough to understand what was said. A number of interpreters make this point (Bock 660; Picirilli, *Paul* 44; Robertson, *Acts* 390; Marshall, *Acts* 355). That seems to be the case, especially in retrospect of the event. Though some try to find contradictions in these accounts, Picirilli (*Paul* 44) is correct in saying "the three accounts are not really discrepant."

The role Ananias of Damascus played in the conversion story (vv. 12-16) is shortened from its original (9:10-17). One must remember where Paul is and his circumstances as he tells this. In all likelihood, Luke gave us Ananias' personal recollection in the original incident, while here is Paul's recall. Both are consistent with what happened, but Paul adds a few details about Ananias, perhaps in compliment for his role in assisting the apostle. Paul adds that he was a very pious and dedicated man, who was well-known and respected among all the Jews in Damascus (v. 12). He was instrumental in the healing of Paul's eyesight (v. 13). He conveyed God's plan for Paul as he had been instructed (vv. 14-15). He baptized Paul (v. 16).

Ananias used an interesting expression in moving Paul to the next step of obedience as a new believer when he asked, "And why tarriest thou?" (v. 16). The words (Greek *ti melleis*) can mean either "why do you delay?" or "what are you going to do now?" The question can be understood as rhetorical (Schnabel 905) or reproachful (Marshall, *Acts* 357), but the idea is that it is time for Paul to take the next step in following the Lord. Ananias is urging Paul forward. He needed to be baptized and begin his life as a believer.

This last phrase "be baptized, and wash away thy sins, calling on the name of the Lord" is often used as a proof-text for baptismal regeneration. There is no question that baptism was very important and in the Acts record practiced immediately after conversion, as it should continue to be today. Baptism pictures the entire salvation model of Christ's death, burial, and resurrection and the believer's identification with Him in that experience via saving faith (Rom. 6:3-6). Rightly practiced and understood, baptism is a powerful Christian symbol and ritual of all that is meant by authentic saving faith. It should never be devalued or marginalized in the believer's life. But neither water nor the ritual washes away sin. It is the Lord Himself who alone has that power (Mk. 2:7-10; Rom. 10:9-10) and that is the focus of the phrase "calling on the name of the Lord" (v. 16).

4. His vision in Jerusalem and commission from the Lord (22:17-21)

17 And it came to pass, that, when I was come again to Jerusalem, even while I prayed in the temple, I was in a trance;
18 And say him saying unto me, Make haste, and get thee quickly out of Jerusalem: for they will not receive thy testimony concerning me.
19 And I said, Lord, they know that I imprisoned and beat in every synagogue them that believed on thee:
20 And when the blood of thy martyr Stephen was shed, I also was standing by, and consenting unto his death, and kept the raiment of them that slew him.

21 And he said unto me, Depart: for I will send thee far hence unto the Gentiles.

We are aware of Paul's first visit to Jerusalem following his conversion (9:26-27; Gal. 1:18) but here is the first time we are informed of the vision he had while he was there. The vision occurred while Paul was in the Temple, and he mentions it here at least partly because he has been accused of defiling the Temple (21:28). For all Christian Jews in the early days of the N. T. era, there was a time of trying to understand the integration of the gospel with the practices of Judaism as they knew it. The disciples in Jerusalem used the Temple areas to teach and minister (chs. 1-6). This did not cease until the Temple was destroyed in A.D. 70.

In the vision Paul encountered the Lord. He saw Him and heard His voice, informing him that he should leave Jerusalem quickly, for his witness there (at that time) would not be accepted (vv. 17-18). Paul responded in protest (vv. 19-20).

In recounting his actions prior to his conversion, Paul is making the argument that he was well-known for these actions. Something powerful had to happen for him to become a believer. That was something only God could bring about; therefore, they ought to listen to him. The vision experience should reinforce the fact of divine intervention in his life. He himself had once stood where they now stand in relation to the followers of Jesus. If they would hear his testimony and be open to its truth, they would think differently, too. But our hopes often exceed reality.

The visionary experience is similar to others, like Moses (Ex. 3:2—4:17) and

311

Isaiah (Isa. 6:1-13). Theirs and Paul's involved a personal, private encounter with the living God. He informed them of His will concerning them, which included rejection by the people to whom they were sent. Those called by God in this way protested (meekly), as if they knew better than God (Polhill, *Acts* 462). Our personal plans often seem better than God's plans. Such is the limitation of our understanding.

Paul's reference to Stephen is significant in a number of ways (v. 20). It is prefaced by Paul's recounting how he pressed the issue against the believers in the synagogues. It was there he would have encountered Stephen and could not win the argument (6:8-14), so he had joined with others to have him killed. Paul confesses his complicity in the matter with a graphic depiction of the shed blood of Stephen as a martyr, of his own personal consent, and of his participation in his death by stoning. One cannot help wondering if the memory still haunted him.

The Lord's response to Paul's protest was direct and sharp: "Depart" (Greek imperative, "Go"). The idea is that he was to obey the Lord's direction without further delay. The Lord had already told him that his witness in Jerusalem would not be received (v. 18). To stay would be fruitless. His work lay in a totally different direction. Until that point, his witness had only been to Jews. God's design for him was to carry the gospel to the Gentiles (v. 21). These are the very words spoken to him by the Lord. We can be sure these words had echoed in his mind repeatedly since that day in the Temple. Paul now rehearses this vivid calling in speaking to the crowd at the Temple. His ministry as apostle to the Gentiles (Eph. 3:1-7; 1 Tim. 2:7) was

specifically given him by the Lord. That calling was an integral part of his commission as a witness (1:8), and it included his proclamation of the gospel and his writing of the major portion of the N. T.

Here is Paul's first personal testimony about his conversion. Its factualness stands in harmony with Luke's record of it (9:1-19) and Paul's testimony given later (26:1-18). I am of the opinion that Acts is not the only record where he recalls his experience. It appears to me that Romans 7:7-25 is, also, autobiographical insofar as Paul details further his inner struggles with the demands of the O. T. Law and the guilt it engendered (for an overview see Forlines, *Romans* 169-171). It may, in fact, be a key to understanding what Jesus said to him in the phrase "It is hard for thee to kick against the pricks" (Acts 9:5).

To understand the radical change in Paul's life when he met Christ, we must understand the extent to which he considered himself to be blameless in his zeal to keep the Law (Phil. 3:6). Blameless does not mean sinless, as he himself confesses in Romans 7:7. Paul details that the Law brought the knowledge of sin that produced guilt and condemnation (Rom. 7:7, 13) as well as a hopeless death (Rom. 7:8-9, 11). These were indeed the "pricks" of conscience prodded by the righteousness of the Law and the conviction of the Holy Spirit. His inward struggles were all the more intensified when he heard the gospel of Christ and its reward of justification probably from Stephen in the synagogue debates (6:9-10). In this regard, Paul stood in direct contrast with the testimony and message of Stephen as well as those he persecuted in his mad pursuit against believers (Acts 22:19).

With deference toward those who differ, I am in agreement with Forlines (*Romans* 172) that the Romans text depicts the struggles of an unsaved person experiencing the condemnation of the Law. However, as much as the text may be autobiographical of Paul, there is a larger sense in which the same struggles of Paul personally were typical of all Jews who were zealous after the Law. Paul, in effect, is Israel. His testimony, in all it implies as to the time and place (near the Temple) where he gives it in Acts 22:1-21, is analogous to what should be the testimony of the covenant nation of Israel. Indeed, Paul claimed that his conversion was to be a "pattern" (1 Tim. 1:16). Certainly, in this sense, he was the pattern of what should have been the vast majority acceptance of Jesus of Nazareth as the promised Messiah.

However, Paul's story is conflicted as was that of the Jews. Jesus "came unto His own and His own received Him not" (Jn. 1:11). Many did receive Him but most did not. Paul was the recipient of God's boundless mercy (1 Tim. 1:13), as are we all, in that God has historically been patient and merciful with Israel. Perhaps that is one reason Paul was so intent on preaching the gospel to "the Jew first" (Rom. 1:16).

Summary
(21:17—22:21)

The long journey from Ephesus to Jerusalem was finally completed. It had included a change in plans, when they learned of a plot against Paul (20:3), and stops to encourage believers at Troas and Miletus. Paul's speech to the Ephesian elders was something of a farewell speech, but it was filled with spiritual counsel to prepare them for leadership. In every city, the Holy Spirit had repeatedly warned Paul of trials ahead when he got to Jerusalem. However, he did not regard the warnings as preventative but preparatory in nature. Even as he shared this with others along the way, he was not deterred from his mission—even if it meant laying down his life for Christ. Even his fellow-laborers came to concede the point and committed Paul's safe keeping to the Lord.

Paul was accompanied by several fellow-laborers who had borne the burdens and victories of the ministry. They carried with them a much-needed offering from the Pauline churches for the suffering saints in Judaea.

Upon arrival in Jerusalem, they were welcomed with open arms. The church there rejoiced in the reports of the successful witness of the gospel. However, the leaders in Jerusalem had discerned potential trouble, growing out of a misunderstanding on the part of some Jewish believers about Paul's practice in regard to the correlation of the gospel and the Law. They advised Paul to address this problem by joining in with others in a certain vow that was accompanied by ceremonial cleansing and offerings in the Temple. To this Paul readily agreed and went about the observance.

But all went sideways when enemies of the gospel from Asia (Ephesus) saw Paul in the Temple and incited a riot against him. He was almost beaten to death in one of the court areas of the Temple but was rescued by the Roman soldiers who happened to be stationed nearby. As he was being dragged from the area and taken into custody, Paul succeeded in getting permission to speak (from the stairway) to the crowd below that had just tried to kill him. His intention was not to hurl angry vindictive words back to them but to tell his story—the story of how he had once stood where they did in belief and practice. He was one of them. But he encountered the living Messiah, who changed his life and commissioned him to carry the gospel to the Gentiles.

Application: Teaching and Preaching the Passage

Exegetical Outline of the Text: 1. Report to James and the Elders in Jerusalem (21:17-20a). 2. Counsel and Recommendation to Paul About Potential Conflicts (21:20b-26). 3. Accusation and Assault of Paul in the Temple Court (21:27-30). 4. Rescue by the Roman Soldiers (21:31-40a). 5. Paul's Testimony to the Crowd in the Temple Court (21:40b—22:21).

With the completion of the third missionary journey and arrival in Jerusalem, the Acts narrative shifts to the six testimonial trials of the apostle, finally culminating with the extended and detailed story of the journey to Rome. Teaching and preaching the text must include the specific places and people where his testimony was given. The first testimonial was given before the Jewish crowd in the Temple court area, as recorded in this passage.

Paul's main defense was his personal testimony of his life before his conversion, his encounter with the living Christ, and the Lord's calling on his life. Luke records this three times, and it is an excellent model to study carefully. One's testimony is, in fact, the best witness (or should be) of his Christian life. It is important, therefore, that believers take time to think through the key elements of their conversion to Christ and be able to succinctly and clearly tell about it when appropriate.

The theme of the providence of God is especially clear, as God's hand of guidance and protection are revealed time and again. This can be seen in this text with the presence of the Roman soldiers who quickly came to Paul's rescue and the openness of the Roman tribune to Paul's questions.

Paul's personal observance of the Law raises the issue of how believers today are to understand the O. T. law. It is clear that the law was never meant to be the means of salvation but serves as "a schoolmaster to bring us to Christ" (Gal. 3:24). This will entail examining texts from Paul's writings, especially Romans, Galatians, and 1 Corinthians. There are cultural practices, however, that do not violate redemptive principles.

D. Paul's Exchange With the Roman tribune (22:22-29)

22 And they gave him audience unto this word, and *then* lifted up their voices, and said, Away with such a *fellow* from the earth: for it is not fit that he should live.
23 And as they cried out, and cast off *their* clothes, and threw dust into the air,
24 The chief captain commanded him to be brought into the castle, and bade that he should be examined by scourging; that he might know wherefore they cried so against him.
25 And as they bound him with thongs, Paul said unto the centurion that stood by, Is it lawful for

you to scourge a man that is a Roman, and uncondemned?

26 When the centurion heard *that,* he went and told the chief captain, saying, Take heed what thou doest: for this man is a Roman.

27 Then the chief captain came, and said unto him, Tell me, art thou a Roman? He said, Yea.

28 And the chief captain answered, With a great sum obtained I this freedom. And Paul said, But I was *free* born.

29 Then straightway they departed from him which should have examined him: and the chief captain also was afraid, after he knew that he was a Roman, and because he had bound him.

At the mention of the word "Gentiles," the crowd found its voice again, shouting the same mantra of madness for Paul's death (21:36; 22:22). It is not exactly clear just what is meant by the phrase "cast off their clothes" (v. 23). It probably involved taking off the outer cloak, perhaps as an expression of stoning (7:58; 22:20) and symbolically shaking them out as if to shake off the very sound of the words (Bock 663-664; Polhill, *Acts* 464). It could also be an expression of rejection (18:6). Perhaps all of the above was intended. They also threw handfuls of dust in the air, symbolizing the removal of the very dirt tainted by blasphemy where they had walked. These were gestures of outrage (Keener III:3244-3245).

With that the tribune has had enough! The raucous actions and words of the religious crowd make little sense to him. Not only is the crowd getting out of control, but also he has not learned what he needs to know about the man

under arrest. At his command, Paul is taken into the Fortress and prepared for scourging (Greek *mastix*, whipping). This is the same form of punishment given to Jesus (Jn. 19:1). In Paul's case, captain Lysias intended the scourging as a means of extracting the truth from him by torture (vv. 24-25).

In the phrase "bound him with thongs," the word thongs (Greek *himasin*) might mean either thongs (like cords) with which he was bound (if the Greek case is instrumental) or the thongs (that is, the strips of the whip) with which he was to be beaten (if the Greek case is dative). Either is possible, and either would make sense in the situation. Regardless, as Paul was being "stretched forward" on the whipping post, he spoke to the centurion in charge (v. 25). With something of a rhetorical question, Paul informed him that a Roman citizen was not to be treated in such a manner.

Picirilli (*Paul* 13) lists four privileges of Roman citizenship. One, a person could not be condemned or punished without a fair hearing. Two, he could not be scourged. Three, he could appeal his case to the emperor himself. Four, there were certain exemptions from taxes. Three of these privileges come into play in the imprisonment accounts in Acts.

Some commentators raise the question why Paul waited until this moment to appeal to his rights as a Roman citizen. However, it seems obvious that Paul did not have a martyr spirit. Meekly submitting to unlawful torture would benefit no one, especially himself. Besides, the physical impact of such a scourging could leave him crippled and unable to continue in ministry. Anyway, it is easy to see how the treatment he received from both the crowd and the soldiers would have clouded and confused the situation enough that only now was his appeal to citizenship possible and needed. The stark reality of the scourging post, no doubt, galvanized him. For that matter, we should not rule out the Lord's prompting of his thoughts at the time (Lk. 12:11-12). In fact, Paul's clarity, courage, and content of truth in all these trial situations can easily demonstrate the inner influence of the Holy Spirit in his life.

Paul's appeal to his Roman citizenship rights brought an immediate halt to the intended torture. It also became the basis for the exchange that followed between the tribune and Paul. Immediately the centurion halted the intended scourging of Paul and went to update the tribune with this new information. His report to his superior officer was given in the form of a sharp warning ("take heed," v. 26). Violations like this could have serious consequences for all of them.

The tribune came to Paul and asked with incredulity (literally, "you are a Roman?!") if this was true. To which, of course, Paul replied in the affirmative. Then, proudly, the tribune informed Paul that his personal Roman citizenship had been bought with a lot of money. Polhill (*Acts* 465) suggests this remark might have been sarcastic. It is also to be noted that the tribune had probably recently purchased his citizenship, given the name he took, Claudius Lysias (23:26), after emperor Claudius. Citizenship could be purchased under the right circumstances. Paul's response was that his citizenship was his birthright.

Paul's city and province of origin (21:39) did not automatically qualify him for citizenship. How his family was granted this right is the source of much discussion (Polhill, Acts 465-466; Picirilli, *Paul* 11-13; Keener III:3255-3258). One likely scenario is that, given the prominence of his family in Tarsus, his father or grandfather had obtained this as a favor from a Roman nobleman for services rendered (Ramsay, *Traveller* 32).

The tribune's assessment of Paul kept changing—from a supposed rebel Egyptian (21:38), to a Jew who spoke fluent Aramaic and polished Greek (21:39), to a free-born Roman citizen (22:27). It appears that he was perplexed as to what to do with his prisoner. At any rate, he was afraid he might already have gone too far in binding him unlawfully (v. 29). But there was still the matter of accusations against Paul that had to be determined. The situation was far from over.

E. Paul's Testimony Before the Sanhedrin (22:30—23:11)

1. Confrontation with the high priest (22:30—23:5)

30 On the morrow, because he would have known the certainty wherefore he was accused of the Jews, he loosed him for *his* bands, and commanded the chief priests and all their council to appear, and brought Paul down, and set him before them.
23:1 And Paul, earnestly beholding the council, said, Men *and* brethren, I have lived in all good conscience before God until this day.

2 And the high priest Ananias commanded them that stood by him to smite him on the mouth.
3 Then said Paul unto him, God shall smite thee, *thou* whited wall: for sittest thou to judge me after the law, and commandest me to be smitten contrary to the law?
4 And they that stood by said, Revilest thou God's high priest?
5 Then said Paul, I wist not, brethren, that he was the high priest: for it is written, Thou shalt not speak evil of the ruler of thy people.

Again, the chapter break is unfortunate. The time and setting shift to the next day and a called meeting of the Jewish high court, the Sanhedrin. We are not told where exactly the meeting was held, but it was not in the Fortress (23:10). Marshall (*Acts* 360) comments that there is scarcely a passage in Acts whose historicity has been so strongly questioned. The reasons some question it are three. One, a Roman tribune had no right to call a meeting of the Jewish high court. Two, the Sanhedrin members were not present when Paul was being assaulted. Three, in the meeting itself Paul did not answer the charges against him. In fact, no charges were actually made by the court. Therefore, Haenchen (639-643) asserts that here is yet another event Luke constructed for his story.

However, the objections are easily answered by the reality of the situation. First, the tribune needed official reasons for the actions of the crowd against Paul if he was to hold him any longer. Paul was a Roman citizen and had rights that could not be violated. The meeting he called for was tantamount to a pre-trial

hearing to determine the exact charges. If, indeed, the members of the Sanhedrin were not present during the melee, they needed to know the charges as well. It must be remembered that a riot had broken out; it violated the civil peace and the Romans were not tolerant of such at all. If Paul was a threat to the peace, there had to be specific reasons to hold him. The high court might have been corrupt, but it was not foolish.

Second, since no official charges had been lodged against him, the gathering of the Sanhedrin presented an opportunity for Paul to announce the real reason for his treatment at the outset. This was a shrewd move on his part. If they managed to charge him with desecration of the Temple, as the Asian Jews had said (21:27-28), they could escalate this into reasons to have Paul killed. The Sanhedrin had a history of doing just this in relation to Jesus (Mt. 26:60-63) and Stephen (6:13-14). In fact, some on this very council were complicit in those situations. Paul himself knew about the charge against Stephen (22:20) and the potential actions of the high court.

Third, if the matter was to go forward legally, the uncertainty of the charges needed clarifying in the court itself. This could easily account for their acquiescing to the tribune's call for a meeting. It is not farfetched at all to believe the Sanhedrin welcomed the opportunity to meet. The situation required actions that exceeded normal protocol (Bock 668-669).

In a scene reminiscent of earlier trials before this court (4:1-21; 5:17-40; 6:15—7:57), Paul is arraigned (22:30). Although Luke might have condensed the account, it appears that Paul was the first to speak (23:1) as he observed the council. His statement is a shrewd comment intended to preempt the possible charge of desecrating the Temple. It is essentially the same statement he made at the beginning of his testimony before the crowd in the court (22:3-5). He had lived his life as a faithful Jew with all good conscience.

The manner in which he made the statement was, however, taken offensively by the high priest. He had Paul cuffed on the mouth for his verbal outburst (v. 2). The reaction of the high priest was quite "unprofessional" but indicative of both the tension of the situation and the character of Ananias (not to be confused with Annas, 4:6). Josephus (*Antiquities* XX.IX.1) described him as being insolent and temperamental, both confirmed here.

In what may be an expression of Paul's own temperament, his reply to being struck shows that he probably lost his temper momentarily at such treatment (v. 3). First, he called for God to send judgment on him and then defined his character. Paul's labeling the high priest as a "whited wall" is a thinly-veiled reference to Ezekiel 13:10 and the effort of false prophets to appear powerful. Ezekiel (and now Paul) alluded to the appearance of power to be like whitewashing a fence to strengthen it. He does justify his words by referencing a well-known Jewish proverb regarding being innocent before proven guilty (Lev. 19:15). As a highly trained Pharisee himself, Paul knew the Law at least as well, if not better, than Ananias, the Sadducee.

The flagrant action of the high priest in having Paul struck was bad enough, but Paul's outburst of calling for judgment on him ("God shall smite thee") brought rebuke from the other council members (v. 4). This rebuke was similar

to a call for order in a tense meeting. Their appeal was to respect the office held by the man. Sometimes the importance of the position exceeds the character of the person holding it.

It seems Paul gathered himself as he respectfully offered an apology (v. 5). His excuse was that he didn't recognize Ananias as the high priest. How it was possible that he did not is the stuff of discussions. Suggestions range from Paul's poor eyesight, to the high priest not being dressed in his official garments, to Paul's hasty, intemperate reaction, to a reply of irony that the command to strike him would not have come from the high priest. Any of these is possible, but I would suggest that one (or both) of the last two is more likely. It had been a tense exchange. Nor should we think that Paul's apology soothed things over. As the continuing story will show, Ananias was not placated. If anything, his anger was so fueled that he joined in a covert operation to kill Paul.

2. Paul's bold announcement leads to internal division on the Council (23:6-11)

**6 But when Paul perceived that the one part were Sadducees, and the other Pharisees, he cried out in the council, Men *and* brethren, I am a Pharisee, the son of a Pharisee: of the hope and resurrection of the dead I am called in question.
7 And when he had so said, there arose a dissension between the Pharisees and the Sadducees: and the multitude was divided.
8 For the Sadducees say that there is no resurrection, neither**

angel, nor spirit: but the Pharisees confess both.

9 And there arose a great cry: and the scribes *that were* of the Pharisees' part arose, and strove, saying, We find no evil in this man: but if a spirit or an angel hath spoken to him, let us not fight against God.

10 And where there arose a great dissension, the chief captain, fearing lest Paul should have been pulled in pieces of them, commanded the soldiers to go down, and to take him by force from among them, and to bring *him* into the castle.

11 And the night following the Lord stood by him, and said, Be of good cheer, Paul: for as thou hast testified of me in Jerusalem, so must thou bear witness also at Rome.

Paul's observation of the High Council (v. 6) confirmed that it was made up of two different groups with two different theological perspectives, Sadducees and Pharisees. Not only was Paul himself a Pharisee (Phil. 3:5), he saw how this theological difference could work to his advantage in the meeting. However, he did not merely mean what he said as a ploy to "divide and conquer." The ultimate reason for his being "on trial" was the encounter he had with the risen Jesus of Nazareth (22:6-8), which confirmed the truth of "the hope and resurrection of the dead." If he waited for them to drum up some other charges—desecrating the Temple, for example—he would be tried on a false charge. So, again with boldness, he spoke so all could hear that the real

reason for his being there was a matter of theology.

His statement had its intended effect (v. 7); the two groups quickly entered into a heated exchange between themselves over this point. Luke adds an interpretative statement (v. 8) to show why this generated such a division between them.

We are very familiar with these two groups for they are integral to the Gospel accounts of their encounters with Jesus. They are present to one extent or another from the beginning of the ministry of Jesus to His death and resurrection. They certainly have played an ongoing role in the Acts narrative with their opposition to the apostles and the early church (chs. 4-7). The High Council was made up of members of these two groups. The high priestly aristocracy, the Sadducees, made up the majority of the Council (TDNT VII:52-54). Luke asserts they did not believe in a "resurrection, neither angel, nor spirit." Their denial of the resurrection is well-attested (Mt. 22:23-32), but not so much their denial of angels and spirits. In fact, the Sadducees held to the authority of the Pentateuch, which affirms both. (It also affirms the resurrection, when we understand the argument of Jesus about the resurrection when He used Ex. 3:6 to prove that point.) How, then, are we to understand Luke's assertion that they denied angels and spirit? Commentators offer as many as six different explanations (Bock 671-672; Keener III:3291-3294). Most likely is that denying the resurrection, ipso facto, means there is no spiritual afterlife or spirit world where angels and the spirits of those who have died continue to exist (Bock 672). Thus, if existence ceases, there is no resurrection (4:1-2).

It is essentially a denial of the authority of the very Pentateuch they claimed to embrace, as Jesus had argued when He said, "Ye do err not knowing the Scriptures nor the power of God" (Mt. 22:29).

On the other hand, the Pharisees embraced all these as spiritual realities, "the Pharisees confess both" (Meyer 430; TDNT IX:45-46). Even with the differences, the theological gap between a Pharisee and Christian was not that wide. In fact, Paul himself is an example of a Pharisee whose core belief in the resurrection was verified with the appearance of Jesus to him. Interestingly, the gospel accounts do not portray either the Sadducees or the Pharisees in a favorable light, with a couple of individual exceptions (Jn. 3:1-2; 19:38). But Luke is more favorable to the Pharisees in the Acts narrative. This may be because of his relationship with Paul.

What began as a heated exchange between the Sadducees and Pharisees (v. 7) escalated even more into a "great cry" (Greek *krauge*, clamor) as they "strove" (Greek <u>diamachomai</u>, to fight fiercely) against each other (v. 9). The Pharisees became Paul's advocates regarding his spiritual experience. This does not mean they were arguing for the resurrection of Jesus and the integrity of the gospel; but, in effect, and perhaps even unwittingly, they were not far from that. They were clearly affirming Paul's innocence of anything worthy of conviction by the Council, a conclusion that would be agreed to in all the coming trials.

Apparently, Lysias and a garrison of soldiers were observing the actions of the Council as things got out of hand (v. 10). Lysias was looking for some formal charge that would explain the mob's previous actions and for which he could continue to hold Paul (22:30). He was still responsible for Paul and intervened again to rescue him from possibly being killed. He ordered his soldiers into the meeting and forcibly removed Paul from the Council, escorting him back to the Fortress of Antonia to be kept in protective custody.

Paul might have wondered how all of this would turn out as indicated by the vision he experienced the next night (v. 11). We are not told if this was a private revelation to Paul, but Luke was made privy to the experience and recorded it. With words of encouragement ("Be of good cheer"), the Lord appeared to Paul and reassured him of his faithful testimony in Jerusalem and the "witness" (1:8) he must bear in Rome. Implied, of course, is the fact that his work was not complete and his future was secured, at least until he could bear witness in Rome. It has been said that we are invincible in this life until the Lord is finished with us. The record in Acts does not look beyond this horizon.

F. The Murder Plot Against Paul (23:12-35)

1. The perpetrators and their plan (23:12-15)

12 And when it was day, certain of the Jews banded together, and bound themselves under a curse, saying that they would neither eat nor drink till they had killed Paul.
13 And they were more than forty which had made this conspiracy.
14 And they came to the chief priests and elders, and said, We have bound ourselves under a

great curse, that we will eat nothing until we have slain Paul.

15 Now therefore ye with the council signify to the chief captain that he bring him down unto you to morrow, as though ye would enquire something more perfectly concerning him: and we, or ever he come near, are ready to kill him.

Ironically, after the Lord gave Paul reassurance, Luke records the plot of some to murder him the next day. Heaven and hell are in battle over the witness of the apostle. The identity of the perpetrators is not given except that there were forty Jews who took a solemn oath to fast from food and drink until Paul was killed (vv. 12-13). When Paul learned of the plot, this word of reassurance from the Lord must have encouraged him.

As long as Paul was under protective custody, he was safe. The perpetrators needed to get him out in the open where they could get to him long enough to kill him. Three times they plainly stated their intention is to kill him (vv. 12, 14-15). To accomplish this they needed help, so they approached the leadership of the Sanhedrin with a proposal for them to call for another meeting with Paul to clarify the issue. More than likely only the Sadducee party of the council was involved in this plot, as the reaction on the previous day shows. The Pharisee party saw no reason to charge Paul, much less to kill him.

It is significant that the perpetrators were able to gain such quick and easy access to the chief priests. Apparently, these were not mere back-alley criminals who were willing to do anything for a price. They knew enough and were well-known enough to gain a hearing from the most powerful religious men in the land. The intent of the perpetrators was clearly stated (v. 15). While Paul was being escorted to the council by the Roman guard, they would attack him and kill him. This meant they were willing to sacrifice their own lives in the process, for the Romans would certainly defend him. It is doubtful that any of them would survive. Fanaticism that is born out of hell is willing to pay the price. And the chief priests agreed to the plot, as the next development shows.

2. The plot revealed (23:16-22)

16 And when Paul's sister's son heard of their lying in wait, he went and entered into the castle, and told Paul.

17 Then Paul called one of the centurions unto *him*, and said, Bring this young man unto the chief captain: for he hath a certain thing to tell him.

18 So he took him, and brought *him* to the chief captain, and said, Paul the prisoner called me unto *him*, and prayed me to bring this young man unto thee, who hath something to say unto thee.

19 Then the chief captain took him by the hand, and went *with him* aside privately, and asked *him*, What is that thou hast to tell me?

20 And he said, The Jews have agreed to desire thee that thou wouldest bring down Paul to morrow into the council, as though they would enquire somewhat of him more perfectly.

21 But do not thou yield unto them: for there lie in wait for him of them more than forty men, which have bound themselves with an oath, that they will neither eat nor drink till they have killed him: and now are they ready, looking for a promise from thee.

22 So the chief captain *then* let the young man depart, and charged *him, See thou* tell no man that thou hast shewed these things unto me.

It must be regarded as the providence of God (as nearly all writers agree) that Paul had a relative who was in just the right place at just the right time to learn of the plot. Here is the only direct N. T. reference to Paul's immediate family. Twice the nephew is called a "young man" (vv. 17-18), the word (Greek *neanias*) meaning he was either a teenager or in his early twenties. He was old enough to be taken seriously. Dutifully he went to see Paul, who was under guard in the Fortress (v.16). Paul's status as a Roman citizen and the fact that he was not officially charged with a crime would have allowed family and friends access to visit him.

Without delay Paul asked the centurion in charge to escort Paul's nephew to the tribune with this information (v. 17). The indication is that Paul was held in high regard by the centurion since he responded so quickly. It seems Paul did not tell him any of the details, but what Paul said and apparently how he said it meant that it should be heard by the tribune immediately. Men's lives would be at stake if the plot were to hatch. With that the nephew was taken immediately to see the high-ranking tribune.

With what must be regarded as an expression of kindness (Keener III:3316-3317), the tribune "took him by the hand" and pulled him aside to talk privately (v. 19). One cannot miss the respect shown by the Roman guards, as seen in Luke's description of their role in the story. This stands in stark contrast to Paul's treatment at the hands of his own countrymen. In detail, the young man told exactly what the plot entailed (vv. 20-22). The chief captain received the information and dismissed Paul's nephew with the instruction for him not to breathe another word of it to anyone. Lysias' next move shows how seriously he regarded the information.

3. Hasty transfer of Paul to Caesarea (23:23-35)

a. The guard assembled and the Tribune's letter (23:23-30)

23 And he called unto *him* two centurions, saying, Make ready two hundred soldiers to go to Caesarea, and horsemen threescore and ten, and spearmen two hundred, at the third hour of the night;

24 And provide *them* beasts, that they may set Paul on, and bring *him* safe unto Felix the governor.

25 And he wrote a letter after this manner:

26 Claudius Lysias unto the most excellent governor Felix *sendeth* greeting.

27 This man was taken of the Jews, and should have been killed of them: then came I with an army, and rescued him, having understood that he was a Roman.

28 And when I would have known the cause wherefore they accused him, I brought him forth into their council:

29 Whom I perceived to be accused of questions of their law, but to

have nothing laid to his charge worthy of death or of bonds.
30 And when it was told me how that the Jews laid wait for the man, I sent straightway to thee, and gave commandment to his accusers also to say before thee what *they had* against him. Farewell.

Without delay, the tribune moved to deal with the situation. The Jews' plot was tantamount to insurrection, and to delay was to court disaster. He needed to remove the cause of their hatred and pull the plug on the potential uprising. Calling two centurions to carry out his orders, he commanded that an armed escort of foot soldiers, spearmen, and cavalry be assembled and ready to leave Jerusalem at nine p.m. ("the third hour of the night"). They were also to provide horses. As Robertson (*Acts* 407) points out, these were not only for Paul but for supplies, gear, and the soldiers to whom he was chained. It was some seventy miles to Caesarea, so a change of horses would be required. There were four hundred and seventy men put on the detail with orders to "bring him safe unto Felix the governor" (v. 23). Nearly one half of the Roman cohort garrisoned at Jerusalem escorted one man to safety. Although this was a severe reduction in military strength in the powderkeg of Jerusalem, it was only for a short time and the situation would be under control enough to risk the brief interlude.

Luke must have obtained a copy of the letter written by Lysias, for he duplicated it word for word (vv. 25-30). Marshall (*Acts* 370) thinks it is a representation and not a duplication. Keener (III:3332) rightly points out, however, that an official letter was required to accompany such a prisoner and would become part of his legal dossier. It would have been read in open court and provided to those who were part of the defendant's defense team. In this case, Paul always defended himself without the assistance of a professional lawyer or presenter. This means that Paul would have been furnished a copy of the letter written by Lysias and, therefore, that Luke could use it as the source of his information. The phrase "after this manner" (v. 25) does not mean, then, a representative summary but the form of the letter itself. Originally, it would have been written in Latin, but Luke translated it into Greek for his record.

The letter itself shows respectful deference to the governor (procurator), recounts a brief history of the arrest, then explains the reasons for the transfer to Caesarea. It should be pointed out that Lysias exaggerated the truth somewhat, in his own favor, about his knowledge of Paul's Roman citizenship (v. 27). He did not know this until after he had rescued Paul from the mob (22:27-28). But in his mind that little detail was unimportant. And it has no bearing on the story. While not excusing the error, one can see why he would favor his side in the matter. Lysias also made clear that there were no official charges levied against Paul (v. 29), but his life had been put in danger with the revealing of the plot to kill him (v. 30). To protect Paul as a Roman citizen, he ordered him transferred to safety and ordered his accusers to appear before the governor.

b. Paul transported to Caesarea under heavy security (23:31-35)

31 Then the soldiers, as it was commanded them, took Paul, and brought *him* by night to Antipatris. 32 On the morrow they left the horsemen to go with him, and returned to the castle: 33 Who, when they came to Caesarea and delivered the epistle to the governor, presented Paul also before him. 34 And when the governor had read *the letter*, he asked of what province he was. And when he understood that *he was* of Cilicia; 35 I will hear thee, said he, when thine accusers are also come. And he commanded him to be kept in Herod's judgment hall.

The city of Antipatris was about halfway to Caesarea, some thirty-five miles northwest of Jerusalem, on the border of Judaea and Samaria. It was a military station built by Herod the Great and named after his father, Antipater. Normally, foot soldiers marched about twenty miles in one day, but this must have been a forced march; the wording suggests they traveled all night to get there. Not only was it necessary to get Paul out of harm's way, but the soldiers would need to return to Jerusalem to reestablish the strength of the military presence (v. 32).

Some writers seem to belabor the point of the forced night march (Keener III: 3340-3341; Marshall, *Acts* 372; Polhill, *Acts* 475-476) as though it were not possible or at least that the account is abbreviated. But Luke is clear that Paul was escorted all the way to Antipatris by the soldiers "as it was commanded them" (v. 31). Having done so they returned to Jerusalem the next day. Only the cavalry took Paul the rest of the way to Caesarea (v. 32). Any military veteran today can testify of such marches as fairly routine. The Roman military was legendary for their stamina. There is no need to read sympathy for the soldiers into the story of the march to Antipatris.

Upon arrival at Caesarea, both the prisoner and the official letter were presented to Felix, the Roman governor (procurator). Whatever else may be exposed later about Felix, he acted with proper legal and professional protocol in the initial treatment of Paul. The inquiry about Paul's home province (v. 34) was not the passing of pleasantries. It was a matter of legal jurisdiction. When he learned Paul was from Cilicia, he had options and a choice to make. As Keener (III:3345-3346) and Polhill (*Acts* 477) point out, at that time Cilicia was a part of his jurisdiction but he could defer the case to another if he chose. He could even transfer the trial to Cilicia if he chose to do so but this would have strained his relationship politically with the Jews. Instead he chose to hear the matter himself when Paul's accusers came to Caesarea. In the meantime, he directed that Paul be kept in Herod's judgment hall (Latin *praetorium*). This was one of many palaces built by Herod the Great; at the time it was used as the official Roman headquarters. In all likelihood Felix himself lived there and conducted the affairs of state from his offices in the building.

In retrospect one cannot help wondering how long the conspirators kept their oath not to eat or drink until they had killed Paul.

Summary
(22:22—23:35)

The fanaticism of the angry crowd in Jerusalem is somewhat parallel to the idolatrous crowd at Ephesus; both had basically the same intent: to kill Paul. The Roman tribune needed to quell the potential of a riot as well as to find out the reason for the hostility toward Paul, so he ordered him scourged to get the truth from him. In this setting, Paul appealed to his rights as a Roman citizen to avoid scourging. Again, the providence of God may be seen in securing this right for Paul long before he was even born.

The revelation of Paul's Roman citizenship brought about a new level of respectful treatment shown him. Even so, the tribune needed to know the reason to continue to hold Paul in custody, so he asked the Jewish Sanhedrin to convene for a hearing. Wisely, Paul preempted any false charges by asserting his Jewish heritage and beliefs as a Pharisee. It was a shrewd and calculated move on his part that prevented the court from doing to him what it had done to Stephen. Again, Paul was rescued from harm by the Roman soldiers.

Among the Jews hostile to Paul, some forty men conspired, with a suicidal vow, to kill Paul. They conspired with the high priest to have Paul brought again to the high court, and they intended to overpower the soldiers enough to murder him as he was being escorted. Providentially, again, Paul's own nephew learned of the plot and reported it to the tribune. Because of the chaos that might take place, that very night the tribune ordered nearly half of the Roman cohort to escort Paul under heavy guard

from Jerusalem to Caesarea and more secure surroundings.

Paul arrived safely at Caesarea under heavy guard and with an official letter; there he was arraigned before the Roman governor (procurator), Felix. Although Felix could have referred the case to others, Felix decided to hear it himself. Again, we see the hand of God in protection of Paul and opening the door of opportunity for him to speak to powerful leaders about the gospel of Christ.

Application: Teaching and Preaching the Passage

Exegetical Outline of the Text: 1. Exchange With the Tribune (22:22-29). 2. Arraigned Before the Sanhedrin (22:3—23:11). 3. The Plot to Kill Paul (23:12-22). 4. Paul Transferred to Caesarea (23:13-35).

There are many directions that can be taken in teaching and preaching this text. For example, it lends itself to a study of the providential hand of God. One can see this in the tribune's being amicable toward Paul; in Paul's rights as a Roman citizen, secured even before he was born; in Paul's own schooling to become a Pharisee and so to recognize the possibility of a resurrection; in Paul's nephew's learning of the plot to kill him, etc. This is especially true in seeing how the imprisonments and trials put him in opportunities to witness he might not have had under less stressful circumstances.

The brief explanatory note Luke inserts about what Sadducees and Pharisees believed opens the door for study in their background and in how these groups interacted with the believers in Acts. Many of the Pharisees

325

became believers, but there is no record that any Sadducees were saved.

In the midst of these incredible trials, the Lord appeared to Paul in a vision to reassure him of his protection and future. While visions today are certainly possible when the Lord chooses, there are many other ways He uses to reassure and encourage His people in times of trial. This principle deserves study and application to today's circumstances.

G. Paul's Defense Before Felix, the Governor (24:1-27)

1. The formal accusation (24:1-9)

1 And after five days Ananias the high priest descended with the elders, and *with* a certain orator *named* Tertullus, who informed the governor against Paul.
2 And when he had called forth, Tertullus began to accuse *him*, saying, Seeing that by thee we enjoy great quietness, and that very worthy deeds are done unto this nation by thy providence,
3 We accept *it* always, and in all places, most noble Felix, with all thankfulness.
4 Nothwithstanding, that I be not further tedious unto thee, I pray thee that thou wouldest hear us of thy clemency a few words.
5 For we have found this man *a* pestilent *fellow*, and a mover of sedition among all the Jews throughout the world, and a ringleader of the sect of the Nazarenes:
6 Who also hath gone about to profane the temple: whom we took, and would have judged according to our law.

7 But the chief captain Lysias came *upon us*, and with great violence took *him* away out of our hands,
8 Commanding his accusers to come unto thee: by examining of whom thyself mayest take knowledge of all things, whereof we accuse him.
9 And the Jews also assented, saying that these things were so.

The appearances before the Roman governors presented a different setting and protocols for Paul's defense testimonials. Bock (688) cites experts in Roman legal proceedings, showing the historical accuracy of Luke's account and especially in the recording of Paul's testimonials. Keener (IV:3352) confirms that Luke was probably present to hear and record Paul's words or, at least, got them directly from Paul himself after the fact. This makes for impeccable integrity in the narrative.

It took five days (v. 1) for the high priest, Ananias, and representative elders from the Sanhedrin to make the seventy-mile trip to Caesarea. They brought with them a skilled orator/lawyer to plead the case. It's unclear whether Tertullus was a Roman or a Jew, but his job was to lodge a formal legal complaint against Paul and persuade the governor to make a judgment in their favor. His skill is noteworthy.

First, Tertullus offered necessary and complimentary courtesies toward the governor. As to their accuracy, history records that the administration of Felix had limited success (Keener IV:3364-3365). This was not, however, a proceeding to analyze his political regime but a trial to secure his favor for the Jews and against Paul. Tertullus skillfully lodged four legal charges against Paul (Bock 691). Schnabel (954-955) says two; Marshall (*Acts* 375) and Polhill (*Acts* 480) identify three.

First, he accused Paul of being a "pestilent fellow" (Greek *loimos*, plague, pestilence). The idea is that Paul presented a public menace like a plague would—a vivid description. Details follow.

Second, he charged Paul with being a seditionist (Greek *stasis*, insurrection) wherever he went ("among all Jews throughout the world"). This might have been the most serious charge. The Romans did not suffer fools well when it came to threats to the public peace. The *Pax Romana* was the law of the empire and was enforced at the cost of blood if necessary. Felix was noted for putting down one insurrection after another in Judaea (Polhill, *Acts* 480). Plus, wherever Paul had been there were uprisings and attempted legal proceedings against him. One only had to recall what happened at Antioch in Pisidia, Iconium, Lystra, Philippi, Thessalonica, Ephesus, and now in Jerusalem for them to charge him with this. Tertullus had done his homework. Of course, Paul was not the cause of the uproars; those who were intolerant of his gospel message caused them. To be sure, there was no mention of Gallio's assessment (18:14-16), nor were there any witnesses to prove this charge, a charge that had major implications against the Christian community at large.

Third, he was charged with being the leader of "the sect of the Nazarenes." The term "Nazarene" is used six times in Acts and is taken from the home town of Jesus and reflects His own self-identification (22:8). Nazareth was not a place of high regard in the N. T. world (Jn. 1:46) but fit perfectly the motif of the Messianic humility of Jesus. Like the term "Christian" (11:26), it was used derisively. That which was least esteemed in the eyes of the world was most esteemed by the followers of Christ (1 Cor. 1:27). This is yet another irony in Acts.

This charge derived from the previous one and was probably the ultimate target of Tertullus' prosecution. Paul was a key leader, of course, so this charge was essentially true but intended to be used against him. The reasoning was that Jesus of Nazareth was condemned some twenty-seven years previously for the same sedition as Paul was being charged with. Therefore, not only was Paul guilty but the whole sect of the Nazarenes was, too. In other words, Paul was leading a group devoted to a person whom the Romans condemned because He was hailed as their King. Now Paul was perpetuating the same teachings and posed an ongoing threat to the public peace.

Fourth, Tertullus charged Paul with profaning the Temple. This derived from the Asian Jews who accused him of bringing a Gentile into the Temple (21:28-29), but they were strangely absent from these proceedings (vv. 20-21). It must be remembered that variations of the Temple charge were also lodged against Jesus (Mt. 26:60-61) and Stephen (7:48-54). Of course, the Temple charge was totally false, but selfish agendas seldom concern themselves with truth. The idea here is that such a violation totally disrupted Jewish ceremonial practices and was one of the most serious offenses that could be committed against Jewish law. Furthermore, to profane the Temple posed yet another threat to the peace.

Proof of this last charge, as Tertullus explained, was seen in the fact that Paul was in the process of being arrested and dealt with according to Jewish procedures when the tribune intervened aggressively, removing Paul from their custody. This happened twice, once in the Temple court area and then before the Sanhedrin. While Schnabel (956) does not see this as a criticism of Lysias, it is, at least, a thinly veiled complaint (Keener IV:3383-3384). The implication is that if Lysias had not intervened the Jews would have disposed of the issue and avoided any further problems. That is probably true, but we can see the providential hand of God in rescuing Paul from the mob and the Jewish high court.

Tertullus concluded his presentation with an appeal to Felix that his judicial cross-examination of the accused would support his charges. Included in that would be the testimony of witnesses, as the next verse asserts (v. 9). The case was brilliantly presented and was intended to make it hard for Paul to defend himself.

2. Paul's answer to the charges by Tertullus (24:10-21)

10 Then Paul, after that the governor had beckoned unto him to speak, answered, Forasmuch as I know that thou hast been of many years a judge unto this nation, I do the more cheerfully answer for myself:
11 Because thou mayest understand, that there are yet but twelve days since I went up to Jerusalem for to worship.
12 And they neither found me in the Temple disputing with any man, neither raising up the people, neither in the synagogues, nor in the city:
13 Neither can they prove the things whereof they now accuse me.
14 But I confess unto thee, that after the way which they call heresy, so worship I the God of my fathers, believing all things which are written in the law and in the prophets:
15 And have hope toward God, which they themselves also allow, that there shall be a resurrection of the dead, both of the just and the unjust.
16 And herein do I exercise myself, to have always a conscience void of offence toward God, and *toward* men.
17 Now after many years I came to bring alms to my nation, and offerings.
18 Whereupon certain Jews from Asia found me purified in the temple, neither with multitude, nor with tumult.
19 Who ought to have been here before thee, and object, if they had ought against me.
20 Or else let these same *here* say, if they have found any evil doing in my, while I stood before the council,
21 Except it be for this one voice, that I cried standing among them, Touching the resurrection of the dead I am called in question by you this day.

Paul's ability to defend himself was no less brilliant than Tertullus' presentation of the charges. With courteous deference, he too acknowledged the administration of Felix (v. 10) and then addressed the charges. He succinctly addressed the main charges against him, appealing for evidence and witnesses to prove their points. Of course, there were none. Theirs were trumped up charges that could not be verified. But he acknowledged the real reason for their opposition: namely, his belief in the resurrection.

His reply can be summarized as follows. First, he was not guilty of causing any disturbance in Jerusalem (vv. 11-12). It had only been twelve days since he arrived. This reference to the time involved has received some discussion by commentators (Meyer 443-444; Polhill, *Acts* 482; Schnabel 957; Bruce, *Acts* 443), since the time from 21:26 to 24:11 adds up to more than twelve days. The best understanding is that Paul was referring to the time from his arrival in Jerusalem until his arrest in the Temple court. Paul was apparently implying that this was insufficient time to foment a rebellion. Besides, he was there to worship, as the evidence of his purification observance proved.

Second, they had offered no proof of their charges (v. 13), which were only words. Third, he was, indeed, a follower of "the way" that embraced the teachings of the O. T. Law and prophets, in particular its teachings about the resurrection (vv. 14-15). This was the heart of the issue. Fourth, he came to Jerusalem bringing financial help for his people (v. 17), a reference to the offering he had sponsored during the third missionary journey. Fifth, he was alone in the Temple observing ceremonial purification when accosted by Asian Jews who were not there to testify before Felix but should have been if their charge was to be seriously considered

(vv. 18-19). Sixth, he could not be charged with any "evil doing," but he would admit to his loud confession, before the Sanhedrin, of his belief in the resurrection (vv. 20-21).

Point by point Paul had answered their charges and shown them to be false and empty. He did acknowledge twice his belief in the resurrection (vv. 15, 21). This, of course, was the heart of the gospel.

3. The response of Felix (24:22-23)

22 And when Felix heard these things, having more perfect knowledge of *that* way, he deferred them, and said, When Lysias the chief captain shall come down, I will know the uttermost of your matter.
23 And he commanded a centurion to keep Paul, and to let *him* have liberty, and that he should forbid none of his acquaintance to minister or come unto him.

Felix had options regarding a decision. He could convict Paul but the evidence did not warrant that. He could release him for lack of evidence, but that would not set well with these high ranking Jews. Or he could postpone a decision on the pretext of needing more information, which is what he decided to do: "he deferred them" or put them off for the time being.

His decision to postpone was based on two considerations. He wanted input from the tribune, Lysias, and he had "more perfect knowledge of that way." We are never told if Lysias ever came to Caesarea to address the case. Actually he had already written his opinion of the matter (23:29). But what did Felix know about "that way" (Christianity) and how did he get his information? The phrase "having more perfect knowledge" (literally, "more accurately knowing") apparently means that he knew more about the Christian way than the Sanhedrin (and Tertullus) thought he knew. Implied is that Felix knew Christians were not seditionists and troublemakers. This would negate Tertullus' argument.

But where did he get his information about "the way"? Suggestions include that his position as governor of Judaea would require some degree of information about Christians, since there were thousands of them all over the province. He might also have been informed of the decision of Gallio in Corinth. Plus, his wife Drusilla was Jewish and a daughter of Herod Agrippa I (12:1-3, 20-23). She could have been a source of information, since the Herod family was always aware of the Christians. Cannot we see, again, the providential hand of God here? Whatever the source of Felix' information, God had directed him previously to know enough about Christians that he had some degree of reasonableness about them. Whoever was the source of his information had not so prejudiced his thinking that he regarded Christians as immediate threats.

Probably because of Paul's Roman citizenship Felix gave him considerable liberties. Though assigned to be guarded by a centurion, family and friends had open access to him. Such an arrangement was regarded as "military custody" (Polhill, *Acts* 485). The acquaintances that had access to Paul would have included Luke, Philip, Aristarchus, Trophimus, Timothy, and perhaps James.

4. Further audience with Felix and Drusilla (24:24-27)

**24 And after certain days, when Felix came with his wife Drusilla, which was a Jewess, he sent for Paul, and heard him concerning the faith in Christ.
25 And as he reasoned of righteousness, temperance, and judgment to come, Felix trembled, and answered, Go thy way for this time; when I have a convenient season, I will call for thee.
26 He hoped also that money should have been given him of Paul, that he might loose him: wherefore he sent for him the oftener, and communed with him.
27 But after two years Porcius Festus came into Felix' room: and Felix, willing to shew the Jews a pleasure, left Paul bound.**

Apparently, having one of the apostles of "the way" incarcerated and available for further discussion was convenience enough for Felix to meet with Paul privately. There might have been other reasons but he wanted to know more. This time he was accompanied by his Jewish wife, Drusilla. According to Josephus (*Antiquities.* XX.VII.2), Drusilla was so beautiful that, though she was married at the time, Felix was so smitten when he met her that he was determined to have her as his own wife. She had been married when she was fourteen to one Azizus, a king of a petty state in Syria and was in an unhappy marriage. Josephus (*Antiquities* XX.VII.2) records that Felix manipulated the situation, using the promise to make her "happy"—an intentional pun since his name in Latin meant "happy." She was sixteen when she married Felix and barely twenty at this meeting with Paul. Such is the stuff of political gossip (Keener IV:3431-3432; Polhill, *Acts* 486). It is certainly possible that she was the one who mostly desired to hear the apostle.

Whatever the motivations were for the private meeting, Felix and Drusilla might have gotten more than they bargained for. Boldly, Paul presented the case for faith in Jesus as the Christ (v. 24), then moved on to three other subjects that were inherent in biblical truth and Christian life: namely, "righteousness, temperance, and judgment to come." These were subjects that were especially appropriate for the governor and his wife to hear.

The theme of "righteousness" (Greek *diakaiosune*) would cover the concepts of a holy God, man's sinfulness and inability to measure up, and God's provision for righteousness through Jesus Christ (Rom. 3:19-25). It would also extend to a lifestyle of justice, fairness, and uprightness. The theme of "temperance" (Greek *egkrateia*) has to do with moral self-control, especially regarding one's pleasures and desires. This would have included the enabling of the Holy Spirit that accompanies personal faith in Christ (Gal. 5:22-23). The theme of "judgment to come" was not a reference to a legal decision by Felix but to future universal judgment by the almighty God (17:31; 2 Thess. 1:7-10; Rom. 14:10-12). As Robertson (*Acts* 422) aptly concludes, "Paul...discoursed 'righteousness' which they did not possess, 'self-control' which they did not exhibit, and 'the judgment to come' which was certain to overtake them."

The reaction of Felix to Paul's message was telling, in that "he trembled"; literally, he "became afraid" (Greek *emphobos*, terrified). Was he "under conviction"? That seems likely. The situation, and Felix' reaction, were similar to another incident involving the Herod family (and including one who got another man's wife!), when John the Baptist pointed out the adultery of Herod (Mt. 14:1-12). Felix dismissed the apostle with the promise of later discussions. How many folks under conviction have so reasoned and postponed their way into hell!

Luke records that Felix had other intentions (v. 26). He did meet with Paul several more times; but he was greedy as well as lustful in that he expected bribe money. Perhaps he thought that Paul's reference to bringing money to aid the believers in Judaea (v. 17) made him a wealthy target to pad his wallet. Although Roman law forbad the taking of bribes (Schnabel 967), it was a widespread practice. (That has not changed. Powerful people know how to skirt the law and often do.) Felix's initial denial did not prevent further attempts to extort money from Paul. It appears that further discussions with him were not so profound.

Felix did not make a judicial decision about Paul but left him incarcerated for two more years (v. 27). It was a delay tactic probably motivated to get money but also as a political favor to the Jews. He had no legal basis to keep Paul imprisoned but neither did he want to ruffle the feathers of high-ranking Jewish officials.

Corruption and brutality were the political undoing of Felix. He mismanaged one too many situations of unrest in Caesarea. A delegation of high-ranking Jews took their complaint all the way to Rome, which resulted in Felix's dismissal from office (Polhill, *Acts* 487; Schnabel 968). He was replaced by Porcius Festus, who inherited the political prisoner, the apostle Paul.

Summary
(24:1-27)

It was five days before the high priest (Ananias), some of the senior officials of the Sanhedrin, and their orator-advocate, Tertullus, arrived in Caesarea to pursue charges against Paul before Felix. With brilliant oratory and concise words, Tertullus made the case against Paul, followed by the affirming testimony of the Jewish delegates. If they thought they had proven their point, and that Paul would soon be turned over to them, they were sadly mistaken. They had no evidence or eye witnesses to sustain serious charges, nor had they counted on Paul's own brilliance and ability to defend himself against the charges.

After hearing both sides, Felix knew the Jews had no strong case against Paul, but he chose to postpone his decision. It was a political move on his part. He kept Paul imprisoned, but with considerable liberty. In the days following, he and his wife Drusilla made time for an audience with their highly-regarded prisoner, who boldly shared the gospel of Christ and its lifestyle principles. The spiritual power and reasoning of the apostle saw Felix respond in intense fear, even though he did not savingly believe. Instead, he chose to try to manipulate the situation for personal gain, wanting Paul to pay money for political favor. Paul, of course, did not oblige him. Two years later, Paul was still imprisoned in Caesarea when a new political administration assumed power.

Application: Teaching and Preaching the Passage

Exegetical Outline of the Text: 1. Tertullus Declares the Charges Against Paul (24:1-9). 2. Paul Defends Against the Charges (24:10-21). 3. Felix Defers Judgment (24:22-23). 4. Felix and Drusilla Decide to Hear Paul (24:24-26). 5. Felix Delays Paul's Release (24:27).

The apologetic theme of Acts shows that believers faced a variety of situations where they gave testimony of faith in Christ. Some were in answer to genuine inquiries about faith in Christ, while others responded to dangerous enemies who sought to kill the witnesses. In fact, in some cases believers did give their lives for the cause of Christ. The trials Paul faces in these closing chapters of Acts include enemies of the gospel who desire to kill the apostle and stop the witness of the gospel. Jesus knew this would happen and spoke to this situation (Mt. 10:17-20; Lk. 12:11-12). Believers today face tests of their faith on different levels. Some in third-world countries even face death. The response of Paul in each of these trial situations is a great model to follow.

Sometimes legal issues require that a believer avail himself of the expertise of other believers who have prepared themselves in the law of the land. As cultures become increasingly hostile to Christianity this is a growing need. Churches should especially be wise and prepared for potential legal issues.

God used the tough times Paul faced to put him in witness situations that he might not otherwise have had. That included the immediate interventions of the Lord in delivering Paul the very night of the plan to kill him as well as the two-year delay caused by his imprisonment at Caesarea. It was probably during that two-year delay that Luke was able to do the research necessary for the writing of Luke and Acts. The providential hand of God can be seen in all these circumstances, both guiding and sustaining Paul. So it is with us today. A great study is the providence of God in the lives of believers. It has been said that for every one time we are aware of His providential care there are a thousand we are not aware of.

H. Paul's Defense Before Festus the Governor and Agrippa the King (25:1—26:32)

1. Paul's first defense before Festus, the governor (25:1-12)

1 Now when Festus was come into the province, after three days he ascended from Caesarea to Jerusalem.
2 Then the high priest and the chief of the Jews informed him against Paul, and besought him,
3 And desired favour against him, that he would send for him to Jerusalem, laying wait in the way to kill him.
4 But Festus answered, that Paul should be kept at Caesarea, and that he himself would depart shortly *thither.*
5 Let them therefore, said he, which among you are able, go down with *me,* and accuse this man, if there be any wickedness in him.
6 And when he had tarried among them more than ten days, he went down unto Caesarea; and the next day sitting on the judgment seat commanded Paul to be brought.

7 And when he was come, the Jews which came down from Jerusalem stood round about, and laid many and grievous complaints against Paul, which they could not prove.
8 While he answered for himself, Neither against the law of the Jews, neither against the temple, nor yet against Caesar, have I offended any thing at all.
9 But Festus, willing to do the Jews a pleasure, answered Paul, and said, Wilt thou go up to Jerusalem, and there be judged of these things before me?
10 Then said Paul, I stand at Caesar's judgment seat, where I ought to be judged: to the Jews have I done no wrong, as thou very well knowest.
11 For if I be an offender, or have committed any thing worthy of death, I refuse not to die: but if there be none of these things whereof these accuse me, no man may deliver me unto them. I appeal unto Caesar.
12 Then Festus, when he had conferred with the council, answered, Hast thou appealed unto Caesar? unto Caesar shalt thou go.

The revolving doors of political Rome resulted in the removal of Felix from being the procurator (see commentary above) and the installation of Porcius Festus as governor of Judaea. Not much is known of him aside from the Acts record and two brief references in Josephus (*Antiquities* XX.VIII.9-10; *Wars* II.XIV.1). Apparently, he was fairminded as well as tough on rebellion, succeeding in putting down a number of these when he came into office. His administration lasted only a short time (A.D. 58/59-62), because of an illness that resulted in his death. His reputation for being tough on rebellions might have sparked the hopes of the Sanhedrin regarding Paul, since that was one of their false charges against him. The Acts record of him is not so kind, as he is shown to be more interested in political favors than making just decisions.

Soon after installation in office, Festus paid a courtesy visit to Jerusalem (v. 1). The office of the high priest was then occupied by Ishmael ben Phiabi (Bock 700; Josephus, *Antiquities* XX.VII.8-9). There would still have been a number of the elders on the high court who would have been involved in the case against Paul. During a meeting of Festus with the powerful elite of the Sanhedrin, they brought up the "loose end" of what to do with Paul (vv. 2-3). They "informed him" in that they reviewed the charges and the fact that a decision had been deferred on the matter. Even the new high priest shouldered the same old vendetta. Bitterness and resentment can often linger for years.

Luke tells us that it was their intention to have him brought back to Jerusalem and, on the way, to ambush the guards and kill Paul. We are not told of Luke's source of this information, but there could easily have been a Christian on the court as Nicodemus had been (Jn. 3:1-3). At risk of speculation, it stands to reason that this piece of information might have compelled Paul to refuse to go back to Jerusalem (v. 9). Even if he did not know this at the time, the Jews' motives, and the risk, would have been fairly obvious.

The previous conspiracy to kill Paul while in custody (23:12-15) was hatched by an outside group and presented to the high court. This time the high court itself adopted the same plan. They would have employed the assistance of thugs to carry out their plan, but they were the ones who hatched it up. The devil never sleeps and has a long list of helpers.

Although it appears that Festus was not aware of the conspiracy to kill Paul (as commentators agree), he might very well have suspicioned such an attempt. He had just traveled the road himself and would have been aware that the terrain was conducive to ambush. However, he was probably less concerned about security than about convenience and legal propriety (Keener IV:3452-3453). He was decisive in denying the favor and put the onus on the Council to press its case in Caesarea if they desired (vv. 4-5). While this was his initial response, later he would take a posture of favoritism and deference.

Festus remained in Jerusalem for several more days (v. 6) before returning to Caesarea. The time there would have given him opportunity to get acquainted with the people he needed to know, as well as with the political and religious culture to which he had been assigned. Apparently, a delegation of the high court went promptly to Caesarea to address Paul's case, as Festus had indicated. The next day after Festus' return, he arranged for the hearing.

With Festus seated on the "judgment seat" (Greek *bema*), the Jewish court delegation surrounded Paul and began to charge him (v. 7), again without being able to prove any crime. Paul responded to each of them with insistence (v. 8) of his innocence. From his summary it appears that these were essentially the same as before (24:5-8). Paul's reference to Caesar should be noted. He had not made that reference previously. This may indicate that he had planned his appeal before the hearing started, knowing that he might need to do just that.

The response of Festus to the situation is, in effect, the same as Felix's: a deferral for the sake of political convenience. Luke regards Festus' motive as a desire to curry political favor with the Jewish elite (v. 9). For that reason Festus wants to accommodate their desire to have Paul extradited to Jerusalem. In truth, Paul should have been exonerated of the charges long ago, but he is still in custody because of these same political tactics. Festus is caught between doing the Jews a favor and knowing Paul is a Roman citizen with rights that must be respected. Instead of making the decision he should, he puts the onus on Paul to decide so it would appear that he was absolved of any responsibility. The whole thing reminds us of the reticence of Pilate over Jesus and his dramatization of his political innocence in washing his hands (Mt. 27:19-25). Justice often takes a back seat to political favoritism.

There was no hesitation in Paul's reply (v. 10), which included a candid assessment of what Festus was doing ("as thou very well knowest"). Paul used his privilege as a Roman citizen in appealing to be heard before Caesar. In doing so, he wisely avoided going to Jerusalem, with it danger and obvious outcome. Fitzmyer (745) labels the Jewish high court as an "incompetent tribunal."

Reaffirming his innocence (v. 11), Paul confessed that if he had, indeed, broken any law he was willing to accept the consequences, including dying if necessary. But he declared clearly that he was not guilty of any. Furthermore, he asserted his rights as a Roman citizen

to appeal, meaning that no one (including Festus) could override his right and hand him over to the Jews. In doing this, Paul was making a legal maneuver around the authority of the governor (Bock 703). Perhaps he sensed that Festus was on the verge of caving in to the Jews. With the formality it required, Paul appealed unto Caesar. (The appeal was known as the *provocatio*.)

The reply of Festus is both an approval of Paul's appeal and a dodging of his own legal responsibilities (v. 12). It was right for him to confer with his legal counsel (Greek *sumboulion*, Festus' advisory council, not the Jewish Council), for there were different possibilities in the situation (Bruce, *Acts* 454). He phrases his response in such a way as to place the responsibility for the decision on Paul rather than on himself. In doing so, he wants to be seen as having to submit to the appeal without any recourse. This is correct in part but only because of his own "straddling the fence." He sits in the judgment seat but he lacks the nerve to render justice. His judgment statement is recorded: "Hast thou appealed unto Caesar? Unto Caesar shalt thou go."

Paul's appeal to Caesar is the stuff of much discussion by commentators (Bock 703-704; Schnabel 992-993; Keener IV:3462-3468). There are numerous implications. The Caesar at the time was Nero and at the time in his rule Christians were not targeted for persecution. That would all change in a few years. Furthermore, Paul was placing his safe-keeping and to a certain extent that of Christianity, in the hands of Rome. That action, however, was simply a legal maneuver; ultimately, the care and keeping of the church is in the Lord's Hands (Mt. 16:18). In essence,

Paul was saying that Christianity was no threat to the government, as falsely charged; and Paul was willing to make that case before Caesar (Rom. 13:1-4; 1 Tim. 2:1-4).

Paul had intended to go to Rome (19:21), but under different circumstances. Regardless, the providential hand of God is evident, for now Paul will be going under protective custody, at the expense of the government, and given an audience before the highest authority of the empire. It was the means by which God was fulfilling His promise that Paul would bear witness to "kings" (9:15; 23:11). The personal trials Paul had to go through were actually doors of opportunity for witness. We do not always understand such things until we look back. We live our lives looking forward. We understand our lives looking backward.

2. Paul's second defense before Festus, Agrippa II, and Bernice (25:13—26:32)

a. The inquiry of Festus to Agrippa about Paul (25:13-22)

13 And after certain days king Agrippa and Bernice came unto Caesarea to salute Festus.
14 And when they had been there many days, Festus declared Paul's cause unto the king, saying, There is a certain man left in bonds by Felix:
15 About whom, when I was at Jerusalem, the chief priests and the elders of the Jews informed *me*, desiring *to have* judgment against him.
16 To whom I answered, It is not the manner of the Romans to deliver any man to die, before that he which is accused have the accusers face to face, and have licence to answer for himself concerning the crime laid against him.
17 Therefore, when they were come hither, without any delay on the morrow I sat on the judgment seat, and commanded the man to be brought forth.
18 Against whom when the accusers stood up, they brought none accusation of such things as I supposed:
19 But had certain questions against him of their own superstition, and of one Jesus, which was dead, whom Paul affirmed to be alive.
20 And because I doubted of such manner of questions, I asked *him* whether he would go to Jerusalem, and there be judged of these matters.
21 But when Paul had appealed to be reserved unto the hearing of Augustus, I commanded him to be kept till I might send him unto Caesar.
22 Then Agrippa said unto Festus, I would also hear the man myself. To morrow, said he, thou shalt hear him.

The visit of King Agrippa II and his sister Bernice to Festus might have been more than just a political courtesy call. Josephus (*Antiquities* XX.IX.4, 7) documents that Agrippa had been given authority over the Temple in Jerusalem and the appointment of high priests (Schnabel 994). This gave him motive to know more of the situation about Paul. Although technically the decision had been made to send him to Rome, political prisoners have disappeared over lesser things. Festus might, indeed, have seen the visit as a way out of the situation; hence his detailed explanation about Paul (Bruce, *Acts* 456). What other prisoners would have been the subject of such extensive discussion?

Bernice (formally "Julia Berenice") is specifically named as accompanying Agrippa. She was the full sister of Agrippa (by the same mother) and the older sister of Drusilla (24:24). She had two previous marriages but was widowed at the time. She was living in the palace with Agrippa who was a year older than she. Rumors were rife that they were engaged in an incestuous relationship but Keener (IV:3474) details how this was almost certainly false. However, his conclusion is based on the cultural impropriety of such a relationship. That does not mean that it was not so, especially with the Herod family who seemed to revel in moral impropriety (Polhill, *Acts* 493). To quell the rumors she had married, but that marriage did not last long either. In spite of her personal troubles, she did become active in advocating for peace with Rome during the Judean rebellion in the late A.D. 60s, culminating with the destruction of Jerusalem in A.D. 70. She was a survivor, albeit a very conflicted one. She and Agrippa were in their early thirties when they heard Paul. He was probably near sixty.

Agrippa II was the son of Agrippa I (12:1), the great grandson of Herod the Great, and the last of the Herods of the N. T. He was placed into position by Claudius in A.D. 50, who advanced his power and territorial rule to cover much of Judaea (Jones 218-219). It is interesting to note that Luke calls his father "Herod" (12:1, 19-21), never "Agrippa,"

and never calls Agrippa II "Herod." This is probably intentional in that Luke portrays the father as a persecutor and Agrippa II as a supporter of Christians. In no way does that mean he was a believer; rather he was caught in the political scheming of the whole situation.

It had been politically convenient for Agrippa and Bernice to have a brother-in-law (Felix) as procurator of Judaea. But there appears to have been personal tensions between them because of Bernice's jealousy of Drusilla's beauty. Josephus (*Antiquities* XX.VII.2) records that "she did indeed exceed all other women in beauty." But they would not have been disappointed with the change in leadership when Festus took the position.

The point of these brief personal profiles is that the people to whom Paul proclaimed the gospel were the political movers and shakers of his day. But they were also people in personal conflict and turmoil and with little moral compass. If there ever were people who needed to hear the gospel, they certainly did.

Whether Agrippa brought up the subject or Festus preempted the question, Festus began with a summary of the situation regarding Paul to Agrippa (v. 14). He reviewed the events accurately (vv. 15-16), adding information about the Roman law and right of trial before one's accusers. No doubt wanting to appear to be judicial and decisive, Festus padded the account with his timely actions (v. 17). However, when the Jews presented the case (v. 18), he had found no legal cause to charge Paul. (Of course, that was when he should have disposed of the whole matter and released Paul.)

What he did find out was, in his opinion, a matter of "superstition" (Greek *deisidaimonia*, religious belief; cf. 17:22). Paul asserted his belief in the resurrection of "one Jesus" (v. 19). The concept of a resurrection of the dead was totally foreign to Romans. Although Festus was paying a back-handed compliment to Paul, who had been a faithful witness, he was being sarcastic. But he was being factual. The resurrection was exactly the core of the issue as far as Paul was concerned.

It is interesting that the use of the name "Jesus" and the resurrection event seems to have been forgotten by now among the Romans. There were records of Pilate's involvement that could have been accessed. Of course, it is possible that Festus did not want to investigate any farther. One cannot help wondering if Agrippa knew of his family's involvement in the case. He certainly would have known about his father's killing of James (12:1) and his own "untimely" death.

Festus candidly confessed to Agrippa that he was not an expert in religious matters. He was probably confessing that he was at a loss over what exactly to do (Bock 711). He wanted Paul to return to Jerusalem where he could address the religious court (v. 20). His uncertainty clearly shows. He would have granted this change of venue but Paul had appealed to Caesar (v. 21). Here Caesar is identified as, literally, "the revered one" (Greek *ho Sebastos*), which is the Greek equivalent of the Latin *Augustus*, a title taken by whatever Caesar was in power at the time. It means "worthy of worship, revered, august" and would be equivalent to "His Majesty" in today's appropriate settings.

It is sometimes translated as "the Emperor" (ESV, NASB).

After Festus spoke, Agrippa expressed his interest in the case (v. 22). Did it stir his curiosity about Paul and his message, or did it present an opportunity for him to pad his political resumé with a certain amount of political cronyism with Festus? Perhaps it even stirred his interest in some faint memories of his family's legacy with Christians. Either way, all would soon be clearer.

One cannot help wondering about Luke's source of information about this exchange between Festus and Agrippa, especially since it is so detailed and personal. Some of the conversation is worded in first person terms. Surprisingly, Marshall (*Acts* 386) states, "It must be assumed that here we have a clear example of Luke's policy of narrating what is likely to have been said on such an occasion...for which he had no concrete evidence." Meyer (457) sees it as entirely "drawn up by Luke himself as a free composition." But that would be unlike Luke, given that all his previous information have been found to be fully trustworthy. Fitzmyer (748) and Bock (706) appeal to Luke's Pauline sources for the information. Lenski (1004) analyzes the literary level of the conversation and concludes that this was exactly the type of language Festus would have used. Furthermore, these high-level officials would have had attendants (v. 23) who waited at their beck and call, among whom there very well could have been believers—especially in the entourage of Agrippa and Bernice. We may not have some of Luke's sources listed for us but that does not mean at all that he was making any of this up. Again, his claim to use "eyewitnesses" (Lk. 1:2) is neither far-fetched nor imaginary.

b. The political assembly to hear Paul (25:23-27)

23 And on the morrow, when Agrippa was come, and Bernice, with great pomp, and was entered into the place of hearing, with the chief captains, and principal men of the city, at Festus' commandment Paul was brought forth.
24 And Festus said, King Agrippa, and all men which are here present with us, ye see this man, about whom all the multitude of the Jews have dealt with me, both at Jerusalem, and *also* here, crying that he ought not to live any longer.
25 But when I found that he had committed nothing worthy of death, and that he himself appealed to Augustus, I have determined to send him.
26 Of whom I have no certain thing to write unto my lord. Wherefore I have brought him forth before you, and specially before thee, O king Agrippa, that, after examination had, I might have somewhat to write.
27 For it seemeth to me unreasonable to send a prisoner, and not withal to signify the crimes *laid* against him.

The most powerful and privileged of the entire province of Judaea were assembled to help the Roman governor write a letter (v. 27). Was there ever anything more ironic? Paul's last testimonial defense in the Acts narrative takes place before such an assembly. It is a fitting climax to the apologetic trial motif of the record regarding Paul, but it is an even greater testimony to the providential hand of God to arrange such an opportunity to witness. Luke records in detail those who are gathered (v. 23).

Agrippa and Bernice are escorted into the "place of hearing" with royal pomp and circumstance. The room would have been large enough to accommodate the crowd and provide for the hearing. There were also "chief captains" (Greek *chiliarchoi*) or tribunes. There were five cohorts of Roman soldiers stationed in Caesarea, each cohort consisting of one thousand men over which a tribune was positioned (Polhill, *Acts* 495). Listed also are the "principal men of the city." These were the leading citizens who were of great notoriety in Caesarea. Represented then were those of political power, financial influence, and military might. Whether they had been apprised of the reason for their invitation is not clear, but that did not matter. Neither were they concerned about being summoned the very next day to the meeting. It was enough that Festus "asked" them to come. "It is a grand occasion, a meeting of royals" (Bock 712).

When all are in place, at the command of Festus, Paul is escorted from his prison room, bound in chains between two soldiers. What could be more contrastive! The pomp and circumstance of the rich and powerful compared to the simplicity of the apostle. When he appears, one can almost see the surprise on the faces of some, the passive eyes of toughened military leaders, and the giddy excitement of the Herods who have yet another follower of Jesus before them. Whether they were aware of it or not, it was their family's legacy to have been the Judaean kings of the N. T. era of the Messiah. If any thought Paul would be intimidated by their presence they were sadly mistaken.

There were two parts to the address of Festus to the assembly. First, he gives the background why "this man" is there (v. 24). Note that Festus does not tell Paul's name even though it will be required for the official letter he must write. The reference to Paul as "this man" reminds us of Pilate's reference to Jesus, "Behold the man" (Jn. 19:5). Festus reviews the intense efforts of the Jews to get him to deliver Paul to them. But he has heard the case and determined that no crimes worthy of death had been committed by the prisoner. One cannot help wondering if those sitting in the audience, especially the tribunes, then wondered what the big issue was all about. Either the man was guilty or not. If not why was he not set free? Here is the second time Festus affirms Paul's innocence (v. 18). In doing so, he adds that Paul has appealed his case to the "August One" (v. 21), and that he has determined to send him to Rome (v. 25).

The second part of his address (vv. 26-27) is that he needs help in writing the letter of appeal to Caesar. This legal document (known as the *littera dimissoria*, Schnabel 1001) was required in such appeal cases. It had to contain four elements: a notice of appeal, the name of the person lodging the appeal, the sentence being contested, and the name and identities of the parties involved. Three of the four are obvious, but "the sentence being contested" would have to read that there was none. The man had been found innocent of the charges. And Paul was not contesting the charge of being innocent. This was the dilemma Festus faced. It was this part that he

needed help with, especially the assistance of Agrippa who knew the religious side better than he. Keener (IV:3489) aptly states, "He needs a sensitive way to word the Jewish charges without unnecessarily compromising Roman justice." If there ever was a kangaroo court, this was it. But the case is going to the most powerful man in the Roman world.

c. Paul's defense testimonial (26:1-23)

Paul's final testimonial defense is the climax of the trial motif of Acts. In these trials, Christianity is personified in the life of Paul and set forth before various audiences for witness. First, before the mob in Jerusalem (21:40b—22:21), then before the Sanhedrin (22:30—23:9), and finally before both the Roman and Jewish political powers in Felix, Festus, and Agrippa. All of Paul's defenses carry the same themes, centered on the reality of the resurrected Jesus of Nazareth and Paul's personal encounter with Him. The careful recording of his defenses gives us a key model for the apologetics of Christianity.

(1) Paul's expression of appreciation (26:1-3)

1 Then Agrippa said unto Paul, Thou art permitted to speak for thyself. Then Paul stretched forth the hand, and answered for himself:
2 I think myself happy, king Agrippa, because I shall answer for myself this day before thee touching all the things whereof I am accused of the Jews:

3 Especially *because I know* thee to be expert in all customs and questions which are among the Jews: wherefore I beseech thee to hear me patiently.

Although Festus had called the meeting, he deferred to Agrippa to initiate the exchange with Paul. Perhaps that was out of courtesy, but it may also imply his lack of expertise in the matter as well as his desire to distance himself from his responsibilities. Paul's hand gesture is typical of his abilities as a speaker (21:40).

It was common courtesy to express gratitude and sincere compliments to the court in such a setting, but it was also a means of disarming those who would hear him. Paul expressed confidence in being able to speak for himself regarding the charges (v. 2) as well as confidence in Agrippa's personal knowledge of Jewish religious beliefs and practices. With that said, Paul asked for patience to hear what he had to say (v. 3). This implies he had determined ahead of time what he wanted to communicate. No doubt Paul was aware of the high-level significance of the audience to whom he was speaking.

(2) Paul's past life in Judaism (26:4-11)

4 My manner of life from my youth, which was at the first among mine own nation at Jerusalem, know all the Jews;
5 Which knew me from the beginning, if they would testify, that after the most straitest sect of our religion I lived a Pharisee.

6 And now I stand and am judged for the hope of the promise made of God, unto our fathers:
7 Unto which *promise* our twelve tribes, instantly serving *God* day and night, hope to come. For which hope's sake, king Agrippa, I am accused of the Jews.
8 Why should it be thought a thing incredible with you, that God should raise the dead?
9 I verily thought with myself, that I ought to do many things contrary to the name of Jesus of Nazareth.
10 Which thing I also did in Jerusalem: and many of the saints did I shut up in prison, having received authority from the chief priests; and when they were put to death, I gave my voice against *them*.
11 And I punished them oft in every synagogue, and compelled *them* to blaspheme; and being exceedingly mad against them, I persecuted *them* even unto strange cities.

The theme of this part of Paul's defense is the same as before, documenting his Jewish identity and training as a Pharisee (vv. 4-5). It was this doctrinal training as a Pharisee that prepared him to embrace the O. T. concept of the hope of the resurrection (vv. 6-7). He had been taught that God could do anything, including raising the dead. Any number of O. T. stories and teachings about God would have established this truth. And it was a point that Agrippa would have known as well (vv. 7-8). In other words, even before his encounter with Jesus, Paul had been taught and personally embraced the O. T. teaching that God *could* raise the dead. The Jews embraced this truth and prayed for its fulfillment (Lk. 2:37). It was the centerpiece of their hope in the Messiah. Therefore, if Paul had come to believe this, why would it be used against him?

Paul does not ever explain his motives for persecuting the followers of Christ before his conversion. He only confesses that he did and that he did it with unholy passion (vv. 9-11). He does relate a few details of that time period, including the imprisonment of some, the death of others, the torturous efforts to get believers to "blaspheme," probably meaning to curse, revile, and deny faith in Jesus Christ (Bock 715; Fitzmyer 758). All this was done with his support and approval.

He describes his zeal for these efforts against the followers of Christ as "being exceedingly mad" (Greek *emmainomai*, be frenzied, frantic, enraged). He raged in anger against them—"a grand heresy hunt" (Robertson, *Acts* 447). His efforts took him into synagogues and cities beyond Judaea (v. 11).

The picture Paul paints of himself to this point is one that portrays him as the last person who would become a follower of Jesus of Nazareth. Even though the biblical truth that God was able to raise the dead had been deeply implanted in him early in his life, he denied its reality when confronted with those who declared that Jesus was the Messiah and had been raised from the dead. There is a subtle hint, here, that Agrippa himself was now in the same boat that Paul had been in (vv. 7-8). Paul specifically makes personal reference to Agrippa six times in the course of his defense (vv. 2, 7, 19, 26, 28-29).

(3) Paul's encounter with the risen Jesus of Nazareth (26:12-18)

12 Whereupon as I went to Damascus with authority and commission from the chief priests,
13 At midday, O king, I saw in the way a light from heaven, above the brightness of the sun, shining round about me and them which journeyed with me.
14 And when we were fallen to the earth, I heard a voice speaking unto me, and saying in the Hebrew tongue, Saul, Saul, why persecutest thou me? *it is* **hard for thee to kick against the pricks.**
15 And I said, Who art thou, Lord? And he said, I am Jesus whom thou persecutest.
16 But rise, and stand upon thy feet: for I have appeared unto thee for this purpose, to make thee a minister and a witness both of these things which thou hast seen, and of those thing in the which I will appear unto thee;
17 Delivering thee from the people, and *from* **the Gentiles, unto whom now I send thee.**
18 To open their eyes, *and* **to turn them from darkness to light, and** *from* **the power of Satan unto God, that they may receive forgiveness of sins, and inheritance among them which are sanctified by faith that is in me.**

Paul's encounter with the living Messiah was the event that changed everything about his life. He describes it this time, condensing the details recorded previously. The most important feature in this account is his commission (vv. 16-18) to be a "minister" (Greek *huperetes*, steward) and "witness" (Greek *martus*). This point explains why he did what he did among the Gentiles in the cities where he went and why he was standing before Festus and Agrippa now.

Especially telling is the purpose of his commission from the Lord, stated in verse 18, to preach to the *Gentiles*, adding a detail found only here. This commission is defined with three infinitives. First, "to *open* their eyes" speaks of spiritual enlightenment. Paul's own physical blindness and healing when he encountered Christ and was later restored is analogous to the spiritual blindness of people in sin who then come to the light of truth in Christ. This also is like the spiritual blindness of those who are not followers of Christ but are given light and life in Christ (2 Cor. 4:4-6).

Second, "to *turn* them from darkness to light" is a matter of spiritual liberation—a profound concept that includes the analogy of man's sinfulness pictured as darkness and the sinlessness of God Himself pictured as light (1 Jn. 1:5-7). This includes liberation from Satan, as the enslaver, to God, who liberates (Eph. 2:1-3; Rom. 8:1-2).

Third, for the Gentiles to "*receive* forgiveness of sins and inheritance" is a matter of reward. This includes the understanding that the purpose of Christ was to provide forgiveness for all men (Rom. 3:23-26) and eternal reward in heaven in perfect relationship with God (Rom. 8:17-18; Eph. 2:1-7).

Paul's final word here regards how these spiritual benefits are received and by whom. They are granted to all those who place their faith in this risen Christ. And this comes in a way that sanctifies (Greek *hagiazo*, to set apart) those who

savingly believe and grants them forgiveness and reward. Of course, the opportunity for that salvation included all those who were hearing Paul that day. As Polhill (*Acts* 504) observes, "One could hardly give a more succinct presentation of the gospel."

(4) Paul's obedience to "the heavenly vision" (26:19-23)

19 Whereupon, O king Agrippa, I was not disobedient unto the heavenly vision:
20 But shewed first unto them of Damascus, and at Jerusalem, and throughout all the coasts of Judaea, and *then* to the Gentiles, that they should repent and turn to God, and do works meet for repentance.
21 For these causes the Jews caught me in the temple, and went about to kill *me*.
22 Having therefore obtained help of God, I continue unto this day, witnessing both to small and great, saying none other things than those which the prophets and Moses did say should come:
23 That Christ should suffer, *and* that he should be the first that should rise from the dead, and should shew light unto the people, and to the Gentiles.

Making yet another personal reference to Agrippa, Paul expressed his own full obedience to "the heavenly vision" (v. 19). This vision became his life quest, and he fully gave himself to it. Significantly, he mentions the progress of his obedient witness, beginning from Damascus immediately following his conversion and extending through the last missionary journey (v. 20). Included in that extended witness was the appeal for repentance in turning away from sin and turning to God. One only has to check Paul's recorded messages to confirm the theme of repentance (17:30; 1 Thess. 1:9-10).

It was in his obedience to God that the Asian Jews who had come to Jerusalem for Pentecost accosted him in the temple and aroused a crowd that went about to kill him (v. 21). It was by the help of God he was spared and still alive. And mentioning this connected Paul's narrative to his being before Festus and Agrippa at that very moment (v. 22). His point is clear. He was simply obeying what he believed God had called him to do, and that was in complete agreement with the core teachings of the Jews and his own training. His appearance before them that day represented his continuing obedience to witness to all men of all social standing, "small and great."

Referencing "the prophets and Moses" as biblical authority (v. 22), Paul expands on his personal experience about the resurrected Messiah as confirming what has been written in the Scriptures. For Jews the Scriptures were the ultimate authority. While Festus would be ignorant of this point, Agrippa and Bernice would not. Again, Paul communicates to the audience that he had them in mind when he said "light to the people (Jews) and to the Gentiles" (v. 23). He was, in effect, giving "an invitation" as part of his message.

d. The reaction to Paul's defense (26:24-32)

(1) Reaction from Festus (26:24-26)

**24 And as he thus spake for himself, Festus said with a loud voice, Paul, thou art beside thyself; much learning doth make thee mad.
25 But he said, I am not mad, most noble Festus; but speak forth the words of truth and soberness.
26 For the king knoweth of these things, before whom also I speak freely: for I am persuaded that none of these things are hidden from him; for this thing was not done in a corner.**

The responses of Festus and Agrippa to Paul's defense present an interesting and dramatic exchange between prisoner and judges. Stott (376-377) has arranged them according to their order to capture the essence of the way they took place.

At the third mention of the resurrection (vv. 8, 15, 23), Festus had all he could stand. The phrase "as he [Paul] thus spake for himself" (Greek present participle, indicating progressive action) indicates that Festus interrupted Paul as he was speaking. This is also indicated by Festus' raising his voice. Of course, Festus was in charge of the proceedings so he had the right to say whatever he wanted. Paul had made his defense anyway.

Festus calls Paul's name for the first time and begins with a one-word (in Greek) affirmation: "thou art beside thyself," literally, "you are mad!" Festus accuses Paul of losing his mind. His reasoning was that Paul's learning and belief in the resurrection has altered his perception of reality. To him and most all Romans, belief in the resurrection was an insane belief. Schnabel (1015) and Polhill (*Acts* 507) do not think his statement was meant to be offensive. Bock (722), Marshall (*Acts* 398), and Robertson (*Acts* 452) disagree, suggesting that, If anything, Festus' statement was a back-handed compliment. He might have been complimenting Paul's learning and brilliance, but to him Paul had been removed from reality.

If Paul understood the statement as an insult he did not respond discourteously but respectfully, calling Festus, "most noble Festus," i.e., "Excellency" (Lk. 1:3). He reassured him that he was in full control of his mental capacities and spoke "truth and soberness" in contrast to insanity.

Furthermore, Paul calls Agrippa to bear witness (v. 26) to what he has said, for the king is fully aware of what Paul believed. Agrippa would have known of the O. T. teachings to which Paul referred, including its teaching of the resurrection. But more than that, Paul asserts that Agrippa is well aware of the story of the resurrection of Jesus and about His followers now known as Christians. The phrase "not done in a corner" was an idiom referring to something that was not hidden from the public. It was sometimes used of esoteric groups who isolated themselves and claimed special insights and knowledge (Keener IV:3543-3544). In this case, Paul specifically observes that "*this thing* was not done in a corner." What thing? Certainly it refers to the resurrection event itself, as well as to the witness of the followers of Jesus who believed in and re-told the story thousands of times. By the time of Agrippa's rule, Christians numbered in the thousands in Judaea alone. Such evidence could hardly be overlooked.

(2) Exchange with Agrippa (26:27-29)

**27 King Agrippa, believest thou the prophets? I know that thou believest.
28 Then Agrippa said unto Paul, Almost thou persuadest me to be a Christian.
29 And Paul said, I would to God, that not only thou, but also all that hear me this day, were both almost, and altogether such as I am, except these bonds.**

In what must have been a very personal and bold appeal, Paul addresses Agrippa directly regarding the state of his personal faith (v. 27). In referencing the prophets, Paul means the authority of the O. T. Scriptures regarding the Messianic prophecies. He is appealing to Agrippa for him to reach a logical conclusion regarding what Paul has just proclaimed. Clearly he is seeking Agrippa's conversion to Jesus Christ (Longenecker 350; Schnabel 1016). That is exactly what Paul has always done when proclaiming the gospel, especially to those who knew the O. T. Scriptures. It is truth that cannot be ignored. It is a logic that cannot be denied: avoided, yes; but not denied.

Paul's statement, "I know that thou believest" probably is an assertion based on an assumption. He is not announcing Agrippa's conversion, but he assumes that Agrippa, at least to a certain extent, accepts as truth the teachings of the O. T. prophets. Like Paul, this would have been part of his Jewish identity and cultural upbringing, however politicized it might have been as a result of his family heritage. Therefore, as Paul sees it, Agrippa ought to believe in Jesus and become a Christ-follower, too. Men and women with far less spiritual light than Agrippa had come to authentic faith in Christ.

The response of Agrippa has been the basis of countless sermons and at least one famous hymn. But just what did Agrippa say and mean by his response, "Almost thou persuadest me to be a Christian" (v. 28)? I believe the place to begin to understand his response is to consider, first, what must have been his thought process that led to his response. He has understood clearly what Paul meant by his belief in the resurrection. His own personal background (see above) has informed him of this. Furthermore, he knows the reports of the resurrection event itself and the undeniable numbers of people who have become followers of Christ. He may never have considered the personal ramifications of this information previously, but Paul has made it so logically clear that it cannot be denied. And Paul has pressed him for a decision. He has backed Agrippa into a corner.

However, the public setting has created for Agrippa a very uncomfortable venue. His political colleague, Festus, has just belittled the idea of a resurrection. Seated all around are political and civic dignitaries of the highest social levels. These are men and women who are dressed in their finest. He and Bernice are the beneficiaries of every privilege of royalty, including moral indulgences of every whim and without accountability. Agrippa has achieved his rank and status by skillfully playing the games of his political world. To become a Christian might be spiritually logical, but it would be politically dangerous. In stark contrast, Paul himself, as a Christian, has been imprisoned and

stands before them in chains. If Agrippa becomes a Christian he may end up where Paul is. He is definitely in an awkward position (Polhill, *Acts* 508; Bruce, *Acts* 471).

The wording of his verbal response is clear but the intent not so much. The phrase literally reads "In (or with) a little, you are persuading me to become a Christian." Fitzmyer (764-765) sees the possibility of Agrippa meaning that with a little more time and effort he could become a Christian like Paul. To say that might be, or sound like, a jest; but sincerity lay just beneath the surface. Robertson (*Acts* 454), Bock (723), and Schnabel (1017) agree that the tone is somewhat earnest but sarcastic.

Bruce (*Acts* 471), Stott (376), and Polhill (*Acts* 508-509) see his reply as insincere and entirely sarcastic; in that case it should be phrased as a question, "Do you think that in such a short time you can persuade me to be a (play the) Christian?"

I tend to agree with the first interpretation, that Agrippa is caught somewhere between earnestness and sarcasm. He cannot deny the truth but he can avoid it. He has been privileged with all the benefits of royalty and skillfully maneuvered his way to the top to sit with the powerful and wealthy. He and Bernice have lived as they chose without moral accountability. But now he is faced with deeper truths about the Messianic King and the undeniable authority of the prophets. Although he has known this previously, he has never addressed the personal implications of it. Thus, he is conflicted and with sarcastic bravado his response was to cover his thoughts and avoid his responsibility. In that case, the words mean something like, "Why, with a little more you'll make me a Christian!"

In this sense, Agrippa represented Judaism. He was faced with the truth of the O. T. Scriptures, but he was conflicted over his ties with the world's elite. God had intended for the Jews to be His witnesses to the world, ultimately through the Messiah (Isa. 43:10). But Judaism had become so politicized and its religious purpose so clouded that it operated somewhere between earnestness and sarcasm. The apostles, converted priests and Pharisees, the Berean Jews, Apollos—all the Jews who came to Christ—were earnest in their faith. The Herods represented the sarcastic elite who saw Christians as threats to their way of life. This was the tragic response of the Jews in the Acts record (Polhill, *Acts* 509).

Paul's reply to Agrippa began with a courteous expression of prayer with the phrase "I would to God." One can almost hear the quiet sincerity of his voice. Next is a play on Agrippa's own words (v. 29), but in complete sincerity not sarcasm. The phrase translated "both almost and altogether" literally reads, "both in a little and in much." The NASB translates it "whether in a short or long time." The idea is that Paul desired the conversion of Agrippa regardless what or how long it took. Those who carry the burden of unsaved family and friends know this feeling.

Added to this is the expansion of Paul's appeal to everyone present. Paul desired all to come to faith in Christ whether it took a short time or a long time to accomplish that. The only caveat is seen in the expression of his desire for the removal of "these bonds." One can picture Paul lifting his hands, shackled to Roman soldiers at his side. It was his desire that all come to know the risen Christ as he did but without the threat of imprisonment. In what is clearly a statement that Christianity presents no overt civil threat, as falsely imposed on him, Paul asserts his desire that all become believers "such as I am." Paul has not responded to either Festus or Agrippa with curtness or sarcasm.

(3) The decision to send Paul to Rome (26:30-32)

30 And when he had thus spoken, the king rose up, and the governor, and Bernice, and they that sat with them:
31 And when they were gone aside, they talked between themselves, saying, This man doeth nothing worthy of death or of bonds.
32 Then said Agrippa unto Festus, This man might have been set at liberty, if he had not appealed unto Caesar.

There was an extent to which God's promise to Paul, that he would bear witness to kings and rulers (9:15), had now been fulfilled. But there was another stage of witness to come, as the next scene will indicate. Paul's last words brought everything to conclusion. "The entertainment was over" (Robertson, *Acts* 454). When Agrippa, Bernice, and Festus rose, all the others rose, too, and filed out of the meeting room. However, Festus, Agrippa, and their advisory council (25:23) huddled together in conference, discussing what to do with Paul now. After all, that was the purpose of the meeting in the first place (25:25-27). Their unanimous conclusion was that Paul was innocent of the charges and could have been set free. Their conclusion was also a commentary on the effectiveness of Paul's defense testimonial. It had been very successful.

The only problem that remained was the fact that Paul had officially appealed his case to Caesar, and Festus had granted that appeal (25:12). The question about how Luke knew of this conversation is easily answered; the judges would have informed Paul of their conclusion when they determined that he would have to go to Rome (Bock 724). However, the question arises why they could not reconsider the appeal. There were two reasons. First, to do so would reflect on the ineptness of Festus in the matter. It certainly would not bode well for him with the Jews whom he sought to please (25:9). Plus, with Agrippa's declaration of Paul's innocence he now had what he needed for the letter (25:26-27). Second, the legal process had been set in motion and the prestige of Rome's Caesar was involved. It was no light thing to stop that process. If Caesar was to decide the case then so be it. In taking this approach, both of them deflected the responsibility away from themselves. Nobody could touch them with the case against Paul anymore.

Even so, in all the political wrangling the providential hand of God can be seen. It was by these unsaved men and these means that the Lord influenced the decision for Paul to bear witness to the highest political authority of the Roman world. The rest of Acts records the eventful journey.

Summary
(25:1—26:32)

The trial motif in Acts reaches its climax with Paul's defense testimonial before Festus, Agrippa, Bernice, and the assembled political and civic elite of Judaea in Caesarea. Getting Paul into that situation had resulted from both the miscarriage of justice by men and the providential hand of God. In the process, Paul had been given opportunity to witness to Felix and his wife Drusilla.

In what must have been a testing of the apostle's patience, he was left imprisoned in Caesarea for two years because Felix curried the favor of the Jews. When Felix was removed from office, Festus was appointed to replace him and inherited the situation with Paul. While making a political courtesy call to Jerusalem the new High Priest brings up Paul's case, asking Festus to help resolve the problem by extraditing Paul back to Jerusalem. The intention was to kill him along the way. For whatever reasons, Festus did not consent to the request but did set a date to reopen the case. When the hearing was finished the Jews had not proved their case and Paul had ably defended himself again. But Festus was willing to curry the favor of the Jews, as his predecessor had, and wanted Paul to return to Jerusalem for further questioning. It is likely that Paul knew what would happen if he went to Jerusalem, so he exercised his right as a Roman citizen to appeal his case to Caesar.

While he is waiting for the process of transfer to begin, Herod Agrippa and his sister Bernice pay Festus a political courtesy call to greet the new governor. During their visit Festus broaches the subject of Paul's case to Agrippa. In considerable detail, he gives Agrippa an update and solicits his help with it. Being Jewish and knowing the religious side of things, Agrippa is seen as an ally in the matter. A hearing for Paul is set, and it is to be held before the assembled military and civic elite of the area. Thus the stage is set for what may be Paul's greatest defense testimonial and one of the great apologetic statements of Christianity in Acts.

Paul's defense was so clearly stated and compelling that he was judged innocent of the charges against him. In the process, Paul made a direct appeal to the entire assembly, particularly Agrippa, to become believers in Jesus who had arisen from the dead. Festus scorned the idea of the resurrection and Agrippa avoided it. After the hearing, it was concluded that Paul could have been set free if he had not made an official appeal to Caesar. It was determined that he would be sent to Rome for that purpose. That way, these political leaders could not be accused of dealing with Paul. Their political expediency was more important to them than justice. But, again, the unjust acts of men became the providential hand of God to open yet another door of witness for the apostle Paul.

Application: Teaching and Preaching the Passage

Exegetical Outline of the Text: 1. Paul's Defense Before Festus and the Jews (25:1-12). 2. Festus and Agrippa Discuss Paul's Case (25:13-27). 3. Paul's Defense Testimonial Before the Political Assembly in Caesarea (26:1-29). 4. The Decision to Send Paul to Rome (26:30-32).

The providential hand of God that influenced men to come together in Caesarea assembled an incredible audience to hear Paul's testimony. Paul stood before men and women in powerful and influential positions in this world. But they were personally needy people.

Their lifestyles reflected their values, skewed by selfishness and pleasures of the flesh. Royal vestments were masks for empty lives. They were public successes but private failures. They were people in positions but without moral principles. Their wealth and power afforded them anything they wanted. But what they needed was what the gospel provided: peace with God and peace in their hearts. No matter who they are or how lofty they become in this world, all men and women need Christ.

The providential hand of God that brings us into contact with others around us—others who need God—is no less incredible. We may not be given an opportunity to stand before the assembled heads of state and share the gospel. But one's family, friends, co-workers, neighbors, and others may be the "assembly" the Lord places us before, to bear witness for Him. That is no less an opportunity than what was afforded to Paul. This theme is found repeatedly in Acts and makes a great basis for study and teaching.

Paul's personal conversion is recorded three times in the Acts record. Each recording adds a few details, never contradictory, that give us a full picture. Paul later said that his conversion was a pattern for others (1 Tim. 1:16) who would believe on Christ. Apparently one's conversion testimony is important. It behooves us as Christ-followers to be able to tell succinctly and clearly how we got saved. Doing this well requires personal reflection and open honesty about this life-changing decision.

Even when Paul was spoken to sarcastically by Festus and Agrippa, he did not respond in kind. It would have hurt his testimony to do so, and it would not have helped his case. How we respond is more important than how others speak to us. The Scriptures reference our words and attitudes many times. Paul modeled for us the right kind of response to what others say.

Perhaps one of the greatest truths from this section relates to the time that seems to be wasted keeping Paul imprisoned though he was innocent of all charges. Luke saw this, instead, as a time for research and writing. For Paul it was a time to pray and study the situation carefully to determine the words of his defense. Psalm 37:23 says, "The *steps* of a good man are ordered by the Lord: and he delighteth in his way." What the Lord orders may include "the *stops*" of a good man, too.

I. The Voyage to Rome (27:1—28:15)

1. From Caesarea to Fair Havens (27:1-8)

**1 And when it was determined that we should sail into Italy, they delivered Paul and certain other prisoners unto *one* named Julius, a centurion of Augustus' band.
2 And entering into a ship of Adramyttium, we launched, meaning to sail by the coasts of Asia; one Aristarchus, a Macedonian of Thessalonica, being with us.
3 And the next *day* we touched at Sidon. And Julius courteously entreated Paul, and gave *him* liberty to go unto his friends to refresh himself.
4 And when we had launched from thence, we sailed under Cyprus, because the winds were contrary.
5 And when we had sailed over the sea of Cilicia and Pamphylia, we came to Myra, *a city* of Lycia.
6 And there the centurion found a ship of Alexandria sailing into Italy; and he put us therein.
7 And when we had sailed slowly many days, and scarce were come against Cnidus, the wind not suffering us, we sailed under Crete, over against Salmone;
8 And, hardly passing it, came unto a place which is called The fair havens; nigh whereunto was the city of Lasea.**

Even a casual reading of Luke's eyewitness record of the trip to Rome shows his careful documentation and nautical awareness, although Robertson (*Acts* 456) concludes that he "writes like a landsman not a sailor." Sailing terms abound. Ports-of-call are specifically listed. Ships are named and specific shipping terms are used. Some of the passengers are named. Even concerns about the seasonal weather and prevailing winds are well documented. The accuracy of the record has been well-attested by many, including James Smith in *The Voyage and Shipwreck of St. Paul.* Furthermore, that Luke was an eyewitness to the events is evident from the repeated "we" references. Apparently, he kept a detailed journal of the trip. Although Paul had experienced other sea voyages and even shipwrecks (2 Cor. 11:25), this trip has gone down in history as a result of Luke's dramatic account.

Some writers have questioned the reality and factualness of the story as it occurs in Acts. Haenchen (708-711)

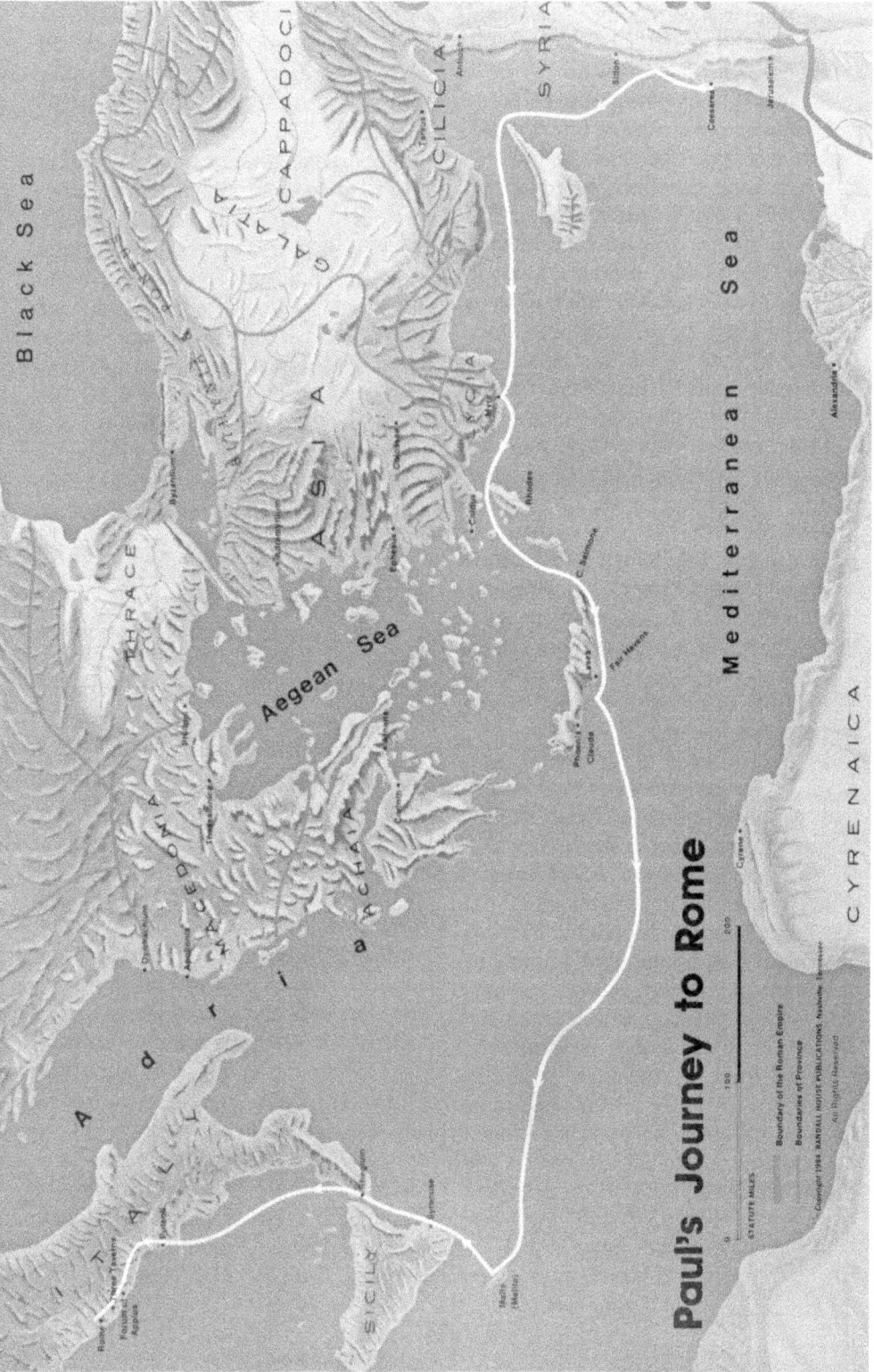

Paul's Journey to Rome

asserts that it is yet another Lucan construct about his hero, Paul. Consequently, in the account, Paul is always portrayed in the limelight as giving advice, always right, miraculously delivered from snakebite, and so on. Haenchen regards this as a borrowed shipwreck story with the character of Paul inserted and embellished, a literary construct by Luke to present Paul as "the unshaken favourite of God who strides from triumph to triumph." Fitzmyer (767-768) lists others who have the same view and agrees that the involvements of Paul were inserted by Luke to fit his literary purposes.

I mention this view only to show the skepticism that exists about the accuracy of the Scriptures and the integrity of Luke as the author of Acts. On the contrary, I agree fully with Marshall (*Acts* 402), who insists that it is completely improbable that Luke either invented the story or took it from another source. There are absolutely no reasons the story could not have happened exactly as Luke recorded it.

What does need to be seriously considered is the providence of God at work in the episode. It was God's will for Paul to go to Rome. Neither storm, nor shipwreck, nor snakebite would prevent that. Apparently Paul was aware of that, too, and courageously endured the tests. Why should it be thought improbable that these things did, indeed, happen? Why should Paul's presence of mind and wisdom in the situations be considered unlikely? After all, he himself had a lot of sailing experience, was already familiar with some of the ports mentioned, and, as an apostle had been gifted with divine abilities and protection to accomplish the ministry God had given him. God certainly could have stilled the storm (Mt. 8:23-27) and given them

smooth sailing all the way. However, His hand of blessing is just as surely displayed in preserving Paul and the others through the storm and shipwreck (Keener IV:3567).

Apparently, arrangements for the trip to Rome were completed in a timely manner. Since Rome had no harbor, Luke more correctly states they were destined for "Italy." The ship's crew are not listed but some of the passengers are noted, including Aristarchus of Thessalonica, possibly the same "fellow-prisoner" as in Colossians 4:10 and Philemon 24. Luke is certainly there as seen in the multiple "we" references. Paul, as a Roman citizen, would be dealt with differently from the other prisoners, to a certain extent. The reference to "certain other prisoners" is probably to men who have been sentenced to death and will provide entertainment in the gladiatorial games in the Colosseum in Rome (Ramsay, *Traveller* 314; Schnabel 1033).

All the prisoners, including Paul, were delivered to a centurion named Julius, charged to deliver them to Rome. He would have been given a detail of soldiers (v. 31) to accompany him but not an entire century of men. Julius was assigned to a unit known as "Augustus' band" or "the Revered One's (Emperor's) cohort." Roman legions had distinctive flag standards and names (as in today's military). It was common to name a legion after the emperor in his honor. This was probably an auxiliary or reserve unit known to have been kept in Syria at that time. Julius himself could have been taken from any legion and assigned to this unit for escort purposes (Keener IV:3570-3572; Polhill, *Acts* 515; Ramsay, *Traveller* 314-315).

The ships used on the journey were private vessels, usually hauling cargo and passengers according to their routes. Anyone could ride if the fare was paid. Apparently there was no ship available, at the time, sailing directly to Italy; so they had to take what was available. The first ship had Adramyttium, near Troas, as its home port. That would be its destination. Judging from the stops it made it was a coasting vessel and not suited for travel in the open sea.

They boarded ship in the man-made harbor at Caesarea and made their way up the coast to Sidon, some seventy nautical miles northward. After putting into port, the centurion gave Paul leave to visit "friends" (v. 3), who were undoubtedly Christians (Polhill, *Acts* 516; Keener IV:3577-3578). The visit was refreshing to Paul, both for the fellowship and in obtaining the food and supplies for the trip. Who has not had gracious and generous friends so make provisions for us as we traveled? One remembers that it had been at Tyre that some of the brethren warned Paul about going to Jerusalem (21:3-4). Tyre was only a few miles away. One cannot help wondering if some of those who warned Paul earlier were there to see him and be updated on how things had worked out.

With the resumption of the sea voyage, the ship ran into the prevailing northwesterly winds that made the trip slow and demanding as they were sailing directly into the wind. The phrase "we sailed under Cyprus" (v. 4) means "in the lee of Cyprus" as they sailed along the east coast (not the south coast) of the island, using it for some shelter from the wind (Smith 68). They finally made port at Myra on the southernmost part of the province of Asia.

Myra was directly north of Alexandria, Egypt (across the Mediterranean), and was a common port for grain vessels bound for Italy. Grain was essential food for the stability of the empire and its transport was closely regulated and guarded by the government. A Roman guard with a centurion accompanied such vessels for security. It was here the centurion, Julius, found a vessel headed for Italy and secured it for his charges. All were transferred to it (v. 6).

Grain ships were usually large vessels. It was common for them to be over one hundred feet in length and to carry in excess of a thousand tons (Keener IV:3584-3585; Polhill, *Acts* 517; Bock 733). In addition to the cargo (v. 18), two-hundred and seventy-six persons (v. 37) were boarded for the remainder of the trip. Those included the ship's crew, the soldiers, those who accompanied Paul, and the prisoners—most of whom were in shackles (v. 1).

When they launched from Myra (v. 7), they immediately encountered the headwinds that slowed their trip. They were blown off the normal route and tracked southward, sailing along the south side of the island of Crete (v. 7), where they finally made the port of "Fair Havens" (v. 8), named for its harbor that gave respite from the prevailing winds. It should be noted that Luke details the whereabouts of certain places. These have all been documented in later research, showing the accuracy of the account (Ramsay; Smith). By now the mariners were weary from fighting the winds and waves.

2. The storm and shipwreck (27:9-44)

a. The decision to sail (27:9-12)

9 Now when much time was spent, and when sailing was not dangerous, because the fast was now already past, Paul admonished *them,*
10 And said unto them, Sirs, I perceive that this voyage will be with hurt and much damage, not only of the lading and ship, but also of our lives.
11 Nevertheless the centurion believed the master and owner of the ship, more than those things which were spoken by Paul.
12 And because the haven was not commodious to winter in, the more part advised to depart thence also, it by any means they might attain to Phenice, *and there* **to winter;** *which is* **an haven of Crete, and lieth toward the south west and north west.**

Travel on the Mediterranean Sea from mid-September through early November was considered to be dangerous (Keener IV:3593-3597). After that, all travel ceased until the last of February or early March. The voyage had already been delayed for several days (v. 9) and the window of opportunity to continue the voyage was closing fast. The reference to "the fast" means the Day of Atonement, which had already come and gone. Commentators favor the date of October 5, A.D. 59 (Polhill, *Acts* 518; Schnabel 1037; Smith 260) for The Day of Atonement and the year of the voyage. Keener (IV:3597-3598) charts the possible dates and progression of the voyage.

It appears that the centurion grew impatient with the delays and held a consultation to determine whether the trip should be resumed. Paul was allowed to give his opinion; he warned of trouble and loss if they continued (v. 10). It should be remembered that Paul had been on many sea voyages and experienced a number of disasters (2 Cor. 11:25-26). So had Luke. Paul's advice was more than just a gut feeling, it was based on experience and common sense. His later advice (vv. 21-26) stems from divine communication (Barrett, *Acts* 401).

Paul's opinion was heard but rejected by the ship's owner, who probably was the captain of the vessel as well, and the sailing master (Keener IV:3602-3603). These were the professionals who should know what to do. There is no doubt the ship was under contract to deliver its cargo of grain (v. 38), so time was money. What businessmen have not had to take risks to deliver on their commitments? The centurion had the authority to make the final decision, so he did. They would sail when given the approval of the ship's captain.

In spite of its name, "Fair Havens" was not desirable enough to spend the winter there, but not far away lay the port of "Phenice" (Phoenix, modern Loutro), well suited for their purpose (v. 12). It was only some forty nautical miles farther west and surely they could get there (at least that was their thinking). With the decision made, they needed only a break in the weather to launch.

b. The storm "Euroclydon" (27:13-20)

13 And when the south wind blew softly, supposing that they had obtained *their* purpose, loosing *thence*, they sailed close by Crete.
14 But not long after there arose against it a tempestuous wind, called Euroclydon.
15 And when the ship was caught, and could not bear up into the wind, we let *her* drive.
16 And running under a certain island which is called Clauda, we had much work to come by the boat:
17 Which when they had taken up, they used helps, undergirding the ship; and, fearing lest they should fall into the quicksands, strake sail, and so were driven.
18 And we being exceedingly tossed with a tempest, the next *day* they lightened the ship;
19 And the third *day* we cast out with our own hands the tackling of the ship.
20 And when neither sun nor stars in many days appeared, and no small tempest lay on *us*, all hope that we should be saved was then taken away.

Perhaps the ship's crew was impatient and that was combined with the flirtatious brush of a south wind. At any rate, they decided it was time to make the run for Phoenix. By sailing close to shore (v. 13), they should be able to make the short distance in a few hours, and they could remain there until the spring sailing season resumed.

What happened next is well documented (Smith 101-103; Ramsay, *Traveller* 262-263; Polhill, *Acts* 520). Some of the mountains on Crete tower to over seven thousand feet and influence the weather systems, especially the wind. But when the wind cascades over the mountain it rushes like a hurricane to the ocean. Anyone who has lived on the lee side of mountains knows about this effect. As the ship rounded Cape Matala, the ship was struck broadside by a "tempestuous wind" nicknamed *Euroclydon*. The word translated *tempestuous* (Greek *tuphonikos*, whence our "typhoon") means hurricane-like or typhoon-like (Moulton and Milligan 646). The so-called nickname is spelled differently in various Greek manuscripts; it is probably a hybrid combination of words for east wind and north wind, and so a "nor'easter." When it struck they were unable to continue on a northwesterly course, so they would have shortened their sails, battened down the hatches, and let the ship be driven by the wind (v. 15).

The Island of Clauda (modern Gozzo) was some twenty-five miles to the southeast, indicating how far off course they were blown before they were able to identify where they were. Near there they were able to save "the boat" (v. 16), which was the life boat or dinghy that trailed behind the ship. They realized they were at the mercy of the storm and began survival tactics, attempting to prevent the ship from breaking up. They undergirded the ship with cables or heavy ropes. This meant they ran these under and around the ship horizontally to tighten the outer planking of the ship (v. 17)—a method called "frapping." The twisting and wrenching of the wooden ship would break its spine unless it was secured.

To the south, still some three hundred and fifty miles away off the North African coast, lay an area called "The Syrtis" (Greek *he surtis*, translated "the quicksands," KJV) that was known for its sandbars and shoals. At that point, to run aground there was their greatest fear as they perceived that the fierceness of the storm threatened to blow them that far south. To slow their drift in that direction, they "strake sail." There is some question as to what exactly is meant here. Bruce (*Acts* 486) takes it to mean they lowered a sea anchor. Ramsay (*Traveller* 264) believes it to mean they lowered the mainsail, leaving only a smaller storm sail out for some control. Keener (IV:3616) suggests it meant to lower anchors with large stones attached to serve as drags. Why not all of the above? Desperate conditions call for desperate measures. Regardless, they were still at the storm's mercy and driven by the wind.

The following day they jettisoned the excess cargo (v. 18). That might have included some of the grain. The third day (v. 19) they jettisoned "the tackling of the ship." Schnabel (1041) thinks this is excess rigging and equipment. But Luke notes that some of the passengers, including himself, had to assist the crew as they all helped "with our own hands." Marshall (*Acts* 409) is puzzled about this. Smith (116) takes Luke to refer to the huge spar used for the mainsail which was midship; removing it would give the ship more balance. Its size and weight required all hands available to help. That would be the meaning of helping "with our own hands." They would still have the foresail to maneuver. With that they had done all they could.

Still the storm did not abate for several more days. The cloud cover was so thick they could not see the sun by day or the stars by night. They could not therefore take a sighting to determine where they were. The sea raged around them and they no doubt worked continually to keep the ship afloat. With the extended weariness and strain came a sense of hopelessness. All hands on board seemed to lapse into despair, fearing that they would not "be saved"—that is, survive (v. 20). All but one despaired, that is.

c. Encouraging words from Paul (27:21-26)

21 But after long abstinence Paul stood forth in the midst of them, and said, Sirs, ye should have hearkened unto me, and not have loosed from Crete, and to have gained this harm and loss.
22 And now I exhort you to be of good cheer: for there shall be no loss of *any man's* life among you, but of the ship.
23 For there stood by me this night the angel of God, whose I am, and whom I serve,
24 Saying, Fear not, Paul: thou must be brought before Caesar: and lo, God hath given thee all them that sail with thee.
25 Wherefore, sirs, be of good cheer: for I believe God, that it shall be even as it was told me.
26 Howbeit we must be cast upon a certain island.

With the storm at its height and morale at its lowest, no one had any appetite for food as indicated by the phrase "long abstinence" (v. 21). This is easily understood to be the result of seasickness, fear, anxiety—not to mention the difficulty of preparing meals under such circumstances. When all seemed completely lost, Paul positioned himself among the men so he could offer words of hope. There is much discussion among commentators about the reality of this. Haenchen (709), for example, comments that the whole scene is unreal and contrived. How could Paul speak on the deck of a storm-tossed ship above the howling wind? As Keener (IV:3624-3625) points out, there would have been lulls in the storm and Paul could have spoken during one such time. For that matter, he might have spoken below deck to men huddled tightly together against the wind and water (Bock 737; Smith 265). Some of the cargo had been thrown into the sea (v. 18), so some room was made below deck. But there is no need to assume that all two hundred and seventy-six men were gathered together in one place. Some might have been scattered here and there, performing their duties while Paul spoke to those who could hear. The word would have been passed to the rest.

With a very human "I told you so" he prefaced his remarks (v. 21). But it was more than an expression of egotism. More likely it was to communicate confidence that they needed to listen to him now since he had been right before. Who among us has not given in to saying "I told you so"? His word to them promised hope and the saving of their lives, but he acknowledged that the ship would be lost (v. 22)—a word of "good cheer" and encouragement. The loss of the ship and the valuable cargo would be bad indeed, but the loss of all hands was not to be compared. When faced with the choice of life or some material thing, most people will choose life. People who are struggling in the storms of life always need a word of encouragement.

And Paul's source for this information was...? Without apology or qualification Paul attributes his information to "the angel of God" (v. 23), who had appeared to him in the night. With the exception of his personal companions, the men to whom Paul is speaking are pagans—hardened sailors, soldiers, and prisoners. Even men like these are known to call on their deities at such a time as these faced (Jon. 1:5-6). The difference here is that Paul identifies the God who appeared to him and affirmed that he belonged to his God. With the confidence of one who has heard from Heaven, the apostle reassured them that God had just promised him that he would make it to Rome to stand before Caesar (23:11). That plan also included the survival of all on board (v. 24). Paul added his own expression of confidence, that he believed what God had told him, and repeated his word to "be of good cheer." They were recipients of the promise, too.

His final words here (v. 26) are that they would "be cast upon a certain island"—literally "fall upon" or "run aground." Normally for a ship to run aground is not good news, but in this case, combined with the encouragement of survival, it was a far better alternative than sinking in the open sea. Of course, Paul's prediction remained to be confirmed. Nor did his words of encouragement have any effect on the raging seas around them. Storms do not always immediately calm around us. In Paul's case the storm had ceased within him and his words of cheer were intended to do the same for them.

It should be noted that Paul was not the "divine man" who miraculously calmed the storm as Jesus could and did (Mt. 8:26-27). He had endured the same thrashing and strain as all the others. He was probably as seasick as they. But he was God's man who had been promised by the Lord that he would stand before Caesar and that these men would survive the storm. In effect he and they would not die until God had finished His purpose.

Marshall (*Acts* 410) observes that there is a parallel between this scene and the intercession of Abraham for Lot in the city of Sodom (Gen. 18:22-33), when he pleaded with God to spare the others in the city for the sake of the righteous. Be that as it may, there are blessings for even the unrighteous who live on the perimeters of God's people (Mt. 15:27). There is no question but that the Lord spared the lives of the people on *this* ship because of the presence of Paul.

d. The shipwreck and escape to land (27:27-44)

27 But when the fourteenth night was come, as we were driven up and down in Adria, about midnight the shipmen deemed that they drew near to some country;
28 And sounded, and found *it* twenty fathoms: and when they had gone a little further, they sounded again, and found *it* fifteen fathoms.
29 Then fearing lest we should have fallen upon rocks, they cast four anchors out of the stern, and wished for the day.
30 And as the shipmen were about to flee out of the ship, when they had let down the boat into the sea, under colour as though they would
have cast anchors out of the fore-ship,
31 Paul said to the centurion and to the soldiers, Except these abide in the ship, ye cannot be saved.
32 Then the soldiers cut off the ropes of the boat, and let her fall off.
33 And while the day was coming on, Paul besought *them* all to take meat, saying, This day is the fourteenth day that ye have tarried and continued fasting, having taken nothing.
34 Wherefore I pray you to take *some* meat: for this is for your health: for there shall not an hair fall from the head of any of you.
35 And when he had thus spoken, he took bread, and gave thanks to God in presence of them all: and when he had broken *it*, he began to eat.
36 Then were they all of good cheer, and they also took *some* meat.
37 And we were in all in the ship two hundred threescore and sixteen souls.
38 And when they had eaten enough, they lightened the ship, and cast out the wheat into the sea.
39 And when it was day, they knew not the land: but they discovered a certain creek with a shore, into the which they were minded, if it were possible, to thrust in the ship.
40 And when they had taken up the anchors, they committed *themselves* unto the sea, and loosed the rudder bands, and hoised up the mainsail to the wind, and made toward the shore.

41 And falling into a place where two seas met, they ran the ship aground; and the forepart stuck fast, and remained unmoveable, but the hinder part was broken with the violence of the waves.
42 And the soldiers' counsel was to kill the prisoners, lest any of them should swim out, and escape.
43 But the centurion, willing to save Paul, kept them from *their* purpose; and commanded that they which could swim should cast *themselves* first *into the sea*, and get to land:
44 And the rest, some on boards, and some on *broken pieces* of the ship. And so it came to pass, that they escaped all safe to land.

Smith (125-128) and Ramsay (*Traveller* 330) document carefully the direction and rate of drift for a ship under these circumstances. By their calculations after thirteen days of drifting under these conditions they had drifted northwest and would have been only three miles off the coast of "Melita" (modern Malta)—confirming the accuracy of Luke's account. Modern day St. Paul's bay, on the island, has been determined to be the site of the shipwreck as recorded (Smith 128; Ramsay, *Traveller* 341).

The sound of waves crashing alerted the crew to the shoals or rocks, so they took "soundings" to determine the depth of the ocean (vv. 27-28). Soundings were taken using ropes that were weighted on the ends and marked in "fathoms." A fathom was measured by the extending of the arms horizontally, usually measuring about six feet. Thus a fathom is six feet. A sounding of twenty fathoms then was about one hundred and twenty feet deep (v. 28). Their soundings showed the depth was getting shallower, so they determined to cast out anchors from the "stern" (the rear) of the ship to keep it from drifting onto rocks (v. 29). With the stern anchored and the action of the waves rolling into shore, this would position the bow (the front) of the ship pointed toward land.

Having anchored the ship and sensing they could make it to land, the crew decided it was time for them to abandon ship (v. 30). It was still dark and they could make their getaway. The dinghy or lifeboat had been taken on board and lashed down (v. 16). They loosened it and put it back into the water under the pretext of securing anchors to the bow of the ship ("under colour" is Greek *prophasis*, pretense). Anchoring the bow was a smart idea that would have stabilized the ship more but that was not their intent. Apparently Luke overheard them and recorded their real intent. Theirs was a complete disregard for the rest of those on board. Apparently, they did not believe the words of Paul. That is not surprising; hardened hearts sometimes take a while to soften.

When the intent of the crew was discovered, Paul directly warned the centurion and connected everyone's survival to remaining in the ship (v. 31). While this had been part of the words of encouragement he had previously spoken (vv. 21-26), the expertise of the crew in assisting the others was essential. If they were allowed to get away the rest of them would be in jeopardy. The actions of the soldiers in cutting away the dinghy shows their respect for what Paul said and may very well have saved the day. If they had kept the dinghy until morning and tried to use it to ferry passengers ashore, there might have been chaos in determining who would go first. There were two hundred and seventy-six souls on board. That would require a huge effort in itself and the ship might not last that long, given the continued violence of the storm (Keener IV:3639; Schnabel 1045).

Paul's fourth intervention in the event is his counsel for them all to eat something ("meat" is Greek *trophe*, food). His reasoning is sound; they have not had much to eat in a while and food is necessary for their "health" (Greek *soteria*, literally "salvation" in the sense of survival). Much energy would be needed for the coming escape to shore. Furthermore, he repeated that no one would perish, as meant by the clause "there shall not an hair fall from the head of any of you."

Paul's act of giving thanks to God was more than just a routine prayer over a meal. It was an open expression of gratitude for preservation thus far and the promise of safety the rest of the way. The scene is striking in that it reminds us of the Lord's Supper when Jesus did the same thing with the apostles the night of His betrayal (Mt. 26:26). This might not have meant anything to those who knew nothing of the Lord's Supper, but it did to the few believers who were there. It reminded them of God's presence through the storm (Polhill, *Acts* 527). Plus, it signaled to the others the authenticity of Paul's words of faith and blessing.

When he finished his simple prayer Paul broke the loaf of bread and began eating. The rest followed suit and were encouraged (v. 36). Who has not found refreshing in a meal and the assurance of God's blessings? Luke has from the beginning of his narrative been focused

on numbers when necessary. Now he records the number of those on board as two hundred and seventy-six souls (v. 37). It would have been easy enough at the meal to take a roll call of all who were on board. This indicates that the vessel was probably overloaded, but there were no government regulations about that in those days. (Josephus, *Life* 3, records a sea voyage he took to Rome when he was twenty-six years old and suffered a shipwreck, too. The ship held six hundred people.) The number Luke records shows that there were a lot of people involved. Polhill (*Acts* 528) comments, "It was no small affair." God's providential hand of protection extended to all on board, not just to Paul and his companions. Given the severity of the storm, it would not have been unusual for some men to have been lost overboard with the wild pitching and tossing of the ship. That all were saved reinforces the literalness of God's promise (v. 22).

When all had finished eating (v. 38), they threw the grain overboard, apparently with the intent to lighten the ship, so they could run it as far aground on the beach as possible when the time came. The decision would have been made by the owner and captain of the vessel. The indication is that the grain had been kept in sacks for transport, so the offloading was more easily facilitated. All this was done while it was still night.

Daylight came (v. 39) and without doubt the men searched the shoreline with anxious eyes. Nothing they saw looked familiar enough for them to identify where they were. The main port on Malta was further west but the storm had blown them to the northeast side of the island. They would have recognized the main port, but they were not there. As they scanned the shoreline, a plan about what to do when the time came developed. The shoreline had a break in it where a creek flowed from inland into the sea. There was a sandy beach ("a shore") where they just might be able to steer the ship and run it aground on the shore (v. 39). Note the conditional phrase "if it were possible." Even with all the sailing expertise they had, they were at the mercy of the wind and waves. But it was a plan they hoped to pull off and make it to shore. Smith (140-145) and Ramsay (*Traveller* 340-341) have well-documented the general features that were still extant when they investigated the area.

With everything in place and committed to the plan, they began its execution (v. 40). There were three actions done simultaneously. 1. They removed the four stern anchors, probably cutting them away. 2. They unlashed the rudders, which were large paddles on either side of the stern for maneuvering. These were lowered into the water. 3. They raised a sail (Greek *artemon*), translated as "mainsail" in the KJV, but probably the foresail to be used for steerage. Having done so, they committed themselves to the wind and waves as they frantically tried to maneuver the ship to the beach.

With limited control of the ship they were not able to get to the beach. Instead they ran aground on a point, a shoal or a promontory that extended out into the sea. The wording suggests that the action was intentional as they saw they could not make the beach and chose, instead, the shoal. It would have water on both sides and a natural boundary that showed where the bay water and the main ocean met—thus

the description "where two seas met" (v. 41). One only has to observe harbors and bays today to get the idea. The promontory is today called "St. Paul's Bank" (Keener IV:3652). It was close enough to shore to offer hope of escape.

The grounding of the vessel was so powerful that the front of the ship, "the forepart" or bow, wedged tightly. The rear of the ship was pounded mercilessly by the violent waves and bit by bit was being broken apart (v. 41). They did not have long before the entire ship would be torn apart.

It was then the soldiers starting making plans to kill the prisoners to prevent their escape (v. 42). This included Paul. They were responsible and, according to law, if the prisoners escaped the soldiers would suffer the penalty assigned to the prisoners (Schnabel 1048). The prisoners would have been chained together. If they tried to swim while chained they would have drowned. If they unchained them they risked their escape. In the world of that day, their reasoning was cruel but understandable.

The decision of the centurion not to kill the prisoners was motivated by his desire to protect and spare Paul (v. 43). By now his respect for Paul has grown to the point of deferring to him for some of the decisions being made, especially this one. It may be that the centurion does not want to anger Paul's deity (Keener IV:3654). It may be that he sees the wisdom of Paul in claiming the need for all to assist in the escape. Whatever his reasoning, it is again clear that because of Paul all the prisoners are spared (Polhill, *Acts* 530).

With the decision made not to kill the prisoners, the order was given by the centurion for those who could swim to go first, followed by the others who would have to find something to help them swim (vv. 43-44). Schnabel (1049) notes the sense and order of the plan as: crew and passengers who could swim go first, to be followed by the rest who could use some means of flotation. That's exactly what they did and it succeeded completely, just as Paul (and the Lord) had said (vv. 24, 34).

Keener (IV:3659-3660) raises the question how Luke could have preserved his notes under these conditions. He gives a number of possible scenarios. It must be remembered that these are not ignorant or inexperienced people. Watertight skins, bottles, and pots using sealants of various types were common means of protecting important papers.

3. On the island of Melita (Malta) (28:1-10)

**1   And when they were escaped, then they knew that the island was called Melita.
2   And the barbarous people shewed us no little kindness: for they kindled a fire, and received us every one, because of the present rain, and because of the cold.
3   And when Paul had gathered a bundle of sticks, and laid *them* on the fire, there came a viper out of the heat, and fastened on his hand.
4   And when the barbarians saw the *venomous* beast hang on his hand, they said among themselves, No doubt this man is a murderer, whom, though he hath escaped the sea, yet vengeance suffereth not to live.
5   And he shook off the beast into the fire, and felt no harm.
6   Howbeit they looked when he should have swollen, or fallen down dead suddenly: but after they had looked a great while, and saw no harm come to him, they changed their minds, and said that he was a god.
7   In the same quarters were possessions of the chief man of the island, whose name was Publius; who received us, and lodged us three days courteously.
8   And it came to pass, that the father of Publius lay sick of a fever and of a bloody flux: to whom Paul entered in, and prayed, and laid his hands on him, and healed him.
9   So when this was done, others also, which had diseases in the island, came, and were healed:
10 Who also honoured us with many honours; and when we departed, they laded *us* with such things as were necessary.**

Paul, his companions, and all the rest of the ship's passengers and crew had survived the storm and the shipwreck. When finally on shore they learned that they were on the island of "Melita" (modern Malta). This was probably established when they met some of the people; one of the first questions they would have asked would have been, "Where are we?" In yet another evidence of God's providence, not only were they safe but the island was on the route to Italy, too.

Luke's identification of the native people of Malta as "barbarians" (v. 2) is merely a cultural-linguistic reference to distinguish them from people who spoke Greek (Schnabel 1049; Bock 742). Hospitality and kindness were usually a part of most cultures such as these, especially toward ships and sailors. They were an integral part of their economy in trade, but hospitality was not necessarily displayed for its monetary benefit. Social interaction was an important part of life that reflected on everything (Wight 69-79).

Their kindness toward the shipwreck victims was immediately shown by their building a fire against the cold of the wind, rain, and water-soaked clothes. With the large number of men on the beach there could have been several fires kindled but Luke notes only one since his focus was on what happened next. Paul was not above helping with the chores (as is typical of those in ministry). When he picked up a bundle of sticks to put on the fire, a "viper" or snake (Greek *echidna*, usually a poisonous snake) that had been nestled among them was awakened from its cold stupor and bit him (v. 3). In fact, its bite caused it to fasten on his hand as the teeth stuck in the skin and flesh. Paul had to shake it loose and drop it in the fire (v. 5).

Many attempts have been made to identify the viper. To deny the reality of the situation by appealing to the fact there are no snakes on Malta today is disingenuous. That does not mean there were none then, or that there were not any poisonous snakes then (Smith 151). The native people would have known well what kind of snake it was and when they saw it bite Paul, they believed it was poisonous. I am not inclined to ambivalence about their opinion (Schnabel 1051), nor was Luke. The island natives expected Paul to suffer and die from its bite (v. 4). Their assumption was that the snakebite was evidence of divine retribution and that Paul must have been a murderer. His luck in escaping the storm and shipwreck had just run out!

Such views of divine retribution appear in many cultures all over the world.

Even though any snakebite is painful, a poisonous snake's bite can be deadly. But Paul was not adversely affected in any way; there was not even any swelling of his hand, much less a paralysis that resulted in death (vv. 5-6). The island natives (as well as others of his own group?) watched carefully for a long time, but there were no negative aftereffects. This resulted in a complete reversal of their opinion about him. He had been judged a murderer who would suffer divine retribution, but now they considered him to be a god. This same effect had occurred in Lystra (14:8-18) following the healing of the lame man. Paul's innocence had again been verified (in the eyes of the people of Malta). It does not appear that Paul was aware of their new appraisal of him, for there is no record of his response. Given his response in Lystra, it seems likely that he would have tried to correct their notion had he known.

So, why did Paul not die from the snakebite? For the same reason he did not die in Jerusalem, Caesarea, the storm, and the shipwreck. God had promised him that he would stand before Caesar and that had not happened yet. One can also apply rightly the special promise of protection found in Luke 10:19 and Mark 16:17-18 in this situation. (For comments on the authenticity of the text in Mark see Picirilli, *Mark* 21-22).

Word soon spread to the chief official of the island, a man with the Roman name of Publius. It is possible that he was the procurator (governor), although Luke is not specific. Polhill (*Acts* 533) reports that archaeological inscriptions have been found on Malta bearing the same title for the "chief man" or "first man." The capital city was Melita at the time and Publius' offices would have been there. The shipwreck could be seen from there. His "quarters" (v. 7) may refer to his personal home where he lodged some of the travelers for three days. Just who Luke means by "us" is not clear; he probably did not mean to include the prisoners, the soldiers who guarded them, or the ship's crew. More likely, he meant the centurion, Paul, Luke, the ship's owner, and the sailing master. It does appear likely that the others were also provided for, and it would have been the responsibility of the centurion, consulting with Publius, to see to that. The island was under Roman jurisdiction.

It appears that while they were staying with Publius they learned of his father's illness (v. 8). Luke's description again shows his interest in medical situations. The symptoms indicate dysentery and fever, perhaps caused by goat's milk and known as "Malta fever" (Polhill, *Acts* 533-534; Bock 744). Although some writers do not think that Luke's details about medical matter lead to the conclusion that he was a physician (Bock 744), it seems strange to deny this since Paul himself said Luke was a physician (Col. 4:14). Bruce (*Acts* 500) insists on Luke's medical skills. Upon learning of the father's illness, Paul was instrumental in his healing. Four actions are associated with the healing. 1. "He entered in": that is, he went to the place where he was. 2. "He prayed": that is, he called upon the Lord on his behalf. 3. He "laid his hands on him": that is, Paul touched him in compassion. 4. He "healed him," that is, the Lord touched the man's body through Paul. Again, Paul is not "the divine man" but a man

of God who is the instrument to heal and relieve the suffering of the sick. The situation may remind us of the same kind of descriptions used when Jesus healed people. The circumstances are relatively unimportant; what is Christlike is the healing of the sick. Paul had been used in apostolic miracles previously (14:8-10; 19:12).

The healing of Publius' father was soon known and others on the island came to Paul for healing (v. 9). Although we are not told specifically that Paul proclaimed the gospel there, it can be reasonably assumed that he did (Longenecker 361). Meyer (500) references traditional sources that say Publius was saved, became the first Bishop of Malta for thirty-one years, and was martyred in Athens. There may be many "silent" stories like this that are not included in the Acts record.

The hospitality of the people of Malta extended to honoring them in many ways. Luke does not tell us how, except that they provided the necessities required for travel when the shipwrecked crew and passengers left. It is clear that the Christians had ministered to needs and provided a positive basis for the proclamation of the gospel. The good will generated by compassion is always acceptable and appreciated.

4. From Melita (Malta) to Rome (28:11-15)

11 And after three months we departed in a ship of Alexandria, which had wintered in the isle, whose sign was Castor and Pollux. 12 And landing at Syracuse, we tarried *there* three days. 13 And from thence we fetched a compass, and came to Rhegium:

and after one day the south wind blew, and we came the next day to Puteoli:
14 Where we found brethren, and were desired to tarry with then seven days: and so we went toward Rome.
15 And from thence, when the brethren heard of us, they came to meet us as far as Appi forum, and The three taverns: whom when Paul saw, he thanked God, and took courage.

The three months wintering on the island of Malta may be figured from their arrival toward the end of October (27:9) to the beginning of February. Even that was a little early to leave, since sea travel did not usually begin until early March. The early departure was probably because of the crew of the ship they found wintering there and with which they made travel arrangements. That ship, too, was a grain ship out of Alexandria (Robertson, *Acts* 482). Luke adds a word to identify the ship, giving its sign as "Castor and Pollux" (Greek *Dioskouroi*, literally "the twins"). The KJV gives the names instead of the single term. In mythology, Castor and Pollux were the twin sons of Zeus and Leda and were regarded as protectors of those who sailed the seas (Bock 744-745). Their figureheads were often carved on ship's bows, given the frequency of sea travel and mythological beliefs. It may be that Luke saw the irony and recorded the name of the ship that honored idolatrous gods, who afforded no protection to sailors, in contrast to the Lord God, who had actually delivered Paul and all the others from the storm and shipwreck.

The first leg of the journey was some eighty nautical miles northeast to Syracuse, which lay on the southeastern tip of Sicily (v. 12). Here they spent three days, either for trade or awaiting fairer southerly winds. It was then some seventy nautical miles due north to Rhegium from Syracuse, but something delayed them. The meaning of the words "fetched a compass" (v. 13) is debatable (and involves some manuscript differences): either to "weigh anchor" or to "make a circuit" (Metzger 443). Robertson (*Acts* 482) insists on the latter meaning (as do most versions); they had to maneuver in such a way (tack against the wind) that it took longer to reach Rhegium (Polhill, *Acts* 535-536).

They left Rhegium when the south wind blew, and this time (compare 27:13) it did not deceive them. The distance from there to Puteoli was some one hundred and eighty nautical miles and took two days (v. 13). When they landed at Puteoli, they were only one hundred and thirty miles from Rome by land, a journey of about ten days. In Puteoli, they found a community of believers and were allowed to stay with them for seven days (v. 14). This is again a remarkable indication of the centurion's courtesy to Paul and his companions. Paul was still a prisoner and would have been bound in chains to soldiers but he was allowed freedoms beyond the usual treatment. Schnabel (1055) suggests that there might have been wealthy Christians in Puteoli who accommodated the entire company, including the prisoners, expressing hospitality and replenishing their supplies. Such would not be unthinkable.

Luke concludes this portion of the journey by saying, "and so we went toward Rome." Literally, this sentence reads, "and so we came to (or arrived in) Rome." Of course, they were not yet in the city proper, but they were in Italy and apparently in the outskirts of Rome. Luke's sentence is an expression of triumph and accomplishment. Given the events of the last few years and the intensity of the last few months one can imagine the feeling of accomplishment and gratitude expressed by the phrase. God had fulfilled His promise to this point. There was no reason the rest would not take place.

Paul's letter to the Roman believers had been written a few years previously and its contents would have been the subject of much discussion among believers in the churches in Rome (Forlines, *Romans* 2)—as the epistle remains the subject of much discussion today. The Christians of the area churches would be familiar with Paul; many of them were his friends and converts (Rom. 16:1-15). At some point, someone had spread the word of Paul's arrival in the area, perhaps during their seven-day layover at Puteoli. Efforts were made to meet him as he made his way to the city of Rome (v. 15). Two places are named. Appii Forum (the Forum of Appius) was a market town some forty miles southeast of Rome on the well-traveled road, the Via Appia. Three Taverns was a station area some twenty miles farther in. At the greetings of fellow believers, Paul (and the other believers with him) were greatly encouraged. The Roman Christians' welcome expressed solidarity with Paul even though he was a prisoner. But he was not one who had committed crimes for which he deserved punishment. He was a "prisoner of Jesus Christ" (Phil. 1:12-14; Col. 4:18; Philem. 1). Who has not

found great encouragement in the company of fellow believers!

J. Imprisoned in Rome (28:16-31)

1. Arrangements for the Apostle Paul (28:16)

16 And when we came to Rome, the centurion delivered the prisoners to the captain of the guard: but Paul was suffered to dwell by himself with a soldier that kept him.

The entire company would have entered the city of Rome from the southeast on the Via Appia. It was a mixed company of soldiers, prisoners, and Paul's few companions. The prisoners were delivered to the "captain of the guard," the commander of the Praetorian Guard. This elite unit of Roman soldiers was assigned to guard the emperor and maintain order in Rome proper and Italy at large. Originally established under Augustus, the group included nine cohorts (a thousand men each), but it had been increased to twelve under Claudius. It was also charged with processing prisoners from the provinces; hence the reference here (Keener IV: 3723-3725).

The last of the "we" references in Acts is found here (v. 16), but Luke apparently remained with Paul. Paul was kept in light military custody, as indicated by the fact that he was chained to a single soldier (v. 20). But he was allowed to stay in his own rented quarters (v. 30)—probably within the garrison—apart from the other prisoners. He was still regarded as a prisoner, but his liberties were probably because of his citizenship status and the letter from

Festus detailing his legal status (Schnabel 1066; Keener IV:3726).

2. Meeting with Jewish leaders (28:17-29)

17 And it came to pass, that after three days Paul called the chief of the Jews together: and when they were come together, he said unto them, Men *and* brethren, though I have committed nothing against the people, or customs of our fathers, yet was I delivered prisoner from Jerusalem into the hands of the Romans.
18 Who, when they had examined me, would have let *me* go, because there was no cause of death in me.
19 But when the Jews spake against *it*, I was constrained to appeal unto Caesar; not that I had ought to accuse my nation of.
20 For this cause therefore have I called for you, to see *you*, and to speak with *you*: because that for the hope of Israel I am bound with this chain.
21 And they said unto him, We neither received letters out of Judaea concerning thee, neither any of the brethren that came shewed or spake any harm of thee.
22 But we desire to hear of thee what thou thinkest: for as concerning this sect, we know that every where it is spoken against.
23 And when they had appointed him a day, there came many to him into *his* lodging; to whom he expounded and testified the kingdom of God, persuading them concerning Jesus, both out of the law of Moses, and *out of* the prophets, from morning till evening.
24 And some believed the things which were spoken, and some believed not.
25 And when they agreed not among themselves, they departed, after that Paul had spoken one word, Well spake the Holy Ghost by Esaias the prophet unto our fathers,
26 Saying, Go unto this people, and say, Hearing ye shall hear, and shall not understand; and seeing ye shall see, and not perceive.
27 For the heart of this people is waxed gross, and their ears are dull of hearing, and their eyes have they closed; lest they should see with *their* eyes, and hear with *their* ears, and understand with *their* heart, and should be converted, and I should heal them.
28 Be it known therefore unto you, that the salvation of God is sent unto the Gentiles, and *that* they will hear it.
29 And when he had said these words, the Jews departed, and had great reasoning among themselves.

The Christians of Rome and some of the surrounding cities had already expressed their gladness over Paul's arrival (vv. 14-15). Now it was time for him to meet with the Jewish leaders and explain his presence and all the circumstances. Not only would he have wanted to explain his "chain" (v. 20), he had long since committed himself to proclaiming the gospel to the "Jews first" (Rom. 1:16). Since he could not go to the synagogues, he called for the leaders ("the chief of the Jews") of the synagogues to meet with him (v. 17). Of course, they would have gone to the place where he was kept under guard.

Paul summarized for them that he had been examined and legally proven innocent of the accusations against him. He would have been released but there were threats against his life that constrained him to appeal to Caesar (vv. 17-19). In spite of that he had no cause to complain against his people. This implies that he would not press any legal charges of malicious prosecution (Schnabel 1068). In his explanation of the situation, Paul went to the heart of things by saying that the real issue was his personal belief in "the hope of Israel" (v. 20). By this, of course, he meant belief in the Messiah and the resurrection (23:6; 26:6).

The response of the Jewish leaders was that they had not heard of or received any word regarding Paul (v. 21). Some commentators find this highly suspect (Haenchen 726-728). However, the lack of any such communication is entirely likely for several reasons (Polhill, *Acts* 540; Schnabel 1069; Bruce, *Acts* 506). First, word from Judaea might not have had time to get to Rome since the approval of Festus to send Paul. They had left Judaea late in the sailing season and arrived early in Rome. If the Jews had sent communications they might still be in route. Second, in view of the troubles the Jews experienced when they were expelled from Rome previously (18:2), they might have turned a blind eye to any reports. Third, the Judaean Jews might have altogether abandoned the case against Paul seeing that he had been sent to Rome. Fourth, if the case against Paul was going to be advanced, the high priest and representatives from Jerusalem would have to come to Rome, and that had not happened.

In response to Paul, the leaders expressed an interest in hearing what he had to say (v. 22). They had indeed heard of "this sect" (a Christian Judaism) and the widespread opposition to it. Of course, they would have had a recent encounter with Christians a few years previously with the uprising that led to the edict of Claudius. And they unwittingly acknowledged how expansive the witness of Christianity had become, characterizing it as being spoken against *everywhere*. Apparently, the experience of Paul was shared by others who took the gospel to the Jews.

At a set date, a large number of Jewish leaders came to Paul's quarters to hear him (vv. 23-28). Paul did what he had always done. He appealed to the Jews, out of the Scriptures and from his own experience, that Jesus was the Messiah. His presentation was no meager summary but an extended exposition ("from morning till evening"). His method was the same as usual; he "persuaded" them about the gospel. There must have been detailed and intense exchanges in the process.

The result was typical of what had always been the case when the gospel was proclaimed to Jews, with few exceptions (2:37; 17:10-12). Some did savingly believe in the Messiah. Others rejected that claim and argued against it (v. 24). This led to a very serious indictment from Paul, using the words of the prophet Isaiah (Isa. 6:9-10) to characterize them (Shires 32, 79). This pronouncement was also a signal that Paul would turn his attention to the Gentiles who would receive the message of the gospel more openly (v. 28).

The conclusion of his remarks did not end the discussions. Though the Jews left the place where Paul was incarcerated, they continued to address what he had said (v. 29). Paul had been faithful to proclaim the gospel and give its O. T. basis. Those texts would be discussed by the Jewish leaders in Rome for days and months to come. As with the Bereans (17:1-12), the more they searched the Scriptures the more the gospel would be understood. Indeed, the gospel will continue to be discussed until Jesus comes again.

3. Imprisoned but not silenced (28:30-31)

30 And Paul dwelt two whole years in his own hired house, and received all that came in unto him, 31 Preaching the kingdom of God, and teaching those things which concern the Lord Jesus Christ, with all confidence, no man forbidding him.

It is entirely fitting that Acts began (2:14-39) and concludes with the presentation of the gospel. With all the people and events detailed in its contents, the central theme is the gospel of Jesus Christ. Here is the genius and intent of Luke.

The ending of Acts (vv. 30-31) seems abrupt, considering it was the conclusion of two volumes, not just one (the Gospel of Luke being the first). Paul was kept imprisoned for two more years in Rome, although he was able to stay in his own rented quarters. Implied is that he had some source of income for what was needed in housing and personal supplies. This would have come from the churches where he ministered and from the Christians he knew in Rome. He was also given liberties to receive all visitors who came to see him, and there

were probably many who did this. He was still chained to a Roman soldier the entire time. One can only imagine the conversations the soldiers heard and the personal exchanges they would have had with Paul. If the epistle to the Philippians is any indicator, there were some of these who were saved (Phil. 1:13; 4:22).

Luke notes that Paul was not prevented from active ministry. Here is yet another indication that the Roman officials saw nothing threatening to civil order about the message of the gospel. What incited trouble in other places, primarily, was the prejudiced reactions of Jewish leaders.

Paul continued the proclamation of the "kingdom of God." This would have included the teachings of Jesus about the kingdom of God in the sovereign rule of God, the community of believers in relationship, and the final return of Christ in the consummation of all things.

Paul also taught about the person of Jesus Christ. This would have included the Messianic promises of the O. T. regarding Him, His birth and life, and then His death, burial, resurrection, and final return. In other words, these two broad areas constitute the contents of Paul's epistles. We also know that four of his epistles were written during this time. Paul was imprisoned but not silenced.

Summary (27:1—28:31)

The journey to Rome takes up a lot of the Acts narrative. Its detail is written in first person as one of the main "we" sections of Acts. Luke covers it in four main parts. The first part was the initial trip from Caesarea to Myra, during which time they began to encounter trouble with the prevailing winds. The centurion secured the services of a grain ship out of Alexandria, Egypt, bound for Italy.

The second part of the trip covers the raging storm they encountered. With difficulty they had made it to Fair Havens on the island of Crete but determined they could not stay there for the off-season. Here Paul advised them to wait until later to continue the trip, warning them of hurt and loss; but his counsel was not heeded. Almost immediately after setting sail they were broadsided by a nor'easter and began a fight for their lives. During the height of the storm, when everyone had lost hope of survival, Paul spoke words of encouragement, assuring them that the Lord had promised him they would all survive. His words included the foresight that they would be shipwrecked on an island. Things happened exactly as he said.

The third part of the trip is taken up with the details of the shipwreck and their escape to land. In the providence of God the ship had drifted toward Italy and wound up on the coast of Melita (modern Malta). Their escape from the doomed ship after running it aground was nothing short of miraculous. Paul advised that the prisoners, including himself, not be killed to prevent their escape. By this time the centurion had come to respect Paul's advice and followed it. With the ship breaking up all around them, they all made it to land where they were treated kindly by the people of Malta, who built fires to warm the men.

Incredibly, Paul was bitten by a venomous snake while he was putting wood on the fire. The locals believed he was a murderer who had escaped the raging sea only to be caught by divine justice. But he suffered no ill effects from the snakebite. Their opinion of Paul changed, viewing him as a god and not a criminal. That was not the case, of course; but Paul had experienced this before.

Their stay on Malta was not without incident. They were hosted by the "chief man" of the island, probably a Roman official. While there Paul was instrumental in the healing of Publius' father. This opened the door for many others to come with their needs. While Luke does not report the proclamation of the gospel there, tradition has it that Publius was saved and the gospel was planted on Malta.

The fourth part of the trip involves the final leg of the journey to Rome. Finding another ship from Alexandria, they secured its services. They arrived at the seaport of Puteoli in Italy in a few days, where they were hosted by other Christians. This begins the overland part of the trip to Rome. Along the way they were met and encouraged by other believers. Upon arrival in the city all the prisoners were turned over to the Praetorian Guard. Paul was shown further courtesy and allowed to secure his own rented quarters.

The last part of the Acts narrative tells about Paul's meeting with the Jewish leaders in Rome, to whom he explained his "chains" and set a time for an in-depth presentation of the gospel to them. The result was that some were saved and others rejected the message. Thus Acts concludes with a mixed response by the Jews to the gospel. Paul characterized them with words from the prophet Isaiah and declared that if they refused the gospel the Gentiles would not.

Abruptly, it seems, Luke concludes his narrative with Paul imprisoned for two more years while awaiting his opportunity to speak to Caesar. He was allowed to be at liberty to live in his own rented house though he was still in custody. Further, he was able to receive all who came to speak with him, and so he continued to preach and teach the gospel of Jesus Christ.

Application: Teaching and Preaching the Passage

Exegetical Outline of the Text: 1. The Start of the Journey to Rome (27:1-8). 2. The Storm on the Journey to Rome (27:9-26). 3. The Shipwreck on the Journey to Rome (27:27-44). 4. The Survival of Everyone for the Journey to Rome (28:1-10). 5. The Success of the Journey to Rome (28:11-14). 6. The Security of Paul in Rome (28:15-31).

The orders to send Paul to Rome came quickly and the trip began, even though the timing was uncertain because of the risks of late-season travel on the Mediterranean. Paul and his companions were part of a much larger group of men, most of whom were prisoners on their way to the Colosseum in Rome. It was a strange company for Christians. But that was part of God's plan as well. There may be other destinations the Lord has for us but part of that journey includes the people we encounter. To be sure, they would never forget Paul. Their lives were spared because of God's providential protection and plan for his life. The same is true for us. We are the only "Bibles" some will ever read. It behooves us to be aware of God's plan for us and be faithful to Him among those we encounter.

Just as Paul and his companions were not delivered *from* the storm but were delivered *through* the storm, so are we. "Storms" are to be expected in this world and some are very severe. The believer is not spared from them but through them. Just as Paul was encouraged by the Lord during the storm so God's truth encourages us too. This makes an excellent theme for teaching and preaching, using the storm analogy. All who live long enough will have their own "storm stories."

Paul and the entire company from the shipwreck found refreshing hospitality from people who were considered by some to be "barbarians." Compassion and good deeds are often found among people in general because these qualities reflect the needs of the human heart and life. These should be appreciated for what they are. We often have opportunities to minister to the needs of hurting people just as Paul did with the sick folks of the island. We may not have his apostolic gift to perform miracles, but we can pray for and encourage others.

Mercy ministries are often the basis for missionary efforts. When we minister to the physical needs of the sick and hurting, doors of opportunity are often opened for the gospel. The church has been the historic leader in mercy ministries, providing hospitals, food, counseling, housing, and a thousand other mercies to minister to people impacted by sin.

Conclusion

There is a sense of completion when we reach the conclusion of Acts. The genius of Luke is that he has traced the witness of the church and its leaders from Jerusalem to Rome (1:8), using selected historical events to chart its movement. The record has established a fixed pattern, that until Jesus returns the church is to continue its witness to "the uttermost part of the earth." The providential hand of God has been evident at every turn: instructing, leading, directing, and delivering those who faithfully follow Him. The power of the Holy Spirit, as promised, has enabled His witnesses to proclaim the gospel persuasively and effectively, resulting in the conversion of thousands and in the establishment of hundreds of churches throughout the Roman empire. Followers of Christ, known as those of "the way," continued to do what Jesus "began to do and teach" (1:1). Luke's conclusion seems intentional, ending not with Paul but with a final reference to the Lord Jesus Christ. His record began with Jesus and ends with Him. How fitting that is! Jesus is "Alpha and Omega, the beginning and the ending" (Rev. 1:8).

Even so, at the end of the account there is also a sense that something has been left out. As when we hear an unfinished musical composition, we want to know what happened to Paul. He had been declared innocent several times by those in legal authority. He survived the storm, the shipwreck, and the snakebite. But Luke has left him awaiting yet another hearing, this time before Caesar himself, telling us that he would wait this way for at least two more years. And he has given us no record of the decision. Our sense of justice is that surely God will not permit Paul to suffer further at the hands of unjust men. But history shows that God does permit the righteous to suffer for His own purposes (Heb. 11:36-40).

There are many opinions as to why Luke terminated the Acts record as he did. They are all grist for the mill (Bock 757-758). Although some interpreters think Luke wrote his account *after* the death of Paul, it may be that for one reason or another—to complete his writing for Theophilus (Lk. 1:3; Acts 1:1), for example—Luke had to finish the writing before Paul's hearing before Caesar. For that matter, in one sense his purpose to account for what happened to the followers of Jesus after His resurrection has been accomplished.

Still, the matter of Paul seems unfinished, something like a "loose end." But there are other "loose ends" in the narrative. What happened to Peter, to Barnabas, to Silas, to Timothy? Luke never purposed to tell *everything*, only the main things according to his basic plan (1:8). Given that point, perhaps Luke intentionally left us with an "open narrative." There really was no need to finish the narrative; other witnesses would continue giving out the gospel until the return of Christ.

Although Luke concludes as he does, we are not left totally in the dark about Paul's future. Commentators have gathered the shards of evidence regarding Paul from his own writings and from the testimony of others (Bruce, *Paul* 441-446; Polhill, *Acts* 547-548; Bock 758-760; Keener IV:3764-3771). The main possibilities, with many variations, are as follows.

First, he might have been found guilty by Nero and executed. This is unlikely given the documentation of his case. But Nero was a loose cannon emotionally and was capable of whims that no one could challenge.

Second, Paul could have been released and resumed his missionary ministry. This is likely when the pieces and implications of his plans prior to his imprisonment and his post-imprisonment (Titus, 1 Timothy) writings are analyzed. Eusebius, with qualification, affirmed his release. If he was released it would have been prior to A.D. 64, when Nero declared Christianity "religio illiciti" and began the persecution. If this were the case, Paul would have been arrested and imprisoned a second time, concluding with his execution.

Third, Paul could have been exiled, as Clement of Rome asserted. However, there are more questions than answers with this possibility. Where was his exile? How long? What were its conditions? On what legal grounds? Clement does not answer the questions. This outcome seems unlikely but remains a possibility.

Fourth, he could have been kept under military arrest and restricted even more. Some see a close connection between this scenario and the difficulty of Onesiphorus' finding him in Rome (2 Tim. 1:16-17). But when Paul wrote his last letter to Timothy, he knew he was about to die (2 Tim. 4:6-8). This does not seem to be a likely possibility.

In conclusion, our interest in the Book of Acts must not focus only on Paul. It would be a disservice to Luke, as well as to all the other great men and women about whom he has written if we forget about them because we lament the way the Acts narrative ends. Contained here are the stories of some of the "great cloud of witnesses" that challenge each generation of Christ-followers to the same calling of faith.

Immeasurably greater is the fact that the Book of Acts is preeminently about the Lord Jesus Christ. Men and women who savingly believed in Him were willing to give their all to obey His calling and take the gospel to the "uttermost part of the earth." The record begins and ends with Him—as it should.

ACTS

BIBLIOGRAPHY: WORKS CITED IN THIS COMMENTARY

Reference Works (cited by the following abbreviations)

EDT. *Evangelical Dictionary of Theology*, ed. Walter Elwell (Baker, 1984).

EHB. *Eerdmans Handbook to the Bible*, eds. David and Pat Alexander (Eerdmans, 1973).

ESV. *ESV Study Bible: English Standard Version* (Crossway Bibles, 2008).

TDNT. *Theological Dictionary of the New Testament*, (10 volumes), ed. Gerhard Kittel, trans. and ed. Geoffrey W. Bromiley (Eerdmans, 1964-1976).

Books and Other Works (cited by author's last name)

Abasciano, Brian, "On the Translation of Acts 13:48," Society of Evangelical Arminians website: http://evangelicalarminians.org/brian-abasciano-on-the-translation-of-acts-1348/, accessed 2/28/18.

Allen, Leslie C., *The Books of Joel, Obadiah, Jonah, and Micah; The New International Commentary on the Old Testament*, ed., R. K. Harrison (Eerdmans, 1976).

Barnes, Albert, *Notes on the New Testament, Explanatory and Practical: Acts* (Baker Book House, 1972).

Barnhouse, Donald Grey, *Acts, An Expositional Commentary* (Zondervan, 1979).

Barrett, C. K., *The Acts of the Apostles: A Shorter Commentary* (T & T Clark, 2002).

Barrett, C. K., *Essays on Paul* (Westminster Press, 1982).

Berkhof, L., *Systematic Theology* (Eerdmans, 1941).

Berry, George Ricker, *Berry's Interlinear Greek-English New Testament With a Greek-English Lexicon and New Testament Synonyms, King James Version* (Guardian Press, 1976).

Bock, Darrell L., *Baker Exegetical Commentary on the New Testament: Acts*; Robert W. Yarbrough and Robert H Stein, eds. (Baker Academic, 2007).

Bruce, F. F., *The New International Commentary on the New Testament: The Book of Acts*, rev. ed. (Eerdmans, 1988).

Bruce, F. F., *Paul: Apostle of the Heart Set Free* (Eerdmans, 1977).

Cadbury, Henry J., *The Book of Acts in History* (Harper and Brothers, 1955).

Cadbury, Henry J., *The Making of Luke—Acts, with a New Introduction by Paul N. Anderson* (Hendrickson, 1999).

Calvin, John, *Calvin's Commentaries, The Acts of the* Apostles, two vols.; trans. John W. Frasier and W. J. G. McDonald (Eerdmans, 1965-1966).

Carson, D. A., *Showing the Spirit: A Theological Exposition of 1 Corinthians 12-14* (Baker, 1987).

Crabtree, Jeffrey A., *The Randall House Bible Commentary: The Book of Matthew* (Randall House, 2015).

Dodd, C. H., *Apostolic Preaching and Its Development, Three Lectures* (Hodder and Stoughton, 1936).

ACTS

Earle, Ralph, *Beacon Bible Commentary: The Acts of the Apostles* (Beacon Hill, 1965).

Edersheim, Alfred, *The Life and Times of Jesus the Messiah* (Eerdmans, 1974; three vols. in one).

Forlines, F. Leroy, *Classical Arminianism: A Theology of Salvation* (Randall House, 2011).

Forlines, Leroy, *The Randall House Bible Commentary: Romans* (Randall House, 1987).

Forlines, Leroy, *The Quest for Truth: Answering Life's Inescapable Questions* (Randall House, 2001).

Fitzmyer, Joseph A., *The Acts of the Apostles: A New Translation With Introduction and Commentary: The Anchor Yale Bible*, William Foxwell Albright, David Noel Freedman, gen. eds. (Yale University Press, 1998).

Geldenhuys, Norval, *The New International Commentary on the New Testament: Commentary on the Gospel of Luke: The English Text With Introduction Exposition and Notes* (Eerdmans, 1975).

Ger, Steven, *The Book of Acts: Witnesses to the World*; Mal Couch and Ed Hindson, gen. eds. (Amg Publishers, 2004).

Gower, Ralph, *The New Manners and Customs of Bible Times* (Moody, 1987).

Grudem, Wayne, gen ed; Stanley N. Gundry, series ed., *Are Miraculous Gifts for Today?* (Zondervan, 1996).

Gundry, Robert H., *A Survey of the New Testament*, rev. ed. (Zondervan, 1981).

Haenchen, Ernst, *The Acts of the Apostles: A Commentary*; trans. from the 14th German edition (1965) by Bernard Noble and Gerald Shinn (Westminster, 1971).

Harnack, Adolf, *New Testament Studies, Vol. III: The Acts of the Apostles,* trans. by J. R. Wilkinson (Williams & Norgate, 1909).

Harrison, Everett F., *Acts: The Expanding Church* (Moody, 1975).

Harrison, Paul V., "Commentary on the Book of James," in *The Randall House Bible Commentary: James, 1, 2 Peter, and Jude* (Randall House, 1992).

Hiebert, D. Edmond, *An Introduction to the New Testament, Volume One: The Gospels and Acts* (Moody 1975).

Hughes, R. Kent, *Preaching the Word: Acts, The Church Afire* (Crossway, 1996).

Irenaeus, *The Writings of Irenaeus* (Aeterna, 2015).

Jones, A. H. M., *The Herods of Judaea* (Oxford, 1967).

Josephus, Flavius, *Complete Works* (includes, as cited, the *Life* of Flavius Josephus, the *Antiquities* of the Jews, The *Wars* of the Jews, and other works), trans. by William Whiston (Kregel, 1960).

Kaiser, Walter Jr., *The Messiah in the Old Testament* (Zondervan, 1995).

Keener, Craig S., *Acts: An Exegetical Commentary,* four vols. (Baker Academic, 2012-2015).

Kent, Homer A. Jr., *Jerusalem to Rome: Studies in Acts* (Baker Academic, 1972).

Knowling, R. J., "The Acts of the Apostles," in *The Expositor's Greek Testament*, ed. W. Robertson Nicoll (Eerdmans, 1983).

ACTS

Lenski, R. C .H., *The Interpretation of the Acts of the Apostles* (Augsburg, 1961).

Leupold, H. C., *Exposition of the Psalms* (Baker Book House, 1986).

Lightfoot, J. B., *The Acts of the Apostles: A Newly Discovered Commentary; The Lightfoot Legacy Set,* vol. 1; eds., Ben Witherington III and Todd D. Still (IVP Academic, 2014).

Logau, Friedrich Von, *Poetic Aphorisms: Retribution*; trans. Henry Wadsworth Longfellow (1846).

Longenecker, Richard N., *The Expositor's Bible Commentary With the New International Version: Acts* (Zondervan, 1995).

Marberry, Thomas L., "Commentary on the Book of Galatians," in *The Randall House Bible Commentary: Galatians through Colossians* (Randall House, 1988).

Marberry, Thomas L., and Craig Shaw, "Commentary on the Books of 1, 2, 3 John," in *The Randall House Bible Commentary: 1, 2, 3 John and Revelation* (Randall House, 2010).

Marshall, I. Howard, *Tyndale New Testament Commentaries: The Acts of the Apostles* (Eerdmans, 1980).

Marshall, I. Howard, *The New International Commentary on the New Testament: The Epistles of John* (Eerdmans, 1978).

Metzger, Bruce M., *A Textual Commentary on the Greek New Testament* (Second Edition): *A Companion Volume to the United Bible Societies Greek New Testament* (Fourth Revised Edition) (United Bible Societies, 1971).

Meyer, Henrich August Wilhelm, *Critical and Exegetical Handbook to The Acts of the Apostles*; trans from the fourth ed. of the German by Rev. Paton J. Gloag, trans, rev. and ed. by William P. Dickson, with preface, index, and supplementary notes to the American ed. by Rev. William Ormiston (Hendrickson, 1983).

Moo, Douglas J., "The Law of Christ as the Fulfillment of the Law of Moses: A Modified Lutheran View," in *Five Views on Law and Gospel*; series ed. Stephen N. Gundry (Zondervan 1996).

Morgan, G. Campbell, *The Acts of the Apostles* (Revell, 1924).

Morris, Leon, *The New International Commentary on the New Testament, The Gospel According to John, The English Text With Introduction, Exposition and Notes* (Eerdmans, 1971).

Moulton, James Hope, and George Milligan, *The Vocabulary of the Greek Testament Illustrated From the Papyri and Other Non-Literary Sources* (Eerdmans, 1930).

Ogg, George, *The Chronology of the Life of Paul* (Wipf and Stock, 1968).

Oswalt, John, *The New International Commentary on the Old Testament: The Book of Isaiah Chapters 1-39*; gen. ed. R. K. Harrison (Eerdmans, 1986).

Outlaw, W. Stanley, *The Randall House Bible Commentary: Hebrews* (Randall House, 2005).

Picirilli, Robert E., "Commentary on the Books of 1 and 2 Peter," in *The Randall House Bible Commentary: James, 1, 2 Peter and Jude* (Randall House, 1992).

ACTS

Picirilli, Robert E., *Discipleship: The Expression of Saving Faith* (Randall House, 2013).

Picirilli, Robert E., *Free Will Revisited: A Respectful Response to Luther, Calvin, and Edwards* (Wipf & Stock, 2017).

Picirilli, Robert E., *Grace, Faith, Free Will: Contrasting Views of Salvation: Calvinism & Arminianism* (Randall House, 2002).

Picirilli, Robert E., *Paul the Apostle* (Moody, 1986).

Picirilli, Robert E., *The Randall House Bible Commentary: 1, 2 Corinthians* (Randall House, 1987).

Picirilli, Robert E., *The Randall House Bible Commentary: The Gospel of Mark* (Randall House, 2003).

Polhill, John B., *The New American Commentary, An Exegetical and Theological Exposition of Holy Scripture: Acts* (vol. 26); gen. ed. David S. Dockery (B&H, 1992).

Polhill, John B., *Paul and His Letters* (Broadman, 1999).

Ramsay, William M., *St. Paul the Traveller and Roman Citizen* (Broadman, 1979).

Ramsay, William Mitchell, *Luke the Physician, and Other Studies in the History of Religion* (Hodder and Stoughton, 1908).

Ramsay, William Mitchell, *The Cities of St. Paul: Their Influence on His Life and Thought: The Cities of Eastern Asia Minor* (Hodder and Stoughton, 1908).

Ridderbos, H. N., *The Speeches of Peter in the Acts of the Apostles* (Tyndale, 1962).

Robertson, A. T., *Word Pictures in the New Testament: Acts* (Broadman, 1930).

Robertson, A. T., *Making Good in the Ministry; A Sketch of John Mark* (Baker, 1918).

Saucy, Robert L., *Are Miraculous Gifts for Today: Four Views* (Zondervan, 1996).

Schaff, Philip, *The Creeds of Christendom With a History and Critical Notes* (David S. Schaff, 1905).

Schnabel, Eckhard J., *Zondervan Exegetical Commentary on the New Testament: Acts*; Clinton E. Arnold, ed., (Zondervan, 2012).

Shires, Henry M., *Finding the Old Testament in the New* (Westminster 1974).

Smith, James, *The Voyage and Shipwreck of St. Paul with Dissertations on the Sources of the Writings of St. Luke and the Ships and Navigation of the Ancients* (Longman, Brown, Green, and Longmans, 1848).

Soards, Marion L., *The Speeches in Acts: Their Content, Context, and Concerns* (Westminster/John Knox, 1994).

Sproul, R. C., *St. Andrew's Expositional Commentary: Acts* (Crossway, 2010).

Stallings, Jack W., *The Randall House Bible Commentary: The Gospel of John* (Randall House, 1989).

Stott, John R. W., *The Bible Speaks Today: The Message of Acts: The Spirit, the Church & the World* (Inter-Varsity, 1990).

Strickland, Wayne G., "The Inauguration of the Law of Christ With the Gospel of Christ: A Dispensational View," in *Five Views on Law and Gospel,* series editor, Stephen N. Gundry (Zondervan 1996).

ACTS

Tenney, Merrill C., *New Testament Survey* (Eerdmans, 1961).

Thayer, Joseph Henry, *Greek-English Lexicon of the New Testament: Being Grimm's Wilke's Clavis Novi Testamenti Translated Revised and Enlarged* (Zondervan, 1975).

Walker, Thomas, *Acts of the Apostles* (Kregel, 1965).

Warfield, Benjamin Brekinridge, *The Inspiration and Authority of the Bible* (Presbyterian and Reformed, 1948).

Wenham, G. J., *The New International Commentary on the Old Testament: The Book of Leviticus*, gen. ed., R. K. Harrison (Eerdmans, 1979).

Wight, Fred, *Manners and Customs of Bible Lands* (Moody, 1953).

Wolters, Albert M., *Creation Regained: Biblical Basics for a Reformational Worldview*; second ed. (Eerdmans, 2005).

Wright, Tom [N. T.], *What St. Paul Really Said* (Lion, 1997).

Wright, N. T., *Paul in Fresh Perspective* (Fortress, 2009).

Wright, N. T. *Justification, God's Plan and Paul's Vision* (IVP Academic, 2009).

www.ingramcontent.com/pod-product-compliance
Lightning Source LLC
Chambersburg PA
CBHW020406100426
42812CB00001B/224

THE RANDALL HOUSE
BIBLE COMMENTARY
SERIES

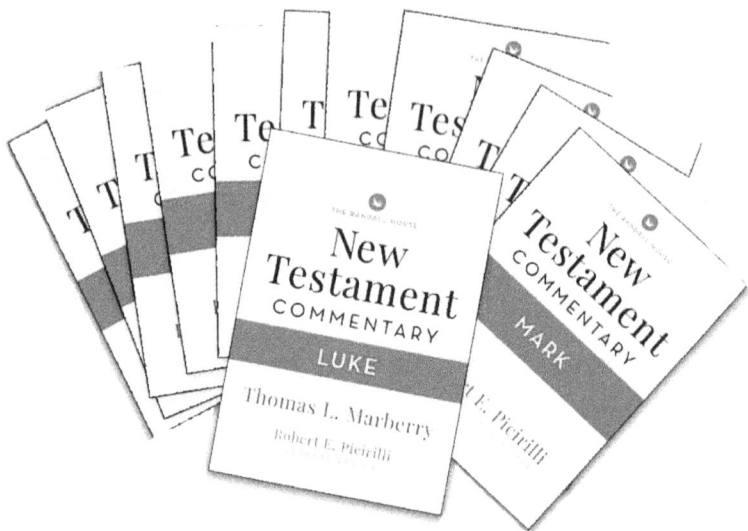

The *Randall House Bible Commentary* series is a must have for pastors and students alike. With Robert Picirilli as General Editor and all Free Will Baptist contributors, the *Randall House Bible Commentary* series is a great addition to any library.

Full set (12 Volumes)
includes 12 matching dust jackets

To order call **1-800-877-7030** or
visit our website at **www.d6.family/store**

D6 FAMILY MINISTRY